POLICE ADMINISTRATION:
An Introduction

ALFRED R. STONE

STUART M. DeLUCA

PRENTICE HALL, Englewood Cliffs, New Jersey 07632

Library of Congress Cataloging in Publication Data
Stone, Alfred R.
   Police administration.

   Bibliography: p.
   Includes indexes.
   1. Police administration—United States. I. DeLuca,
Stuart M. II. Title.
HV7935.S76 1985   351.74   84-13030
ISBN 0-471-86898-1

Printed in the United States of America

10 9 8 7 6 5 4 3 2 1

FOREWORD

Among all the law enforcement agencies in the United States, large and small, there is one common characteristic: every last one of them has an administrator. In fact, some of them have several administrators.

I mention this because somehow the administrators are so often overlooked when the quality of police service is being discussed. There are plenty of ideas for improving the patrol force, for raising the quality of criminal investigations, for making police agencies more effective and efficient. But in my experience, all these schemes are fruitless unless the quality and performance of the administrator is considered.

Part of the problem, I suppose, is the long-standing tradition (which is really not much more than a habit) of choosing administrators on the basis of seniority: whoever has lasted longest gets the best job. If experience and ability were identical, this would be as good a way as any to select people for administrative positions. Unfortunately, it appears that some people profit much less than others from experience.

There have been earlier textbooks designed to improve the quality of police administration. Without discrediting the contributions of Wilson and McLaren, Eastman, and several others, I have felt for many years that there was a great need for a text that would first address the genuine needs of administrators in all kinds and sizes of police agencies—not just the large urban departments—and second, that would present a blend of proven theory and current, practical information. The present text, in my opinion, comes closer to the ideal than any other work that has come to my attention.

I have known Al Stone for some 30 years. He has had ample experience in every aspect of law enforcement, and has made countless contributions (mostly unrecognized) to the field. As a personnel training officer for the Texas Department of Public Safety, he has helped a generation of young officers enter the field with the best practical education available anywhere.

Stuart DeLuca brings an entirely different kind of background to the endeavor. He has a rare talent for expressing in clear, concise language the principles of police science.

Together, these gentlemen have produced a text that may come to be seen as a landmark in the field. It is comprehensive in scope, contemporary in approach, and unusually coherent in its presentation of both the principles of administration and their practical applications. I commend their work to your examination in the hope, which I share with the authors, that the student will find it both useful and stimulating.

Wilson E. Speir
Southwest Texas State University,
San Marcos, Texas

PREFACE

This text is intended to provide an overview of the principal duties and responsibilities of the police administrator. In most cases, police administration is offered to first- and second-year students, so we have assumed only a minimal familiarity with basic concepts of law enforcement on the part of the student.

The practice of managing a law enforcement agency is fraught with serious difficulties. One segment of the community demands more, and more effective, police services to take criminals off the streets; another segment of the community insists on paring public expenditures to the bone regardless of the consequences; yet another segment of the community calls for greater sensitivity and compassion on the part of the police toward disadvantaged, socially alienated minorities, who, for whatever reasons, seem to provide a disproportionate share of the police agency's workload. And when the beleaguered administrator looks within the agency for support, he or she finds subordinates who are too often poorly motivated, undisciplined, and clamoring for more pay and benefits.

Police administrators themselves are often poorly prepared for their awesome responsibilites. Within the past decade, both pre-service training (primarily in colleges) and continuing education programs have begun to develop a generation of young law enforcement professionals who are far better equipped than their predecessors. However, the long-standing traditions of promotion from within and emphasis on seniority (even when qualified by competitive examinations) continue to produce ranks of supervisors, mid-level managers, and upper-level administrators whose most outstanding trait is that they have survived. Some are dynamic, innovative leaders, but these are at least as rare in law enforcement as in any other field of endeavor.

We do not expect the student who completes a course in police administration to go out into the world and be hired as a police chief. Rather, most of the students who use this book will face at least two or three more years of pre-service education, then will enter the police service at the bottom: as a rookie police officer. Those who find police work to be a satisfying, challenging career, and who do not wash out along the way, have a good chance of being promoted to sergeant after four or five years; with that promotion will come their first taste of managerial responsibility. Further promotions will come slowly; with luck and diligence, the student who reads these words today might hope to attain a mid-level managerial position some 12 to 15 years from now. It is also probable that this text will be used in continuing education courses or police academy training seminars to prepare officers to take administrative positions in the near future, or to assist those who already hold managerial jobs and who could use a little help in coping with the unfamiliar terrain. Nevertheless, we assume that for most of the readers of this text direct experience with administrative responsibility lies somewhere in the future.

Why then should students study police administration so early in their careers? There are several reasons.

- An understanding of the principles of police administration and organization will enable the subordinate officer to better understand the way his or her agency operates; in short, learning the principles of leadership helps one to be a good follower.
- The study of police administration provides a broad perspective over the entirety of a police agency, more so than any other subject except perhaps a course in the principles of criminal justice; thus, the course helps a young officer to understand how his or her duties are related to the other operations of the agency.
- The fundamental concepts of good administration, once learned, are unlikely to be wholly forgotten even over a period of a decade or more; the young officer will have ample opportunities to compare the principles learned in this course with the realities of organization and administrative practice found in his or her agency.

Some of the practical advice and specific procedures we will discuss in this text might be obsolete by the time today's student settles into a desk job (although, again, this should not be true for the reader who is already an administrator or about to become one). Nevertheless, we have conscientiously tried to maintain a balance between theoretical concepts and their practical applications. We feel strongly that a theory alone, no matter how precisely formulated or how thoroughly validated, means very little. On the other hand, a book full of "recipes" and detailed guidelines for administrative practice, without a theoretical framework to make sense of the mass of detail, does not give the student a fair opportunity to apply the principles of sound administration to the particular situation with which he or she must deal. Whether we have succeeded in maintaining the proper balance between theory and practice, the reader must judge.

The text is divided into five parts. Part I is an introduction to basic concepts and theories of management, derived largely from business administration practices and applied to the specific requirements of law enforcement. Part II presents both theoretical and practical approaches to the management of the buildings, equipment, and other material resources required by a police agency.

Part III covers the theory and practice of managing police personnel, including recruitment, selection, training, promotion, leadership, and discipline.

Part IV treats the basic principles of organization and administration of police patrol, traffic law enforcement, criminal investigation, and other essential law enforcement operations.

An epilogue, "Police and the Community," concludes the text with some observatons on the relationships between à law enforcement agency and the public it serves.

The 17 chapters in the text are intended to cover every aspect of police administration in sufficient depth and detail that it would be possible for the student to take an administrative job immediately upon completing the course. Naturally, there is a great deal more that an administrator must know in order to be successful, and much of that knowledge can come only from experience, including trial-and-error experimentation with different techniques. For some of the most difficult administrative problems, there is no one right answer, but rather a range of possible solutions. We can only hope to suggest that range, and perhaps point the student toward sources of more detailed information where appropriate. As for the rest, the novice administrator will soon learn what works and what does not in his or her environment.

Our world has been made considerably easier, during the development of this text, by the help that we have gratefully received from the following:

Major Kenneth Maurer, Tucson (Ariz.) Police Dept.; Chief Travis L. Lynch, Macon (Ga.) Police Dept.; Chief Ernie Gallaher, Pendleton (Ore.) Police Dept.; Chief Chris Wiggins, Durango (Colo.) Police Dept.; Chief Bill R. Myers, Birmingham (Ala.) Police Dept.; the Planning and Research Division, Mesa (Ariz.) Police Dept.; Chief Alan E. Gollihue, Portsmouth (Va.) Police Dept.; Chief Byron R. Rookstad, Cheyenne (Wyo.) Police Dept.; Sheriff Charles Sharpe, Cumberland County, Maine; Chief W. W. Perrett, Tacoma (Wash.) Police Dept.; Chief C. E. Swindall, Montgomery (Ala.) Police Dept.; Lt. Frank Barker, Las Vegas Metropolitan Police Dept.; Chief Daryl F. Gates, Los Angeles Police Dept.; Deputy Superintendent Dennis E. Nowicki, Chicago Police Dept.; and Captain R. Hampton, Fort Smith (Ark.) Police Dept.

Also, Marcia Werner and Marty Lewis of Quality Composing, Austin, created the typography for most of the "in-basket exercise" materials; and Sue Bryant of the Texas Dept. of Highways and Public Transportation provided a number of photographs and documents.

We are grateful also to those who read and commented upon the manuscript for this book in various drafts. They are: Andrew P. Dantschisch, Robert E. Snow, Charles D. Hale, Robert B. Tegarden, Howard Abadinsky, Erik Beckman, B. W. Adams, Jr., Wilson E. Speir.

CONTENTS

DATA BANK
CITY
POLICE DEPARTMENT

AT THE END OF EACH CHAPTER IN THIS BOOK, THERE IS A simulation exercise for the student to complete. The exercise consists of one or more documents that might be found in the in basket on an administrator's desk. These documents—interoffice memos, letters, and so forth—introduce or represent management problems for which a solution must be found or a decision must be made. The student's task will be to solve the problem or make the decision, based on the information given in the simulated documents, as if the student were the administrator.

The student will be directed to take various roles, representing different levels of management in the police agency—from chief of police to lieutenant—in a hypothetical agency, the City Police Department, in the fictitious community of City, State. The following Data Bank contains basic information about City and its police department that the student will need as background for the administrative decisions to be made in the in-basket exercises.

CITY, STATE

City is a growing urban center with a current population of 132,000. In recent years City's growth rate has been about 5 percent per year, which means that the population will double in about 14 years (assuming that the growth rate continues). This rapid growth has brought a number of problems to City: overcrowding in its deteriorating older areas, rapid expansion of its boundaries as new suburban developments are built, and a constant need for public services—including law enforcement—to catch up to the population growth.

City was founded in 1856 as an agricultural trading center on the Gray River. The river was the main transportation link to larger markets downstream and brought a steady flow of traffic from farther upriver. During the late nineteenth century, a variety of small industries located along the river where transportation and water for industrial processes were readily available. Although the river is no longer important for transportation, the riverfront is still primarily an industrial area with smoky factories (metal processing, a brickworks, a brewery, and so forth), warehouses, and low-rent tenements. The commercial heart of City continues to thrive and, in fact, has prospered as the town has grown into a modern urban center. Banking and retail trade have kept the downtown area vibrant in spite of increasing competition from outlying shopping malls.

The railroad replaced the river as the primary transportation link around the turn of the century. Before World War I, the regional rail yards just north of City employed hundreds of workers in their shops. Now the rail yard is an industrial park, occupied by a variety of small factories and warehouses. A third, much newer industrial area is located near the City Municipal Airport on City's southwest corner.

The old residential areas around the fringes of City's commercial district went through a long decline, from World War II until the early 1970s, when young people began to reclaim the old homes and restore them—or, in some cases, convert them into offices and shops. Meanwhile, the principal residential areas shifted to the suburbs, especially City's gently rolling hills to the west. For the most part, residential development has continued westward; the newest and most fashionable suburban developments are along City's western flanks.

The establishment of an Army Air Corps base north of City, to the east of the railroad district, attracted another element to City's population during World War II. After the war, Wingtip Air Force Base was made a permanent installation; during the Korean War, Wingtip became a closed, high-security base. Local gossips assume that the base has something to do with nuclear weapons, but the subject is not openly discussed even among the military families who live around the base's perimeter.

Yet another population center within City is the university area on the south side, east of the airport. City University is a private, four-year college with an enrollment of about 2500 students, most of whom live on the campus or in the fraternity houses and cooperative dormitories nearby. College faculty members also tend to live in the area, which is characterized by graceful, well-maintained homes built mostly during the 1920s. A new, upper-middle-class suburb, University Heights, has been developed southwest of the university area in recent years.

Overall, City's population is highly representative of the national population. About 22 percent of the City population has less than a poverty-level income, as computed by the federal Department of Commerce. Sixty-nine percent are classified as middle income, and 9 percent have a high income. City's ethnic composition is as follows:

White/Anglo	62.9 percent
Black	17.3 percent
Hispanic	14.7 percent
Native American	1.6 percent
Oriental	3.0 percent
Other, unclassified	0.5 percent

The only incorporated suburb adjacent to City is Riverside, across the Gray River to the southeast. Riverside is actually older than City; it was first settled in the 1830s and incorporated in 1848 but, for reasons that have never been clear, Riverside never grew to prosperity as City did. Riverside today, with a population of 8500, is a town of struggling, marginal industries, dilapidated warehouses, and a comparatively transient working-class population, of whom about 65 percent are black or Hispanic. There are no other incorporated communities in County, of which City is the county seat. There are, however, four unincorporated villages, two to the west of City, one to the northeast, and one to the south.

The following maps show (1) the public streets and main physical features of City, (2) the pattern of land use, and (3) the City Police Department's patrol beats. The maps were prepared by the City Planning Department, are current, and are presumed to be accurate.

CITY POLICE DEPARTMENT

The first official police agency was established in City in 1861 with the hiring of a town marshal and two deputies. After the Civil War, the marshal's office expanded with the growing population. In 1875, the marshal was fired for incompetence, along with 6 of his 24 deputies, and the force was reorganized as the City Police Department. The first chief, "Boss" Howtzer, established four patrols of eight men each in the four municipal

wards that existed then. The patrols soon came under the influence of the ward political leaders; with each new municipal administration came massive firings of the entire police force. Somehow, "Boss" Howtzer survived these periodic upheavals and remained as police chief until his retirement in 1903.

City's second chief, G. A. Theery, lasted only six years, during which he attempted to reform the agency and uproot the corruption and graft that were common at the time. These efforts, despite the support of the reform-minded mayor and the city's elite, succeeded only in confusing the lines of political influence by eliminating the ward organization. In its place, Theery established a "modern" system of foot and horse patrols operating from a single police headquarters. Theery also established City Police Department's first criminalistics laboratory, detective bureau, and a telegraphic call box system to keep headquarters in touch with the patrolmen on their beats.

Theery's successor in 1909 was L. O. "Howdy" Pottner. Pottner's appointment was highly controversial, since he had no prior law enforcement experience but was considered a crony of the town's political leaders. Nevertheless, Pottner proved to be a surprisingly capable administrator, and his excellent political connections enabled him to fend off corrupting influences without any major scandals. Although Pottner was not regarded as an innovator, he did introduce the agency's first motorized patrols (in 1932), and he strongly supported the continued development of the crime lab and detective bureau. He also instituted new, scientific management techniques of patrol scheduling, bookkeeping, and central purchasing. When he retired in 1935, City Police Department was widely regarded as a model of scientific law enforcement administration.

The agency's fourth chief was Pottner's former assistant, Les Goodman. Goodman's credentials were impeccable: He was a career police officer who had risen through the ranks to the post of assistant chief. Unfortunately, Goodman proved to be a mediocre leader who commanded neither the respect nor the affection of his troops. During the Depression and World War II, vice flourished in City while Goodman occupied himself with endless policy manuals, organization charts, order memoranda, and idle threats of disciplinary crackdowns. He remained in office only because the city administration during this period was both incompetent and corrupt.

Immediately after the war, in 1946, Goodman was allowed to retire. He was replaced by the flamboyant young chief of detectives, Captain Marv Ellis. Ellis soon established his reputation as a dynamic leader and strict disciplinarian by firing nearly half the police force, including several of his former colleagues, for corruption. Most of the remaining members of the force were shuffled into new positions as Ellis completely reorganized the agency. A civil service system was installed, with elaborate grievance procedures, competitive promotional examinations, and so on. A war on vice was declared; by 1950, it was generally agreed that Ellis had "cleaned up" City with a vengeance. Thereafter, no major reorganizations were carried out, but Ellis kept up the pressure on organized crime and established a small intelligence unit to keep track of subversives and political radicals. During the turbulent 1960s, he was proud of his department's ability to identify and suppress rabble-rousers before any serious trouble could develop. As a whole, the department enjoyed high morale (thanks to Ellis's leadership skills) and a reputation for strict discipline, integrity, and a no-holds-barred attitude toward crime.

Ellis died of a heart attack in the midst of a staff meeting last year. The search for his successor took several months; it became obvious that none of his experienced subordinates could fill his shoes. The search committee, composed of several leading citizens, a sociologist at City University, and the city manager, finally chose E. Z. Abel, who was then deputy chief of police in a city of 500,000 population in California. Chief Abel took office on the first of the year. He found an agency that was essentially sound but highly traditional in structure and drifting from its nearly year-long lack of leadership.

The following pages present the information that was available to Chief Abel when he took command of City Police Department. All data are current and accurate. Throughout the course of this book, changes may be made in City Police Department's organization and practices. Some changes will be made by Chief Abel or his subordinates, and you will often participate in making these changes. You may wish to keep a separate record of the changes so that your decisions will be based on up-to-date information.

We should emphasize again that City and its police department are entirely fictitious. All names of personnel, businesses, and locations are also fictitious, and any resemblance to real persons or places is purely coincidental.

Citizens of City

City Council

City Manager

Chief of Police — Secretary

Patrol Bureau — Captain

- First Watch: 1 Lt., 4 Sgts., 10 P.O.s
- Second Watch: 1 Lt., 4 Sgts., 10 P.O.s
- School Crossing Guards: 1 Sgt.
- Third Watch: 1 Lt., 4 Sgts., 10 P.O.s
- Relief Watch: 5 Sgts., 12 P.O.s

Detective Bureau — Captain

- Crimes Against Persons Secn.: 1 Lt., 3 Sgts.
- Crimes Against Property: 1 Lt., 4 Sgts.
- Fraud & Forgery: 1 Lt., 2 Sgts.
- Crime Prevention: 1 Lt.
  - Community Relations: 1 Sgt.
  - Juvenile Division: 1 Sgt., 3 P.O.s

Organized Crime Bureau — Captain

- Vice Secn.: 1 Lt., 3 Sgts.
- Narcotics Section: 1 Lt., 2 Sgts.
- Intelligence Section: 2 Lts., 1 Sgt.

Technical Services Bureau — Captain — Sec.

- Communicns.: 1 Lt., 4 Sgts., 16 Disps.
- Rec. & Ident. Section: 1 Lt., 2 Sgts., 8 Clerks
- Crime Lab: 1 Lt., 1 Sgt., 3 Technicns.
- Fleet Opers.: 2 Sgts.
- Traffic Law Enforcement: 1 Lt., 3 Sgts., 6 P.O.s
- Jail Operations: 1 Lt.
  - Booking Desk: 4 Sgts.
  - Jail: 16 Jailers
  - Women's Unit: 4 Matrons

Administrative Services Bureau — Asst. Chief — Sec.

- Budget & Accountg.: 1 Lt., 4 Clerks
- Personnel & Train'g: 1 Lt., 2 Sgts.
- Public Info.: 1 Lt., 1 Sgt.
- Parking Enforcm't: 1 Sgt., 8 Metermaids
- Property & Evidence: 2 Sgts.

Personnel Summary:

Commissioned Personnel:

Chief, Assistant Chief 2
Captains 4
Lieutenants 19
Sergeants 57
Patrol Officers 51
Sub — total, Commissioned 133

Civilian Personnel:

Secretaties 3   Crime Lab Technicians 3
Clerks 12   Meter Maids 8
Dispatchers 16
Jailers 16   Sub — total, Civilian 62
Matrons 4   Total Budgeted 195

```
                        CITY POLICE DEPARTMENT
                          PERSONNEL ROSTER

   Name                      Yrs Svc       Age      Current Assmt

   Abel, E Z                    0          52       Chief of Police
   Williamson, Earl            43          62       Asst Chief/Ch Admin Svcs

   CAPTAINS:
   Avery, Mike                 32          50       Ch Patrol Bur
   Bowen, Thomas               26          46       Ch Detectives
   Edwards, Frank              24          41       Ch Organized Cr
   Lewis, Michael              35          53       Ch Technical Svcs

   LIEUTENANTS:
   Alexander, Joseph           16          35       Patrol, 1st Watch
   Boudreau, Robert            27          46       Records & ID
   Brooks, Raymond             18          36       Det., Fraud & Forgery
   Clements, Larry             11          32       Patrol, 3rd Watch
   Courtney, Sam               14          33       Org Cr, Narcotics
   Cox, Ralph                  20          42       Org Cr, Intelligence
   Davis, Dale                 10          34       Public Information
   Goodman, Les, Jr            28          51       Communications
   Guthrie, James              18          37       Patrol, 2nd Watch
   Hubbard, Mark                9          30       Org Cr, Intelligence
   Lawrence, Wm                32          53       Det., Cr Agst Persons
   Lusk, Dennis                18          39       Personnel & Training
   Rader, John                 14          34       Org Cr, Vice
   Smith, Charles              17          35       Crime Prevention
   Stockton, Douglas           12          33       Crime Lab
   Thomas, Lloyd               32          52       Jail Operations
   Ullrich, Roland             16          36       Budget & Acctg
   Washington, Henry           19          38       Det., Cr Agst Property
   Young, Joe                  22          42       Traffic Law Enf

   SENIOR SERGEANTS:
   Abbey, Joe                  11          42       Det., Cr Agst Persons
   Abbott, Gregory             26          45       Communications
   Alexander, Henry            17          38       Org Cr, Vice
   Bailey, Dale                24          46       Patrol, IA*
   Brooks, Lee                 23          44       Det., Fraud & Forgery
   Cantrell, Gary              18          39       Traffic Law Enf
   Davis, Charles              21          45       Jail, Booking Desk
   Fletcher, Richard           12          32       Patrol, IIID
   Gifford, Edward             13          31       Org Cr, Narcotics
   Gordon, Robert              24          44       Parking Enf
   Goss, Nelson                20          41       Patrol, IIIC
   Griffin, Mike               29          53       Property & Evidence
   Koonce, Ralph               14          34       Det., Juvenile
   Lancaster, Donald           15          36       Personnel & Training
   Land, Wm                    12          33       Crime Lab
   Matthews, Bert              15          35       Fleet Operations
   Smith, Albert               30          52       Property & Evidence
   Smith, James                 8          29       Patrol, Relief
   Thomas, Michael             14          32       Records & ID
   Thompson, Scott             10          31       Jail, Booking Desk

   SERGEANTS:
   Alvarez, Manuel             12          33       Patrol, IIIB
   Amos, Guy                   16          42       School Crossg Guards
   Andersen, Robert             7          26       Patrol, ID
   Anderson, Jeffrey            9          29       Det., Cr Agst Property
   Bailey, Kenneth              6          26       Traffic Law Enf
   Baker, Jack                 12          30       Jail, Booking Desk
   Bedford, Russell             8          29       Public Information
   Berger, Paul                 6          27       Org Cr, Vice
   Blanton, George              7          29       Org Cr, Narcotics
   Bowden, Wm                   8          30       Patrol, Relief
   Brandt, Arthur              14          32       Det., Cr Agst Persons
   Breit, Eugene               20          38       Org Cr, Intelligence
```

Name			
Brooks, Edward	7	26	Patrol, IIB
Brown, Raymond	9	32	Patrol, IIA
Cooke, Robert	7	28	Patrol, IB
Davis, John	5	29	Fleet Operations
Feldman, Wm	8	30	Det., Fraud & Forgery
Giles, George	11	32	Det., Cr Agst Property
Greer, Duane	8	28	Patrol, Relief
Hobbs, Jeffrey	6	27	Patrol, IID
James, Lloyd C.	9	31	Community Relations
Jones, Melvin	7	28	Patrol, IIC
Lang, Richard	13	31	Communications
MacIntyre, David	10	31	Det., Cr Agst Persons
Mackey, Anthony	8	29	Org Cr, Vice
McBride, Edward	6	26	Patrol, Relief
McCarty, Ernest	7	30	Communications
Nicholson, Daniel	5	26	Patrol, IC
Overton, James	15	37	Jail, Booking Desk
Ruiz, Carlos	10	31	Personnel & Training
Turner, Richard	7	28	Patrol, IIIA
Sloan, William	8	29	Traffic Law Enf
Stratton, Mike	6	27	Patrol, Relief
Thompson, Paul	8	30	Communications
Wade, Louis	14	32	Records & ID
Williamson, Robert	7	28	Det., Cr Agst Property

(1 position vacant in Detective Bureau, Cr Agst Property Section)

SENIOR PATROL OFFICERS:

Name			
Amberg, Thomas	11	32	Patrol, IIA
Bentley, Scott	6	28	Patrol, IB
Cantu, Juan	8	29	Patrol, IIID
Chambers, Norman	4	25	Traffic Law Enf
Darileck, Jerry	18	36	Patrol, IIB
Goodwin, Thomas	9	28	Patrol, ID
Griffith, Thomas	5	26	Patrol, Relief
Hayes, Oscar	6	27	Patrol, IIIC
Martin, Ted	4	25	Patrol, IC
Rainey, George	22	42	Juvenile

PATROL OFFICERS:

Name			
Aaron, Wm	2	23	Patrol, ID
Abernathy, Glen	4	25	Patrol, IIIA
Anderson, Beth	6	28	Juvenile
Barnett, Gerald	0	21	Patrol, IIID
Barrerra, Ricardo	2	24	Patrol, IID
Berman, Steve	3	23	Patrol, IA
Brown, John	2	23	Traffic Law Enf
Bryant, Howard	0	21	Patrol, IIC
Calderon, Marco	1	22	Patrol, IC
Castaneda, Jesus (Jay)	2	24	Patrol, IIIB
Chadwick, John	1	22	Traffic Law Enf
Chamberlain, Steve	5	27	Patrol, Relief
Chapman, Edwin	2	24	Patrol, IIA
Clark, John	1	22	Patrol, Relief
Davidson, Roland	1	21	Patrol, IID
Devaney, Charles	3	24	Patrol, IB
Edwards, Robert	0	22	Patrol, Relief
Faulkner, Mark	0	21	Traffic Law Enf
Foster, Edward	2	24	Patrol, IA
Fowler, John	5	27	Patrol, IIB
Garrison, Michael	3	24	Patrol, IIIB
Gentry, Richard	4	26	Traffic Law Enf
Gibson, James	2	23	Patrol, Relief
Gilbert, Ted	1	22	Patrol, Relief
Gonzalez, Gloria	0	21	Patrol, IIC
Hall, Gary	0	20	Patrol, IIIA
Hall, Wallace	3	33	Patrol, IIIC
Hill, David	2	22	Patrol, ID
Knox, James	2	23	Patrol, Relief
Lawrence, Michael	0	24	Patrol, Relief

```
Martinez, Hector        4    23    Patrol, IIIC
McPherson, Edward        3    24    Patrol, IC
Nash, Earl               7    28    Patrol, Relief
Reese, Lester           10    32    Traffic Law Enf
Roberts, Joel            2    23    Patrol, IIID
Robinson, Davis          0    21    Patrol, IIC
Rush, George             0    22    Patrol, Relief
Schiller, Arnold         2    24    Patrol, IID
Wallace, Martha          6    32    Juvenile
```

(2 positions vacant in Patrol Bureau, Relief Watch)

Non-Commissioned Personnel

```
SECRETARIES:
Bell, Shirley                       Captain, Technical Svcs
Brannen, Elizabeth                  Chief of Police
Malone, Debra                       Asst Chief


CLERKS:
Ayers, Lorene                       Records & ID
Barnes, Judy
Emerson, Diane
Fleming, Marlene
Lara, Guadalupe
Lyons, Mattie
Scales, Cindy
Torres, Yolanda


Bratton, Donna                      Budget & Acctg
Gates, Laurel
Griffith, Susan
Martinez, Sylvia

DISPATCHERS:
Acevedo, Orelia                     Communications
Allen, Cynthia
Anderson, Louise
Bell, Frank
Chandler, Anthony
Chavez, Maria
Clayton, Sue
DeLeon, Beatriz
Gustafson, Cheryl
Hall, Margaret
Hamilton, Suzanne
Heath, Jill
Morgan, Robert
Mullen, Joe
Potter, Joanne
Robinson, Gladys

JAILERS:
Alvarez, Rafael                     Jail Operations
Barkley, Patrick
Barnes, Michael
Bernard, Mike
Blake, Keith
Blakely, Ralph
Brown, Norman
Campbell, Michael
Campbell, Wm
Ford, Walter
Gonzalez, Leonardo
McGregor, Larry
(4 positions vacant in Jail Operations)
```

```
JAIL MATRONS:
Barker, Annette                          Jail Operations
Camacho, Juanita
Howell, Mary
Lewis, Georgia

CRIME LAB TECHNICIANS:
Dolan, Marvin                            Crime Lab
Gomez, Susan
Pearson, Carl

METER MAIDS:
Alvarado, Lupe                           Parking Enf
Ault, Nancy
Bell, Anne
Driscoll, Peggy
Evans, Bonnie
Herrera, Carmen
Singleton, Tina
Tucker, Mary
```

* Patrol Bureau assignments are shown as I, II, or III Watch and District A, B, C, or D; thus, IIA = Second Watch, District A.

CITY POLICE DEPARTMENT
Interoffice Memorandum

FROM:	D. Lusk, Lt., Personnel
TO:	Chief Abel
SUBJECT: Personnel	DATE: 23 Jan 19--

SIR: Here is the information you requested last week.

	Commissioned	Civilian	Total
Anglo male	114	13	127
Anglo female	2	29	31
Black male	6	3	9
Black female	0	1	1
Hispanic male	7	2	9
Hispanic female	1	10	11
Other ethnic groups	0	0	0
Totals	130	58	188
Vacant positions	3	4	7
Total authorized	133	62	195

D. Lusk, Lt.
Personnel

CITY POLICE DEPARTMENT	
Interoffice Memorandum	
FROM: B. Matthews, Sgt., Fleet Garage	
TO: Chief Abel	
SUBJECT: Fleet Status Report	DATE: 25 Jan 19--

SIR:

Attached is the information you requested. It is a list of all vehicles owned by City PD and their current operating status.

"In svc" means that the vehicle is presently in use, except for minor repair or routine maintenance (2 working days or less). "Out of svc" means that the vehicle is not usable but is being repaired and will be returned to service (2 working days or more). "Wrecked" means not repairable but parts may be salvaged.

Please let me know if you want more information. Thank you.

B. Matthews, Sgt.
Fleet Operations

CITY POLICE DEPARTMENT FLEET STATUS REPORT

UNIT NO.	TYPE VEHICLE	AGE	ASSIGNED TO	STATUS
X-1	4-dr sedan	1 yr	Chief	In service
X-2	4-dr sedan	1 yr	Assistant chief	In service
X-3	4-dr sedan	3 yr	Captain Avery	In service
X-4	4-dr sedan	3 yr	Captain Bowen	In service
X-5	2-dr sedan	6 yr	Captain Edwards	In service
X-6	4-dr sedan	4 yr	Captain Lewis	In service
L-7	4-dr sedan	3 yr	Patrol lieutenants	In service
L-8	4-dr sedan	4 yr	Administrative lieutenants	In service
L-9	2-dr sedan	6 yr	Administrative	Out of service
L-10	4-dr sedan	2 yr	Patrol lieutenants	In service
L-11	2-dr sedan	New	Detective lieutenants	In service
L-12	4-dr sedan	3 yr	Detective lieutenants	In service
L-13	4-dr sedan	5 yr	Detective lieutenants	In service
L-14	4-dr sedan	5 yr	Administrative	Out of service
L-15	2-dr sedan	4 yr	Technical Services	In service
L-16	Station wagon	New	Crime lab	In service
L-17	4-dr sedan	4 yr	Unassigned	Out of service
L-18	2-dr sedan	2 yr	Jail Op. lieutenant	In service
S-19	Station wagon	2 yr	Patrol sergeant	In service
S-20	Squad car	4 yr	Patrol sergeant	In service
S-21	4-dr sedan	3 yr	Detective sergeant	In service
S-22	4-dr sedan	New	Detective sergeant	In service
S-23	2-dr sedan	7 yr	Detective sergeant	In service
S-24	2-dr sedan	6 yr	Detective sergeant	Out of service
S-25	Station wagon	2 yr	Patrol sergeant	In service
S-26	Squad car	3 yr	Patrol sergeant	In service

UNIT NO.	TYPE VEHICLE	AGE	ASSIGNED TO	STATUS
S-27	Squad car	3 yr	Patrol sergeant	In service
S-28	Squad car	3 yr	Patrol sergeant	Wrecked
S-29	Squad car	4 yr	Patrol sergeant	In service
S-30	Squad car	4 yr	Patrol sergeant	In service
S-31	Squad car	4 yr	Patrol sergeant	Out of service
S-32	Squad car	6 yr	Patrol sergeant	In service
S-33	Squad car	?	Vehicle wrecked in collision	
S-34	Squad car	7 yr	Patrol sergeant	In service
S-35	4-dr sedan	5 yr	Detective sergeant	In service
S-36	4-dr sedan	5 yr	Detective sergeant	In service
S-37	4-dr sedan	3 yr	Detective sergeant	In service
S-38	4-dr sedan	3 yr	Org. crime	In service
S-39	2-dr sedan	1 yr	Org. crime	In service
S-40	4-dr sedan	1 yr	Org. crime	In service
S-41	Van	3 yr	Org. crime	In service
S-42	Pickup truck	4 yr	Org. crime	In service
S-43	Convertible	2 yr	Org. crime	Out of service
S-44	4-dr sedan	5 yr	Detective sergeant	In service
S-45	2-dr sedan	5 yr	Detective sergeant	In service
S-46	4-dr sedan	6 yr	Technical services	In service
S-47	4-dr sedan	7 yr	Unassigned	In service
S-48	4-dr sedan	5 yr	Unassigned	In service
S-49	Squad car	2 yr	Traffic sergeant	In service
S-50	Squad car	5 yr	Crime lab	In service
S-51	Squad car	2 yr	Traffic sergeant	Out of service
S-52	Squad car	3 yr	Personnel	In service
S-53	Squad car	3 yr	Unassigned	Out of service
S-54	4-dr sedan	3 yr	Administrative sergeant	In service
S-55	Wrecker truck	8 yr	Fleet garage operations	In service
M-1	Motorcycle (2-wheel)	2 yr	Traffic	In service
M-2	Motorcycle (2-wheel)	2 yr	Traffic	In service
M-3	Motorcycle (2-wheel)	2 yr	Traffic	Out of service
M-4	Motorcycle (3-wheel)	4 yr	Parking	In service
M-5	Motorcycle (3-wheel)	5 yr	Parking	In service
A-1	Squad car	New	Patrol A	In service
A-2	Squad car	New	Patrol A	In service
B-6	Squad car	1 yr	Patrol B	In service
B-7	Squad car	New	Patrol B	In service
C-11	Squad car	1 yr	Patrol C	In service
C-12	Squad car	2 yr	Patrol C	In service
C-13	Squad car	2 yr	Vehicle wrecked in collision	
D-21	Squad car	2 yr	Patrol D	In service
D-22	Squad car	2 yr	Patrol D	In service
D-23	Squad car	2 yr	Patrol D	In service
A-31	Squad car	3 yr	Patrol relief watch	In service
A-32	Squad car	3 yr	Unassigned	In service
A-33	Squad car	3 yr	Patrol C	In service
A-34	Squad car	3 yr	Unassigned	Out of service
A-35	Squad car	4 yr	Unassigned	In service
J-10	Armored van	8 yr	Jail	In service
J-12	Armored bus	10 yr	Jail	In service
W-2	Wrecker truck	7 yr	Fleet garage operations	In service

END OF REPORT

PART ONE
PRINCIPLES OF ADMINISTRATION

1 A BRIEF HISTORY OF POLICE AGENCIES

ANY ORGANIZATION, REGARDLESS OF ITS PURPOSE OR SIZE, must have a certain minimum amount of structure in order to carry out its task successfully. It does not matter whether the task is simple or complicated, or whether the organization consists of two people or twenty thousand—except that the more complicated the task and the more people who must cooperate in order to get the job done, the more elaborate the organization is likely to be.

Consider, for example, a simple, routine task that you can accomplish entirely by yourself: preparing a meal. First you must decide what to eat, and then you must gather the various foods you will need. Next you must decide how to prepare the foods—whether to boil, fry, bake, or otherwise process it, or simply to eat it in its present state. Your choice of the manner of preparation also may influence the resources you will need: If you decide to fry some meat, for example, you will need a frying pan, perhaps some cooking oil, and a stove or other source of concentrated heat. Then you must actually perform the work of preparing the meal. If several steps are involved, you must coordinate them so that all the foods are properly cooked and everything is ready at the same time.

In this simple example, you will have performed each of the major functions involved in any large, complex organization, such as a business corporation, government bureaucracy, or—the kind of organization we will discuss in this book—a police agency. These major functions can be defined as follows:

1. **Goal definition and policy setting.** The choice of what foods to prepare and how to prepare them.
2. **Resource acquisition and allocation.** The gathering of the foods you have chosen and the decision to use such resources as cooking oil, the stove, and so on.
3. **Task assignment.** The decision to perform some steps on the stove and others on the table or counter, and the decisions made as to the order in which various steps must be taken.
4. **Task performance.** The actual work of preparing the meal.
5. **Evaluation and modification.** Checking to see that the various steps are being carried out properly and making adjustments to correct any errors or deficiencies.

Routine, everyday household tasks are so much a part of our commonplace experience that they are performed largely out of habit, without thinking in terms of a series of specialized functions. But when several people must work together to carry out a task that is too big or complicated for one person to do alone, such an analysis is necessary. It is the only way to ensure that each person knows what to do and how to do it, and that each person has the necessary resources to carry out his or her tasks.

When people work together in more or less permanent cooperative organizations, these same functions must be performed regularly. In theory, each member of an organization could perform every function independently of the others, but centuries of human experience have demonstrated that greater **efficiency** (accomplishing the most work with the smallest possible expenditure of resources, including human effort) can be obtained if the various functions are divided among the people in the organization. Such specialization permits each individual to do what he or she does best, using native talents, training, and experience to best advantage.

However, there are many different ways that the five basic functions listed earlier can be divided among a group of people. The study of the different ways to divide and distribute these functions is the science of management.

For example, one person could act as a solitary leader, carrying out all of the functions except task performance; the rest of the group could be assigned to perform the various tasks but have no role in making decisions. This is not an unusual arrangement in small groups with limited, well-defined tasks. A basketball team consists of five players (who perform the "tasks" of playing the game) and a single coach or manager (who performs all other functions).

The most common arrangement in any reasonably large and complicated task involving a number of people over a long period of time is the system that has evolved in business corporations, which we call the **corporate model** (although, actually, it can be traced back to earlier military, governmental, and religious organizations). In the corporate model, the five basic functions are allocated as follows:

Administration (sometimes called executive level or upper-level management)
1. Goal definition and policy setting
2. Resource acquisition and allocation

Midlevel Management
3. Task assignment (with some responsibility for evaluation and modification)

Supervisors
4. Evaluation and modification (with some responsibility for task assignment)

Operating Personnel
5. Task performance

This four-level structure is a greatly simplified representation of what actually takes place in any corporate organization. In some organizations, portions of the responsibility for a given function may be assigned to two or more different levels of the structure. Midlevel managers and supervisors also have the additional function of serving as *communication channels*, transmitting the goals and policies of the administrative level to the operational level (so that the latter will know what to do and how to do it) and, simultaneously, transmitting information about the work that has been accomplished from the operational level to the administrators (so that they will know how well their goals are being achieved, how well policies are being applied, and what additional resources may be needed). In very large, complex organizations, this communications function can so overwhelm the five basic functions that everyone is busy shuttling information back and forth, and little real work is ever done. On the other hand, if the communications function is neglected, the administrators will not know the results of their goals and policies while the operational personnel will be confused and uncertain about what they are supposed to do.

In modern police agencies, we can see the corporate model at work. The administrative level is occupied by the chief of police or agency head, who may have several deputies or assistants to help carry out the administrative functions. The middle management level is occupied by the heads of the various major elements of the agency, often called bureaus or divisions; these personnel usually hold the rank of major or captain. The supervisory role is carried out by lieutenants and sergeants, each of whom has a specific responsibility to supervise a given type of work or group of operating personnel. Finally, the operational personnel are the patrol officers, sometimes sergeants (if they have no supervisory duties), and civilian clerks, secretaries, laboratory technicians, jailers, and so on.

In Chapter 2, we will discuss in more detail the different responsibilities and functions of each level of the corporate model, and we will describe some variations that are found in police agencies. For now, our point is that this basic structure is nearly universal, not only in police agencies, but in almost every permanent form of organization: supermarkets, universities, executive departments of government, multinational corporations, even the so-called cooperative factories in Communist nations.

The primary value of this model is that it gives us a tool to analyze any type of organization and to understand how the organization is functioning—or, perhaps, why it is not functioning well. The corporate model was not discovered as a fact of nature, nor was it invented overnight. It has evolved over many centuries in response to changes in human needs and the social environment. Police agencies have developed their own distinctive versions of the corporate model only in the past century and, in many cases, the process of development has been painful. It is still going on, and probably will continue to do so for the foreseeable future.

Before we can begin to analyze the management of modern police agencies, we need to gain a better understanding of current practices by reviewing a little history.

THE EVOLUTION OF THE AMERICAN POLICE SERVICE

Just as our laws are derived from British legal traditions, our concept of criminal law and of the police service is based on British history and culture. In most of the world, there is no clear distinction between the police function and the military function; the police operate as merely a local or specialized branch of the military. But in medieval England, for a variety of historical reasons, the idea arose of a community peace-keeping function entirely separate from the military function.

After the Norman invasion of England in 1066 AD, many villages had a **shire reeve**, or head man, appointed by the local noble to maintain order and settle disputes. The Normans, under their king, William the Conqueror, reinforced and broadened the shire reeve's authority. He was not only the local police officer, but also something like a modern justice of the peace. Later, as a growing population crowded into the cities, a **bailiff** was appointed to keep track of the citizens and to discourage outsiders from causing trouble, and a **sergeans** was appointed to guard the city's gates. In rural villages, the local noble's army enforced the laws under the direction of the shire reeve. Whenever the troops went out on patrol, the stable keeper, or **constable**, was left in charge.

Each of these ancient positions had limited law enforcement responsibilities that were gradually expanded and refined over the centuries. The duty of the shire reeve became the basis for the modern **sheriff** (a position that no longer exists in England but that was adopted in this country); the bailiff became attached directly to the local courts, as a keeper of the peace, jailer, or marshal; the role of the sergeans was assumed by **watchmen** while the title was absorbed into the military in its modern form, *sergeant*. The constable continued to function as an important law enforcement officer in small villages.

When British colonies were established in North America, they were governed primarily by the military. After the American Revolution, bitter memories of military oppression left the public mistrustful of any sort of permanent law enforcement agency. This distrust is clearly reflected in the Bill of Rights, 5 of whose 10 major sections (the Fourth, Fifth, Sixth, Eighth, and Tenth Amendments to the Constitution) were designed specifically to limit the police powers of the federal government. The Fourteenth Amendment, adopted in 1868, extended those limitations to the states.

For many years after the Revolution, the police function simply did not exist. When a crime was committed, the victim's family or neighbors would attempt to find the criminal and bring him or her to court. In some of the larger cities, merchants organized a night watch, either rotating guard duty among themselves or hiring night watchmen. After the War of 1812, the practice of hiring a night watch became quite common in the larger cities. There was no central administration of the watchmen, who were often transients looking for a few days' (or nights') easy work. They had no police authority. On the other hand, if they shot or beat a presumed thief, no one objected.

Both day and night watches were established by the city governments in New York, Boston, Philadelphia, and a few other large cities about 1820. There still was no central administration. However, by the mid-1820s, true police agencies began to develop. In the southern cities—Baltimore, Richmond, Atlanta, and several others—troops of police were organized mostly to capture runaway slaves.[1] In the northern cities, police troops were established to deal with the frequent riots that had begun to occur as a result of massive immigration and the rapid concentration of unskilled labor in the new factories.[2] In either case, the police did not function as individual patrol officers. They were not uniformed, they carried weapons only while they were under the immediate supervision of their commanders, and their principal function was to maintain order by brute force. Apprehending violators of the law was simply not part of their job. A few cities, notably Philadelphia and Washington, D.C., established separate detective agencies in the 1840s to carry out the law enforcement function.[3]

By 1850, the urban police function had begun to undergo several crucial changes. An officer was required to wear a uniform and was allowed to carry weapons.[4] More important, in a few cities the police began to operate in patrols, taking over the function of the old day and night watches. For the first time, the police were given the duty of preventing crime by their mere physical presence wherever crimes were thought likely to occur.

The use of police patrols necessarily meant the decentralization of the police. Previously, the police troops remained at a central headquarters until they were called out to chase a runaway slave or to suppress a riot. This kind of centralization was impractical if patrol officers were to cover an entire city. Instead, several subheadquarters were established, one in each district or **precinct** of the city. Patrol officers reported to their precinct headquarters at the beginning and end of each day's work, or **watch**. In some cities, reserve troops were also stationed in each precinct headquarters. An officer's working day might include eight hours on patrol plus another six or eight hours at precinct headquarters, on reserve.

At the end of the Civil War, this decentralized structure was the standard pattern in all urban police agencies. In smaller towns, the police function might be carried out by a town marshal or constable (the former usually appointed, the latter usually elected). In rural areas, law enforcement was the responsibility of the sheriff, an elected official. There were no state or federal police agencies, although the Treasury Department formed a Secret Service during the Civil War to suppress counterfeiting.

The urban police agencies usually were organized under a police chief, appointed by the city's elected officials, or under a police commission, a supervisory board elected by the public. In theory, the chief or the commission held authority over the entire agency. In fact, however, the precinct captains held all effective power. Orders and policies issued by the chief or commission could be, and often were, simply ignored by the precinct captains. The captains hired, promoted, and fired their own personnel, assigned them to their beats, and provided all supervision.

During the 1870s, police work was a very low-status occupation. Officers were poorly paid and given no training; there were no pensions, paid holidays, or other benefits. The work was tedious and sometimes dangerous, and the hours were incredibly long. The public generally held the police in low esteem. Consequently, the job was attractive only to men who could find no other work, and that usually meant large numbers of recent immigrants. For most of them, policing was a temporary occupation until they could find something better. For others, it was a relatively undemanding, but also not very promising, way to earn a meager living.

The precinct captains themselves came under the influence of local politicians. Political parties in the larger cities were organized geographically into **wards** that had boundaries similar to those of the precincts. Each ward had its **ward boss**, a functionary whose job was to ensure that the party's candidates won every local election. One way to reward loyal party followers was to secure them, or their unemployable relatives, government jobs—and the most plentiful jobs were in the police force. Thus, the precinct captains relied on the ward bosses to supply them with manpower. If the party in power lost an election, the new administration typically fired the entire police force and installed its own followers.[5]

During this same period, America underwent one of its periodic waves of moral crusading. Church leaders and idealistic reformers were determined to improve the social conditions in the cities, which were, to be sure, much in need of improvement. To achieve their objectives, the reformers pressured state legislatures and local governments to prohibit what the reformers considered immoral social behavior. Hundreds of laws were passed to forbid such vices as gambling, prostitution, public drunkenness, conducting business on Sundays, vagrancy, loitering, begging, selling liquor to minors, and so forth. The police were charged with the responsibility of enforcing all these new laws.

But the police were completely incompetent to handle such a major expansion of their duties. They had had little enough success in dealing with serious crimes. At best, the police were able to prevent some property crimes and public disorders merely by their presence on the streets. Major crimes against persons, such as murders, usually were solved only if the perpetrator's identity was widely known. Such crimes as rape, assault, and kidnapping were simply regarded as "not police problems" but as private matters to be settled by the victims' families.

Before long, the police found a way to accommodate their new duties. Moral offenses were not a serious problem in the rural areas and upper-class neighborhoods, where social pressure was a far more effective force than the law (as it is to this day). In the lower-class and working-class neighborhoods where police patrols were concentrated, and where the ward bosses had their greatest power, the public was not enthusiastic about the moralistic laws anyway. Their own life-styles and ethnic cultures were much more tolerant of so-called vices than was the strict Protestant culture of the upper-middle and upper classes. Thus the new vice laws created a golden opportunity for the police. Instead of arresting prostitutes, gamblers, and other vice offenders, the police readily accepted bribes from them. In effect, the police wound up "licensing" crime rather than suppressing it. Offenders (as defined by the laws) were allowed to operate as long as they paid tribute to the police and avoided flagrant scandal. An offender who crossed the police, of course, could expect to be arrested at once.

This system fit well with the prevailing political structure. The ward bosses decided which criminals would be allowed to operate, depending on their party loyalties, and distributed bribes to the police, judges, and any other officials whose tolerance was required. By the mid-1870s, many police officers, from patrolmen to precinct captains—and even a few police chiefs—received two or three times their annual salaries in bribes.[6]

The First Reform Effort

The church leaders and other reformers did not fail to notice the extent of police corruption that their moralistic laws had produced. Their response, beginning in the 1880s, was to demand improvements in the police force. At first, they tried to institute modest reforms such as centralized selection of police recruits and promotions on the basis of competitive testing. However, these measures were easily thwarted; the ward bosses and precinct captains simply gave favored candidates a copy of the test, or otherwise helped them to cheat. In some cities, patrolmen's jobs were obtained not by competitive examination but by paying a fixed fee to the precinct captain.[7]

The reform crusaders stepped up their efforts, calling on state legislatures to deal with the urban corruption. In New York, the legislature formed an investigative committee chaired by State Senator Clarence Lexow, in 1894. The committee compiled massive evidence of police abuses, corruption, and crime. However, no specific remedies emerged from the legislature.

At about the same time, a handful of reform-minded individuals appeared within the ranks of police agencies. Allan Pinkerton, who is best remembered as the founder of the Pinkerton Detective Agency, served briefly as chief of the Chicago Police Department and tried to establish the idea that policing should be an honest occupation for talented individuals of unblemished integrity—in short, that it should be a profession. Pinkerton's ideas were not very successful in Chicago, but his concept of professionalism was attractive to other reform-minded police administrators.

Several hundred police administrators joined forces in the National Police Chiefs Union in 1893, which became the International Association of Chiefs of Police (IACP) in 1901. This organization served as the forum and training ground for the slow but steady growth of the concept of police professionalism.[8] Although different reformers held different ideas about police professionalism, the most widely shared definition included these elements:

1. Law enforcement is an honorable occupation that serves a vital need in society; without effective policing, a society is doomed to anarchy.
2. Police officers must be carefully selected persons of great integrity, talent, and trained ability; in order to attract and retain such people, salaries and other benefits must be sufficiently high, and applicants must be evaluated on an objective, competitive basis.
3. The primary responsibility of the police is to prevent crime through techniques such as patrol; when prevention fails, the police have an obligation to enforce the law by apprehending the offender, using any scientific or other aids or methods available.
4. Corruption or graft within the police ranks is intolerable.
5. All citizens must be treated with respect and due regard for their constitutional rights; there must be no hint of favoritism or discrimination by the police; anyone who commits a crime, however minor, must be subject to the penalties provided by law.

This concept of professionalism was very appealing to the upper-middle- and upper-class citizens who supported the era of moral reform. New laws were passed, increasing salaries and benefits for the police, requiring competitive testing for new recruits and for promotions, and placing greater administrative powers in the hands of police chiefs and commissions.

The most difficult task, however, was to remove the police from the control of the ward bosses. One after another, the reform-minded police chiefs faced immovable obstacles and either resigned in frustration or were fired for their ineffectiveness. The power of the ward bosses could not be swept away merely by issuing orders. The precinct captains and their favored subordinates were not at all inclined to accept the reforms that could cost them their supplementary incomes and privileges—or even their jobs. For their own protection, they formed "associations" that were not quite unions, but that served most of the same functions as unions.

Among the reform-minded police chiefs or commissioners whose efforts met with all-out resistance and eventual failure were Theodore Roosevelt, who was briefly commissioner of the New York City Police Department, and August K. Vollmer, who served at various times as chief of the Los

Angeles, Berkeley, and Oakland police departments before withdrawing to the sanctuary of a professorship at the University of California at Berkeley. However, Vollmer did not abandon the cause; as professor of criminology, he taught an entire generation of young men and women, many of whom became leaders in the long struggle for police reform.

Although police reform was unpopular among the rank-and-file police officers, it was spectacularly popular with the general public. Even among the immigrants, ethnic minorities, and working-class people who generally provided the base of support for the corrupt political machines, the idea of a well-trained, competent, nonpartisan police force was most appealing. Thus the reform campaign, despite its many setbacks, continued through the end of the nineteenth century and the beginning of the twentieth.

Outside of the major cities, criminal law enforcement remained largely in the hands of county sheriffs, constables, and village marshals. These officials were generally elected by the public for two-year terms or were appointed by local officials (and thus served only as long as the appointing officials did). Their success in winning and holding office had little to do with police professionalism and, in fact, they were not generally effective in carrying out their law enforcement duties.

At the federal level, the desire for more effective criminal law enforcement led to the establishment of the Bureau of Investigation in the Justice Department in 1908. At first the Bureau was given no real police authority; its job was to conduct investigations for the Justice Department's lawyers. Soon the agency was dominated by partisan politicians who subverted it into a corrupt secret police agency. In 1924, President Calvin Coolidge appointed a young Washington lawyer, J. Edgar Hoover, to take over and reorganize the discredited Bureau. Hoover drew heavily on the support of reform-minded, politically influential citizens in transforming the Bureau into a crime-fighting agency that relied on the latest scientific aids to investigation and a carefully maintained reputation for integrity. He had little success in promoting similar reforms in major urban police departments.

The Second Generation of Reform

At the end of the 1920s, the status of the urban police in America was not much better than it had been at the turn of the century. However, the reformers had accomplished more than they may have realized: They had trained a whole new generation of young men who became the reform leaders of the 1930s and beyond. Among them were Lewis J. Valentine, Fred Kohler, Orlando W. Wilson, Herbert T. Jenkins, Eliot Ness, Virgil W. Peterson, Quinn Tamm, Franklin M. Kreml, William H. Parker, Clarence M. Kelly, Patrick V. Murphy, and A. C. Germann, several of whom are still active in police administration or in teaching police science.[9]

The young reformers, most of whom were college graduates, rose through the police ranks quickly or were appointed directly to upper-level administrative positions. By 1935, many of them were in a position to bring about the reforms they and their teachers had advocated.

The agenda of the second-generation reformers was not very different from the concept of police professionalism that had originated before the turn of the century. The young reformers sought absolute independence and freedom from political interference, and they called for a drastic upgrading of the quality of police personnel through better salaries and benefits, objective and competitive testing, and more thorough training. They believed that the traditional precinct headquarters must be abolished; in its place they would have specialized crime-fighting units, operating from a central headquarters, using scientific methods to attack specific types of crime. They also wanted to free the police from the distracting burden of various non-law-enforcement duties, such as issuing taxicab licenses or inspecting boilers, that had accumulated over the years.

There is a popular impression that the 1930s, the decade of the Great Depression and of Prohibition, was an era of total lawlessness in which America's cities were turned into playgrounds for ruthless gangsters. In fact, of course, the condition of the cities was never quite as desperate and dramatic as Hollywood movies and television programs have portrayed it. However, Prohibition did give organized crime a golden opportunity to reach new pinnacles of wealth and corruption; at the same time, public attention was focussed on crime as never before. One result was a rapid increase in public support for more effective law enforcement. The reformers capitalized on this shift in public attitudes, forcing politicians to adopt large parts of the reform agenda and insulating the police from political influence.

The reformers also were largely successful in upgrading the quality of police personnel through better recruitment, selection, and training methods. Unfortunately, these measures had an unanticipated consequence. The "objective" standards and tests inadvertently favored the dominant ethnic group at the expense of blacks, Southern Europeans, and Hispanics. The descendants of earlier immigrant families, especially the Irish and Germans, gained a virtual monopoly on policing and were able to maintain their grip through such devices as civil service procedures and pension benefits (which strongly favored those who remained in law enforcement for 20 or 30 years). Ultimately, the idea of police professionalism was co-opted by the pseudounions, such as the Patrolmen's Benevolent Association and the Fraternal Order of Police, and was used to protect the police from truly objective outside scrutiny.

The use of specialized crime-fighting units to centralize police authority also backfired. The first such specialized units were vice squads, answerable only to the police chief or commissioner and given citywide authority to combat vice. In many cities, the vice squads adopted the same crime-licensing tactics of the old precincts. Several reformist leaders were badly embarrassed, and hounded out of office, when their highly touted vice squads proved to be hopelessly corrupt. Nevertheless, the use of specialized squads continued and became a central feature of police agency organization. Nearly every category of crime was represented by a special unit: homicide, sexual assault, burglary, robbery, theft, fraud, and so on. The larger the agency, the more specialized the units became.

As specific crime-fighting duties were taken away from the general patrol force, few new responsibilities were added. By far the most important exception is the responsibility for traffic law enforcement, which was given to the patrol force in the 1920s and became an overwhelming burden in the 1930s. However, with the exception of traffic enforcement, the patrol force had little to do other than to patrol their beats, presumably to prevent crime. By 1940, the increasingly widespread use of motorized patrols and two-way radios—both of which were supposed to make patrol officers more responsive and effective—actually further reduced their effectiveness. Previously, patrol officers on foot were expected to be continually alert to any suspicious activities or signs of crime and were supposed to be familiar with the people in the neighborhoods they patrolled. But the patrol officers cruising in squad cars were assigned a much larger territory, had almost no contact with the people in the patrol area, and had little opportunity to observe potentially suspicious activities. Instead, motorized patrol officers were reduced to receiving complaints (relayed by radio), interviewing complainants, and passing along reports to the detectives. In general, patrol officers were neither expected nor encouraged to do anything more, such as investigate the crimes that occurred in their patrol areas.

Another of the reformers' goals, the elimination of the precinct stations, was rarely achieved. There is a persistent public notion that the local police station contributes to a neighborhood's safety. The precinct captains and their supporters were able to muster public sentiment in favor of keeping most of the precinct stations open. However, the decline of the ward bosses' power and the increasing availability of modern communications such as the telephone gave the central administrators considerably better control over the precinct captains.

Another goal, the elimination of non-law-enforcement duties, met with only marginal success. In many cities, the police had been assigned dozens of non-law-enforcement tasks, and some of the earlier reformers had brought these burdens on themselves by arguing that the police had a larger role in society than merely catching criminals. Some of the reformers had sought to act directly on social problems that are associated with crime, such as unemployment, poor housing, alcoholism, and broken families. A few police agencies went so far as to provide temporary housing for unemployed workers, to distribute food and clothing to the poor, and even to operate job-placement agencies. In the 1930s and afterward, the second-generation reformers argued that these activities interfered with the real function of the police. Unfortunately, for every non-law-enforcement duty the police were able to turn over to some other agency, or drop altogether, they seemed to gain at least two more. Traffic control, which is only peripherally a matter of criminal law enforcement, has become firmly fixed in the minds of the public—and of the police themselves—as a major police responsibility. Juvenile delinquency prevention programs, the organization of marching bands and parade drill units, licensing of pets and bicycles, licensing and inspection of taxicabs and their drivers, and dozens of other miscellaneous duties are still borne by many police agencies.

Another aim of the reformers, to instill a sense of military pride and discipline in the patrol force, proved to be utterly futile. Even when military-style ranks were adopted and recruits were trained in close-order drill and other militaristic rituals, the essentially nonmilitary nature of the American police undermined the reformers' efforts. To this day, many police authorities regard police service as **paramilitary**, but in fact there is only the slightest similarity between modern police service and the military.

When World War II ended, many thousands of young men came home to find that there were not enough civilian jobs to go around. However, their military experience was welcomed by the police agencies, which were undergoing rapid expansion to catch up to the population growth. The influx of new recruits, used to military-style discipline and imbued with a strong sense of patriotism, greatly strengthened the power of the reform-minded administrators. The recruits, after all, bore little loyalty for the old political machines and their corruption. The young officers often responded enthusiastically to the call for professionalism and dedication to public service.

Thus the reform movement gained momentum during the postwar years. The concept of police professionalism gradually trickled down from the colleges and urban police departments to the smaller agencies. Journal articles and books by several of the reform leaders set out the doctrines of police professionalism, and their ideas were adopted as standards for police practice. There were still glaring setbacks. The police in Chicago, New York City, Detroit, San Francisco, Houston, New Orleans, Pittsburgh, and Los Angeles all suffered the embarrassment of scandal from time to time.

Still, by the early 1960s most Americans regarded their local police departments more favorably and held their police officers in higher esteem than ever before. Graft, corruption, and the abuse of power were considered exceptions to the rule, the "rotten apple in the barrel," as Los Angeles Chief William Parker liked to put it. For the young men who had entered police service just after World War II, the 1950s represented a golden age of policing, a period of domestic tranquility during which it was easy to be proud of one's badge and uniform.

But that peace was soon to be shattered. In the southern states, the black civil rights movements strained the existing social order to the bursting point. The police were caught between the demand for order (which was commonly interpreted to mean keeping the blacks in their segregated place) and the demand for law, as defined by government functionaries and judges in far-off Washington. The cause of professional law enforcement was not helped by news reports, sometimes televised, of police officers using cattle prods, attack dogs, and fire hoses against demonstrators. By the mid-1960s, demonstrations were widespread in the south and the north, east and west, on college campuses and in ghetto streets, for civil rights and against the war in Viet Nam. Most of the demonstrations were peaceful from beginning to end, and the police in most cases performed admirably under trying circumstances. But the exceptions—the demonstrations that turned into riots, the police who responded violently to provocation—were shocking and bewildering to the general public.

The bloody decade brought into question the entire idea of police professionalism. To some observers it seemed that the police had gained status by aligning themselves with an oppressive, elite "establishment" whose sole purpose was to protect its privileges at the expense of blacks and young people. At a time when the cry for social reform was ringing in the air, the police found themselves in the position of guardians of the existing social order, whether or not they personally supported it (which, in fact, they most often did). From the police point of view, the civil rights and antiwar protestors were radical troublemakers intent on subverting social order. The protestors' deliberate use of provocative rhetoric and occasional terrorist violence reinforced the fears of the police that they were, indeed, the last line of defense before Armageddon.

Presidents Johnson and Nixon appointed one high-level commission after another to examine the root causes of the riots and disorders. One after another, the commissions concluded that the police were more a part of the problem than a part of the solution. The more thoughtful police officials were simply bewildered; rank-and-file officers felt betrayed, defensive, and increasingly embittered. The society they had sworn to protect seemed to be turning against them.

The final casualty of the 1960s was the police reform movement. The demand for community control of the police, heard in most of the larger cities, sounded dangerously like a reversion to the days of corruption and local political interference. The demand for safeguards against police brutality and abuses of police power—demands that were echoed by the Supreme Court in a series of decisions, most notably the *Gideon*, *Escobedo*, and *Miranda* decisions—seemed to hamstring the police, preventing them from discharging their most vital function, the war against crime. The demand for relaxed entry standards, to enable more blacks and other minorities to enter the police service, seemed to undermine the century-long struggle to upgrade the quality of police personnel. The most crucial gains won in some eight decades of the struggle for reform seemed to be swept aside. Even the champions of the second-generation reformers—Patrick Murphy, O. W. Wilson, Clarence Kelly, J. Edgar Hoover, William Parker, and others—were ignored, discredited, or hustled into the limbo of retirement.

For a brief while, at the beginning of the 1970s, the police star seemed to shine again. President Nixon called for a resurgence of "law and order," a new war against "crime in the streets." In 1968, Congress passed the Omnibus Crime Control and Safe Streets Act, the first major federal effort to support local law enforcement. Among other things, the act created the Law Enforcement Assistance Administration and allotted millions of dollars to bolster local police budgets and to carry forward the drive toward professionalism. But Nixon's call for law and order took on ironic overtones as his own administration was torn apart by scandal and he finally resigned in disgrace in 1974.

America seemed to pause to catch its breath after the turbulent 1960s and the Watergate scandals. During the rest of the 1970s, the police experienced no further cataclysmic changes either in the society they attempted to serve or in their own ranks. The demand for community control of the police, and other radical measures, quickly subsided. The police learned to live with the Supreme Court decisions and new laws that, at first, seemed to devastate their ability to fight crime. The Law Enforcement Assistance Administration doled out its grants, enabling the police to modernize its equipment and try out new ideas.

Some of the new ideas made little headway. For example, several communities experimented with nonmilitary uniforms that featured sports jackets and pocket patches in place of the traditional military-style jacket and metal badge. Other new ideas were essentially refinements of traditional practices, such as the formation of specially trained tactical squads and Special Weapons and Tactics (SWAT) units to respond to crises. A few new ideas, such as patrol-oriented investigation and team policing, required extensive changes in police organization and techniques; these were, of course, the ideas that were adopted most slowly.

In retrospect, the American concept of the police function can be seen as an outgrowth of the English traditions of criminal law enforcement, but adapted to the unique circumstances of our own history. The American police service began in the early nineteenth century as a crime prevention service, to which various law enforcement and non-law-enforcement functions were added over the years. The system broke down in the late nineteenth century because of political interference and corruption. Since then, the police service has undergone a century-long struggle to achieve respectability, competence, independence, and effectiveness. As historian Samuel Walker remarks:

The history of the police . . . becomes intelligible when we think of it in terms of its halting progress along the scale of professionalism.[10]

The concept of professionalism has been the organizing principle throughout the successive periods of police reform. Yet, as Robert Fogelson points out:

The [professional] model was so vague, its meaning susceptible to so many different interpretations, that it united law enforcement figures who were divided on just about everything else.[11]

Thus, professionalism has been the rallying cry, but it could not serve as a yardstick for reform efforts because it is a yardstick of unknown length. There never has been a clear sense of what a truly professional police force would look like, or of what the police must do to become fully professional. When examined too closely, the whole idea of professionalism seems to disappear; it is a thin tissue of generalized goals and contradictory notions.

One of the basic principles of the corporate model that we mentioned earlier is that an organization's goals must be completely clear. Otherwise, neither the administrator nor the operating personnel can know whether the goals are being achieved. Therefore, before we proceed any further to discuss how a police agency should be managed, we should stop to consider just what it is supposed to do.

THE POLICE ROLE TODAY

If you were asked to define the function of a law enforcement agency, you probably would answer that its function is to enforce the laws. But it is not that simple; two more questions would quickly follow: Which laws? and What do you mean by "enforce"?

The Concept of Law Enforcement

A crime is a violation of a law. Any legislative body—the Congress, state legislature, city council or, in some states, county commission—may enact any law (so long as it does not conflict with the Constitution) and, in so doing, may designate any violation of the law as a crime. There are perhaps 20,000 or 30,000 different laws at the federal, state, and local levels in the United States that define crimes.

Any sort of human behavior can be designated as a crime. The deliberate taking of a human life (murder) is a crime everywhere in this country, except under certain circumstances defined in the law. The taking of property without the owner's permission may or may not be a crime, depending on the nature of the property, the circumstances under which it was taken, and the relationship (if any) between the taker and the owner. At one time, it was a crime in Boston to bathe without a doctor's prescription.[12]

There are also many laws that do not concern crimes. They involve relationships between private individuals, or the internal workings of government. In general, the police have no responsibility nor authority with regard to noncriminal laws. Therefore, our first answer (not necessarily our final answer) to the question Which laws? might be, "All criminal laws that have been enacted by the appropriate legislature and that are valid under the Constitution."

The enforcement of the laws—including criminal laws—is the duty of every citizen, not just of the police. The concept of democratic self-government is based on the belief that people who participate in making the laws, directly or indirectly, will be more inclined to obey them and to report violations to the proper authorities. Unfortunately, it is difficult and sometimes dangerous for the average citizen to play an active part in law enforcement. Therefore, the duty of enforcing certain laws is partly assigned to a particular group of people—the police—and they are given the authority to act on behalf of the entire citizenry. However, it is not always very clear exactly what authority the police may have and what methods they are allowed to use to discharge that authority.

"Enforcing the law" means, at a minimum, that all citizens are required to obey all laws, and that anyone who fails to obey a law is subject to some form of punishment. Our society takes rather elaborate precautions to ensure that punishment is given only to those who in fact have violated a law. Thus, a person accused of a violation is entitled to answer the accusation in a public forum, and the burden of proving the accusation is placed on the accuser. In all criminal cases, the state (that is, the government) acts as the accuser.

The first step in enforcing the law is to identify those persons who are thought to have committed violations. Next, evidence must be gathered to prove that the accused person is guilty. The accused and the evidence must be brought to the public forum, or court, and the accused must have every opportunity to answer the accusation. Either a judge trained in the law or a jury of citizens must decide that the accused is actually guilty; then and only then may punishment be decided.

Only some of the steps in this process have been assigned to the police: the identification of violators, the gathering of evidence, and the presentation of the accused in court. The rest of the process is left to other parts of government: an attorney representing the state, and the court; if the violator is found guilty and punishment is set, another part of government, the corrections system, is responsible for seeing that the punishment is carried out.

Thus, our initial answer to the question What do you mean by "enforce"? is, *to identify and apprehend accused violators, to gather evidence of the violation, and to present both the accused and the evidence to a court.*

However, as our review of police history suggests, this is not the only function of the police. In fact, "enforcing the law" might not be the most important function of a law enforcement agency.

The Concept of Police Service

Law enforcement, as we have just defined it, is a complex task that requires the expenditure of a good deal of time and energy that might be saved if people could be prevented from committing crimes in the first place. If we knew in advance which individuals were going to commit crimes, or where crimes were going to be committed, it would be a simple matter to restrain the prospective violators. Actually, this was the first duty assigned to the police and their predecessors, the watchmen: to prevent violators from committing offenses by physically restraining them.

Unfortunately, in today's very complex society, it is nearly impossible to identify prospective criminals in advance, and it is not practical to station guards at every place where crimes might occur. Prospective criminals cannot be identified in advance because they are not clearly different from other citizens; *any* citizen might commit a crime. Actually, only a tiny percentage of the total population (about 1 or 2 percent) commit serious crimes, and even these individuals devote only a small part of their lives to criminal behavior. It simply makes no sense to impose severe restraints on all citizens merely to keep a handful from committing crimes.

Of course, those who do commit crimes go to some effort to keep from being identified as violators. The presence of a guard at a particular place may prevent a crime from taking place there, but does not necessarily prevent a crime from taking place somewhere else. Thus, the most that can be accomplished by stationing guards is to protect the places that would be most tempting to prospective criminals, such as places where valuable goods are stored.

As you can see, then, perfect crime prevention is not possible. Prospective violators cannot be distinguished from ordinary citizens, and all the places where crimes might occur cannot be guarded.

Logically, if the police were perfectly successful in preventing crimes, there would be no need for law enforcement. Even if the police were imperfectly successful but managed to prevent almost all crimes, the enforcement function could be reduced to a minimal level. But the fact is that police crime-prevention efforts have had only a marginal effect on the incidence of crime; greater and greater resources have had to be devoted to law enforcement. In this sense, *enforcement always represents the failure of prevention*. However, this does not mean that the police are always at fault, even though they usually get the blame. Not only is perfect prevention inherently impossible, but the police do not have complete control over the resources that they are able to apply to this task.

It is important to remember that law enforcement and crime prevention are two separate, distinct functions. They are often confused in the minds of the public, and even in the minds of the police. This confusion is compounded when people argue that law enforcement contributes to prevention by discouraging potential violators. The argument may be correct, but it is somewhat irrelevant; preventing crime is preventing crime, and enforcing the law is enforcing the law. These are two separate functions that must be discharged in very different ways.

Law enforcement and crime prevention are not the only functions assigned to the police. A third function is the source of endless trouble: the maintenance of social order.

Remember that a legislature may define any sort of behavior as unlawful. Legislatures enact laws to prohibit behavior that is regarded as harmful to social order. Murder is a crime *not* because it is harmful to the immediate victim, but because it disrupts the peaceful relationships that must exist in society if people are to live in reasonable comfort and safety. As far as the criminal law is concerned, the victim is not the individual who has been harmed by a violator, but, instead, society as a whole.

But legislators cannot be expected to imagine, and therefore to prohibit in advance, every sort of human behavior that might be socially disruptive. "Social order" itself is a vaguely defined state; whether it is disrupted depends not only on the actions of individuals, but on the reactions of other people. Some behavior might be disruptive under certain circumstances but not under other circumstances. For example, if a person turns on a radio and plays rock music at high volume, is that socially disruptive? It certainly would be if the person is in a church where a religious service is going on; it might not be if the person is on a public beach.

In order to write a law that will prohibit social disruption, legislators must try to imagine and define exactly what circumstances will be regarded as a violation. If a law is written too broadly or is too vague, it is likely to be ignored by many people and will be enforced only at great expense in terms of the time and effort of the police and the judiciary.

During the nineteenth century, many social-order laws were written in very broad terms, and the police were expected to exercise discretion in deciding whether specific behavior was disruptive. The results were not very satisfactory. In many cases, the police took advantage of their discretionary authority to overlook violations committed by their friends and abused their authority to harrass and intimidate anyone they happened to dislike.

Over the years, such vague, general laws have either been stricken from the books or overturned by the courts. According to the courts, the Constitution forbids vague laws on the grounds that every citizen has a right to know in advance whether certain behavior is illegal. If a law is so vague that a reasonable person cannot tell whether the behavior is permitted or prohibited, the law is not valid. Furthermore, the police have no authority to interfere with the freedom of anyone unless the person has violated a specific law. Thus, the police have no authority to "maintain social order" *except when a criminal act has taken place.* The use of police power to intimidate or discourage people whose behavior may be obnoxious or objectionable to others, but not specifically illegal, has been drastically reduced.

Thus, the proper functions of the police are limited to only two:

- Preventing crimes by observing prospective violators (when they can be identified) and by guarding places where crimes are most likely to occur.
- Enforcing the criminal laws by identifying and apprehending accused violators and by gathering evidence concerning violations.

The call for police professionalism is essentially a call for the police to discharge both of these functions as effectively as possible.

The Concept of Police Professionalism

Sociologists have concluded that a true profession has certain characteristics that distinguish it from other occupations. Those characteristics are as follows.[13]

A Social Grant of Authority.   The members of a profession have a special privilege or authority, sometimes granted to them exclusively, to practice their occupation. Although society has not granted the police an exclusive privilege to enforce the laws—in general, all citizens have the right to arrest a suspected offender, to register a complaint, or to gather evidence of a violation—only the police have an obligation to perform these tasks on behalf of the whole society. Furthermore, the police do have special privileges to carry sidearms, to use certain other weapons, and to use certain other "tools of the trade" such as nightsticks, handcuffs, sirens, and so on.

Autonomy of Practice.   The members of a profession exercise a high degree of discretion; what they do and how they do it are not subject to the criticism of people outside of their own occupational group. One of the major goals of the police reform movement has been to secure autonomy for the police *agency* but to remove it from the individual police *officer*. The idea is that the police agency must be free of political interference and must be the sole judge, subject to the law and court rulings, of proper law enforcement techniques and procedures. However, the individual officer is supposed to have almost no discretion in following the procedures, policies, and regulations of the agency.

In fact, however, most police officers work alone or in the company of no more than one or two of their peers. It is customary among police officers to develop informal understandings among themselves as to which policies and rules they will observe and which they will overlook. Furthermore, the nature of police work unavoidably requires individual officers to exercise a great deal of discretion. An officer must decide whether to issue a ticket to a speeding driver, or merely to warn the driver, or to ignore the violation altogether. Even when the offense is more serious, officers must decide whether to believe the testimony of a victim or witness, what kinds of evidence to seek, when to arrest a suspected offender, and what charges to file. Each of these decisions can have profound consequences for the people involved, but with rare exceptions an officer's decisions are not reviewed and criticized by anyone outside of the police agency.

Systematic Body of Knowledge.   The members of a profession are expected to have special competence because they have acquired a systematic body of knowledge, including theories that explain the functioning of their work and rare skills that can be acquired only by special training. The existence of books like this one and college classes in police science imply that there is a body of knowledge about police matters. There are also theories concerning the causes and effects of crime; however, these theories do not seem to be as systematic and conclusive as, for instance, theories about the causes and effects of infectious diseases. As for special training, the majority of police agencies in the United States require new officers to have no more than a high school diploma and two or three weeks of **basic training**. Nevertheless, the number and complexity of the special skills a police officer is expected to possess have risen in recent years, and so have the amount and quality of the training given to police officers.

Self-regulation. The members of a profession are expected to govern themselves by controlling the entry of newcomers into their occupation and by enforcing a self-imposed code of ethics or discipline. Police agencies do, in fact, regulate the entry of new members through selective recruitment, screening, and testing procedures. Most agencies also have some sort of internal inspection system to investigate complaints of improper conduct, and most agencies administer discipline when an officer is found to have behaved improperly. Unfortunately, among police officers themselves, self-regulation does not appear to be very effective. Several studies have found that individual police officers are reluctant to criticize one another even when there are blatant improprieties. Instead, the tendency among police officers is to protect one another.[14] This tendency undermines the self-regulatory system and sustains a widespread belief among the public that the police are unable and unwilling to discipline themselves. Often there are demands for civilian review boards or comparable outside agencies to exercise disciplinary authority over the police. In the few cases where such a mechanism has been established, it has been sabotaged by the relentless hostility and uncooperative attitude of the police—or, what is just as bad, the "independent" agency has been captured by partisan political groups.[15]

Service Orientation. Although the members of a profession are expected to be paid for their work like anyone else, they are also expected to be concerned primarily with performing an essential service to society. When necessary, they should willingly set aside their personal interests in order to provide that service. From the very beginning of the police reform movement, policing has been represented as a noble endeavor and a vital service to the public. Unfortunately, studies of police behavior and attitudes suggest that this ideal is not universally accepted by the police themselves. Lower-ranking officers frequently regard policing as "just a job, a way of earning a living," and not a very attractive job at that.[16] Some researchers have found that police officers regard the public with suspicion and hostility. Fogelson has described the common attitude among police officers as "occupational paranoia."[17]

According to some sociologists, there is no clear-cut distinction between "professional" and "nonprofessional" occupations but, instead, a scale or continuum between "fully professional" and "completely nonprofessional." Overall, the police appear to rank somewhere in the middle, about the same as public school teachers or accountants. This may seem discouraging to the advocates of professionalism, but actually it represents a great deal of progress over the past century. Furthermore, there is no inherent reason that dedicated police officers, given adequate leadership, cannot raise their occupation a few more notches up the scale of professionalism.

CHIEF ABEL'S IN BASKET

Instructions

In this exercise you are to assume the role of City Police Chief E. Z. Abel. The documents below have been selected from Chief Abel's in basket. Read them with care. If you need more information about City or its police department, refer to the data bank in the front of the book. After you have studied the documents, complete these steps:

1. State the problem or problems that these documents present to Chief Abel.
2. List as many alternative solutions as you can.
3. Select the solution you think would be best, and give your reasons for choosing it.

CITY, STATE
CITY HALL
INTEROFFICE MEMORANDUM

FROM: Harley Muven, Director, Transportation Dept.
TO: E. Z. Abel, Chief, Police Dept.
SUBJECT: Parking Meter Enforcement
DATE: January 10, 19--

Allow me to call to your attention the continuing decline in parking meter revenue we have experienced. City has about 9,500 parking meters that should produce $5,225,000 in revenue each year. Our actual peak year was 1978, when the meters produced $4,876,392 in revenue. Last year's revenue dropped to $4,178,394.65.

The eight Meter Maids on your payroll are expected to issue an average of 20 citations per day at $3.00 apiece, producing an average of $105,600 in revenue annually. Last year, however, they actually produced only $75,211 total, which is not even enough to cover their salaries.

I know you will want to take action now to remedy this situation before you begin budget preparation in March. Otherwise it will be hard for me to endorse your budget for this important function.

Harley Muven, Director

Sudsworthy

Distributing Co.

"Since 1892"

1904 Teakwood Street • 555-4567
City, State 65903

January 11, 19--

Chief E. Z. Abel
City Police Dept.
308 E. 6th St.
City, State 65901

Dear Chief Abel:

I am an honest businessman trying to make a living and keep
my people employed. I also pay a lot of taxes that go to your
salaries. I do not like having my men harrassed by your officers.

Yesterday one of your officers gave my driver, Otis Dunkle,
a ticket for illegal parking at 1501 E. River St. Otis was
unloading his truck and was not away from the truck more than
5 min. The truck was parked in the street because some idiot had
parked his car in the loading zone. This happens to us all the
time. It is the third time in the past 2 weeks that one of my
drivers has got a ticket. I cannot afford to keep paying these
$10 tickets all the time.

We didn't have this kind of problem when Chief Ellis ran the
dept. He always told his people not to give us tickets when our
men were just unloading their trucks. I do not see why I should
continue to support the Police Association with ads in their
magazine and tickets to the annual dance if we are not going to
get the same kind of consideration. If something is not done about
this, I will talk to the City Council about it.

Yours truly,

Amos Sudsworthy

Amos Sudsworthy

CITY, STATE
City Hall

City Council Memorandum

TO: Chief Abel, Police Dept.
DATE: Jan. 9, 19--

Dear Chief Abel:

    I have received a number of complaints about the apparent lack of enforcement of parking laws in the Warehouse District. People tell me that it is almost impossible to drive along Teakwood, Vine, and Walnut streets, and the cross-streets from 19th to Basin, because of the illegally-parked trucks blocking the street. This has gotten to be a problem even on Industrial. Obviously this is a very dangerous situation, as well as being an inconvenience to motorists. It also discourages people from patronizing the businesses along these streets. Please let me know what you plan to do about this.

Paul Iticoe, Member
City Council

IN REVIEW

1. The five basic functions in any organization are:
   (a) Task performance.
   (b) Resource acquisition and allocation.
   (c) Self-regulation.
   (d) Goal definition and policy setting.
   (e) Task assignment.
   (f) Professionalism.
   (g) Evaluation and modification.

2. Efficiency means:
   (a) Performing the most work in a given amount of time.
   (b) Reducing the number of employees in an agency.
   (c) Performing all five basic functions perfectly.
   (d) Accomplishing the most work with the smallest possible expenditure of resources.
   (e) Exercising individual discretion.

3. In addition to performing one or more of the five basic functions, the _____ must act as communication channels.

4. True or False: The Bill of Rights reflects the English tradition of relying on the military for law enforcement.

5. During the 1850s, the urban police began to take over the crime-prevention function of:
   (a) The day and night watches.
   (b) The military.
   (c) The sheriffs.
   (d) The detectives.
   (e) The state militia.

6. After the Civil War, most urban police agencies became corrupt because:
   (a) Local politicians controlled the precinct captains.
   (b) Unpopular vice laws encouraged graft.
   (c) The police themselves were generally untrained, poorly paid, and ineffective.
   (d) There was no strong central administration of the police.
   (e) All of the above.
   (f) None of the above.

7. True or False: The first generation of police reformers had few successes, but they did succeed in training a new generation of reform-minded administrators.

8. The history of the police in America can be seen as a history of:
   (a) Incompetence and corruption.
   (b) The long struggle for professionalism.
   (c) Patriotic service and courage.
   (d) Constant conflict between the police and the public.
   (e) Dismal failure in controlling crime.

9. Enforcing the law means:
   (a) Punishing all known violators for their offenses.
   (b) Preventing violations by physically restraining prospective offenders.
   (c) Identifying and apprehending accused violators, gathering evidence of violations, and presenting the accused and the evidence to the courts.
   (d) Maintaining social order.
   (e) Determining which citizens are likely offenders and keeping them under surveillance to discourage them from violating the laws.
   (f) None of the above.
   (g) All of the above.

10. Which of the following is *not* a characteristic of a profession?
    (a) Social grant of authority.
    (b) Autonomy of practice.
    (c) Systematic body of knowledge.
    (d) High level of compensation.
    (e) Self-regulation.
    (f) Service orientation.

REFERENCES

1. Samuel Walker, *A Critical History of Police Reform*, Lexington, Mass.: Lexington Books—D. C. Heath, 1977, page 4.

2. Walker, page 4.

3. Robert Fogelson, *Big City Police*, Cambridge, Mass.: Harvard Univ. Press, 1977, page 15.

4. Walker, pages 12–13.

5. Fogelson, pages 18–19.

6. Fogelson, page 21.

7. Fogelson, page 26.

8. Walker, page 48.

9. Fogelson, page 141.

10. Walker, page x.

11. Fogelson, page 157.

12. Barbara Seulig, *You Can't Eat Peanuts in Church and Other Little-Known Laws*, Garden City, N.Y.: Doubleday, 1975, page 13.

13. Alan P. Bates and Joseph Julian, *Sociology: Understanding Social Behavior*, Boston: Houghton Mifflin, 1975, pages 206–212; also Fredric D. Wolinsky, *The Sociology of Health*, Boston: Little, Brown, 1980, pages 255–268.

14. Harlan Hahn, "A Profile of Urban Police," in Jack Goldsmith and Sharon S. Goldsmith, eds., *The Police Community*, Pacific Palisades, Calif.: Palisades Publishers, 1974, pages 19–21.

15. Fogelson, page 285.

16. Alex Nicholas, *New York Cops Talk Back*, New York: Wiley, 1976; also William Ker Muir, Jr., *Police: Streetcorner Politicians*, Chicago: Univ. of Chicago Press, 1977.

17. Fogelson, pages 238–242.

2 CONCEPTS OF MANAGEMENT

Kansas City Police Computer Operations Center

BEFORE THE TURN OF THE CENTURY, MANAGEMENT HAD never been considered as a particular discipline or body of skills and knowledge. In fact, until the Industrial Revolution, there were very few enterprises of any sort that involved more than a handful of people. The exceptions—government, the military, and the clergy—had each developed its own unique system of management and organization.

Industrial capitalism, which began in the seventeenth century and became the dominant economic system in the Western nations in the nineteenth century, required ever larger and more complex forms of organization and thus more skilled and knowledgeable management. At the same time, the triumph of science and technology contributed to a widespread belief that every sort of problem or human need could be resolved through the rational application of scientific principles.

Around 1880 a young factory worker, Frederick W. Taylor, observed that some of his colleagues in the machine shop produced more work with less effort than did others. This observation certainly was not original, but Taylor resolved to study the matter more closely. He soon concluded that the more productive workers did not necessarily work harder; in fact, some of them did not seem to be working as hard as their less productive co-workers. But the more productive workers had arranged their work in such a way that they lost as little time as possible in wasted movement—reaching for materials or tools, placing pieces on a machine, and so forth. Taylor found that he, too, could increase his productivity just by planning and organizing his work a little better.

Based on this limited observation and experience, Taylor concluded that every job might be planned and arranged in one particular way that would be more productive than any other possible arrangement. When he explained his ideas to his superiors, he was encouraged to try them out.

First, Taylor analyzed each job, dividing it into the smallest possible steps. He then tried various arrangements of the individual steps, placing the necessary tools and materials where they could be reached with the least possible effort exactly when they were needed. He also timed each step, using a stopwatch and, when necessary, rearranged the work to reduce the time it would take. Not every experiment succeeded on the first attempt, but before long Taylor was able to double and triple the productivity of every worker in the factory merely by defining and prescribing the "one best way" to perform each job.

At first, many of the workers were resentful of Taylor's methods. They were used to working in whatever way they pleased and at whatever pace they found comfortable. However, Taylor's methods proved to make their work more productive with less effort. Since many factory workers were paid on a piece rate, a set amount for each piece of work they accomplished, their increased productivity paid off immediately in larger paychecks.

Taylor began to publish his theories of **scientific management** about the turn of the century and attracted a great deal of attention. His techniques of job analysis and planning were significant in themselves, but even more important was the idea that the management of a business could be improved by the application of science and theory.[1] Taylor was the first of many management theorists.

**THEORIES
OF MANAGEMENT**

**Scientific Management
Theories**

Taylor's theories attracted a number of followers, one of whom was Frank Gilbreth. Gilbreth adopted Taylor's system of time and motion studies and the theory that there was one best way to perform every job. He also developed a method of depicting all the individual steps in a particular job through the use of a work-flow process chart, a device that later proved to be indispensable in computer system design and programming.

Perhaps Gilbreth's most important contribution, however, was to take Taylor's theories out of the factory and apply them to all kinds of work. Gilbreth trained a staff of efficiency experts and sent them with their stopwatches and clipboards into file rooms, offices, department stores, laboratories, and every type of work environment. He advised architects and industrial engineers on the design of production lines, office furniture and equipment, and even private homes. The modern kitchen, with its arrangement of appliances, cabinets, and countertops for the efficient storage and preparation of food, is a direct product of Gilbreth's theories.[2]

Meanwhile, other theorists tackled a whole range of management problems. C. B. Thompson developed new methods of accounting that gave managers a clearer picture of their businesses' financial status. Harrington Emerson applied Taylor's and Gilbreth's job analysis techniques to giant, complex industrial systems such as railroads. Henry L. Gantt created more sophisticated methods of recording complex work processes. By the 1920s the concept of scientific management and efficiency was firmly established in American business and had begun to have a profound influence on other kinds of enterprises, including government.

The early police reformers were not directly affected by the scientific management movement until after World War I but, even before then, police administrators had begun to seek ways to make policing more efficient. Efficiency became a primary goal of the second-generation reformers.

The theories of scientific management were not universally admired. Critics complained that scientific management ignored the human factor in work, and that the methods advocated by Taylor and Gilbreth treated workers as if they were just another factory machine. Elton Mayo, a professor of business administration at Harvard University, was one of those critics.

**Human Relations
Management Theories**

Mayo set out to learn whether Taylor's and Gilbreth's methods really resulted in increased productivity and whether there really was only one best way to perform any given job. Mayo was invited to assist in a series of experiments at the Hawthorne plant of the Western Electric Company in Chicago. The experiments were designed to apply the principles of scientific management by varying different aspects of the work environment, such as the lighting level and the number and duration of rest periods, to determine which measures would increase productivity the most.

To the astonishment of the experimenters, *every* change in the work environment produced at least a short-term increase in productivity. When light levels were increased, productivity rose; when light levels were decreased, productivity rose again! In each case, productivity soon dropped back to its previous level. In another series of experiments, women assembly-line workers were given rest periods of varying duration and frequency. Each change in the schedule resulted in an increase in productivity. Even restoring the original schedule brought increased productivity. The experimenters were baffled.

Mayo solved the riddle of Hawthorne by interviewing the workers at great length. He discovered that they were responding as a group to the mere fact that the experiments were being conducted. The experimenters had asked the workers to cooperate, and so they did! This discovery that almost any change in the work environment, especially if it is introduced as an experiment, will produce at least a temporary increase in productivity, has since become known as the Hawthorne effect. According to Mayo and others who have studied this phenomenon, the explanation for the Hawthorne effect is not that the workers feel pressure to work harder because they are being watched, but instead that they feel encouraged to work harder because they are being given special attention and recognition.

Furthermore, Mayo found that the increased productivity was not the result of individual decisions made by the workers, but instead was a product of group interaction. The workers encouraged one another to accomplish more work and, as far as possible, they helped one another.

This discovery led Mayo to examine more closely the conventional working environment in factories and offices. Once again, he found that workers as a group set their own production standards, deciding how much work they would accomplish in a given period of time. Slower workers were encouraged and assisted to keep up with the rest of the group, while faster workers were pressured into slowing down so that they would not show up their co-workers.

Mayo's discoveries led him to a generalization: In any working situation, the interpersonal relationships among the workers are at least as significant in determining productivity as the physical environment, work methods, or procedures dictated by scientific management. This generalization became the foundation of the human relations theory of management.

Mayo went on to make many other discoveries about human relations in the work place. Taylor, Gilbreth, and the other scientific management theorists had assumed that people work only to earn money and that a larger paycheck would be a sufficient incentive to motivate workers to work harder. Mayo found that human motivation was much more complex. He showed that many workers paid on a piece rate basis could have earned more money by working just a little harder but did not. In part, workers voluntarily submitted to the productivity standards set by their working group; but, besides that, most workers seemed to feel that it was more important to function at a pace they found comfortable, rather than exhausting themselves just to earn another dollar or two. The paycheck, according to Mayo, was an important motivator but not the only one.

Mayo also concluded that the worker's perception of the importance of his or her job was a significant motivating factor. Workers who believed that their jobs were unimportant, no matter how well they were paid, tended to perform poorly; people who believed that their jobs were important—either to the economic success of their employer or to society as a whole—tended to perform well no matter how poorly they were paid. Furthermore, Mayo found that most people judged the value of their work according to the value put on it by their co-workers, friends, family members, and neighbors—that is, by the various social groups of which they were members.[3]

Elton Mayo's discoveries and his explanations for them had a great impact on the business world. Unfortunately, that impact was blunted by the difficulty of applying his theories. Taylor, Gilbreth, and their followers had offered concrete rules, specific procedures, and visible evidence of their methods' success. Mayo offered insights into human relationships and motivations that were not easily translated into specific actions to be taken by managers.

The human relations theories had even less impact in the world of law enforcement. The reform-minded police administrators were intent on introducing discipline, efficiency, and uniformity. If anything, they were more interested in breaking up group relationships such as the informal arrangements among patrol officers, precinct captains, and ward bosses that had allowed widespread corruption and incompetence to flourish. There was an effort to convince police officers that their work was socially significant, as part of the campaign for professionalism; however, this effort to boost morale was intended mainly to reinforce the need for tight discipline and strict integrity, not to give the individual officer a greater sense of personal satisfaction.

Overall, Mayo's theories and those of his followers came to be treated as a sort of footnote to management theory. Managers sought to increase productivity by introducing more efficient work methods, by offering better pay, by stricter supervision—and, oh, yes, by paying some attention to human relations. Meanwhile, another group of theorists had come forward, pushing the human relations theories even further into the background.

Organizational Theories

This third group of management theorists concentrated not on the individual workers or the working environment but on the relationships among all the elements in an organization.

Max Weber, a German sociologist, provided the most comprehensive theory of organizational management. He believed that the most efficient form of organization was the **bureaucracy**, in which the overall work of an organization is divided into sets of specific tasks that are assigned to the individual units of the organization. This theory applies to every sort of enterprise, whether private business or government. Briefly, Weber's theory of bureaucratic organization includes the following elements:

1. Each unit of an organization should be assigned one particular type of work, or set of closely related tasks, to be performed more or less continuously.
2. The units of the organization should be arranged into a hierarchy of offices, each having responsibility for a specific type of work *and* for the

work of all its subordinate offices, and each office should have exactly the authority it needs to carry out these responsibilities.

3. Each person in an organization should be assigned to the office he or she is most competent to fill, and competence should be determined by objective means such as standardized tests or competition among applicants.

4. All of the relationships among the organizational units, and thus among the people who fill the various offices, should be regulated by a formal, uniform, and consistent set of rules and policies; each office should have authority to set the rules and policies for its subordinate offices, subject to the authority of higher offices.

5. The exact procedures to be followed for the completion of every task should be determined in advance and established by the appropriate authority.

6. All work should be reported by means of written documents, reviewed by supervising authorities as necessary, and kept in permanent files for future reference.[4]

Stated in these stark terms, Weber's theory seems harsh and authoritarian, but it was not meant to be. Weber himself thought that his theory, properly applied, would produce "precision, speed, unambiguity, knowledge of the files, continuity, discretion, unity, strict subordination, reduction of friction and of material and personal costs . . ."[5]—in short, the kind of efficiency that a business manager can appreciate.

Weber's bureaucratic theory was made to order for the police reformers, and it was quickly adopted by the young police administrators of the 1930s. Above all, the theory promised an end to individual discretion and nonconformity; it seemed to show how to achieve a high degree of regularity in even the most complex endeavors.

Many other organization theorists followed in Weber's footsteps, especially during the 1930s and 1940s. They drew freely from military traditions, the hierarchical patterns of religious organizations and, in particular, the basic pattern we defined in Chapter 1 as the corporate model. They blended these time-tested ideas with those of Weber along with the concepts of efficiency developed by Taylor, Gilbreth, and their followers, and produced what has become the standard model for nearly all governmental organizations and businesses. Only in the last 15 or 20 years have these principles of organization come under serious challenge. Suddenly it has become very fashionable to criticize the Weber-style bureaucratic organization as excessively rigid, authoritarian, and unresponsive to changing human needs. Whether these criticisms are valid—and to a large extent, they probably are—the fact remains that, for its time, Weber's theory of organization was a major step forward.

One of the most significant additions to organizational theory is the systems approach theory, developed in the 1950s and 1960s as an outgrowth of the design of computer systems. Briefly, the systems approach treats an organization not as a collection of separate elements, but as a single entity through which resources flow in order to produce something. This approach emphasizes the complex relationships and interactions among the various parts of an organization. For example, a decision to manufacture a new product might be made at the highest level of administration. However, the decision affects many different elements of the organization. The purchasing department must obtain the raw materials to make the product, the production department must assign the necessary workers and machinery (or perhaps even build a new factory), the marketing department must arrange for suitable packaging and advertising, and the sales department must train the sales staff to sell the product. If all these effects are not taken into account when the decision is first made, the results might be disastrous.

The systems approach has been popular not only in the computer industry but also in many other industries. It has been adapted to several federal agencies, especially those that provide social welfare services where extremely complex social interactions must be taken into account. However, efforts to apply the systems theory to police administration have been limited and less successful.

Behavioral Theories of Management

The long-neglected ideas of Elton Mayo and his followers in the human-relations school of management were revived during the 1960s and gained new influence in the 1970s as the basis for another set of management theories. These theories largely take for granted the kinds of organizational structures and work procedures advocated by the scientific management and organizational theorists of the past. Instead of seeking ways to make work more routine and efficient, the new theorists look for ways to make workers more productive by tapping their unused potential.

In 1943 psychologist Abraham Maslow published a theory of human motivation that attempted to explain virtually all behavior in terms of a relatively small set of universal human needs. According to Maslow, every person has essentially the same needs, although they may be expressed in different ways. All people must have food, drink, shelter from a harsh environment, and other basic physical elements of life. All people need to be free of pain or discomfort, and all people feel a need for physical security.

In addition to these physical needs, Maslow theorized that people also have a universal set of psychological needs: a need for friendship, affection, affiliation (the sense of belonging to a worthwhile group), self-respect, self-confidence, and the fulfillment of one's personal potential, or *self-actualization*.

Furthermore, according to Maslow, these needs exist in a hierarchical structure. Basic physical needs must be satisfied first because, if they are not, the person's very existence is threatened. Once these needs have been satisfied, a person seeks to achieve a degree of physical security; after that, social-emotional needs (affection, affiliation, and the like) must be satisfied. Next on the hierarchy are the needs for self-esteem and self-confidence; highest of all is the need for self-actualization.[6]

The practical significance of Maslow's work is that it seems to explain why people react differently to certain incentives. A person who is hungry will be highly motivated by the prospect of earning some food but, once the hunger has been satisfied, an offer of more food would not motivate the person to perform any further work. Of course, ordinarily people are paid in money, not food, and one of the great advantages of money is that it can be used to buy many different things. Indirectly, money can even be used to buy psychologically gratifying experiences such as works of art, entertainment, or travel.

People also differ in the way their needs are expressed and in the degree to which they require satisfaction. Some people are perfectly content to accept a quantity of material goods—food, shelter, clothing, and so on— that other people would consider completely inadequate. Many artists, for example, voluntarily maintain a rather low material standard of living in order to continue practicing their art, as a form of self-expression, in spite of the lack of financial compensation. In effect, they have suppressed some of their physical and social needs in order to satisfy their psychological needs.

Another psychologist, Douglas McGregor, built on Maslow's work in the late 1950s. McGregor pointed out that there is a fundamental conflict between the assumptions held by conventional management theorists and those held by Maslow and other behavioral theorists. The conventional theorists have always assumed that most people do not want to work and would not work if they could avoid it. According to this assumption, which McGregor called Theory X, people must be forced to work and must be closely supervised to make sure that they keep working. Also, if Theory X is true, most people have no desire to hold and exercise responsibility, even for their own welfare, but would much prefer to enjoy the security of being cared for by someone else and being told what to do.

McGregor believed that there was ample evidence to support just the opposite view, which he called Theory Y: that work is natural to all people, that most people want to accept responsibility for themselves and for their own work once they have clear goals in mind, and that most people enjoy facing a challenge if they have a reasonable chance to meet it and if there is some reward for doing so.[7] According to McGregor, managers who rely on Theory Y should place much less emphasis on authority and accountability—the heart of Weber's bureaucratic model—and much more emphasis on helping workers to find personal satisfaction in their work.

A number of other behavioral theorists have contributed useful ideas to management science in the past two decades. The general theme in all cases has been to apply the knowledge gained from the behavioral sciences, especially psychology and sociology, to improve the productivity of business or government enterprises and to increase the satisfaction felt by workers.[8] Robert R. Blake and Jane S. Mouton have tried with some success to bring together all these theories into a single, systematic approach to management, which they call grid organizational development. Briefly, their idea is that every organization has two dominant concerns: the concern for *production* (or, more broadly, for meeting the organization's overall goals) and the concern for the *welfare* (both physical and psychological) of the organization's members, including employees. However, organizations vary in the amount of attention that is paid to each of these concerns. Some managers are so obsessed with production that they neglect the welfare of the people in the organization, while other managers are so determined to "keep everyone happy" that production suffers. Blake and Mouton believe that managers should use specific strategies to balance these two concerns so that they actually reinforce each other:

increased production brings greater rewards (both material and psychological), while more satisfied workers are naturally more productive.[9]

Management by Objectives

Finally, another set of management theories begins with the idea that people are both more productive and more content when they know precisely what is expected of them and when they are working toward specific, challenging goals, especially if they have helped to set those goals. These theories, which have been developed by a number of theorists over the last 20 years, are known collectively as **management by objectives**, or **MBO**.

According to the MBO theory, the most important task of management is to decide what the organization's goals will be and to define those goals in specific terms that can be understood by every worker. As far as possible, the workers themselves should participate in setting goals, since people are likely to feel a stronger commitment to achieving a goal that they have set for themselves. Once objectives have been set, everyone in the organization should be informed of their progress toward meeting them. There should be periodic assessments of progress at which time the goals might be amended to take into consideration factors that have changed since the original goal-setting. Most MBO theorists agree that these **feedback** provisions and regular evaluations are just as important as the goal-setting process itself.[10]

Contingency Theory of Management

Every one of the different management theories we have discussed has been put into practice by business and government managers. They have all proven successful in some cases, unsuccessful in others. For the practical manager faced with immediate problems, this creates a dilemma; *which* theory should he or she adopt?

According to Roy R. Roberg and other advocates of the **contingency theory**, the only possible answer is that it depends.

The contingency theory is based on the idea that there is no one universal best way to organize and operate a complex enterprise. Instead, managers must be responsive to the particular situation that faces them. They must choose management techniques that are appropriate to the needs of the organization itself, the people in the organization, and the outside world that the organization intends to serve.[11] The primary task of the manager is not to choose and apply slavishly any one system or theory but, instead, to integrate the needs of the individual with the needs of the organization by selecting and using any system that meets those needs.

Roberg distinguishes between "mechanistic" and "organic" organizations. A mechanistic organization is one that is managed according to a rigid, highly authoritarian system, such as Weber's bureaucratic model. There is little room for personal preferences and the individual characteristics of the people in the organization. This organization can be successful in certain cases, for instance, when the organization's principal task is to carry out highly routine, standardized work; for example, a factory that produces products on a continuous, conveyor-belt basis.

However, organizations like police agencies whose goals are diverse, with constant interaction between the organization's members and the outside world, and with continual changes in the demands being made on the organization, are less likely to succeed with a mechanistic system. Instead, Roberg advocates an organic system that "grows out of the situation." This system has as little structure as possible, it allows for and rewards individual initiative and discretion within limits that are set as far apart as possible, and it actively seeks opportunities for change and improvement in response to changing internal and external conditions.[12] Roberg believes that police agencies, if they are to be successful, must develop a more organic approach to their organizational structure and management than they have had in the past.

The challenges of contingency theory and organic management are very great. An organic system requires managers to be sensitive to the demands of the outside world and to the needs of the people in the organization, without losing sight of the organization's own ultimate goals. These managers must know a lot about many different theories and techniques of management and about which techniques are appropriate to which circumstances. If individual initiative and discretion are encouraged, mistakes inevitably will be made by lower-level personnel. Somehow the manager must make sure that when mistakes are made, the consequences will not be disastrous (especially for some innocent citizen) and that the person who made the mistake learns from it.

Most important, the successful manager must have a keen, clear understanding of his or her own role in the organization and of the responsibility he or she must bear.

THE ROLE OF THE MANAGER

Duties of Management

In 1937, one of the scientific management theorists, Luther Gulick, attempted to define and list all the duties of a manager. He summarized them in the acronym, POSDCORB, which stands for Planning, Organizing, Staffing, Directing, Coordinating, Reporting, and Budgeting.[13] Since then, many other theorists have attempted to improve on Gulick's list by making minor changes or by redefining various terms. Some of the lists are so long and elaborate that few managers could ever hope to get around to all the duties they are supposed to discharge. We will try to avoid this pitfall by simplifying the matter. Instead of listing every conceivable task a manager might undertake, we describe three general categories of managerial responsibilities.

Prospective Duties. The first responsibility of the manager is to anticipate the future: to decide what is to be done, how it may best be done, and what resources will be needed to do it. In this category are the recognized duties of planning and budgeting, which we will discuss in much greater detail in Chapters 4 and 5. Organizing is also partly a prospective duty, since it involves deciding which people and skills will be required to perform each task.

Perhaps the most important prospective duty of the manager is policy-making. A manager makes policy when he or she decides how a given task or job is to be performed. Policies usually are expressed in the form of orders, rules, regulations, and directives. Some police agencies have developed elaborate schemes for expressing policies as a hierarchy of orders, some of which (general orders) are supposed to serve as universal rules for all personnel at all times, while others (special orders) are supposed to apply only to particular situations or cases. These elaborate schemes usually break down. Some people in the organization never receive some orders, and many orders are simply ignored by most personnel.

Generally, managers are well advised to *avoid* making policies, in whatever form, whenever possible. Once a rule is made, it must be enforced. Otherwise, respect for all rules will decline, inconsistencies and injustices will occur, and personnel will become increasingly confused. No manager can hope to anticipate every situation in which the operating personnel will find themselves; thus, policies are likely to be riddled with exceptions and contradictions. The operating personnel will be forced to try to decide whether a particular rule made months or years ago applies to the immediate situation. Some policies must be made to set realistic standards of performance, to give order to such routine events as the work schedule, and to ensure that all personnel abide by legal requirements in matters such as arrests, property searches, and the use of force. However, it is much better for the manager to make policies that set broad limits on the discretion of personnel rather than trying to make rules that restrict personnel to the one correct way of performing their jobs.

Current Duties.   Once the manager has decided what is to be done, how it is to be done, and what resources will be needed, it is the manager's job to acquire and organize those resources (including people). Most of these current duties are routine in nature: setting up periodic work schedules, transferring personnel from one unit to another, administering the payroll and purchasing systems, and so on. Because these duties are routine, they demand very little creativity on the part of the manager. Once the routine has been established, doing the work is relatively easy (though it may be tedious and time-consuming). There is a danger that the manager will occupy more and more of his or her time with these routine, nondemanding chores at the expense of the other duties that are actually more important to the organization's success. Therefore, whenever possible, the manager should shift the burden of routine duties to subordinates: clerks, assistants, and so on.

Retrospective Duties.   The third part of the manager's job is to find out whether the tasks that were planned in advance have actually been performed and with what results. These "backward-looking" chores are perhaps the most often neglected part of the manager's duties. Too many managers assume that once they have given an order, the job is done. Eventually they may discover that the order has not been followed, but by that time it is too late. The manager must constantly supervise, not in the sense of "cracking the whip" over subordinates but in the proper sense of "looking over" the work being performed to make sure that it is being done properly. The goals and plans made previously serve as the standard of current performance. If the standards are not being met, the manager must determine whether the fault lies in the personnel (inability or unwillingness to do the work), the plans themselves (unrealistic expectations or inadequate resources), or some change in the environment that has made the plans unworkable. Adjustments and corrections then must be made, and new goals and plans must be set. Thus the manager's retrospective duties provide the basis for a continual renewal of the prospective duties: there is a complete cycle, and ideally the organization moves steadily forward toward its ultimate objectives.

This summary of the manager's duties is not intended to define every task that a manager performs. We will describe many tasks that are ordinarily assigned to management personnel in a police agency. However, in any police agency, there may be duties assigned to managerial and supervisory personnel in addition to those we will describe. Lower-level supervisors almost always have some operational duties; for example, a sergeant may be expected to serve as a backup patrol officer in addition to supervising a patrol squad, or may have clerical duties at the police station. Since most police agencies are chronically short of personnel, there is a natural tendency to distribute routine chores to anyone whose time does not appear to be fully occupied. Even executive-level administrators should be willing to perform some operational-level duties, if only to ensure that they have continuing, personal experience with the day-to-day reality of police work. However, remember that the most essential duties of the manager are prospective and retrospective, planning for the future and evaluating past performance, and that it is dangerously easy to let these crucial tasks be overwhelmed with routine and trivial chores that could be performed just as well by someone else.

The Leadership Function

It is not too difficult to compile lists of the various jobs that managers must perform, but it has proven to be very difficult to describe how managers should perform their work. Many management theorists agree that managers must exercise something called **leadership**, but there is little agreement on what leadership is, what it looks like, or how managers should exercise it.

Leadership has been defined as "the ability to cause other people to do things." Presumably, the "things" done are those desired by the leader but not necessarily by the people who are caused to do them; otherwise, leadership would require nothing more than getting out of the way. If we adopt McGregor's Theory X view of management, the definition makes good sense: a leader's (manager's) job is to influence people to do things that they otherwise would not want to do. However, this does not mean that a leader must operate only by physical force and intimidation. Anthropologists George Maclay and Humphry Knipe have found that not only all human societies, but many nonhuman groups, exhibit patterns of **dominance** in which certain individuals are accepted as leaders within their own group. According to Maclay and Knipe, physical force is rarely used to achieve or to maintain dominance, because if a leader must resort to violence to maintain authority, there is constant turmoil in the group and valuable members are needlessly injured.[14]

A somewhat more subtle idea of leadership is that it involves "the ability to cause people to want to do things that the leader wants to have done."

This implies that the leader psychologically manipulates the group's members, persuading them to change their own desires until the leader's desires are satisfied. People may be made to think that they are acting voluntarily. Most theories of motivation start with the premise that ordinarily people would not want to do certain things, but somehow the leader must persuade them to want what he or she wants.[15]

McGregor's Theory Y suggests that neither coercion nor manipulation may be necessary. If people actually want to do the things that need to be done, the leader's only task is to make sure that the subordinates know what is needed. Of course, there is a little more to it than that. There may be confusion or uncertainty about what tasks are necessary or about the best way to perform the tasks. There may also be conflicts among the subordinates as to what they really want. For example, two patrol officers patrolling the same beat might have very different ideas about how they should relate to the people in the neighborhood, how they should respond to suspicious activities or complaints of crimes, and so on. The leader, therefore, must work to remove confusion and uncertainty wherever it exists and to resolve the subordinates' conflicting needs and desires.[16]

Some theorists have taken a different approach to the subject of leadership. Instead of trying to define its nature, they have tried to discover the common characteristics and personality traits of individuals who are generally regarded as successful leaders. Unfortunately, different theorists have compiled lists of traits that, when combined, include hundreds of different "characteristics of leaders."

More recent theorists have tried to simplify these lists by determining which traits were truly universal among leaders. According to Roberg, "In 1971, [Edwin] Ghiselli . . . concluded that the most important trait for successful managers is supervisory ability, followed closely by the desire for occupational achievement."[17] But if leadership is supposed to be a prerequisite of supervisory ability, and supervisory ability is a characteristic of leadership, we know nothing more than we did when we began—except the assertion that successful managers want to succeed.

Some behavioral scientists have suggested that there may be no universal leadership traits, but that leaders may operate successfully in any of several different styles. Robert Tannenbaum and Warren H. Schmidt have described a continuum of leadership styles, from highly authoritarian to highly democratic, according to the amount of freedom and discretion allowed to subordinates. A highly authoritarian leader simply makes decisions and issues orders; at the other extreme, a highly democratic leader makes very few decisions, but allows subordinates to do their work however they see fit. Between these extremes are several different styles. The point is that no one style is universally effective. The most successful leaders consider a number of variables, including their own personalities, the abilities and personalities of their subordinates, and the nature of the demands made on their organizations.[18] Thus, a leader might function in a highly authoritarian style at one time, but in a more democratic style at another time. For example, the chief of a small police department might allow the patrol officers to set their own duty schedule, requiring only that a minimum number of officers be on duty at any time. However, the same chief might decide and announce detailed regulations to govern the procedures for a drug raid, without consulting subordinates and without giving them any opportunity for discussion or debate.

Behavioral scientists also have considered the possibility that the nature of leadership and the traits or style of the leader may represent only half the picture, and perhaps not the more important half. The other half may be the nature, traits, or style of followers. The whole subject of followership has only begun to be explored.

Some sociologists believe that every group chooses its own leaders with only minimal regard for the official position a person happens to hold, and that these decisions—usually made informally or even unconsciously—are based on the group's perceptions of its needs, not so much on the abilities of the leader.

For example, it is not unusual for a police captain, who is supposed to hold authority over an entire bureau, to find that his or her orders are frequently ignored unless they are transmitted to the lower-ranking personnel by a respected lieutenant. In effect, the group has chosen the lieutenant as its leader and rejected the leadership of the captain. On the other hand, it is also common for a lieutenant to find that he or she has almost no influence on direct subordinates unless every order is endorsed and confirmed by the captain. In this case, the group has rejected the lieutenant's leadership. The personal qualities and abilities of the captain and the lieutenant might be essentially the same; the difference lies in the group's perception of their superiors and of their needs. However, we know very little about how groups choose their leaders or whether the choices generally are good or bad.

CAPTAIN BOWEN'S IN BASKET

Instructions

In this exercise, you are to assume the role of Captain Thomas Bowen, Chief, Detective Bureau. The documents below have been selected from Captain Bowen's in basket. Read them with care. If you need more information about City or its police department, refer to the data bank in the front of the book. After you have studied the documents, complete these steps:

1. State the problem or problems that these documents present to Captain Bowen.
2. List as many alternative solutions as you can.
3. Select the solution you think would be best, and give your reasons for choosing it.

CITY POLICE DEPARTMENT
Interoffice Memorandum

FROM:
C. Smith, Lt., Crime Prevention

TO:
T. Bowen, Capt., Detective Bureau

SUBJECT:
Request for Disciplinary Action

DATE:
14 Jan 19--

SIR:

    I hereby request that disciplinary action be taken against Sr. Sgt. Ralph Koonce, Juvenile Div. The disciplinary action I recommend is: (1) official reprimand placed in permanent personnel file, and (2) penalty of 25 points deducted from Sgt. Koonce's next Personnel Evaluation. The reasons for this request are as follows:

    1. Insubordination. In accordance with City PD General Policy Manual, Sec. 134, Para. G-5. Sgt. Koonce deliberately and maliciously contradicted a direct order, given by me to one of his subordinate officers, in my presence and in the presence of other persons.

Page 2

    2. Failure to Perform a Required Duty. In accordance with City PD General Policy Manual, Sec. 132, Para. E-1, E-2, and E-4. Sgt. Koonce failed to post a correct, current duty roster for his subordinates, failed to require his subordinates to observe a regular work schedule, and failed to report to me the fact that one of his subordinates was absent without prior authorization.

    According to General Policy Manual, Sec. 24, Para. F, a formal disciplinary hearing is not required unless Sgt. Koonce objects to the penalties recommended. If a hearing is held, I will be prepared to present a detailed report on the incidents mentioned above and witnesses will be available as required.

        Charles Smith, Lt.,
        Crime Prevention Section

CITY POLICE DEPARTMENT
Interoffice Memorandum

FROM:
R. Koonce, Sr. Sgt., Juvenile Div.

TO:
T. Bowen, Capt., Detective Bureau

SUBJECT:
Disagreement with Lt. Smith

DATE:
16 Jan 19--

SIR:

    I understand that Lt. Smith has requested disciplinary action against me because of the incident that occurred yesterday. Before you decide what action to take, I hope you will consider my side of it.

    Last weekend, two of my people, Sr. Patrol Officer Rainey and Patrol Officer Anderson, spent approximately 15 hours each on their off-duty time counselling with two youth gangs in West City. P.O. Anderson had received a tip that these gangs were planning an all-out war over the weekend. I am convinced that their action, taken on their own initiative at a time when I was not available (I was out of town over the weekend), prevented serious violence. Under the circumstances, of course, they had no opportunity to receive advance authorization for overtime, and the Department's rules therefore do not permit me to pay for their extra work.

-2-

I thought it would be only fair to reward their initiative and good work by allowing them to take compensatory time off on Tuesday, Wednesday, and Thursday mornings. Ordinarily our workload on weekday mornings is not very heavy, anyway; it consists mostly of catching up on paperwork. However, I did not change the official duty roster to show that the officers would be off-duty on the three mornings because that would have meant changing the payroll forms and they would have been charged with personal leave time. It seemed to me that the simplest solution was to leave the roster alone.

On Tuesday morning, while I was out of the office to attend a meeting with the county social workers, Lt. Smith came into the office looking for Off. Rainey. Patrol Officer Wallace informed him that Officers Rainey and Anderson had taken the morning off, and she explained why.

Lt. Smith returned Tuesday afternoon and accused the two officers of being absent without leave. I told Lt. Smith that this was not true, and told him that I had given them permission to take compensatory time off, even though Dept. policy does not officially provide for this. Lt. Smith grew very angry and accused me of incompetence. He ordered Officers Rainey and Anderson to make up the time by working Tuesday evening and said they would have to be at their desks Wednesday morning or face disciplinary action. I pointed out that there was no rule that would require the officers to "make up" the time they had taken off. As for Wednesday and Thursday mornings, I said the officers had earned the time off and should take it. At this point, Lt. Smith accused me of insubordination and said he would file a complaint against me.

Captain, if I handled this matter improperly, I apologize. I should not have lost my temper during the argument with Lt. Smith, and I regret any improper remarks I may have made in the heat of the moment. However, if I am supposed to be in charge of this Section, I think I should have the authority to make reasonable adjustments in the duty schedule. As you know, our work does not always fit into a regular 8-to-5, five-day-a-week schedule. None of my officers have ever complained about putting in overtime whether or not they got paid for it. In this case, I thought these two officers deserved some compensation for their efforts.

Ralph Koonce, Sr. Sgt.,
Juvenile Division

IN REVIEW

1. Match the following management theorists with the types of theory they helped to develop:

    (a) Elton Mayo   i.   Behavioral theory
    (b) Frank Gilbreth   ii.   Organizational theory
    (c) Jane S. Mouton   iii. Scientific management theory
    (d) Douglas McGregor   iv.   Human relations theory
    (e) Frederick W. Taylor
    (f) Max Weber

2. A characteristic of scientific management theory is:

    (a) The belief that the personal satisfaction of the workers is more important than productivity.
    (b) The belief that there is one best way to perform every job.
    (c) The belief that workers set their own performance standards as a group.
    (d) The belief that advanced technology can solve all management problems.
    (e) The belief that proper organizational structure is the key to greater efficiency.

3. What is the Hawthorne effect?
   (a) The use of time and motion studies to increase efficiency.
   (b) The tendency of workers to allow their social relationships to interfere with their job performance.
   (c) A temporary increase in productivity that usually occurs whenever there is any change in the work environment.
   (d) The decrease in productivity that usually occurs when there are unexpected changes in the work environment.
   (e) The loss of motivation that occurs once a worker's material needs are satisfied.

4. A bureaucracy is:
   (a) An organization that is divided into a number of subunits, arranged hierarchically, each of which is responsible for performing specific tasks.
   (b) An organization that is incapable of responding to changes in external demands.
   (c) A manager who is more concerned with productivity than with the personal needs and desires of subordinates.
   (d) Any governmental agency, as distinguished from a business or other private organization.
   (e) A German theory of human motivation.

5. Indicate which of the following statements would be characteristic of Theory X and which would be characteristic of Theory Y:
   (a) Most people do not want to work and would not work if they could avoid it.
   (b) Most people, given a choice, prefer the security of being told what to do, rather than taking responsibility for their own welfare.
   (c) Most people enjoy facing a challenge if they have a reasonable opportunity to meet it and if there is some reward for doing so.
   (d) Most people must be closely supervised to make sure that they keep working.
   (e) Most people prefer to accept responsibility for themselves and for their own work.
   (f) Work is natural to almost everyone.

6. True or False: According to the contingency theory, every manager must choose the one management system or technique that is likely to be successful no matter what changes may occur in the situation.

7. Indicate which of the following tasks, usually performed by managers, are prospective duties(P), current duties (C), and retrospective duties (R):
   (a) Evaluating the performance of workers.
   (b) Preparing a budget.
   (c) Making out payroll checks.
   (d) Developing and issuing policies or rules.
   (e) Transferring personnel from one unit to another.

8. True or False: Most theories of motivation begin with the premise that people ordinarily would not want to do certain things, and there-

fore the leader must somehow persuade them to do what he or she wants.

9. According to some behavioral scientists, most groups:
    (a) Do not want or need a leader.
    (b) Will do whatever their leader wants, regardless of whether it meets their own needs and desires.
    (c) Prefer a leader who always tells them what to do.
    (d) Are unable to choose their leader wisely.
    (e) Choose their own leader regardless of the person's official position in the organization.

10. True or False: The most important responsibility of a manger is to anticipate every situation that might arise, so that appropriate rules and policies can be issued to prevent subordinates from making mistakes.

REFERENCES

1. Ernest Dale, *Management: Theory and Practice*, 3rd ed., New York: McGraw-Hill, 1973, pages 114–117.

2. Dale, pages 117–120.

3. Dale, pages 136–143.

4. Alan O. Bates and Joseph Julian, *Sociology: Understanding Social Behavior*, Boston: Houghton Mifflin, 1975, pages 223–224.

5. Max Weber, *Theory of Social and Economic Organization*, tr. A. M. Henderson and Talcott Parsons, New York: Oxford Univ. Press, 1947, page 333.

6. Abraham H. Maslow, *Motivation and Personality*, New York: Harper & Row, 1954.

7. Douglas M. McGregor, *The Human Side of Enterprise*, New York: McGraw-Hill, 1960.

8. Dale, pages 179–183.

9. Robert R. Blake and Jane Srygley Mouton, *The New Managerial Grid*, 2nd ed., Houston: Gulf Publishing Co., 1978.

10. Roy R. Roberg, *Police Management and Organizational Behavior*, St. Paul: West Publishing, 1979, pages 91–92, 98, and 114.

11. Roberg, pages 43–47.

12. Roberg, pages 208–211.

13. Luther Gulick, "Notes on the Theory of Organization," in Luther Gulick and Lyndall Urwick, eds., *Papers on the Science of Administration*, New York: Institute of Public Administration, 1937.

14. George Maclay and Humphry Knipe, *The Dominant Man*, New York: Delacorte, 1972.

15. Dale, pages 459–465.

16. Roberg, pages 160–161.

17. Roberg, pages 159–160.

18. Roberg, pages 165–169.

3 ORGANIZATION OF POLICE AGENCIES

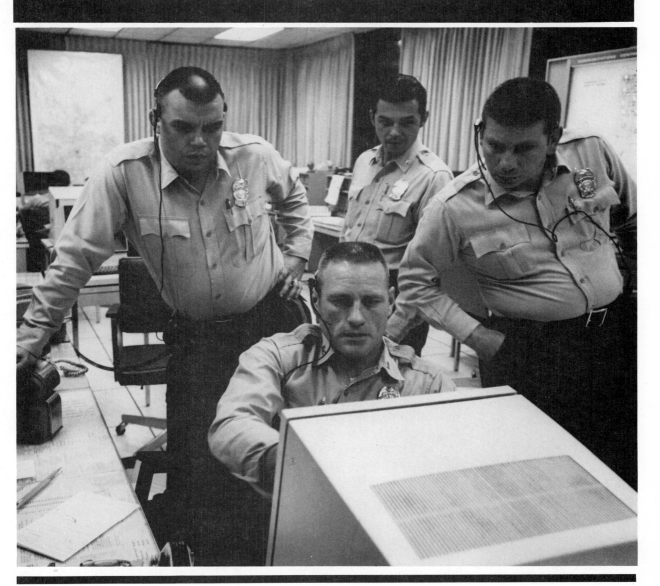

ANY ACTIVITY THAT INVOLVES MORE THAN TWO OR THREE people over any relatively long period of time demands some sort of organization. Even if the people involved are determined to avoid a formal structure (for example, a communal group dedicated to a belief in perfect democracy), there seems to be an inescapable tendency for one person to become dominant, either because of that person's superior skill and knowledge or because the other members of the group prefer to rely on the dominant person's leadership. Once there is a leader, the group has a structure: at the very least, it consists of the leader at the top and the rest of the members at the bottom. If the group is so large or its activities are so complicated that the leader is unable to supervise everyone at once, subleaders may be given the authority and responsibility for portions of the group's overall task.

It is important to understand that this tendency toward hierarchical structure appears to be universal in human societies. It is not a feature of any one ideology or culture. In fact, anthropologists say that the same kind of hierarchical structure appears in groups of social animals other than humans; even some flocks of birds and schools of fish exhibit approximately the same structure.[1] However, this does not mean that an organizational structure, in order to be successful, must be so rigidly authoritarian that the people at lower levels feel oppressed and exploited. Instead, the principles of hierarchical structure must be recognized and observed, but applied in such a way that every individual in the organization feels that his or her contribution is needed and valued.

THE THEORY OF HIERARCHICAL ORGANIZATION

We introduced the principles of organization in Chapter 2, so they do not need to be repeated here. However, some points do require further clarification.

Authority and Responsibility

The word **authority** means that a person has a right or privilege to perform some action, to require others to perform some action, or to make certain kinds of decisions. In principle, all legal authority rests in society as a whole. The rights and privileges held by any particular individual or group of individuals have been granted by the rest of society, and this grant must serve some need or purpose of the whole society. Thus, the authority of government derives from the "consent of the governed" or the desire of the people in general to have a government. By the same token, the people have an inherent right to limit the authority they grant, by setting restrictions or conditions on it.

Every grant of authority carries with it an equal **responsibility**: an obligation for the person to perform the authorized duty, to observe the limits or restrictions set by the people, and ultimately to serve the public need or purpose for which authority has been granted.

In accord with this principle, both the authority and the responsibility to make laws have been granted by the members of our society to the various legislatures: the Congress, state legislatures, city councils, and, in some states, county commissions or boards of supervisors. The authority and responsibility to enforce the laws have been granted to various executive bodies: the president, the governors, the mayors or city managers, and again the county commissions or boards of supervisors. To a certain extent, the city councils in some cities also serve an executive function. These grants of authority and responsibility, and the terms and conditions that limit these grants, are contained in the federal and state constitutions, city charters, and, in most states, the state laws establishing local governments.

Any grant of authority, with its accompanying responsibility, can be **delegated** to another person, just as society as a whole granted the authority in the first place. However, when authority is delegated, the person or agency to whom it was originally granted remains responsible for its proper exercise and has the right to revoke the delegation at any time. There can be a series of such delegations as different parts of a task are passed along and divided into smaller and smaller segments. No matter how long the chain of delegations may be, the ultimate authority always rests with the person or agency at the beginning of the chain. Usually this person is represented as being at the top of a triangle or pyramid; authority is said to flow downward from the top of the pyramid toward the bottom, while responsibility is said to flow upward from the bottom to the top.

Management theorists often point out that it is unfair and ineffective to delegate responsibility for a particular task without also delegating the authority to carry it out. Actually, it is not only unfair and unwise: it is impossible. Authority and responsibility are bound together like the two sides of a coin. Unfortunately, it sometimes happens that a person in authority will try to shift the blame to subordinates when something goes wrong by claiming that the subordinates had responsibility for taking some action. However, if it is clear that the subordinates never had the authority to act, then they could not have had the responsibility to act.

When responsibility and authority are granted or delegated, the person who receives the grant or delegation also must be **accountable** to the person (or agency, or society as a whole) who made the grant or delegation. **Accountability** simply means that each person in the organization may be called on at any time to show that he or she has exercised the authority properly.

The Chain of Command

The fact that authority and responsibility are delegated to the various parts of an organization creates a **chain of command**. The chain of command is the route or channel along which authority and responsibility have been subdivided and parcelled out among the elements of the organization. (See Figure 3.1.)

For example, the chief of police has both authority and responsibility for everything done by the entire agency. Obviously the chief is not expected to personally perform every task. The chief's authority and responsibility for law enforcement operations might be delegated to a Deputy Chief of Operations, who in turn might delegate the authority and responsibility for criminal investigations to the captain in charge of the Detective Bureau. The captain, in turn, delegates the authority and responsibility for investigating certain crimes to the lieutenant in charge of, say, the Crimes Against Persons Section, and the lieutenant delegates the authority and responsibility for investigating specific cases to the several detective sergeants in

Figure 3-1 The chain of command.

that section. The chain of command, then, begins with the chief and passes through the deputy chief, captain, and lieutenant to the sergeants.

Unity of Command

Traditional organization theorists have maintained that there must be **unity of command**, that each person in an organization must be accountable to one and only one higher official. The reason for this rule is that if a person is placed under the authority of two different officials, they might give conflicting orders that would confuse and immobilize the subordinate.

As a general rule, the principle of unity of command is valid and ought to be observed. However, it is sometimes the source of as much confusion as it prevents. For example, in some very large metropolitan police agencies, detectives are assigned to the various precinct headquarters. To whom are the detectives accountable: to the precinct commanders or to the chief of detectives for the whole department? Most agencies, following the principle of unity of command, place the precinct detectives under the authority of the departmental chief of detectives. But this puts the detectives in the position of resident aliens in the precinct stations. Since they are not accountable to the precinct commanders and must carry out assignments from the departmental headquarters, they are not available to assist in precinct-level operations and they are not necessarily bound by the precinct commander's rules and policies. On the other hand, making the detectives answerable only to the precinct commander diminishes the role of the chief of detectives to that of a technical adviser and breeds inconsistency in the investigative policies and procedures followed from one precinct to the next.

The traditional answer to this dilemma is that the precinct commander should go through channels and ask the chief of detectives for the assistance of the precinct detectives or for their compliance with precinct rules and policies. That way, the authority of the chief of detectives is not diminished, but in a sense is delegated to the precinct commander, and an acceptable degree of cooperation and coordination can be achieved. In practice, however, the procedure of going through channels to obtain coordination often fails, and it is frequently more time-consuming and troublesome than it is worth.

A more practical solution is to frankly place the detectives under dual jurisdiction, but to state explicitly the areas of policy and procedure for which each commanding officer has authority. The chief of detectives might retain authority for developing investigative procedures and policies, for transferring personnel from one precinct or section to another, for recommending promotions, and so on. Meanwhile, the precinct commander might have authority to assign work schedules, to assign cases for investigation within the precinct, and to enforce precinct-level rules and policies that apply to all personnel. Inevitably, there will be occasions when the chief of detectives and the precinct commander issue conflicting or ambiguous orders. However, these two officials should be able to resolve these conflicts between themselves; if they cannot, they should refer the matter to the next higher authority in the chain of command.

A more serious problem develops when personnel in different chains of command are required to work together. Often there is no time or opportunity for questions of authority to be resolved by rational compromise. For example, if a regular patrol officer and a traffic division officer arrive simultaneously at the scene of a serious accident, their immediate life-saving duties do not allow time for them to debate over which of them should take charge. The responsibility in such a situation may be established in advance, by agency policy. If it is not, the two officers should be willing to work together cooperatively without concern for which of them has the right to take charge; such matters can be settled after the immediate task is completed.

If we seem to be belaboring a point that ought to be a matter of common sense, it is only because there have been far too many instances of the sort described by Roy Roberg:

In one incident, [a student of Roberg's] was the first officer to arrive on the scene of a traffic accident in which one of the cars had overturned and pinned the driver inside. The officer could not free the accident victim from the car. Not knowing the extent of the injuries, and fearing that the car might catch fire and explode, the officer immediately radioed for an ambulance and a fire truck to help free the victim. The firemen, after some effort, removed the victim from the car and the ambulance took the victim to the hospital. Instead of receiving praise for his efforts, the officer was later reprimanded by the department for not going through channels and receiving permission from his immediate superior (sergeant) to call for the ambulance and fire truck.[2]

What is most discouraging about this incident is that the reprimand was an official one, from the department itself (which in effect means from some higher level of authority), and not just from a misguided sergeant. No doubt the reprimanded officer's experience became common knowledge among the rest of the patrol force. One wonders how many future accident victims might die while a confused officer tries desperately to locate a superior officer to authorize what obviously must be done at once.

Coordination and the Span of Control

The principles of the chain of command and of unity of command define the manner in which people are arranged into a hierarchical order of authority and responsibility. If everyone performed his or her tasks independently, these principles probably would be sufficient to describe an ideal organization.

In some simple enterprises, a very simple organizational structure is quite adequate. For example, in a factory that produces a single product more or less continuously, the workers on the assembly line each have a particular job to do, each line foreman supervises a group of workers doing essentially the same job, and each supervisor is responsible for a group of foremen whose workers perform a clearly defined portion of the overall work. As long as everyone does his or her job properly, the entire operation should proceed smoothly and efficiently.

Police work, however, is vastly more complicated. The "workers" at the end of the chain of command have not one task but many different tasks to perform at different times. Some tasks can be performed by individual workers while other tasks require the joint efforts of several people, not all of whom are necessarily accountable to the same supervisor. The tasks themselves are not always routine; many of them require a variety of skills and the exercise of mature judgment and discretion.

In the single-product factory, the task of **coordination**, bringing various parts into the proper order or relationship, is easily performed by a shop supervisor who assigns the workers to their different tasks and sees that raw materials are delivered to each work station at the proper time. But coordination is not so easy to achieve in a police agency. In theory, the responsibility for coordinating any two elements in an organization rests with the person who has authority over both of them. For example, if the chief of detectives has authority over both the Crimes Against Persons Section and the Property Crimes Section, it is the chief's responsibility to coordinate the activities of the two sections so that every new case is assigned to one section or the other, each section knows what procedures to employ in each type of case, and cases that involve both crimes against persons and property crimes (an armed robbery and assault, for instance) are properly investigated by the most competent person. Similarly, any operation that involves both detectives and patrol officers should be coordinated by the official who has authority over both: usually the deputy chief of operations or some equivalent official.

The difficulty is that in any organization large enough to have a deputy chief of operations, that individual could not hope to take charge personally of every case that might require the cooperative efforts of both patrol officers and detectives. Even in a comparatively small agency, one that has, say, eight detectives divided equally into two sections, it would be unrealistic to expect the chief of detectives (usually a captain) to supervise every case that requires some degree of coordination. Instead, the usual practice is to try to establish coordination by rules and policies set in advance.

The danger in relying on formal rules, as we have said earlier, is that no set of rules will anticipate every circumstance that may arise. The result is a mass of rules so complicated and elaborate that no one can understand or remember them. When a situation occurs that demands coordination between two units, the people most immediately involved will first try to decide which rules apply; failing that, they will appeal for help to their respective supervisors, who may have to appeal to a higher level of authority to resolve the impasse. Meanwhile, no work is being done and the official with the authority for coordination will have to make the final decision.

Most of the time, this cumbersome procedure is accepted as a necessary product of the principle of unity of command. Most officials are relieved of the need to make nearly all routine decisions, since these are resolved in formal rules and policies, and the period of confusion and lost production while unusual situations are resolved ordinarily has no serious consequences. However, police work does involve life-and-death crises sometimes, and there may be no opportunity for the work to wait while someone resolves questions of coordination.

A better solution, once again, is to encourage all personnel to coordinate their own work, to cooperate with one another to the maximum extent possible, and to *avoid* referring jurisdictional questions to their superiors. Some formal rules are necessary, of course, but their intent should be to establish broad guidelines and general principles for coordination. The emphasis always should be on getting the job done first, and afterward straightening out any questions of authority, jurisdiction, or procedure. If mistakes are made, they should be brought to the attention of supervisors and the personnel involved should be corrected—not to punish them for the mistake or for exercising discretion and initiative, but to help them avoid similar mistakes in the future. Such after-the-fact evaluation and correction is an important duty of every supervisor; it is a far more potent method of coordinating the work of subordinates than any volume of rules and policies.

One of the traditional concerns of organization theorists is the extent of a supervisor's or manager's **span of control**, which simply means the number of people or organizational elements that are accountable to one person. In order for the supervisor or manager to be aware of the subordinates' work, to coordinate their activities, to evaluate and correct their performance, and so on, the span of control must be reasonably small. For example, the chief of police in a small agency may have no great difficulty in supervising the department's 25 employees organized into two main sections. However, as the agency grows and is divided into more and more sections, a point may be reached at which the chief is attempting to control the activities of 200 people in 20 major sections. There would not be enough time in the day for the chief to learn what has been done in all the sections, let alone to make important decisions and resolve conflicts. The chief's span of control has gotten too large. The solution is to insert an intermediate level of management, such as three deputy chiefs, each of whom assumes responsibility for several of the sections. Now the chief merely has to keep track of the activities of the three deputy chiefs, evaluating and correcting their work, and resolving disputes or conflicts among them. (See Figure 3.2.)

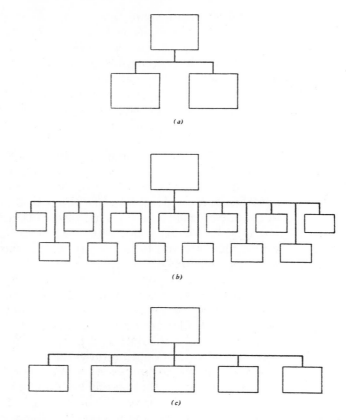

Figure 3-2 The span of control. (*a*) Very narrow. (*b*) Very broad. (*c*) Moderately broad.

Of course, as this example illustrates, any reduction in the span of control for an individual manager is obtained at the expense of inserting a new level of management into the organization. The chain of command is thereby made longer, further removing the workers at the bottom of the pyramid from the ultimate source of authority and further removing the person at the top of the pyramid from intimate, day-to-day knowledge of activities at the operational level. Management theorists have debated for years which is worse: a **flat structure** in which the manager's span of control is extended too far or a **tall structure** in which the chain of command is too long. Although there can be no absolute, universal formula, most theorists have concluded that the best structure is as flat as possible, provided no one manager has too great a span of control. (See Figure 3.3.)

How great is "too great"? At one time, management theorists believed that there was a simple answer: No manager should be responsible for more than six subordinates (or six organizational elements). However, cases were found where a manager easily supervised twice or three times that many people, and other cases were found where a manager was over-taxed with only two or three subordinates. Today, most theorists reject any magic number but rely instead on the consideration of three factors:

● **The nature of the work.** Routine work performed more or less continu-ously will require few decisions on the part of the manager, and there-

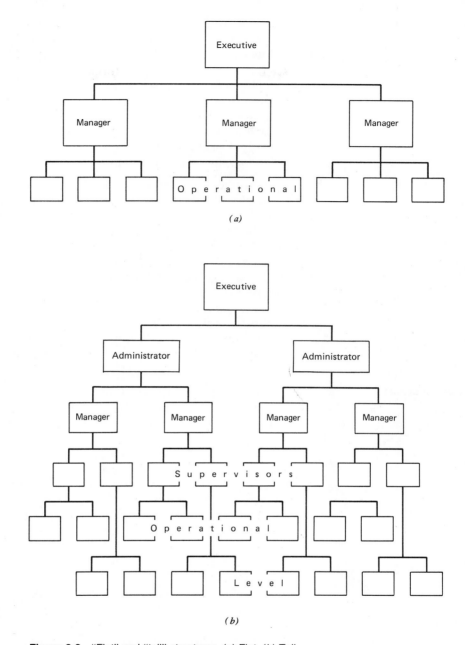

Figure 3-3 "Flat" and "tall" structures. (*a*) Flat. (*b*) Tall.

fore a manager can control a greater number of subordinates. Work that varies in content, that requires the exercise of discretion and judgment, or that is relatively complex will require closer supervision by the manager, and therefore the span of control must be reduced.

- **The character of the workers.** If employees are highly skilled, intelligent, well-trained, and highly motivated, they will require little supervision regardless of the nature of their work, and therefore the manager's span of control can be enlarged. If workers are poorly skilled and unenthusiastic about their work, close supervision will be required and the span of control must be reduced.

- **The character and personality of the manager.** Some managers seem to be able to be everywhere, to keep track of thousands of details about their subordinates' jobs and performances, to make decisions quickly, and through it all to remain alert and relaxed. Other managers agonize over decisions, or feel compelled to immerse themselves in the details of each individual job, or hesitate to make any demands on their subordinates. Certainly, the first manager would be able to handle a much larger span of control than the second.

Again, there is no firm rule that dictates the ideal span of control. The nature of police work is such that, even given exceptionally well-qualified personnel and unusually competent managers, it is unlikely that anyone would be able to provide adequate direct supervision of more than about 10 subordinates at the operational level or more than 5 at the administrative level. On the other hand, any manager who supervises fewer than five subordinates, except perhaps at the highest administrative level, probably is not being overworked and the organizational structure probably is taller than necessary.

Unfortunately, the effort to organize an agency so that the span of control is appropriate for every supervisor often conflicts with the tendency of many police administrators to overspecialize.

Specialization

The fundamental purpose of any organization is to divide the tasks that make up the total enterprise among the people who are available to perform them, so that each person is assigned to the job for which he or she is best qualified.

A basketball team could not function effectively if it were made up of five centers or five guards or five forwards. But one center, two guards, and two forwards, if they work together harmoniously and if each is skillful at his or her task, should be able to win any given game. Some basketball teams specialize even further: One forward may be especially skilled at driving under the basket for a lay-up shot while another may be better at long jump shots.

Specialization is often carried to a considerable degree in other sports. A certain football player may be not just a defensive tackle, but specifically a defensive left tackle who only plays when the other team is likely to pass.

As we discussed in Chapter 1, there was little if any specialization in the earliest police agencies. Police officers were either troops or commanders. After the Civil War, more advanced ideas of crime-prevention patrols and criminal investigation brought about a degree of specialization: An officer might be assigned to patrol, or to investigate crimes, or to supervise other officers. Intermediate supervisory ranks such as patrol lieutenant and precinct captain were established. Later still, the first wave of police reform around the turn of the century involved greater degrees of specialization. Separate units were established to deal with particular types of crime or to provide specific services. Since then, the tendency toward specialization has continued and if anything has grown stronger over the years.

The advantages of specialization are frequently cited by management theorists and authorities on police administration. Specialization is supposed to enable a person to make the best use of individual skills and interests, to learn a great deal about a specialty through repeated experience, and to develop a high level of motivation through pride in one's special expertise. Also, specialization is supposed to enable administrators to assign responsibility more clearly, since every task becomes the duty of one or another specific unit, and to organize training more effectively, since specialized individuals need to be given only the training required for their particular specialty.[3]

The disadvantages of specialization are less often mentioned. The most significant disadvantage is that specialization narrows the range of competencies of every individual in the agency. A detective may know everything there is to know about, say, auto thefts but almost nothing about homicides. If the detective is assigned to a case that involves both crimes, the homicide may be improperly investigated or the detective must ask for help from a homicide detective.

Even a more limited degree of specialization has the same disadvantage. For example, in many traditional police agencies, the patrol officers are neither expected nor encouraged to know anything about criminalistics techniques. Their responsibility at a crime scene is merely to obtain a preliminary report by interviewing the complainant or victim, then to notify the detectives, protect the crime scene from contamination, and assist the evidence technicians when they arrive. These policies mean that much of the patrol officers' time is wasted. At least one additional person (a detective) and often three or four (evidence technicians, photographers, etc.) must be involved in every routine investigation. Almost always, valuable evidence is lost or overlooked.[4] At the very least, valuable time is lost—time in which the perpetrator may escape beyond the agency's reach.

Excessive specialization complicates the already difficult task of coordinating the activities of police personnel, and it leads to inefficient allocations of personnel. One section of the agency may have little or no work to do while another section is overburdened, but it may be impossible to shift people from the first section to the second because the people have not been trained in the appropriate specialty.

Some degree of specialization is obviously necessary. You would not expect a criminalistics technician to issue parking tickets. In general, specialization is most practical in the administrative and technical sections of a police agency, where the work often requires particular skills or training and where the tasks are continuous or repetitive in nature (such as checking and filing reports or keeping financial accounts). Even here, it is desirable to see that employees who perform similar or related work are cross-trained so they can assist one another or fill in if there is a shift in work load or someone is absent. Cross-training also promotes better coordination and cooperation since employees have a better understanding of one another's jobs.

Among operational personnel—those engaged directly in crime prevention and law enforcement duties—we believe that specialization should be avoided where possible and kept to a minimum where it is necessary. There should be no rigid lines of demarcation between regular patrol officers, traffic patrol officers, investigators, and other officers. Any police officer who is called on, or who sees an opportunity, to perform any police service for the public—whether it involves investigating a crime, arresting an offender, or directing traffic—should do so without hesitation, to the limits of his or her abilities. All personnel should be trained in advanced techniques and specialized areas of law enforcement such as traffic control or criminal investigation and should be discouraged from committing themselves and their careers exclusively to one specialty.

Certainly, differences in talent and personal preferences ought to be accommodated, and some officers will be better at certain tasks than at others. However, there is no known limit to the ability of the human brain to absorb new knowledge. Effective, ongoing training programs should be designed to expand every officer's repertoire of skills over the whole spectrum of law enforcement responsibilities, rather than narrowing each officer's range of competencies.

From an organizational point of view, the tendency to specialize should be resisted. Officers performing related work should be grouped into units of sufficient size to permit flexibility in work assignments and to maintain an optimal span of control for supervisors. It makes little sense for a medium-sized agency to divide its Detective Bureau into six or seven specialized units, each containing only two or three investigators supervised by a lieutenant. A better arrangement would be to consolidate the units into at most two, cross-train the officers in the various investigative specialties, and rotate case assignments to give each investigator experience in different kinds of cases. Those officers who have developed special expertise in a particular area should assist their supervisors in cross-training their colleagues and should readily give technical advice when it is needed. If nothing else, this arrangement ensures that the agency's overall abilities are not impaired if an officer with a particular specialty leaves the department or is temporarily absent.

There is still a place for individuals with unique specialties within a more generalized operational structure. For example, most smaller agencies do not need a full-time polygraph specialist. However, a patrol officer or detective could be given advanced training in polygraph techniques and then could be assigned to conduct all polygraph interviews and interrogations. The rest of the officer's time would be spent on ordinary patrol or investigative duties. Such a part-time specialist also should train other members of the department in his or her specialty, acting as a technical advisor and resource person to the agency.

ORGANIZING A POLICE AGENCY

Few individuals will ever have the opportunity to establish and organize an entire police agency from scratch. Such opportunities usually arise only when a town is newly incorporated and hires its first police chief, who may be the only salaried employee in the agency.

However, small agencies generally grow if the community they serve grows. Medium-sized and even larger agencies periodically must be reorganized to accommodate changes in the community's size, population, political system, or its needs and desires for police services. An agency may have internal needs that require reorganization, too. Rapid growth in the number of personnel, changes in the availability of special skills, or changing ideas about the police service and the agency's responsibilities may make reorganization desirable. Fortunately, the procedures that should be followed in organizing a new agency or in reorganizing an existing one are essentially the same.

Terminology: Ranks, Functions, and Elements

Before we discuss how to organize a police agency, we should establish a standard vocabulary for the various parts of the organization. There is often a great deal of confusion when two different police agencies are compared because there is no standardized terminology in use among all law enforcement agencies. What one agency may call a unit may be equivalent to another agency's section while the first agency's section is more or less the same as someone else's bureau.

Adding to the confusion is the traditional use of military-style ranks. As traditions go, this is not a very old one. It extends back to about the post-Civil War period, around the same time that military-style uniforms were first introduced to law enforcement, and for much the same reason: to instill pride and discipline by drawing on military traditions. It is by no means clear that military-style ranks are necessary or appropriate in the police service at all; in fact, the usefulness of rank designations in the military itself may be disappearing rapidly as weapons and military tactics become more sophisticated and more dependent on highly specialized personnel.

Nevertheless, it does not appear likely that the use of military-style ranks will disappear from the police service anytime soon. Because rank designations vary from one agency to another, we list in Table 3.1 the terms we use in this book, the more or less equivalent terms used by some agencies, and a rough description of what the title means.

In addition to the ranks listed in Table 3.1, some agencies use the ranks of senior patrol officer and senior sergeant. These ranks may be intermediate between patrol officer and sergeant, or sergeant and lieutenant; or they may merely indicate that the individual has remained at the same rank long enough to deserve a higher salary. In some agencies, intermediate ranks are awarded to individuals who show exceptional promise and initiative, and who are expected to exert leadership among their colleagues. Other agencies use the "senior" designation to indicate that the individual, while competent in his or her present position, is not likely to be promoted to any higher rank but is being rewarded for faithful service.

There is often confusion over the fact that most police officers have two titles: their rank and their functional, or office, title. Rank indicates nothing more than a person's salary level and general range of authority and responsibility. Functional titles indicate what a person does for the agency and approximately where he or she fits into the agency's hierarchy. There is virtually an infinite list of possible functional titles, since there is a title for every position in an agency, and agencies are free to make up their own titles. The list in Table 3.2 is by no means exhaustive; it merely includes some of the more common functional titles that we use here.

In addition to the titles in Table 3.2, there may be a number of other functional titles, such as juvenile officer, training officer, and field training supervisor, whose meaning is (more or less) evident from the title itself.

Table 3.1 Police Rank Designations

Our Terminology	Equivalent Term	Description
Chief of Police	Director of Public Safety[a] Commissioner[a]	Executive head of police agency, appointed by city government (or, in a few cases, elected).
Deputy Chief	Assistant Chief Major	Second-highest administrator, head of a major element of the agency.
Captain	Commander	Head of a major element, if there are no deputy chiefs; head of a precinct, district, or bureau.
Lieutenant	Same	Head of an element with a specific area of responsibility: a unit, section, watch, shift.
Sergeant	Same	Head of a group of personnel (unit, watch, or shift); in some units, such as detectives, the lowest-level operating personnel.
Patrol officer	Officer; patrolman, patrolwoman	Operational personnel; the lowest-ranking commissioned officer.
(Not used)	Corporal	Intermediate rank between officer and sergeant.
(Not used)	Cadet	Probationary patrol officer; temporary rank given to new recruits during or just after training, while assigned to on-the-job training.

[a]These titles are sometimes used to designate officials who are responsible for overseeing the police department and other public safety agencies such as the fire department and ambulance service. Often these officials are elected and do not take an active, day-to-day part in law enforcement operations.

The important point to remember is that these functional titles do not necessarily reflect a person's rank or vice versa.

In this and the preceding chapters, we have referred to the various parts of a police agency by various terms. Again, there is no uniform terminology used by all police agencies. In Table 3.3 we compare the terms we use with some of the roughly equivalent terms used by many agencies.

Table 3.2 Functional Titles

Our Terminology	Equivalent Terms	Description
Patrol officer[a]	Uniformed officer; patrolman, patrolwoman	Any low-ranking police officer assigned to general police duty such as patrol.
Traffic officer	Traffic patrolman	A patrol officer assigned exclusively to traffic law enforcement.
Detective	Investigator, detective sergeant, plainclothesman, inspector (rarely)	Any officer assigned to criminal investigation duties; usually does not wear a uniform.
Evidence technician	Criminalist	Any person, either a police officer or civilian, who assists in locating, collecting, and evaluating evidence.
Supervisor	Same	A sergeant, lieutenant, or (sometimes) captain who directly supervises operational personnel.
Chief of—	Head of— Section (or unit) commander	The supervisor of a functional element such as a bureau, section, or unit.
Commander	Chief of— Head of— Commanding officer	The manager (usually ranked captain or higher) of a major functional element such as a precinct, bureau, division.
Ranking officer	Commander	The officer, regardless of rank or title, who has the authority and responsibility for a given task; usually the highest-ranking officer present in a situation.
Manager, administrator	Supervisor	Every officer above the operational level.
Executive		Chief of police; highest-ranking person within the agency.

[a]We capitalize Patrol Officer when we mean the rank of a given individual and lowercase patrol officer when we mean the function.

Function Analysis

Once the various parts of an agency have been identified, the police administrator is ready to consider the best way to arrange them into an effective organizational structure. The different categories of elements listed in Table 3.3 are the "boxes" into which the functions and ranks listed in Tables 3.2 and 3.1 must fit.

Table 3.3 Elements of a Police Agency

Our Terminology	Equivalent Terms	Description
Division	Bureau, section	One of the two to five major parts of the agency, headed by a deputy chief, major, or captain.
Bureau	Division, section, office	One of the parts of a division, including several smaller units, headed by a captain or lieutenant.
Section	Unit, office, watch, detail, division	One of the parts of a bureau; may be divided into smaller parts; headed by a lieutenant or sergeant.
Unit	Section, office, watch, detail, shift, squad	One of the parts of a section; not divided further by function, may be divided by time of day; headed by a lieutenant or sergeant.
Precinct	District, sector	A geographic section of a city with its own police subheadquarters (station).
District	Precinct, area	A geographic section of a city, used to assign patrol and other personnel, but with no permanent station.
Sector	District, area	A part of a district or precinct containing two or more adjacent patrol areas.
Area, beat	Sector, section, route	Part of a district or sector to which a patrol officer (or squad of patrol officers) is assigned.
Shift, watch	Same	A unit of time: a part of the working day, which is not necessarily divided into equal parts.
Squad, team	Patrol, unit	Several officers who work together in a coordinated activity.

One more step must be performed before any decisions about structure are made: the administrator must know what tasks are to be performed by the agency.

Every police agency's list of functions is unique to that agency, since it is derived from the needs of the community and from the laws and ordinances that grant authority to it. However, there is enough similarity among all American police agencies to permit some generalizations. In the next list, Table 3.4, we have tried to include every specific function that is common to most police agencies, including municipal police departments, sheriff's departments, and state police. Some agencies might have additional functions not listed here, and others may omit some of these functions. We have not attempted to include non-law enforcement functions such as ambulance service, funeral escorts, and so forth.

Table 3.4   Functions of a Police Agency

Function	Purpose	Description of Tasks
I. Law Enforcement Functions		
1. Receipt and disposition of citizens' complaints	1. To ensure that complaints of crime, prospective crime, emergency, etc., receive prompt attention	1. Receive complaint, record on standard form; assign police officer to respond as needed.
2. Response to crime-in-progress and other emergencies	2. To protect lives and property; to apprehend offender if possible	2. Proceed rapidly to scene of incident; determine nature of incident; obtain additional help if needed; act to protect lives and property and to arrest any suspected offenders found at the scene.
3. Preliminary investigation	3. To determine the nature of the incident and identity of offenders if known	3. Interview complainant, victim, or witnesses; record condition of the crime scene; gather and preserve evidence found at scene.
4. Continuing investigation	4. To determine the identity and whereabouts and to apprehend suspected offender	4. Interview witnesses, interrogate suspects, gather and preserve evidence away from the crime scene; apprehend and arrest suspected offender.
5. Analysis and development of evidence	5. To identify, characterize, and rationalize physical evidence	5. Apply criminalistics techniques to physical evidence, as needed; prepare reports; prepare exhibits for presentation in court.
6. Polygraphic interrogation	6. To test the veracity of witness, suspect	6. Apply polygraphic techniques; interpret and report findings; prepare court presentations.
7. Investigation of organized crimes	7. To determine the identity of persons involved in organized crime; to gather evidence against organized criminals	7. Observe sites and persons believed to be involved in organized crime; penetrate criminal organizations by use of undercover techniques, by locating cooperative and knowledgeable informants, and by legally acceptable surveillance techniques.
8. Preparation of case reports	8. To organize and present evidence for use by prosecutors	8. Prepare a written statement of the nature of the crime and of the evidence; deliver the report to prosecutors; confer with prosecutors on any improvements needed in the report.
9. Presentation of evidence in court	9. To present evidence against accused offenders	9. Testify in court proceedings, such as hearings and trials, on the evidence produced by an investigation.
II. Traffic Law Enforcement Functions		
10. Direction of traffic	10. To ensure the safe movement of vehicles and pedestrians	10. Direct traffic in and around congested areas; coordinate the traffic flow with traffic control devices and other officers.

(Continued)

Table 3.4 *(Continued)*

Function	Purpose	Description of Tasks
11. Detection and apprehension of traffic violators	11. To discourage violations; to protect other citizens from unsafe and illegal acts of violators	11. Observe motorists and pedestrians, using appropriate devices such as radar speed detectors; apprehend violators; identify violators and their vehicles; issue verbal or written warnings or citations as appropriate; arrest violators who present an imminent danger to others (such as reckless or intoxicated driver).
12. Investigation of accidents	12. To protect the lives or property of citizens; to relieve traffic congestion; to create legal record of incident	12. Proceed rapidly to scene of reported accident; observe need for, and obtain, assistance if hazard exists; establish traffic control around accident site; interview drivers and witnesses; record conditions at scene; arrange for and supervise removal of disabled vehicles.
13. Enforcement of parking regulations	13. To ensure safe traffic movement; to protect revenue from meters; to provide citizens with fair access to convenient parking areas	13. Observe legal parking areas adjacent to roads; place citations on illegally parked vehicles; arrange for and supervise removal of vehicles parked in a hazardous or obstructive location; instruct motorists to move away from improper parking locations.
III. Crime Prevention Functions		
14. Preventive patrol	14. To observe criminal acts, behavior, or conditions that might lead to criminal acts or that create a hazard to lives or property; to discourage persons from committing crimes; to identify and apprehend offenders	14. Observe the activities of suspicious persons and places where criminal behavior frequently occurs; observe hazardous conditions and remove the hazard or report it to appropriate authorities.
15. Traffic patrol	15. To discourage motorists from violating traffic laws	15. Conspicuously patrol streets, highways, intersections where traffic law violations and accidents occur most often.
16. Public education	16. To encourage all citizens to obey all criminal and traffic laws and to protect themselves from offenders	16. Advise public, individually or in groups, of the requirements of the laws, reasons for the laws, consequences of violating the law, and methods of protecting themselves and property.
IV. Family Protection Services		
17. Juvenile crime prevention	17. To discourage juveniles from engaging in crime	17. Observe juvenile groups and individuals; advise them as to the requirements of the laws and consequences of committing crimes; encourage constructive youth activities.
18. Apprehension of juvenile offenders	18. To identify and apprehend juvenile offenders; to promote rapid, effective reformative treatment	18. Interview witnesses who have knowledge of juveniles engaged in criminal activities; gather evidence concerning juvenile crimes; apprehend suspected juvenile

Table 3.4 *(Continued)*

Function	Purpose	Description of Tasks
		offenders and present them, with evidence, to appropriate court or other officials.
19. Truancy law enforcement	19. To ensure that juveniles and parents obey school attendance laws	19. Obtain names and likely whereabouts of truant students from school officials; locate and apprehend truant students; notify and counsel parents; refer chronic offenders to juvenile court or other appropriate officials.
20. Child protective law enforcement	20. To protect the lives and welfare of children	20. Respond promptly to all complaints or reports of possible child abuse, neglect, mistreatment, or exploitation; gather evidence of offenses; assist child welfare authorities in taking legal steps against abusive adults; when necessary, arrest abusive adults and assume custody of abused children.
21. Family crisis intervention	21. To protect the lives and welfare of all persons; to reduce disturbances of the peace; to assist family members in obtaining needed assistance	21. Intervene in family disturbances to the extent necessary to protect the lives of all persons present; counsel and advise citizens to obtain appropriate help in resolving their problems constructively; if necessary, restrain or arrest belligerent family members.
V. Operational Supervision Functions		
22. Patrol supervision	22. To ensure that patrol functions are discharged properly	22. Assign officers to patrol shifts and beats; create and maintain work schedules; observe patrol officers in the field; receive, review, and correct all routine field reports; inform patrol officers of applicable policies, regulations, crime and hazard conditions on their beats; instruct officers in policing techniques; assist in conducting potentially dangerous activities.
23. Investigative supervision	23. To ensure that investigative functions are performed properly	23. Assign officers to investigative duties; create and maintain a work schedule; assign cases to investigators; receive, review, and correct all investigative reports; ensure that officers observe all applicable policies and regulations; inform officers of current crime trends and conditions; assist officers in applying appropriate investigative techniques, in preparing case reports and other documents, and in preparing court testimony.
VI. Technical Support Functions		
24. Communications	24. To maintain continuous communication with all field units and to provide all other communications services needed	24. Operate telephone, radio, and other communications systems.

(Continued)

Table 3.4 *(Continued)*

Function	Purpose	Description of Tasks
25. Document entry	25. To ensure that all reports and documents are complete and accurate; to place all documents correctly in files	25. Receive incoming reports and documents; review them for completeness and accuracy; return incomplete or inaccurate documents to originator for correction; create cross-index entries for each new document; place new documents in correct file position.
26. Document retrieval	26. To provide agency personnel with needed documents	26. On proper request, retrieve any needed document from files, record its removal, and transmit to requesting officer; assist personnel in identifying and locating needed documents.
27. Public records service	27. To provide needed documents to citizens	27. Receive requests from citizens; determine whether release of document is authorized by law and agency policy; if so, retrieve document from files, record its removal, and transmit it (or a copy) to citizen.
28. Vehicle servicing and maintenance	28. To ensure that all police vehicles are available for use when needed	28. Service all patrol vehicles at end of each shift and all other vehicles on regular basis; perform all needed repairs on vehicles; provide field repair and towing for disabled vehicles; maintain records of all maintenance and repairs; maintain and repair vehicle-related equipment (siren, radio, etc.).
29. Evidence and property service	29. To maintain legal custody of all personal property in agency's possession; to maintain legal chain of custody of evidence	29. Provide secure storage for all nonevidence personal property (found property, recovered stolen property, prisoners' property); maintain records of all personal property in agency's possession; provide legally secure storage for all physical evidence.
30. Jail	30. To maintain custody of prisoners according to law and agency regulations; to maintain records of persons in custody	30. Receive prisoners; record prisoners' identity, physical condition, and personal property; detain prisoners in a secure place; provide prisoners with food, clothing, medical care, recreation, access to visitors, communication with legal counsel, and other services required by law and agency policy; maintain records of current location of each prisoner until final release is authorized by appropriate official.
31. Crime analysis	31. To assist agency personnel in detecting and understanding crime trends and patterns	31. Receive and review all crime reports; analyze crime reports to determine trends or patterns in criminal behavior; report analyses to administrative and operational personnel.
VII. Administrative Support Functions		
32. Personnel recruitment and selection	32. To provide the agency with needed personnel	32. Inform the public of the availability and benefits of employment in police service; conduct recruitment campaigns aimed at specific population segments; select qualified

Table 3.4 *(Continued)*

Function	Purpose	Description of Tasks
		applicants in a manner consistent with laws and Civil Service regulations; provide administrators with lists of eligible recruits; advise and assist recruits during entry process.
33. Personnel training	33. To ensure that all agency personnel have needed skills and knowledge	33. Establish and conduct training programs for recruits, in-service personnel, and personnel eligible for promotion; maintain records of training; assist personnel in taking advantage of external training opportunities.
34. Personnel records	34. To maintain accurate records of employment of all personnel	34. Create a permanent file upon entry of each new employee; enter information concerning training completed, rank and duty assignments, promotions, awards, current salary, and all other matters as agency policy requires; locate and retrieve files on proper request of administrators.
35. Accounting	35. To create and maintain complete and accurate records of agency's finances	35. Receive and record all receipts; prepare and issue all disbursements (payroll and purchase vouchers or checks); transfer funds to and from proper depositories (banks); keep a current record of the budgeted and expended funds in each of the agency's accounts.
36. Purchasing	36. To ensure that the agency acquires needed supplies and equipment at best price	36. Prepare descriptions and specifications of needed items; issue requests for bids; receive and review bids; issue purchase order to lowest qualified bidder; receive purchased items, determine that they meet specifications, and deliver them to ordering unit or store for future use.
37. Inventory	37. To ensure that all agency property is accounted for	37. Periodically perform a count of supplies and equipment; determine the location and condition of equipment having a useful life of one year or more; report discrepancies (equipment not located) to administrators.
38. Building maintenance	38. To ensure that the agency's buildings and equipment are properly maintained	38. Clean all buildings on regular basis; repair facilities and equipment as needed.
39. Public information	39. To inform the news media of significant events and activities; to answer inquiries from news media or the public	39. Inform the news media of all events, agency actions, and related matters that are likely to be considered newsworthy; answer inquiries or relay them to appropriate personnel; prepare and disseminate information about agency activities and matters of continuing public interest; assist crime prevention personnel in publicizing information about crime prevention.

(Continued)

Table 3.4 *(Continued)*

Function	Purpose	Description of Tasks
40. Planning	40. To assist administrators in developing policies; to determine future needs for personnel, other resources	40. Review all aspects of agency's operations and performance of all elements of agency; identify needs for change in policies, resource allocations, or methods of operation; prepare program plans and research reports for administrators' use.
41. Budget preparation	41. To prepare a fiscal budget for future use	41. Solicit and receive budget requests from each element of the agency; develop a consolidated budget for approval by administrators and submission to parent government.
42. Budget supervision and execution	42. To ensure that budgeted funds are spent as planned	42. Periodically review current accounts of all agency elements; advise administrators of any deviations from approved current budget; prepare and execute budget amendments authorized by appropriate officials.

A list of functions similar to that in Table 3.4 can be developed for any police agency. Once the list has been compiled, the next step is to match the list of functions to the personnel available. To do this, the administrator must know three things:

- How many people are available? What is the total number of employees, both full time and part time? Are some of them available only at certain times of the day or only on certain days of the week?
- What competencies do the personnel have? How many are certified police officers (if there is a state certification program)? How many have completed college preparation programs or advanced training in such areas as investigation, evidence collection, traffic law enforcement, crisis intervention, and so forth? How many have had actual working experience in one of these special areas, or in supervision or management?
- What changes can be made in the number of personnel and their competencies? Are funds available to hire more people? If so, what competencies are most needed, and can they be obtained by hiring the right people? Can present personnel be given additional training to expand or change their competencies, and how long will the additional training take?

For a newly organized department, the answers to these questions will depend almost entirely on the size of the budget, which in turn is dictated by the overall availability of tax revenues and other funds to the government. A new police chief establishing a department in a newly incorporated city of, say, 10,000 people could not expect to hire 150 certified police officers and 75 civilians; a total staff of 10 would be much more reasonable.

For an existing agency, the number of people available and their competencies usually are determined by the agency's previous budgets, organizational structure, and personnel practices. Unless the agency has been chronically underfunded and the governing body (that is, the city council or other parent government) indicates a willingness to make more money available, the administrator cannot count on being able to add a large number of new people. Except in unusual circumstances, it is not practical to fire many of the existing personnel in order to replace them with others who have the desired competencies. To some extent, **attrition**, the normal loss of personnel through death, retirement, and resignation, will provide some opportunities to bring in new people with new competencies. However, the attrition rate in most police agencies is something less than 10 percent per year. Furthermore, there is a strong tradition in policing that upper-level vacancies are filled by the promotion of people already in the agency; thus, for the most part, new employees are hired only at the lowest level. If they have any special competencies that may be desired at higher levels, it will be several years before they work their way up to those levels through promotions.

In short, the administrator's options are somewhat limited. Personnel can be reassigned to new functions if their present competencies are compatible with their new duties, or they can be retrained to equip them for new functions. Usually reassigned personnel are less productive for a while than they would be otherwise, since they must learn the details of their new jobs. There also may be a period of reduced morale, since people often resist being reassigned unless their new job is perceived as a promotion. Sometimes a temporary loss of morale and productivity is an acceptable price to pay if the anticipated gains from reorganization are sufficiently high. However, the administrator must realize that these costs will be borne and that the benefits may not appear for months or even years.

With all these factors in mind, the administrator must complete the task of organizing, or reorganizing, the agency. Every function must be assigned to someone, and everyone must have a specific function.

Assigning functions to specific organizational elements is a matter for the administrator's judgment and, to some extent, for trial-and-error experimentation; if an organizational structure clearly is not working, usually there is no good reason not to change it. The procedure for assigning functions to organizational elements is fairly simple:

1. First, list on a sheet of ruled notebook paper or graph paper all functions of the agency, as in Table 3.4, but adapted to the needs of the actual agency.
2. Across the top of the sheet, establish column headings for each of the kinds of personnel that are available to the agency, showing the number of each kind.
3. Assign each function to one or more of the kinds of personnel. (See Figure 3.4 for an example.)

This **functional assignment matrix** should be regarded as only tentative, since assignments may be shuffled around somewhat. However, every function must be assigned to someone, and every person in the organization must be assigned to one or more specific functions.

Next, the administrator must group related functions into organizational elements. Personnel who are to perform the same function usually should be assigned to the same element; these groupings are obvious from the

Group	Function	Asst. Chief (2)	Captain (5)	Lieutenant (12)	Sr. Sgt. (6)	Det. Sgt. (18)	Sergeant (11)	Sr. Patrol Off. (21)	Patrol Off. (49)	Secretary (3)	Clerk (3)	Bookkpr. (4)	Criminalistics (4)	Evidence Tech. (2)	Comm. Svc. Aide (8)	Parking Officer (6)	Jail Attendant (18)	Animal Control Off. (3)	Dispatchers (12)	Janitors (6)	#
Patrol	Receive complaints	A	A						42										X		1
	Complaint response	A	A					X	42												2
	Prelim. invest'g'n	A	A					X	42												3
Inv.	Cont'g invest'g'n	A	B			10		X													4
	Evidence collection	A	B			X		X						X							5
	Evidence analysis	A	B										X	X							6
	Polygraph operator	A	B		1																7
	Case review	A	B	2																	8
Traffic	Direct traffic	A	A						7												9
	Violator appreh'n	A	A					X	X												10
	Accident invest'g'n	A	A						7												11
	Parking Enforcem't.	A	A						X							X					12
Patrol	Prev. Patrol: car	A	A					18	30												13
	Prev. Patrol: cycle	A	A					2	6												14
	Prev. Patrol: foot	A	A						6												15
Community Svcs.	Crime prev/educ'n.	B	C				1	1							1						16
	Juvenile offenses	B	C				2								2						17
	Family offenses	B	C		1		1								3						18
	Org. crime/spec. cr.	B	C	1		3															19
Sup.	Patrol supervision	A	A	2	1		3														20
	Inv. supervision	A	B	3	1																21
Technical Svcs.	Communications	B	D	2			1												X		22
	Records & ID	B	D	1							6										23
	Vehicle maint.	B	E				1														24
	Evidence/Property	B	D				1								1						25
	Jail	B	E				1										X				26
	Planning & analysis	B	D			2															27
Admin. Svcs.	Personnel	B	E	1																	28
	Training	B	E	(1)																	29
	Accounting	B	E									3									30
	Purchasing/Stores	B	E									1									31
	Bldg maint.	B	E																	X	32
	Public information	B	D	1											2						33
Misc.	Internal affairs	Chf	—	1	1																34
	Animal control	B	D															X			35
	License issuance	B	D								2										36

Figure 3-4 Functional Assignment Matrix

functional assignment matrix. Again, judgment must be exercised in grouping related functions into specific elements. Figure 3.5 shows how these groupings can be developed.

Finally, the elements are arranged into a hierarchical structure to provide for authority, responsibility, and accountability. At this point it may be necessary to add specific elements for supervision and management. The most common way to represent the organizational structure is to draw an **organizational chart**, such as the one illustrated in Figure 3.6.

It is important to realize that there is no one right way to organize a police agency. The organizational chart often will resemble the charts of many other police agencies and the administrator will wonder whether the effort of going through all the steps we have outlined has been wasted, since the results are so predictable. However, the real value of this procedure lies in the series of rational analyses and decisions that the administrator must make.

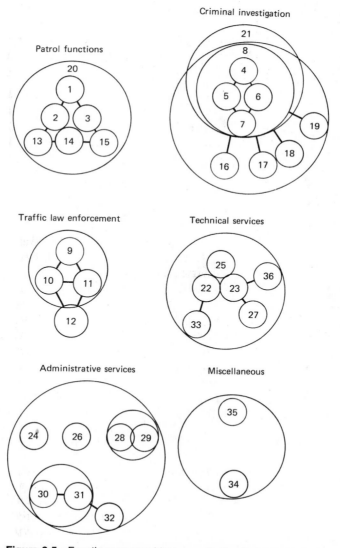

Figure 3-5 Functions grouped into organizational elements.

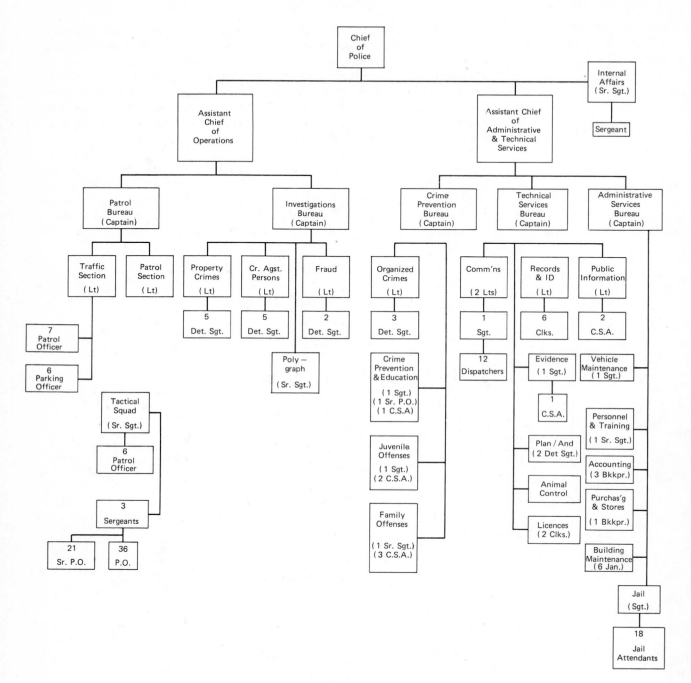

Figure 3-6 An organization chart.

EXAMPLES OF POLICE AGENCY ORGANIZATION

In Figures 3.7 to 3.15, organizational charts for several typical police agencies are shown. The charts represent agencies of different sizes and with somewhat different functions. We have grouped the charts by agency size. Studying these charts will show how different administrators, given similar situations, have arrived at somewhat different solutions to the problem of organizing a police agency. However, it is also clear that the majority of police agencies are organized along similar lines, largely because of the strong and pervasive traditions of American policing.

Figure 3-7 Organization chart of the Montgomery, Alabama Police Department. (Courtesy MPD.)

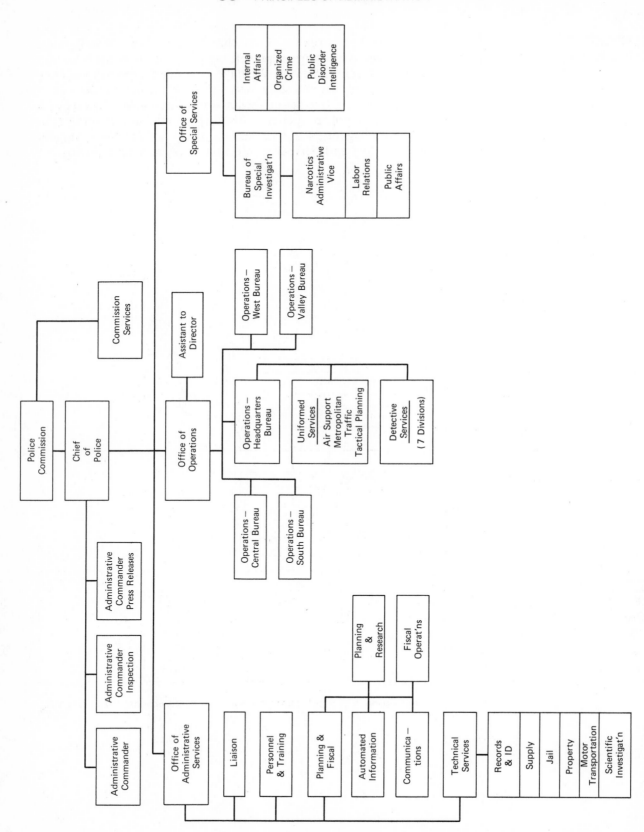

Figure 3-8 Organization chart of the Los Angeles Police Department. (Courtesy LAPD.)

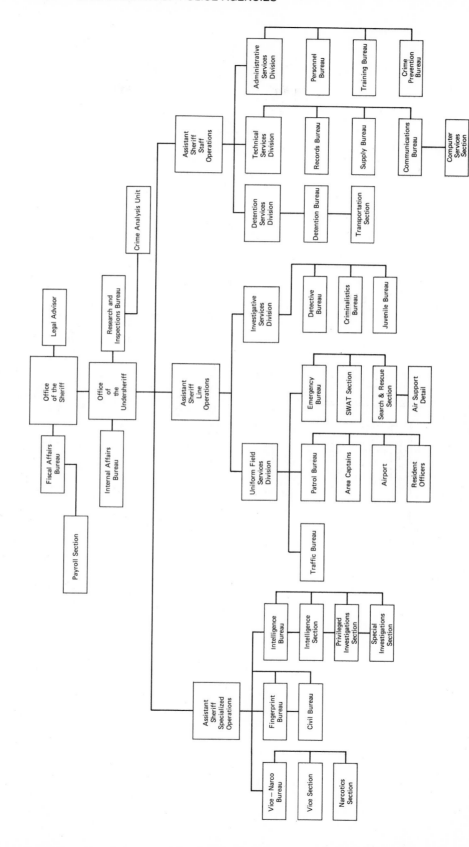

Figure 3-9 Organization chart of the Las Vegas Metropolitan Police Department. (Courtesy LVMPD.)

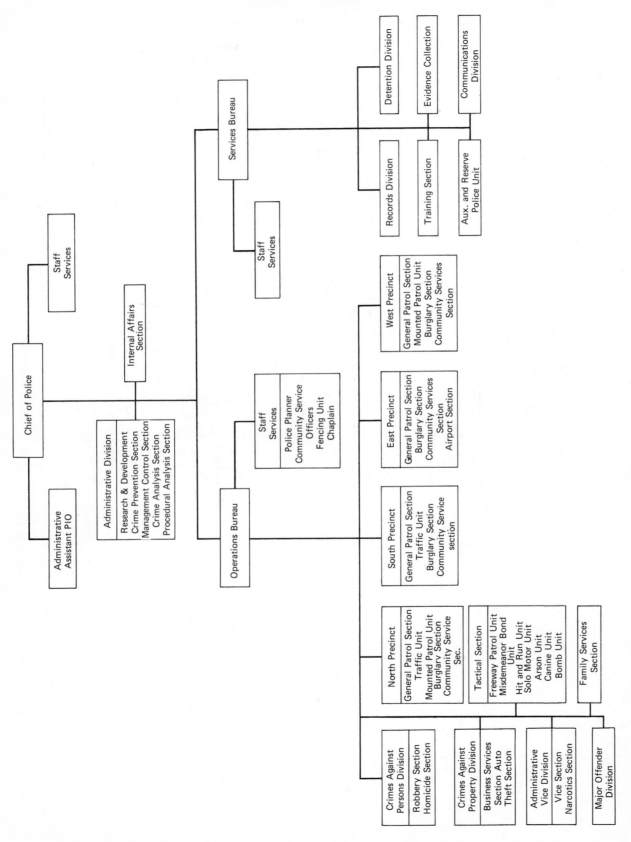

Figure 3-10 Organization chart of the Birmingham, Alabama Police Department. (Courtesy BPD.)

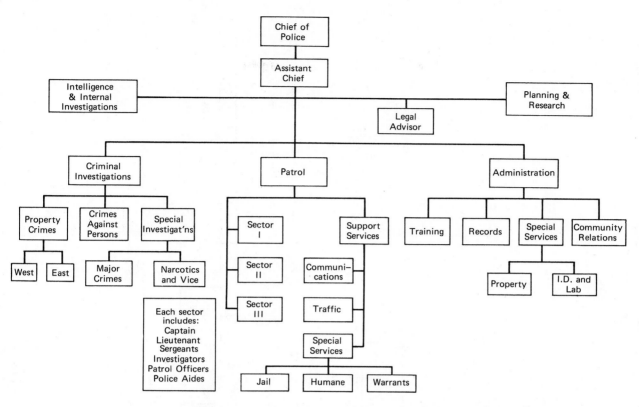

Figure 3-11 Organization chart of the Mesa, Arizona Police Department. (Courtesy MPD.)

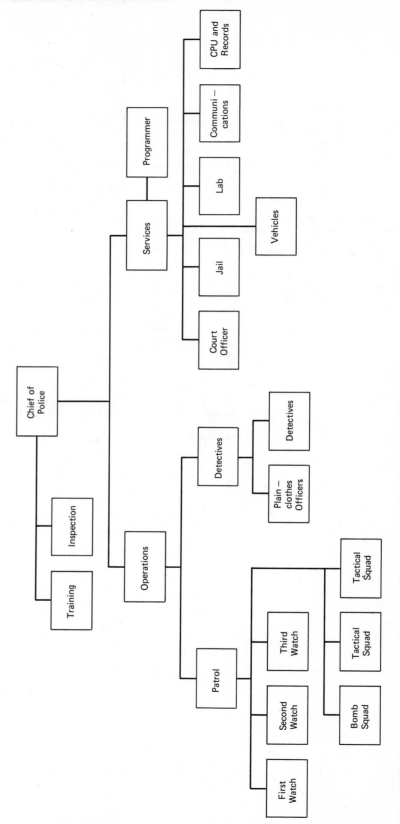

Figure 3-12 Organization chart of the Cheyenne, Wyoming Police Department, (Courtesy CPD.)

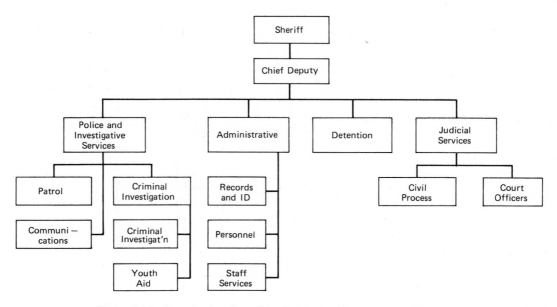

Figure 3-13 Organization chart of the Cumberland County, Maine Sheriff's Department. (Courtesy CCSD.)

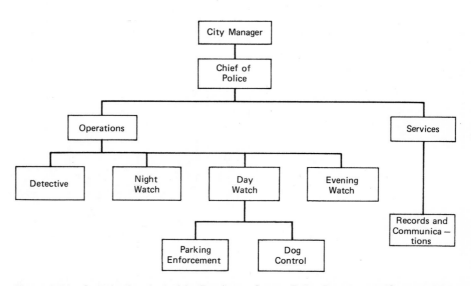

Figure 3-14 Organization chart of the Pendleton, Oregon Police Department. (Courtesy PPD.)

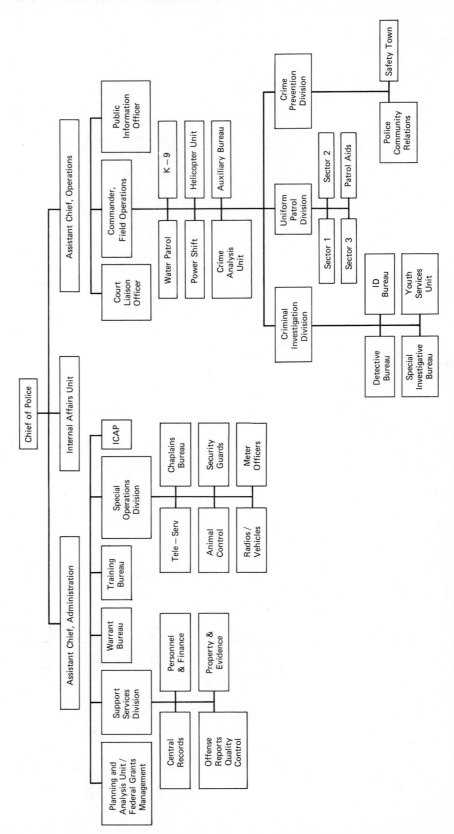

Figure 3-15 Organization chart of the Portsmouth, Virginia Police Department (Courtesy PPD.)

**UNCONVENTIONAL
ORGANIZATIONAL
PLANS**

In recent years, a number of police agencies have tested organizational structures that are significantly different from those we have just discussed. In some cases, the experiments have been quite successful; in other cases, they have not. However, the mere fact that the experiments were made indicates that police administrators are more willing to try variations on traditional themes than they have been in the past. The two broad categories of unconventional plans that we discuss here are only examples of the directions some agencies have taken.

**Patrol-Oriented
Investigation**

In a conventional police agency structure, the job of investigating crimes is divided between the patrol officers and the detectives. Typically, patrol officers respond to the initial report of a crime, take a preliminary report by interviewing the victim or witnesses and, if there appears to be any physical evidence at the crime scene, call evidence technicians and detectives to make a more thorough investigation. Once these tasks have been completed, the investigation is turned over to the detectives and the patrol officer has no further role in the case.

Critics have claimed that this common practice wastes the talents of personnel. They say that specialist detectives are not significantly more effective in solving crimes than are properly trained patrol officers.[5] Giving patrol officers a larger role in criminal investigation requires some changes in organizational structure. A thorough investigation may require an hour or more at the crime scene, with additional time spent on the follow-up investigation, case reporting, and so on. In order to give patrol officers the time to spend on investigations, they must be freed from routine patrol duties.

One approach is simply to increase the number of patrol officers assigned to each sector. Most officers are assigned to a specific beat, in the conventional manner; however, there are also patrol officers who have no specific beat assignment. When one officer becomes involved in a lengthy investigation, one of the unassigned officers takes over the beat. Or the extra patrol officers can be designated as patrol officer investigators, who are dispatched to respond to any complaint that is likely to require extensive investigation. When they are not involved in an investigation, the patrol officer investigators perform routine patrol duties.

The increased number of patrol officers usually is obtained by sharply decreasing the number of specialist detectives. Instead of three or more sections of detectives, there may be only one or at most two. Instead of dividing each section into several highly specialized units (the fraud unit, sex crimes unit, auto theft unit, etc.), the sections remain undivided. The detectives serve as resource advisers to the patrol officers, offering guidance and assistance in complicated investigations and taking charge of only the most difficult or complicated cases.

An organizational chart for an agency that has adopted a patrol-oriented investigation structure is shown in Figure 3.16.

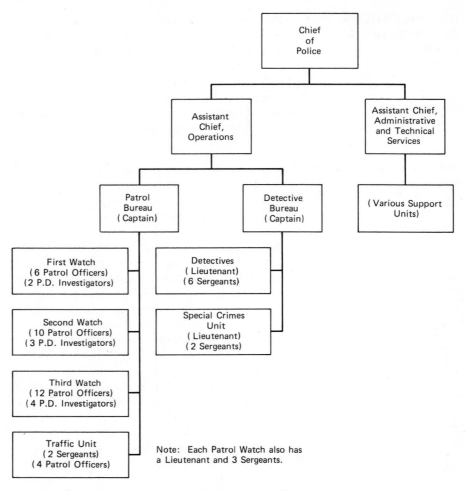

Figure 3-16 An organizational chart for a patrol-oriented investigative structure.

Team Policing

The idea behind the concept of team policing is also to make better use of the patrol force and to improve law enforcement service by maintaining a closer relationship between the police personnel and the community they serve. Unfortunately, the term **team policing** has become popularized as the sign of an innovative, progressive police agency. Several different organizational structures have been tried as variations on the theme of team policing. The result is that the term no longer has a clear, definite meaning; to some extent, team policing may mean whatever someone chooses to make it mean.

For example, the original concept of team policing was to attack crime more effectively by assigning a team of officers, usually consisting of one or more patrol officers, a detective, and sometimes other specialists, to assume responsibility for all crimes that occur in a given area. But another approach to team policing involves forming several teams (each consisting of a patrol officer, a detective, and sometimes another specialist) for each area; whenever a complaint is received, the entire team responds as a unit to perform whatever investigation is needed. This second approach, in practice, usually amounts to putting detectives in patrol cars.

The relative merits and disadvantages of various forms of team policing have been the subject of vigorous debate in law enforcement for the past decade. For now, we merely point out that this unconventional approach to police agency organizational structure exists. Later, especially in Chapter 14, we will have more to say about team policing, the various forms of it, and some of the implications for both patrol and investigative functions. Figure 3.17 shows the organizational charts for two different types of team policing structures.

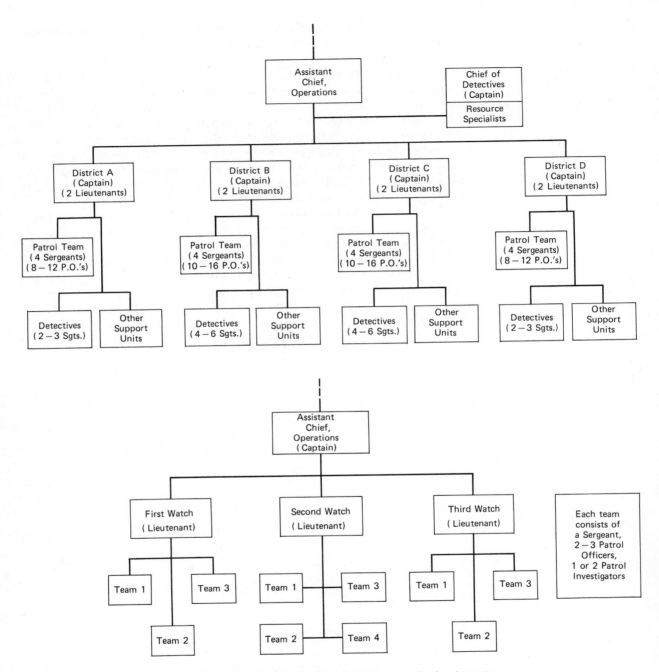

Figure 3-17 Two types of team-policing organizational structures.

CAPTAIN LEWIS'S IN BASKET

Instructions

In this exercise, you are to assume the role of Captain Michael Lewis, Chief of Technical Services. The documents below have been selected from Captain Lewis's in basket. Read them with care. If you need more information about City or its police department, refer to the data bank in the front of the book. After you have studied the documents, complete these steps:

1. State the problem or problems these documents present to Captain Lewis.
2. List as many alternative solutions as you can.
3. Select the solution you think would be best, and give your reasons for choosing it.

CITY POLICE DEPARTMENT
Interoffice Memorandum

FROM: M. Avery, Capt. Patrol Bureau

TO: M. Lewis, Capt., Technical Services

SUBJECT: Interference in Patrol affairs   DATE: 21 Jan 19--

Captain Lewis:

Please inform your people that they have no authority to issue orders or instructions to Patrol personnel. Thank you.

Mike Avery

CITY POLICE DEPARTMENT
Interoffice Memorandum

FROM: Joe Young, Lt.

TO: M. Lewis, Capt., Technical

SUBJECT: Rush-hour traffic monitoring plan   DATE: 21 Jan 19--

SIR:
I regret to report that the Patrol Bureau has refused to cooperate in the Rush-Hour Traffic Monitoring Plan that you approved last week. As I said in my proposal for this plan, the Traffic Section does not have the people to carry out the plan by ourselves. I met yesterday with all three of the Patrol watch lieutenants and they said that they would not assist us in carrying out this plan because they are already too busy during the rush hours. It appears that we will have to drop the plan.

                              Joe Young, Lt.
                              Traffic Section

CITY POLICE DEPARTMENT
Interoffice Memorandum

FROM: L. Thomas, Lt., Jail Operations

TO: M. Lewis, Capt., Chief of Technical Services Bureau

SUBJECT: Unauthorized Removal of Prisoners   DATE: 22 Jan 19--

SIR:
    Last Saturday morning at 0245 hours, Patrol Officer Martha Wallace of the Juvenile Division came to the Jail and insisted on removing a prisoner from our custody. The prisoner was a 16-yr-old female being held on a narcotics charge. The prisoner had not yet been presented to the Municipal Judge because she was arrested late Friday night. The arresting officer was Sgt. Gifford, Narcotics Division.
    Officer Wallace said that the arrest was a "mistake" and that charges would be dropped. However, she did not have the proper signed documents authorizing this release.
    The booking officer, Sgt. Overton, called me at home and asked for instructions. I told him not to release the prisoner without proper authorization. Besides, the female prisoner was the only female in custody and I had already schedule matrons for the entire weekend, and would have to pay them whether we had any prisoners or not. Officer Wallace became very abusive. It is clear that she was exceeding her authority in this case. Please correct this situation or relieve me of responsibility.
                                        - L. Thomas, Lt., Jail Operations

IN REVIEW

1. Every grant of authority carries with it an equal responsibility. This means that:
    (a) The person who has the right to perform a function also has an obligation to perform it.
    (b) No one has the right to question an order or policy issued by a person in authority.
    (c) A person in authority must delegate responsibility to subordinates in order to be sure that all work is done properly.
    (d) Subordinates, since they have no authority, also are not responsible when they make mistakes.
    (e) The principle of unity of command must not be violated.

2. The responsibility for coordinating any two elements in an organization rests with:
    (a) The Chief of Police.
    (b) The executive.
    (c) The person who has authority over both of them.
    (d) The subordinate.
    (e) None of the above.

3. True or False: Subordinates should be encouraged to avoid referring questions of coordination to their superiors.

4. The usual method of reducing an administrator's span of control is to:
    (a) Decrease the size of the agency.
    (b) Insert a new level of managers or supervisors into the organization's structure.
    (c) Expand the administrator's authority.

    (d)   Make the structure "flatter."
    (e)   Shorten the chain of command.

5. Cross-training is one method of:
    (a)   Ensuring the accountability of subordinates.
    (b)   Increasing specialization.
    (c)   Reducing the length of the chain of command.
    (d)   Avoiding some of the undesirable effects of specialization.
    (e)   Reducing the cost of training programs.

6. Once a list of an agency's functions has been compiled, the administrator must match the list to the personnel available. To do this, the administrator must know:
    (a)   The competencies of the available personnel.
    (b)   What changes can be made in the number of personnel and their competencies.
    (c)   The number of available personnel.
    (d)   All of the above.
    (e)   None of the above.

7. True or False: Reassigning personnel often results in a temporary loss of morale and productivity, but this cost may be offset by the eventual benefits of reorganization.

8. Patrol officers who have no specific beat assignment are most likely to be members of an agency whose organizational structure is based on the concept of:
    (a)   Team policing.
    (b)   Patrol-oriented investigation.
    (c)   Decentralization.
    (d)   Specialization.
    (e)   Functional organization.

9. The advocates of the team policing concept claim that this organizational structure will:
    (a)   Improve the relationship between the police and the community.
    (b)   Eliminate crime.
    (c)   Regain the advantages of local political control over police precincts.
    (d)   Increase the use of detectives.
    (e)   Reduce the need for police officers.

10. In organizing a police agency, the most important principle is that:
    (a)   There can be only one chain of command.
    (b)   Every member of the agency must have one, and only one, function to perform.
    (c)   All ranks and functional titles must be standardized to avoid confusion.
    (d)   Every function must be performed by someone, everyone must have at least one specific function, and there must be a reason for every assignment.
    (e)   Administrators must not be permitted to delegate their responsibilities.

REFERENCES

1. George Maclay and Humphry Knipe, *The Dominant Man*, New York: Delacorte, 1972.

2. Roy R. Roberg, *Police Management and Organizational Behavior*, St. Paul: West Publishing, 1979, page 199.

3. O. W. Wilson and Roy C. McLaren, *Police Administration*, 3rd ed., New York: McGraw-Hill, 1972, pages 80–81.

4. Alfred R. Stone and Stuart M. DeLuca, *Investigating Crimes*, Boston: Houghton Mifflin, 1980, pages 42–43.

5. Peter W. Greenwood, Jan M. Chaiken, and Joan Petersilia, *The Criminal Investigation Process*, Lexington, Mass.: D. C. Heath, 1977.

4 RESEARCH AND PLANNING

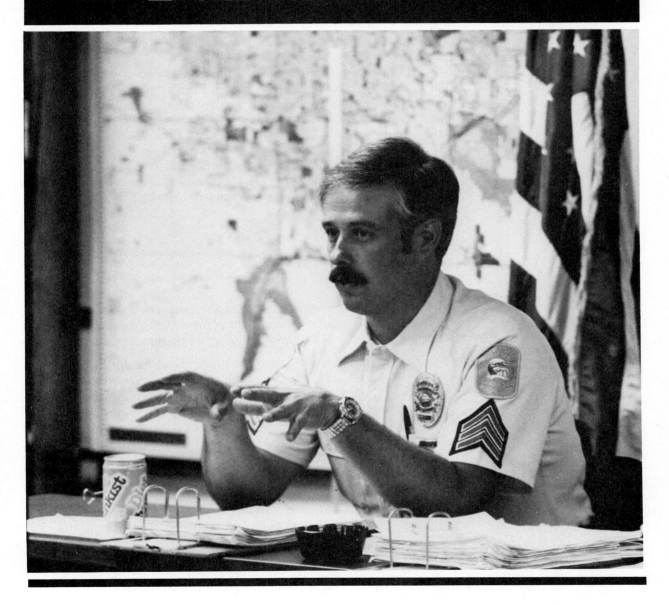

ONE OF THE MOST FREQUENT CRITICISMS OF POLICE agencies is that they fail to plan for the future. Too often, according to the critics, police administrators are content to operate on a day-to-day basis without regard for the long-range needs and direction of their agencies. As a result, they are often faced with crises that demand immediate attention but that could have been foreseen and perhaps avoided, if appropriate steps had been planned in advance.

Planning is an indispensable human activity; all people plan, at least for themselves. Setting an alarm clock at night is an act of planning. Buying groceries once a week requires planning. Putting money into a savings account or signing a loan agreement to buy a car represent forms of planning.

In its broadest sense, planning is "the design of a desired future and of effective ways of bringing it about."[1] It is a continuous process: The plans we have made in the past are subject to revision, and new plans are being made for the future because of new information about our current status or new ideas of what the future may hold for us.

Left to itself, the future will not turn out the way we might like. Present conditions may continue indefinitely or they might get worse. A supreme optimist might refuse to plan anything on the assumption, or hope, that future conditions will be better than those of the present. However, an administrator who is responsible for the operations of an agency that protects the public's lives and property cannot afford such blind optimism. Planning is an essential management function that is "directed toward producing one or more future states that are desired and that are not expected to occur unless something is done."[2]

A THEORY OF PLANNING

The Role of Research

As management theorist Arthur B. Toan, Jr., points out, "One of the most interesting and disquieting things about plans is that they rarely work out quite as anticipated."[3] There are a number of reasons for this to be true:

- Planning requires predictions to be made about the future, and these predictions are likely to be less than perfectly accurate.
- Planning is based on perceptions about current conditions, and these may be based on inaccurate or incomplete information.
- Planning is based on current objectives, or notions of what is desirable, and these can change over time so that before a plan is fully accomplished its objective may have been discarded.
- The actions chosen to carry out a plan may have results different from those that were expected.

It should be apparent from this list that all plans must be based on knowledge—knowledge about current conditions, about the future, and about the effects of current actions—and that the accuracy and completeness of this knowledge will have a considerable bearing on the success of plans. This knowledge must be carefully assembled from a variety of sources; it does not simply come into existence by itself.

Research is the systematic gathering of knowledge. To most people, research means one of two things: either conducting scientific experiments in a laboratory filled with exotic equipment or poring over dusty volumes in the dark recesses of a library. In fact, these stereotypes represent only two forms of research; there are several others. Briefly, these are the forms of research that are most often useful to police administrators:

- **Observation.** Events, people, or natural phenomena can be observed, described, and counted, and the results of observations can be compared.
- **Experimentation.** Processes, techniques, or actions can be carried out under controlled conditions and the results can be observed to determine whether the researcher's ideas about what will happen are correct.
- **Review of previous research.** Previous researchers' observations, the results of past experiments, and other researchers' theories or generalizations can be studied and compared to determine what is already known about a problem or subject.
- **Forecasting.** Predictions can be made about future conditions on the basis of observations of current conditions and apparent trends or patterns of change.

Of these four forms of research, the one most often used by police agencies is observation. Most police agencies amass a tremendous volume of records and documents concerning current activities and conditions. These records and documents, although they are not often considered in this way, actually represent observations of events, people, and (to a lesser extent) natural phenomena. A detective who looks through a file of criminal modus operandi (method of operation) records is conducting research, comparing observations of past criminal behavior to current cases. Ordinarily, a police agency's records are considered important only because they might be needed to demonstrate that the agency has acted in a lawful and responsible manner. However, these same records contain immensely valuable information that can contribute to the agency's planning for the future.

Experimentation, on the other hand, is rarely used as a method of research by police agencies. Most administrators believe that they cannot afford to divert their already limited personnel and other resources into experimental activities that may or may not succeed. An experiment that fails might attract public or political criticism—or, worse yet, might result in damage to some citizens. However, without experimentation, new ideas about police techniques and procedures would never be implemented. A reasonable degree of caution certainly is necessary; an administrator who recklessly endangers public lives and property by trying every new idea that comes along could only be regarded as irresponsible. However, it may be just as irresponsible to ignore promising new ideas, if they can be tested safely, only because "we've never done that before."

Police administrators also fail to take advantage of previous research as well as they might. Information about current police practices, crime conditions in almost every community in the country, and the results of research on police techniques can be found in dozens of journals, magazines, and books. Not all of this information is useful; much of it is poorly developed and presented. Nevertheless, a responsible administrator should be aware of the information available and should be willing to devote time and energy to finding information that may shed new light on current problems.

A **forecast** is a statement of expectations for the future based on historical experience, and it can be one of the most valuable forms of research for the police administrator. Forecasting future trends is an art and science in itself, practiced primarily by mathematicians and economists. However, relatively simple forecasts can be made by anyone who has learned the proper techniques.

For example, if records of past experience indicate that the volume of automotive traffic in a city has grown by an average of 2.5 percent per year over the past five years, it is reasonable to assume that this trend will continue over the next five years. This would mean that the volume of traffic five years from now will be 113 percent of the current volume. Such a simple forecast could be valuable to the administrator in planning for the number of personnel who will be needed in the future or changes in traffic law enforcement practices, for example.

Most large cities have their own forecasters in the city planning department whose job is to predict the city's future population, economic conditions, patterns of growth, and so forth. Economic and **demographic** (population measurement) forecasters also can be found in various college departments, especially in schools of business administration and economics; in private research bureaus; and in state and federal agencies. Detailed economic and demographic forecasts are published by these agencies and may be obtained directly from the source or through a public or university library. The U.S. Bureau of the Census, a part of the Department of Commerce, and the Bureau of Labor Statistics in the Department of Labor publish thousands of detailed economic and demographic studies for individual cities and counties. Police administrators should obtain this information and use it in making their own plans.[4]

Of course, even the best forecast is no guarantee that conditions or events at some future date will occur exactly as predicted. That is one reason plans must be revised and updated frequently. By and large, forecasts for the near future are more likely to be accurate than those for the distant future. Unfortunately, the long-range forecasts are more likely to be important to the administrator, since they are necessary for long-range planning; short-range plans are more often based on the assumption that current conditions will continue without any major changes. This is not a dilemma that can be solved; it is merely one of the uncertainties of life that every administrator must accept.

All four of the forms of research we have discussed can contribute to the planning process. What matters most is not the type of research, but that administrators base their plans on accurate, complete knowledge, obtained in a systematic way.

The Responsibility for Planning

Ultimately, of course, it is one of the overall responsibilities of the executive—the chief of police or equivalent position—to see that planning is carried out. In smaller agencies, nearly all planning is actually done by the executive, since everyone else is occupied with other vital functions. All too often, the executive is also "too busy" and somehow never gets around to planning at all.

Larger police agencies sometimes go to the opposite extreme. They set up elaborate planning departments staffed with computer programmers, information specialists, and other experts. The Planning Department analyzes data, projects future trends, and prepares bewildering charts and proposals. Eventually the planners prepare a master plan that calls for the entire department to be reorganized over the next 5 or 10 years. This plan is copied and distributed to the agency's upper-level administrators, who point out the impracticalities and inconsistencies in the master plan, which is then filed away and never seen again.

Practical planning is not only possible, it is absolutely necessary. However, the responsibility for planning cannot be delegated to a separate planning department and then forgotten. The planning process must be carried out by the people who will be responsible for putting the plans into action: the working administrators of the agency. If the agency is large enough to afford a staff of planning experts and specialists, they can be immensely helpful in carrying out detailed research, in preparing forecasts, and in assisting the agency's other personnel during the planning process. However, every police officer from the patrol force to the chief should have some part in that process.

Types of Plans

A plan can be anything that represents a conscious decision to influence some future action or condition: setting an alarm clock, for example. More formal kinds of plans, such as we consider in this chapter, vary according to:

- The scope and nature of the action that is to be taken according to the plan.
- The period of time encompassed in the plan.
- The number of times the plan, or minor variations of it, will be repeated.
- The definiteness of the plan.

Some management theorists consider all policies, standard operating procedures, and rules to be "standing plans," in the sense that they represent conscious decisions that are intended to influence future acts.[5] For example, a policy or set of regulations that describes the proper procedures for issuing a traffic citation could be regarded as a "standing plan for the issuance of traffic citations." However, for our purposes we will set aside the standing plan as a special case. The kinds of plans that will concern us are designed not just to standardize employees' work performance, but to deal with unusual future events or to bring about desirable changes in an agency. We discuss four types of plans: operational plans, contingency plans, programmatic plans, and strategic plans.

Operational Plans.   An operational plan is one that concerns a limited scope of actions, encompasses a relatively short period of time, and may be repeated with some variations. Its purpose is to provide for the coordination of several persons, activities, or processes to achieve a particular desired outcome.

The most common operational plans are schedules of people, things, and processes. For example, a work schedule or duty roster lists the various jobs that are to be performed or the work that is to be done at different times and shows which personnel are assigned to each job or work period. The desired outcome, of course, is that all the work is to be completed. Similarly, a schedule for the processing of the agency's payroll is an operational plan. Various supervisors and managers must report to the accounting office the number of hours each employee has worked; the personnel office must report the correct salary rate for each employee; the salaries, deductions for benefits and taxes, compensation for overtime, and so forth must be calculated; and, finally, the checks must be prepared and distributed. Without a schedule, there is no assurance that everyone would be paid on time.

Another type of operational plan involves the coordination of personnel in carrying out complex actions to achieve a specific, limited purpose such as a felony arrest, a raid on a suspected crime site, or a surveillance action.[6] This plan does not have to be recorded in any elaborate form, but it should be outlined on paper in advance and a record should be kept for future reference. The purpose of the plan is to ensure that everyone involved in the operation knows what to do and when to do it, and that as far as possible everything that might occur during the operation has been taken into consideration.

Contingency Plans.   A police agency's responsibilities are much broader than those of most governmental units. To some degree, the police must be prepared for almost anything that might happen to endanger citizens' lives and property. Most police departments are expected to assume responsibility for both security and rescue operations in all sorts of emergencies, from violent weather to riots to plane crashes. Such events are so infrequent that it is impractical to establish standardized policies and operational plans to deal with them. But once an event occurs, it is too late for thoughtful, deliberate planning; the police must respond immediately in an efficiently coordinated manner. Thus, plans must be made well in advance and kept ready in case they are needed. They will go into effect only if certain events occur; that is, the plans are contingent on the event or condition and thus are known as contingency plans.

It is impossible to give detailed recommendations as to the number and variety of contingency plans a department should maintain. But at the very least, even a small police department should have contingency plans to deal with the following kinds of events:

I.   Natural disasters
  A.   A storm (hurricane, flood, tornado, earthquake) that causes widespread property damage, personal injuries, and disruption of communications.
  B.   A major fire or explosion in a commercial district.
  C.   A major fire or explosion in a residential district.

II.   Transportation disasters
  A.   A commercial aircraft crash:
    1.   At the local airport.
    2.   Away from the airport, in a commercial, residential, or undeveloped area.

    B.   A multivehicle collision on a major highway or arterial street.
    C.   A railroad derailment or accident:
       1.   Involving passengers.
       2.   Involving bulk freight (coal, grain, etc.).
       3.   Involving hazardous cargo (chemicals, radioactive material, gases).
    D.   A pipeline or petroleum storage tank explosion or major leakage.

III.   Public events and civil disorders
    A.   A protest demonstration:
       1.   In a confined area.
       2.   Involving a large area or parade.
    B.   A riotous attack on, or invasion of, a public building.
    C.   An actual or threatened bombing of a public building.
    D.   A potentially riotous disturbance at a public event.
    E.   A parade or other public appearance of a celebrity or controversial person requiring special security.

IV.   Miscellaneous events
    A.   An aircraft hijacking.
    B.   Kidnapping or hostage-taking of a public figure or group of individuals.
    C.   A barricaded sniper.

Each contingency plan should describe in as much detail as possible the kind of event it is intended to cover and all the circumstances that can be anticipated. A single plan might cover a number of variations. For example, the police procedures outlined in a plan for a disturbance at a public event (number III-D above) would vary depending on whether the event is a dance, rock concert, street party, or sports event and also would vary depending on whether the event is taking place inside a dance hall, in a stadium, or in a city park. Each contingency plan should specify:

1.   Who will decide that the plan is to be implemented.
2.   Who will be in charge of carrying out the plan (the commanding officer).
3.   What departmental units and personnel will be assigned to the operation, in what capacities, and how they are to be informed.
4.   Where personnel are to assemble for instructions, distribution of special equipment, and deployment.
5.   What actions may be taken at the discretion of individual personnel and what actions are to be taken only on the instructions of the commanding officer.
6.   Who will serve as subcommanders or intermediate officers.
7.   When and by whom the operation will be terminated, and how personnel will be informed.

A great deal of time will be required to develop a complete set of contingency plans if none exist. However, once the plans have been developed, reviewed by all the administrators who are likely to be involved in carrying them out, and approved, they can be retained on file indefinitely. At least once a year, the file should be reviewed; any plans that are clearly out of date should be pulled and revised, and new plans should be drafted to cover situations that were not previously anticipated.

Programmatic Plans. The most important plans for any organization, including a police agency, are those that specify a course of action that, if successfully accomplished, will contribute in an important way to carrying out the organization's basic purpose or function. These plans represent the agency's program for fulfilling its function; they are crucial to the success of the whole organization. Yet this is the kind of planning that is rarely done well, and often not done at all, by police agencies.

Programmatic plans involve a series of complex actions to be undertaken by a number of people over a relatively long period of time, usually no less than six months and sometimes as much as two to five years.

The most common type of programmatic plan is the budget. In its simplest form, a **budget** is merely a statement of the financial resources one expects to have over a given period of time and how those resources are to be used. Virtually all police agencies are required to prepare a budget on an annual basis to obtain operating funds from the parent government. Because budgeting is such an essential process, we devote a separate chapter to it; for now, we merely wish to point out that a budget is a plan.

A programmatic plan can be designed to do nothing more than to maintain the status quo, the current level of accomplishment in fulfilling the agency's basic functions. It is easy for administrators to persuade themselves that the status quo is entirely satisfactory or that improving current conditions would be either impossible or not worth the extra effort. At the opposite extreme, administrators sometimes develop plans for an ideal world in which their resources are limitless and all contemplated activities are successful. In most cases, a better approach avoids both extremes. An administrator should plan for specific changes that bring the organization closer to ideal conditions by adopting a realistic estimate of resources and courses of action that are likely to be successful in a reasonable period of time.[7]

Planning for constructive change is one of the most challenging, and potentially most rewarding, tasks a manager can undertake. Most managers feel a great sense of pride and satisfaction when they see their plans successfully put into effect, bringing about measurable progress toward their agency's fundamental purpose. It is not unlike the feeling that athletes get when they have won an important victory: It is the payoff for the creativity and hard work they have devoted to their efforts.

Programmatic plans can take one of two basic forms: the project and the program. A **project** involves the introduction of a single, specific change in an organization over a limited period of time. Once the change has been introduced and the project ends, a new situation may exist that will continue indefinitely thereafter. For example, a project might involve installing a computer-assisted dispatching system in the police communications network. First the system must be designed, proper equipment must be chosen and purchased, and space must be found to house it. While the equipment is being installed and tested, the existing dispatching system will continue to be used but the communications personnel will be trained on the new system. Perhaps for a while both systems will be operated in parallel, or perhaps the new system will be introduced in stages. Eventually the old system will be discontinued and the new equipment will take over; at that point, which may be six months or a year after the first steps, the project would end.

A project also can be used to experiment with a new idea, technique, or type of equipment. At the end of a predetermined period of time, the project is evaluated and a decision is made to discontinue the innovation, to install it permanently, or to continue the testing period, perhaps with some modification. For example, a police department might decide to experiment with the use of two-wheel motorcycles for traffic patrol. Initially perhaps only a few motorcycles would be purchased and assigned to use in one section of the city. After six months or a year, the experiment would be evaluated; either more cycles would be bought and assigned throughout the city, or the use of motorcycles would be assigned to another part of town for further testing.

A project can be used when the need for a particular kind of activity is likely to be temporary. A police department might conduct an anti-shoplifting campaign just before the Christmas shopping season, for instance.

Finally, a project can be used when there is an ongoing need for a certain kind of activity but the agency does not have adequate resources to carry it out continuously. For example, a police department might conduct a short-term campaign to educate the public about burglary prevention, the dangers of driving while intoxicated, or any number of other matters. Few agencies could afford to devote officers full time on a permanent basis to such projects, but personnel may be able to spend a few weeks on each campaign. Often a series of short-term projects of this sort can be linked together to form a continuous effort.

A **program** is also a type of programmatic plan that is designed to meet a specific need through a specific course of action, with the desired results stated in advance, and a program should be designed for a specific period of time. The difference between a project and a program is that the latter is intended from the beginning to be a permanent part of the organization. Changes may be introduced from time to time, but ordinarily a program continues from year to year until the need for it no longer exists. Furthermore, a program is designed to fulfill one of the basic, permanent functions of the agency. Conversely, each of the agency's basic functions or purposes should be represented by a particular program. Each program should be designed to bring about desired changes that will enable the agency to fulfill its purposes more completely and effectively in the future, taking into account reasonable expectations of future resources and the kinds of activities that will be feasible.

A program can be composed of a single set of actions that are carried out continuously, or it can be made up of a series of separate projects. For example, a department's crime prevention program might consist entirely of the patrol bureau's routine patrol activity, or this activity could be supplemented with a series of short-term projects, each aimed at reducing the incidence of a particular type of crime.

Program planning and budgeting are so closely related that we will have a great deal more to say about programs and how they are developed in the next chapter.

Strategic Plans.   Every police agency—indeed, every organization of any sort—undergoes change more or less continuously. The programmatic plans we have just discussed are intended to bring about desired changes, to improve an agency's ability to serve its community. However, it is not always easy to see how a number of individual programs and projects fit together into an overall plan of progress. What is needed is a strategic plan, a master plan for the entire organization, showing how all the bits and pieces of programmatic planning are interrelated and coordinated to achieve, over a substantial period of time (perhaps 5 to 10 years), large-scale improvement in the whole organization.

A strategic plan, because it covers such a long period of time, is most vulnerable to unpredictable future changes. By the same token, it is most dependent on accurate knowledge of current conditions and accurate forecasts of future conditions. One way to avoid the possibility that a strategic plan will become obsolete is to take into consideration several different possible futures.

For example, if the agency's present personnel strength is one commissioned officer for every 1250 citizens in the community, the strategic plan might call for increasing overall strength to a ratio of 1:1000. However, the actual number of officers would vary according to the rate of population growth in the community. The strategic plan should take these variations into account. Thus, the plan might show the personnel levels for three different growth rates:

Present Personnel: 100
Present Population: 125,000
Personnel/Population Ratio: 1:1250

If Growth Rate Is	Population in 5 Years Will Be	Personnel in 5 Years
1% per year	131,400	131
2.5% per year	141,400	141
5% per year	159,500	160

(to achieve personnel/population ratio of 1:1000)

The strategic plan should contain a number of projections of the same sort showing how personnel needs, the community's need for police services, and so forth are likely to change over the period of time encompassed by the plan and how the agency proposes to respond to these changes. The value of a strategic plan, or master plan, is that it can serve as the overall guide to the development of specific program and project plans, and each year's budget can be compared to the predictions given in the strategic plan. Of course, like any other long-range plan, the strategic plan itself should be reviewed and updated periodically, at least every two years; otherwise it is likely to become obsolete and useless except as a historical curiosity.

THE PLANNING PROCESS

Perhaps one reason many police administrators do not plan well, or do not plan at all, is that they are intimidated by what seems to be a hopelessly complicated and mysterious planning process. Actually, planning need not be complicated or mysterious if the administrator follows an orderly, logical procedure. However, planning is undeniably time-consuming, and the better it is done, the more time it takes. It can and should be done on a group basis, with various parts of the process carried out by different individuals, so that no one must invest a disproportionate amount of time in the whole process.

Briefly, there are six steps in the planning process:

1. Needs assessment.
2. Goal and objective setting.
3. Defining alternative methods.
4. Cost-benefit assessment.
5. Selection of a methodology.
6. Defining the evaluation method.

Needs Assessment

Before any plan can be designed to bring about some action or condition in the future, first it must be determined that the action or condition does not already exist and that it is desirable. In other words, **needs assessment** requires the administrator to ask, "What should we do (or have) that we do not already do (or have)?"

Management scholars William H. Newman and E. Kirby Warren compare this step with the diagnostic process in medicine. They warn, "Accurate diagnosis is the essential first phase of sound decision-making. Unless the diagnosis is correct, subsequent planning will be misdirected and wasteful."[8] They suggest a number of ways to make an accurate diagnosis:

- Compare existing conditions with some basic value, such as a statement of the organization's purpose.
- Compare existing conditions with conditions in another, comparable organization.
- Compare existing conditions with long-term goals.

Each of these comparisons may reveal a gap between the existing condition and the desired condition. For example, suppose one of the basic purposes of the City Police Department is to promote traffic safety and reduce, to the minimum attainable, deaths and injuries due to traffic accidents. How well is City Police Department serving this purpose? According to the agency's records, last year there were 36 traffic deaths, or 2.73 per 10,000 population and 624 traffic injuries, or 47.27 per 10,000 population. Is that acceptable or not? The city of Springdale has about the same population as City. Last year, there were 21 traffic deaths and 476 injuries in Springdale; clearly, then, City is not doing as well as Springdale. How well should City be doing if it is to serve its ultimate purpose to the best of its ability? One way to measure progress is to set a realistic but challenging goal. In this case, City Police Department might decide that traffic deaths should be reduced to not more than 1 per 10,000 population per year, and injuries from traffic accidents to not more than 25 per 10,000 population per year.

These comparisons can be quite dramatic:

	Traffic Deaths		Traffic Injuries	
	Number	**Ratio[a]**	**Number**	**Ratio[a]**
City, current[b]	36	2.73	624	47.27
Springdale, current	21	1.62	476	36.62
City, long-term goal	13	1.00	330	25.00

[a]Per 10,000 population.
[b]Most recent year's records.

There are several things that you should notice about this simple example. First, information has been collected from various sources; in this case, from the two police departments. The accuracy of a diagnosis based on this information will be no greater than the accuracy of the information itself. Most police departments routinely keep all sorts of records; unless the records are correct, important administrative decisions are likely to be wrong.

Also, it is tempting to look for needs only where the information is readily available. If City Police Department did not keep records of traffic deaths and injuries or if the records were not readily accessible, the administrator might never think of this as a possible area of need—*unless* a deliberate effort is made to evaluate the entire agency's performance, in comparison with basic values and long-term goals, from time to time. When this is done, deficiencies in the information system are likely to be revealed when the administrator discovers that necessary information is not available.

Notice too that we have not indicated how the agency's basic values and long-term goals were produced, or by whom, or where they came from. In fact, they can come from many sources: the parent government, statewide or national law enforcement advisory groups, planning agencies, public demands, or the administrator's own personal values and beliefs. Wherever the values and long-term goals come from, they are useless as a basis for comparison unless they are expressed in specific terms. In our example, the value statement is fairly vague: "to promote traffic safety and to reduce, to the minimum attainable, deaths and injuries due to traffic accidents." In the absence of any comparison, one might argue that the current death and injury rates are the "minimum attainable" and that City Police Department is satisfying this goal. But the long-term goal is stated in precise terms and there is no room for argument: the current conditions are far short of the goal.

Finally, notice that in this example we have not tried to suggest *why* there is a gap between current and desired conditions. To use Newman and Warren's medical analogy, we have identified only the "symptoms" but not the underlying cause of the "illness." Sometimes that is as much as can be done, and many problems can be treated "symptomatically." If you relieve or eliminate the symptoms, it is reasonable to assume that the underlying illness is controlled if not "cured." If City Police Department took *any* action that resulted in a reduced traffic death and injury rate, no one would care whether the real cause of the problem had been corrected. In fact, often the real cause of a problem cannot be discovered or is not accessible for "treatment." Most sociologists are convinced that a large part of the crime problem in our society is the result of fundamental social conditions such as poverty and ethnic discrimination. Although this theory may or may not be correct, it hardly matters from the police administrator's point of view since the police are not able to change these social conditions. The police can only treat the symptoms, the crimes themselves.

Not all problems can be treated symptomatically. For example, a police administrator might find that the agency is experiencing an abnormally high rate of personnel turnover. Instead of an acceptable rate of 8 to 10 percent per year, the rate has climbed to 15 percent. Before any action can be taken to correct the problem, the causes of the problem must be discovered. If young officers with less than five years' experience are quitting to go into some other kind of work, that would suggest problems with the agency's recruitment and selection process. If young officers are leaving to join another police agency that pays better, that would suggest an urgent need to adjust the salary schedule. But if the increased turnover rate can be attributed to an unusual number of older, experienced officers who happen to be reaching the normal retirement age at the same time, the administrator's response would be entirely different. Perhaps it would be necessary to bring in experienced personnel from another agency (possibly by offering higher salaries) to fill the middle-management ranks, or perhaps less-experienced younger officers can be quickly trained and promoted. In any case, the turnover problem should not be treated symptomatically (for example, by rushing to the City Council for an immediate across-the-board pay raise) until the root cause can be determined.

Once a need has been defined—that is, the administrator has determined that some current condition falls short of what is desirable—the next step is to decide the extent to which the undesirable condition should be corrected within a given period of time.

Goal and Objective Setting

All of an organization's goals and objectives ultimately are derived from its basic values and purposes. As we saw earlier, basic values usually are stated in such general terms that, by themselves, they cannot be applied directly to immediate problems; first they must be restated in specific terms. A specific statement of an agency's basic values or purposes is an expression of a **goal** toward which the agency is working. In the example of City's traffic death and injury rates, the goal is to reduce deaths to a ratio of 1 per 10,000 population and to reduce injuries to a ratio of 25 per 10,000 population. The obvious advantage in stating a goal in such specific terms is that progress toward meeting it can be measured and particular activities can be designed to achieve it. Such a goal is sometimes called an **operational definition** of an agency's values: it defines the value in measurable terms.

Once values and goals have been operationally defined, it is possible to assess needs in comparable terms and to determine the root causes for those needs. For example, careful study of the pattern of traffic accidents in City might point to three major causes of the unacceptable death and injury rates:

1. More than 25 percent of deaths and more than 30 percent of injuries occur in accidents on the Central Expressway, and the majority of these accidents occur outside of the Loop Expressway.

2. More than 65 percent of the accidents resulting in a death and more than 45 percent of accidents resulting in injuries involve a person who is driving while intoxicated (DWI). About 35 percent of the DWI drivers are males under 30 years of age who are either military personnel assigned to Wingtip AFB or students at City University.

3. Of the accidents resulting in death or injury other than those on the Expressway, and other than those involving drunken drivers, the majority occur at street intersections where there are traffic signals. Nearly all such accidents involve a driver who fails to observe the signal and yield the right of way.

This information suggests the directions that City Police Department might take to achieve its goals. Apparently there are several interrelated causes of the present unacceptable condition. The next step for the planner or administrator is to translate these findings into objectives that can be attained within a reasonable period of time. Setting objectives is an exercise in judgment based on the planner's own past experience, the experience of others, and creative imagination. Objectives must be stated in measurable terms, and they should be high enough to challenge the organization but not so high that success will be impossible. In our example, the following goals might be set:

1. The number of serious accidents on the Central Expressway outside of the Loop Expressway will be reduced by 15 percent in one year and 25 percent in two years.

2. The number of accidents involving DWI drivers who are military personnel or students will be reduced by 25 percent each year over the next two years.

3. The number of accidents at major intersections controlled by traffic signals will be reduced by at least 10 percent each year over the next two years.

The administrator can check these specific objectives against the long-term goals by simply computing how well the goals will be achieved if the objectives are achieved. In this case, if all three objectives are met, the result after two years would be 12 fatalities (0.91 per 10,000 population) and 201 injuries (15.23 per 10,000), which is better than the long-term goal. However, these calculations assume that there is no overlap among the three causes of traffic accidents. In fact, it is very likely that some of the expressway and intersection accidents involve drinking drivers. Still, even if there is some overlap, the attainment of the three specific objectives listed above would mean that City Police Department's ultimate goals would be met.

The next question that must be answered is how best to achieve these objectives.

Defining Alternative Methods

Almost any objective might be reached by a number of different methods, in the same way that you could get from where you are to where you want to be by any of several different routes. The search for the best method is one of the most creative parts of the planning process since it relies largely on the ingenuity, experience, and knowledge of the planner.[9]

There are three sources of alternative methods to reach a given objective:

1.   What has worked in the past.
2.   What other, similar organizations have done.
3.   What the planner can imagine.

The search for alternative methods should not be limited. The idea is to produce the maximum possible number of alternatives, no matter how impractical or unrealistic they might appear at first. Often a ridiculous idea can be modified or adapted until it is made practical, or it may suggest another approach that is practical.

A separate list of alternative solutions should be made for each objective, even though some methods might contribute to two or more related objectives. In our example, the planner might list the following methods of attaining the second objective:

A.   Intensively patrol taverns and other drinking places frequented by military personnel and students, especially during high-accident-frequency periods.
B.   Equip all patrol units with field breath analyzer kits and train all officers in field sobriety testing and DWI arrest techniques.
C.   Conduct a public education campaign on the dangers of DWI and on City Police Department's strict-enforcement policy.
D.   Ask the City Council for an ordinance requiring tavern operators to limit the sale of alcohol to one drink per hour per patron during the evening.
E.   Ask tavern operators to inform the police whenever a patron who may be intoxicated leaves the tavern.
F.   Ask City University officials to change their current policy, which forbids alcoholic beverages on campus and at school-related events; if students drink on campus, they are less likely to drink away from campus and drive home.
G.   Ask Wingtip AFB officials to cooperate by imposing stiff penalties on any personnel who return to the base intoxicated, especially if they are driving.

These examples certainly do not exhaust the possibilities. You should be able to add several more alternative solutions to this list. The more alternatives one can develop, the greater the likelihood that the most effective, successful method will be chosen to meet the plan's objectives.

In looking over the list of alternative methods, notice that some would be much more expensive or difficult to implement than others. Some methods also might be more likely to produce beneficial results than others. Of course, an expensive solution that works may be preferable to an inexpensive solution that does not work. The next step in the planning process involves just such considerations.

Cost-Benefit Assessment   Every activity an agency undertakes involves some cost and, if the activity is worthwhile, produces some benefit. The administrator's hope is to produce the maximum possible benefit for the minimum possible cost. Cost-benefit analysis or assessment simply means comparing the costs and benefits of alternative activities.

In carrying out this analysis, it is important to include all costs, even though some of the resources needed to carry out an activity might already be available. If you assign patrol officers to a new activity, they will no longer be available to do what they are now doing; either that activity must be dropped (at the expense of whatever benefit it may have produced) or the officers must be replaced. However, some indirect costs such as administrators' salaries and general overhead can be omitted from the analysis since these costs generally do not change regardless of the agency's activities.

Let us see what a cost-benefit analysis for our seven proposed activities might show:

Objective 2.   Reduce the number of accidents involving DWIs by 25 percent per year for each of two years.

Activity	Estimated Costs	Estimated Benefits[a]
A	3 patrol officers × 6 hours a day × 313 days per year at $12 an hour per officer = $67,608	60%
B	Breath analysis kits, 20 at $250 + training program, 40 officers × 24 hours of training at $12 an hour per officer = $16,520	40%
C	Campaign development, 2 officers × 80 hours at $12 an hour per officer + literature and materials, $5000 + implementation, 2 officers × 500 hours at $12 an hour per officer = $16,420	20%
D	Administrative time to develop ordinance and obtain Council action, 40 hours at $30 an hour = $1200	5%
E	Development of literature, 1 officer × 8 hours at $12 an hour + distribution of literature, 2 officers × 10 hours at $12 an hour = $436	5%
F	Administrative time to consult with City University officials, 4 hours at $30 = $120	5%
G	Administrative time to consult with Wingtip AFB officials, 4 hours at $30 = $120	2.5%

[a]The benefits are shown as a percentage of the total objective that each activity is likely to produce. These estimates are based on past experience and intuition and may later prove to be incorrect. In this example, if Activity A is carried out, 60 percent of the objective should be achieved.

The analysis in this example can be converted into a dollar cost for each percentage of the objective that each activity is expected to produce:

Activity A	$67,608/60% =	$1,126.80
Activity B	16,520/40% =	413.00
Activity C	16,420/20% =	821.00

Activity D	1,200/5% =	240.00
Activity E	436/5% =	87.20
Activity F	120/5% =	24.00
Activity G	$120/2.5% =	$48.00

In this example, no single activity is expected to attain the entire objective, but two or more activities could be combined. If Activities A and B were combined, the predicted benefit would be 100 percent of the objective at a total cost of $84,128 or $841.28 per percent. Or you could combine Activity A with all of the others *except* B; this would cost $85,904 and would meet 97.5 percent of the objective at a cost of $881.07 per percent. No other combination of proposed activities would be expected to achieve more than 90 percent of the objective.

Once the costs and benefits for each proposed activity have been calculated, the choice of activities to be implemented may seem obvious. Sometimes, in fact, cost-benefit analysis points to one alternative as the obvious choice. More often, as in this case, other considerations may affect the planners' decisions.

Selection of a Methodology

The estimates of cost are based on factors that should be easily known and accurately estimated such as the number of people needed to carry out an activity, their salaries (and related expenses such as the cost of operating their vehicles), and the number of hours they are likely to spend on the activity. The estimate of benefits, of course, is not always so clear-cut. Unless the same activity has been carried out in the past, there may be very little experience on which to base an estimate. However, the estimate always should be based on an assumption that the activity will be successful. For instance, in the cost-benefit analysis for activity G above, we would assume that the Wingtip AFB officials will agree to cooperate. Even so, the activity will have relatively little effect because the military personnel would soon find ways to avoid getting in trouble with their superiors, but probably would continue drinking away from the base.

Before actually choosing an activity, the administrator must consider whether there actually is a reasonably high probability that an activity will be successful. If the Wingtip AFB officials are not likely to cooperate, the expense of activity G, though relatively small, would be completely wasted. Similarly, activity D is not very expensive, but is it likely that the City Council would pass an ordinance limiting the sale of liquor? How vigorously would tavern and restaurant owners object? If the ordinance were passed, how would it be enforced? Would City Police Department then have to increase patrol activities to enforce the new law?

Activity E, on the other hand, involves soliciting the tavern owners' cooperation. If completely successful, this activity would produce about the same benefit as activity D but at much lower cost. The planner must consider whether, in fact, the tavern owners probably would be responsive to this idea.

The administrator also must consider the effects of each activity on the other operations of the agency. The tavern patrols proposed in activity A would require three patrol officers for six hours each day. If regular patrol officers are diverted from their beats for this purpose, other types of criminal activity might increase. If the taverns are concentrated on one or two patrol beats, the officers assigned to those beats might spend nearly all their time on tavern patrols and the rest of their duties might be neglected. Or additional officers may have to be hired just to perform the tavern patrols, and such specialization usually is not desirable.

Ultimately, the administrator's choice of methodology must be based on experience, knowledge of other agencies' successful practices, understanding of the community, intuition, and judgment. Whatever decision is made, it should never be regarded as final and immutable. If a particular activity does not work the way the administrator thought it would, it should be discarded and replaced.

First, however, the administrator must have some way of knowing whether the activity works.

Defining the Evaluation Method

Whenever a plan is first developed, it should contain an explicit statement of the methods that will be used to evaluate its success. Usually the method of evaluation is implied by the objectives set for the program. In the example we have been using, the objective was to reduce the number of accidents involving drunken drivers by 25 percent each year for two years. The method of evaluating this program, then, would be to study the accident records at the end of each year to determine whether DWI-related accidents have been reduced by 25 percent.

If a program involves several related activities, it may be desirable to evaluate whether each activity is contributing as much benefit as was predicted. Again, the method of evaluation should be specified in advance, when the activity first begins. However, it is sometimes impossible to tell which activity has caused a certain kind of event *not* to happen. In our example, if DWI-related accidents were reduced by 25 percent, it would be difficult to know which of several related activities were responsible.

Almost always, careful evaluation will show that some programs are successful, perhaps even more so than was expected, while others are not entirely successful. At that point, the evaluation becomes, in effect, a needs assessment for the next round of planning and the process has come full circle.

LIEUTENANT LUSK'S IN BASKET

Instructions

In this exercise, you are to assume the role of Lieutenant Dennis Lusk, Personnel and Training Officer for the City Police Department. The documents below have been selected from Lieutenant Lusk's in basket. Read them with care. If you need more information about City or its police department, refer to the data bank in the front of the book. After you have studied the documents, complete these steps:

1. Determine whether Lieutenant Lusk has enough information to complete the assignment given to him by Chief Abel. If not, what additional information does he need and where could he obtain it?

2. Using only the information given in these documents, complete Lieutenant Lusk's assignment as best you can.

CITY POLICE DEPARTMENT
Interoffice Memorandum

FROM: Chief Abel

TO: Lt. Lusk, Pers. & Trng.

SUBJECT: Personnel Needs Projections   DATE: 28 Jan 19--

Dennis:

     In a few weeks it will be time to begin work on next year's budget. Before we start, I would like to have a better idea of where the Dept. is heading and what our needs will be in future years. I have asked the City Planning Office and some of our own people to supply the information attached to this memo. Please analyze this information and give me a projection of our personnel needs for each of the next five years, showing not only the total number of personnel we will need but also the number in each of these categories:

         1. Patrol officers
         2. Detectives
         3. Administrative and technical support

     Please give this assignment a high priority. I would like to have this data no later than February 15. Thanks.

                             E. Z. Abel, Chief.

CITY POLICE DEPARTMENT
Interoffice Memorandum

FROM: M. Avery, Capt., Patrol Bureau

TO: Chief Abel

SUBJECT: Requested data   DATE: 25 Jan 19--

SIR:

     Our present authorized strength is 42 patrol officers, 17 sergeants, and 3 lieutenants. We have two P.O. positions vacant in the Relief Watch. There has been no increase in our authorized strength over the past 3 years.

     Last year our officers responded to 142,687 requests for police services. The breakdown by type is as follows:

Type of Incident	Number	Percent
Crime report, felony	6,278	04.4
Crime report, misdemeanor	25,142	17.6
Crime report, unfounded	3,194	02.2
Traffic accident	3,825	02.7
Family & other disturbances (noncriminal)	16,226	11.4
Traffic:		
Citations issued	21,084	14.8

PAGE 2.

Miscellaneous other	8,113	05.7
Investigation, suspicious activity, etc.	11,995	08.4
Assist Fire Dept., EMS	4,348	03.0
Crime prevention (bldg. inspections, etc.)	5,474	03.8
Miscellaneous, unclassifiable	37,007	26.0
TOTAL:	142,687	100.0

     Last year there were 32 job-related injuries among patrol officers, of which 11 were a result of assaults on officers. A total of 45 working days was lost due to injuries, including 21 days lost due to injuries from assaults. No City police officer was killed in the line of duty last year.

     Please advice whether the above information is sufficient.

         M. Avery, Captain
         Patrol Bureau

CITY, STATE
CITY HALL
INTEROFFICE MEMORANDUM

FROM: Dr. Crystal Gazer, Dir., Ofc. of Planning & Budgets

TO: Chief Abel, Police Dept.

SUBJECT: Requested Data

DATE: January 22, 19--

Here is the information you requested:

	3 Yrs. Ago.	2 Yrs. Ago.	Last Year
Total City population	120,000	125,800	132,000
Population segments:			
Anglo, number	74,345	80,764	83,028
Anglo, percent	61.8	64.2	62.9
Black, number	20,331	21,386	22,836
Black, percent	16.9	17.0	17.3
Hispanic, number	17,925	18,367	19,404
Hispanic, percent	14.9	14.6	14.7
Other, number	7,699	5,284	6,732
Other, percent	6.4	4.2	5.1
Employment:			
Not in labor force:			
number	70,376	73,216	76,956
percent	58.5	58.2	58.3
Unemployed seeking work:			
number	7,699	11,574	9,900
percent	6.4	9.2	7.5
Military (active duty):			
number	6,200	5,850	5,600
percent	5.2	4.7	4.2
Agricultural workers:			
number	2,045	2,013	1,848
percent	1.7	1.6	1.4
Industrial workers, laborers:			
number	22,015	21,124	19,404
percent	18.3	16.8	14.7
Office, service, and technical workers:			
number	9,143	9,812	11,484
percent	7.6	7.8	8.7
Professional and other:			
number	2,767	2,139	6,864
percent	2.3	1.7	5.2

I hope this is all you need. If not, let me know.

Crystal Gazer

Crystal Gazer, Ph.D.
Director, Planning & Budget

CITY POLICE DEPARTMENT
Interoffice Memorandum

FROM:	T. Bowen, Capt., Chief of Detectives
TO:	Chief Abel
SUBJECT:	Detective Activity Report DATE: 26 Jan 19--

SIR:

    As requested, here is a summary of the activity of the Detective Bureau for the past 2 years.

Crime Index Type	Number Cases	Cleared by Arrest	Conviction Obtained
Homicide (murder, voluntary manslaughter)	23	18	12*
Aggravated assault	267	221	164*
Rape, sexual assault	135	64	31
Robbery	398	183	128
Burglary	1,818	615	459
Theft	2,897	1,479	973
Theft of motor vehicle	469	143	102

Page 2.

Arson	35	11	9*
Fraud, forgery	211	63	41
Miscellaneous other	25	23	19
Total Felony Cases:	6,278	2,820	1,938

* Includes cases that ended in conviction during first 2 weeks of this year. In addition, 11 cases are pending trial.

    In addition to the above, the Detective Bureau was involved in 4,248 cases that were determined to be misdemeanor offenses. Of these, detectives performed arrests in 1,003 cases and obtained convictions in 784 cases.

Thomas Bowen, Captain,
Chief of Detectives

```
┌─────────────────────────────────────────────────────────────────────────┐
│                      CITY POLICE DEPARTMENT                               │
│                      Interoffice Memorandum                              │
├─────────────────────────────────────────────────────────────────────────┤
│ FROM:      Capt. Frank Edwards, OCB                                       │
├─────────────────────────────────────────────────────────────────────────┤
│ TO:        Chief Abel                                                     │
├──────────────────────────────────────────────────┬──────────────────────┤
│ SUBJECT:   CONFIDENTIAL REPORT                    │ DATE: 27 Jan 19--     │
├──────────────────────────────────────────────────┴──────────────────────┤
│                                                                           │
│         THIS INFORMATION IS CONFIDENTIAL. ACCESS TO THIS INFORMATION IS   │
│         RESTRICTED TO AUTHORIZED PERSONNEL.                               │
│                                                                           │
│         SIR:  Here is the summary of Organized Crime Bureau activity:     │
│                                                                           │
```

Activity	Last Yr	2 Yrs Ago	3 Yrs Ago
Vice (incl. prostitution)			
Cases made	124	118	128
Persons arrested	372	493	406
Convictions	276	259	310
Narcotics:			
Cases made	438	815	652
Persons arrested	593	1,801	825
Convictions	502	1,629	756
Value of drugs seized ($000s)	8,500	9,250	7,890
Intelligence:			

```
         CONFIDENTIAL REPORT*****ACCESS RESTRICTED              PAGE 2 of 2.
```

Documents filed	23,496	18,943	19,672
Field interviews	4,104	5,627	5,396
Surveillances	160	139	1,528
Cases referred to other CPD units	12	47	82

As you know, this information is highly sensitive and must be treated as confidential. Please let me know if you require a verbal explanation or additional details.

```
                                          Frank Edwards, Captain
                                          Organized Crime Bureau
```

IN REVIEW

1. Plans often do not work out as anticipated because:
   (a) Employees are unable or unwilling to do their jobs properly.
   (b) Most police agencies cannot afford the highly specialized experts needed to make successful plans.
   (c) Plans usually are based on less than perfectly accurate information and predictions.
   (d) Administrators are not competent to develop good plans.
   (e) Most planners are unrealistic about the resources that will be available to carry out their plans.

2. _____ is a form of research in which processes, techniques, or actions are carried out under controlled conditions to determine whether the researcher's ideas about what will happen are correct.

3. The role of a police agency's planning unit should be:
   (a) To perform detailed research and to assist administrators during the planning process.
   (b) To develop all plans for the agency, relieving administrators of this time-consuming burden.
   (c) To evaluate and criticize plans made by the agency's administrators.
   (d) All of the above.
   (e) None of the above.

4. A work schedule is an example of:
   (a) A standing plan.
   (b) A contingency plan.
   (c) A strategic plan.
   (d) An operational plan.
   (e) A programmatic plan.

5. A contingency plan is any plan that:
   (a) Is developed by an outside consultant or separate planning unit.
   (b) Is implemented only when a certain event occurs.
   (c) Involves substantial changes in an agency's organizational structure.
   (d) Is automatically discontinued after a specified period of time.
   (e) Does not require the participation of upper-level administrators in the planning process.

6. A budget is an example of:
   (a) An operational plan.
   (b) A contingency plan.
   (c) A programmatic plan.
   (d) A standing plan.
   (e) A strategic plan.

7. A programmatic plan that involves the introduction of a single, specific change in an organization over a limited period of time is:
   (a) A project.
   (b) A budget.
   (c) A program.
   (d) A forecast.
   (e) An experiment.

8. A _____ plan is intended to show how all the separate programs and projects are interrelated and coordinated to achieve large-scale improvements in an organization over a substantial period of time.

9. An operational definition:
   (a) Serves as a comparison of current conditions with a desired future condition.
   (b) Expresses an agency's values in measurable terms.
   (c) States a specific objective to be achieved in a specific period of time.
   (d) Is a type of operational plan.
   (e) Defines the cost-benefit ratio for an activity.

10. True or False: Once a cost-benefit assessment has been made, the choice of the best alternative method of achieving an objective is automatically determined.

REFERENCES

1. Russell L. Ackoff, *A Concept of Corporate Planning*, New York: Wiley-Interscience, 1970, page 1.
2. Ackoff, page 3.
3. Arthur B. Troan, Jr., *Using Information to Manage*, New York: Ronald Press, 1968, page 25.
4. For more information about forecasting, see John C. Chambers, Satinder K. Mullick, and Donald D. Smith, *An Executive's Guide to Forecasting*, New York: Wiley, 1974; and William Ascher, *Forecasting: Appraisal for Policy-makers and Planners*, Baltimore: Johns Hopkins Univ. Press, 1978.
5. Herbert C. Hicks and C. Ray Gullett, *The Management of Organizations*, 3rd ed., New York: McGraw-Hill, 1976, pages 271−278.
6. Alfred R. Stone and Stuart M. DeLuca, *Investigating Crimes*, Boston: Houghton Mifflin, 1980, pages 387−388 and 434.
7. Ackoff, pages 8−20.
8. William H. Newman and E. Kirby Warren, *The Process of Management*, 4th ed., Englewood Cliffs, N.J.: Prentice-Hall, 1977, page 230.
9. Newman and Warren, page 246.

5 BUDGETING

THERE IS ONE KIND OF PLAN THAT EVERY POLICE AGENCY must develop periodically, usually on an annual basis: the agency budget. For some administrators, budgeting is a distasteful, frustrating chore that is undertaken only because the agency's parent government requires it. In most states and municipalities, a governmental department cannot receive funds from the public treasury until it has submitted a budget and the budget has been approved by the legislature, city council, county commissioners, or other governing body. Sometimes this process is marked by strident public controversy and hot competition among department heads or between the police administrators and the legislature.

Budgeting can, and should, be an orderly, rational process whereby an agency's programmatic plans and goals are weighed against competing claims for resources and the public's will is expressed in terms of an allocation of those resources. Much depends on whether the budget itself is based on solid facts and considered judgments of what is necessary and desirable. Developing such a budget is the subject of this chapter.

THE PURPOSE OF BUDGETING

Even if it were not necessary to submit a budget in order to obtain funds from the parent government, police administrators would find the budgeting process an indispensable tool of management. William H. Newman and E. Kirby Warren point out, "The greatest strength of budgeting is probably its use of a single common denominator—dollars—for many diverse activities and things."[1] By reducing all of an agency's resource requirements to a single, easily compared quantity, conflicting claims can be evaluated and reasonable decisions can be made as to which activities and what things are truly needed.

Once a budget has been adopted, it serves as the standard for the control of expenditures. Funds can be spent only for the purposes stated in the budget; if the budget is executed properly, expenses cannot exceed resources and all resources are used for their intended purpose. Without a budget, there is no standard of accountability, no way to determine whether funds are being used properly or whether the resources one expects to receive in the future will be adequate.

Finally, a budget serves as a standard for evaluating the efficiency of many different kinds of activities. In the previous chapter, we showed how cost-benefit analysis can be used to compare different activities that have been proposed. The same kind of analysis can be applied to current activities by comparing the budgeted cost with the actual benefit being produced. This kind of analysis often plays an important role in the needs assessment stage of the planning process.

TYPES OF BUDGETS

Any budget consists of a statement of expected or required income—the funds an agency expects to receive in the future or will need in order to operate—and a statement of expected or proposed expenses—how the organization plans to use its funds. Ordinarily a police agency's budget should show that its income and its expenses will be precisely equal over the budget period (which we will assume to be one year).

The expense portion of a budget usually is divided into two parts: the capital budget and the operating budget. The **capital budget** lists expenditures for things such as buildings, durable equipment that will last several years (including vehicles), and anything else that has a useful life beyond the immediate budget period. These costs can be prorated over the entire useful life of the object to be bought, so that the true annual cost can be compared meaningfully with other current costs. However, there are different ways to treat capital expenditures in a budget, as we will see shortly.

The **operating budget** includes the expenses that occur regularly and continuously such as personnel costs, utilities, and other routine costs and any items that are not expected to last beyond the immediate budget period such as office supplies or nondurable equipment.

Some government agencies also have special fund budgets in addition to their operating and capital budgets. A **special fund budget** is used when certain revenues are required to be spent only for a certain purpose. For example, federal taxes on gasoline, tires, and other automotive products go into a special Federal Highway Trust Fund. Money from this fund can be used only for highway construction and maintenance and for the support of public transportation. Special funds are not always a concern to police administrators, but there may be instances when funds from a state grant or other source are dedicated to a particular use such as traffic law enforcement or crime prevention.

Capital Budget Formats

Capital expenditures are separated from operating expenditures simply because the objects bought on a capital basis are expected to last beyond the budget period. If the whole cost of a capital expenditure were shown in one year, a comparison between the two types of expenditures would be misleading. Furthermore, most capital expenditures are funded by borrowing money, usually through the sale of bonds, so that the cost of the object can be spread out over its expected useful life and the government is not burdened with the entire cost in a single budget period.

Nevertheless, the parent government (and the public) should know the total cost of everything that is to be bought. The capital budget, then, includes a list of things that are to be purchased during the budget period and their expected useful life. If the expense is to be funded out of bond revenues, that fact should be shown in the budget. However, the amount is not included in the operating budget. Instead, the operating budget should include only the cost of repaying the debt during the immediate budget period.

For example, suppose the police agency needs a new headquarters building. The building will cost $5 million and is expected to be used by the police for 25 years. If bonds are sold to pay for this building, the interest on the bonds will be 10 percent per year. The average payment of principal and interest will be $468,000 per year (the total cost being $11,700,000); this figure should be shown in the operating budget as the current year's **debt service** for the building.

Not all capital expenditures, even large ones such as the cost of a new building, are funded through debt. Some states, including Texas, and many cities do not permit their government to borrow money except for certain limited purposes; they are required by law to spend in any one budget period only as much as they expect to receive in taxes and other revenues. Also, a city or county government might be unable to sell its bonds at an acceptable interest rate, or may be unable to persuade its citizens to approve the issuance of new bonds. Or a city might have a windfall of revenue, perhaps from the sale of some city-owned land that is no longer needed, or funds from the state or federal government might be available to finance a needed capital item. For any of these reasons, in our example of the new building, the city might decide to pay outright the entire $5 million cost. In this case, the capital budget shows both the total cost and the **amortized** cost, which is the total divided by the expected useful life. In our example, the amortized cost of a $5 million building that will last 25 years would be $200,000. However, this figure is not added to the operating budget, since no current funds will be needed each year.

Vehicles, furniture, and equipment of every sort may be included in the capital budget, if their useful life is expected to be greater than the budget period. These items are often bought out of current funds, but the expenditure should be amortized over the useful life of each item. Both the total cost and the amortized cost should be shown in the capital budget, but neither amount should be added to the operating budget.

Often a capital budget shows the amortized cost of previous years' capital expenses, throughout the useful life of each item.

There is still another way that capital expenditures can be treated. When an agency buys, say, a squad car for $10,000, the administrator expects the vehicle to last for perhaps four years. At the end of that time, the squad car will have to be replaced, since it will no longer be serviceable. Even though the original cost of the squad car has already been paid, it would be a good idea to save up the money for its replacement. One way to do this is to show the current expense for the vehicle in the capital budget but, instead of amortizing the vehicle's cost, the cost can be **depreciated** by adding to the operating budget a portion of the replacement cost. In this case, the depreciation would be shown as $2500 per year. Even though this is shown as an expense on the operating budget, the money would not actually be spent; it would be set aside to be used when a new vehicle is needed.

Most agencies, if they have been in existence for a number of years and they are reasonably stable in size, reach a point at which their annual capital expenditures for equipment, vehicles, furniture, and so on are about the same from year to year. The amounts set aside in the operating budget for depreciation then should be sufficient to cover the actual capital expenditures for each year.

Operating Budget Formats

Operating budgets are generally more complex than capital budgets because there are so many different kinds of things, from people to paperclips, that must be included. Experts in accounting and management have devised a number of ways to list these expenditures so that reasonable comparisons can be made among the costs of different kinds of activities. Robert D. Lee, Jr., and Ronald W. Johnson have listed three basic types of operating budget formats.[2]

Object-of-expenditure Budgets (Figure 5.1).   Only the things or types of things to be purchased are stated, along with their cost. For example, the budget might list, in part:

ANNUAL BUDGET—CITY OF PORTSMOUTH, VIRGINIA

DEPT.: PUBLIC SAFETY—POLICE
FUNCTION: POLICING, INVESTIGATION AND TRAFFIC CONTROL

FUND: GENERAL FUND
CODE: 09010

DEPARTMENTAL DETAIL

CATE-GORY-SUB-GROUP	CLASSIFICATION	PERSONNEL CUR-RENT	PERSONNEL PROS'D. DEPT.	PERSONNEL RCMD. MGR.	ACTUAL EXPENDITURE 78-79	ESTIMATED EXPENDITURE 79-80	PROPOSED BY DEPARTMENT 80-81	RECOMMENDED BY MANAGER 80-81	FINAL BUDGET 80-81
110	**Personal Services**								
111-01	Police chief	1	1	1		31,610	33,473	35,542	35,542
111-02	Assistant chief	2	2	2		52,157	54,414	58,892	58,892
111-07	Field operations commander	1	1	1		21,701	22,974	24,386	24,386
111-09	Captain	8	8	8		163,137	168,399	178,882	178,882
111-13	Lieutenant	11	11	11		206,840	213,098	225,938	225,938
111-15	Sergeant	28	28	28		453,979	474,622	500,733	500,733
111-20	Police officer	156	156	156		2,049,798	2,154,819	2,287,607	2,287,607
111-21	Police planning analyst	1	1	1		16,198	17,186	18,775	18,775
111-23	Property and evidence clerk	1	2	2		11,523	18,886	20,074	20,074
111-28	Administrative assistant	1	1	1		15,485	16,150	17,176	17,176
111-30	Secretary	1	1	1		11,437	12,418	13,195	13,195
111-31	Senior clerk	1	1	1		9,576	10,152	10,795	10,795
111-32	Supervising clerk	1	1	1		10,716	11,299	12,021	12,021
111-33	Clerk stenographer	2	2	2		15,988	16,410	17,461	17,461
111-34	Senior account clerk	1	1	1		9,465	9,719	10,334	10,334
111-35	Fingerprint technician	1	1	1		9,288	9,848	10,469	10,469
111-36	Intermediate clerk typist	12	15	13		87,255	113,120	106,476	106,476
111-39	Clerk typist	1				6,843			
111-47	Court pay					50,000	55,000	55,000	55,000
111-48	Field training officer allowance					5,040	10,920	10,920	10,920
111-51	Janitor	1	2	1		8,104	15,091	9,058	9,058
111-52	Special assignment					71,550	90,000	85,000	85,000
	Subtotal	231	235	232	3,099,335	3,317,690	3,527,998	3,708,734	3,708,734
	CETA Personnel								
181-37	Intermediate clerk typist CETA	2	3	3		12,773	15,214	15,214	15,214
181-40	Clerk typist	1	1	1			6,924	6,924	6,924
191-37	Intermediate clerk typist CETA	4	2	2		25,294	12,835	12,835	12,835
191-40	Clerk typist CETA	3				25,294			
191-43	Janitor—CETA	1				6,412			
	Total	241	241	238	3,099,335	3,387,463	3,562,971	3,743,707	3,743,707

(Continued)

ANNUAL BUDGET (Continued)

DEPT.: PUBLIC SAFETY–POLICE
FUNCTION: POLICING, INVESTIGATION AND TRAFFIC CONTROL
FUND: GENERAL FUND
CODE: 09010

DEPARTMENTAL DETAIL

CATE-GORY-SUB-GROUP	CLASSIFICATION	PERSONNEL CUR-RENT	PERSONNEL PROS'D. DEPT.	PERSONNEL RCMD. MGR.	ACTUAL EXPENDITURE 78-79	ESTIMATED EXPENDITURE 79-80	PROPOSED BY DEPARTMENT 80-81	RECOMMENDED BY MANAGER 80-81	FINAL BUDGET 80-81
210	**Contractual services**								
211-00	Telephone service					32,246	32,246	32,246	32,246
213-00	Travel and expenses					5,000	6,500	5,200	5,200
221-00	Repairs office equipment					2,000	2,000	1,500	1,500
222-00	Repairs other equipment (video)						2,000	1,500	1,500
225-00	Training expense					10,000	14,908	12,000	12,000
231-01	Contractual services—other					18,000	21,178	19,000	19,000
231-02	Police community relations					32,760	32,550	32,550	32,550
231-03	Vehicle equipment rental					8,450	7,200	7,200	7,200
232-00	Medical costs					7,986	7,986	7,986	7,986
235-00	Data processing charges				241,269	101,712	121,365	131,631	131,631
	Total					218,154	247,933	250,813	250,813
310	**Fixed and Sundry Charges**								
311-00	Rental equipment garage					552,555	630,520	598,634	598,634
321-00	Clothing allowance detective					37,380	42,720	42,720	42,720
325-00	Parking rental					3,840	5,760	5,760	5,760
327-00	Membership dues					350	350	350	350
333-00	Maintenance K-9 corps					15,786	18,370	16,000	16,000
340-09	Fees, other					1,800	1,800	1,800	1,800
346-00	Coronor fees					5,500	5,500	5,500	5,500
	Total				581,785	617,211	705,020	670,764	670,764
410	**Materials and Supplies**								
411-00	Office and printing					29,700	32,670	30,000	30,000
411-03	Micro film supplies						2,800	1,500	1,500
416-00	Laboratory supplies					19,702	25,242	23,000	23,000
429-04	Uniform cost					35,376	41,542	37,500	37,500
429-12	Weapons and ammunition					13,731	23,531	16,000	16,000
	Total				94,995	98,509	125,785	108,000	108,000
520	**Equipment**								
521-01	Equipment other					4,155	437	437	437
522-01	Office machines						1,600		
	Total				187	4,155	2,037	437	437
	Total Budget.				4,017,571	4,325,492	4,643,746	4,773,721	4,773,721

Figure 5-1 An object-of-expenditure budget. Only the items to be purchased (including personnel salaries) are listed, without showing their purpose. (Courtesy Portsmouth, Virginia Police Department.)

Personnel

Salaries, 124 persons	$1,860,000
Benefits at 11.75%	218,550
Subtotal, Personnel	$2,078,550
Utilities	$ 360,000

Vehicles

Depreciation, 42 autos	$ 111,300
Depreciation, 4 trucks	14,480
Operating costs, maintenance	258,750
Subtotal, Vehicles	$ 384,530

This is the simplest type of operating budget, but it also provides the least information. There is nothing to show how many of the personnel will be captains, how many lieutenants, and so forth, nor does it show what these people will be doing. It is not clear from the single line, "operating costs, maintenance," what the average annual mileage per vehicle is likely to be, how much the administrator expects fuel to cost, and how much is likely to be spent on repairs and routine upkeep; nor does the budget show what the vehicles will be used to do, or by whom. Of course, much of this information could be included in a separate document, but that would reduce the primary value of the budget: to allow expenditures for different kinds of activities to be compared.

Performance Budgets. In addition to the things to be purchased, the purpose of each item can be shown in terms of the function it is to perform. For example, instead of merely showing the total number of personnel to be employed and their total salaries, the figures might be broken down as follows:

PERSONNEL

Chief of Police $ 32,000

Executive head of agency; responsible for management of all agency functions.

Division Chiefs (Captains) (4) $ 108,000

Administrators of principal agency functions: patrol, investigation, technical support, and administrative services.

Bureau Chiefs (Lieutenants) (15) $ 330,000

Managers of agency's operational units; supervisors of agency personnel and activities at operating level.

Sergeants (38) $ 665,000

Supervisors of operational personnel in patrol bureau (14); perform operational functions in other bureaus (24).

Patrol Officers (46) $ 552,000

Operating personnel in patrol bureau and traffic section; provide 24-hour-per-day patrol, complaint response, and routine law-enforcement services on 12 patrol beats.

Civilian Personnel (20) $ 173,000

Radio communications operators (8) provide 24-hour-per-day communications services; jail staff (6) assist in providing security and custodial services to prisoners; clerical staff (6) perform essential secretarial and bookkeeping services.

Subtotal, Salaries $1,860,000

Personnel Benefits

Employer contribution to Social Security (6.5%), pension plan (5%), group insurance plan (0.25%); total, 11.5%. $ 218,550

This example does not exhaust the possibilities of what can be shown in a performance budget. For instance, the item for patrol officers might include the number of police services rendered per year (based on an average of previous years, plus an increase if more officers are to be hired). However, the example does indicate the greater amount of detail that a performance budget offers, as compared to an object-of-expenditure budget. The added detail makes it possible for decision makers, both within the agency and in the parent government, to choose between, say, adding two more sergeants to the Investigation Bureau or four more patrol officers to the Patrol Bureau.

A performance budget, although it offers more information than an object-of-expenditure budget, still concentrates on the things and people to be bought without showing how those things and people will be used to provide services or benefits to the public.

Program Budgets (Figure 5.2).   In a **program budget**, expenditures are grouped according to the agency's major programs and subprograms. It is then possible to see not only how much money is to be spent, but how activities are planned and coordinated to achieve specific goals.

A program budget, if it is done properly, is much more detailed than either an object-of-expenditure or performance budget. Naturally, this means that a program budget is also more complicated and time-consuming to prepare. The time and effort are well spent, though, if the result enables

(a)   OFFICE OF THE CHIEF OF POLICE
Activity 2010

	PAYROLL			
100	Personal services		$395,270	
110	Fringe benefits		40,840	
		Subtotal 100	436,110	
	SERVICES			
236	Maintenance of office equipment		200	Typewriters
284	Memberships and subscriptions		480	Listing available
293	Motor pool		5,300	
294	Radio services		720	
		Subtotal 200	6,700	
	SUPPLIES AND COMMODITIES			
311	Office supplies		250	Expendable office supplies
321	Food		300	Coffee service
341	Books, periodicals, records		5,400	Legal advisor
		Subtotal 300	5,950	
		Activity Total	$448,760	

(b) ADMINISTRATIVE STAFF
Activity 2011

	PAYROLL		
100	Personal services	$168,850	
110	Fringe benefits	29,250	
	Subtotal 100	198,100	
	SERVICES		
236	Maintenance of office equipment	100	Typewriters
	Subtotal 200	100	
	SUPPLIES AND COMMODITIES		
311	Office supplies	670	
312	Printing and reproduction	2,400	Maps
314	Postage	1,630	Trust account
341	Books, periodicals, records	1,000	Library
358	Arts and crafts supplies	300	
359	Other supplies	400	
	Subtotal 300	6,400	
	Activity Total	$204,600	

(c) PATROL
Activity 2021

	PAYROLL		
100	Personal services	$7,189,275	
110	Fringe benefits	1,454,014	
	Subtotal 100	8,643,289	
	SERVICES		
223	Damage claims and awards	10,500	Small claims
234	Maintenance of equipment	3,500	Binoculars, equip. repair, CB's
235	Remodeling and alterations	2,000	Front desk, security intercom
236	Maintenance of office equipment	500	Office typewriter
251	Rents, land and buildings	9,600	Adam I
252	Rents—equipment	5,720	Copiers
284	Memberships and subscriptions	370	Listing available
286	Miscellaneous	3,200	El Presidio, police training
293	Motor pool service	1,083,290	
294	Radio services	81,060	
	Subtotal 200	1,199,740	
	SUPPLIES AND COMMODITIES		
311	Office supplies	1,300	
312	Printing and reproduction	400	Misc. reports
351	Operation and maintenance (grounds)	200	Adam I
352	Operation and maintenance (buildings)	400	Adam I, Heliport
355	Small equipment and tools	2,500	Calculators, recorders
359	Other supplies	11,220	First aid, chemical fuses, misc. supplies
	Subtotal 300	14,320	

(Continued)

(c) PATROL
Activity 2021 *(Continued)*

	CAPITAL		
451	Office furniture	1,260	Desk, chairs
452	Office equipment	610	Transcriber
475	Replacement of equipment	3,370	Typewriters
	Subtotal 400	5,240	
	Activity Total	$9,862,589	

(d) DETECTIVES
Activity 2031

	PAYROLL		
100	Salaries	$2,186,450	
110	Fringe benefits	359,680	
	Subtotal 100	2,546,130	
	SERVICES		
202	Nonlocal travel	3,000	Investigative travel
219	Professional services	1,000	Buy money
234	Maintenance of equipment	200	
236	Maintenance of office equipment	2,300	Recorders, typewriter
252	Rents	3,000	Copier
284	Memberships and subscriptions	280	List available
293	Motor pool services	246,720	
294	Radio services	22,560	
	Subtotal 200	279,060	
	SUPPLIES AND COMMODITIES		
311	Office supplies	350	
321	Food	100	Host for seminars meeting
355	Small equipment and tools	500	Accessories to modify equipment
359	Other supplies	5,500	Misc. supplies, robbery camera supplies
	Subtotal 300	6,450	
	CAPITAL		
453	Other office equipment	200	1 filing cabinet
471	Portable machines and equipment	650	Slide projector and 16-mm viewer
	Subtotal 400	850	
	Activity Total	$2,832,490	

Figure 5-2 In these four program budgets, expenditures are grouped by organizational elements, which are explained in some detail in another part of the budget presentation. (Courtesy Tucson, Arizona Police Department.)

the agency administrators and the parent governing body to make better decisions about the allocation of scarce resources.

In practice, the type of budget and its format usually are dictated by the parent government. The police administrator often must follow detailed instructions from the city's or county's budget officer or the state legislature's budget committee. However, there is nothing to prevent the police agency from preparing its budget in the format it finds most useful for internal planning purposes, and then adapting the figures to the format required for submission. In a small city or county, where the police department often is the largest single agency, the administrator may be able to persuade the parent government to adopt the budget format he or she prefers.

PREPARING THE BUDGET

The way a budget is prepared and presented reflects the amount of thoughtful planning that has gone into it. A budget is a plan; it is either a well-conceived, organized, logical plan, or it is a hastily thrown-together one.

The Budget Cycle

The preparation of the budget is the first step in the **budget cycle**, the series of events that take place during the entire budget period. The second step in the cycle is the adoption of the budget; the third step, implementation or execution of the budget; fourth and last, review and evaluation of the previous budget. These cycles necessarily overlap to some extent, since the current year's budget is being executed while the previous year's budget is reviewed and the succeeding year's budget is being prepared and adopted. Thus, the budget cycles for three consecutive years might look like this:

	Last Year	This Year	Next Year
September	I	A	—
October	I	A	—
November	I	A	—
December	I	A	—
January	E	I	P
February	E	I	P
March	E	I	P
April	—	I	P
May	—	I	P
June	—	I	P
July	—	I	P
August	—	I	P
September	—	I	A
October	—	I	A
November	—	I	A
December	—	I	A
January	—	E	I
February	—	E	I
March	—	E	I

Note. P = Preparation; A = Adoption; I = Implementation; and E = Evaluation.

Each of the four stages of the budget cycle is important in itself, and each can contribute to the ability of an administrator to manage the agency and to plan for the future. As always, the key to success is good planning, which in this case means careful, thorough preparation of the budget.

**Methods of
Budget Preparation**

The most common procedure for preparing a budget is the **incremental method**. An *increment* is simply the amount of an increase or decrease. When a budget is prepared according to this method, the current level of expenditure for each item is used as a base that needs no justification. However, any increase or decrease from that base must be explained. For example:

Personnel	Current	Proposed
Salaries, 124	$1,860,000	$1,860,000
4 Patrol officers (Traffic Section)		46,000
2 Dispatchers (night shift)		16,500
3 Clerk-typists (Records Section)		25,500
Subtotal, Salaries	$1,860,000	$1,948,000
Benefits, 11.75%	218,550	228,890
Increase in group insurance, 0.25%		4,870
Total Personnel Cost	$2,078,550	$2,181,760

The principal advantage of the incremental method is that it focuses attention on the changes from the previous budgets that an agency is requesting. Much more often than not, these changes are an increase over the previous level of expenditure, and increases are understandably the major concern of the parent government. The danger in this procedure is that past practices and activities are likely to continue indefinitely, whether or not they are still appropriate, because it is not necessary to justify them. What is even worse, personnel and equipment previously budgeted for one purpose may be applied to some entirely different purpose or activity without this significant change being reflected in the budget.

The incremental method is most often used in preparing an object-of-expenditure budget, although it can be used in developing a performance or even a program budget. However, there are much better methods of preparation for the more detailed formats.

One alternative is the **zero-base budget method**. This method can be used to prepare either a performance or program budget. Each category of expense in a performance budget, or each type of activity in a program budget, is presented as if it were being proposed for the very first time— that is, as if it were at "base zero." Thus, an explanation or justification must be given for every expenditure, usually in the form of a statement of the expected benefit or level of performance. The usual procedure is to show three or more possible levels of activity, with the anticipated costs and benefits of each. In theory, this allows the parent government to decide exactly how much should be spent to buy a given level of service. For example, taking just one item from our sample budget, presented in the performance format:

PATROL OFFICERS

Level I.   Provide crime-prevention patrols and routine law-enforcement services on 12 patrol beats for 18 hours a day (rely on county sheriff for service at other times); 24 officers plus 4 relief officers, total 28. No patrol officers assigned to Traffic Section. $336,000

CITY OF TACOMA
DEPARTMENTAL SUMMARY

DEPARTMENT					YEAR **1981**	PAGE NO.

FUND CATEGORY	PERSONAL SERVICES	MAINTENANCE & OPERATION	CAPITAL OUTLAY	OTHER	TOTAL	PERSON-NEL
ACTUAL EXPENDITURES - 1979 INITIAL APPROPRIATION - 1980 REAPPROPRIATION FROM - 1979 ADDITIONAL APPROPRIATION - 1980						
TOTAL APPROPRIATION - 1980						
ESTIMATED EXPENDITURES - 1981						

PROGRAM NUMBER	PROGRAM/DIVISION	EMPLOYEES		ACTUAL	BUDGET	ESTIMATE
		1980	1981	YEAR 1979	YEAR 1980	YEAR 1981

Figure 5-3 *(Continued)*

CITY OF TACOMA

PROGRAM TITLE	DEPARTMENT	YEAR **1981**	PAGE

PROGRAM INDICATORS

OUTPUT STATEMENT OR UNIT MEASURED	ACTUAL 1979	FIRST 5 MONTHS 1980	BUDGET ESTIMATE 1980	REVISED ESTIMATE 1980	ESTIMATE 1981

COMMENTS

SERVICE LEVEL CATEGORY

NEW SERVICE . . . . ————	MAINTAIN EXISTING SERVICE . . . . ————
INCREASE SERVICE . . . . ————	DECREASE EXISTING SERVICE . . . . ————

PB-3 (06 80)

Figure 5-3 *(Continued)*

CITY OF TACOMA
PROGRAM SUMMARY

FUNCTIONAL CATEGORY	PROGRAM CATEGORY	PROGRAM NO.	PAGE
PROGRAM TITLE	FUND & DEPARTMENT	BARS NO.	YEAR **1981**

	PERSONAL SERVICES	MAINTENANCE & OPERATION	CAPITAL OUTLAY	OTHER	TOTAL	PERSON-NEL
ACTUAL - 1979						
INITIAL APPROPRIATION - 1980						
REAPPROPRIATION FROM - 1979						
ADDITIONAL APPROPRIATION - 1980						
TOTAL APPROPRIATION - 1980						
ESTIMATED EXPENDITURES - 1981						

PROGRAM DESCRIPTION AND OBJECTIVES

PB-2 (5/79)

Figure 5-3 *(Continued)*

CITY OF TACOMA
REQUEST FOR CAPITAL OUTLAY

PAGE _____ OF _____

DEPARTMENT:	REQUEST NO.
BUDGET LEVEL	ACCOUNT NO.

1. QUANTITY | **2. DETAILED DESCRIPTION OF EQUIPMENT REQUESTED.**

3. EXPLAIN THE NECESSITY FOR OR BENEFITS EXPECTED FROM THE ACQUISITION OF THIS EQUIPMENT.

4. CHECK THE APPROPRIATE SQUARE.
  ☐ REPLACEMENT EQUIPMENT   ☐ ADDITIONAL EQUIPMENT

5. IF REPLACEMENT EQUIPMENT WHAT IS THE ESTIMATED TRADE-IN OR SALVAGE VALUE OF THE PRESENT EQUIPMENT, OR WHAT DISPOSITION CAN BE MADE OF THE PRESENT?

6. ESTIMATED COSTS

IN (B) AND/OR (C) INDICATE THE ADDITIONAL COSTS TO THE PURCHASE PRICE THAT WILL BE REQUIRED TO PLACE ITEM INTO SERVICE.

	UNIT COST	TOTAL COST
A. PURCHASE PRICE		
B. LABOR AND MATERIAL		
C. OTHER		
D. LESS TRADE - IN		
TOTAL COST		

7. SUBMITTED BY:	DATE	**8. PRIORITY NO.**

9. STAFF COMMENTS (SUBMITTING DEPARTMENTS LEAVE BLANK)	**10. APPROVAL:**

B-6 (5/79)

Figure 5-3 Presentation forms for a zero-base budget. In addition to the summary, separate budgets must be prepared for each program at each of two or more possible levels of expenditure. (Courtesy Tacoma, Washington Police Department.)

Level II. Provide crime-prevention patrols and routine law-enforcement services on 10 patrol beats for 24 hours a day; 30 officers plus 6 relief officers, total 36. No patrol officers assigned to Traffic Section. $432,000

Level III. Provide crime-prevention and law-enforcement services on 12 patrol beats, 24 hours a day; 36 officers plus 8 relief officers, total 44; plus 2 patrol officers assigned to Traffic Section, total 46 (current level of service). $552,000

Level IV. 12 patrol beats (36 officers) plus 8 relief officers; plus 6 patrol officers assigned to Traffic Section for increased coverage during rush hours and high-accident-rate periods; total 50. $600,000

In a similar manner, proposed expenditures for personnel benefits, vehicles, and all other types of equipment and supplies would be shown at each of several possible levels of activity. In the example above, two levels have been shown below the current level of activity. Level I represents the administrator's concept of the absolute minimal level of operation that could be tolerated. Level II represents a reduction from the current level, but not so drastic as level I. Level III is the current level, and Level IV represents an increase in activity. Additional levels could be proposed as well, up to the point at which further expenditures would be wasteful. In preparing a zero base budget, most administrators show the current level as level II, with one lower level and one higher level.

The brief example above, showing four possible levels of activity, indicates the considerable complexity that a zero-base budget involves. Often no real purpose is served by treating all of an agency's activities as if they did not exist. In theory, the parent government might decide not to fund any patrol officers at all (level zero), but in fact that is quite unlikely. Furthermore, presenting this information in a performance budget format can lead to great confusion. For example, the parent government might decide to fund the patrol officers at level III but the vehicles at level II—which would mean that some of the patrol officers would have no vehicles in which to patrol! This difficulty is reduced by using a program format budget, but even so, the presentation of several levels of activity can cause confusion.

Another problem in the zero-base method is that inappropriate measures of performance often appear. In the examples we have been using, there are currently eight civilians employed as radio dispatchers and they provide 24-hour-a-day service. Presumably, then, there are three 8-hour shifts with two people on duty on each shift and two who serve as a relief shift for people on their day off. In our example of an incremental budget, the agency is requesting two more dispatchers for the night shift. Since it is unlikely that the night shift is getting twice as many calls as the other shifts, the likely explanation for this request is that the new employees will be assigned to the night shift and the present night-shift dispatchers will be reassigned to one of the day shifts. If we were to present the budget for the Communications Section in a zero-base format, it might look like this:

Level I. 2 dispatchers, providing telephone response and radio operation services for 43,800 calls a year. $16,500

Level II. 8 dispatchers, providing telephone response and radio operation services for 175,200 calls a year. $66,000

Level III. 10 dispatchers, providing telephone response and radio operation services for 219,000 calls a year. $82,500

Here, the level of activity has been shown for each proposed level of expenditure, and the administrator could reasonably explain that in past years the agency has handled an average of about 10 calls per hour; thus, the number of dispatchers, multiplied by the number of hours they are on duty, multiplied by 10 calls an hour, gives a projected number of calls handled. However, the dispatchers are going to be paid the same no matter how many calls they handle. Furthermore, the police department has no control over how many calls it receives; reducing the dispatching staff to two persons will not cause the number of calls for police service to be reduced from 175,200 to 43,800, nor will adding two dispatchers cause the number of calls to increase. What the police agency is buying is a certain number of hours of the dispatchers' services, and that is the appropriate measure of benefit.

The zero-base budget method has been popular in recent years among many state governments and federal agencies. However, it is one of the most difficult of all types of budgets to prepare well. If it is not done well, the results can be confusing and misleading. The various levels of activity can be manipulated by administrators to show whatever they want to show; the current level can be shown as "level I" (the minimum reasonable level), with all other levels showing a higher expenditure. Or the lower levels can be portrayed as so unappealing that the parent government would not dare reduce the current level of expenditures. Or an arbitrary decision may be made by the parent government that level I must represent at least a 10 percent reduction from the current level, and Level II may not show more than a 5 percent increase from current expenses. These restrictions may discourage administrators from trying to manipulate the levels, but they also may prevent reasonable proposals from being presented.[3]

A third alternative method of preparing a budget is the **planning-programming-budgeting system**, or PPBS.

The original PPB system was developed by the Rand Corporation and first used by the U.S. Department of Defense in the mid-1960s. Later, other federal agencies adopted variations of the PPB system, which President Johnson especially favored, and it has been adopted by some state and local governments.

As the name suggests, a PPB system is particularly appropriate for a program budget format. In essence, a PPB system simply carries the planning process, much as we described it in Chapter 4, a step further to include the budget preparation process. Once a program has been planned, the analysis of the program's cost forms the basis for the program's budget. The budget for an entire agency consists of the separate budgets for all of its programs. The justification or explanation of each program also serves as the justification for the expenditure.

Ideally, every cost should be assigned to one program or another. However, this leads to a difficulty, since some costs are shared among several programs. There are three common solutions to this problem:

1. Every cost can be allocated to one or more programs; shared costs are allocated according to the proportion that each program is responsible

for the cost. For example, if the chief of the Technical Services Division manages five separate bureaus, his or her salary can be divided evenly and each bureau's program budget can include one-fifth of the chief's salary; or the salary might be divided according to the amount of time the chief devotes to each bureau. The same principle can be applied to the cost of utilities, office supplies, and anything else that is shared among several programs.

2. Costs can be divided into two types: direct costs, which are attributable to one program, and indirect costs, which are shared among several programs. Each program's budget includes all of its own direct costs plus a portion of the total indirect costs. The proportion may be based on the number of personnel in each program, the proportion of each program's direct costs to the agency's total budget, or any other reasonable formula. In this case, the administrators' salaries, utilities, office supplies, and all other shared costs would be lumped together as indirect costs.

3. Instead of charging each program for its share of the agency's indirect costs, these costs can be presented separately as the agency's administrative program. This is the simplest solution; the only danger is that program managers may try to reduce their own budgets by shifting more and more items to the administrative program, until eventually the administrative program contains most of the agency's expenditures.

The PPB system almost requires every manager and supervisor in the agency to contribute to the budget preparation process. Each supervisor can be asked to prepare a proposed budget for his or her program. These program budgets are then reviewed by section or bureau managers, who make adjustments or corrections. Each section's or bureau's program budgets are then submitted to divisional administrators, who review them for accuracy and, if necessary, make further adjustments or corrections. The divisional budgets are then consolidated into the agency budget, which is submitted to the parent government.

A program budget, by its very nature, includes the most important feature of a performance budget: the statement of the activity, function, or benefit that is to be obtained for each expenditure. A program budget also should show a comparison of proposed expenditures with current costs, either in an incremental format or in a zero-base format. Thus the program budget incorporates the most useful features of each type of budget while adding an important new feature: the presentation of all costs in relation to the goals that each program is expected to achieve.

Once again, we can see what a small portion of a program budget might look like for our hypothetical agency:

32. TRAFFIC LAW ENFORCEMENT SECTION

Program Purpose.
(1) To reduce traffic deaths and injuries, and property damage from traffic accidents, to the lowest levels attainable.
(2) To promote the safe and rapid flow of vehicular and pedestrian traffic.
(3) To encourage motorists and pedestrians to observe traffic laws.
(4) To identify and cite violators of traffic laws.

Program Objectives

(1) To reduce traffic deaths by 10%, injuries from accidents by 20%, and property damage from accidents by 25%.

(2) To improve traffic flow during rush hours, increasing average vehicle speed through the downtown area from the current 8 to 12 miles per hour.

(3) To conduct a traffic safety campaign in local junior and senior high schools, providing 6 hours of instruction to a total of 200 students.

(4) To reduce the incidence of speeding by 20% through use of radar speed detectors and to reduce the incidence of DWI by 25%.

Program Methods

(1) Staff will consult with City Streets and Bridges Department and with consultants from U.S. Department of Transportation to identify roadway and intersection features that contribute to accidents and to determine other causes of accidents. Staff will implement consultants' recommendations to the extent possible.

(2) Four downtown intersections have been identified as the most congested during the evening rush hour (4:30 to 6:30 PM). Officers will be stationed at these intersections during weekday rush hours to direct traffic, thereby increasing traffic flow. Other officers will be assigned to monitor traffic movement on Central Expressway and major arterials to coordinate traffic flow. The average motorist's time in congested traffic will be reduced by 10 minutes, which corresponds to an increase from an average 8 miles per hour through the downtown area to 12 miles per hour.

(3) Two officers will develop a traffic safety presentation for each ninth grade social science class in City's high schools and each eighth grade civics class in junior high schools. Total enrollment in these 6 classes is 200 students.

(4) Two radar speed detectors will be purchased; Traffic Section officers will be trained in their use and assigned an average of 4 hours per day to locations selected because of a high accident rate, special safety problem (such as school zones), or records showing numerous speeding violations. Afternoon and evening shift patrol officers will concentrate on areas with large numbers of drinking establishments and locations where numerous drunken drivers have been observed. All suspected drunken drivers will be stopped and checked.

Program Budget

Capital Expenditures	Current	Proposed
4 patrol cars at $10,000	-0-	$40,000
2 radar speed detectors	-0-	2,500
4 handheld radios	-0-	3,000
Total capital expenditures	-0-	$45,500

Note. e.g.   No capital expenditures are budgeted for the current year. Four patrol cars are needed for additional officers. Two radar speed detectors are needed for program method No. 4 above. Four handheld radios are needed for use by officers directing traffic at intersections (program method No. 2 above) to enable them to coordinate traffic flow with mobile officers.

Operating Expenses	Current	Proposed
Lieutenant (Chief of Section)	$20,750	$ 21,250
Sergeant	16,875	17,250
2 Patrol officers	24,000	24,750
4 Patrol officers	—	46,000
Subtotal, salaries	$61,625	$109,250
Personnel benefits 11.75%	7,241	—
Personnel benefits 12.0%	—	13,110
Total personnel costs	$68,866	$122,360

Vehicle Operation and Maintenance

3 patrol cars, 18,000 miles at $0.22 per mile	$11,880	—
7 patrol cars, 18,000 miles at $0.24 per mile	—	$ 30,240

Note. Mileage is based on Traffic Section's experience over past 5 years. Cost per mile figure is provided by the Vehicle Maintenance Section and includes $0.18 per mile for fuel and $0.04 per mile for maintenance; fuel for next year is expected to cost $0.20 per mile.

Consumable materials and supplies	$ 5,200	$ 8,500
Literature, printing, etc.	500	2,500

Note. Includes materials for distribution as part of junior/senior high school traffic education program.

Total operating expenses	$86,446	$163,600

In studying this example, notice that the program budget includes capital expenditures for the proposed budget period. These expenditures are not amortized, nor is debt service included in the operating expense budget. The only purpose in showing the capital expenditures is to relate them to the program. Debt service or depreciation might not be considered a direct program cost, but may be included in the agency's total administrative costs, which then might be divided proportionally among all programs and added as an indirect cost to each program's operating budget.

Also, in this example an explanation is given for each significant change from the current budget. Presumably the explanation for current items has been given in previous program budgets, and no real purpose would be served by repeating the explanations here. Anyone who wants to know exactly what functions are performed by the lieutenant, sergeant, and the two patrol officers who are already on the staff should get this information from previous budgets. However, any significant changes in these officers' duties would have to be shown and explained here, just as the duties of the additional four officers have been explained.

The sample may seem excessively detailed, especially when one considers that the Traffic Law Enforcement Program is probably one of 40 or 50 separate programs in a medium-sized agency and a comparable budget presentation would be needed for each and every program. Eventually the mass of detail could reach a point at which the budget is almost incomprehensible, and that certainly is not desired. The program budget statement should be just detailed enough that the administrator and the parent government can understand what the program intends to do, what those activities are expected to cost, and what choices can be made among different activities. In this example, the City Council might decide not to fund the requested four additional patrol officers and thus would not need to buy the extra patrol cars and radios. Or the City Council could decide to fund only two additional officers, cars and radios. Or they could agree to everything proposed here except the educational program, which would eliminate the extra $2000 for literature.

Finally, a program budget should contain a single, summary statement of all of the agency's programs and their current and proposed costs. In the summary statement, capital expenditures can be amortized if that is how the parent government prefers to handle them, or the debt service or depreciation figures can be added to the total budget (if they have not been included in indirect costs). The summary statement should include a listing of all programs, showing their current and proposed capital and operating expenses. It may also be desirable to rearrange the summary figures into an object-of-expenditure listing, to show the total amounts being spent on personnel, equipment, supplies, and so on.

Using the PPB system is no small task. However, it is a task that can be divided among all of the agency's managers and supervisors, which is often hard to do with other budget formats. Once a program budget has been done the first time, it will be easier in succeeding years since each new budget will contain the programs that are being continued (and that require no additional explanation), excluding those that have been discontinued, and adding in detail any new ones that are proposed for the coming year.[4]

Budget Adoption

Once the budget has been approved by the agency's chief executive, the preparation phase of the budget cycle ends and the adoption phase begins.

The details of the adoption process vary enormously from place to place. Usually the budget must be submitted first to the parent government's chief executive (such as the City Manager, the County Commissioner, or the Governor). It is then reviewed in detail by the administrative staff. The chief executive may order changes, such as a reduction in the total amount, or may suggest specific items that are unlikely to be approved and therefore should be omitted. Once these adjustments and corrections are made, the police department's budget is consolidated with all the other city, county, or state agency budgets. In some cases, the capital expenditure budget and operating expense budget will become two completely separate documents, especially if all capital expenditures are financed through the sale of bonds or some other form of debt.

The consolidated budget is then presented to the legislative body (city council, board of commissioners or supervisors, or state legislature). The legislature may have its own separate staff to review the budget. Usually there are public hearings during which the representatives of each agency must appear to defend their proposals.

Many police administrators resent the budget adoption process. Rarely will a budget go through the entire process without changes. Items or whole programs may be sharply reduced or eliminated altogether. The legislature may even insist on increasing an item or program that the police administrator considers unnecessary or undesirable. Even when the administrator is confident that the budget has been prepared with careful attention to detail, and that every item in it is justified, the prospect of having to defend the budget in public hearings or debates is enough to make anyone uncomfortable. Of course, a poorly prepared budget gives the administrator even more reason to dread the adoption process.

Police administrators often dismiss the budget adoption process and the decisions made by city, county, or state officials, as "purely political." Indeed they are! Elected officials generally respond to what they perceive to be the wishes of the public. If their perceptions of the public's wishes are correct, and if they are honest in attempting to represent the wishes of the

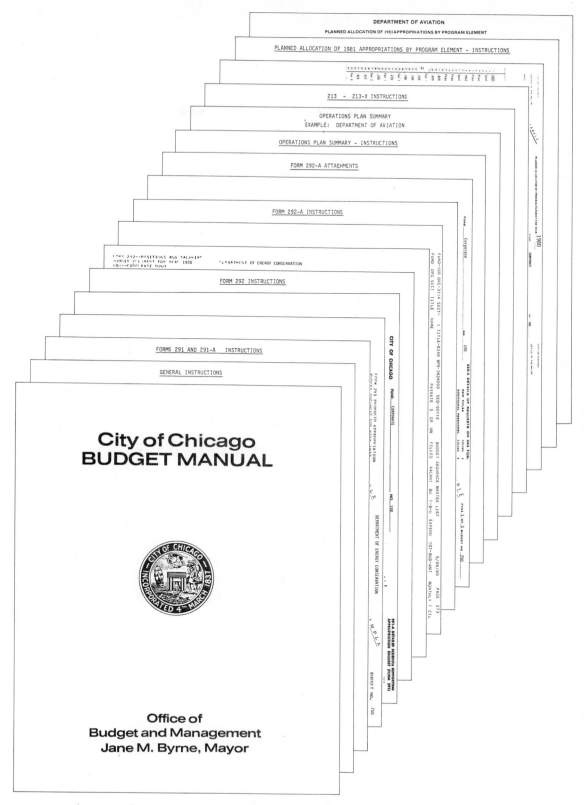

Figure 5-4 Budget preparation manual. (Courtesy Chicago Police Department.)

majority (not just the interests of some special interest group), then they are fulfilling their proper duty in a democratic government.

Nothing is accomplished by the administrator who ignores the budget adoption process, who merely submits the budget and hopes for the best. An intelligent, reasonable presentation of a well-prepared budget may or may not succeed, but at the least it will help to inform the public about the police department's needs and intentions. A careless presentation will merely persuade the public that the department is ineffective and poorly managed.

Some administrators routinely "pad" their budgets by 10 or 20 percent, on the theory that the legislature can then cut the excess without damaging the essential items in the budget. Unfortunately, legislators often detect this sort of trickery and lose respect for administrators who use it.

Eventually, a budget will be approved and adopted; otherwise the police department would cease to exist. The adoption of the budget completes the second phase of the budget cycle, often just a few weeks—and sometimes only a day or two—before the new budget period begins.

Budget Execution

The implementation, or execution, of the budget is one of the executive's most important responsibilities. The chief administrator of a governmental agency can be held personally accountable for every penny of public money that the agency spends. In most relatively small police agencies, the chief executive usually acts as the primary budget administrator; in larger agencies, the day-to-day work is delegated to a budget officer or finance office, but the ultimate responsibility is still the chief's.

The budget, as adopted by the parent governing body, determines exactly how much money can be spent and for what purposes. The items listed in the budget become budget **accounts**, and the money credited to an account can be spent only for the purposes stated in the budget. Once all the money has been spent, nothing more can be spent on that item unless funds are transferred to the account from some other account.

There are three basic ways that money can be paid out of a budget account, or **disbursed**.

Payroll Payments. In most governmental agencies, the largest account and the largest part of the budget is the payroll, or payments to employees. Payroll payments are made on a regular, scheduled basis; the budget or accounting office is informed by the agency's supervisors of the people who are to be paid, the personnel office (in most cases) confirms the amount to be paid, and the accounting office prepares and distributes the payroll checks. The accounting office also makes various deductions from each employee's pay check, to pay federal (and sometimes state) income taxes, the employee's share of Social Security and, depending on what benefits the agency offers its employees, things such as pension contributions, group insurance premiums, and union dues. These deductions are held in the payroll account, or transferred to their own separate accounts, until they are paid out.

Transfer Payments. Funds can be transferred from one account to another. For example, as we just said, payroll deductions are transferred from the payroll account to any of several other accounts. This may be merely a bookkeeping action: The funds are subtracted from one account (a page in a ledger) and added to another. However, federal income taxes and Social Security payments, and some other deductions, must be transferred periodically to federally approved banks. Technically, this is still only a transfer, since the bank accounts that hold these deposits are legally under the control of the employer.

Purchases. Any object or service can be purchased if funds for that purpose are available in the budget. Some accounts are restricted to specific purchases; for example, a capital account may be used only to buy the items whose purchase has been approved. Most accounts are established for general categories of things to be purchased such as office supplies, communications equipment, postage and shipping services, and utilities. We will discuss in Chapter 10 the procedures that are commonly used to make purchases. Briefly, the guiding principle is that no purchase may be made until it has been approved in advance by the administrator who has the authority to give this approval, and the accounting or budget office has confirmed that there are funds in the appropriate account to pay for the purchase.

For every purchase, there should be a permanent record showing who requested the item, who approved it, who confirmed that budgeted funds were available, who determined that the item should be bought from a certain vendor, when the purchase was made, when the vendor demanded payment, and when payment was made. The records also should show, of course, what was bought and how much was paid. These records not only ensure that purchases are made properly but also that administrators have the information they need to make purchases wisely and efficiently.

Budget Review

At the end of the budget period, ideally every account should be empty, except depository accounts such as those that hold federal income taxes and Social Security contributions which may not be due until two or three months later. In practice, not all of the budgeted funds will be spent in some accounts. Usually these unexpended funds are simply "given back" to the parent government. However, some cities and a few states allow their agencies to "carry over" unexpended funds into the next budget period or permit the money to be spent on capital items that were not previously budgeted.

Many administrators routinely check all their budget accounts about three months before the end of the budget period. If there appear to be any funds that are not going to be expended, the administrator transfers the money to some other account where it can be spent before the budget period ends. This practice may be limited, since some governments prohibit any budget transfers of more than, say, 10 percent of the original budgeted amount, and some prohibit any transfers at all during the last three months of the budget year. Furthermore, spending a lot of money near the end of the year may attract unfavorable attention from the parent government, since it is usually regarded as a sign of sloppy budget management.

Once the budget period is over, a new budget period begins. The previous period is then subject to review and evaluation.

Internally, the agency's own accounting staff, or better yet a separate auditing staff (if the agency is large enough to have a separate staff for this function), conducts a **sample audit**, a check of a random sample of purchase vouchers, payroll records, and other records of disbursements, to make sure that all disbursements were made and recorded properly. If any serious discrepancies are found, a complete audit of the entire year's records may be necessary. A complete audit ought to be performed not less than once every five years in any case. Most agencies also should have an external audit, performed by accountants who are not employees of the agency, not less than once every two years; some governments are required by law to have an external audit conducted every year.

The purpose of the audit is not so much to detect cheating or stealing (although a properly conducted audit will do so), but, more important, to test the agency's disbursement and record-keeping procedures for any weaknesses or errors. A small error, if it is repeated frequently over a long period of time, could cause an agency to lose a great deal of money. Too often small errors go undetected, even when purchases must be reviewed and approved several times before a disbursement is made, simply because everyone assumes that the erroneous information must be correct—or someone else would have caught it!

FUNDING

Throughout most of this chapter, we have discussed mainly the procedures for spending money: developing the capital and operating expense budgets, handling disbursements, and so on. We have paid little attention to the question of where the money will come from. The reason is that virtually all police agencies are funded out of the general tax revenue of their parent governments and no other source. City police departments obtain their funds from the city's local taxes, county governments fund the sheriff's office out of county taxes, and state police agencies are funded out of statewide general taxes. Usually all of these taxes are in the form of property and sales taxes. Some states and a few cities also use local income taxes to support law enforcement.

However, there are other sources of funds that could be used by police agencies. For example, federal community development funds, allocated to the states and cities, can be used for certain capital expenditures such as the construction of police buildings. Obtaining funds from these sources is not easy; the funding agencies have strict rules and guidelines concerning what kinds of things can be funded and how application must be made. The police administrator should consult with the parent government's budget officer about these funds and how to apply for them.

Most states have established a separate fund, often under the administration of a separate agency, to promote the development of law enforcement and other public safety agencies. At one time, these funds were derived mainly from the federal government, through the Law Enforcement Assistance Administration (LEAA) (which was set up under the Omnibus Crime Control and Safe Streets Act of 1968). However, the LEAA was severely cut back by President Jimmy Carter in 1979, and very little federal money has been available to the states for law enforcement purposes since then. Nevertheless, many states continued the planning and funding agencies that had been established to handle LEAA grants, using state funds instead of federal funds.

Typically, a state law enforcement or criminal justice planning agency has a limited amount of money that it can disburse to local law enforcement agencies (and other public safety or criminal justice agencies). The state agency develops a plan to improve the entire state's criminal justice system; the specific activities within the state plan are assigned priorities according to their relative importance. Grants can be awarded to local police agencies if their proposed programs or projects meet the criteria given in the state plan.

Applying for one of these grants is not as difficult as many police administrators expect it to be. The first step is to obtain a copy of the state plan. The administrator then compares the local agency's own programs with the state plan, to see whether any local programs meet the state criteria. If so, and if the kind of activity planned locally has been given a reasonably high priority, there is a good chance that a grant can be obtained. A formal application must be submitted to the state planning agency, whose staff usually will assist the administrator in filling out the forms and gathering supporting documents. The application is then reviewed by the planning agency's staff to make sure it meets the technical requirements and that the proposed activity is eligible for funding. After this review, the application is forwarded to an advisory board, which makes the final decision on whether a grant should be awarded. In some states, other agencies such as regional planning councils also must review and approve criminal justice grant applications; again, the state planning agency's staff will assist the police administrator in getting the application through this procedure.

Most administrators who apply for funding from a state planning agency or other source do so only for programs or projects that cannot be funded locally, either because they are just too expensive for the local government to undertake or because there is not enough public support for the proposed activity. Ordinarily it is not a good idea to seek these external funds for activities of an ongoing nature or for anything that could be funded locally. There is never any guarantee that the external source will continue to provide funds from year to year. However, external funding is an excellent way to start new or experimental projects; if they are successful and attract public support, it will be that much easier to include them in the local budget after a year or two.

In addition to funds from state criminal justice planning agencies, external funds are sometimes available from various federal agencies. Earlier we mentioned federal community development funds, which generally are limited to capital improvements such as new buildings. However, there may be funds available from other federal sources for specific projects. Also, some philanthropic foundations have funds that are available to police agencies. There are catalogs and guides, usually available at a public library, that describe the various kinds of federal grants and private charitable organizations, what kinds of activities they are interested in funding, and how application should be made. Generally, federal and foundation grants are more difficult to get than state grants, but if a worthwhile program cannot be funded in any other way, the administrator should explore this possibility.

LIEUTENANT ULLRICH'S IN BASKET

Instructions

In this exercise, you are to assume the role of Lieutenant Roland Ullrich, chief of the City Police Department Budget and Accounting Office. The documents below have been selected from Lieutenant Ullrich's in basket. Read them with care. If you need more information about City or its police department, refer to the data bank in the front of the book. After you have studied these documents, complete these steps:

1. List any additional information you would need to complete the tasks assigned to Lieutenant Ullrich, and where that information might be obtained.
2. Using only the information given here, complete the assignment given by Chief Abel as best you can.

CITY POLICE DEPARTMENT		
Interoffice Memorandum		
FROM: Chief Abel		
TO: Lt. Ullrich, Budget & Accounting		
SUBJECT: Budget Preparation for Next Year	DATE:	3 Feb 19--

The City Manager has informed me that we are supposed to have our proposed budget in his office no later than May 15. I have looked over our budget for last year and consider it completely inadequate in form. I think it is time for our department to adopt more modern, sophisticated management practices in this important area.

Please prepare a proposed Budget Preparation Procedure, including a set of instructions and any standardized forms that may be necessary, for use by the Department's administrators and managers. Your proposal will be reviewed by the Bureau Chiefs and myself, and if approved will be used to prepare this year's budget. To give us time to review your ideas and complete the budgeting process within the deadline, I need your proposal within 10 days.

E. Z. Abel,
Chief

BUDGET PREPARATION INSTRUCTIONS

From: CITY DEPT. OF FINANCE

To: ALL DEPARTMENT HEADS & BUDGET OFFICERS

There will be NO major changes in the budget preparation process this year. A summary of your budget must be submitted on FORM BgSm-4/73, a copy of which is attached. Proposed CAPITAL EXPENDITURES must be submitted on FORM BgCP-3/78.

DO NOT include Building rent, utilities, equipment depreciation, or charges for the use of the Central Data Processing System. These expenses will be added to your budget by my staff.

The Personnel Benefit Rates are AS FOLLOWS:

ALL Employees EXCEPT Fire & P.D.:
Social Security (FICA)	6.5%
Municipal Employees' Pension	5.25%
TOTAL:	11.75%

P.D. & F.D. ONLY:
Social Security (FICA)	6.5%
Public Safety Employees' Pension Fund	5.0%
Public Safety Employees' Assoc., employer contr'b'n	1.0%
TOTAL:	12.5%

You may use last year's salary schedules as the basis for calculation. We will propose a 3.2% across-the-board wage raise for all employees, including public safety. This amount should be ADDED TO the automatic year-of-service raises in the schedule. The City Manager has decided NOT to request ANY MERIT INCREASES this year, so DO NOT include them in your budget!!

As always, call my office if you need assistance.

Oliver Bucksman, Director
Dept. of Finance

CITY BUDGET PROPOSAL   BUDGET SUMMARY   FORM BgSm-4/73

CATEGORY OF EXPENDITURE	CURRENT YEAR BUDGETED		ACTUAL		PROPOSED NEXT YEAR REQUESTED		
100. PERSONNEL:	NUMBER		NUMBER		NUMBER		
101. Full-time Salaries							
102. Part-time Salaries							
103. Overtime							
105. Other							
108. Benefits at 11.75%							
109. Benefits at 12.5%							
110. SUBTOTAL:							
200. MAINTENANCE & EQPT. OPERATION:							
300. TELEPHONE, TELEGRAPH:							
400. POSTAGE & SHIPPING:							
500. TRAVEL:							
501. Local mileage reimbursement							
502. Out-of-town travel, mileage							
503. Out-of-town, lodging & food							
505. SUBTOTAL:							
600. NON-CAPITAL EQUIPMENT:							
700. SUPPLIES & MATERIALS:							
800. PRINTING & COPYING:							
900. CONTRACT SERVICES & OTHER:							
TOTAL, CATEGORIES 200-900:							
TOTAL, ALL CATEGORIES:							

Prepared by:_____ Submitted by:_____

AGENCY:_____ REVENUE/FUNDS:_____

CITY BUDGET PROPOSAL   CAPITAL EXPENDITURES   FORM BgCp-3/78

CATEGORY DESCRIPTION OF ITEM	Estimated Cost	Estimated Life	AMORTIZED ANNUAL COST	
C-100. LAND:				
C-200. BUILDINGS:				
C-202. NEW BUILDINGS:				
C-206. IMPROVEMENTS & ADDITIONS:				
C-300. VEHICLES:				
C-400. EQUIPMENT:				
C-402. DATA PROCESSING:				
C-405. OTHER EQPT.:				
C-500. OTHER:				
TOTAL, ALL CATEGORIES:				

Prepared by:_____ Submitted by:_____

AGENCY:_____ REVENUE/FUNDS:_____

CITY POLICE DEPARTMENT
Annual Salary Schedule

Rank/Title	YEARS OF SERVICE					
	0	1	2	3–5	6–9	10+
Chief	33,975	35,675	37,460	39,334	43,267	47,594
Assistant Chief	29,415	32,357	33,975	35,675	39,243	43,167
Captain	23,100	24,255	25,468	26,741	29,415	32,357
Lieutenant	20,953	22,000	23,100	24,255	26,680	29,348
Senior Sergeant	19,005	19,955	20,953	22,000	24,200	26,620
Sergeant	16,417	17,238	18,100	19,005	21,856	25,134
Senior Patrol	14,181	14,890	15,635	16,417	18,880	21,712
Patrol Officer	12,250	12,863	13,506	14,181	16,308	18,754
Civilian Employees						
Lab Technician	11,951	12,549	13,176	14,164	16,289	18,732
Dispatcher, Administrative Assistant	8,769	9,207	9,667	10,392	11,951	13,744
Secretary	6,433	6,755	7,093	7,625	8,769	10,084
Clerk	5,835	6,127	6,433	6,915	7,952	9,154
Jailer	5,292	5,557	5,835	6,273	7,214	8,296
Jail Matron, Meter Maid	4,800	5,040	5,292	5,689	6,542	7,523

IN REVIEW

1. True or False: If it were not necessary to submit a budget in order to obtain funds from the parent government, police administrators would have no reason to prepare one.

2. A budget serves as a standard for:
   (a) Evaluating the efficiency of different kinds of activities.
   (b) Comparing conflicting claims on scarce resources.
   (c) The control of expenditures.
   (d) All of the above.
   (e) None of the above.

3. Debt service, the expense of repaying borrowed money with interest, usually is an item in:
   (a) The capital budget.
   (b) The operating budget.
   (c) The special funds budget.
   (d) The transfer accounts.
   (e) The revenue budget.

4. Depreciation is:
   (a) The reduced value of revenues caused by inflation.
   (b) A capital expense.
   (c) The transfer of funds from the capital budget to the operating budget.
   (d) An annual charge for the replacement cost of capital items.
   (e) The interest paid on borrowed funds.

5. An operating budget that shows only the items to be purchased and their cost is:
   (a) An object-of-expenditure budget.
   (b) A capital budget.
   (c) An incremental budget.
   (d) A program budget.
   (e) A zero-base budget.

6. List the four stages of the budget cycle in proper order.

7. The principal advantage of the incremental method of preparing a budget is that:
   (a) It shows how each item contributes to the agency's activities and programs.
   (b) It is very simple to prepare.
   (c) It allows previous activities to be continued without requiring further explanation.
   (d) It focuses attention on the changes from previous budgets.
   (e) It provides more detailed information than any other budgeting method.

8. An indirect cost is:
   (a) An expense that is shared among all of an agency's programs.
   (b) An expense that has been assigned to a particular program.
   (c) An expense that is not included in the current year's budget.
   (d) The current portion of a capital expense.
   (e) An operating expense that is transferred to a federally approved depository bank.

9. True or False: Police administrators are correct in their belief that the budget adoption process is "purely political."

10. The three types of disbursements are:
    (a) Accounts   (e) Payroll payments
    (b) Transfers   (f) Purchases
    (c) Depreciation   (g) Deposits
    (d) Amortization   (h) Audits

REFERENCES

1. William H. Newman and E. Kirby Warren, *The Process of Management*, 4th ed., Englewood Cliffs, N.J.: Prentice-Hall, 1977, page 484.

2. Robert D. Lee, Jr., and Ronald W. Johnson, *Public Budgeting Systems*, Baltimore: University Park Press, 1973, pages 228–254.

3. Lee and Johnson, pages 108–109.

4. Lee and Johnson, pages 144–147.

PART TWO
THE MANAGEMENT OF MATERIAL RESOURCES

6 POLICE BUILDINGS

MANAGING A POLICE DEPARTMENT EFFICIENTLY, OR ANY other enterprise for that matter, means making the best use of the available resources. Those resources include time, things, and people. This section of the text concerns the management of things.

The largest and often most visible thing a police agency uses is the building or buildings it occupies. Buildings serve a great many different purposes: They are places to store and protect equipment, supplies, records, and even people (such as prisoners); they are places where people meet to interact with one another and transact business.

Police administrators do not often have an opportunity to design and build a new police building. Most police buildings, like other publicly owned structures, are designed to last as long as possible, since this reduces the effective cost of the building. Unfortunately, this also means that the building often outlasts its usefulness. A police building that was designed and built 30 or 40 years ago may not meet today's needs; it may be too small for the number of people who must use it, or it may be in the wrong location, or it may be arranged inconveniently. But public officials are extremely reluctant to abandon and replace a building for any of those reasons if the structure is still sound. Instead, the building may be enlarged somewhat to make room for a larger staff, without resolving the other problems of an obsolete building. Or, more often, the replacement is postponed until the obsolete building is no longer serviceable at all.

There are ways that an obsolete building can be managed to make it more efficient in serving today's needs, and we will discuss some of those methods later. Furthermore, occasionally an entirely new building will be built, either to replace an existing one or to meet the needs of a new agency. In either case, the administrator should take full advantage of the opportunity to make a new building as functional and useful as possible, since the opportunity may not come again for several decades.

The worst course for any police administrator to take is to abandon the planning and design of a new building to outside experts, including architects. The police administrator does not need to know much about architecture or structural engineering; those matters can be left to the hired experts. On the other hand, it is unwise to assume that the architects and engineers will know anything about police operations and the physical facilities needed by an efficient police force. Those matters require the police administrator's knowledge, experience, and attention. Together, the administrator and the architectural experts can design a building that is both architecturally sound and operationally satisfactory.

The first step in achieving this ideal is, of course, planning. In fact, a great deal of planning must go on before any thought is given to the shape, arrangement, or size of the building itself. If the planning procedures described in Chapters 4 and 5 have been followed, the administrator is already well-prepared to begin the specific planning for a new building.

BUILDING DESIGN: THE PLANNING PROCESS

Planning anything is largely a matter of making choices: what you want to have happen, when it should happen, what it should look like, and so forth. In the case of planning a building, there are a vast number of choices to be made, and some of the choices necessarily affect other choices (even if the relationship is not apparent at first). For example, one of the first choices to be made for a new building is the site where it is to be built. If the site is not large enough to allow a building of the necessary size on one floor, then a multistory building will be required. This means that extra space must be set aside for stairways and, if the building will be more than two or three stories high, elevator shafts. Similarly, the foundation and supporting structure must be sturdier.

Because choices are so interrelated, it is a good idea to postpone making any hard and fast decisions until fairly late in the planning process. First, information must be gathered, analyzed, and compared. For each choice to be made, as many alternatives as possible should be considered, and the influence of one choice on all the others should be examined. Choices also should be examined according to a set of **planning criteria** that have been established in advance and that define an ideal police building.

Clearly, the planning process is time-consuming. Six months is not long enough to properly plan a new building. Furthermore, everyone who will occupy and use the building should have some role in the planning process. The choices made in the design of the building will affect the way the building is used—and thus how the police department functions—for years to come.

Nearly every member of the department should help to gather and provide the information on which important decisions will be based. Field and operational personnel—patrol officers, technicians, and clerks—should be given an opportunity to contribute their own suggestions and ideas. First-line supervisors should provide the basic information about personnel patterns and physical requirements for each unit in the agency. Higher-level managers such as division and bureau chiefs should correlate the information from lower levels and add their own perceptions of what is needed for each unit to function most effectively. Finally, all of the agency's upper-level administrators should participate in making choices and design decisions; these decisions then should be reviewed by the chief executive, who may add his or her own suggestions and ideas.

Of course, all these choices and decisions are not made in a void, and we do not mean to suggest that the planners are free to make whatever choices they like. Almost always, the design of a new building is subject to various factors imposed on the project from outside. For example, sometimes a city council will inform the police department, "We will set aside a certain amount of money for your new building, and not a penny more." In this case, the budget for the building will have to be considered as a constraint on the design.

Local government is not the only source of design constraints, nor is the budget the only sort of limitation. In one case that has come to our attention, a metropolitan police department was considering a new building to replace its existing, obsolete headquarters. Before specific plans could be made, however, a bond issue would have to be approved by the voters. In recent years, bond issues have been difficult to pass under any circumstances, so the police administrators were concerned about whether the voters would approve their new building. One of the influential political organizations in the city told the chief of police, "We will support your building only if it does not contain a new jail. We do not want money to be spent on jails, so you will have to make do with the old one." This meant that the new building would have to be built on the same site as the old one, so that the existing jail could be left intact. Ideally, the police building might have been built in another part of town or on a site with more room available. In this case, the police administrators decided to accept the constraint. As matters turned out, the bond issue passed by a narrow margin and probably would not have passed without the support of that political organization. So, by accepting a design constraint imposed by a group that had no official role in the planning process, the police administrators were able to save the entire project.

Basic Planning Criteria

Planning criteria are the standards against which all decisions and design choices will be evaluated. Thus, the criteria serve to define what the agency regards as desirable in a building. Each planning criterion is important in itself; in addition, the criteria should be ranked according to their priority, so that conflicting design choices can be resolved on the basis of which criterion has the greater priority.

The planning criteria for a police building reflect the philosophy of the police agency. According to the National Clearinghouse for Criminal Justice Planning and Architecture:

> . . . a police station is one of the most important public buildings in a community. In its design and architectural character a police facility often has a significant impact on the image of law enforcement in the community. It can also have a direct influence on the morale and operational efficiency of police department employees . . . . Those who pass by or enter the building should be reminded of the community's commitment to modern law enforcement standards.[1]

Some of the criteria that should influence the choice of police building designs are examined.

Flexibility. Every police agency experiences changes over a period of time. When the period of time is the typical life span of a building—30 or 40 years or more—the extent of change can be substantial. Consequently, a building should be designed to adapt to those changes. It should be relatively easy to rearrange spaces in the building for new uses that were not foreseeable when the building was first designed. For example, 50 years ago few police agencies had or needed well-equipped photographic laboratories. Today, this facility is necessary for many kinds of criminalistics investigations, and photography is used routinely in all sorts of police operations. Fifty years from now, some other technology, perhaps based on video recording, may replace photography. Although a modern police building might need a photo lab with its stainless steel sinks, floor drain, light-proof doors, and other specialized fittings, the designers should realize that all of these features might be obsolete and unnecessary at some future time.

The number of people who must be served by a building changes constantly. If the community is growing, it is virtually certain that the police agency will expand, and allowance must be made for future expansion. If the community is declining, the building might contain more space than will be needed in the future, in which case it should be possible to adapt the space for some other use.

Flexibility, then, means that the building as a whole and all of its component parts should be adaptable to different uses, and consideration must be given to the building's future expansion if that is likely.

Public Accessibility.   A police building is a public facility, owned by the public through its government. It exists only to serve the public. Citizens may need to come into the police building for any number of reasons: They may wish to report a crime, give information as witnesses, inquire about a friend or relative who is a suspect in a crime, or obtain records of a traffic accident or other police matter. Juveniles and their parents may need to meet with juvenile officers. Journalists may need to interview officers and administrators. Volunteers may need to meet at the police building in order to carry out their programs in support of law enforcement. Neighborhood groups may need to gather for a crime prevention lecture by a police officer.

In short, the building should be designed so that members of the public have convenient access to police personnel and to those areas where public services are delivered. Nothing about the building should discourage public access. It should not be intimidating, remote, uncomfortable, impersonal, or frightening. Convenient access must be provided for citizens who are physically handicapped, too. The citizens coming into a police building may be emotionally upset, embarrassed, or reluctant; the building's design should contribute to a comforting, civil, and respectful atmosphere.

Serviceability.   A police building is one of very few public buildings that is typically in use 24 hours a day, throughout the year, with heavy traffic loads at almost all hours of the day. Some of the people using the building may be violent, emotionally agitated, or physically ill. A few people may express hostility by attacking the building and its fixtures. Consequently, police buildings must be designed to withstand heavy use and abuse, while still retaining the attractiveness and comfort that provide an inviting atmosphere to the public. Building surface materials (walls and floor coverings), fixtures (lighting, water fountains and other plumbing, handrails, and so on), and equipment (including furniture) should be selected for durability under hard use. The building itself should be designed to minimize maintenance requirements by reducing, or even eliminating, hard-to-clean devices and surfaces.

Serviceability also means that the building should be economical to operate. The energy needed for lighting, electrical equipment, heating, air conditioning, and hot water should be conserved as much as possible.

All of the building's working areas should be designed to promote efficient operations. Each working area should be planned for maximum efficiency and convenience in itself. In addition, the relationships among the working areas should allow the department's employees to interact with one another as conveniently and efficiently as possible.

Aesthetic Qualities.   In the past, police officials have not always paid attention to the attractiveness of their physical surroundings. This may be a serious mistake. Many psychological studies have demonstrated that human behavior reflects the environment in which people find themselves. Attractive surroundings encourage people to act toward one another in a pleasant, harmonious way. Both public and working areas of a police building should be designed with bright, eye-appealing colors and textures.

Areas where more serious, emotionally upsetting interactions are likely to occur should be designed with more subdued, relaxing, and inviting qualities. Even in areas where high security is required, an effort should be made to preserve an atmosphere of dignity and respect for the individual. Police administrators should study contemporary designs for office buildings, schools, hospitals, banks, and other facilities whose operational needs are similar to theirs. This is also one area in which the advice of architectural experts should be sought early in the planning process.

Security.   There are so many misconceptions about the security needs of police buildings that we discuss the subject in some detail.

In the past, security has often been given the highest priority as a design criterion. Too often, the result has been a monumental structure resembling a medieval fortress. Such a building often is inflexible, uninviting to the public, difficult to clean, expensive to operate, inefficient in its working areas, and ugly.

We do not mean to suggest that security needs should be ignored or overlooked. However, they should be assessed realistically. The first question to be asked is, "Security from what?" What are the dangers to be avoided? What kinds of events might occur in a police building that would not occur anywhere else? How likely are these events? Who might cause them to occur?

In the most general terms, the dangers are three: attacks against people, attacks against property, and attacks against the operations of the agency. There is also one danger that is peculiar to police buildings: the escape of persons who are being detained (that is, prisoners).

Attacks against people might mean either personal attack or the use of weapons against police officers, civilian employees, or innocent bystanders. The most likely source of these attacks would be a violent prisoner. Another possible source would be hostile or mentally deranged citizens who are not known to be criminal. The use of weapons by prisoners can be avoided simply by maintaining a firm policy of searching every prisoner when he or she is brought into the building. Personal attacks by prisoners can be controlled by the standard techniques of personal restraint and by detaining prisoners in areas that are separated from other areas by architectural barriers such as locked doors.

Attacks by nonprisoners are harder to control, but they are also considerably less likely to occur. The danger can be controlled by limiting public access to those specific personnel and areas where interaction with the public must take place and by providing the personnel in those areas with protected spaces within easy reach in the event of threat.

Attacks against police property can take a great variety of forms. Buildings and vehicles can be vandalized; working areas can be attacked by fire, bomb, or weapons. Records are especially vulnerable to destruction; both paper records and other forms, such as magnetic recordings of computer data, can be destroyed by fire, water, contamination, or physical attack. Records and other police property also can be stolen or damaged by tampering. Criminal evidence in police custody can be made worthless if there is even the mere suspicion of tampering.

The likelihood of any of these dangers is hard to estimate. In this case, a better measure of the need for security is the intrinsic value of the property that might be attacked. The building itself and its ordinary furniture and equipment can be replaced if damage occurs. There is some expense and inconvenience, of course, but the cost might be considerably less than the expense of taking extreme precautions to avoid every conceivable danger.

Records, weapons, and certain other police equipment, and criminal evidence in police custody, represent a much higher value. These items, if lost or destroyed, often cannot be replaced; in the case of police weapons, any loss into criminal hands could represent a serious danger to the whole community. All such property must be protected by placing it out of the reach of anyone other than employees of the department and by using protective architectural devices (such as fireproof barriers) wherever possible.

A related security need is protection *from* some police property. Chemicals used in the criminalistics and photography labs are often toxic, flammable, or explosive. Ammunition stored for police weapons is, of course, explosive. These items must be protected from attack and at the same time the building and personnel must be protected from them. Limited access and architectural barriers are the most practical measures.

Attacks against police operations might mean efforts to disrupt police communications or data recording systems, physical interference with police activities, and harassment of police and civilian personnel. The people most likely to attack police operations are criminals (whether or not they are prisoners at the time) and hostile or emotionally unstable citizens. Actually, attacks of this kind are not very common, and they are more likely to occur as the result of a spontaneous response to a police activity, such as an arrest, rather than as a conscious plan to disrupt the police agency. The best protective measure is to plan and conduct every police operation in a manner that is least likely to provoke a physical confrontation or to be emotionally upsetting to the individuals involved. Creating a fortress-like atmosphere in a police building and maintaining attitudes of suspicion and hostility toward the public are more likely to provoke than to prevent attacks.

When security hazards are carefully considered in terms of the potential object of attack, source of attack, and likelihood of attack, and these hazards are weighed against competing considerations such as the necessity of public access, a fairly simple pattern emerges. This pattern suggests that the building design should provide for different levels or degrees of security; in physical terms, the building might be divided into security zones that are given different architectural treatment. (See Figure 6.1.)

Zone 1. Maximum public accessibility, minimum protection from attack. This zone includes the public lobby, service counters, meeting rooms, witness interview rooms, juvenile counselling rooms, and any other area in which unrestricted access between agency personnel and the public is necessary. Aside from the selection of materials and equipment that are capable of withstanding heavy use and possible abuse, no obvious security measures are necessary. Police personnel should not be present in the public areas except to give information or directions to citizens, to receive visitors, or to carry out specific activities that involve the public. Personnel at service counters should be protected by bullet-resistant glass and protective barriers, but these devices need not be obvious.

Zone 2. Limited public access. This zone includes all areas to which some

(Drawing not to scale)

Figure 6-1 Security zones. Each unit is placed in a part of the building with appropriate security design. (Note that the drawing is not to any scale.)

members of the public require access on occasion, but the general public is excluded. Most administrative offices, classrooms, interview rooms, prisoners' visiting rooms, and similar areas should be included in this zone. Security is maintained primarily by permitting access only to individuals who are known to the police personnel and who have sufficient reason to enter the restricted zone. Anyone who might pose a threat to police personnel or property should be accompanied by a police officer at all times.

Zone 3. No public access. This zone, often called the *security core* of the building, includes all records facilities, the communications center, evidence storage, and other sensitive facilities. With few exceptions, no citizen should have access to this zone, and any citizen who enters it must be accompanied by a police officer at all times. Architectural devices such as fireproof walls or bullet-resistant glass should be used to protect irreplaceable property and to prevent disruption of vital police operations.

Zone 4. Maximum security area. This zone includes any police facility that is a likely target of attack or that is potentially dangerous in itself. The jail, criminalistics lab, armory or weapons storage area, and any area in which toxic or explosive chemicals are stored should be in this zone. With the exception of the jail, only police personnel should be permitted in this zone under any circumstances. In a large agency, there may be restrictions on which police personnel may enter this zone.

The placement of a particular facility or work area into one zone or another (for example, whether the communications center should be in Zone 3 or Zone 4) is a matter for the building planners to decide. In some cases, there may be a range of architectural treatments that blurs the distinctions between zones; parts of Zone 2 may be essentially as secure as parts of Zone 3, for example.

Once the specific planning criteria have been defined and given appropriate priorities, the planners must consider the basic physical requirements for the new building.

Physical Requirements

There are two ways to approach the design of a new building. The more common way is to begin with the maximum overall building size that the budget and other constraints will allow, then divide the total space among the various components of the agency. All too often, this method results in many mistakes. Some components are assigned to areas that are too small to accommodate their present personnel, much less future expansion; other components are given more space than they really need. Proper physical relationships among the various components are overlooked because of the pressure to squeeze every existing operation into the available space.

A far better method is to determine first the physical needs of each component, then add them together to determine the optimum overall building size. If the total is greater than the maximum space that the budget will allow (which is very likely), adjustments and compromises can be made. Nevertheless, it is much more likely that the building will be efficiently arranged if this method is used.

The first step is to survey the space requirements of each component of the agency. This can be done simply by sending a brief questionnaire to the supervisor or manager of each program and operating unit in the agency, with instructions to consult with their subordinate personnel. The questionnaire should contain questions concerning three things:

1. The number of personnel in the unit at present and the projected number of personnel at specific points in the future (say, in 5 and 10 years).
2. The activities and operations carried out by the unit's personnel, especially the specific activities that are conducted in the police building. The unit's working hours also should be determined; areas that must be accessible at all hours may need to be located in a different part of the building from areas that are in use only during the day, for instance.
3. The furniture and equipment used by the unit, especially if there are any special requirements such as high-voltage electricity, plumbing, and so on.

Once the questionnaires have been completed, they should be reviewed by management and administrative personnel to correct any errors or discrepancies and to ensure that the information is complete.

The questionnaires serve as the basis for two important planning steps: the allocation of space (based on the total number of employees in each unit, with allowance for future planned expansion, plus the amount of working space required by each unit) and the arrangement of the individual spaces to promote efficient interactions. The latter step is accomplished by developing an **interaction matrix**, a chart that shows how the personnel of each unit relate to one another and to the public.

An interaction matrix is not especially complicated or difficult to develop. The personnel in each of the agency's components are listed in one column; next to that column is a grid with a space for each interaction to be indicated. Figure 6.2 illustrates an interaction matrix that might be constructed for the City Police Department. Each space on the grid represents the intersection of two rows; each row ends at the column containing the list of the agency's personnel. For example, the chart shows the types of interactions that most frequently occur between the chief of police and the various members of the public, along the row that extends diagonally upward from the chief's position in the left-hand column; interactions between the chief and other members of the department are shown along the row that extends diagonally downward from the chief's position.

Each type of interaction is represented by a symbol. Empty spaces indicate that little or no interaction takes place between the personnel on those two rows. Interaction does not always mean face-to-face encounters; where some or all of the interaction takes place through telephone calls or correspondence, that information should be presented too.

Carefully analyzed, the interaction matrix tells the planners a great deal about the physical requirements of the building. For example, personnel who have heavy face-to-face interaction should be directly accessible to one another; otherwise, their work will be inconvenient and inefficient. On the other hand, personnel who interact only by telephone, or who do not interact with one another at all, might be located in different parts of the building without this interfering with their work.

BUILDING ALTERNATIVES

Until recently, nearly all police buildings in the United States were surprisingly similar in their concept and design. In large communities and small ones, the central police station contained every kind of program and facility the agency had. In major metropolitan areas, where the agency's jurisdiction was divided into a number of precincts or districts, each precinct or district station was a complete, independent replica of the central downtown headquarters: It contained essentially the same facilities and programs on a smaller scale.

Police facilities do not have to be designed with such "cookie-cutter" duplication, nor do all programs and facilities have to be crammed into one building whether they fit or not. Communities differ in the kinds of police programs they require, and thus police agencies differ in their physical needs. Small agencies (which comprise the majority of police agencies) generally need, and can afford, only one comprehensive police building. However, there are alternatives that should be considered by medium-

CITY POLICE DEPARTMENT INTERACTION MATRIX

Public:				
General				
Witnesses*				
Suspects				
Juveniles				
Press				

Aministrative:				
Chief				
Assistant chief				

Captains:				
Patrol				
Detectives				
Organized crime				
Technical services				
Secretaries				

Patrol Bureau:				
Watch lieutenants				
Sergeants				
Patrol officers				
School guards				

Detective Bureau:				
Lieutenants				
Sergeants				

Crime prevention:				
Lieutenant				
Community relations sergeant				
Juvenile officers				

Organized Crime:				
Lieutenants				
Sergeants				

Technical Services:				
Communications				
Records and identification				
Crime lab technicians:				
Fleet operations				

Traffic law enforcement:				
Lieutenant				
Sergeants				
Patrol officers				

Jail:				
Lieutenant				
Booking sergeants				
Jailers				
Prisoners				

Administrative Services:				
Budget and accounting				
Personnel and training				
Public information				
Parking enforcement				
Property and evidence				

*Witnesses include complainants and informants.

Key to symbols:

▨ Heavy face—to—face interaction

▧ Light face—to—face interaction

⊡ Interaction by telephone computer terminal

⊠ Interaction by correspondence

Figure 6-2 An interaction matrix for the City Police Department.

sized and larger agencies. Even the smallest agencies should seriously consider the possibility of sharing some specialized facilities with neighboring agencies, thereby avoiding wasteful duplication and underutilization.

The Independent Police Station

A conventional police building contains all of the administrative offices and operational facilities that the police agency requires. We use the term **independent police station** for this facility.[2]

An independent police station can be divided into several distinct areas:

Public areas	Space for the general public to enter, to interact with police personnel (obtaining records, being interviewed, etc.), and in some cases to meet (volunteer organizations, community crime prevention meetings).
Administrative	Offices for administrative police officials; supervisors' offices and work spaces; records storage; work space for functions such as accounting and personnel.
Operational	Work spaces for operating personnel including patrol, investigative, and special units (juvenile, organized crime, etc.).
Technical support	Work spaces for functions such as communications, records and identification, criminalistics, photography, fleet maintenance.
Prisoner custody	Jail or detention and related facilities.
Personnel training	Briefing, classroom training, physical training, vehicle training, firearms training, and other special training facilities.

The extent to which each of these areas must be developed depends (1) on the size of the agency and of the community it serves and (2) on the kinds of programs it conducts. Every independent police station, even the very smallest, must devote some space to each of these six areas.

The Specialized Building Network

One alternative for medium-sized and larger agencies is to distribute the various programs and functions among several buildings at different sites. At first, this may seem expensive and inconvenient, since it implies a certain amount of travel by agency personnel among the various sites. However, careful allocation of programs to different facilities can reduce the inconvenience to a minimum, and it can be more than outweighed by the convenience and efficiency of placing each type of program in a facility at the location where it is best suited.

A specialized building network could be developed on a single site (what might be called a "campus plan"), thus avoiding some of the inconvenience of travel between sites. However, the campus plan, unless it occupies a very large site, negates the advantages of having certain facilities placed in the locations where they are most needed.

Any number of different arrangements of building networks might be practical, depending on local needs and preferences. However, a typical arrangement might divide the agency's facilities into seven types:

Administrative and technical services center	Houses all central administrative offices plus some central operating programs (such as an organized crime unit) and most technical support units (such as communications, criminalistics).
Community police station	Houses subunits or branches of all operating programs (patrol, investigation, etc.) and some technical support services (such as duplicated records that are significant only for the area served); similar to a conventional precinct station but without duplicating administrative, technical support, and prisoner custody facilities.
Neighborhood police station	Sometimes called a "store-front" or "walk-in" police station; intended primarily for community relations and crime prevention; limited operational use; no technical support or prisoner-holding facilities.
Maintenance and supply center	Warehouse for police supplies and stored property; maintenance shops for vehicles and equipment.
Training center	Often called a police academy, includes classrooms, specialized training facilities, materials production facilities.
Adult detention center	Complete jail for adult prisoners.
Juvenile detention center	Complete facility for holding juveniles on a temporary basis (not intended for long-term detention after sentencing).

One great advantage of a specialized building network, aside from the fact that each type of facility can be placed where it is most needed and designed for its specific purpose, is that neighboring agencies often can share some of the facilities. For example, several small police agencies in one county, or even in adjacent counties, could pool their funds to build one maintenance and supply center, one adult detention center, one juvenile detention center, and one training center, rather than each agency attempting to build and maintain all of these special facilities. In a metropolitan area, several suburban police departments could build a single administrative and technical services center and scatter a number of community police stations throughout their areas of jurisdiction. It might seem peculiar to have the police chiefs from three or four different cities occupying offices in one building, but the advantages of lower building costs and in promoting interagency cooperation would be enormous.

Multiagency Facilities   Another way to reduce costs through facility sharing is to house several different governmental agencies in the same building.

In fact, it is quite common for small police agencies to occupy only a few rooms in the city hall or county courthouse. In slightly larger communities, the police and fire departments frequently are in the same building. The reason is primarily economic: It costs much less to consolidate several spaces into one building than it would to construct several small buildings.

However, the same principle applies even in large communities, and there are other significant advantages to the police agency in sharing a building with other agencies. No matter how successful a police agency's

Figure 6-3 A combined police–fire station. Shared facilities are common in small towns, but even in urban areas there are attractive economies in interdepartmental sharing. (Adapted from Tucson, Arizona Police Department.)

community relations program may be, there are still people who are extremely reluctant to walk into a police building even when they have good reason to seek help. Some people are intimidated by the authority of the law, while others may fear that they will be subjected to some embarrassment or discomfort. But if the building also houses other community service agencies, much of the intimidation is removed.

Furthermore, as we will emphasize repeatedly, it is vital to a police agency's functions for it to act as an integrated part of the community. One of the best ways to demonstrate this principle is through a direct, physical association with other community service organizations.

There is no inherent reason that a police agency must share its building only with other municipal agencies (or, for a sheriff's department, only with other county agencies). The fact that each governmental level in the United States has its own law enforcement apparatus is mostly an accident of history, not a reflection of rational decisions. It is perfectly feasible, and often very practical, for the municipal police, county sheriff, and state highway patrol or police to share facilities. Usually one governmental body owns the building and the others rent the space they need or pay a proportional share of the costs. Again, considerable savings can be achieved through such sharing, by arranging facilities to serve common needs while avoiding wasteful duplication.

A few examples of multiagency facilities will illustrate some of the possibilities:

Public safety administrative center	Houses administrative offices, technical support, and some operational units for police, fire, and Emergency Medical Services (EMS).
Public safety services center	Houses police operational units plus fire station and perhaps EMS station.
Community services center	Houses police operational units plus various community service agencies such as welfare office, employment office, public library.
Regional law enforcement center	Houses all units of municipal police and county sheriff, plus local office of state police or highway patrol; some technical support facilities shared among all agencies; could house two or more local police agencies.

These examples do not exhaust the possibilities, but merely illustrate them.

RECYCLING EXISTING FACILITIES

As we said earlier, police agencies do not often have the opportunity to build new facilities. Since public buildings are expensive, they are designed to last as long as possible, even if that means they outlast their usefulness. Many police agencies find themselves stuck in overcrowded, inefficient buildings, inconveniently located on inappropriate sites, with little hope of getting the money to put up a new building somewhere else.

The alternative is to remodel the existing structure or to put some other building to a new use. Often this is much less expensive than constructing an entirely new building (although this is not always true), and the results can be surprisingly successful.

Remodeling an Existing Police Building

The most obvious reason to remodel an existing structure (usually an independent police station) is to relieve overcrowding. Other reasons include the deterioration of the building through heavy use or abuse, and sometimes inadequate maintenance, and the need to accommodate changes in the physical requirements of police programs such as the addition of a photo lab or the downgrading of a jail to a temporary holding facility.

Before any effort is made to plan a remodeling, a qualified structural engineer should be hired to evaluate the soundness of the building. There is little to be gained by trying to remodel a building that is likely to fall down in a few years; in some cases, the effort to remodel could hasten the building's demise. There is also the possibility that an unfavorable engineering report will stimulate the local government to consider more seriously the need for a new building.

If the building is structurally sound, the engineer also should be able to evaluate the kinds of remodeling that would be practical. Entirely different construction techniques have been used at different times in the past. In some old buildings, every interior wall is part of the load-bearing structure; removing or relocating a wall could literally cause the roof to fall in. In other buildings, the structure is supported by an arrangement of interior columns (piers and beams); walls can be moved about or removed entirely at little cost or trouble. In yet other buildings, only the framework in the exterior walls is load-bearing; both the interior and exterior walls, and to some extent interior columns, can be rearranged at will.

It may seem unlikely that overcrowding can be relieved without adding to a building's overall size, but that is often the case. In many older buildings, valuable space is wastefully used for unnecessary circulation areas (corridors and lobbies), storage, and inefficient arrangements of work spaces. For example, 20 people may feel cramped in 12 separate offices, but 24 people may have more than adequate working room in exactly the same amount of space if the walls between the offices are removed. Similarly, several small, inconvenient storage spaces might be consolidated into one larger, efficient space.

In general, the key to successfully remodeling an existing facility is to remove every wall that is not absolutely necessary for efficient operation (or to support the building) and arrange every work area for the best possible use of the space.

With these principles in mind, the agency's planners and an architect should proceed exactly as if a new building were being designed. The same planning process should be used, except that there are more constraints to be taken into consideration.

One difficulty in remodeling an existing building is that the agency must continue to function during the rebuilding. Usually a police agency cannot shut down for several weeks while its building is being renovated. There are two possible solutions to this problem. First, it might be possible to relocate the agency temporarily during the reconstruction. The second solution is to schedule the construction carefully as a series of phases involving different areas of the building, so that only a portion of the agency must be relocated (either to another part of the building or into temporary quarters elsewhere). The first solution is preferable since it means only two moves: first to the temporary quarters and then back into the remodeled building. Phased construction, unfortunately, is the solution usually chosen because it may not require the expense of renting temporary quarters. However, it means that every unit in the agency must be shifted two or three times, and everyone will undergo a long period of severe crowding, inconvenience, and the unpleasantness of trying to work in the middle of a construction zone for several months. Whichever solution is chosen, the agency officials must work closely with the architect and contractor to ensure that the disruption is kept to a minimum, that all vital operations are maintained, and that security is not violated in sensitive areas.

Converting Other Facilities to Police Use

There is nothing about a police facility that makes it substantially different from any other kind of building, except perhaps the unusual security needs of a jail. Any structurally sound building can be converted to police use. If constructing a new building is not feasible and the existing building is not suitable for remodeling, police officials should give careful thought to the possibility of finding some other existing building that can be converted.

The present use of the building is not important. A warehouse, office building, grocery store, school, even a church or a drive-in restaurant could be successfully converted into a practical, efficient police facility. Any building that is a candidate for conversion should meet three important criteria:

- The building must be structurally sound.
- It must contain at least as much space as the agency needs immediately and should contain ample room for future expansion.
- It must be in a suitable location for the kind of police operations that are to be housed.

Converting an existing building is often the most practical approach when a network of specialized facilities is needed. By placing the various functions of the police agency into different kinds of buildings, usually in different parts of town, a great deal of flexibility is attained. A maintenance and supply facility could be built in the warehouse or industrial district. An administrative and technical services center can be housed in an office building or department store in the downtown business district. A community police station might occupy a former grocery store or large restaurant, a former school building, even a former church. A neighborhood police station could occupy a storefront, a drive-in restaurant, even a gas station. A school building, church, or small factory could be converted into a police academy or an adult or juvenile detention center.

Shopping centers and industrial office-warehouse complexes should not be overlooked as possible sites for police facilities. A shopping center might be an ideal location for a community police station; what better way to integrate the police department into the fabric of the community! Even if there is no existing space that would be suitable, commercial property developers are often willing to build any kind of facility that is needed, at their own expense, in return for a long-term lease (five years or more). This could be a perfect solution for an agency whose parent government is unable or unwilling to issue bonds for major capital expenditures, but whose budget could tolerate the cost of leased space. It might even be possible to sell the old police building at a high enough price to pay in advance the lease on a new facility for the first several years.

If it is true that a police facility reflects "the community's commitment to modern law enforcement standards," then it is an important part of the police administrator's responsibilities to see that the agency's facilities are adequate to its operational needs and responsive to the needs and interests of the community. Police officers and civilian employees who are crowded into outmoded, inefficient, and unattractive facilities cannot serve the public to the best of their ability, and the public cannot have pride and confidence in a police department housed in shabby quarters.

ASSISTANT CHIEF WILLIAMSON'S IN BASKET

Instructions

In this exercise, you are to assume the role of Assistant Chief of Police Earl Williamson, who is chief of Administrative Services. The documents below have been selected from Chief Williamson's in basket. Read them with care. If you need more information about City or its police department, refer to the data bank in the front of the book. After you have studied the documents, complete these steps:

1. State the problem or problems these documents present to Chief Williamson.
2. List as many alternative solutions as you can.
3. Select the solution you think would be best, and give your reasons for choosing it.

CITY POLICE DEPARTMENT		
Interoffice Memorandum		
FROM: Chief Abel		
TO: Capt. Lewis		
SUBJECT: Attached letter	DATE:	12 Mar 19--

EARL: Mike really dropped the ball on this! Please draft another letter for my signature, explaining to Ms. Prizzen that the jail is designed for security, etc., etc., not for convenience, etc., etc. Thanks. E.Z.A.

PUTNAM, INNA, PRIZZEN
ATTORNEYS AT LAW
326 W. EIGHTEENTH STREET
CITY, STATE

March 7, 19--

Chief E. Z. Abel
City Police Department
308 E. Sixth Street
City, State

Dear Chief Abel:

I wish to protest the totally inadequate attorney-client consultation facilities in your jail. In my opinion, these facilities are so poor that they compromise the rights of defendants to adequate legal counsel. Unless corrective steps are taken, I will have no choice but to present the matter to the Court.

I realize that, since I am new to City, I could be accused of overreacting to conditions that are taken for granted in this community. My partners do not practice criminal law, and did not prepare me for this experience. When I made my first jail visit this morning, I was simply shocked.

First of all, the consulting room is entirely too small. Two other attorneys were already there, meeting with their clients. My client and I had to stand and wait for a vacant chair. Needless to say, privacy was impossible, and attorney-client confidentiality was seriously eroded. The glass partition (which I suppose is bulletproof) and telephone-type intercom system further intrude on attorney-client communications and prevent the exchange of documents.

Also, I resent having to climb three flights of stairs at the back of the police station to reach the crowded, dingy, filthy visiting room. I don't know what my older, less agile colleagues do. By the time I got up there, I was in no condition to render the kind of service my client has a right to expect.

These deplorable conditions must be corrected immediately. The situation is a disgrace to our fine community.

Respectfully yours,

(Ms.) Wanda N. Prizzen,
Attorney

CITY POLICE DEPARTMENT

308 E. 6TH STREET
CITY, STATE

March 12, 19--

Ms. Wanda N. Prizzen, Attorney
Putnam Inna Prizzen, Attorneys
326 W. 8th St.
City, State

Dear Ms. Prizzen:

Thank you for your constructive comments concerning our
jail. We appreciate your interest in our problems.

As you know, our City Police building is quite old and
overcrowded. We are not always able to provide the quality
of facilities that we would like. The jail, which has not
been remodelled since 1954, is less than ideal.
Nevertheless, this is the first time we have received a
complaint about the attorney's visiting room. We added this
room because of Court rulings, by reducing the size of the
regular visiting room.

If you feel that improvements are needed, I suggest you
discuss the situation with a member of the City Council,
since they control our budget. We would like to make many
improvements, but we are always told that the money is not
available. Maybe you could do something about that.

Thank you again for your interest. Please let me know
if there is anything else I can do for you.

Sincerely,

E. Z. Abel, Chief
(by M. Lewis, Capt.,
Technical Services)

CITY POLICE DEPARTMENT
Interoffice Memorandum

FROM: M. Lewis

TO: Chief Williamson

SUBJECT: Vandalism to Patrol cars   DATE: 15 Mar 19--

SIR: Last night 2 more of our Patrol cars were parked at the PD Vehicle Service garage at 12th & Nutmeg Sts. and were damaged by vandals. One car had its windshield and 2 side windows smashed, and both cars had all 4 tires slashed. This is the third time this has happened, and it really is cutting down the number of vehicles we can put on the street.

Fleet Operations has assured me that the fence around the Garage and parking area is locked at night, but there is no one there and no real security. We have got to do something about this. Maybe we could hire a private guard or buy a dog. Part of the problem is that the place is so crowded, we have to put some of the cars up by the fence.

Ever since we bought the Garage from a private mechanic 5 years ago, we have had this kind of problem.

                         M. Lewis, Captain
                         Technical Services

CITY POLICE DEPARTMENT
Interoffice Memorandum

FROM: W. Lawrence, Lt., Crimes Against Persons

TO: E. Williamson, Asst. Chief

SUBJECT: Need for expanded interview room   DATE: 16 Mar 19--

SIR:

Captain Bowen suggested that I submit this request directly to you, and said he would speak to you about it. The Detective Bureau desperately needs more space to interview suspects and witnesses.

Our one little interview room is in almost constant use. When it is being used for suspect interrogation, witnesses and victims must be interviewed in our office, which is also crowded and noisy. Often a detective holding a suspect must wait an hour or more to use the interview room, which is inconvenient and potentially dangerous, especially when there are also witnesses and victims in the office.

Organized Crime has two interview rooms with an observation window between them, and built-in audio recording system. Our one tiny interview room has no one-way window and no recording system. We should have facilities at least equal to those of OCB. In fact, we

Page 2

need three or four interview rooms. We have asked to use the OCB interview rooms when ours is busy, but we have always been told that each request must go through channels. By the time we refer it to Capt. Bowen and he refers it to Capt. Edwards, it is too late. It would help if we could at least have some clarification of policy on this.

We could add at least one more interview room by reducing the lobby space in front of the 2nd floor stairs. This is not an ideal solution, but it would sure help.

        W. Lawrence, Lt.,
        Crimes Against Persons

CHIEF WILLIAMSON:

    Here are the floor plans you asked for, of our present building.

Let me know if you need anything more.

                            Roland Ullrich, Lt.,

                            Budget & Accounting Sec.

EL — Elevator

CL — Closet / storage

M, W — Rest rooms

1 — Building utilities

    Ia — Workshop
    Ib — Water heater
    Ic — Emergency generator
    Id — Boiler (heating)

2 — Employee lounge

3 — Crime lab

    3a — Lieutenant's office
    3b — Photo lab

4 — School crossing guards

5 — Parking enforcement

6 — Property / evidence

    6a — Sergeant's office

7 — Communications

    7a — Lieutenant's office
    7b — Sergeant's office

8 — Juvenile division

    8a — Sergeant's office
    8b — Interview room

9 — Community relations

10 — Crime prevention

11 — Public information

Basement

Scale:

(a)

First (Ground) Floor

(b)

EL — Elevator

CL — Closet

M — Men's room
(public)

W — Women's room
(public)

1 — Armory

2 — Patrol lieutenant's office

3 — Patrol captain

4 — Patrol staff room

5 — Briefing room

6 — Personnel and training

7 — Men's lockers

7A — Men's showers

8 — Budget and accounting

9 — Women's lockers

9A — Women's showers

10 — Records and identification

11 — Judge's chamber

12 — Municipal courtroom

13 — Court clerk's office

14 — Display area

Scale:

EL — Elevator

CL — Closet

M — Men's room

W — Women's room

1 — Chief's office

    la — Secretary
    lb — Bathroom

2 — Captain, detectives

3 — Captain, organized crime

4 — Conference room

5 — Narcotics section

6a — Interview room
6b — Observation

7 — Assistant chief,
    Administrative services

    7a — Secretary

8 — Intelligence section

9 — Vice section

    9a — Lieutenant's office

10 — Crimes against property

11 — Captain, technical
    services

    11a — Secretary

12 — Crimes against persons

13 — Interview room

14 — Criminalistics
    equipment and
    evidence

15 — Fraud and forgery
    section

16 — Traffic law
    enforcement

Second Floor

(c)

Scale:

Third Floor — Jail

(d)

EL — Elevator

1 — Booking desk

    la — Sergeant's office

2 — Visitor's room

    2a — Prisoners

3 — Matrons' office

4 — Attorney consultation room

    4a — Prisoners

5a — Men's showers

5b — Women's showers

6 — Juvenile holding

    6a — Group cell and dayroom
    6b — Single cells

7 — Women's jail

    7a — Dayroom
    7b — Single cells
    7c — 2—person cells

8a — Infirmary treatment

8b — Infirmary examination

9a — Lieutenant's office

9b — Jail operations office

10 — Jailers' lounge

11 — Men's dayroom

12 — Kitchen

    12a — Cold storage

13 — Men's group cells

14 — Men's single cells

Scale:

IN REVIEW

1. True or False: The planning and design of a new building should be entrusted to qualified experts such as architects and engineers. It is too complicated and too time-consuming for police administrators to get involved.

2. Which of the following items might be a planning constraint?
   (a) The site for the new building.
   (b) The budget for the building.
   (c) Community attitudes about the police department.
   (d) State laws regarding jail and prison design.
   (e) All of the above.
   (f) None of the above.

3. A police building should be designed for flexibility because:
   (a) The agency is certain to expand in the future.
   (b) The building may have to be shared with other agencies.
   (c) Most police programs outlive their usefulness.
   (d) All police agencies experience change over time.
   (e) None of the above.

4. True or False: A police building should be accessible to the public, but citizens should be discouraged from coming into the building unless they have serious police business.

5. *Serviceability* means that a police building:
   (a) Should be easy to clean and maintain and economical to operate.
   (b) Should have nothing that could be damaged by vandals or criminals.
   (c) Should have every aspect planned to accommodate efficient police operations even if this means that the building is not very attractive.
   (d) All of the above.
   (e) None of the above.

6. True or False: Every part of a police building must be designed for maximum security, to withstand any attack that might occur.

7. A police building might be divided into several **zones** for the following purpose:
   (a) To economize on utilities such as heat and electricity.
   (b) To prevent the public from interfering with police operations.
   (c) To provide appropriate levels of security for each police function.
   (d) To prevent prisoners from escaping.
   (e) To make routine cleaning and maintenance easier.

8. A survey should be taken for the following purpose:
   (a) To determine employees' attitudes toward the agency.
   (b) To determine the needs for physical space.
   (c) To determine the kinds of interactions that need to be prevented by proper security.
   (d) To determine employees' preferences concerning furnishings and decor.
   (e) To determine the public's willingness to pay for a new police building.

9. **A specialized building network** might include:
   (a) Two or more independent police stations.
   (b) A communications center.
   (c) An administrative and technical services center.
   (d) One or more community police stations.
   (e) A maintenance and supply facility.
   (f) One or more detention facilities.
   (g) A police academy.
   (h) All of the above.
   (i) None of the above.

10. True or False: Remodeling an existing building usually is not practical because older buildings were not designed for prolonged use.

REFERENCES

A diligent search of police literature and architectural sources has revealed a surprising lack of information on the subject of this chapter. One useful and widely circulated document is:

National Clearinghouse for Criminal Justice Planning and Architecture, *Guidelines for the Planning and Design of Police Programs and Facilities*, Urbana, Ill.: The Univ. of Illinois, 1973.

We are indebted to Joseph Stoeltje, AIA, of Wilson, Stoeltje, and Martin, Architects, Austin, Texas for providing us with much valuable information during a personal interview in his office, December 2, 1981.

1. National Clearinghouse, *Guidelines*, page D-3.1.
2. National Clearinghouse, *Guidelines*, page D-3f.

7 POLICE VEHICLES

IF THERE IS ANY ONE THING THAT DISTINGUISHES MODERN law enforcement from the police practices of the nineteenth century, it is certainly the use of the automobile. It would be difficult to imagine a police force today that did not rely on automotive patrol as the primary tool in combatting crime.

Automobiles were first introduced in American police agencies after World War I. Before then, police officers patrolled almost entirely on foot in urban areas or on horseback in rural and semirural areas. Bicycles were used by some municipal police departments after about 1895, but they were not common.

At first automobiles were not used for patrol, but merely to transport officers to their beats or to deliver squads of five or six officers to the scene of a disturbance; thus the obsolete term "squad car" applied to the basic police vehicle. Apparently the idea of using the automobile as a moving platform from which an officer could continuously observe activities along a patrol beat was first developed in Detroit (which may have been the first city to employ motor vehicles for law enforcement) during the early 1920s. Those early auto patrols were not very impressive. The vehicles were balky, difficult to operate, and slow. There was no convenient method to communicate with a patrolling officer; he had to stop the vehicle every so often to call headquarters by telephone or by use of a police call box. The same lack of communication was a problem for foot patrols too, of course, but foot patrolmen covered comparatively smaller beats and generally were within reach of a call box.

The automotive patrol first became reasonably practical when it became possible to install a mobile radio in each vehicle. This, too, was a Detroit innovation, in the mid-20s.[1]

The combination of the automobile and the mobile radio seemed so powerful that it quickly dominated law enforcement practices and has continued to do so to the present day. Only in recent years have law enforcement authorities begun to question the efficiency of this most basic of crime-prevention tools. Doubts have been raised about whether a police officer riding around the streets, presumably observing activities of the citizenry while listening to radio calls and keeping an eye on traffic (to avoid being involved in an accident), is in fact performing a worthwhile service. A careful study of standard patrol techniques in Kansas City, Missouri, reported in 1974, indicated that the answer might be no.[2] We will discuss this study further in Chapter 14.

Despite the discouraging results of the Kansas City study, police departments have not abandoned the use of patrol cars. The fact remains that the patrol vehicle is nearly indispensable to law enforcement because of its many functions other than serving as a mobile platform for preventive observation.

THE FUNCTIONS OF POLICE VEHICLES

The term **police vehicle** immediately brings to mind the familiar marked patrol car. Actually, there are several kinds of vehicles used by most police agencies; each kind has its own distinctive functions and purposes.

Patrol Vehicle

In the most basic sense, the function of the patrol vehicle is to transport one or two patrol officers from place to place within their assigned beat or district; to transport and protect the equipment they may need from time to time; and occasionally to transport a witness, prisoner, or other person.

At one time, the use of unmarked, inconspicuous patrol cars was popular, on the theory that criminals would never know where the police were at any given time. A few police agencies still cling to this practice, but the prevailing theory in law enforcement today is just the opposite: A patrol car is most effective if it is highly conspicuous. Conventional patrol car markings include the use of two contrasting colors of body paint (usually either black and white or blue and white, although brown is also popular in some of the western states) and the word "police" in large letters on each side of the vehicle and on the rear trunk lid. A reproduction of a police badge or shield may be displayed on the side doors. Patrol cars are also usually fitted with flashing lights (red, blue, and sometimes white), a siren, and sometimes a public-address speaker (often combined with the siren) on the roof. Occasionally flashing lights are installed on the front bumper, front fenders, dashboard, rear deck, or other locations.

Some agencies add a slogan such as "We Protect and Serve" on the side doors or rear of the car. Other agencies put the police emergency telephone number on the fenders or side doors. Whether these markings contribute anything other than a cluttered appearance may be questionable.

One additional marking, however, is important: the vehicle's unique, assigned unit number. The unit number should be highly visible from every direction. It should appear on each side, the rear deck, and in large letters or numbers on the vehicle's roof. The value of this last marking will be obvious when we discuss police aircraft.

A patrol car need not be gaudy in appearance, but it should be immediately recognizable from any direction, at a distance of at least five blocks, even at night or in inclement weather.

Whether a patrol car should carry one officer or two continues to be extremely controversial. We examine this subject in Chapter 14, but for now we simply point out that a one-person patrol vehicle may need to be equipped and arranged in a somewhat different fashion from a two-person vehicle. For example, in a one-officer vehicle the driver must have ready access to the controls for the siren, lights, radio, and any other equipment that may be needed while the vehicle is in motion. In a two-officer vehicle, the operation of this equipment might be divided between the driver and second officer.

A patrol car serves as, among other things, a mobile office for the patrol officer. There must be provision for the storage of report forms, blank paper, writing instruments, maps, and other printed materials. Some patrol cars are outfitted with a small desk. One of the most recent innovations in police science, the mobile computer terminal, may eliminate the need for some of this material, but then space must be found for the terminal itself.

It is standard practice in most agencies to equip each patrol car with a shotgun or other weapon (in addition to the sidearm each officer wears).

By far the single most important piece of equipment next to the vehicle itself is the police radio. Usually the main section of the radio—the combination transmitter and receiver—is stored in the trunk or underneath a seat. A small "control head," containing the operating controls for volume, channel selection, and so on, is attached to the dashboard or the hump between the seats, within easy reach of the driver and, in the case of a two-person car, of the second officer. The radio's speaker may be mounted in the dash or suspended under it.

Often more than one radio is installed in a patrol car. There may be a scanner (a receiver that monitors several channels) to enable the patrol officer to hear calls for the fire department, ambulance service, or neighboring police departments; or there may be a second police radio enabling the officer to both hear and respond to such calls. There also may be a Citizens Band radio (see Chapter 9), a commercial broadcast receiver (for AM and FM broadcasts), a Weather Service broadcast receiver, and sometimes other types of radios.

The trunk of the patrol car should contain a variety of other kinds of police equipment, depending on the particular law enforcement and emergency services that an agency's patrol officers are expected to provide. For example, there might be a fingerprint kit, evidence collection kit, and photographic equipment if patrol officers are expected to perform fairly extensive preliminary investigations at crime scenes. Most patrol cars also should carry well-stocked first-aid kits and basic rescue equipment such as pry bars and collapsible stretchers. In communities where severe weather is common, there should be a small, flat shovel, a set of snow chains, and other portable devices for helping motorists out of thick mud or snow. All patrol cars should carry portable electric flares, reflectors, a fire extinguisher, a chain (capable of being used to tow a disabled vehicle), and at least 100 feet of strong rope. Portable barricades, a battery-powered high-intensity spotlight, blankets, and other emergency gear might be added to the list.

Obviously, a patrol car's trunk can become a very crowded place! In fact, few patrol cars carry everything we have listed. The point is that all of these items might be needed in an emergency or to render routine police services. Decisions must be made as to which equipment will be carried in all patrol cars and which will be carried in other police vehicles or not at all. These decisions should be made by agency administrators in consultation with field officers and should be based on officers' actual experience as well as the administrators' policies and expectations.

Command Vehicles

A command vehicle is a general-purpose vehicle, usually a standard sedan. It is used primarily to transport agency administrators, plainclothes officers (investigators), and nonuniformed supervisors, along with any specialized equipment they might need. Occasionally a command vehicle, especially when it is being used by an investigator, may be used to transport a witness, prisoner, or other person.

The standard practice among nearly all police agencies in the United States is to leave command vehicles unmarked. Usually a command vehicle is equipped with a siren mounted under the front hood and some kind of portable flashing light that can be set on the dashboard or attached to the roof by magnets when it is needed. The police radio usually is mounted out of sight, under the dashboard or in the glove compartment.

This practice is probably unnecessary and may be unwise. A command vehicle does not have to be as readily identifiable as a patrol car, but there might be good reasons to make the command vehicle more recognizable. At the scene of a crime, major traffic accident, public disturbance, or other police business, a semimarked command vehicle will be more easily identified both by the public and by other police officers. The markings may be unobtrusive: black lettering, perhaps 2 inches high, on the side doors and rear deck; a small reproduction of a police shield on the side doors; a flashing light permanently mounted on the dashboard and on the shelf behind the rear seat; and unit numbers on the front or rear fenders. If nothing else, these markings will increase the public's awareness of the presence of the police in the community and will reassure citizens that appropriate police attention is being given in emergencies.

Undercover Vehicles

Whether command vehicles should be unmarked or semimarked, there clearly is a need for most law enforcement agencies to maintain some vehicles that are not recognizable as police equipment. These vehicles are used for undercover investigations and covert surveillance. They ordinarily contain no police equipment other than a police radio that is fully concealed in the glove compartment or under the driver's seat.

An undercover vehicle, if it is to serve its purpose, must be completely inconspicuous. It should not be the same kind of automobile that is ordinarily used as a patrol or command vehicle. Older-model sedans, convertibles, sports cars, pickup trucks, vans, and station wagons may serve as undercover vehicles. They should not be equipped with sirens, flashing lights (portable or otherwise), tax-exempt license plates, police parking lot stickers, or anything else that can be recognized as police-related. Any police equipment such as weapons or emergency gear should be kept in a locked trunk, preferably under a false floor or in a padlocked crate. Police officers who use an undercover vehicle must be careful not to leave any law enforcement equipment or materials (such as report forms or stolen car lists) in the car. An undercover vehicle loses most of its usefulness, and may actually pose a danger to the police officers who use it, if it is identified by the criminal element in the community.

Single-Purpose Police Vehicles

Some kinds of police services require the use of special-purpose vehicles; in addition, it is sometimes desirable, in the interests of efficiency and economy, to use special-purpose vehicles for a particular type of police function even though a general-purpose vehicle such as a patrol car could be used.

For example, in many metropolitan areas, a **patrol wagon** (sometimes called a paddy wagon) is used for the single purpose of picking up drunks and transients in skid-row neighborhoods. The patrol wagon is simply a van that is outfitted with a metal screen between the driver and the rear compartment and screens or bars over all the windows. Benches are provided in the rear compartment for the passengers while they are transported to jail. The patrol wagon also may be used at the scene of a civil disturbance or a mass arrest, such as a vice raid, when large numbers of prisoners are to be transported.

In some communities, it might be practical for a patrol wagon to transport nearly all prisoners from the point of arrest to a central jail or police station. Where the volume of police activity involves a daily average of perhaps 15 to 30 arrests per shift, one or two patrol wagons could be operated continuously to provide all prisoner transportation. When a patrol officer or investigator makes an arrest, the patrol wagon would be called; in most cases, it should arrive at the arrest scene within 15 minutes and remove the prisoner (on the authority of the arresting officer). The arresting officer could file a preliminary arrest report by radio or mobile computer terminal, or call it in from a public telephone, and be back on the street in less than half an hour. The conventional procedure requires the arresting officer to transport the prisoner to the central jail, remain present during booking, and file all necessary reports in writing before returning to patrol—an elapsed time of an hour to an hour and a half. The patrol wagon used for this purpose might be a station wagon or small (six- to nine-passenger) van, rather than the large van that is often used for mass arrests.

Some police agencies use station wagons and vans with special equipment as mobile criminalistics laboratories, mobile radio command centers, and so on. These special-purpose vehicles are usually expensive to buy, equip, and operate. Unless there is a clear need for them and a well-thought-out plan for their use, the expense is largely a waste. Too often, police agencies buy these vehicles with the best of intentions, but find that the vehicles simply sit in the parking lot day after day because they are not truly needed.

On the other hand, an investment in a special-purpose vehicle is perfectly sensible, even if the vehicle is used only on rare occasions, if it serves a function that could not be handled in any other way. For example, a disaster response vehicle might be used only once in every few years when a major disaster occurs. But if the vehicle is equipped with items such as rescue gear, first-aid supplies, portable generators and lights, folding stretchers or cots, blankets, emergency food, several kinds of mobile radios, and traffic-control equipment (such as flares and barricades), the expense would be justifiable. Of course, the equipment and supplies must be maintained, the vehicle must be ready for use at all times, and someone must be assigned and trained to operate it. Otherwise, when the moment comes for the vehicle to justify its existence, it may be more of a hindrance than a help.

Police Motorcycles

Both two-wheel and three-wheel motorcycles are used by many urban police agencies. In most cases, their use is limited to traffic patrol and crowd-control functions. A motorcycle is capable of carrying one person and a very limited quantity of equipment and materials.

These limitations may be outweighed by the advantages of the motorcycle. Two-wheel motorcycles are extremely maneuverable even in very dense traffic and they are capable of being operated at relatively high speeds. Three-wheel motorcycles are useful primarily for low-speed applications with frequent stops and starts such as parking law enforcement and crowd control. In general, motorcycles are considerably less expensive to operate than even the smallest, most economical automobiles.

On the other hand, motorcycles—especially the two-wheeled ones—are extremely dangerous. Some police agencies have reported that their motorcycle officers have experienced eight times as many accidents resulting in death or injury as their automobile-patrol officers. Two-wheel motorcycles cannot be operated in rainy or otherwise inclement weather not only because of the discomfort to the driver but also because these conditions make the vehicle even more unsafe. Three-wheel motorcycles, especially if they are equipped with canopies, can be operated in poor weather to some extent. However, they too are involved in a disproportionately high number of serious accidents. The reason for the high rate of injuries and deaths, of course, is that a motorcycle offers no protection at all in the event of an accident, and the inherent instability of a two-wheel motorcycle contributes to a high accident rate even when the drivers are well trained and competent.

Police Aircraft

Both fixed-wing and rotary aircraft are used by many police agencies for a variety of purposes.

Fixed-wing aircraft (conventional airplanes, generally with one or two engines) were first used by state police in 1929 and continue to be used by state, county, and rural police agencies. Their most common use is for the transportation of personnel between distant locations. However, they also can be used for observation, rescue searches, traffic surveillance, and other patrol-type functions, especially in rural areas.[3] The major advantages of fixed-wing aircraft are their speed and relatively large load capacity (depending, of course on the aircraft's size). Most small, single-engine airplanes have a cruising speed of 80 to 120 miles per hour, a very considerable advantage over the 55 mph speed limit that applies to ground vehicles. (Most automobiles are capable of being operated at higher speeds, but even in emergencies high-speed operation for sustained periods of time is unreasonably dangerous.) Furthermore, a small aircraft can be operated for three or four hours at a time, and sometimes longer, if it is equipped with high-capacity fuel tanks. This operating limit can be a significant advantage in traffic patrol, rescue searches, searches for fugitives, and similar police activities.

Rotary aircraft (helicopters) have the unique advantage of being able to hover over one location or fly at very slow speeds. They are ideal for surveillance and observation from the air, especially in densely built urban areas. They also are invaluable in some rescue operations where the person to be rescued is inaccessible from the ground and there is no place for an aircraft to land; the helicopter can hover over the rescue site while a rope or basket is lowered, or a rescuer can be dropped down on a rope to complete the operation.

The principal disadvantages of the helicopter are its noisy operation, its high fuel consumption (and therefore high operating expense), and its relatively high risk. If a fixed-wing aircraft has engine problems, usually it can glide to an emergency landing; when a helicopter malfunctions, it may plummet to the ground.

Both fixed-wing and rotary aircraft require specially trained, licensed pilots. Some police agencies prefer to hire experienced pilots and train them as police officers. Other agencies assign experienced police officers (usually on a voluntary basis) to become trained as pilots. In that case, the personnel deserve and may demand promotion to a higher rank or other special compensation. More important, if the special personnel are not available, the aircraft is useless.

Aircraft are comparatively expensive to purchase and to operate. Most helicopters are able to run for no more than an hour or two on a full fuel load, which limits their ability to patrol continuously. Both fixed-wing and rotary aircraft require specialized facilities such as an airport, maintenance hangar, and licensed aircraft mechanics. These costly operations make sense only if the aircraft are used frequently for purposes that cannot be served in any other way with equal efficiency. In fact, studies of helicopter use in several metropolitan areas have demonstrated that a single aircraft, *when properly used*, can perform about as much police work as 10 ground vehicles. We will discuss the use of aircraft in Chapters 14 and 15.

Police Marine Craft

Any community that has a substantial body of water—a river, a lake, ocean beach, and so on—requires a police agency capable of responding to marine emergencies and crimes. This in turn means that the law enforcement agency must have some kind of marine craft.

The kind of craft needed depends mostly on the size of the body of water and the kinds of police functions that are to be served. A city that borders on a major river, such as the Mississippi or the Columbia, will be concerned mainly with shore patrols and rescues; a city in which there is a major port, such as Houston or Boston, requires far more extensive police marine activity. Some major port cities have established separate law enforcement agencies, or harbor patrols, specifically for this purpose.

In some cases, there is no need for marine patrols on a full-time, year-round basis. If the body of water is used primarily for recreation during the warm-weather months, daylight patrols during the recreational season should be sufficient. However, in any city or county where there is a substantial body of water, the police agency should have appropriate marine craft readily available, with trained personnel ready on short notice to handle rescues, searches for drowning victims, and routine police tasks.

SELECTION AND ACQUISITION OF POLICE VEHICLES

Police aircraft and marine craft are so specialized in nature and the types of vehicles available for police use are so varied that there is not a great deal we can say to guide the police administrator in selecting and acquiring this kind of equipment, other than to follow the general rules for property acquisition that we will discuss in Chapter 10. Before any aircraft or marine craft is purchased, there must be a clear plan for its use: not only how it is to be operated, but who will operate it, what kinds of trained personnel will be required, how the equipment will be stored and maintained, and how operating expenses are to be paid.

Police automobiles are another matter. Their general purposes are so much a part of conventional police practice that, unfortunately, they usually are taken for granted. Too little thought is given to the operational requirements of police vehicles. Many agencies routinely buy the same kind of automobiles, often from the same manufacturer and local dealer, year after year without ever re-examining whether the vehicles being bought are the most appropriate and economical ones for the intended purpose.

Standard urban patrol techniques do not vary a great deal from one community to the next, and it is reasonable to suppose that the same kinds of automobiles are equally appropriate in most communities. For many years, the three major U.S. automobile manufacturers offered standardized vehicles with standardized "police packages." These vehicles were simply fleet versions of the company's least-expensive sedan; the same cars offered to taxicab companies, utility companies, and other fleet operators. The only difference between a taxicab and a police car is that the latter may have a larger engine, radiator, and air-conditioning system, and sturdier suspension system, plus some accessories that are intended to meet the special needs of police.

In recent years, even these "police package" features have grown very skimpy. Before the mid-1970s, police agencies could count on the major automakers to provide vehicles with the necessary features for high-speed pursuit driving and the hard day-in-day-out use to which police vehicles are exposed. These vehicles were sometimes called police cruisers in manufacturers' literature and in police circles. Today, a true police cruiser is as readily available as dinosaur eggs. Several factors including government regulations concerning pollution and fuel conservation, the general economic depression of the auto industry at the end of the 1970s, and the rising public demand for smaller and more fuel-efficient cars served to eliminate the traditional police cruiser. In its place the manufacturers offer a limited version of the police package on their standard models, which are smaller, lighter, and less durable than equivalent cars of the past.

From the police officer's point of view, the most serious drawback to the current crop of police vehicles is their comparatively poor performance. They are not capable of the high speeds, hard cornering, and rapid acceleration that the old police cruiser provided. In any type of collision, the newer cars offer considerably less protection; they tend to crumple, if not disintegrate altogether. All in all, the police vehicles of the 1980s are not well-suited to traditional police techniques, including high-speed pursuit.

To make matters worse, there are plenty of cars on the road—both older cars and newer models with high-performance sports designs—that can outperform the newer police cars. In the past, a police officer could reasonably expect to overtake most other vehicles on the road; today this is simply not the case.

The decrease in performance capabilities of vehicles offered by major U.S. manufacturers for police use can be seen even over the relatively brief three-year period from 1979 to 1982. Table 7.1 shows a comparison of six similar models offered by the three major auto companies and tested by the Michigan State Police, under the auspices of the International Association of Chiefs of Police (IACP). We will describe the testing program in greater detail; first, however, an explanation of the table. Each vehicle was given a series of performance tests by experienced test drivers on a test track. For our purposes, we are reproducing here only the test results for three performance factors: acceleration from 0 to 80 miles per hour (measured in seconds; the lower the figure, the better); top speed (the highest speed the car attained with constant acceleration, over a winding test track, after 14 miles); and braking (the deceleration rate, in feet per second per second, averaged over several hard-braking stops from 60 to 0 miles per hour; the higher the figure, the better). Only new vehicles, supplied by the factories

Table 7.1   Comparison of Performance of Similar Vehicles Equipped as Police Patrol Cars, 1979 and 1982

Vehicle/Model/Engine Size	1979	1982	Test
Ford LTD, 351 cu in.	19.78	21.82	Acceleration
	120.5	115.8	Top speed
	22.00	22.63	Braking
Ford Fairmont, 255 cu in.	29.25	25.55	Acceleration
	111.6	107.0	Top speed
	24.21	23.17	Braking
Chevrolet Impala, 350 cu in.	23.80	23.31	Acceleration
	110.4	107.8	Top speed
	23.70	24.00	Braking
Chevrolet Malibu, 305 cu in.	23.97	24.62	Acceleration
	113.4	110.1	Top speed
	24.13	24.62	Braking
Plymouth Gran Fury, 360 cu in.	19.54	21.19	Acceleration
(318 cu in. in 1982)	124.6	116.3	Top speed
	22.48	24.29	Braking
Dodge St. Regis/Diplomat	19.62	21.65	Acceleration
360 cu in. (318 cu in. in 1982)	122.7	115.4	Top speed
	23.47	23.71	Braking

and equipped to the Michigan State Police specifications, were tested. The results shown in this table are for essentially the same model cars with the same equipment. (The model name for the 1979 Dodge was "St. Regis" and for a similar model in 1982 was "Diplomat.")

Table 7.1 shows that, among these six cars, only the Ford Fairmont improved in acceleration by a significant margin; all six vehicles showed a substantial decrease in top speed (the range of decrease being from 2.6 miles per hour for the Chevrolet Impala, which was the slowest car in 1979 and second slowest in 1982, to 8.3 miles per hour for the Plymouth Gran Fury, which offered only a smaller engine in 1982). Four of the six vehicles showed very slightly improved braking in 1982, and one (Plymouth) showed a significant improvement in braking; the Ford Fairmont's braking performance actually deteriorated somewhat.

In short, the automobiles most likely to be purchased for police use gave substantially poorer performances in 1982 than they had a mere three years earlier.

The importance of these statistics lies in the implications for patrol operations. If recent-model patrol cars are not capable of high-speed, high-performance pursuit driving, entirely different police techniques must be developed. (For more detail see Chapter 14.)

Ideally, a police agency should be able to select vehicles that are perfectly suited to their intended use. The police administrator should be able to determine first how the vehicle will be used: the operational requirements. From the definition of operational requirements, the administrator should be able to prepare detailed specifications and standards that the vehicle must meet. Manufacturers and dealers then should be invited to offer vehicles that meet the specifications, at whatever price they consider appropriate. The police agency then should test each offered vehicle to make sure that it actually meets the specifications and standards; vehicles that fail these tests would be disqualified. From those vehicles that meet the tests, the police administrator then could choose on the basis of the best price offered.

Unfortunately, few police administrators have the time or expertise to develop complete statements of operational requirements and from them to develop comprehensive specifications and standards. Only a handful of very large police agencies could afford the extensive testing that would be ideal. Most police agencies assume that the manufacturers themselves have given some thought to the operational requirements of a police patrol vehicle; therefore, the administrator typically copies the vehicle's specifications from manufacturers' brochures. Bids may or may not be solicited from several manufacturers and dealers. If there is any bidding, the police agency usually buys whichever vehicle is offered at the lowest price, without making an independent decision on whether the vehicle meets established specifications. Quite often, especially in smaller communities, only one dealer will bid on the police fleet, since the police department already has indicated which model it favors by using that manufacturers' specifications. (It also happens in some small communities that three or four dealers will "take turns" bidding on the police fleet, a practice that is clearly illegal.)

There is one alternative that ought to be used by nearly all law enforcement agencies. The *Technology Assessment Program of the International Association of Chiefs of Police (TAP/IACP)* publishes an annual report of the vehicle testing program conducted by the Michigan State Police, the source of the information in Table 7.1. Since the Michigan State Police annually buys several hundred new vehicles and has ready access to both the manufacturers and the test-track facilities, the department decided in 1979 to begin its own comprehensive testing program and to share the results with other law enforcement agencies. The information produced by the Michigan State Police testing program is considerably more comprehensive than the sample we have used in our table. Copies of the current test reports are available from TAP/IACP in Gaithersburg, Maryland.[4]

The Michigan test results should not automatically determine which of the tested vehicles will be chosen by a particular police agency. Different agencies do have different needs; in some cases, economical operation may be more important than high-speed performance, while in other cases maneuverability in dense traffic might be most important. Furthermore, the Michigan tests do not include every factor that might be significant to the police administrator. For example, no effort is made to test the durability of the vehicles or their maintenance costs. Some of this information is available from magazines, including the annual automotive issue of *Consumer Reports* and some of the automotive hobbyist magazines. Before a final decision on any fleet of new vehicles is made, as much information from as many different sources as possible ought to be gathered and analyzed.

At present, there is no comparable testing program for police motorcycles. However, most police agencies use relatively few motorcycles and buy them once every several years (while automobiles are used in large numbers and usually purchased new every year or two). Thus it is more practical for motorcycles to be selected and purchased on the basis of more carefully developed specifications and some kind of performance testing.

VEHICLE OPERATION AND MAINTENANCE

Police administrators must assume responsibility for the proper maintenance of the agency's vehicles. Most police vehicles are in constant, hard use. The maintenance procedures that are appropriate to one's private automobile (which usually can be summarized as, "When something breaks, fix it") do not apply to police vehicles.

The key concept, of course, is preventive maintenance. By this we mean that every vehicle should be inspected and serviced on a regular, scheduled basis, whether there is anything apparently wrong with it or not. Often preventive maintenance inspections will result in the discovery of potential problems before they become serious enough to affect the vehicle's performance. Preventive maintenance also helps to ensure that all of a vehicle's complicated mechanical and electrical systems are operating at their optimum level of performance.

The Technology Assessment Program of IACP offers a helpful guide to scheduled preventive maintenance for automobiles in police fleets. The guide is especially useful to administrators whose agencies have a relatively small fleet; large police agencies typically have their own extensive maintenance facilities and trained, full-time mechanics.[5] Most automobiles also come with an owner's manual that specifies the proper interval for routine servicing. These recommendations should be followed scrupulously, except where actual experience with a type of vehicle indicates that more frequent servicing is needed because of the hard use to which the vehicle is subjected.

Proper fleet maintenance is not just a matter of following a preventive maintenance schedule. There also must be some facility where the vehicles can be maintained and repaired when necessary. Some small agencies are able to get by without their own garage, by contracting with a private garage for maintenance services. However, any agency that has 10 or more vehicles should have its own maintenance and repair facility; it is almost certain to give closer attention, better care, and lower vehicle operating costs in the long run, than a contract mechanic.

The officers assigned to drive a police vehicle also bear part of the responsibility for proper maintenance. Aside from showing reasonable care for their assigned vehicle, officers should take the initiative in reporting any signs of trouble to their supervisors or to the agency's fleet maintenance personnel. Every officer should inspect his or her vehicle at the beginning of each shift. The inspection should include the appearance of the exterior and interior of the car; the operation of lights, wipers, and horn; the extent of wear of the tires; and any mechanical component (brakes, transmission, steering, suspension, and so on) that does not appear to be operating properly. Any defects found during the inspection should be corrected before the car goes out onto the street.

The automobile is so much a part of the American way of life that it is not often appreciated as fully as it might be. Motor vehicles have made modern law enforcement practices possible; whether that is entirely good or bad depends on just how successful those practices are. The evidence on that question is not conclusive. However, there is no doubt that police agencies will continue to rely on motor vehicles for the foreseeable future. Aircraft and marine craft are important supplements, but it is hard to imagine a replacement for the patrol and command vehicles as they are presently used in American law enforcement.

CAPTAIN LEWIS'S IN BASKET

Instructions

In this exercise, you are to assume the role of Captain Michael Lewis, chief of the Technical Services Bureau. The documents below have been selected from Captain Lewis's in basket. Read them with care. If you need more information about City or its police department, refer to the data bank in the front of the book. After you have studied the documents, complete these steps:

1. State the problem or problems these documents present to Captain Lewis.
2. List as many alternative solutions as you can.
3. Select the solution you think would be best, and give your reasons for choosing it.

CITY POLICE DEPARTMENT
Interoffice Memorandum

FROM:	E. Z. Abel, Chief	
TO:	Capt. Lewis, Technical Services	
SUBJECT:	Problems with Patrol Fleet	DATE: 10 May 19--

Mike: Please review the attached memo from Avery. I'd like your thoughts on the best way to handle these problems.

EZA

CITY POLICE DEPARTMENT
Interoffice Memorandum

FROM:	M. Avery, Capt., Patrol
TO:	Chief Abel
SUBJECT: Patrol vehicles	DATE: 4 May 19--

SIR:

Attached is a list of Patrol vehicles that are out of service for one reason or another as of today. As you can see, some of these cars are permanently out of service. We are getting to the point that we don't have enough cars available to cover all our beats properly. Also, it seems to take forever to get a car back, when it goes into the shop for repairs. If we don't get some new cars soon, I will have to transfer some of my Patrol people to desk jobs, or put them two in a car. Please advise.

M. Avery, Captain
Patrol Bureau

CITY POLICE DEPARTMENT
Interoffice Memorandum

FROM:	B. Matthews, Sgt., Garage
TO:	Capt. Avery, Patrol
SUBJECT: Condition of Patrol Cars	DATE: 1 May 19--

SIR:

Here is a report on the status of patrol vehicles that are not available for service as of this date.

Sgt. Davis and I are working on these cars every day in addition to servicing all vehicles before each shift. In some cases we are waiting on parts ordered direct from the manufacturer. We salvage parts from wrecked cars when we can, but this isn't always possible. We will let you know if there is any major change in our work schedule that will delay the work on any of these cars. Meanwhile, maybe you could get your people to take a little better care of their equipment and give us guys in the shop a chance. Thank you.

B. Matthews, Sgt.
Fleet Operations

STATUS OF CITY P.D. PATROL VEHICLES

Unit #	Problem or Condition	Estimated Return to Service
L-10	Leaking radiator	2 - 3 weeks
S-31	Collision (pursuit)	Wrecked
S-33	Collision (hit by truck while unit was parked)	Wrecked
A-2	Collision (pursuit)	5 - 6 weeks
C-12	Electrical problem (???)	2 - 3 weeks
C-13	Collision (hit fire engine)	Wrecked
D-22	Idles rough, stalls	3 - 4 days
A -32	Upholstered ripped by prisoner	1 week
A-34	Replace RF fender (collision)	2 weeks

Prepared by B. Matthews, Sgt., Garage

CITY POLICE DEPARTMENT
Interoffice Memorandum

FROM:	Sr. Sgt. Courtney, OC/Intel
TO:	Capt. Lewis, Technical Services
SUBJECT: Replacement of vehicle	DATE: 9 May 19--

SIR:
    Please be advised that the vehicle assigned to me for undercover intelligence operations, Unit #S-43, Chevrolet Corvette convertible, may have become known to the criminal community as a police vehicle. Therefore, this vehicle is no longer acceptable for undercover use. Please arrange to replace it at the earliest possible time.

                                        S. Courtney, Sr. Sgt.
                                        Organized Crimes

IN REVIEW

1. The automotive patrol first became practical when:
   (a) High-speed patrol cruisers were developed.
   (b) Foot patrols were found to be inefficient.
   (c) Mobile radios were installed in automobiles.
   (d) Traffic signals were invented.
   (e) Telephone call boxes came into widespread use.

2. True or False: The patrol vehicle is the only means of providing a mobile platform for preventive observation.

3. The most important equipment in a patrol vehicle is:
   (a) A desk or other writing surface.
   (b) The siren.
   (c) A shotgun or other weapon.
   (d) The radio.
   (e) The unit number.

4. A _____ might be semimarked to make it more easily identifiable.
   (a) Command vehicle
   (b) Patrol vehicle
   (c) Undercover vehicle
   (d) Single-purpose vehicle
   (e) Motorcycle

5. True or False: The greatest disadvantage to the use of motorcycles is that they are more expensive to operate than automobiles.

6. The ideal vehicle for surveillance and observation of large, densely built urban areas is:
   (a) The patrol car.
   (b) The helicopter.
   (c) The command vehicle.
   (d) The bicycle.
   (e) The police cruiser.

7. Largely because of government regulations and economic conditions, the vehicles offered for police use today are _____ the police vehicles of the early 1970s.
   (a) Better than
   (b) Safer than
   (c) Faster than
   (d) About the same as
   (e) Not as good as

8. True or False: Before purchasing new vehicles, the police administrator should obtain the results of objective tests, consumer research, and other information, rather than relying entirely on manufacturers' claims.

9. Police aircraft and marine craft are alike in that:
   (a) They are specially designed for police use.
   (b) They require specially trained personnel for effective operation and maintenance.
   (c) They are too expensive for most police agencies to have.
   (d) They are useful only for limited purposes such as transporting personnel over long distances.
   (e) Their use is resented by most citizens.

10. True or False: Statistics show that police motorcycles, when driven by specially trained officers, are much safer than standard police automobiles.

REFERENCES

1. Alan Burton, *Police Telecommunications*, Springfield, Ill.: Charles C. Thomas, 1973, page 4.

2. *The Kansas City Preventive Patrol Experiment*, Washington, D.C.: The Police Foundation, 1974.

3. George D. Eastman, ed., *Municipal Police Administration*, Washington, D.C.: International City Management Association, 1969, pages 82−83. See also Donald T. Shanahan, *Patrol Administration*, Boston: Holbrook Press, 1975, pages 48−62.

4. Patrol vehicle tests conducted by the Michigan State Police are published by the Technology Assessment Program, International Association of Chiefs of Police, 13 Firstfield Road, Gaithersburg, Maryland 20878. Funds for the tests and publications are provided by the U.S. Department of Justice. Information in this section was drawn from the 1979 and 1982 publications.

5. *A Guide—Scheduled Preventive Maintenance*, Washington, D.C.: Technology Assessment Program, International Association of Chiefs of Police, 1981.

8 PERSONAL EQUIPMENT

LAW ENFORCEMENT OFFICERS PERFORM THEIR VITAL duties on the streets, in public places. This is equally true for plainclothes investigators, undercover agents, and patrol officers. They must carry their working equipment, the tools of their trade, on their persons. In some cases, the very clothes they wear are tools of their trade.

Unfortunately, the police officers' personal equipment, like their vehicles, is too often taken for granted and overlooked as the proper subject of administrative attention, planning, and budgeting. The result is that officers are left to shift for themselves, to accumulate their own collection of equipment that may or may not be suitable to their duties, and certainly will not conform to a reasonable degree of standardization.

Standardization is important for several reasons. First, the equipment used by police officers, regardless of their specific assignment, should be the best available for the tasks they are to perform. Police work is difficult and not infrequently dangerous, both to the officers and to the citizens with whom they interact. Inadequate or inappropriate equipment increases the danger. Second, police officers must work cooperatively with one another; sometimes this means sharing equipment. Since police equipment can be used effectively only with proper training, an officer may be hindered more than helped if a borrowed piece of equipment is unfamiliar. In some cases, the sharing of equipment may be impossible unless there is a high level of standardization. For example, if officers provide their own handguns, and there is no common type of weapon used by all officers, one officer's ammunition may not fit another officer's weapon.

Finally, standardization of police personal equipment helps to enable the public to recognize and identify a police officer without hesitation. In some small police agencies, each officer supplies his or her own uniform, with no well-defined standards. As a result, the uniforms are not—in a word— uniform. Even though all officers may wear the same shoulder patch, badge, and general color scheme, the lack of uniformity can create confusion and mistrust among the public.

It is the responsibility of administrators to ensure that uniforms are uniform and that all personal equipment is standardized as far as possible. This responsibility is not eliminated even when officers are expected to provide some or all of their own equipment; the agency still can specify the types of equipment that are acceptable.

POLICE UNIFORMS

The Standard Duty Uniform

In most police agencies, all commissioned officers wear a standard duty uniform except (1) officers assigned to criminal investigations, (2) officers assigned to undercover investigations, and (3) officers whose duties require a specialized uniform. Higher-level administrators usually wear a uniform in smaller agencies, but generally wear civilian clothes in larger agencies; however, these practices are not universal.

Standard police uniforms are available from uniform manufacturers in a vast array of styles and colors. The choice ultimately is left to the administrators of each agency. Aside from matters of personal taste, the most important consideration in selecting a uniform style is recognizability. The public should be able to identify at a glance, even from a distance, a uniformed police officer, and should be able to distinguish the police officer from a firefighter, postal carrier, delivery person, bus driver, airline pilot, or any of the other people who wear some kind of uniform. It is also helpful, though not so important, for the public to be able to distinguish among city police officers, sheriff's deputies, and state police officers.

The second important consideration is serviceability. Police work is (at least occasionally) physically strenuous. Sometimes an officer is exposed to dirt, blood, grass stains, and abrasive surfaces such as concrete sidewalks and brick walls. A serviceable uniform should be comfortable to wear and easy to clean. It should not restrict the officer's physical movements, and it should be possible to make at least minor repairs in a neat, nearly undetectable manner. The serviceability of the uniform depends on two factors: its style and the fabric of which it is made. A simple, neat style with a minimum of decorative flourishes, tailored out of such fabrics as cotton and polyester, will prove to be most successful.

The climate in which the uniform will be worn also must be considered. A summer uniform, or a year-round uniform in warm climates, might include short-sleeved shirts. A winter uniform might include a general-purpose jacket, such as the Eisenhower jacket (which buttons at the waist) or a modified suit jacket.

The basic components of the standard duty uniform include a shirt, slacks (skirts for female officers are not recommended), a light jacket, a heavy winter jacket, black socks and shoes, and an appropriate cap. Most urban police officers wear a garrison cap; some sheriff's officers and highway patrol officers wear either a western-style hat or a campaign hat ("Smokey Bear" hat). Some city police officers have begun to wear a baseball-type cap that is considerably more practical than the traditional garrison cap. A raincoat or slicker and hat cover complete the basic uniform, to which may be added winter gloves, a winter hat with ear covers, and a reflective jacket or vest for traffic duty at night and in severe weather.

Epaulets (buttoned shoulder flaps), braid, Sam Browne belts (worn diagonally across one shoulder, named for a nineteenth century British general), and other devices that are merely decorative should be omitted from the standard duty uniform, although they might be added to the uniform for special dress occasions. The same thing probably applies to four-in-hand ties that some agencies make a part of the uniform; they serve no useful purpose and may be in the way at times.

A uniform generally requires two belts: one for the slacks and one to hold a pistol and other working equipment. However, some styles of slacks do not require a belt.

Male and female officers' uniforms should be as nearly alike as possible. Skirts should be avoided not only for the sake of uniformity but also because a skirt simply is not a practical garment for police work. Again, however, a skirt could be part of a female officer's dress uniform.

Each officer should have a minimum of three complete basic uniforms, with one of each type of jacket and bad-weather gear. Five complete uniforms would be even better.

The appearance of a police officer's uniform directly reflects the officers' attitudes and the pride that the agency takes in itself. Each officer must be held responsible for his or her appearance. A soiled, worn, or damaged uniform should never be worn; if a uniform becomes damaged in the course of an officer's work, he or she should be allowed to return to the police station, or go home if necessary, to change clothes. Supervisors should be responsible for checking the appearance of their subordinates regularly and for correcting any problems that are observed.

Many smaller departments, as we mentioned before, require their personnel to supply all of their own uniforms. This policy is acceptable if the agency's administrators set and enforce standards that are sufficiently detailed to ensure that the uniforms are identical in appearance.[1] A better policy, followed by most medium-sized and larger agencies, is to provide all officers with a minimum set of uniforms and to pay a monthly uniform allowance that ordinarily covers the cost of cleaning, minor repairs, and the replacement of badly worn or damaged garments.[2] Officers should be allowed to purchase additional uniform items, either directly from the department at cost or from the department's regular suppliers. One advantage to this policy, aside from maintaining standardization, is that the purchase of uniforms in fairly large quantities will help to reduce the cost. A single complete uniform may cost anywhere from $100 to $500, depending on style, fabric, and so forth; however, discounts of as much as 25 percent may be available if large quantities are purchased at one time. The argument that officers will take better care of the uniform if they must purchase it themselves can be avoided if supervisors make frequent inspections and enforce a high standard of appearance.

Special-Purpose Uniforms

The standard duty uniform is appropriate for nearly all patrol, traffic enforcement, and office work. However, it is not entirely suitable to some kinds of special duty.

Agencies whose officers are occasionally called on to participate in ceremonial events may require a special dress uniform. The dress uniform, for the sake of economy, may consist of a standard duty uniform to which various decorative touches are added: epaulets, braid at the shoulders, a dress tie or ascot, leather spats, special belts (such as white Sam Browne belts), even a special dress jacket. Some taste and restraint should be exercised so that the dress uniform does not become too gaudy, nor too far removed from the standard uniform so that officers are not recognizable.

Motorcycle officers and others whose work involves special vehicles or equipment need appropriate uniforms. Motorcycle officers should wear leather boots that cover the shin, for protection of the foot and lower leg. These require slacks with narrow "pipe-stem" legs or jodhpurs (slacks that are loose-fitting above the knee but tight below the knee, originally designed for horse riding). It should go without saying that all motorcycle officers must wear a suitable helmet with goggles or faceplate.

Officers assigned to special weapons teams (sometimes called SWAT, or Special Weapons and Tactics, teams) generally wear military-style fatigue coveralls and combat-type boots, garments that are appropriate for any kind of physical activity. Coveralls are also suitable for aircraft officers and might be worn by marine officers.

Plainclothes Officers

Officers who do not wear a standard uniform nevertheless have an obligation to uphold the agency's standards of public appearance. This applies to all criminal investigators, administrators, and others who wear "plain clothes." Undercover agents, naturally, must wear whatever is appropriate to the environment in which they are working, which may mean clothing that is very far removed from ordinary standards of dress. However, they should be the only exception.

All other police personnel should be expected—in fact, required—to dress in a neat, conventional, and attractive manner at all times. Men should wear a business suit or jacket and matching slacks with a dress shirt and tie. Women should wear either an appropriate slacks suit or jacket, blouse, and skirt; in recent years, a type of women's business suit has become fashionable that is perfectly appropriate. Colors should be subdued and tasteful; extreme styles, even though they may be very fashionable, should be avoided. Plainclothes officers should in fact wear *plain* clothes. If they want to be noticed, they should wear a uniform. Otherwise, it is to their advantage to be unobtrusive and conservative in appearance.

However, it is also important for plainclothes officers (except undercover agents) to be recognizable as law enforcement agents. One useful device, adopted by the federal Secret Service and other federal law enforcement agencies, is a lapel pin. At a distance it is not noticeable, but to anyone up close it immediately identifies the agent. A pin of about half-inch diameter, bearing a miniature police badge or city seal and the name of the agency, would be quite sufficient. In addition, plainclothes officers should carry a full-sized badge in the breast pocket of their jacket, or in a special wallet alongside an identification card bearing their photograph. The old practice of pinning a badge under the lapel or to an inside jacket pocket has been largely abandoned, mostly because it has become the target of ridicule in popular entertainment.

Police Insignia

The recognizability of the police uniform depends almost entirely on its general style and color scheme. However, standardized police insignia contribute greatly to recognizability and impart useful information about the individual officer.

The universal device to identify personnel of a law enforcement agency is the badge. A metal badge should be attached to the front of the hat or cap, and another badge should be worn on, or more often just above, the left breast pocket of the shirt or jacket. Badges are offered by specialty manufacturers in an array of styles; the choice of style is purely a matter of taste, except that all officers in an agency should wear exactly the same style.

An officer's rank and duty assignment may be indicated by cloth patches on the sleeve of the shirt or jacket, or by pins on the shirt collar, jacket lapel, or sometimes on the cap. Nearly all police agencies use the same rank markings as the U.S. Army, except that not all Army ranks are used by most police departments. However, there is nothing to prevent a police department from either eliminating rank markings or adopting its own markings. A police department, after all, is not a military force. Markings are available in various designs to indicate duty assignment or branch of service, such as patrol, traffic, special weapons, tactical squad, and technical services.

Shoulder patches, identifying the agency and perhaps the officer's assignment or branch of service, should be worn on both shoulders of the jacket or shirt.

Every uniformed officer should wear a name tag, usually in the form of a metal or plastic pin worn above the right breast pocket of the shirt or jacket. The name tag ideally contains the officer's badge number, rank, first initial, and full last name. The minimum would be a name tag bearing only the officer's last name. The name tag is particularly important because it allows a citizen to identify the specific officer with whom he or she has had contact, in case further contact is necessary or the citizen has some reason to file a complaint against the officer for improper conduct.

In addition to the name tag, or in place of it, some agencies use a photo identification card, usually worn in a plastic holder attached to the right or left breast pocket. The photo ID card is valuable, especially for plainclothes officers while they are at the police station. However, the photo ID should not be used as a replacement for the uniformed officer's name tag, since the name on the ID is usually not easy to read from a distance of more than a couple of feet.

Other insignia, identification marks, and decorative devices are neither necessary nor advisable, since they tend to clutter up the uniform without adding worthwhile information. Flag patches or lapel pins, for example, may reflect an officer's personal patriotism, but (unless there is evidence to the contrary) most people would assume that all police officers are at least as patriotic as the average citizen. Religious, fraternal, or other insignia should not be worn on a police uniform nor by plainclothes officers since they might give offense unnecessarily to some citizens.

Exceptions may be made for pins or small patches that represent service awards. Many agencies give pins or other insignia for life-saving action, service above and beyond the call of duty, special achievements (such as marksmanship), and so on. Within reason, these devices contribute to morale and encourage professional attitudes. However, a few agencies go overboard, to the point that their officers begin to resemble Bolshevik generals with a chestful of ribbons and medals. These devices should be kept to a minimum, and any pins, medals, ribbons, or patches that are authorized for the uniform should be tasteful and discreet. A police uniform, after all, is not a fancy-dress costume. It is a set of working clothes, and anything that detracts from its serviceability could hamper an officer's performance of vital duties.

PROTECTIVE EQUIPMENT

The hazardous nature of police work, especially certain specialized assignments, requires that every reasonable effort be made to protect the officers' lives and safety. In recent years, several types of protective equipment have been developed and gained widespread use for this purpose.

The routine use of protective body armor, or "bulletproof vests," has generated a certain amount of controversy among police officials. The question has been raised as to whether these devices actually provide as much protection as officers may suppose, and whether the wearing of protective equipment may cause officers to become careless or foolhardy. These are difficult questions to which no hard and fast answers can be found. However, it is certainly true that no protective device offers an absolute guarantee of safety. Even the best body armor provides only limited protection from certain kinds of hazards. Before this equipment came into general use, police agencies had developed a number of procedural rules and policies designed to keep officers safe by avoiding, as much as possible, life-threatening situations. These rules and policies remain by far the best safeguards of officers' lives. Protective equipment cannot substitute for effective, sensible, and cautious police techniques.

With these reservations in mind, four kinds of protective equipment can be considered.

For general police use, body armor has become increasingly popular. Body armor consists of a sleeveless jacket or vest, ordinarily worn under an officer's shirt or jacket. The armor is made of either nylon or Kevlar (a trade name for a type of plastic) fibers, woven into a tight mesh, covered with fabric. The vest is stiff but somewhat flexible; although advertised as lightweight, most vests are in fact fairly heavy and not very comfortable to wear, especially in warm weather.

The purpose of body armor, of course, is to prevent a bullet from penetrating the officer's body. The vest covers only the torso (some vests have a flap that extends over the groin area). Arms, legs, and head receive no protection at all.

Body armor was the first type of police equipment tested by the Technology Assessment Program of the International Association of Chiefs of Police (TAP/IACP, which we mentioned in Chapter 7). In its first report, TAP/IACP commented, "no garment manufactured is 'bulletproof.' The term 'bulletproof vest' has been used since crime shows on radio and TV have become popular. Just about anything worn by a police officer can be 'defeated.' When it is defeated, the results are usually disastrous."[3] According to TAP/IACP, most body armor is designed to withstand penetration of bullets from .22 and .38 caliber weapons, which account for about 85 percent of the handguns distributed among the public.

The tests conducted by TAP/IACP consist of firing various weapons from a standard distance (depending on the type of weapon) directly at a garment that has been attached to a block of clay, which represents the average density of the human torso. If the bullet deforms the vest or penetrates it beyond a depth of about 1¾ inches (44 millimeters, to be precise) the armor is considered to have failed. Armor that successfully resists penetration is considered acceptable at one of four levels, depending on the type of weapons tested. A Level I vest is tested against .22 and .38 caliber bullets; a Level II vest has successfully withstood bullets of 9 millimeter and .357 Magnum calibers; a Level III vest has been successfully tested against 7.62 mm (.308 Winchester) rifles; and a Level IV vest has stood up to a 30.06 armor-piercing bullet.

In the first TAP/IACP body armor tests, conducted by independent laboratories in 1978, more than 100 vests were offered by 16 manufacturers. Unfortunately, more than half of them failed even at the Level I standard of performance. (Curiously, some vests failed the Level I test but passed at higher levels.) Since then, dozens of new models have been tested in an ongoing evaluation program, and the percentage of passes has increased greatly. For example, TAP/IACP reported in November 1981, on three new models of body armor that had passed the Level II tests.

Before any law enforcement agency purchases body armor or declares its use acceptable by its officers, copies of the TAP/IACP test reports should be obtained and studied carefully. Officers who wear this equipment routinely should be given thorough instruction in its use and should know precisely what it will *and will not* do.

Officers should be warned that body armor will not simply deflect a bullet harmlessly. Even the best armor will be deformed more than an inch by many projectiles. This means that the impact of the bullet will be transferred to the wearer's body with about the same force as the round end of a ballpeen hammer swung from a distance of 3 feet. At the very least, the impact will leave a painful bruise. Impact on the rib cage may cause a fracture. Furthermore, the impact is likely to knock the officer off his or her feet. The officer should expect this reaction and be prepared to recover quickly. Only movie superheroes are able to stand up to a hail of bullets without flinching.

A second type of protective equipment is the armored shield. Unlike the vest, the shield is not used routinely, but must be carried whenever the officer feels that danger is imminent. Shields may be made of metal (usually steel) or an impact-resistant plastic such as Lexan. They are used in exactly the same manner that medieval knights used their shields: They are worn or held on the left arm and used to deflect bullets or other projectiles.

In general, a shield provides better protection for the officer's entire body and it is more likely to resist being penetrated by most projectiles. However, there is no such thing as a perfectly bulletproof shield, and there is always the possibility that a ricocheting bullet will find its way around the shield. Furthermore, there is the problem of storing the shield where it is readily accessible when it is needed. Usually there is no room in the interior of a patrol car; the shield must go into the trunk, which may be already crowded with other gear. Finally, since the shield must be carried in or on the left hand, that leaves the officer with only one hand free to use a weapon or other equipment.[4] Because of its limitations, the shield is most useful in special situations such as riot control or terrorist incidents. Even then, it is most effective when it is used in conjunction with body armor for protection against ricochets.

Incidentally, some police equipment manufacturers offer clipboards and notebooks made of bulletproof or bullet resistant material (usually Lexan). These devices are in no sense a substitute for a full shield or body armor, but there may be instances when an officer could use a high-impact clipboard to deflect a projectile or a hand weapon such as a knife.

As we said earlier, body armor offers no protection at all against one of the most critically vulnerable parts of an officer's body: the head. A shield offers only partial protection to the head, depending on how it is held. The only kind of protection that is effective for the head is a helmet. A suitable protective helmet should cover the entire skull, from the base of the neck to the throat. Most motorcycle-type helmets cover only to the jawline in front and to the nape of the neck in back. The helmets worn by automobile racing drivers (especially drivers in Formula I and other open-cockpit vehicles) provide more complete coverage, but they are relatively expensive. The alternative is a helmet designed specifically for police use. It should have a transparent faceplate of high-impact plastic that covers the entire face opening of the helmet; coverage of the eyes alone is not adequate. An ideal helmet would have only a small opening at eye level, with a broad chin piece covering the entire jaw.

A helmet that gives adequate protection is likely to be hot and uncomfortable to wear and restricts both vision and hearing. Officers must be trained to use this equipment properly, and they must realize the limitations of it. Even the best and most expensive helmet will not provide absolute protection against such hazards as a high-powered rifle bullet.

Finally, police officers occasionally may need to use a gas mask, especially if the police themselves are employing some of the nonlethal chemical weapons we will discuss later. Gas masks are used only infrequently; there is little reason for every patrol officer to carry one routinely. On the other hand, when a gas mask is needed, there is no effective substitute. Masks should be available in sufficient quantities for all officers who may need them, rather than supplying them only to special-duty officers such as members of a SWAT team.

Masks are available in a number of types and styles, some for general-purpose protection against almost any airborne hazard and some for very specific uses. Those that are connected to an independent air supply (such as an air tank carried by the wearer) are most effective against any hazard, but also are the most cumbersome and expensive. Filter-type masks are less expensive and far easier to use but offer the least protection and offer no protection at all against some hazards. Unfortunately, only the largest police agencies can afford to provide a selection of different masks for different applications. Smaller agencies should, at a minimum, make sure that their masks provide at least 30 minutes of protection against the kinds of chemicals they are most likely to encounter, including any gas weapons that the agency itself uses.

POLICE WEAPONS

Handguns

Every police officer in the United States carries a handgun of one kind or another. In fact, Great Britain is one of the very few countries in the world where law enforcement officers do not routinely carry handguns as their primary defensive weapon.

The function of the handgun is to protect the officer and innocent citizens from deadly force used by a criminal, by making it possible for the officer to disable the criminal. At times, disabling the criminal results in the criminal's death, an unfortunate but often unavoidable result. Police officials sometimes propose that officers follow a policy of "shooting to disable" rather than "shooting to kill," but in fact such a policy is impractical in too many instances.

A handgun should not be used by a police officer (or anyone else, for that matter) to stop a fleeing suspect, to disable a suspect who is not known to be dangerous, to intimidate any person who is not a criminal subject, or for any other purpose. Warning shots should not be fired into the air or ground; when a weapon is fired, it should be for the specific purpose of protecting life from deadly force. These policies should be established, maintained, and firmly enforced by police administrators.

The .38 caliber revolver has become the most widely used handgun in police service in the United States because of its high reliability and more than adequate effectiveness. Some officers prefer an automatic weapon, because it is able to fire at a rapid rate and an ammunition clip can be reloaded much more quickly than a revolver's cylinder. However, the automatic pistol has a tendency to jam, and misfired rounds must be manually removed before another round can be fired. It is also possible to load a revolver with two or more different types of rounds (such as standard load, Magnum, and soft-nose) and select the round to be used in a given situation.[5]

The effectiveness of a handgun or rifle bullet generally is measurable in terms of its impact (the total force it exerts on the target) and its penetrating power. These two factors are only somewhat interdependent. For example, a .22 caliber bullet has considerably less impact than a .38 caliber round but may have about the same penetrating power. Likewise, a .45 caliber bullet has considerably more impact than a .38, but somewhat less penetrating power. Ammunition for a .357 Magnum has both more impact and more penetrating power; in fact, many police authorities consider the .357 Magnum to be too powerful for urban police work, since it is almost certain to be lethal.

A short (4-inch) barrel is considered preferable to a longer barrel because the holster is less cumbersome and because it is less likely that a criminal grappling with an officer at close quarters will be able to grab the barrel and pull the weapon out of the officer's hand. A longer barrel does give greater accuracy, but the difference usually is not great enough to be an important consideration.

Standardization of handguns should be an inflexible policy of the police agency. As we pointed out earlier, there might be situations in which officers would need to share ammunition, which is impossible if they carry different types of handguns. Furthermore, every officer should be trained and competent in the use of every type of weapon used by the agency. Finally, most police agencies supply the ammunition for their officers' weapons, and stocking several different types of ammunition is unnecessarily costly.[6]

Officers should be held responsible for seeing that their weapons, especially their handguns, are cleaned and maintained in perfect working order. Repairs, when needed, might be performed by an agency employee or, if none is available, at the agency's expense.

Every officer should be required to fire practice rounds from his or her handgun, and all other assigned weapons, on a regular basis and should be required to qualify on a practice range (that is, meet specific standards of marksmanship) at least every six months.

Finally, the practice of carrying a concealed second or backup weapon should be forbidden. If proper police techniques are followed, it is extremely unlikely that an officer will be disarmed or unable to use his or her regular weapon. If that unlikely event does occur, it is even less likely that the officer will have the opportunity to reach and use a concealed backup weapon. Too often, backup weapons are actually used as "throw-down guns"—put in the grasp or near the body of an unarmed suspect who has been shot, to make it appear that the suspect was armed. This despicable practice must not be tolerated.

Rifles and Shotguns

Municipal police officers rarely have a need for a high-powered, long-range rifle. However, there are situations in which the greater impact and accuracy of a large firearm might be needed, and for those situations a standard-barrel shotgun is appropriate. Patrol officers should carry a shotgun in their vehicles.

Rural police (sheriff's officers or state troopers) are more likely to need a rifle for its greater accuracy over longer distances. The type of weapon selected is a matter of weighing the various advantages and disadvantages of many different models. However, the choice should be made by the agency's administrators and standardized for the entire agency, whether the agency actually purchases the weapons or they are bought by individual officers.

Few police officers will ever have any reason to use some of the more exotic firearms such as machine guns or armor-piercing rifles. If these weapons are acquired by an agency, they should be reserved for use by special weapons teams or other officers who have the extensive training needed to make effective use of them.

Nonlethal Weapons

Handguns, shotguns, and rifles all must be classified as lethal weapons because of the high probability that their use will cause the death of the target, even if the officer's intention is merely to disable the subject.

Quite often, lethal force is neither necessary nor desirable, but some force must be used to discourage or disable the subject. For example, a mentally deranged person is as much a hazard to himself as to innocent bystanders, but there is no legal reason to kill the person. A person wanted in connection with a crime may have to be subdued by force, but there is no need or desire on the part of the police to kill the suspect. Citizens involved in a disturbance or demonstration may have to be discouraged or subdued, but lethal force usually is not justified.

In these situations, it would be extremely desirable for the police to have an effective but nonlethal weapon. Unfortunately, none of the nonlethal weapons available to the police have proven to be very effective.

There are four major types of nonlethal weapons, classified by their basic principle of operation: impact, chemical, electrical, and noxious. There are also some miscellaneous devices that do not fit into any of these categories.

The most common impact weapon is the familiar police baton (also known as the nightstick or billy club), a wooden stick usually about 18 to 24 inches in length. Most municipal police departments consider the baton a basic part of the patrol officer's equipment. In fact, the baton has very limited uses. It is properly used either to prod or to push individuals in the direction an officer wishes them to go. A baton also can be used to ward off blows from a fist or from a knife or other handheld weapon.

The baton should not be used to strike a person because the impact of a baton swung with some force is more than enough to cause serious permanent injury. Under no circumstances should a baton ever be swung at a person's head or face, or brought down on a person's back at the base of the neck; such a blow is very likely to be lethal. Many agencies have adopted the policy that a baton may not be used at all unless it is held firmly in both hands and must not be used by poking one end into a person's face or midsection. Batons filled with metal pellets or reinforcing bars are not permitted by most law enforcement agencies. Batons made of somewhat flexible rubber or plastic are permitted by some agencies, but subject to the same limitations as wooden batons.

Several types of nonlethal impact projectile weapons have been developed for police use, but none have proven to be both safe and effective. These weapons include the stun gun, which fires bags of metal pellets; the broomstick gun, which fires short wooden dowels; the ricochet gun, which fires soft plastic pellets that are supposed to be fired toward the ground at the feet of rioters; and the Blake impact gun, which fires soft metal (aluminum) or rubber balls. Each type of weapon has serious drawbacks. Most are very inaccurate, and are as likely to injure innocent bystanders as rioters. They are too inaccurate to be used against individual subjects. Despite being intended as nonlethal weapons, all are likely to cause serious injury or death even when properly used.

Probably the only reasonably effective impact weapon is the water cannon, which sprays a high-powered stream of water. The chances of causing serious injury or death are low unless the subjects struck by the water are forced off their feet or propelled into a barrier such as a plate-glass window. The primary disadvantage of the water cannon is its cost, which is quite high, and the fairly rare occasions when it is likely to be used; it is of little use against individual subjects. Any ordinary fire department pumper truck can be used as a water cannon, if the fire fighters are willing to work under direct police supervision or if police officers have been specially trained to operate the equipment. In some communities, the use of fire trucks for this purpose is offensive to many citizens, and fire fighters are reluctant to permit it because of the resentment toward them that may be generated.

Chemical nonlethal weapons consist of several types of gas that can be disseminated by cannisters, grenades, or projectiles from special guns. These weapons are best known by the term **tear gas**. The two types of chemical most widely used as tear gas are CN (alphachloroacetophenone) and CS (orthochlorobenzal malononitrile). The former is more common; it was developed by the military in World War I and has been used ever since. CS, which was developed in the late 1950s, is now considered much more effective than CN and has the particular advantage of being less likely to cause permanent eye or skin injury. CS gas is also longer lasting because the gas particles tend to cling to clothing and other rough or textured surfaces (including, in some cases, the subjects' hair). Two other types of chemical weapons, known as DM and HC, are not regarded as suitable for police use, the former because it is extremely dangerous and the latter because it is not very effective.

The method of delivering a chemical or gas may be at least as important as the type of chemical. The most widely used delivery systems are gas grenades and cannisters. The former are essentially like military incendiary grenades: The gas is contained in a small, barrel-shaped vessel sealed with a lever-type trigger. A pin is pulled to make the trigger operable; the grenade is then hurled, releasing the trigger, and a few seconds later the gas is released. The most serious problem with a gas grenade is that it can be picked up and hurled right back at the police officers.

Cannisters or cartridges are fired from a large-bore shotgun. Some cartridges are designed to explode on impact; others are designed to release a stream of gas. The explosive-type cartridge may cause serious injury and, if fired into a confined area, may start a fire. The other type of cannister, like a grenade, can be picked up and thrown back at the user.

The proper use of a gas weapon demands care and skill. Consideration must be given to the wind direction and any other condition that might affect the dispersal of the gas. As much as possible, the user should avoid letting gas drift beyond the target area, where it may injure or annoy innocent citizens. It is also quite likely that the gas will drift or be blown back into the officers' faces. Whenever gas weapons are used, all officers should wear gas masks. If the target is a building or enclosed area, gas weapons should be used with extra care, precision, and restraint. If one grenade or cannister will release enough gas to fill a room, there is no need to use two or three grenades.

Another type of chemical weapon is the aerosol spray, the most familiar of which is **Chemical Mace**. The chemical is similar in nature and in effect to CS gas; it is delivered by aiming a spray nozzle on an aerosol can and spraying the target. In principle, Chemical Mace and similar aerosol sprays should disorient and temporarily disable the subject. However, there are several difficulties. First, the spray must be aimed directly into the target's face from a distance of no more than a couple of feet. Second, individuals vary in their sensitivity to the chemical; some people are not bothered by it very much, while others may be permanently blinded by a heavy dose. Third, since it is unlikely that a subject will stand still and wait to be sprayed, an officer who produces an aerosol can may expect to be met with violent resistance—perhaps more violent than would have been exhibited otherwise. In some cases, subjects have wrestled the can away from the officer or simply deflected the spray back into the officer's face.

Nevertheless, Chemical Mace and similar aerosol sprays can be effective if used with discretion and skill. Once the subject has been sprayed and has reacted to the spray (usually by closing his or her eyes, coughing violently, and trying to cover his or her face), the officer should put the spray can away and take control of the subject by hand, applying handcuffs or other suitable restraint as necessary. Continued spraying of a disabled or unresisting subject is unnecessary and abusive. As soon as the prisoner is firmly under control, his or her face, neck, arms, hands, and other exposed skin areas should be flushed with water to dilute the spray chemical, which otherwise continues to give an unpleasant stinging sensation. It is especially important to wash the chemical out of the prisoner's eyes and nose to avoid permanent injury.[7]

Two kinds of electrical nonlethal weapons have been used by police agencies. The first of these is the electrified baton, often called a cattle prod. The device consists of a hollow baton or tube that contains electrical batteries and electrical contacts on one end. When the baton is pressed against a subject, an electric shock is transmitted. The shock is not ordinarily dangerous but it is painful. In rare cases, it can be lethal if used on a person with a weak heart or a chronic neurological condition such as epilepsy. Furthermore, it is not a very effective way to subdue a prisoner, since the painful shock is likely to make the prisoner more enraged and violent than ever.

The Taser is an ingenious device that has been invented as a nonlethal substitute for the pistol. Instead of firing bullets, the specially designed Taser handgun or rifle fires a pair of small metal barbs, not unlike fishhooks. The barbs remain connected to the gun by a pair of lightweight copper wires. When the barbs strike the target, they are supposed to catch on the subject's clothing, hair, or skin. A strong, low-amperage electrical charge is sent through the wires. The charge is strong enough to cause the subject to be paralyzed until the current is turned off.

The disadvantages of the Taser system are several. First, the gun's range is supposed to be up to 500 feet, which means that a rather strong explosive charge is needed to propel the barbs and their trailing wires. If used at closer range, the explosive charge itself could be dangerous or the barbs could be propelled at high enough velocity to penetrate the target's skin and cause serious damage. At longer ranges, more than about 25 feet, the Taser is not very accurate; at long range the barbs may not strike the target with enough impact to catch. Also, the electrical charge may have varying effects on different individuals and could be lethal in some instances.

Noxious nonlethal weapons include any of several devices that are intended to create such a nuisance that the target will become disoriented or will submit in order to end the annoyance. Some of the noxious-type weapons that have been tested include blindingly bright lights, high-intensity noises, and smoke grenades that release a gas with an obnoxious odor. None of these devices have proven to be very effective against most subjects, and all are likely to be at least as obnoxious to the user (that is, the police officers) as they are to the target subjects.

Finally, there are several miscellaneous devices that have been proposed as nonlethal weapons. Animal control authorities have used tranquilizer darts with great success to capture dangerous animals, and it has been suggested that the police use such a device against criminal subjects or rioters. Unfortunately, there is no way to estimate in advance how much tranquilizer will be needed to subdue a violent subject; too little is ineffective and too much may be lethal. The tranquilizers also are fairly slow-acting. These are not serious problems when the target is an animal, but they are great disadvantages when human targets are involved.

Several kinds of foam and liquid agents have been developed for crowd control purposes. In most cases, the idea is to make the street, sidewalk, or other surface so slippery that the crowd will be unable to stay on their feet. One product of this sort is called Instant Banana Peel. Some of these agents are quite effective but not terribly useful. If the rioters are unable to stay on their feet, the same will be true for the police officers who are trying to disperse the crowd or take criminal subjects into their control.[8]

In summary, then, all of the so-called nonlethal weapons are either not very effective, or not very useful, or if they are both effective and useful, they are not very nonlethal. Gas and aerosol weapons can be used effectively under proper conditions when used with restraint and skill. The standard police baton is an effective device for hand use as a prod or to ward off a blow. The water cannon also can be used effectively. However, the indiscriminate or careless use of any of these weapons is likely to cause serious injuries or fatalities and may create the appearance of unnecessarily brutal police actions.

POLICE SERVICE EQUIPMENT

In addition to the handgun and baton, one other item of police equipment is nearly universal in American law enforcement: the bracelet-type handcuffs. This kind of device is so familiar that little needs to be said about it, except once again to urge uniformity and standardization.

Most police officers will need to be equipped with various kinds of specialized tools for their particular assignments. Officers who may be assigned to investigate traffic accidents should have a measuring wheel or tape. The measuring wheel is especially handy because it can be used by one person, it can measure a curved or zig-zag line, and it is not limited in the length of line it can measure. A measuring tape, on the other hand, is more accurate and may be less cumbersome to store and carry.

Officers (including patrol officers in many agencies) who may be assigned to investigate reported crimes should be equipped with an assortment of evidence containers and basic gear such as a fingerprint kit, brushes, tweezers, and a handheld vacuum cleaner.[9]

Officers assigned to traffic law enforcement should be equipped with a radar speed-measuring unit. Several types of radar units are widely available; the selection of a particular unit depends mainly on the traffic patrol techniques favored by the agency. Probably the most commonly used type is the dashboard-mounted unit, which (depending on the design of the radar transmitter) may be used either in stationary or moving patrol vehicles, and which may be capable of reading the speed of traffic in either direction (that is, oncoming cars or cars approaching from the rear). The dashboard-mounted unit also is much less conspicuous than the other type of bidirectional radar, which is mounted on the side of the vehicle.

Perhaps the most versatile type of radar unit is the hand held or radar gun type. The gun can be kept out of sight until a target vehicle approaches, then aimed and triggered to give an immediate reading. This technique makes radar-detection receivers in citizens' cars almost useless, and it avoids the problem of incorrect identification of the target. However, if the radar gun is not used correctly, it will give false speed indications.

One of the most valuable types of equipment in all police work is the camera. Every patrol officer and investigator should be equipped with at least a small snapshot or instant camera for general use at traffic accident and crime scenes. More sophisticated cameras should be used for full investigations of crimes; some agencies prefer to assign photographic specialists to this duty, although any police officer might be trained to be a competent investigative photographer.

The biggest problem with all photographic equipment is that it is somewhat difficult to use and generally rather expensive. A new kind of equipment has been developed that could represent a major breakthrough. These are various types of ultracompact video tape recorders, with both the camera mechanism and the recorder in a single, handheld housing not much larger than a conventional 8-mm movie camera. The great advantage of the ultracompact video recorder is that the tape cassette requires no chemical processing; it can be removed from the camera and viewed on a standard television set. The tape cassettes are relatively inexpensive and can be reused several times. The combined camera-recorder is somewhat more expensive than a conventional still camera (generally the video equipment costs around $1000 to $1500).

All patrol vehicles should be equipped with an extensive first aid kit for immediate care of injured persons when it is impractical to wait for emergency medical personnel; and a small fire extinguisher. As a matter of good police practice, officers should not be expected to act as emergency medical technicians or fire fighters. However, they should be prepared, trained, and equipped to render any emergency assistance that may be necessary to protect lives and property until the proper personnel arrive.

The quality of service provided by a law enforcement agency depends, in the final instance, on the quality of the people employed and deployed by the agency. Well-trained and highly motivated officers do not need an elaborate arsenal of exotic, costly equipment. However, they do need a carefully conceived, standardized set of working tools. It is the responsibility of administrators at every level to see that their officers are properly equipped, whether with uniforms and equipment supplied by the agency, or with gear purchased by the individual officers. Standards must be established and maintained to ensure that all equipment is both appropriate and uniform. These responsibilities are just as important a part of the planning and budgeting process as the design of a new building or the purchase of a fleet of vehicles.

ASSISTANT CHIEF WILLIAMSON'S IN BASKET

Instructions

In this exercise, you are to assume the role of Assistant Chief Earl Williamson, chief of Administrative Services. The documents below have been selected from Chief Williamson's in basket. Read them with care. If you need more information about City or its police department, refer to the data bank in the front of the book. After you have studied the documents, complete these steps:

1. State the problem or problems these documents present to Chief Williamson.
2. List as many alternative solutions as you can.
3. Select the solution you think would be best, and give your reasons for choosing it.

CITY PD

REQUESTING SECTION	ORGANIZED CRIMES--INTELLIGENCE		
REQUESTING OFFICER Lt. Hubbard		APPROVED BY Capt. Edwards	
APPR. BUDGET R. Ullrich, Lt.	DATE 4 Jun 19--	FUND 32-002A	
APPR. CHIEF/ADMIN. SVCS.		DATE	

BUDGET CLASS	DESCRIPTION OF ITEM	QUAN.	COST EA.	TOTAL
025A	AK-16 automatic repeating rifle	2	$765.00	$ 1,530.00
027G	AK-16 ammunition, 10,000 rounds	1	2,500.00	2,500.00
	TOTAL:			$ 4,030.00

INSTRUCTIONS: On the reverse side of this form, if bids have been taken list bidders and the amount of each bid. If bids have not been taken, list vendors and state reason for not taking bids.

BID LIST

BIDDER/VENDOR	ADDRESS	AMT. OF BID
Manny Marx Rifles	327 W. Columbia Blvd., City	$ 4,030.00

NOTE: Price quoted is manufacturer's list price less 20% discount from Manny Marx. This is the best price we can get.

CERTIFICATION: I hereby certify that the prices quoted above or the bids stated above were obtained by me and are accurate.

DATE: ____27 May 19--____   OFFICER: __M. Hubbard, Lt., OC/I__

CITY PD

REQUESTING SECTION	PATROL BUREAU		
REQUESTING OFFICER M. Avery, Capt.		APPROVED BY M. Avery, Capt.	
APPR. BUDGET NOT APPROVED	DATE 2 Jun 19--	FUND NOT AVAILABLE	
APPR. CHIEF/ADMIN. SVCS.		DATE	

BUDGET CLASS	DESCRIPTION OF ITEM	QUAN.	COST EA.	TOTAL
010C	Baton, 15-in., oak, #331	6	$ 23.95	$ 143.70
010C	Baton, 18-in., walnut, #306	8	31.45	251.60
010C	Baton, 6-in., walnut w. metal insert, #25M	2	27.95	55.90
	TOTAL:			$ 451.20

INSTRUCTIONS: On the reverse side of this form, if bids have been taken list bidders and the amount of each bid. If bids have not been taken, list vendors and state reason for not taking bids.

BID LIST

PURCHASE REQUISITION NO. 42995

BIDDER/VENDOR	ADDRESS	AMT. OF BID
Redlite Police Eqpt. Co.	9215 S. Military Ave., Farwest, Calif. 90099	$ 451.20

CERTIFICATION: I hereby certify that the prices quoted above or the bids stated above were obtained by me and are accurate.

DATE: 22 May 19-- OFFICER: M. Avery, Capt., Patrol

CHIEF WILLIAMSON:
   These items are not in my budget but I think we should get them anyway. They are to replace batons that have been lost or broken over the past several months. Thanks.
   Mike Avery

CITY POLICE DEPARTMENT
Interoffice Memorandum

FROM: E. Z. Abel, Chief

TO: All Bureau Chiefs

SUBJECT: Attached memorandum DATE: 5 Jun 19--

   Please review the attached proposal from Lt. Rader. We have talked about setting up a SWAT team before but have not gotten into the details. I think Rader's ideas merit some consideration but I want to know what problems you foresee in your respective areas. Please reply by the end of the week. Thanks.

   EZA

CITY POLICE DEPARTMENT
Interoffice Memorandum

FROM:	Lt. J. Rader, OC/Vice
TO:	Chief Abel
SUBJECT:	Need for Special Weapons Team

DATE: 3 Jun 19--

SIR:

Captain Edwards suggested that I transmit this proposal directly to you. I have already discussed it with some of the other people in OC and Investigations and they generally agree. We think it is time for City PD to establish a Special Weapons Team to deal with some of the situations that are happening on the street.

Basically what we have in mind is a group of 15 or 20 men specially trained for hostage situations, terrorists, mental cases, bomb threats, kidnappings, VIP protection, riots, large-scale vice or drug raids, civil disasters, nuclear incidents (because of the presence of Wingtip AFB), and other possible events that would be beyond the abilities of Patrol and other regular units. These men would be elite troops with a minimum of 250 hours of advanced training in hand-to-hand combat (especially martial arts techniques), urban guerilla warfare, electronic countermeasures, riot control, search-and-rescue, emergency medical training, counter-terrorist tactics, and, of course, special weapons.

All members of the SWT would continue their present duties except that they would need to be released about 10 hours per week for training.

Page 2.

They would be available 24 hours a day for SWT duty. We probably would need a special "hotline" telephone system to call out the SWT.

I think we could get enough people to volunteer for SWT even if there is no budget for special pay. However, we should at least have a special SWT uniform, or special insignia for the regular uniform and maybe a special tie or lapel pin for plainclothes officers assigned to SWT. Also, of course, we will need appropriate weapons and equipment for the various kinds of tasks described above. I will prepare a budget proposal upon request.

I am aware that none of the kinds of events listed above have happened in City in the last few years. However, we did have a hostage situation several years ago, and we all remember the riots at City University about ten years ago. Considering the international situation and the rise of urban terrorism in other parts of the country, it is only a matter of time before these things happen in City, and we think that City PD ought to be prepared. As soon as you give the word, we will begin signing up volunteers.

John Rader, Lieutenant
OC/Vice

IN REVIEW

1. True or False: Police equipment should be standardized so that all officers can be trained to use it properly.

2. Which of the following is *not* an important consideration in selecting a style of uniform?
   (a) Recognizability.
   (b) Serviceability.
   (c) Standardization.
   (d) Fashionableness.
   (e) Cost.

3. True or False: Officers should not be expected to assume responsibility for cleaning and maintenance of uniforms since it is up to the agency to maintain a good appearance.

4. Appropriate police insignia might include:
   (a) A metal badge.
   (b) Shoulder patches identifying the agency.
   (c) A plastic name tag or photo ID, or both.
   (d) Patches or pins indicating rank and branch of service.
   (e) All of the above.
   (f) None of the above.

5. Bulletproof vests (body armor) are valuable because:
   (a) They provide a limited degree of protection under certain circumstances.
   (b) They protect an officer from almost any kind of weapon.
   (c) They keep officers from becoming careless.
   (d) They eliminate the need to remember and follow a lot of complicated police procedures.
   (e) They are easier to wear than most other kinds of protective devices.

6. A _____ type of body armor is certified to protect only against .22 and .38 caliber weapons.
   (a) Plastic shield
   (b) Level I
   (c) Level II
   (d) Level III
   (e) Standard

7. True or False: The proper function of a police handgun is only to disable a person who is using or threatening to use deadly force against an officer or citizen.

8. Officers should not be permitted to carry:
   (a) A backup handgun.
   (b) A rifle.
   (c) A shotgun.
   (d) An automatic pistol.
   (e) A baton.

9. Match the following nonlethal weapons with their basic principle of operation:
   (a) Aerosol spray   A. Impact
   (b) Water cannon   B. Chemical
   (c) Baton   C. Electrical
   (d) Taser   D. Noxious
   (e) Stun gun
   (f) CS gas
   (g) Cattle prod
   (h) Noise generator

10. True or False: Photography at an accident or crime scene should be entirely the responsibility of a qualified specialist.

REFERENCES

1. O. W. Wilson, *Police Planning*, 2nd ed., Springfield, Ill.: Charles C. Thomas, 1962, page 223.

2. George D. Eastman, ed., *Municipal Police Administration*, Washington, D.C.: International City Management Association, 1969, page 284.

3. *Police Body Armor*, Gaithersburg, Md.: Technology Assessment Program, International Association of Chiefs of Police, December 1978, page 11.

4. Wilson, page 222.

5. Wilson, page 221.

6. Eastman, page 285.

7. Donald T. Shanahan, *Patrol Administration*, Boston: Holbrook Press, 1975, pages 431–432.

8. Shanahan, pages 423–430.

9. Alfred R. Stone and Stuart M. DeLuca, *Investigating Crimes*, Boston: Houghton Mifflin, 1980, pages 130–152.

9 POLICE INFORMATION SYSTEMS

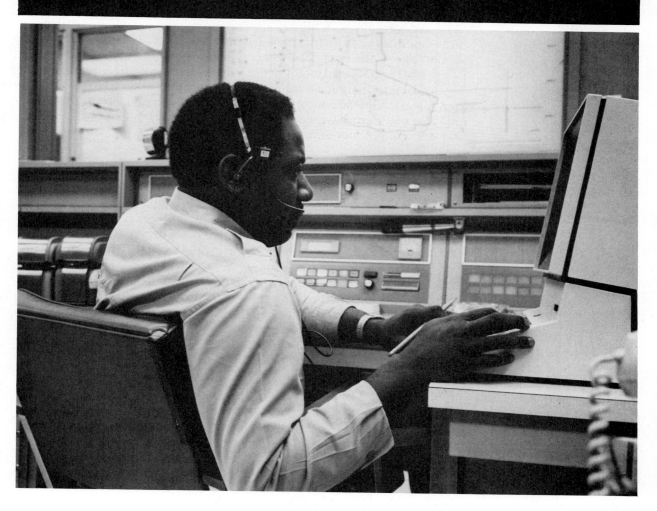

EVERY ACTION TAKEN BY A POLICE AGENCY DEPENDS ON the collection, recording, storage, retrieval, and distribution of information. In an important sense, a law enforcement agency can be regarded primarily as a large information-processing system.

Information about criminal activity comes either from direct observation by police officers or, much more often, from citizens who have observed or been victimized by the criminal. This initial *report* of a crime (or, more rarely, of a potential crime that has not yet been committed) becomes the basis for an *investigation* to learn as much as possible about the circumstances of the crime and of the criminal. The object of the investigation, of course, is to determine the identity of the criminal and to assemble enough *facts* about the crime to persuade a judge or jury that the criminal has been accurately identified. At the same time, the *identification* of the criminal is a necessary step toward his or her apprehension, the legal purpose of which is to ensure that the accused criminal will be presented before a court for trial. *Knowledge* of the criminal's whereabouts is therefore crucial.

Each of the italicized words in the preceding paragraph represents a type or form of information. In addition, there are many other types of information that concern the police: plans, beliefs, ideas, hunches, policies, and so on. For our purposes, we can define **information** very broadly, as the content and product of human minds.

THE NATURE OF INFORMATION SYSTEMS

Information held in a single person's mind is useful only to that person and only so long as he or she has access to the memory of it. People are able to expand the usefulness of information by storing it outside of their own memories (for example, in the form of drawings, paintings, or written words) or by transmitting it to other persons (for example, by speech or by distributing the drawings, paintings, or written words). These activities are two basic forms of **communication**: the transfer of information over time or space, or both.[1] All communication involves four elements: the transmitter (the source), the information (the content), the receiver, and a **medium** or method (drawing, painting, writing, or speech). In some instances, the transmitter and receiver may be the same person, as when a person makes a note and later reads it.

A useful communications system (Figure 9.1) also must include a provision for **feedback**, a means by which the receiver can respond to the information in a way that is perceptible to the transmitter.[2] For example, when you speak to another person, usually the other person will speak back to you to let you know that the **message** (a unit of information) was received.

An **information system** is a set of communications systems designed to collect, sort, store, retrieve, assemble, and distribute information for some particular purpose. In the case of a law enforcement agency, the purpose is, of course, to detect crimes, identify and apprehend the perpetrators, and bring them to justice.

Unfortunately, law enforcement agencies in the past have not always recognized the importance of establishing a sound, well-planned information system as an integrated whole. Instead, several piecemeal information systems have developed in most agencies, with a good deal of overlap and

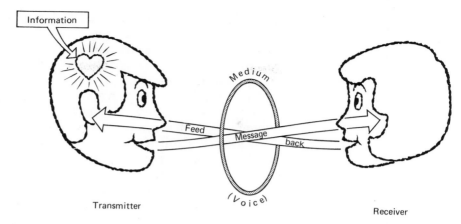

Figure 9-1 A communications system: the information, the transmitter, the medium of transmission, the message, the receiver, and feedback.

duplication, significant gaps, and resulting inefficiencies. Inefficiency is evil enough when it merely wastes money or other resources, but when the waste involves an essential resource such as information, the evil is compounded.

The first carefully designed police information systems did not even exist until the end of the nineteenth century, when the concept of scientific investigation began to take hold and, more or less at the same time, legal reforms to improve the criminal justice system placed greater demands on the police to keep accurate records. At the turn of the century, the newly formed International Association of Chiefs of Police attempted without success to establish a uniform system of recording crimes and the disposition of criminal cases. This system did not actually come about until 1930.[3] Even today, the **Uniform Crime Reporting System (UCRS)** is not completely uniform and is not used by all law enforcement agencies in the United States. As late as 1942, O. W. Wilson's suggestion that police departments consolidate their records into a single, centralized file was regarded as a radical notion (although it has come to be the conventional wisdom).[4] Previously, each officer kept his own file of criminal cases and the only centralized records were those of a primarily administrative nature.

Police communications systems have been fragmented in the past partly for lack of suitable technology. The first telegraphic call boxes were put into use by American police departments in the 1880s; they were further developed and refined over the next 40 years until they finally were replaced with telephone call boxes. The latter were first introduced about 1890 but were not widely used because they were expensive and unreliable. However, police stations did install telephones to receive calls from the public in the late 1880s.

The most significant development in police communication was the development of the mobile radio in the 1920s. Other communication technologies have been added from time to time; the old telegraphic call boxes disappeared in the 1920s but telegraphic communication, in the form of teletype, was reborn about 1930. In the late 1960s a national teletype system, dedicated specifically to law enforcement use, finally was established. At about the same time, state police agencies and the larger metropolitan police departments had begun to establish computerized information-processing systems, and these were tied together over the national teletype system.

Each of these information and communications systems developed independently of the others. Wilson and other authorities have insisted since the mid-1930s that central records bureaus and radio rooms should be at least adjacent to one another, but that still is not the case in many medium-sized and larger departments. It is usually the case in smaller departments simply because one person is employed as both radio dispatcher and records clerk. The combination of computerized data banks and the teletype network remains virtually the only case of a partially integrated, systematic application of both information processing and communications technologies to police work.

Here, we try to describe a police information system that is fully integrated. To the best of our knowledge, no such system actually exists, although some agencies have made creditable progress toward that end.

The basic elements and components of an integrated police information system are diagrammed in Figure 9.2. Messages enter the police system from several sources: the general public, other governmental agencies, and other law enforcement agencies. Police field units (patrol officers and investigators) and police staff units (administrative and technical support

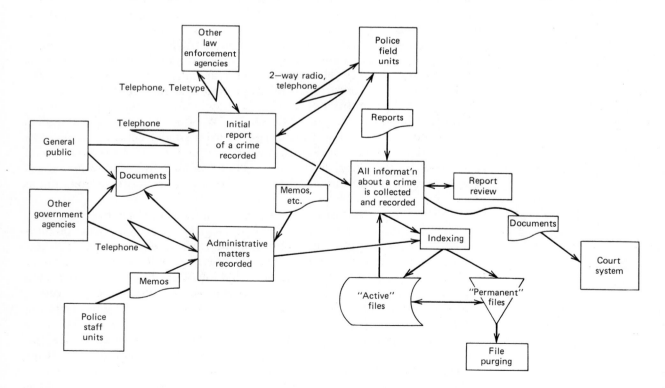

personnel) also generate messages within the system. These messages, from whatever source, are of two major types: administrative matters and information regarding crimes (and other police matters). The messages may take any of several forms, including written documents (letters, periodicals, memoranda), telephone calls, and teletype messages; communication between the police headquarters and the field units usually is in the form of radio calls or telephone calls.

Incoming messages, of whatever type, are first recorded, then acted on by delivering the message to the proper personnel. In the case of police matters, the field units' major responsibility is to gather more information, which is once again communicated back to a central point for recording (most often in the form of written reports).

After a message has been recorded, regardless of its type or form, it must be stored for future use. Some types of messages, such as reports from field units, must be reviewed to make sure that the report is complete, accurate, and in the proper form. Before any message is stored, it must be indexed: A record must be made of the message's location in the storage files. Messages then may be stored either in an active file, if it is likely to be retrieved for further use in the near future, or in a permanent file if it is uncertain that the message will be needed soon. Periodically the permanent files must be "purged," which means that obsolete and useless messages are discarded, to keep the file from becoming overloaded. Finally, some messages are transmitted from the police system to the court system; these messages are generally in the form of written documents.

In the rest of this chapter, we will see how these elements can be developed and arranged to meet the administrative and operational needs of a contemporary law enforcement agency.

MANAGEMENT INFORMATION SYSTEMS

The managers of any enterprise must receive a constant stream of information about the condition of the enterprise, the use being made of resources, and the activities of the people involved in it. This is no less true for a police agency than for a steel mill, an army, or a shoe store.

Managers are decision makers. They must have information on which to base their decisions. They must know what resources are available to them, what conditions exist in the organization and its environment, and what the results have been from the last set of decisions they made. Much of this information must come from within the organization itself.

With so much information being bandied about, there is a considerable likelihood that problems will arise. One problem is that the manager may receive inaccurate, obsolete, or otherwise useless information. Another problem is that useful information will be transmitted to the wrong person and not to the person who needs it. Similarly, a manager may receive so much information, all of it useful and necessary, that he or she has no time to digest and act on all of it. These problems exist in almost every organization. Preventing or correcting them can be accomplished only by designing an efficient management information system.

First, consider what kinds of information might be produced by a police agency or introduced into it from the outside. For now, we consider only administrative matters; later we will examine police matters.

The general public might transmit information about any number of administrative matters. A citizen might complain that the police department's budget is too high (or too low!), or that too many (or too few) patrol officers are assigned to a particular neighborhood. Publishers regularly send police departments their magazines, journals, newsletters, books, catalogs, and other literature, either at the request of someone in the agency or unsolicited. Businesses send police departments flyers, brochures, and catalogs of merchandise that the agency might wish to purchase. Correspondence between the police department and the general public might concern announcements of job openings, promotions, and other personnel actions; negotiations involving the purchase of equipment or property; announcements of newly established police policies that may affect the community; and so on. In fact, almost every aspect of a police agency might result in communications between the agency and some member of the public.

Communications between a police department and other governmental agencies usually involve a smaller range of matters. The agency may receive messages from its parent government concerning newly established policies, procedures, and administrative actions that affect all agencies. There are many communications between the police department and its parent government concerning budget, purchases, personnel, and other transactions. Police departments occasionally receive or transmit correspondence with other governmental agencies (besides the parent government) on miscellaneous matters such as sharing information about the community or about the agency's administrative practices.

Communications with other law enforcement agencies are almost entirely concerned with police matters. Police agencies also sometimes (not as often as they might) share information about administrative practices and policies.

Within the police agency itself, information about administrative matters is generated continuously by every employee. Administrators issue statements of policy, guidelines for particular procedures, and directives that describe actions to be taken by subordinates. Field units produce reports of their activities. The personnel office generates reports of all kinds of personnel actions: job vacancies, appointments, promotions, disciplinary actions, leaves and vacations, tests for promotion, training courses offered and completed, and so on. The accounting office produces reports on budget balances, expenditures, revenues received, and other financial matters. The purchasing office produces estimates of the cost of items to be bought, invitations to bid, specifications, reports of bids, purchase vouchers, and similar documents.

Not every type of administrative message must be transmitted to every administrator. The key factors in designing an effective information system are the answers to three questions: (1) *who* needs to know (2) *what*, and (3) *when* do they need to know it? Determining the correct answers to these questions is in itself an important management decision. Agency officials should decide what kinds of information are to be transmitted to each person, in what form, and by what means. Or, to look at the problem from another perspective, officials must decide what kinds of information to collect internally and where the information (whether generated internally or externally) is to be sent.

All information received from external sources should go through one central receiving point, where the nature of the message and its destination are recorded. The personnel at the central receiving point (usually the clerks in a mail room) should be given a set of policies to determine where each type of message is to be delivered. Messages that do not fit the standard policies should be reviewed by a supervisor or sent to whichever administrative unit seems most appropriate.

Similarly, information produced within the agency should be recorded and distributed according to an established procedure. Usually the person who generates a message will determine who is to receive it. However, many types of administrative messages will require essentially the same treatment, which should be determined by a standard policy. For example, messages concerning the agency's operating policies should be distributed to all field and operational units in the same form and by the same methods. Often the form of a message is as meaningful as its contents; for example, a statement of policy distributed to all field units as an "executive order" means something very different from a statement delivered to only the field supervisors in the form of an "interoffice memorandum."

Again, not all administrative messages should be delivered to all administrative personnel. The reason is not to limit the amount of information available to administrators, but instead to avoid burying them in a mass of unnecessary information. Within reason, all administrative information should be available to anyone who has an interest in seeing it. Some kinds of information, such as records of disciplinary actions against personnel, should be restricted in the interests of individual privacy and security, but those restrictions should be very few. State and federal laws regard most police administrative records as **public records** that must be made available to any interested citizen. It would be bizarre if an agency prohibited its own employees from examining records that must be shown to anyone who walks in off the street.

The form of nearly all administrative records is the written or printed document. In the not-so-distant future, much of this paperwork will be replaced by computerized data bases and individual display terminals, but for the present most law enforcement agencies rely on the medium of the written word for the majority of administrative communications.

The next most important form of administrative communications is the telephone message. Unfortunately, since these communications are almost never recorded, the content is lost to everyone except the parties to the conversation. Very few police agencies adhere to the sensible practice of maintaining detailed telephone logs. Telephone logs need not be elaborate or complicated. A standard form may be used, permitting several conversations to be recorded on a single sheet. Only the most basic information needs to be recorded: who was called, by whom, the date and time of the call, and the substance of the matters discussed. Each employee should keep his or her own log; completed logs for each day, week, or other appropriate period should be filed in a central place. The purpose of maintaining telephone logs is not to check up on employees, but simply to ensure that important information is not lost.

POLICE SERVICE INFORMATION SYSTEMS

The management information systems needed by a police agency are not particularly different from those needed by any other governmental agency. However, a law enforcement agency has an additional set of information needs: those that concern police matters.

Police service information systems must serve a number of different, though related, purposes. First, records of police activities are needed by administrators so that they can make appropriate management decisions. Administrative officials must decide how many personnel are needed for each of the various police tasks and functions; this information, of course, provides the basis for planning and budgeting. Administrators also need to know the circumstances and outcomes of police activities so that appropriate policies and procedures can be devised.

Second, police activities are subject to a broad range of legal restrictions and controls. Police officers, in the exercise of their official duties, may pose a threat to the constitutional rights and privileges of citizens. In addition, citizens who are involved in disputes with one another may need to know something about actions taken by the police; for example, a driver involved in an automobile accident might decide to sue the other driver, and the official police report of the accident might supply important evidence for the civil suit. In short, records of police activities often have important legal implications, aside from the basic function of helping to control crime.

Finally, records of police activities are indispensable to the basic police role. From the time that the police first become aware that a crime has been committed until the accused perpetrator is turned over to the courts, and sometimes beyond, every action of the police depends largely on the record of what has been done before. A complete record of the police activities in identifying and apprehending an accused criminal is necessary to secure a conviction in a criminal trial. According to some authorities, the difference between successful and unsuccessful prosecution of a suspect often can be traced to the quality of the police reports submitted to the prosecutors.[5]

Each type of police activity or function may require its own information system. For example, if a police agency is required to issue licenses to taxicab drivers, liquor dealers, operators of steam boilers, ambulance services, and so on, separate records must be kept for each type of license issuance. The same is true for noncriminal police services such as inspecting boilers, escorting funeral processions, and operating an emergency medical service. However, we assume that the record-keeping requirements for these non-law-enforcement activities are relatively modest, straightforward, and completely separate from crime-related police activities.

The Case Report

All crime-related records begin with the **case report** (sometimes called the incident report or complaint report), the first record that a crime has been, or may have been, committed. Every official action of the police department (other than the non-law-enforcement services already discussed) should be recorded on a standard case report form, even if it does not clearly involve criminal activity; for example, traffic accident investigations, runaway child cases, search and rescue cases, and other noncriminal matters. The case report should be initiated by whichever employee of the agency, whether police officer or civilian telephone operator, first becomes aware of a situation that requires a police response. Each case report should bear a unique serial number.

If serial numbers are issued in chronological sequence from some central control point, it is fairly simple to keep track of the case reports and ensure that none are missing. The serial number should be issued at the moment the case report is initiated; this helps to determine the order in which complaints and requests for service were received. When officers in the field initiate a case based on their own observation, they must immediately report (by radio or telephone) the actions they have taken, and the dispatcher or telephone operator should immediately initiate a case report and assign it a serial number.

All complaints and cases should be recorded on standard forms. Larger agencies often use a series of different forms for each type of criminal and noncriminal case; there may be separate forms for traffic accidents, traffic violations, homicides, burglaries, bad checks and documents, robberies, missing persons, and so on. Each form can be designed to contain exactly the information that is needed for follow-up police work. If a case involves two or more different types of crimes (for example, a burglary and homicide), both forms should be used but one should be regarded as the master report and only one serial number should be assigned.

Medium-sized and smaller agencies have less need for a multitude of report forms. A single form can be used for all crimes against property, another for crimes against persons, a third for traffic accidents and violations, and a fourth for miscellaneous matters. The use of multipurpose forms not only eliminates the problem of deciding which form to use, but reduces the cost of maintaining an adequate supply of all the forms.

All case reports should be filed in one place, in strict serial-number order. All other reports and documents relating to each case should be filed with the original case report and should bear the same serial number.

The complete case report usually is written by the police officer who is assigned to investigate an incident. This assignment is made by the dispatcher (or telephone operator) or by a supervising official, when the case is not initiated by the police officer in the field. Since the majority of cases are initiated as the result of a complaint received, usually by telephone, in the communications center, a record of the telephone operators' and dispatchers' actions must be kept. The record usually is in the form of a **complaint card** or *dispatch card*, which summarizes the information received from the complainant and indicates when the complaint was received, when an officer was assigned to investigate, and (in brief) what the officer found. The complaint or dispatch card also should bear the case's serial number.[6]

At one time, the common practice in police agencies was to record complaints (whether received by telephone or otherwise) in a *log book* or *police blotter* kept on the front desk of the police station. This procedure simplifies the issuance of serial numbers, but has little else to recommend it. A few small police departments still follow this traditional practice, but nearly all agencies have adopted a card system instead.

Other Police Service Records

Not all police service records are related to specific cases. In many agencies, officers are encouraged to question suspicious persons they encounter on the street and to complete a **field interview report** (often a single card). These reports are filed separately from case reports. Evidence and property inventories (see Chapter 10) also should be kept separately, although a copy should be filed with each case to which the evidence or property pertains. The same is true for arrest records.

Personal Identification Files

Most police agencies also keep extensive files on individual criminals, suspected criminals, suspicious persons who are not known to be active criminals, and persons whose occupations, place of residence, personal habits, or whatever suggest that they might have some knowledge of criminal activities. Both the quantity and quality of these records vary from one agency to another; some of the largest files are almost worthless because the records they contain are incomplete, filled with inaccuracies, and stuffed with irrelevant trivia. However, a well-managed personal identifications file can be immensely valuable to investigators. The file usually contains the types of records indicated below.

Arrest Reports. Duplicate copies of arrest reports should be maintained, apart from case reports, usually by type of crime. These reports are permanently filed after the arrested person has been either convicted or acquitted in court; until that time, arrest reports should be kept in an active file of persons currently under arrest (whether the person is actually in jail or released on bail).

Modus Operandi Records. These records consist of descriptions of the methods of operation used by known criminals. They are usually filed by type of crime.

Vehicle File. A record should be kept of every vehicle that is in any way involved in criminal activity: vehicles owned or used by known criminals, stolen vehicles, and so on.

Accident Reports. Both those accidents that are actually investigated by the police and those that are reported by the individuals involved in them, but not investigated, should be recorded in a central file.

Fingerprint Files. Nearly all police agencies maintain a file of the fingerprints of arrested persons and sometimes of other persons who are not known criminals but whose prints are available to the police. In many communities, taxicab drivers, liquor dealers, and citizens engaged in other lawful occupations are required to be fingerprinted by the police before they are issued a license. The value of such noncriminal fingerprint files is very much open to debate, but the fact is that most police agencies maintain these files on the chance that an unknown set of prints might someday happen to match those of someone in the file.

Photograph Files. Most police agencies also maintain files of photographs of arrested persons, other known or suspected criminals, and various noncriminal citizens such as license applicants.

Current Wants and Warrants File. This file contains the record of every person wanted by the police in connection with a crime (either as a suspect or as a material witness), of persons for whom arrest warrants have been issued by a court, and of vehicles sought by the police (either because they are stolen or because they are thought to have been used in a crime). Only current, outstanding warrants should be kept in an active file. Once the person or vehicle has been found, or there is reason to think that the person or vehicle is no longer wanted, the record should be removed and placed in a permanent file (such as the case report, if that is appropriate).

Indexing

Earlier we said that records in a police information system must be indexed, to create a record of the original record's location in the files. Otherwise, finding the original record when it is needed may involve a time-consuming and possibly futile search.

The index files may contain nothing more than 3 × 5-inch index cards. One set of cards should contain the name of every person who comes to the attention of the police: suspected and known criminals, victims, witnesses, complainants, persons interviewed in the field, and so on. A second set of cards should be made for every location involved in a police matter: crime scenes, residences and known hangouts of suspected and known criminals, traffic accident sites, and so forth. A third set should contain descriptions of vehicles involved in police matters.

Each index card should contain *one* name, location, or vehicle description and a reference to the case report or other complete record to which the card is related. A new card should be made for each entry. Name cards should be filed alphabetically by last name; vehicle cards should be filed either by license number or, in states that issue a new license each year, by the manufacturer's vehicle identification number (VIN) or the state-issued title number. The card also should contain the make, model, original color, and physical description of the vehicle. Location cards should be filed in the same order that addresses are listed in the postal ZIP code directory: named buildings in alphabetical order, followed by named streets in alphabetical order (with addresses on the same street in numerical order), followed by numbered streets. The names of businesses may be filed in alphabetical order and cross-indexed to the street address.

A good, well-maintained indexing system is one of the most crucial elements of an effective police information system. Unfortunately, it is also one of the elements most often overlooked or slighted by smaller agencies whose personnel are too busy to take the time to make index cards.

Summaries and Bulletins

Most police agencies that have 25 or more employees compile and distribute a daily bulletin that contains a summary of the previous day's police activities. Smaller agencies often find that a weekly bulletin is sufficient. The bulletin keeps everyone informed of important events and of crime trends and provides a record for administrative and other purposes of the level of police activities.

The bulletin should be compiled and duplicated in time to distribute it to the first shift as it comes on duty each morning, usually between 6:00 and 8:00 AM. Copies should be distributed to all officers at each shift's roll call and should be placed on the desk of all personnel who work standard office hours.

The contents of the bulletin may vary from one agency to another, but certain items should always be included; they are:

- A list and brief description of all wanted persons, with an indication of whether a warrant has been issued.
- A list and description of all wanted vehicles.
- A summary of the previous day's (or week's) police activities: complaints received, requests for service, calls handled, reports filed by type of crime, arrests or other clearances (dispositions of cases) by type of case, and so on.

The bulletin also might contain some or all of the following items:

- A brief analysis of current crime trends; what types of crimes are increasing in frequency, where particular types of crimes are occurring, and so on.
- A description of significant unsolved crimes, wanted persons, or other matters that deserve special attention.
- Announcements of new administrative policies, guidelines, directives, and so on.
- Announcements of personnel actions of general interest such as promotions, transfers, new appointments, and retirements.

The bulletin is not the place for personal messages or news of social events such as the Police League softball schedule. These matters are more appropriately handled in a separate employee newsletter or by posting on bulletin boards. The bulletin should be treated as an official record.

The daily or weekly bulletin also serves as the source for a monthly compilation of statistical information about police activities and crime trends. For that reason, the crime information in the bulletin should be arranged according to the Uniform Crime Reporting System administered by the Federal Bureau of Investigation. The monthly summaries, prepared from the daily or weekly bulletins, serve in turn as the source for quarterly, semiannual, and annual summary reports that are used for administrative purposes such as planning and budgeting.

The Uniform Crime Reporting System was established in 1909 by the International Association of Chiefs of Police (IACP), but was not widely used until the early 1930s when the FBI agreed to administer it and to organize its own files according to the UCR categories. Since then, the FBI has received regular reports from some 15,000 U.S. agencies, all on a voluntary basis. These reports are compiled, added to the FBI's own records, and published by the Department of Justice each year.[7]

The Uniform Crime Reports (UCRs) are often criticized, and indeed there may be much about them to question. However, they are also the only statistics maintained on a nationwide, continuous, and reasonably uniform basis. They may not be the best statistics possible, but they are the best ones available—provided that local agencies understand that the UCRs are something of a "rubber yardstick." All agencies should submit reports on a regular basis, following the guidelines developed by the FBI and IACP committee that monitors the UCRs. The more agencies that submit reports in a standardized manner, the more likely that the overall statistics will reflect at least the general pattern of criminal and police activity across the nation.

INFORMATION AND COMMUNICATIONS TECHNOLOGIES

Enormous strides have been made in information and communications technologies during the present century, yet law enforcement agencies have been even slower than most governmental bureaucracies in adopting the newest advances. New technologies are often costly, of course, but the main reason for the reluctance of police administrators to improve their information systems seems to be not a lack of funds but a lack of understanding about how new technologies can be applied to police work.

The information and communications technologies most widely used by the police are writing (including printing), photography, the telephone, and the radio (more properly called the radiotelephone). The teletype is also used to some extent by many police agencies, although not always as well as it could be. Most of the larger police agencies have installed computers in the past 20 years, although again they are not always used very well.

Writing

Writing on paper is by far the most prevalent of all communications technologies. Paper documents have the great advantage that they are easy and inexpensive to create, duplicate, distribute, store, and retrieve—provided that the persons using them are literate. Since most adult Americans are reasonably literate, this is not a serious barrier.

The greatest disadvantage to paper documents is their relatively low **packing density**: the volume of information that can be recorded in a given amount of space. The use of standardized forms and codes helps to increase the packing density, but paper documents still tend to be bulky and awkward to store. Furthermore, writing involves the use of "natural" language; it is a means of recording the words that evolve from the spoken language. Language is not always precise. Words may have different meanings, and even numbers (mathematical language) can be used inaccurately. Both writing and reading are fairly time-consuming activities. Most adult Americans are literate, but the ability to use language well, either in writing or in reading, varies considerably from one person to the next. Finally, paper documents must be stored with considerable care to avoid their loss or destruction.

Photography

Photography is used by most police agencies to record the conditions that are found at crime and accident scenes and sometimes to record police activities (for example, to record the procedures used by the police to control a civil disturbance).

The great advantage of photography is that quite a bit of information can be stored in a relatively small space; compared to writing, photography has a much higher packing density. Furthermore, since it happens that humans rely on their visual sense much more than on their other senses, and photography records visual information in much the same way that it would appear to a person actually present at the time a photograph was made, it is generally assumed that photographs represent an accurate account of a scene.

The principal disadvantages of photography are that the equipment is relatively expensive and requires a degree of skill to operate it properly. Some police agencies insist that only specially trained personnel should be given the responsibility for making crime-scene photographs, where skill in using the equipment is especially important. In other agencies, all officers who have crime-investigating duties are given some training in photography, since even poorly made photographs made as early in the investigative process as possible are much better than either no photographs at all or photographs made at a later time when a specialist happens to be available.

Finally, photographs, like written documents, can be inaccurate or misleading. Still photographs represent an event at an instant of time, and the activities shown in the photograph may be misinterpreted if the viewer does not know what went before or after. Since a photograph shows only a two-dimensional view of a three-dimensional scene or event, information about the relative positions of objects in the scene also may be misrepresented. These problems can be partially overcome by the skill of the photographer or by making a series of photographs at different instants in a sequence of events, or at different angles in a scene.

Motion picture photography, by its nature, represents a sequence of events more accurately, since most or all of the sequence can be shown. However, it is still possible to represent an event in a misleading way, either by the choice of angles at which the scene is recorded or by stopping and starting the camera selectively. It is worth noting that most of the special effects in television and theatrical motion pictures are obtained in just this way, to mislead the viewer (for dramatic or creative reasons). For example, a sequence in which a car speeds down a street, squeals around a corner, hurdles over another car, crashes through a solid brick wall, and rolls over several times—after which the driver emerges without a scratch—may actually consist of dozens of short sequences in which several different cars, each specially prepared for its part, were used; the camera may have been operated at a slow speed (to make the car appear to be traveling faster than it was), and special ramps and other devices may have been used. Such a scene may actually have required three or four cars to be totally destroyed, yet the viewer sees only the intact car in the final scene.

Telephones

The minimum equipment for police communications consists of a one-line telephone and a single-channel radiotelephone. When the telephone operator receives a request for police service, the information is then retransmitted orally over the radiotelephone to the nearest available field officer. The telephone operator (or the dispatcher) and the field officer also may exchange additional information over the radio.

The principal advantage of the telephone is that it is readily accessible to almost everyone. In the United States, approximately 99 percent of all homes and businesses contain at least one telephone, and the nationwide telephone system permits almost anyone to place a call within a few seconds from any one telephone to any other. Furthermore, a great deal of information can be conveyed rapidly by means of a telephone conversation.

However, the telephone system is not without some disadvantages. Telephones are used almost exclusively for oral communication, and the spoken word is even more likely to be misunderstood or misinterpreted than the written word (although persons engaged in a telephone conversation can speak back and forth repeatedly until both parties are certain that the correct information has been conveyed). This problem is made somewhat worse by the relatively poor quality of the sound signals carried by the telephone system and by the interference that sometimes affects telephone circuits. Furthermore, the person receiving a telephone call usually has no means of determining the true source of the call; people sometimes intentionally use the telephone to misrepresent their identity or location or to convey false information (such as false alarms). Finally, the telephone technology used in the United States generally permits only a limited number of telephone calls to be received at one time over a particular set of equipment; thus, the equipment may be busy with one set of calls while another, possibly more urgent, call is blocked.

It is highly desirable, in all but the very smallest police agencies (those with fewer than five employees), to have separate telephone lines for emergency and administrative calls. Telephone switchboards are available that permit the administrative lines to be connected to different internal lines (stations, as they are called by telephone engineers, or what most people call extensions). Emergency calls should always be terminated at the switchboard.[8]

Some of the most elaborate police telephone systems are the **911 systems**. American (and some foreign) telephone companies have agreed to use the numbers, 911, exclusively for emergency calls, and special equipment has been designed for 911 systems. That number is published as the sole number for all kinds of emergency services: police, fire department, ambulance service, and so on. At a 911 Center, the operators first determine what kind of emergency service is needed by each caller; calls for the fire department or ambulance service may either be switched to direct lines to those agencies, or the operators may handle all incoming calls in the same manner (usually by initiating a dispatch card) and route the information to the appropriate agency. Many 911 systems serve a countywide area that may contain several law enforcement and other emergency service agencies, in which case the 911 operator also must determine which law enforcement agency is to be notified for each call.

Obviously, a 911 system demands a high degree of cooperation among all the participating agencies, whether the 911 Center operators actually dispatch all calls or simply transfer calls to the various agencies. In some cases, considerable cost savings can be achieved by using the 911 Center as a centralized point for both receiving calls and dispatching. However, a 911 system can be the source of unimaginable confusion if it is not managed properly.

Some of the most sophisticated 911 systems are able to offer a **calling number display** feature. This means that the telephone number from which each call is being placed is displayed on the operator's console. False reports may be detected if the operator asks for the caller's number and the number given is different from the number displayed. Also, if the call is interrupted, the operator may be able to trace the location from which the call came, by referring to a cross-index of telephone numbers. It is even possible for a computerized cross-index to be built into the telephone equipment.

It is not possible, in theory or in practice, to build a telephone system that is capable of handling any number of calls that might be received. Telephone systems are designed to have enough incoming lines so that ordinarily no caller will receive a busy signal during "normal peak periods." A normal peak period is the time of day that is busiest under ordinary circumstances. However, there are bound to be times when all incoming lines are jammed such as during a period of severe weather or a communitywide disaster. Some telephone switchboards can be designed to include an overload feature that automatically switches emergency calls to other lines (the agency's administrative lines or even lines to another agency) when all emergency lines are jammed. The newer switchboards also are capable of "queueing" (which is pronounced like "cueing") incoming calls, so that when all lines are being used, other callers are not given a busy signal but are made to wait until the next nonbusy line is available.[9] Even with these protective devices, it is a good idea for the police telephone system to have at least one completely separate line, with an unpublished number, that can be used for urgent outgoing calls when all the other lines are busy. The number for the separate line also might be given to selected police officials and other authorized persons to use for urgent incoming calls. Dedicated lines (popularly known as hotlines) also should be established among the various public safety and emergency service agencies.

Telephone engineers are the best source of information about the design of a suitable police telephone system. The engineers can conduct studies of telephone usage to determine the most efficient number of lines for normal peak periods and whether special overload protection devices are appropriate. The local telephone service company is not the only source of telephone equipment; switchboards and other equipment, some of it extremely sophisticated, can be purchased from many different manufacturers and dealers.

Radiotelephones

Radio systems designed specifically for police service are offered by a number of manufacturers. These radio systems vary in two important ways: the frequency bandwidth (the portion of the radio frequency spectrum) at which they operate and the number of channels available. There are other differences among the various police radio systems, including a variety of special features, but bandwidth and channel capacity are the most basic.

The Federal Communications Commission (FCC) decides what uses can be made of various parts of the radio frequency spectrum in the United

States and allocates frequency bandwidths to different uses. At present, three bandwidths are available for general police use:

Low band	37 to 46 megahertz (MHz)
High band	154.6 to 159.2 MHz
Ultrahigh frequency (UHF) band	453 to 459 MHz

The different bandwidths have very different operating characteristics. A low-band system requires the least electrical power to transmit a signal over a given area, but it is also the most subject to interference from other radio systems and natural phenomena. A UHF system requires much more power to cover the same area, but the signals tend to penetrate most obstacles; however, UHF signals are sometimes absorbed or reflected by very heavy rainfall, fog, or snow. One advantage of a UHF system is that the mobile antennas are very short, generally only a foot long, and therefore not so noticeable on unmarked police vehicles.[10]

A police radio system consists of three or four major components: the base station, the mobile units, portable units, and any repeaters or relay transmitters that are used.

The base station ordinarily should be located at the agency's communications center, usually in its headquarters facility. In some large metropolitan areas, each district or precinct has its own base station and, in effect, its own independent radio system. Most authorities discourage this practice since it may lead to confusion among the agency's personnel. A better system is to establish a single dispatching center through which all communications must flow. In any case, there should be a backup base station at a different location, in case the principal base station is unavailable because of some catastrophe. Both the main base station and the backup base should be equipped with emergency power batteries and generators (what communications engineers call an "uninterruptible power supply").

The mobile radios used in police vehicles are properly called *transceivers*, since they are combined transmitters and receivers. In some radio systems, the mobile units receive on one frequency and transmit on another. However, this kind of system prevents the mobile personnel from hearing one another's transmissions. A better system (technically called a full duplex system) uses a single frequency for both transmitting and receiving, although generally a transceiver is not able to do both at the same time.

It is very desirable for every mobile unit to be able to receive and transmit over all radio channels used by the agency. When a large agency has a number of channels for different purposes, mobile units that are limited to only a few channels are considerably less expensive; however, the problems of coordinating personnel from several different districts or elements of the agency are compounded when they are not able to communicate with one another over a common channel.

All field personnel, and most headquarters personnel, should be equipped with portable transceivers (popularly called walkie-talkies). Again, it is very desirable for all portable transceivers to be able to operate on every channel used by the agency.

Repeaters, or relay transmitters, are used when it is impractical or impossible for a single central transmitter to cover the agency's entire geographic territory. Usually the central transmitter is located at or near the highest point in town (which may be some distance from the central base station, with either a separate radio link or a wire connection between the two). However, it is very desirable for the central transmitter to be close to the geographic center of the area to be served. In that location, the transmitter may be unable to reach mobile units in remote parts of the community. Anywhere from one to half a dozen repeaters might be needed to ensure that communications are uninterrupted no matter where the mobile units happen to be.

A police radio system may require any number of radio channels. A very small agency might be able to share one channel with other nearby agencies, if the total radio traffic for all of them is quite low. Using a shared frequency encourages the various agencies to work cooperatively and can mean considerable cost savings if a single dispatching center and central transmitter are used by all.

As the number of officers in the field increases, so does the volume of radio traffic. It does not take long for a single-channel system to become overloaded. There is no general rule on the number of field units that can be accommodated by a single-channel system, since that depends also on the number of routine messages generated by each unit and on how quickly the dispatcher is able to dispose of each exchange of messages. Since adding more channels to a radio system is costly (and often requires replacing the entire system), the first step when a channel is approaching its traffic-handling capacity is to improve the efficiency of communications by using codes for routine messages, such as the well-known **ten-codes**, and by standardizing the form of many messages. Compare, for example, these two exchanges between a dispatcher and a patrol unit:

Example 1

Dispatcher: *Unit 34?*
Patrol: *This is Unit 34, go ahead, Central.*
Dispatcher: *Unit 34, what is your present location?*
Patrol: *Uh, let's see, I'm at Fifth and Main right now.*
Dispatcher: *Unit 34, I've got a call from a lady about a prowler, at 111 West Avenue. Check it out for me, would you?*
Patrol: *Roger, that was 111 West Avenue. Unit 34 out.*

Example 2

Dispatcher: *34, 10—20 ("Location").*
Patrol: *34, 500 Main.*
Dispatcher: *34, see the lady, prowler, 111 West Avenue.*
Patrol: *34, 111 West Avenue, 10—4 ("Acknowledged").*

In the first example, the dispatcher and the patrol unit are engaged in a natural conversation that requires several exchanges of radio messages over a period of about 20 seconds. In the second example, the form of the messages has been standardized (the dispatcher always begins with the unit number of the unit being called, and the patrol unit always begins each transmission with the unit number) and codes are used (such as the ten-codes for location and acknowledgment) to make each message as brief as possible; the same information is conveyed in about 10 seconds. If every exchange could be cut in half in this manner, the same radio channel could be used for twice as many calls. In practice, improving the efficiency of radio communications by this large a margin is difficult to achieve, but savings of 25 percent and more are not unusual.

A single dispatcher should be able to handle all communications with about 25 patrol units or as many as 50 nonpatrol units (investigators, special units, and administrators). Thus, an agency with 100 officers on duty at one time, half of whom are on patrol, would need a minimum of three channels.

However, the volume of radio traffic is not the only consideration. If the patrol units are dispersed over a relatively large geographical area and if it is fairly common for police activity to be taking place simultaneously at several different locations, more channels may be needed to avoid confusion and to reduce the complexity of the dispatcher's job.[11] (A few agencies have attempted to use two or more dispatchers on each channel, but this practice generally adds to the confusion.)

The standard practice in most police agencies is to assign channels to different geographic areas, usually the patrol districts. At least one channel should be set aside for use by investigators, administrators, supervisors, and other nonpatrol units; this channel also might be used by patrol officers who are engaged in lengthy conversations with the dispatcher or with one another (for example, during a search operation). Also, it is a common practice in many metropolitan areas to reserve one channel for use by all law enforcement and other public safety agencies in the area.

Thus a police department might require eight or more radio channels; for example:

Channel 1	Patrol district A
Channel 2	Patrol district B
Channel 3	Patrol districts C and D
Channel 4	Patrol district E
Channel 5	Patrol supervisors
Channel 6	Investigators and administrative
Channel 7	Tactical and special units
Channel 8	Metro (all public safety agencies)

Ordinarily, the FCC will grant a license to a police agency for any number of radio channels the agency requires. However, the number of channels in each bandwidth is limited. If nearby agencies are assigned the same channels, they will interfere with one another; interference is especially a problem on the low-band channels. The more channels an agency needs, the more difficult it may be to find sufficient bandwidth to accommodate them. Also, the greater the channel capacity of a radio system, the more expensive the equipment will be. Thus it is desirable not to overdesign the radio system by building in more channel capacity than is really needed.

It is not necessary for all channels to be in the same band. Patrol channels might be in the low band, while administrative and special-unit channels are on UHF. Each type of communication is served by a radio system that is particularly suited to its needs (for example, since communications with patrol units may require more geographic range than communications with administrative and special units, low band may be more economical). At the same time, unauthorized persons listening to the police radio often are unaware of anything but the patrol channels, which increases the security of the administrative and special-unit channels. Of course, the disadvantage in this arrangement is that operating two or more separate radio systems may be much more expensive than operating one system, even when the total number of channels remains the same. Also, unless fairly expensive equipment is used, most mobile and portable units are limited to a single bandwidth; the patrol units would not have access to the administrative and special-unit channels, and vice versa.

All police telephone and radio systems should be connected to a recording system. Tape recording systems designed specifically for this purpose are available from several manufacturers; some have a number of separate tracks for each telephone line and radio channel. Even a small agency can afford to install an ordinary tape recorder to its telephone line and a second one to its radio. The tapes should be kept for at least one week, and longer if any questions arise about any of the conversations that have been recorded.[12]

The selection of telephone and radio equipment is crucial to the development of a sound, efficient police communications system. Thanks to the revolution in communications technology that has taken place in the past 20 years, an incredible variety of equipment is available. This does not make the task of choosing the best, most appropriate system any easier. Some help is available from the Technology Assessment Program of the International Association of Chiefs of Police, which regularly evaluates radio equipment and publishes its findings.[13] In addition, there are independent communications consultants who, for a fee, will research the available technology and design a system for a specific situation. Consultants' services are not cheap, but they might save more than they cost in the long run, if they succeed in designing a system that meets the police agency's immediate needs, allows for future expansion, and promotes efficient police operations.

Teletype

There are two automated telegraph systems in the United States, both similar in operation and both owned by the Western Union Corporation. Both use typewriter-like terminals to transmit and receive messages, and both are switched networks; that is, the user dials the address of the intended receiver, in much the same way as a telephone is dialed, and the message is sent only to that address. Both systems are used by law enforcement agencies in the United States; in fact, some agencies use both systems, with two terminals side by side in the communications center. The TWX system (formerly owned by American Telephone and Telegraph, but bought by Western Union in the early 1970s) offers higher transmission speed, but it is a "closed" network; it does not connect to other teletype systems. The telex system operates at a lower transmission speed, but it is a worldwide system; any telex terminal can be connected to any other, almost anywhere in the world, through the facilities of Western Union and several international communications companies.[14]

The teletype system of most interest to law enforcement agencies is the **National Law Enforcement Telecommunications System (NLETS)**, a telex network operated by the U.S. Department of Justice. It connects all state and federal law enforcement agencies (including some military agencies). Each participating state police agency also serves as the "gateway" to NLETS for local law enforcement agencies. This means that an NLETS terminal in a municipal police department is connected to the NLETS center at the state police headquarters (usually in the state capital); any messages to or from agencies in other states, or federal agencies, pass through the state center.

NLETS can be used simply to exchange messages between police agencies. For example, a local police department may use the system to distribute information about a fugitive suspect or to inquire about whether the police in another city have information concerning certain stolen property. In addition, the NLETS center in most states and the NLETS facilities in several federal agencies provide access to computer data bases of law enforcement information. Personal identification information, criminal histories, reports of wanted persons and vehicles, and vast amounts of similar law enforcement information can be obtained through the NLETS network.

Computers

Before about 1970, computers were so expensive and difficult to operate that only the very largest police agencies could even consider having one. Since then, the size and cost of the equipment has declined steadily at the same time that its capabilities and ease of use have advanced. Now there are computer systems readily available in almost any size and at almost any price.

Most state and federal agencies operate large **mainframe computer** systems and maintain enormous files of information on criminal histories, personal identifications, traffic accidents, and so on. Very few local law enforcement agencies need or could afford such large systems. Municipal police agencies are more likely to need a small system, either a **minicomputer** or a **microcomputer**. A minicomputer consists of a central processing unit (CPU), a control unit (usually a separate console), and several peripheral devices such as magnetic disk drives, magnetic tape drives, and possibly a punched-card or punched-tape reader. Microcomputers, more commonly called personal computers, combine a CPU, control unit, limited permanent and temporary memories, and a terminal for both entering and displaying information, all in one or two pieces of desk-top equipment. (See Figure 9.3.) Most microcomputers are also designed to be used with such peripheral devices as tape recorders and small disk drives (to store programs and data) and printers.

Large, mainframe computer systems usually are designed to carry on several different kinds of operations simultaneously. Through the technique of time-sharing, several different users may be operating entirely different programs at once. Actually, the computer switches from one program or operation to another, but the switching takes place so rapidly that, as far as the users are concerned, everything is happening at the same time.

Some minicomputer systems also are capable of serving several users at the same time, although usually they must all be using the same program. Time-sharing on some minicomputer systems is also possible.

Figure 9-3 A microcomputer. Even small personal computers like this one can be a valuable part of a police agency's information system. (Photo courtesy Tandy Corporation.)

Most microcomputer systems are not capable of time-sharing; in fact, most are designed strictly for use by one person at a time. A few of the more complex microcomputers permit several users to operate one program simultaneously.

The most expensive part of any computer system is its memory. The permanent memory contains the incredibly detailed instructions that cause particular circuits within the equipment to be turned on or off at the correct time, according to the instructions contained in an operating program. Usually the permanent memory is limited; it is just large enough to contain the operating program. Most computers also contain a built-in **random-access memory (RAM)** that is used to store programs and data temporarily. The size of the random-access memory varies according to the system's design; a small personal computer may have only enough RAM for about 4000 bits of data (roughly 800 characters, or perhaps a couple of hundred words). A large mainframe computer might have RAM capacity of several million bits. A computer's RAM capacity is important because it largely determines the complexity of the programs it is capable of using and the volume of data it is able to process at one time.

Because RAM capacity is limited in every computer system, and because it is so expensive, it does not make sense to store programs and data permanently in RAM. Instead, the programs and data are kept separately, on punched cards or tape, magnetic tape, or on magnetic disks. Two types of magnetic disks are used: "hard" disks, usually metal, and "floppy" disks. Hard disks are permanently mounted (either individually or in "stacks" of two or more) in separate cabinets. Each disk typically can hold a couple of million bits of data. Floppy disks consist of a magnetic coating on a thin sheet of acetate contained in a paper envelope; the disk is inserted into a disk drive. A single floppy disk may contain anywhere from a few thousand to about a million bits of data.

This is not the place to go into the details of computer technology, but it is a subject that should become familiar to every police administrator, since the effective use of computers can have as much impact on a police agency's operations as effective scheduling of personnel. In police administration, computers are being used by law enforcement agencies to maintain financial records, prepare payrolls, maintain property inventories, and prepare budgets. Often the police agency has no computer of its own, but must submit the information in written form to another governmental agency (often the city's accounting office) and receive a stack of computer print-outs several days or weeks later. Where this system exists, the police department has lost control over its own administrative records. If a large centralized computer system must be used, at least the police department should have access to it from their own terminals. Terminals may be used to enter information into the computer, control mathematical operations, and receive reports. Through the time-sharing technique, the police department's computer operators can enter, manipulate, and retrieve information as they need it, rather than being forced to wait until someone else runs a batch of data for them.

A better arrangement by far is to install a separate mini- or microcomputer system in the police department. A small system can be connected to the parent government's central computer so that the police agency has access to centralized data banks of financial information, city planning information, and so on. At the same time, the police department is able to do all of its own data processing and keep its own computer files. Terminals may be located at many points within the police department; they do not have to be concentrated in the budget office and communications center.

One of the most important uses of the computer in modern police service is computer-aided dispatching (CAD), a technique that has been developed in just the past few years. Several types of CAD systems have been developed with many variations. In general, a CAD system involves the use of computer terminals by the telephone operators and dispatchers and a remote terminal in each mobile unit. The mobile terminals may be in the form of teletype-like keyboards and printers or keyboards with television-like display screens; in either case, they are connected to the central computer by radio.

When a complaint or request for service is received by telephone, the telephone operator enters the information into the computer. The computer verifies the information (if no such address exists, the computer will let the operator know this), then determines which patrol or other field unit should be assigned to the call. This information is displayed on the dispatcher's terminal. If the dispatcher agrees with the assignment, merely pressing a button causes the information to be transmitted to the appropriate mobile unit. If the dispatcher disagrees, which should occur rarely, the computer's assignment can be overridden manually. Everything we have described so far can take place in much less time than it takes to describe it. The computer keeps a permanent record of every call handled, as well as detailed information about the activities of each field unit. This information can be retrieved in the form of lists, summaries, or (depending on the computer system) graphs and charts.

When a call is transmitted to a mobile unit, the information is stored in the mobile unit's terminal. If the officer is not in the vehicle or is temporarily unavailable, the information waits until the officer acknowledges it; if no acknowledgement is received within a certain time, the computer notifies the dispatcher and proposes another assignment. Also, field personnel can communicate directly with the computer to obtain additional information, such as current wants and warrants on a person or license number, or to file a summary preliminary report of an investigation.

A well-designed CAD system can do much more than just speed up the dispatching process. It can connect every field unit to the agency's central data base and, through it, to regional, state, and national files of police information. At the same time, the CAD system connects every element of the police department into a single nerve system through which every kind of administrative and police service information can flow.

An elaborate CAD system requires at least a large minicomputer; some are based on small mainframe computers. The smaller minicomputers and microcomputers do not have the processing and multiuse capability required for CAD. However, many smaller police agencies could get by with a minicomputer or even a microcomputer to assist the dispatcher, without some of the more elaborate features and without using mobile computer terminals in each field unit. The computer would be used to store information about each call (entered manually by the telephone operator and dispatcher) and would assist the dispatcher by looking up addresses, criminal histories, wants and warrants, and other data base information. The dispatcher still would make case assignments and communicate with field units by radiotelephone.

Computer-aided dispatching systems are available commercially from several manufacturers. Since these systems vary considerably in their capabilities and in the types of computer systems they require, careful consideration must be given to their selection.[15]

Television

Law enforcement agencies have slowly begun to develop innovative and effective uses of television and its ancillary technologies, video tape recording and cable television.

There are several rather obvious uses of broadcast television for purposes such as public information and community relations. Video tape recording also has been used extensively in police training programs. However, there are some other uses of television that are less obvious.

For example, in the late 1960s the Detroit Police Department installed remote-controlled television cameras on several bridges over a major expressway. The cameras continuously fed pictures to monitors at the police headquarters, enabling an officer to observe traffic flow and operate a system of lane control signals to direct traffic.[16]

Some experiments were conducted at about the same time in the use of television cameras for surveillance of public areas such as parks, beaches, and shopping malls. There were protests from some citizens concerned with possible invasions of privacy, but the courts ruled that the presence of cameras *in a public place* was no more invasive than the presence of an actual police officer. Nevertheless, these experiments usually did not last long, partly because of the public outcry over the "Big Brother" implications and partly because of the high cost of leasing special transmission lines to carry signals from the cameras to a central monitoring point.

Television is used increasingly for surveillance in and around police buildings, jails, and other locations where security is a major concern. Also, video tape recordings are now made routinely of persons at the time of arrest, especially for driving while intoxicated or driving under the influence of drugs. On occasion, witnesses and even defendants have been represented in court by video tape recordings of their testimony, if it was impractical for them to appear in court. Video tape recordings of crime and accident scenes have been allowed as evidence in some court cases and are often valuable to investigators even if they are not presented as evidence.

State police agencies and some large metropolitan police departments could use video teleconferencing as a substitute or supplement for meetings of far-flung employees. Video teleconferencing means that individuals at two or more locations communicate by the transmission of both visual and audio information. Video teleconferencing is fairly expensive, mostly because of the cost of transmitting two-way video signals over the telephone or other communications networks. Nevertheless, the cost savings over "live" meetings can be substantial. More important, it may be possible for individuals at different locations to "meet" by teleconference more frequently and more conveniently than meetings in person would permit. Some people are understandably concerned that an electronic meeting will be less effective than a live meeting, but the experience of organizations that have used video teleconferencing is just the opposite: The electronic meeting is somewhat more productive if only because the participants are often better organized and more involved in the proceedings.

Cable television systems offer a means of transmitting television and other signals that can be extraordinarily cost effective. Most people think of a cable system purely as a means for distributing entertainment programs to homes. However, nearly all cable systems built during the past few years, and many older systems, have one or more channels reserved for use by local government. These channels can be used by law enforcement agencies for a variety of purposes. Crime prevention and other public information programs can be transmitted to the general public at little or no cost. Training programs can be transmitted to personnel at several locations at once, or even to officers' homes (so that they can receive training during their off-duty hours).

Similarly there may be cable channels available for law enforcement use that cannot be received by the public. Some large cable systems have institutional channels, or completely separate institutional networks, designed for this purpose. The institutional channels often can be used for two-way transmissions (or at least one-way video and two-way audio), which means that they can be used not only to distribute training programs but also for teleconferencing. In most cases, cable television systems also can be used to carry almost any kind of nontelevision signal, including voice (in effect, a citywide intercom system) and data. The nonvideo channels could be used to connect computer terminals between the police headquarters and precinct stations, or between the police department and other governmental agencies; to connect remote surveillance cameras and other surveillance devices to a central monitoring point; to synchronize and control traffic signals throughout the city from a central computer; and to transmit teletype messages among several law enforcement agencies in the area. These applications represent only a handful of suggestions; the potential for police use of cable television is almost limitless.

POLICE-PUBLIC COMMUNICATIONS SYSTEMS

In this chapter we have been concerned primarily with information systems within a police agency. In addition we have referred to communications systems between the police and other governmental agencies.

Police agencies are also faced with another important communications need: communications between the agency and the public it serves. Of course, there is a good deal of this type of communication. Citizens call in complaints or requests for police service over the telephone, or come in person to the police station to file a complaint or to give information. Field officers routinely communicate with individual citizens, and sometimes with citizens' groups, on the street. Some police agencies make effective use of the mass media (newspapers, radio, and television) to provide the public with information and to solicit information from the public.

With one exception—the telephone—all these forms of police-public communication are usually initiated by the police. When the police department wishes to inform the public or wishes to receive information from the public, the department does the communicating, by whatever means it finds convenient. Additional channels of communication can be opened between the police and the public, to the benefit of both.

For example, it is not difficult and certainly not expensive to encourage the operators of radio-equipped mobile fleets to assist the police by reporting traffic accidents, hazardous conditions, or suspicious incidents. In many cities there are dozens of radio-equipped fleets on the streets at almost all times: taxicabs, delivery trucks, construction crews, utility crews, and individuals with mobile radiotelephones. The operators of these fleets can be contacted and asked for assistance. The police department should conduct a training session for the fleet drivers and dispatchers, explaining what kinds of things they should look for and how to report them.

In hundreds of cities, volunteer citizens' groups have been organized specifically to provide emergency communications by Citizens Band (CB) and other widely used radio systems. The FCC has reserved CB channel 9, and many other amateur frequencies, specifically for emergency messages and assistance to motorists. National organizations such as the Amateur Radio Relay League and REACT International have been established to promote the proper use of CB and amateur radio for emergency communications. (In 1982, REACT International was one of 18 groups to receive the President's Award for Outstanding Volunteer Service.)

The local chapters or affiliates of these national organizations are actually quite autonomous and independent. Some are much more effective than others. Police authorities should welcome the interest of civic-minded volunteers and should strongly encourage their activities. Contact should be made as early as possible with the groups' organizers or leaders to establish a cooperative working relationship. If possible, the police should participate in the training of volunteer emergency monitors and should work with the volunteers to establish reporting procedures, liaison for the communication of problems or grievances, and so forth. All police agency personnel, especially in the communications center, should be fully informed about the groups' purposes and agreed-on operating procedures.

If no volunteer emergency radio group already exists, the police should seriously consider sponsoring one of their own. This has been done with notable success in several communities. Where there is already a police reserve or police buddy program, it might be expanded to incorporate emergency radio monitoring. Not all CB and amateur radio operators will respond favorably, but in almost every community there are plenty of civic-minded citizens, willing and able to serve their community, if they are only asked.

CAPTAIN AVERY'S IN BASKET

Instructions

In this exercise, you are to assume the role of Captain Mike Avery, chief of the Patrol Bureau. The documents below have been selected from Captain Avery's in basket. Read them with care. If you need more information about City or its police department, refer to the data bank in the front of the book. After you have studied the documents, complete the following steps:

1. State the problem or problems these documents present to Captain Avery.
2. List as many alternative solutions as you can.
3. Select the solution(s) you think would be best, and give your reasons.

```
TO: AVERY
FROM: EZA
June 23, 19--
     Mike, sorry about the confusion. I thought you said you
had called the City Manager's office to get the information
about the proposed annexation of the new subdivision west of
the Loop, and I guess you thought I was going to call him.
Anyway, I'll have one of Earl's people get the info, and let
you know what we get.
                                              --EZA
```

CITY POLICE DEPARTMENT	
Interoffice Memorandum	
FROM: Lts. Alexander, Clements, and Guthrie	
TO: Captain Avery, Chief, Patrol Bureau	
SUBJECT: "Rader's Raiders" Proposal	DATE: 11 Jun 19--

SIR

We have heard through the "grapevine" that Lt. Rader of the Vice Squad has proposed a SWAT team, and this is being considered by the Dept. We would like to offer our comments and suggestions on the proposal. We have obtained a copy of the proposal and studied it carefully.

1. We think that any SWAT team should be under the Patrol Bureau, not Organized Crime. Our people are already on the streets and we probably make a lot more arrests than Detectives and OC combined. Besides that, we think most of the "volunteers" will come from Patrol and will work better under the command of people they already know.

2. The idea of calling the SWAT team "Rader's Raiders" is not acceptable to most of the people in Patrol, for obvious reasons.

3. We do not have enough people on the streets now. We could not afford to have Patrol officers released from regular duty 10 hours a week for extra training. This should be done on a paid

Page 2.

overtime basis.

4. Also, 250 hours of training is too much. Our people are already well trained in most of the areas that a SWAT team would need. We think that an additional 24 to 30 hours of intensive training should be enough.

5. If there is any "hotline" telephone to call out the SWAT team at all hours of the day or night, it should be based in a separate Command Center, not in Communications, so there will be no chance of calling people out by mistake. Also, how would Patrol officers who are already on duty be notified of a SWAT call-up? Who will cover their beats while they are in a SWAT situation?

If these problems are solved, we think Patrol will support the SWAT idea, but only if it is put under Patrol's command.

J. ALexander, Lt.
L. Clements, Lt.
J. Guthrie, Lt.
Patrol Bureau

June 24, 19--

Capt. Avery:

Last month you used $3,275.18 in overtime funds. This was $189.75 more than was budgeted for the month. As of June 15, you had already used $1,593.22 of this month's overtime budget. If you don't make up last month's overage from this month, you are going to be short by the end of the fiscal year. Please advise.

R. Ullrich, Lt.
Budget & Accounting

CITY POLICE DEPARTMENT
Interoffice Memorandum

FROM:	T. Bowen, Inv.		
TO:	Mike Avery, Patrol		
SUBJECT:	Improper Action of Patrol	DATE:	24 Jun 19--

Mike:
      I hate to sound like a broken record, but your people have
messed up another investigation. You have got to get your patrol
officers to pay more attention in Roll Call.
      Yesterday Sgt. Abbey, one of my top people, spent 15 minutes
briefing the First Watch on three situations. One was the problem
we've been having around the University with purse snatchings and
muggings. The second was the warrant that is out on our suspect in
the Balthazar murder. The third was a general warning not to go into
"family" situations without a backup. As you know, this is the policy
that was decided last month and announced by Chief Abel.

Page 2.

      At 1430 yesterday afternoon, a patrol unit (C-3) investigated an
assault at University and Rutherford, not three blocks from the
college. We did not get the preliminary report until this morning. We
should have known about this immediately so we could correlate with
other information we have on University-area muggings.
      Also, late yesterday afternoon two of my people were on
stake-out near the suspected hide-out of our suspect in the Balthazar
case. They were on stake-out for seven and 1/2 straight hours. One of
your people (B-2) drove a marked patrol car right up to the stake-out
and proceeded to warn my detectives to "move along"! He finally left
after my people produced their ID's, but obviously the stake-out was
blown. We have been working on this case for four solid months, and I
sure hope the guy doesn't get away just because one of your people
fouled us up.
      · Couldn't we try to get a little more cooperation out of Patrol?
Otherwise, what is the point of having my detectives waste their time
giving briefings at Roll Call?

                        Tom Bowen, Captain
                        Detective Bureau

IN REVIEW

1. Communication is:
   (a) Any electronic means of transmitting information.
   (b) The use of written documents to store information.
   (c) The transfer of information over time or space, or both.
   (d) The proper relationship between administrative and operational
       units of a police department.
   (e) None of the above.

2. True or False: An effective communications system must provide for
   feedback.

3. The *Uniform Crime Reporting System* is:
   (a) A voluntary system for collecting crime statistics from participating agencies.
   (b) A system for recording crimes that have been reported by uniformed police officers.
   (c) A collection of statistics on cases investigated by the FBI.
   (d) A method of comparing state laws so that similar crimes will have the same definitions.
   (e) A computerized data base of criminal case histories.

4. True or False: Police agencies historically have been quick to adopt new communications technologies.

5. A telephone log is:
   (a) A detailed transcript of every conversation involving a police officer.
   (b) A complete list of the department's telephone equipment.
   (c) The names and addresses of persons or agencies who are frequently called by police officers.
   (d) A list of phone calls initiated or received by each officer, with a brief summary of each conversation.
   (e) A cross-reference list of the street address for every phone number in the community.

6. Records must be kept on all police activities because:
   (a) They are needed to make administrative decisions.
   (b) The services rendered by the police usually have legal significance.
   (c) They often influence the agency's future activities.
   (d) All of the above.
   (e) None of the above.

7. True or False: Every field officer should be given a supply of case report forms preprinted with serial numbers so that the forms will not be lost or wasted.

8. Three sets of _____ should be maintained to assist in locating records once they have been filed.
   (a) Personal identification records
   (b) Documents
   (c) Case reports
   (d) Indexes
   (e) Summaries

9. The terms low band, high band, and UHF refer to:
   (a) Three types of computer-assisted dispatching systems.
   (b) Three portions of the radio frequency spectrum that have been set aside for police radio systems.
   (c) The number of channels in a police radio system.
   (d) The maximum distance that a police radio signal can be transmitted.
   (e) The volume of traffic (number of calls) that a police radio system ordinarily handles.

10. True or False: A computer system designed for use by the police must be capable of using the time-sharing technique.

REFERENCES

1. Sam Souryal, *Police Administration and Management*, St. Paul, West Publishing Co., 1977, page 322.

2. George D. Eastman, ed., *Municipal Police Administration*, Washington, D.C.: International City Management Association, 1969, pages 56–57.

3. V. A. Leonard, *The Police Records System*, Springfield, Ill.: Charles C. Thomas, 1970, pages 37–42.

4. O. W. Wilson, *Police Records and Their Installation*, Chicago: Public Administration Service, 1942.

5. Peter W. Greenwood, Jan M. Chaiken, and Joan Petersilia, *The Criminal Investigation Process*, Lexington, Mass.: D.C. Heath, 1977, pages 182–190.

6. Donald G. Hanna and John R. Kleberg, *A Police Records System for the Small Department*, 2nd ed., Springfield, Ill.: Charles C. Thomas, 1974, pages 12–16.

7. United States Dept. of Justice, Federal Bureau of Investigation, *Uniform Crime Reports for the United States*, Washington, D.C.: U.S. Government Printing Office, published annually.

8. Roger W. Reinke, *Design and Operation of Police Communications Systems*, Washington, D.C.: International Association of Chiefs of Police, 1964, page 3.

9. Reinke, pages 10–11.

10. Reinke, page 19.

11. Reinke, pages 12–13.

12. Reinke, page 16.

13. *Police Personal FM Transceiver Report*, Washington, D.C.: Technology Assessment Program, International Association of Chiefs of Police, 1981.

14. James Martin, *Telecommunications and the Computer*, 2nd ed., Englewood Cliffs, N.J.: Prentice-Hall, 1976, page 355.

15. Arthur B. Carroll et al., *Computer Aided Dispatching for Law Enforcement Agencies*, Champaign, Ill.: Community Technology, Inc., not dated; see also Alfred R. Stone and Stuart M. DeLuca, *Investigating Crimes*, Boston: Houghton Mifflin, 1980, pages 232–233.

16. V. A. Leonard, *The Police Communications System*, Springfield, Ill.: Charles C. Thomas, 1970, page 41.

10 POLICE PROPERTY AND EVIDENCE MANAGEMENT

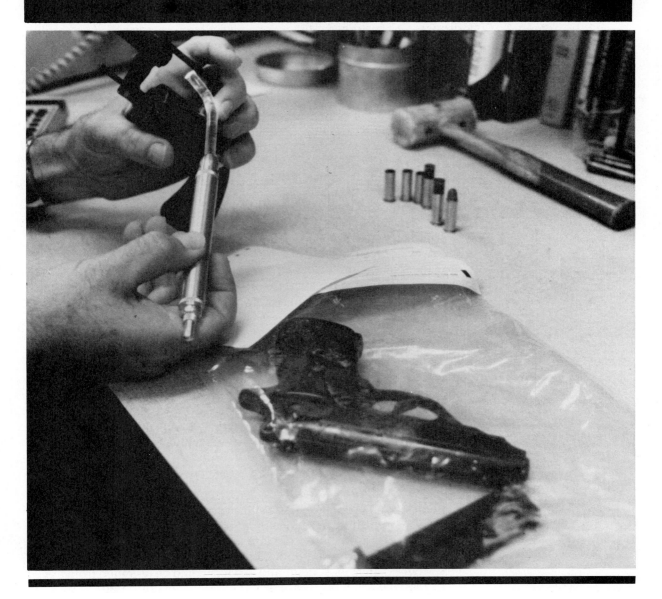

ALL THE THINGS WE HAVE DISCUSSED IN THE PAST FOUR chapters have one characteristic in common: They must be purchased. Buildings, furniture, equipment, vehicles and their accessories, uniforms, weapons, personal equipment, records forms, computers, gasoline and oil for police vehicles, food for jail prisoners—all must be bought from someone.

Once items have been purchased, they must be cared for and used properly; when they are no longer useful or needed, they must be disposed of.

The police also act as custodians of several kinds of property that do not actually belong to them: property that has been found, or whose ownership is unknown or disputed; stolen property that has been recovered; evidence connected with a crime; and the personal belongings of prisoners. As custodians, the police have a legal responsibility to care for such property; especially in the case of evidence the police have a professional interest in keeping secure.

PROPERTY ACQUISITION   The purchasing of materials and services is a continuing, indeed neverending, function of police administration. Usually about one-fourth of a police agency's annual budget is allocated to items that are to be purchased (the rest being devoted to personnel costs, rent, utilities, and other fixed costs).

In private business and in government, purchasing is a highly specialized field. Purchasing agents or managers often have advanced degrees in business administration, special training in purchasing, and years of experience as purchasing clerks or buyers of specific kinds of merchandise. Unfortunately, this level of expertise is not always available to law enforcement agencies.

Some very large police departments have established a centralized purchasing unit (sometimes called the procurement section, materiel acquisition section, or supply section). Medium-sized and moderately large agencies—those with between 100 and 500 employees—often have no specialized purchasing unit, but instead rely entirely on the parent government to provide this function. In smaller agencies, purchases are made by individual administrators or entirely by the chief executive.

The first step in establishing an efficient purchasing system is to designate some one individual as the agency's purchasing agent.[1] In small agencies, this individual may have other duties; however, it is preferable for the person designated as purchasing agent to be someone other than the person responsible for supervising the budget and keeping the agency's accounts.

There are four major steps in the purchasing process, all of which require the participation of the purchasing agent and of other agency administrators:

1. **Requisition.** Every purchase begins when someone in the agency has a need for some item or service that must be acquired from outside. This need is expressed in a standard form, a purchase **requisition**, that describes what is to be obtained.[2]
2. **Selection.** Since most items and services could be obtained from any of several sources, and often at different prices, an effort must be made to

determine the best source for whatever is needed and then to obtain the best possible price for the item or service.

3. **Transaction.** The purchase itself is a legal transaction, a commitment of the agency's funds in exchange for goods or services to be delivered.

4. **Receipt.** Finally, the goods must be received by the agency and either accepted or, if they are not correct, rejected; or the service must be performed to the agency's satisfaction.

The purchase requisition might be prepared by anyone in an agency, subject to whatever limits are imposed by the agency's policies. When the requisition is submitted to the purchasing agent, the item or service to be bought must be described so thoroughly that there is little chance that the wrong thing will be bought. It is the purchasing agent's responsibility to get only what the requisition specifies; if the requisition says merely, "One dozen ½-inch-long screws," it is not the purchasing agent's fault if the screws that are bought have the wrong thickness or thread pattern.

Because the requisition is so important, most agencies require that it be approved by at least one supervisor or administrator before it is sent to the purchasing agent. (See Figure 10.1.)

The purchasing agent's most obvious value comes in the selection part of the process. An experienced and capable purchasing agent should be personally familiar with most of the usual sources for the goods or services needed, and should be able to select the source that is capable of delivering what is needed in the appropriate quantity and quality at the best possible price.

The purchasing agent also must know how to complete the transaction in a manner that is legally correct and that best achieves the agency's goal of obtaining goods and services in a timely fashion, at the least cost for the quality of goods desired.

Finally, the purchasing agent's responsibilities end when the goods are delivered and checked to be sure that they are in proper order, or when the service has been performed to the agency's satisfaction. However, a competent purchasing agent also wants to know whether the agency's personnel are satisfied with items that have been bought, whether expensive equipment performs as it is supposed to, whether the vendor provides prompt and satisfactory maintenance services, whether the warranty is honored, and so on.

Requisitions

Each purchase requisition should carry out some part of the plans contained and reflected in the agency's budget. If a need arises that was not foreseen, and for which the budget has no provision, a decision must be made to amend the budget before the purchase is made. As a general rule, no purchase should be made unless the funds for it have been provided in the budget.

The most important part of any purchase requisition is the specification of what is needed. As we have said, the specification should be sufficiently complete that there is no question about what is needed. On the other hand, the specification should not be so detailed and restrictive that there is only one possible source for an item, since that limits the purchasing agent's chances of seeking the best possible price through competitive bidding.

Act—3

<u>PURCHASE MEMORANDUM</u>

Date _____   Memorandum No. _____

From:

To:

It is requested that the following items be requisitioned for the _____

DIVISION, to be used (or assigned) _____

_____

APPROVED FOR PURCHASE: Requested by: _____
_____   (Signature)

_____   Title:_____

Ordered by: _____ on Requisition No. _____ Date _____

Purchased from Appropriation No. _____

Order Placed With _____ Date Delivered _____

example, if the item to be bought is a part that must be assembled with some equipment that the agency already owns).[3]

Selection

Police officers must be able to rely on the equipment and materials purchased for their use. At the same time, police departments do not have unlimited funds at their disposal; they must get the most out of every dollar they spend. The best way to do this is to make every purchase from the lowest *qualified* bidder.[4] This does not always mean that the lowest price must be used as the only criterion for selection.

Somewhat different procedures are used for different kinds of purchases. The kinds of purchases that occur most often in police agencies are commodities purchases, item orders, and service contracts.

Commodities are goods that are used more or less continuously; they tend to be highly standardized items, usually bought in large quantities. Some examples would be vehicle fuel and motor oil, office supplies and stationery, ammunition, cleaning and maintenance supplies, food for jail prisoners, and photographic supplies. It would be ridiculous to require a separate requisition for a day's supply of gasoline, wait for bids to be taken, and then take a purchase order to the chosen gas station. Instead, fuel and other commodities are purchased in sufficiently large quantities to meet the agency's needs over some period of time, often as much as a year. However, the commodities usually are delivered periodically, as they are consumed, so that the agency does not have to store the entire year's supply at once. For example, if the department has 20 vehicles, each of which consumes on the average 25 gallons of gasoline per day, the department would need a total of 3500 gallons per week, or 182,000 gallons per year. The department might have adequate storage for a week's supply, plus a reserve for higher-than-normal usage or late delivery, and require the vendor to deliver 3500 gallons each week.

Item orders are purchases of individual items or small groups of items on an irregular basis as the goods are actually needed. Many purchases are for single items that may vary in cost from a few cents to several hundred thousand dollars. Each item order is handled as a unique case, as if nothing of the sort had ever been purchased before, except that some goods (such as uniforms) may be standardized and obtained routinely from the same vendor.

Services are work performed by individuals who are not employees of an agency. Police departments may have many occasions to purchase services from individuals; for example, an attorney might be paid a monthly fee, or retainer, for advice about the legal aspects of police activities; similarly, a radio technician might be paid on a contract basis to maintain the agency's radios. Usually services are purchased from nonemployees when there is not enough work to justify hiring someone on a regular basis or when the volume of work varies so greatly and irregularly that it would be inefficient to keep enough employees on the payroll.

In some cases, purchased services do not involve the work of people, but of machines. For example, some businesses offer the use of small computers, xerographic copiers, and other specialized office equipment on a service basis. Instead of buying or leasing the machines, the purchaser merely buys the use of them. The cost might be calculated on the basis of the number of hours (or minutes) the computer is used during a month, or the number of copies made, and so on.

A distinction should be made between a service contract and a **maintenance contract**. The former is an agreement to pay a certain amount for the services of an individual (or, as we have just seen, for a machine) to do certain work. A maintenance contract is an agreement to pay in advance a predetermined fee in return for any repairs or maintenance services that might be needed on a particular piece or type of equipment. Unfortunately, some businesses refer to their maintenance contracts as service contracts, which adds to the confusion.

For any of the three types of purchases, the selection process begins with the compiling of a **source list**, or bidders' list. Experienced purchasing agents maintain a source list for each type of merchandise or service that the agency routinely buys. Lists are constantly updated, with new businesses added and out-of-date information removed. Vendors who have previously delivered unsatisfactory merchandise or services may be removed from the list, either temporarily or permanently. The list is compiled from as many sources of information as the purchasing agent has available: from trade advertising, direct mail advertising, salespersons' calls, telephone directories, trade association directories, and so on.[5]

Once a source list has been compiled, the purchasing agent is prepared to invite bids on the item or items to be purchased. (See Figure 10.2.) The invitation may be on a standardized form, containing the description given in the purchase requisition, plus any other conditions of delivery, agency policies regarding discounts, and so forth. In some cases, the invitation may be given in the form of a letter. Anyone interested in bidding on the purchase is required to reply by a certain time and date.[6]

For items of relatively small value, especially when they are reasonably standardized or when precise specifications are unnecessary, bids may be solicited by telephone and written bids may not be required.[7]

Commodity purchases are almost always made on the basis of written bids because the size of the purchase usually is quite large. Some governments require commodity purchases to be made only after invitations to bidders have been published in newspapers (often in the classified advertising columns) or in official publications. For example, the federal government uses several of its own publications to solicit bids, including the *Federal Register* and the U. S. Department of Commerce's *Business and Commerce Daily*.[8]

If the item to be purchased is unusually expensive, complicated, or involves services as well as goods, a two-step purchasing process may be used. For example, if a police department decides to buy a new computer system, there are a vast number of computer systems that might fit the agency's needs, and probably the department would not have anyone among its employees who would be competent to design such a system and specify the components to be purchased. Instead, a **request for proposals (RFP)** should be issued. The RFP consists of a statement of the general sort of thing that is desired and, in as much detail as possible, what it is expected to accomplish. Interested bidders respond with a detailed proposal, including the design of the system, the required components, and an estimated price.

INVITATION TO BID
CITY OF FORT SMITH
Mail Sealed Bids To → PURCHASING AGENT
P.O. BOX 1908
FORT SMITH, ARKANSAS 72901

Place ___PURCHASING___

Date _____   Bid Opening Date 10 A.M. _____ 19____

ON THE OUTSIDE OF SEALED BID ENVELOPE SHOW:
(1) RETURN ADDRESS OF FIRM
(2) BID OPENING DATE
(3) BID ON _4-DOOR SEDAN_

Bidder agrees to comply with all conditions below and on reverse side of this bid. Purchases made for the City of Fort Smith are exempt from Federal Excise Tax. Do NOT include on your bid. Unit prices and extensions are required. If a trade discount is shown on bid, it should be deducted and net line extension shown. Bidder guarantees product offered will meet or exceed specifications identified in this bid invitation.

BIDDER MUST FILL IN & SIGN

NAME OF FIRM

STREET ADDRESS

CITY   STATE   ZIP

AUTHORIZED SIGNATURE   DATE

TITLE

QUOTE F.O.B. DESTINATION

ITEM NO.	DESCRIPTION AND/OR SPECIFICATIONS	QUANTITY	MFG. & MODEL	UNIT PRICE	EXTENSION
I	Automobiles as per specifications				
	GENERAL: Standard four (4) door sedans with center post. All vehicles bid shall be of a general quality level equivalent to the Chevrolet Impala, Ford L.T.D. II, Pontiac Catalina, or Dodge Monaco. Sedans are to be furnished with all interior and exterior trim and appointments listed by the manufacturer in printed specifications and literature as "Standard Equipment". Vehicles must meet all Federal Safety Emission Regulations.				
	ENGINE: 350 cubic inch displacement, 8 cylinder.				
	TRANSMISSION: Automatic shift specifically recommended by manufacturer for the engine being offered. Shall include a first-gear lock out feature.				
	WHEELBASE: 116 inch				
	SUSPENSION: Heavy-duty designed and engineered for pursuit-type work. Should include heavy-duty front and rear sway bar, torsion bar, heavy duty rear springs and heavy duty shock absorbers 1 3/16″ front and 1 3/8″ rear.				
	STEERING: Power				
	BRAKES: Power disc front metallic-impregnated, drum rear				
	ELECTRICAL: 12 volt with 61-ampere alternator and 80-ampere/hour battery, dual horns and radio noise suppression equipment.				
	AIR CONDITIONING: Factory installed integrated with heater-defroster.				
	GLASS: Tinted.				
	TIRES: Five (5) radial ply BSW (Includes mounted spare).				
	SPEEDOMETER: Calibrated, (0−100 MPH) in 2 mph increments.				
	ACCESSORIES: Glove and truck compartment lights. Interior dome lights NOT to light when doors are opened. Vinyl upholstry—Colors to be compatible with vehicle color.				

By the signature hereon affixed, the bidder hereby certifies that neither the bidder nor the firm, corporation, partnership or institution represented by the bidder, or anyone acting for such firm, corporation or institution has violated the Federal Antitrust Laws, nor communicated directly or indirectly the bid made to any competitor or any other person engaged in such line of business.

DELIVERY IN _____ DAYS
CASH DISCOUNT
_____%_____

Figure 10-2   A bid invitation form. (Courtesy Fort Smith, Arkansas Police Department.)

The responses to an RFP may represent a number of different approaches to the department's needs. The selection process focusses not on the price, but on the quality of the proposed system design: Will it do what the department wants to do, and is it the most efficient and economical of the various designs submitted? Sometimes specific features of one design will be very attractive, while another vendor's overall design comes closer to meeting the agency's needs. Ultimately, the agency (usually with the participation of every administrator who will be affected by the purchase) must choose the vendor whose design comes closest to meeting those needs.

The second step, then, is the negotiation of a contract with the chosen vendor. Changes in the design might be made to incorporate new features (including some that may have been proposed by another vendor) or to delete features that the agency decides are unnecessary. The contract often will specify conditions such as the time of delivery, how the equipment is to be installed, training that is to be provided by the vendor for the agency's employees, and how repair service is to be provided under a warranty. Finally, a fixed price is negotiated and written into the contract.

The Transaction

Once bids have been received and the lowest qualified bidder has been selected, or a contract has been negotiated, the actual purchase is made, usually by issuing a **purchase order** to the successful bidder. The merchandise may not be actually delivered until sometime later. However, a purchase order is a legal, enforceable contract; if either the buyer or the seller fails to complete the transaction, the contract is broken and the other party has recourse to the courts.[9]

Receipt

When the purchased goods are delivered, a responsible person in authority must examine them to be sure that they are the items that were ordered and that they are in proper condition. For items of a routine nature, the delivery inspection may be performed by a clerk; for expensive or unusual items, the inspection should be performed by the purchasing agent and by the person who will actually use the item. If everything is in proper order, a delivery receipt is given and the items are accepted. If anything is not in order, the delivery should be refused. Once the agency has accepted delivery, the department may be obligated to pay for the item even if it later turns out to be defective or unsuitable. Furthermore, once the item has been accepted, it is legally the property of the department and the vendor is not responsible for any losses that might occur as a result of theft, fire, weather, and so on. Thus, as soon as an item has been accepted, it should be moved to the place where it is to be used or, if this is not possible, it should be put into safe storage.

Merchandise, especially commodities that are delivered periodically, may be delivered with an **invoice**, the supplier's claim for payment. Otherwise, the invoice is sent directly to the purchasing agent. All invoices must be checked against the agency's delivery records to make sure that the items in the invoice were in fact received and accepted. Any deviation from the terms of the purchase order must be settled before payment is made (and preferably before the item is put to use). When the invoice is found to be correct, it is forwarded to the department's accounting unit, where it should be checked again by comparison with the purchase order and, if possible, the original requisition.[10]

These routine checks are more important than may be apparent. Careless handling of purchases is one of the largest sources of waste and corruption in both government and private industry. Swindlers frequently mail out large batches of falsified invoices, knowing that careless businesses and government agencies will pay the bill without checking.

Legal Considerations in Police Purchasing

Aside from the legal implications of purchasing we have already discussed, there are some particular legal considerations that apply specifically to police agencies.

The purchasing process usually involves a great deal of money, which means that there is always the possibility of abuse, corruption, or waste. To avoid these problems, legislators and agency administrators devote considerable attention to purchasing procedures. Federal, state, and local laws dictate the kinds of things that may be bought by public agencies; laws and administrative rules specify the exact procedures that must be followed in purchasing them. Most cities and counties have established their own standard purchasing procedures; standardized forms must be used for purchase requisitions, bid invitations, requests for proposals, purchase orders, and so on. Naturally, every police agency must follow the laws of its parent government. For that reason, we have not gone into great detail about these procedures, which may vary from place to place.

There also may be **flow-through requirements**. When an agency receives funds from a source other than its parent government, or when the parent government receives funds from another source and passes them on to the police department, any requirements imposed by the original source of the funds may "flow through" and affect the way those funds are used. For example, the federal government may provide money to a state criminal justice planning agency, which in turn may award a grant to a local police department. The federal grant might have a number of restrictions as to how the funds may be used or may carry some conditions on the purchasing procedures that may be used. These restrictions or conditions apply to the local police department, even though it was not the direct recipient of the federal money.

Flow-through requirements can be extremely complicated, especially when funds pass through two or more levels of government. Often each level adds its own specific restrictions or conditions.[11]

There are also federal and state laws designed to use purchasing procedures for various social purposes. Since governments spend a great deal of money, it is only reasonable to use some of it to achieve the general goals of society. For example, laws or rules may require agencies to purchase goods from minority-owned businesses whenever possible or from businesses in economically depressed areas. Many local governments have formal or informal policies of buying from businesses in the community. Other laws and administrative rules may require purchased goods to meet special qualifications to protect the natural environment, to reduce energy consumption, and so forth.

The real problem for a police administrator is to know what rules apply to a particular purchase, especially since the social welfare requirements also may flow through from higher to lower levels of government. Even if the parent government has an exceptionally well-organized central purchasing office, the police department should have at least one person on its own staff who is familiar with the special requirements of police purchasing.

Donated Equipment and Funds

One other special problem affects police agencies more than most other governmental agencies. Public-spirited citizens occasionally offer to donate equipment, services, or money to their local police department. In some communities, there are established charitable organizations whose primary purpose is to support the local police department by supplementing the funds that are available from local government.

Police officers and administrators often feel uneasy about accepting such contributions. There is a genuine concern that accepting anything from outsiders might compromise the agency's integrity. In some states, there are laws that forbid the police from accepting donations except under extremely strict conditions.

On the other hand, no police department has more money than it needs. Police departments, especially in smaller communities, are chronically strapped for funds; they do not have enough money for all of the necessities, much less the extras that might make police work more enjoyable, more efficient, or even safer.

Unless there are very strict laws to the contrary, police agencies should accept donations, but only on certain conditions.

The first condition is that the donation should not be from a single individual. Donations should be accepted only from organizations that have qualified under state law or the rules of the U.S. Internal Revenue Service for designation as nonprofit organizations. Private foundations or trusts are also acceptable donors, if they are administered by a board of trustees composed of reputable persons.

The second condition is that the donor must attach no restrictions to the contribution. Equipment or merchandise must become the permanent property of the agency, to be used in any way the agency sees fit.

The third condition is that the donation should be publicly acknowledged. Some donors prefer to remain anonymous, and may have practical reasons for doing so, but a police agency should not accept any anonymous donation nor any donation from a known source who insists that the contribution not be made public. The police do not need to seek publicity for every donation, but the fact of the donation, the amount, and the source should be considered public information.

The fourth condition is that the acceptance of a donation must not obligate the agency to do (or fail to do) anything. Some people, out of sincere and honest motives, contribute to the police in the hope of promoting the enforcement of particular laws. For example, funds might be contributed to establish an antiobscenity project. The funds should not be accepted unless the police have already decided to establish such a project. Even after the funds have been accepted, the police agency must be under no obligation to continue the project once proper law enforcement objectives have been achieved. Of course, if funds are contributed for a particular purpose, and then not used for that purpose, they must be returned to the donor and not used for something else.

INVENTORY AND PROPERTY CONTROL

Once goods have been purchased for use by a law enforcement agency, the agency has a responsibility to its parent government, the taxpayers who support it, and to its own personnel to make sure that the goods are properly maintained and used. Waste and unnecessary loss are probably no more common in law enforcement agencies than in any other kind of organization, but there is always room for improvement.

Many police agencies have adopted the policy that each employee is responsible for each piece of equipment assigned to him or her. If a piece of equipment, whether it is a handgun, an automobile, or a computer terminal, is lost or damaged through the employee's negligence, the cost of repair or replacement is charged against the employee's salary. In practice, however, this policy is unenforceable. Negligence is difficult to prove when equipment is lost or damaged in the heat of police action. Even when negligence is clearly established, assessing the cost against an officer's pay (which is usually not very generous to begin with) often results in an excessively severe penalty. A better policy is to treat negligence or abuse of equipment as a disciplinary matter. All personnel should receive thorough training in the use and care of their equipment; supervisors should observe any instances of misuse and take appropriate corrective action.

Inventory Controls

From an administrative perspective, the control of police property is largely a matter of establishing and maintaining proper records of the assignment and use of materials.[12]

Each nonconsumable item (such as furniture) should be marked with the agency's name and a unique serial number; the marking should be done at the time the item is received and accepted. Once an item has been marked, a permanent record should be established, showing when and from whom the item was purchased, along with whatever other information (cost, physical description, and so on) may be desired. The record should indicate to whom the item has been assigned for use or where it is located.

At least once a year, a complete physical inventory of all furniture and equipment should be taken. If the inventory records have been computerized, the computer should be able to provide a printed list of the numbered items, their description, and their assigned location. A clerk then takes the list to each unit of the agency and checks to make sure that every numbered item is actually present. Equipment in use on the streets or elsewhere also must be checked, either by having a clerk go to each location where the equipment should be found or by having the equipment brought to the headquarters for checking. The physical inventory is time-consuming and inconvenient, but it is a necessary procedure to make sure that equipment is not lost or abused.

Consumable items must be handled differently. All commodities should be placed in storage when they are delivered, and there should be some individual responsible for each storage location or facility. When consumable supplies are withdrawn to be used, the person taking them out of storage must leave with the storage supervisor a receipt, showing what has been taken out. From time to time, the storage supervisor should report to the accounting office (or to the purchasing agent) the total amount of supplies that have been withdrawn and how much remains in inventory.

Losses of consumable supplies are most likely to occur after they have been withdrawn from storage. For this reason, the accounting office or the purchasing agent should periodically review all supply receipts to determine whether any units of the agency, or even individual employees, are taking out unreasonable quantities of supplies.

Property Maintenance

Equipment cannot be used properly unless it is in proper working condition. Unfortunately, property maintenance is an area of chronic neglect in many agencies, especially the smaller ones whose budgets are most limited. Once a piece of equipment has been acquired, it is used until it stops working (for whatever reason), and then it is simply discarded or put in storage until funds can be found to repair it.

Any machine, any device that has working parts, requires some sort of maintenance, if only to keep it clean. Weapons, communications equipment, laboratory and photographic equipment, and vehicles all require fairly elaborate maintenance. Information on correct maintenance procedures usually is supplied by manufacturers or can be found in commercially published technical manuals.

The responsibility for maintenance should be clearly assigned. In general, the first responsibility rests with the individual officers and employees who are assigned the use of each type of equipment. It is their responsibility to keep their equipment clean and to report promptly any signs of malfunctions or excessive wear. Employees should not be expected to make repairs themselves, nor to pay for repairs caused by normal use or accidents that are not attributed to their own negligence. Periodic preventive maintenance and repairs are the responsibility of the agency. If the agency is too small to afford full-time repair technicians, maintenance contracts may be negotiated with qualified technicians who may perform repairs either at the department's facilities or in their own shops.

Disposition of Obsolete and Unneeded Equipment

No matter how thorough the maintenance effort, eventually every item of equipment will reach the end of its useful life. Police equipment often becomes outdated and useless to the agency even before it stops working.

When each piece of equipment is obtained, an estimate of its useful life should be made. Nothing lasts forever, and most manufacturers are willing to state the useful life of their products.

It may seem that the most economical way to use equipment is to "run it into the ground"; that is, to use it until its useful life has been exhausted, or until it has broken down to the point that it can no longer be repaired. Actually, that is the least economical practice. It is much better to keep an item in use only until:

(a) Its maintenance costs are equal to or greater than the amortized cost of a new item.

(b) It has reached the end of its designed life expectancy but is still in good working condition.

(c) A new model is available that, because of its greater efficiency, will cost less to operate or maintain than the item it will replace.

For example:

1. The agency has a copying machine that cost $5000 when purchased eight years ago. At the beginning of the ninth year, the machine has required only routine servicing. However, during the ninth year it begins to break down frequently, and each breakdown means an average repair bill of $100. A replacement machine will cost $6000 and may be expected to last five years. Thus, the new machine's amortized cost would be $1200 per year. Since the old machine is costing at least $1200 per year to keep in operation, the new machine should be bought.

2. The agency has a fleet of 10 vehicles, all purchased three years ago at a cost of $7500 each. All have about 100,000 miles on their odometers and have been maintained in good working condition. If they are sold now, as used cars, they are likely to bring $3000 each. If they are kept another year, and used for an average of 30,000 miles each, they are likely to bring only $1500 apiece (assuming that none of them begins to break down, which probably is not a valid assumption).

If the cars are sold now, they will have cost an average of $1500 per year (the original cost of $7500, less the resale value of $3000, divided by three years). If they are kept another year, they still will have cost $1500 per year ($7500, less $1500 resale value, divided by four years). So there is no economic advantage in keeping them another year. They should be sold.

3. The agency has a three-channel radio system, bought and installed 20 years ago at a cost of $50,000 for the base station equipment and $1200 per mobile unit. Today the agency has 60 mobile units. The three-channel system is still in good working order, but the three channels are badly overloaded with traffic; there is frequent interference from other transmitters on adjacent channels; and the system's design does not permit mobile units to hear one another, so mobile-to-mobile messages must be relayed through the dispatcher. A new radio system with four channels, at a higher frequency that is less susceptible to interference, and with mobile-to-mobile capability, will cost $100,000 for the base station and $1000 per mobile unit, or a total of $160,000. The old radio system cannot be sold, since there is no market for obsolete equipment. In this case, the decision is not entirely economic. There is no doubt that the new system will reduce the volume of radio traffic on each channel, reduce time lost due to interference, and increase the efficiency of both dispatching and patrol operations; the end result will be better service to the public. These considerations alone indicate that the old radio system should be replaced.

Once a decision has been made to replace outdated or unneeded equipment, a considerable period of time may pass before the replacement actually occurs. Most police agencies operate on an annual budget; funds for replacement equipment must be written into the next year's budget. Even after the budget has been approved, the purchasing procedures may take several months to complete. From the time a decision is made to purchase new equipment until the equipment is actually delivered may be anywhere from a year to two years.

For that reason, equipment replacement should be done on a scheduled basis. Equipment does not have to be kept until it is falling apart; it is much better to replace it while it is still in good working order and can be sold for a fair price. Therefore, all equipment should be scheduled for replacement *when it is first acquired*. Many kinds of equipment that are used continuously, for example, vehicles, should be replaced on a regular basis; for example, a police department might replace one-third of its fleet each year, so that no vehicle is kept longer than three years.

Equipment that is being replaced should not be simply discarded. If possible, it should be sold for its full, fair market value, either through a negotiated sale (perhaps with another law enforcement agency) or through a public auction. Even equipment that is not in good condition may be sold for its parts or its scrap value. Often the money made from the sale of obsolete equipment is enough to greatly reduce the cost of the replacement equipment.

CONTROL OF NONPOLICE PROPERTY

Law enforcement agencies, more than any other governmental agency, often must act as custodians of property that belongs to someone else. This custodianship is a legal status: The responsibility for the care of someone else's property is not merely a matter of good administrative practice, it is a legal obligation.

There are two broad classes of nonpolice property that a police agency must be concerned with: evidence and nonevidence.

Evidence

The legal meaning of **evidence** is, quite simply, anything that may have some bearing on the facts of a crime. More precise definitions are available in state statutes and in texts on criminal investigation. For our purposes, we are concerned with any tangible item that has been collected in connection with the investigation of a crime, and that must be kept either for laboratory examination or for presentation in court.

We are not presently concerned with the handling of evidence by investigators, laboratory technicians, or other police personnel, but instead with the administrative aspects of custodianship of evidence. In this regard, the proper handling of evidence ought to be simple.

The first requirement is that adequate, appropriate storage facilities must be provided. Second, one or more officers must be assigned the responsibility of caring for all evidence.

Evidence may be in any of a vast array of forms, sizes, and shapes, which makes proper storage difficult. Some evidence might be in the form of a few human hairs and a bit of dust; another item of evidence might be a bicycle, a television set, or an automobile. Obviously, the same storage facilities will not be appropriate for all.

Most evidence should be stored in a single room equipped with shelves and cabinets, and floor space for bulky items. Each item received as evidence must be clearly marked as to its source, the case number to which it applies, and the identity of the officer investigating the case. Small items should be packed in boxes or envelopes, clearly marked on the outside.

The shelves and cabinets in the evidence storage room should be divided by partitions into separate bins, with wire or solid doors on the front of each bin and, best of all, a lock on each bin. All evidence that pertains to a single case should be kept in one bin if possible.

Specialized facilities must be available for some types of evidence. Some materials may need to be refrigerated until (or after) they have been examined in the lab. Drugs and weapons must be kept in a safe or vault. Very bulky items such as a refrigerator or a piece of furniture must be stored on the floor, but they too must be protected against contamination and tampering. A few items, for example, an automobile, cannot be brought into the police building; they should be kept in a garage or at least in a secured area under constant surveillance.

A few police departments have adopted the policy of providing each officer with a small locker in which evidence for his or her cases may be kept. This procedure has few advantages and many disadvantages; evidence from several cases may be mixed together, and the lockers usually are not large enough for even moderately bulky items (a suitcase or a stereo). Centralized storage under the supervision of a designated officer is a more practical approach.

When an item of evidence is delivered to the storage supervisor, a permanent record should be established. The record should include a description of the item, the case number, where the evidence was found, and the signature of the investigating officer. The investigator should keep a copy of the record; another copy should be kept at the storage facility. Each time an item is removed from storage, that fact should be noted on the permanent record; the evidence custodian also should obtain a signed receipt from the person taking the item out, showing where it is being taken and for what purpose. These records may be needed in court, to demonstrate that the chain of custody for each piece of evidence has been properly maintained, and that there is no likelihood that the evidence has been contaminated.[13]

Nonevidence Property

Items that have been found and turned in to the police, stolen property that has been recovered, and items whose ownership is unknown or disputed all must be stored until they can be returned to their proper owners. Again, the police have legal custodianship of this property.

The storage of nonevidence property is not as demanding as it is for evidence. Locked storage bins are not necessary, provided the property is kept in a single room under the control of a responsible officer. The agency does have an obligation to protect the property from loss or damage; this could mean that some items such as food or prescription drugs must be refrigerated, and items of considerable value such as jewelry should be kept in a safe or vault.

Again, a permanent record should be kept of each item of nonevidence property held by the police, indicating its source and any information available about its ownership. No property should be removed for any purpose without a notation being made on the record and a receipt being given by the person taking the property.

Police agencies traditionally have been eager to return nonevidence property to its rightful owners. Unfortunately, sometimes they are too eager. Anything delivered to the police as found property, recovered stolen property, or property of questionable ownership must be turned over to the rightful owner only after that person has established his or her claim to it. If the police turn property over to the wrong person, the department could be sued by the rightful owner. Great caution must be exercised. The best procedure in many cases would be to turn the matter over to the courts. Most states have reasonably simple procedures for the disposition of property whose ownership is uncertain or disputed. Ordinarily, the decision to release the property to the person claiming ownership may be made by a magistrate. Following these procedures will relieve the police of responsibility if an honest mistake is made.

ASSISTANT CHIEF WILLIAMSON'S IN BASKET

Instructions

In this exercise, you are to assume the role of Assistant Chief Earl Williamson, chief of Administrative Services. The documents below have been selected from Chief Williamson's in basket. Read them with care. If you need more information about City or its police department, refer to the data bank in the front of the book. After you have studied the documents, complete these steps:

1. State the problem or problems these documents present to Assistant Chief Williamson.
2. List as many alternative solutions as you can.
3. Select the solution you think would be best, and give your reasons for choosing it.

<table>
<tr><td colspan="2" align="center">**CITY POLICE DEPARTMENT**
Interoffice Memorandum</td></tr>
<tr><td>FROM:</td><td>Sgt. Davis, Garage</td></tr>
<tr><td>TO:</td><td>Chief Williamson</td></tr>
<tr><td>SUBJECT: Auto parts</td><td>DATE: 6 Jul 19--</td></tr>
</table>

SIR:

Yesterday we received a shipment of 50 sets of spark plugs. They were delivered to the Garage by parcel post from the Rex N. Lemmens Auto Parts Co. of Chicago.

In the first place, we only ordered 25 sets of plugs. Also, the plugs they sent were the wrong type for our patrol cars. They are the right ones for the older cars but they do not fit the newer cars.

Should we send them all back or just keep the ones we need for the older cars?

J. Davis, Sgt.
~~Garage~~ Fleet Operations

Balogna's PETROX Service Station

804 N. Juniper
555-0987
Anthony Balogna, Proprietor

July 3, 19--

Chief E. Z. Abel
City Police Department
308 E. 6th St.
City, State

Dear Chief:

I am sorry to inform you that as of August 1, 19--, I will no longer be able to sell gasoline to the PD at a discount.

Mr. Robert Barron, Regional Manager for PETROX Petroleum Co., has informed me that as of August 1 the wholesale price for my gasoline will be increased by at least 5 cents per gallon. In order to keep my prices to my regular customers from being too high, I will have to stop selling it to you, or anybody else, at a discount. Last month your Police Cars bought almost 10,000 gallons of gas at my station, and you can see, the discount of 15% means that I lost nearly $2,000 from what I would have got at the regular price. I can't afford to keep doing this.

I feel really bad about this because City PD has been buying its gas at my station since 1953 at a discount, and I would like very much to continue doing business with you. I hope you will understand why I have to do this.

Sincerely yours,

A. Balogna

A. Balogna, Prop.

CITY POLICE DEPARTMENT
Interoffice Memorandum

FROM:	R. Ullrich, Lt., Budget
TO:	Chief E. Williamson, Admin. Services
SUBJECT: Budget for Fleet Operations	**DATE:** 7 Jul 19--

SIR:

According to my records, Fleet Operations has expended 62.89% of its budget for the current fiscal year for vehicle fuel, lubricants, parts, and supplies, as of June 30. At current rates of expenditure, Fleet will have run over its budget by about 25% at the end of the year.

May I suggest that all unnecessary expenditures be cancelled at once, and as much as possible that all expenditures be deferred until next year. Also, I would suggest that all personnel be advised to reduce fuel consumption as much as possible.

May I point out that Jail Operations has expended only 43.72% of its budget for food, linens, and miscellaneous supplies. Part of the

---

Page Two

surplus from Jail Operations could be transferred to Fleet Operations if you prefer. The actual dollar surplus in Jail is not enough to cover all of the excess expenditure in Fleet, but it would help to some degree. There is also a small surplus (about $1,500) in the Crime Lab budget that could be shifted to Fleet.

Please advise.

R. Ullrich, Lt.
Budget & Accounting
COPY: Capt. Lewis

EARL:

I spoke to you last month about the problem with the garage. Mike Avery says that he still can't get all his cars on the street. I've discussed this with Lewis and he tells me that the garage is having problems getting parts. If we don't get this mess straightened out pretty soon, we're going to have half our patrol on foot beats and the other half on bicycles. Would you please coordinate with Lewis and do something to get our cars back on the streets!

EZA

IN REVIEW

1. The first step in establishing an efficient purchasing system is: _____ .

2. The four major parts of the purchasing process are:
   (a) Selection.
   (b) Receipt.
   (c) Transaction.
   (d) Evaluation.
   (e) Requisition.
   (f) Specifications.
   (g) Advertising.
   (h) Acceptance.

3. True or False: Before a requisition is approved, it should be referred to the accounting unit to make sure that budgeted funds are available.

4. The most important part of any requisition is:
   (a) The specifications.
   (b) The identification of the vendor.
   (c) The signature of the approving administrator.
   (d) The signature of the purchasing agent.
   (e) The price.

5. _____ are goods that are used more or less continuously.
   (a) Services
   (b) Nonconsumables
   (c) Commodities
   (d) Items
   (e) Bidders

6. True or False: The purchase of services requires that the work be done by machines.

7. A request for proposals might be used in the purchase of:
   (a) Commodities.
   (b) Items.
   (c) Services.
   (d) All of the above.
   (e) None of the above.

8. A purchase order is:
   (a) A request for the vendor to give the price for goods.
   (b) A contract.
   (c) A receipt for the delivery of merchandise.
   (d) A payment for goods.
   (e) A statement of administrative policies.

9. True or False: Flow-through requirements apply only to purchases made by the federal or state governments.

10. Nonconsumable items such as equipment should be replaced as soon as:
    (a) It no longer works and cannot be repaired.
    (b) It is more than three years old.
    (c) It can be sold for profit.
    (d) It has reached the end of its design life.
    (e) None of the above.

REFERENCES

1. O. W. Wilson, *Police Planning*, 2nd ed., Springfield, Ill.: Charles C. Thomas, 1962, page 65.

2. Paul V. Farrell, ed., *Aljian's Purchasing Handbook*, 4th ed., New York: McGraw-Hill, 1982, pages 5−3 to 5−7.

3. Farrell, pages 3−29 to 3−30.

4. Farrell, pages 1−5 to 1−6.

5. Farrell, pages 6−10 to 6−23.

6. Farrell, pages 5−7 to 5−10.

7. Farrell, page 5−51.

8. Farrell, pages 20−23 to 20−24.

9. Farrell, pages 5−10 to 5−41.

10. Farrell, pages 5−48 to 5−49.

11. Farrell, pages 20−39 to 20−41.

12. Wilson, page 58.

13. George D. Eastman, ed., *Municipal Police Administration*, Washington, D.C.: International City Management Association, 1969, pages 270−274.

PART THREE
THE MANAGEMENT OF HUMAN RESOURCES

11 PERSONNEL RECRUITMENT AND SELECTION

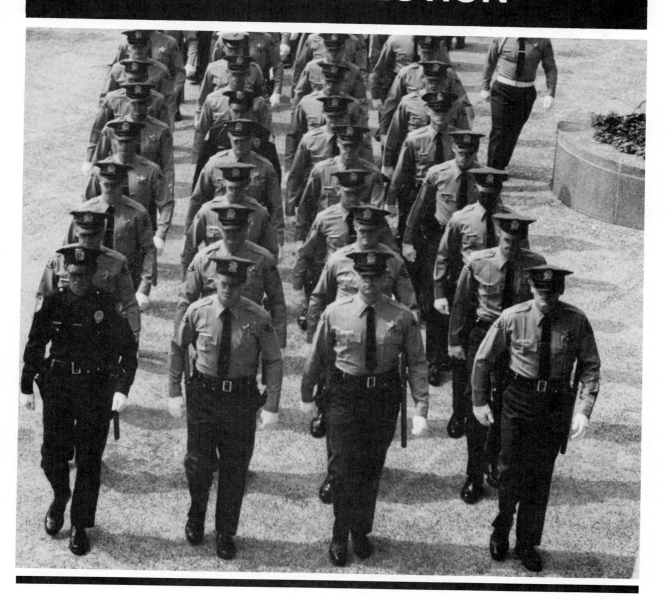

IN PART TWO, WE DISCUSSED THE PHYSICAL RESOURCES that police administrators must manage: the buildings, vehicles, and various kinds of equipment. Here we discuss the management of the most fundamental resource of a police agency: its people.

Since law enforcement has existed as a separate discipline and governmental service for more than 100 years, and policing began well before the modern era of sophisticated equipment and motor vehicles, you might suppose that all the important issues in managing a police agency's human resources were long ago settled. However, that is far from the case. The proper management of police personnel is easily the biggest source of controversy within the law enforcement profession, and between the police establishment and the community it serves.

How do you attract the best-qualified individuals to become police officers? For that matter, what does "best-qualified" mean? How do you select, from among those who apply for a police job, those who are most likely to be successful? Once you have made a choice, how do you determine whether the ones selected are, in fact, successful? How much training should new recruits be given, and what kinds of training? Do experienced officers also need training, and if so, what kinds and how often? How closely should police officers be supervised to make sure that they are doing their jobs properly? What should be done if there is evidence that they are not doing their jobs properly? What can be done to prevent and correct instances of abuse of police authority or of outright police corruption?

These are only a few of the thorny issues that confront police administrators today. On each issue, nearly everyone has an opinion, but very few people are able to back up their opinions with generally accepted facts.

The management of human resources is clearly the greatest challenge in police administration. Unfortunately, as John Furcon points out:

> The percentage of the annual police budget allocated to personnel salaries and benefits usually ranges from 75 to 90 percent of the total. . . . The percentage of the budget related to vehicle fleet purchases is ordinarily far less. Ironically, however, we find that the amount spent on vehicle operation and maintenance is many times the amount expended for personnel selection and development and training activities.[1]

In a world in which, generally speaking, you get what you pay for, Furcon's comment may reflect a disastrous misplacement of priorities. A police department *is* the people who wear its uniform and carry its badge. How they are recruited and selected determines the basic quality of the agency and of the services it provides to its community.

RECRUITING

The majority of police agencies in the United States have no formal recruiting program at all. Many police administrators reason, "Why should we go to the trouble and expense of recruiting when we have very few positions open, and usually there are more applicants than jobs available?"

The problem with this approach is (1) the number of applicants at a given time might not meet the agency's immediate personnel needs, and (2) the quality of applicants may not correspond at all with the agency's requirements.

A few very large agencies, especially those that enjoy an excellent reputation in their communities, have many more applicants than they need; nevertheless, they conduct a continuous recruiting program to attract new applicants. The reason is simply to ensure that not only is the number of applicants adequate, but that applicants of the highest possible quality are available at all times. Furthermore, experience has shown that it is more efficient and less costly in the long run to maintain a constant recruiting effort, even when there are no vacancies at the moment, than it is to start and stop recruiting drives over short periods of time.

Recruiting should not be merely a matter of rounding up warm bodies to fill vacancies. A sophisticated recruiting program is designed to locate, identify, and attract individuals who have the personal characteristics, basic skills, and motivation to become outstanding police officers. These traits are not widely distributed among the general population; finding these individuals demands forethought and diligence. As sociologist Jennie Farley points out, "*Where* employers look for applicants may well determine who they find."[2] She could have added that *how* employers look is just as important.

Before any recruiting program is established, the administrator must be able to answer the question, "What kind of people do we want?" The answer may seem obvious, but it is not. Defining the ideal police officer has proven to be very difficult despite the best efforts of hundreds of police officials and social scientists.

If one were recruiting, say, basketball players, the task would be comparatively simple: Give each prospective applicant a ball, put him or her on a court with several players of known ability, and see how the recruit performs. The Boston Symphony Orchestra has used the technique of having applicants play their instruments while a panel of judges, hidden behind an opaque screen, listen to and evaluate the performance.[3] But in both cases, the standards for selecting basketball players or symphony musicians are relatively clear-cut. The job of police officer is so complex and subtle that it defies any simple analysis.

Recruitment of Entry-Level Personnel

Nearly all American law enforcement agencies have adopted the same basic personnel system as the military services. With rare exceptions, all new personnel enter at the lowest level and are assigned general duties that, in theory, demand only modest skills and experience. Those who perform the entry-level duties successfully may be promoted, sooner or later, to higher-level positions that involve either supervision of the entry-level personnel or more specialized skills. In other words, all new police officers are assigned to patrol; those who prove to be good patrol officers have the opportunity to become, in turn, sergeants, lieutenants, captains, detectives, communications specialists, crime prevention specialists, and so on. It is very rare for an American police agency to hire someone for any position other than patrol officer.

Ironically, the job of patrol officer is actually the most demanding and difficult of all law enforcement jobs. No other police officer is likely to be exposed to the endless variety of challenges that face patrol officers on the street. Nevertheless, the system demands that the best, most effective patrol officers move up to positions that are, in some ways, less demanding (although they involve broader responsibilities). By implication, officers who remain in the patrol force throughout their careers are often regarded as failures.

This system places a tremendous burden on the recruiting and selection process. If new police officers were put in jobs that involve relatively modest demands, they could be given the time and opportunity to prove themselves and to learn what will be expected of them before they were put on the streets. Instead, new officers must be nearly at the peak of their capabilities from their first day on the job. It is simply too dangerous—to the recruit, to other police officers, and to the community—to hire someone as a police officer whose capabilities are uncertain.

Under these circumstances, recruiters must cast their net as widely as possible, hoping to bring the greatest possible number of applicants into the selection process. Since the criteria for selecting successful patrol officers are so difficult to determine, the recruiter can never be certain which individuals are likely to succeed.

The techniques used in police recruiting are not especially different from those used in private industry, the military, and other governmental services. Posters, pamphlets, booklets, and other printed materials are distributed wherever young people are likely to see them. Police personnel speak at high school assemblies, church youth group meetings, and anywhere else prospective recruits might congregate. Radio and television *public service announcements* ("commercials" that are broadcast at no cost to the agency) and appearances on radio and television talk shows also may be effective. All these activities are designed simply to call attention to the fact that the police department is seeking applicants.

The recruiting materials and literature must be developed with care. (See Figure 11.1) They must be attractive to their intended audience, of course; dull and unimaginative posters or public service announcements are not likely to attract anyone. At the same time, recruiting materials must not mislead prospective recruits into false expectations about police work. Jack L. Kuykendall and Peter C. Unsinger have observed, "All too often, applicants get images from the [entertainment] media of what law enforcement is all about, and they are quite shocked when they are informed, or discover, what being a policeman [sic] actually involves."[4]

Consequently, recruiting materials and presentations by recruiters must not only attract qualified applicants, but must serve to correct some of the misconceptions that the public has. People whose knowledge of law enforcement is gained mostly by watching television crime shows will be astonished to learn that police officers are not encouraged to beat up informants, shoot suspects on sight, race at breakneck speed in their patrol vehicles, trick suspects into confessing their crimes, or flirt with citizens who have been stopped for traffic violations. Prospective applicants should be told forthrightly that police work is occasionally dangerous, usually tedious, often frustrating, and sometimes emotionally devastating. It demands great physical stamina, mental alertness, an exceptionally reliable memory, constant attention to minute details, and nearly unshakable emotional stability. It is never glamorous. Once in a while it is extraordinarily, deeply satisfying.

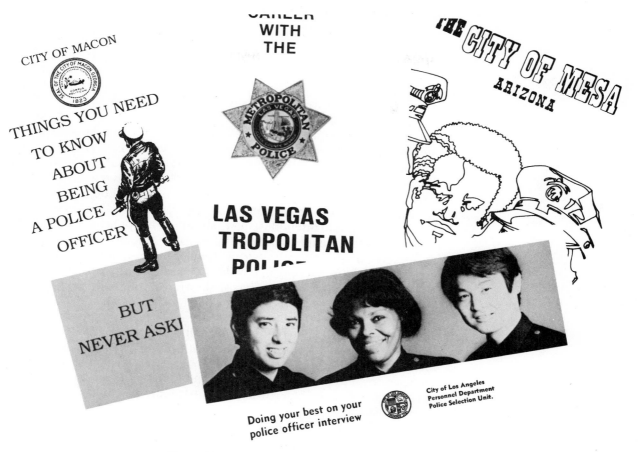

Figure 11-1 Recruiting literature must be not only attractive but also informative and accurate. (Courtesy Los Angeles Police Department, Las Vegas Metropolitan Police Department, Macon, Georgia Police Department and Mesa, Arizona Police Department.)

Recruiters must be candid not to discourage qualified applicants but to discourage those who might apply for the wrong reasons. By the same token, recruiters must be careful never to mislead prospective applicants about matters such as pay, job security, fringe benefits, or the chances for promotion. Human resources expert Robert L. Desatrik warns, "During the recruiting process an organization will foster unrealistic expectations. . . . These bright young people will look around at their competition, perceive that they can reach the top more quickly elsewhere, and resign. . . . Conversely, the ineffective performers will stay as long as possible, knowing that they cannot compete in the open market."[5]

Police recruiters must realize that they are in fact competing with all other employers, both those in governmental services and private industry. Unfortunately, the competition frequently will offer higher starting wages, more attractive fringe benefits and working conditions, and at least equally good chances for advancement. Recruiters may be tempted to emphasize, even exaggerate, whatever slight advantages they have, to the point of misleading recruits who will later be disillusioned and resentful when they learn that they have been misled.

What can recruiters offer that will attract qualified candidates? They should be able to offer wages and other benefits that are not unreasonable for the level of education and experience that are required. More important, recruiters can appeal to the idealism and desire for service to the community that are widespread among young people.

Perhaps the most important factor is the general reputation of the police agency. An agency that enjoys a well-deserved reputation for effectiveness, integrity, and dedication to serving the public will be far more successful in its recruiting than an agency with an unfavorable image. However, it is not sufficient for an agency to cultivate a good image by papering over the truth. In the long run, an agency that wants to enjoy a good reputation must be in fact effective, incorruptible, and dedicated to public service.

Recruiters should attempt to maintain a pool of applicants that will meet the agency's foreseeable personnel needs over at least the next year, even when there are no current vacancies. It is not unreasonable to estimate that of every 10 applicants, only one will be chosen for entry-level training, and that of every 10 trainees only five or six will complete the training and be accepted as permanent employees. Thus for every vacancy to be filled in the future, the recruiter needs to attract 20 or more applicants.[6]

Recruiters must be aware that their ultimate success lies in the future. They must not become so concerned with filling the agency's immediate vacancies that they neglect longer-term needs. For example, many police agencies now require recruits to have a minimum of two years of college; a few agencies require a college degree. But this does not mean that recruiters should concentrate entirely on college students as prospective applicants. They should devote a part of their time to recruiting among high school students, if only to let potential future recruits know what requirements they will have to meet. Even grade-school and junior-high students should be encouraged to consider careers in law enforcement and to prepare themselves in high school and college.

Recruiting College Students

Should a college degree be required of all recruits? The question is controversial among police authorities; the prevailing opinion is that a degree is not essential, but that, all else being equal, a police officer's job performance increases in direct proportion to the amount of his or her formal education.[7] Consequently, many agencies now require at least a year or two of college.

Since college education is relatively specialized, are some college degrees more valuable than others? This, too, is a controversial question. Some police officials place a high premium on academic training in law enforcement, police science, or criminal justice. Other officials take just the opposite approach; they believe that students with degrees in law enforcement will have to be detrained of overly idealistic and unrealistic attitudes. Obviously, the problem is that some officials lack confidence in the academic program! Nevertheless, it is a fact that some police officials prefer graduates with degrees in the liberal arts, sciences, or other fields.

Whatever an agency's preferences may be, recruiting on college campuses will be a major part of the overall recruitment effort. The effort should begin with standard techniques such as the distribution of posters and literature, but that is only the beginning.

Most colleges have a placement office whose specific responsibility is to help students in finding suitable employment after graduation. The police recruiter should work closely with the placement office staff in identifying promising students. Wherever possible, the recruiter should meet with individual instructors whose students are likely prospects.

On-campus recruiting should be a two-step process. First, students who might be interested in law enforcement as a career must be identified. Second, interested students must be screened to be sure that they have the appropriate qualifications for the recruiter's agency, and then they should be encouraged to submit an application.

The first step can be accomplished with the help of the placement office and by techniques such as operating a booth in a high-traffic area, perhaps in the student union. The second step requires personal contact between the recruiter and promising students. This contact might be initiated by a letter from the recruiter to all students who have been identified as prospects. The letter might invite the student to submit a preapplication, or to meet the recruiter at a designated time and place for a brief interview. Students could be invited to a social gathering where they would have the opportunity to meet recruiters for informal discussions, after which individual interviews would be held.

Most of the recruiter's time will be spent answering students' questions. At the same time, the recruiter should evaluate each student in terms of the agency's basic requirements. Students who are clearly unsuitable for law enforcement careers should be candidly discouraged from wasting time that could be better spent preparing for another career. Students who are marginally qualified or whose qualifications are uncertain should be encouraged to take whatever steps are necessary to correct their deficiencies. Students whose qualifications are superior should be identified for follow-up contacts.

It is especially important for promising prospects to receive follow-up attention. One brief on-campus visit or interview is not enough. At the very least, prospective recruits should receive a letter, a week or two after the initial visit, thanking them for their time and encouraging them to keep in touch with the agency. The most promising prospects should be contacted by letter or, if possible, by telephone every few months, to remind them of the agency's interest. They might be encouraged to enroll in the agency's volunteer program or intern program, if this exists. Follow-up contacts should continue until either the student formally applies for a police job or indicates that he or she is no longer interested.

In addition, students who have been identified as promising recruits should be asked to refer the recruiter to any of their friends who might be interested in a police career. These referrals are not only an excellent way to meet other good prospects, but they give the recruiter additional background information about the initial prospect.

Many police departments have organized volunteer programs that are especially appealing to college-age young people who are interested in a career in law enforcement. Some agencies have **police cadets**, unpaid volunteers who assist commissioned officers in a variety of routine tasks; **police aides**, either part-time or full-time paid employees who perform clerical and public service duties; Explorer Scouts, affiliated with the Boy Scouts of America, who carry out special public service projects; or **community service officers**, noncommissioned personnel (usually paid, full-time employees) who assist the police in crime prevention, community relations, and social welfare projects. College-age prospective recruits should be invited to participate in any of these programs as a valuable introduction to law enforcement.

Recruiting Minority Applicants

Strictly speaking, a person is a member of an ethnic minority if he or she belongs to a racial, nationality, or language group that makes up something less than half the population of the community. In that sense, all Americans are members of ethnic minorities, since no one group accounts for more than half of the total population. However, **minority** also has a specific legal meaning. For reasons of history and social policy, the courts and legislatures have defined minority to include certain specific groups who have been the victims of various kinds of discrimination in the past. Those groups are blacks, Hispanics, Native Americans (including the native tribes of Alaska), and Orientals. We use the term minority to mean these specific ethnic groups.

It is illegal to discriminate against any applicant or employee because of his or her gender, age, race, creed, color, national origin, native language, marital status, or other characteristics that are irrelevant to the job. In fact, at the end of the 1970s there were more than 130 federal laws and regulations concerning personnel practices in industry and public employment, and most of those laws and regulations were designed to prevent discrimination.[8] Furthermore, it is poor administrative policy to allow discrimination to persist, since members of minority communities are extremely sensitive to these conditions and reject the authority of any agency that does not recognize and protect their rights as citizens.

However, it is not enough for the police administrator to declare, "We will no longer discriminate against minority individuals. From now on, anyone who meets the standards we have set for new employees will be accepted." The problem is that the standards themselves may be discriminatory, intentionally or not. For example, many police agencies at one time required all recruits to be not less than 5 feet, 10 inches tall; some required recruits to be at least 6 feet tall. Of course, not many women could meet that requirement, and very few Hispanic men could do so. Thus, the requirement discriminated against those two groups.

Over the past two decades, every requirement used by police agencies and other employers to screen applicants has been tested in court or by the administrative procedures of the federal **Equal Employment Opportunity Commission (EEOC)**. Those requirements or standards that are found to be clearly and fairly relevant to the work of the police officer have been allowed to stand. However, requirements that are purely arbitrary or that have no bearing on a person's ability to be a competent police officer have been eliminated or modified to remove their discriminatory effect.

Simply removing unfair standards and treating all applicants equally may not be enough. Because of discriminatory practices in the past, ethnic minorities are seriously **underrepresented** in many police agencies; that is, there are fewer minority police officers than there would be if there had been no discrimination, and there are fewer than there should be in proportion to the number of minority individuals in the general population. Ethnic minorities are especially underrepresented at the higher administrative levels of most police departments. By the late 1960s, the courts and legislatures began to realize that passively ending discrimination would do very little to correct the problem of underrepresentation. A positive effort would be required.

This positive effort must be expressed in the form of an **affirmative action plan**, a statement of the methods that an agency will use to correct minority underrepresentation. Some affirmative action plans have been developed as a result of court orders and have had to be submitted to the EEOC for approval. However, many agencies have developed voluntary plans, which also may be submitted to EEOC for acceptance; later, if an individual complains that an agency's personnel policies are discriminatory, the existence of an EEOC-accepted plan should at least demonstrate the agency's good intentions.

Once a plan has been developed, submitted to the EEOC, and accepted, it must be carried out. The test of any plan is the results that it produces. An affirmative action plan should produce a clear increase in the proportion of minority individuals at all ranks. These results usually are measured against a set of specific goals that are expressed in terms of the percentages of employees of different ethnic backgrounds. For example, an agency might begin with a personnel roster that consists of 92 percent white males, 5 percent black males, 1 percent Hispanic males, and 2 percent females. Its affirmative action plan might call for the following percentages over a five-year period:

	Male (%)			Female (%)
	White	Black	Hispanic	
1st year	88	6	2	4
2nd year	80	10	4	6
3rd year	75	12	8	15
4th year	65	15	10	20
5th year	60	15	12	23

These goals would bring the agency's personnel complement more into line with the proportional minority membership in the community (assuming that the single category of female includes minority women in appropriate proportions). Of course, since women are not a minority but actually a slight majority of the general population, they would still be underrepresented at the end of the five-year period in this plan. However, given the fact that about half of all women do not enter the labor force and that women in general may be somewhat less attracted to careers in law enforcement than are men, these goals may be realistic. (Note that the figures shown here are intended merely for purposes of illustration and do not represent the actual plan of any particular agency.)

Despite much progress in the past two decades, minorities continue to be underrepresented in most police agencies and therefore are a special concern of recruiters. (Photo courtesy Texas Department of Public Safety.)

The use of proportional goals sometimes has been misinterpreted to mean that a police agency is required to meet specific quotas. In fact, a few court decisions have imposed proportional goals as quotas, as a means of evaluating an employer's good faith and efforts to correct underrepresentation. Ordinarily, the percentages are simply goals toward which an agency has committed its efforts.

No police agency has been required to hire only minority individuals or women, or to hire them in preference to all qualified white males. However, some agencies have been required by courts to hire minority or female applicants in preference to *equally qualified* white males until the representation goals have been achieved. If the current goal is to raise the percentage of black males from, say, 5 to 10 percent, then black male applicants would be given preference over white males who have essentially the same qualifications, until the goal is met; after that, all applicants should be considered equally.[9]

Affirmative action plans do not consist only of goals for proportional representation; some EEOC-approved plans do not even contain specific goals. However, a plan must state that all arbitrary standards of selection have been eliminated and that every effort is made to seek, identify, and attract qualified minority applicants.

That brings us back to the subject of recruiting. In principle, the recruitment of minority applicants is no different from the recruitment of anyone else. Recruiters use essentially the same techniques: literature distributed to places where young people are likely to find it, speeches to community organizations, and, when possible, the use of the mass media.

An extra effort must be made to bring the recruiting message to the minority population. If the recruiter is a white male police officer, he may have no idea where young blacks or Hispanics congregate. Recruiters who are actively seeking minority applicants must be willing and able to "speak the language" of their prospects. In some cases, this is literally true; a recruiter who speaks Spanish reasonably well is more likely to be successful with Hispanic young people than a recruiter who does not know the language at all. Even more important than proficiency in another language is the recruiter's understanding of the minority population's culture, social environment, attitudes, and values. Black, Hispanic, Native American, or Oriental young people do not have the same attitudes toward law enforcement, police officers, and careers in policing that middle-class white youths are likely to have. Recruiters who do not personally share their targets' social background must at least be trained to understand it.[10]

Personal contact with the minority community is vital. It is not enough for the recruiter to make a speech at a high school with a high percentage of minority students. The recruiter also must meet with the school administrators and teachers, asking them to identify students who might be good prospects. Similarly, the recruiter should contact coaches, ministers, and leaders of civic organizations, especially those that are youth-oriented, such as the Scouts, YMCA and YWCA, Boys Clubs, and so on.

The police recruiter also must face a difficult fact: the most outstanding minority young people are not likely to be interested in a police career. Since virtually all employers are actively seeking minority applicants, the exceptional young person has almost unlimited opportunities. A career in law enforcement, with its chronically low salaries, mediocre fringe benefits, and generally unfavorable working conditions, is not very appealing. Also, most law enforcement agencies have a far worse reputation in the minority community than they do in the community at large, whether or not the poor reputation is deserved.

There is nothing the recruiter can do about low salaries and poor working conditions. There is very little the recruiter can do about an agency's poor reputation, except to try to correct it by giving factual information in response to misconceptions and distortions. The recruiter must not try to ignore the problem or counteract it with misleading statements, exaggerations, or false propaganda. In particular, the recruiter must be careful not to overstate the agency's progress in carrying out its affirmative action plan; the recruiter should candidly admit the extent of progress in raising minority representation and in opening opportunities for advancement.[11]

Recruiting Women

Women have been employed by American police departments since about 1845, when New York City first hired women as prison matrons. However, until the late 1960s women police officers were employed only for a limited range of duties: They were used as matrons in women's prisons or jails, as plainclothes officers in juvenile, crime prevention, and other specialized units, and occasionally as undercover agents in vice and organized crime units. Many were assigned to essentially social-service, non-law-enforcement duties. Because of their limited roles and lack of exposure to general law enforcement duties, women had virtually no opportunity for advancement in police careers.

Women began to complain about these limitations during the mid-60s, as an outgrowth of the civil rights and women's liberation movements. In 1968, the Indianapolis Police Department became the first in the United States to employ women as general-duty patrol officers.[12] In 1972, the U.S. Supreme Court declared that job discrimination based on gender was unconstitutional, in a case that did not involve a police department, and Congress passed the Equal Rights Amendment, which was never ratified by the states but nevertheless influenced federal and state legislation and both private and public employment practices. The Federal Bureau of Investigation and the U.S. Secret Service immediately began to hire women as regular agents. The metropolitan police in Washington, D.C., St. Louis, and New York City, and the Pennsylvania State Police, also began to employ women as general-duty patrol officers.[13] By the mid-70s, most urban police departments had at least a few women patrol officers. In short, nondiscriminatory employment policies apply to women as well as to minority men.

Assigning women to general patrol duties and making available to them advancement into the higher ranks of law enforcement is not without problems. According to sociologist Susan Ehrlich Martin, about half of the male officers in the Washington, D.C., Metro Police Department were dogmatically opposed to working with female officers, no matter what the law might say. Female officers themselves had great difficulty in adapting to the demands of police patrol work and in relating to their male and female colleagues.[14] Resolving these problems is not the job of the recruiter, but women who are interested in a career in law enforcement will have many questions about these matters, and a recruiter who cannot answer the questions candidly will lose some excellent candidates.

Other than that, recruiting women is not substantially different from recruiting men. As with the recruitment of minority males, the recruiter must make a special effort to go where the candidates are likely to be found; this may include youth organizations that cater to young women, such as the Girl Scouts, Campfire Girls, and YWCA, or women's colleges. However, women are most likely to be found in the same places as men: high schools, youth groups, churches, colleges, and universities. When addressing such groups, the recruiter should make a special effort to make it clear that women are sought as prospective recruits.

Some recruiters are baffled by the "problem" of minority women: should they be treated as women or as members of a minority, or both? Or are they a special category distinct from either one? Probably the best approach is to treat minority women first as members of a minority, since they are likely to identify with the minority group and its culture and values. At the same time, the recruiter must address the candidate's special concerns about the treatment of women.

Ultimately, every prospect must be treated as an individual. The recruiter must learn what his or her interests, concerns, and capabilities are, regardless of gender or ethnic background. After all, the recruiter's job is to attract the most promising individuals, not the most promising "categories."

Recruiting Experienced Personnel

One of the peculiarities of American law enforcement is the absolute refusal of most agencies to consider applicants from other police departments for higher-level positions. A study of police personnel practices, conducted under the auspices of the Police Foundation in 1972, found that about one-fourth of all American police departments have a firm policy of not accepting transfers from other agencies. Among the three-fourths of departments that have no such policy, transfers were still exceedingly rare; less than one-third of the agencies that responded to the survey had ever hired a police officer with previous police experience. Even when agencies do employ officers with previous experience, almost always the new employee must start over as a basic trainee or patrol officer. Out of some 670 American police agencies, only nine had hired an officer with previous experience for any position above the rank of police officer; four of those nine were small police departments whose chief had been previously employed in a nearby urban agency.[15]

Why is it so difficult for police officers to transfer their hard-won skills and experience from one agency to another? Most agencies that have policies against such **lateral entry** claim that there are laws or civil service regulations against it. However, this merely shifts the blame without explaining why these laws or regulations exist. Another common explanation is that experience in one agency has no particular value in another agency, where administrative policies, law enforcement techniques, and the social environment are likely to be completely different. Some police officials insist that an officer with experience in another agency must be completely "retrained" before he or she is competent in their agency.

It is virtually impossible to prove or disprove the validity of these claims. From an objective point of view, the differences in administrative policies and law enforcement techniques from one agency to another, especially if both are in the same state, are not overwhelming. The social environment in most large urban agencies certainly is different from that in small suburban or rural agencies. Nevertheless, it is hard to imagine that a competent, experienced officer could not adapt to the changed environment; certainly, people in other professions adapt to different working conditions when they change jobs. To put it another way, it seems at least equally likely that the training and experience gained by a police officer in one setting would enable him or her to adapt to a new environment more rapidly than a brand new, totally inexperienced recruit will.

The problem may lie not in differences in working conditions, but instead in differences in the standards of recruit selection and training among different agencies. A personnel officer in Agency A has no way of knowing whether an applicant from Agency B has gone through the same kind of selection process and training that Agency A would have given its own recruits. Until recently, a majority of small police agencies have given their recruits no training at all. The solution to this problem may rest partly in the certification programs that are now in effect in all but a few states. **Certification** simply means that an individual must meet certain basic minimum standards and must complete a prescribed training program in order to be employed as a police officer anywhere in the state. We will discuss the details of state certification programs in Chapter 12. The point here is that there is no apparent reason for a police agency to prohibit certified police officers from other agencies from competing for positions. However, there are still some states with no certification program at all, and no two state programs are exactly alike. Thus, an officer qualified in one state may not meet even the minimum qualifications in another state. Until there is a greater degree of standardization from state to state, and police officials generally recognize that certification is a valid means of establishing an officer's credentials as a qualified applicant, it is likely that lateral transfers will continue to be rare.

SELECTION

Recruiters and police administrators have no control over who applies for a job in a police department. Individuals who are obviously unsuitable may be discouraged from submitting an application, but it is not always obvious whether an applicant is qualified or not. Thus an applicant's suitability for employment must be determined through some process of evaluation.

Even if there were only one position to be filled and only one applicant for that position, some kind of evaluation process would be necessary to ensure that the applicant is qualified for the position. In fact, there are usually several applicants for every vacancy, and therefore it is necessary to determine which applicant is best suited to the position. This is done through a process of selection.

At one time, police departments were free to use whatever selection criteria they liked. Some of the criteria were entirely arbitrary; they were based solely on the personal prejudices and whims of the agencies' administrators. Other criteria were based on vague notions and unproven theories about what makes a good patrol officer. For example, the 1972 Police Foundation study of American police personnel practices found that various agencies had the following minimum requirements for new recruits (among others):

Must be between the ages of 21 and 34.

Must be between 5 ft, 8 in. and 6 ft, 5 in. tall.

Must weigh between 146 and 229 pounds.

Must have 20/20 vision (not worse than 20/50 uncorrected).

Must be able to swim.

Must not be color blind.

Must be a resident of the city (or other jurisdiction) for six months before applying.

Must be a registered voter.

Must have a valid driver's license.

At first glance, each of the criteria listed above seems fairly reasonable. However, *none* of these standards was used by all police agencies; some agencies had much less specific standards, while others had much stricter criteria. In addition, more than a dozen different written tests were used by one agency or another to determine applicants' intelligence, educational achievement, adaptability, mental alertness, mental maturity, or other psychological qualities.[16] Nearly all agencies required applicants to pass a physical examination performed by a physician, but the items covered by the examination varied from one agency to another. Many agencies also required applicants to pass a physical agility test that consisted of anything from lifting weights to performing pushups and other calisthenics to running an obstacle course. Some agencies required applicants to pass an examination by a psychiatrist or psychologist.[17]

Most agencies used the same selection criteria for all applicants. As we pointed out earlier, this automatically meant that most women and many minority males were disqualified because they could not meet the height, weight, and physical agility standards. Eventually the courts ruled that an employer could use any standard it wanted, even if the standard discriminated against some prospective employees, *provided* the employer could prove that the standard was a reasonably accurate method of determining whether a person could perform the work that the employees would be expected to perform. Criteria that were not clearly job-related could not be used, even if there was no proof that they were discriminatory.

When police departments began trying to implement the court rulings, they discovered a serious problem: No one knew exactly what qualities in an applicant are most likely to predict the applicant's future success as a police officer. In fact, as police officials and social scientists attempted to develop new, job-related selection criteria, they found that they could not agree on even a simple definition of what makes a successful police officer, or of what "successful police officer" means. Does it mean someone who makes a lot of arrests? Or does it mean someone whose preventive patrol techniques are so good that a high volume of arrests is not needed?[18]

A police department must screen out those applicants who are unfit in the sense that they are incapable of becoming competent police officers. At the same time, the department is interested in screening in or selecting those applicants who are most likely to become not just competent, but superior police officers. Any standards or criteria used to screen out or screen in applicants must be clearly related to the job of the police officer, and they should have **predictive validity**; that is, they should accurately determine whether an individual is likely to become a competent police officer. All this must be accomplished despite the fact that there is no universally agreed-upon definition of what a "competent police officer" is or does, or of what qualities in an applicant are likely to produce competence.[19]

Despite this dilemma, police departments must continue to hire new personnel, and they must continue to select from the applicants available to them. If there are no perfect methods of selection, the only recourse is to use the best available methods (even though imperfect) and continually seek to improve them.

The Multiple-Hurdle Procedure

The traditional method of selecting recruits from a group of applicants involves the use of a series of separate tests. An applicant's failure to pass any one test immediately disqualifies the person from further consideration.

First, applicants are informed of the agency's basic minimum qualifications: factors such as minimum age, minimum educational attainment, height and weight standards, and residency requirements. These are all factors that an applicant can judge for himself or herself; if the agency requires a minimum height of 5 feet, 8 inches, a person who is 5 feet, 4 inches tall will not bother to apply.

All applicants who meet the basic minimum standards are then put through a series of tests. The tests actually used vary from one agency to the next, and the order in which the tests are applied also varies. However, a typical sequence might begin with a written test that the applicant must pass with a specified minimum score. Those who fail the written test are immediately dismissed. Those who pass the written test are then given a thorough physical examination; those who pass it are required to complete a physical agility test. After that, some agencies use either a written psychological test or applicants are interviewed by a clinical psychologist or psychiatrist. Each test or "hurdle" produces a clear, pass-or-fail decision; those who fail any one test are not allowed to continue.

The last two steps in the multiple-hurdle process usually are an oral interview with anywhere from one to seven police officials and a background investigation conducted by the agency's investigative personnel. We will have more to say about these two steps later.

The biggest advantage of the multiple-hurdle process is its efficiency. The various hurdles can be arranged in a sequence according to their relative cost and difficulty. Administering the written intelligence test is relatively inexpensive and simple, while conducting a background investigation is expensive and time-consuming. The more costly steps are not wasted on applicants who are certain to be disqualified anyway. Second, each unsuccessful applicant knows (or should know) where he or she failed and, in some cases, may be able to correct the deficiency and successfully take the tests another time.

However, there are several disadvantages to the multiple-hurdle procedure. Applicants vary in their ability to take certain kinds of tests, especially written tests, regardless of their potential capabilities. An applicant might fail a test on a bad day that he or she would have passed on another day. Usually the multiple-hurdle process makes no provision for second chances; an applicant who fails any one test must start over.

Some of the tests that are commonly used in multiple-hurdle procedures are of questionable value. As late as 1975, many police departments continued to use written intelligence tests that were originally developed for the testing of U.S. Army recruits—in World War I. There is very little evidence that even the newest intelligence and psychological tests have a direct relationship to the job of patrol officer, although there is no question that patrol officers must have above-average intelligence and must be emotionally stable. Psychological interviews, and even the medical examination performed by a physician, may involve subjective judgments that have no proven relationship to an individual's ability to perform the job of police officer. For example, some physicians would automatically fail an applicant who has a heart murmur; others would require that the applicant undergo lengthy and expensive cardiovascular testing to determine whether the heart murmur poses a health threat; still other physicians would consider a slight heart murmur in an otherwise healthy young person to be irrelevant.

Finally, the multiple-hurdle process ignores the widely held belief that no single set of qualities or personal characteristics can be used to define the ideal patrol officer. Some successful patrol officers are more intelligent than others; some are more physically vigorous than others; some are more

APPLICATION FOR EMPLOYMENT

CITY AND COUNTY OF MONTGOMERY

"An Equal Opportunity Employer

PERSONNEL DEPARTMENT

City Hall

Montgomery, Alabama 36102

	Accepted	Rejected
Citz.		
Ed.		
Exp.		
Res.		
Other		

Title of Position: _____

INSTRUCTIONS:
ALL BLANKS MUST BE
FILLED IN COMPLETELY

Name: (Type or print name)

Mr.

Mrs.

Miss

_____ First _____ Middle _____ Last _____ Race _____ Age _____

Address _____ House No. _____ Street _____ City _____ State _____ Zip _____ Tel. No. _____

How long have you lived in Alabama immediately prior to date of application _____ Yr. _____ Mo. _____

Are you a U.S. citizen? _____

Date of Birth _____ Place of Birth _____ City _____ County _____ State _____

PERSONAL DATA: Height _____ft.____in. Weight _____lbs. What is the condition of your health? _____

Marital Status: Single ☐; Married ☐; Separated ☐; Widowed ☐; Number of dependents under 18. _____

Do you have any physical handicaps? _____ . If so, attach a description to this application. Do you object to having your present employer questioned about your work? _____ . Have you ever been discharged or forced to resign from a position? _____ . If so, attach a complete explanation to this application. Have you ever been convicted of any law violation other than a minor traffic violation? _____ . If so, give name and location of court, date, nature of charge and disposition. _____

SOCIAL SECURITY NO. _____

EDUCATION	Circle Highest Grade you Completed	Date Completed
Grammar and High School	1 2 3 4 5 6 7 8 9 10 11 12	
College or University (name of schools)	1 2 3 4 5 6 7 Degrees	
	Major	
Business, Trade or Correspondence School		
	Courses Studied	
List your professional certificate or license		

List three reliable persons, not relatives or employers, who know you well enough to give information about you:

	Address	Occupation

WORK HISTORY

Beginning with your PRESENT or most recent employment, list in REVERSE ORDER periods of employment. Each time you chaged jobs or your title changed should be listed as a separate period. Give complete information, especially about the kind of work you did. (Use extra sheet if necessary). Applicant must be specific and accurate in stating their experience and training for this position.

EMPLOYMENT RECORD: List all employment.

Employment Dates	Occupation and Description of Duties	Employer's Name and Address	Salary Received	Reason For Leaving
FROM				
TO				
TOTAL MOS.				
FROM				
TO				
TOTAL MOS.				
FROM				
TO				
TOTAL MOS				
FROM				
TO				
TOTAL MOS.				
FROM				
TO				
TOTAL MOS.				
FROM				
TO				
TOTAL MOS.				
FROM				
TO				
TOTAL MOS.				
FROM				
TO				
TOTAL MOS.				

6. Show other experience by using additional sheets.

I hereby certify that all statements made hereon and attached hereto are true and correct to the best of my knowledge. Any false statement may be cause for denying me the right to examination or employment.

Date _____   Signature _____

Figure 11-2 A police employment application form. This short form is used to screen applicants. Later, applicants must complete a more detailed form. (Courtesy Montgomery, Alabama Police Department.)

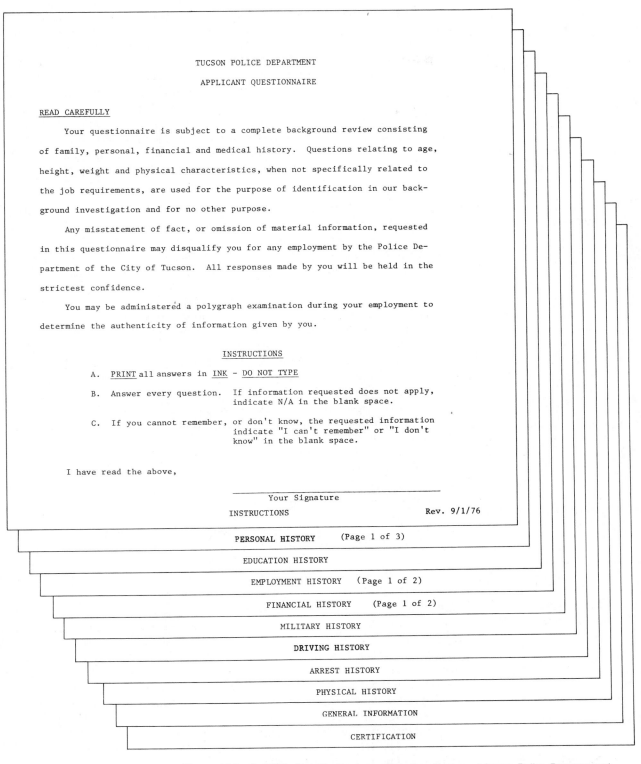

TUCSON POLICE DEPARTMENT

APPLICANT QUESTIONNAIRE

READ CAREFULLY

Your questionnaire is subject to a complete background review consisting of family, personal, financial and medical history. Questions relating to age, height, weight and physical characteristics, when not specifically related to the job requirements, are used for the purpose of identification in our background investigation and for no other purpose.

Any misstatement of fact, or omission of material information, requested in this questionnaire may disqualify you for any employment by the Police Department of the City of Tucson. All responses made by you will be held in the strictest confidence.

You may be administered a polygraph examination during your employment to determine the authenticity of information given by you.

INSTRUCTIONS

A. PRINT all answers in INK - DO NOT TYPE

B. Answer every question. If information requested does not apply, indicate N/A in the blank space.

C. If you cannot remember, or don't know, the requested information indicate "I can't remember" or "I don't know" in the blank space.

I have read the above,

_____
Your Signature

INSTRUCTIONS   Rev. 9/1/76

PERSONAL HISTORY   (Page 1 of 3)

EDUCATION HISTORY

EMPLOYMENT HISTORY   (Page 1 of 2)

FINANCIAL HISTORY   (Page 1 of 2)

MILITARY HISTORY

DRIVING HISTORY

ARREST HISTORY

PHYSICAL HISTORY

GENERAL INFORMATION

CERTIFICATION

Figure 11-3 A detailed application form. (Courtesy Tucson, Arizona, Police Department.)

emotionally stable than others. Certainly, a person who is significantly deficient in any of those three areas would not be fit for consideration. However, a person might be only marginally qualified in one or more areas, yet so highly qualified in another area that the deficiencies are not that important. An arbitrary pass-or-fail cutoff point on consecutive tests would not allow an applicant to compensate for a minor deficiency in one area. Furthermore, most people, given proper training and guidance, can improve their intellectual, physical, and emotional performance. Young people, especially those from a relatively deprived social and economic background, are particularly likely to show deficiencies that can be corrected in a well-conceived and properly executed training program.

The Multiple Assessment Procedure

Some of the disadvantages of the multiple-hurdle process can be avoided by eliminating the use of a single set of pass-or-fail standards and, instead, considering the overall performance of each applicant on a series of tests. Often the tests are the same ones used in the multiple-hurdle procedure. However, each applicant receives a numerical score on each test, and the scores may be weighted according to their relative importance. For example, the scores on a physical agility test might range from 0 to 10, while the scores on a written intelligence test might range from 0 to 25. After an applicant has completed all the tests, his or her scores are added together. Sometimes each applicant's average score is computed. In any case, all of the applicants who complete the test series are ranked according to their total or average scores.

This procedure allows an applicant to make up for a low score on one test by getting a high score on another test. If weighting formulas are used, greater emphasis can be placed on the characteristics that are presumed to be most significant.

After all applicants have been ranked according to their scores, oral interviews are conducted beginning with the highest-ranked applicant and continuing down the rankings as far as necessary to fill the available vacancies. Usually more applicants are interviewed than will be hired, since some recruits are certain to drop out during training. Some agencies also have a cutoff point below which they will not go; only applicants ranked in the top half, or top third, are interviewed even if this leaves some unfilled vacancies.

The Assessment Center Method

The newest selection procedure is an expanded form of the multiple-assessment procedure; it is called the **assessment center method**. Usually all applicants are brought to a single location and put through a series of assessment tests; however, according to psychologist Robert J. Filer, "An assessment center is a method. . . ; it is not a place."[20]

Many of the same testing procedures and techniques that are used in the multiple-hurdle and multiple-assessment procedures are also used in the assessment center method. In addition, applicants are required to complete several **performance tests** in which they are expected to demonstrate their ability to perform tasks similar to those actually performed by police officers. The performance tests often take the form of simulated police activities. Some of these simulation tests are similar to the in-basket exercises in this text. Other simulations involve situational testing. Filer describes a situational test used by some Colorado police departments:

The applicant [was] brought to the testing room and given a gun belt to wear. He or she was then briefly instructed in handcuffing and frisking procedure and was handed a card on which minimal instructions were typed. An example would be, "You are driving on patrol in the downtown area when you notice a young man (approximately 25 years of age) prying at a parking meter with a screwdriver. It is 4:45 p.m. Do your duty."

When the applicant had read and understood the card, he or she entered the room in which [a police officer playing the part of] an irate citizen was kicking and prying at the parking meter. The "theme" that the [actor] followed in this situation was that he had been looking for a parking place for 15 minutes and that, when he finally found one, his nickel jammed in the meter. . . . Once the applicant had completed one situation, he was handed instructions for the next until all three situations were completed.[21]

An important aspect of the assessment center method is that each applicant is rated not by one evaluator, but by several, and the applicant's final score on performance tests is a composite of the several evaluators' ratings. Written tests and other testing procedures with specific, fixed scores also may be used, and applicants' scores may be averaged or weighted in various ways. However, the idea behind the assessment center method is to treat the applicant as a whole person and to evaluate a number of possible areas of strengths and weaknesses, rather than merely to set arbitrary pass-or-fail criteria. The advantage of the assessment center method is that it allows applicants to be rated on their overall performance on both objective tests and situational tests. The use of several evaluators whose ratings are combined in some manner helps to overcome the possibility that a single evaluator might be biased for or against an applicant.

However, the assessment center method is, as you might expect, a very costly procedure. The testing process is more time-consuming than either of the other procedures we have discussed, and it requires teams of well-trained evaluators. There are no well-established standards against which to measure the applicants' performance on simulations and situational tests.

Nevertheless, some of the assessment center techniques appear to be promising. As more experience with this procedure is gained, it should be possible to determine whether applicants who successfully enter the police ranks through an assessment center turn out to be competent police officers.

Oral Interviews

Nearly all police agencies use oral interviews as the last or next-to-last step in the selection process. The rationale for the oral interview is that every new police officer should be acceptable in overall personality and behavior. This unavoidably involves a subjective judgment on the part of the officers who conduct the interview, and often it is a judgment made in a surprisingly short period of time. When many applicants are being processed, interviews may last only three to five minutes, which means that the judgments may be based on no more than superficial impressions.

The oral interview is only as valuable as the skill of the interviewers can make it. For that reason, the members of an oral interview board should be chosen carefully, rather than being assigned at random or on the basis of such factors as official title or seniority. The board should consist of five to seven members, including the personnel officer, one or two senior administrators, one or two midlevel supervisors (sergeants or lieutenants), and one or two experienced patrol officers chosen from different units. A smaller board cannot represent all elements of the agency, while a board that is too large will merely confuse and intimidate the applicants.

Interview board members should meet well in advance of the interview period to discuss and agree on what they intend to accomplish. Board members should compile a list of questions, perhaps 15 or 20, that will be put to each candidate.

The questions should not be random or arbitrary. Questions that call for a simple "yes-no" answer should be used only to confirm basic minimum qualifications or background data. Most of the questions should call for a more open-ended, exploratory response from the candidate: questions that ask, "Why do you . . . ? or, "How would you . . . ?" or, "What would you do if . . . ?" Follow-up questions should be used if the applicant's responses are incomplete or ambiguous or if the applicant simply fails to address the original question.

Questions must not concern matters such as the applicant's ethnic background, nationality, marital status, sexual preferences, or other matters that are not clearly job-related and that could imply discrimination on the part of the agency.[22]

Finally, applicants should be given an opportunity to ask questions, too, and the interviewers should answer them as fully as possible. Often the questions asked by an applicant are as revealing as the answers to the board's questions. For example, an applicant who is overly concerned with salary, prompt promotions, fringe benefits, and pension plans may be more interested in a secure job than in serving the public.

It is essential for the interview board to be provided in advance with copies of each candidate's background records, including the original application form and the results of all of the tests that each candidate has completed. Board members should have ample time to study the background packages, so that each applicant is not met as a stranger.

Immediately after each interview, the board should be given time to discuss the members' impressions. Each board member should keep a score sheet on which to record ratings of the applicant during the interview. During the discussion period, board members should decide on their final ratings and make a group judgment on the applicant.

**Background
Investigations**

Those applicants who have passed every test and have been approved by the oral interview board should be given a thorough background investigation. In larger agencies, this task is often assigned to a special unit composed of experienced investigators assigned to the personnel office. In smaller agencies, the investigations may have to be performed by regular detectives whenever they are able to find the time.

The background investigation should be a two-step process. The first step consists of a routine screening. Local, state, and federal criminal records files such as the **National Crime Information Center (NCIC)** and drivers' license records are checked to determine whether an applicant has an unfavorable history. Nearly all agencies disqualify an applicant with a past felony conviction, certain misdemeanor convictions, or an excessive number of traffic violations.[23]

Many agencies also conduct a credit check, on the theory that individuals who are unable to manage their personal finances are likely to be irresponsible. However, this information must be judged carefully. Credit reporting agencies are not always scrupulous about maintaining accurate records, and an unfavorable record could be due to special circumstances (a serious illness in the family or some other misfortune) that were beyond the individual's control.

If nothing unsatisfactory turns up in the routine screening, a candidate is subject to a more complete investigation. Neighbors, relatives, former employers, and other potential information sources are interviewed to learn as much as possible about the candidate's personal background and reputation. A standard set of interview questions should be developed to focus the investigator's attention on matters that have some bearing on the applicant's ability to be a competent police officer. Questions that could imply improper discrimination, or plain snooping into matters that are none of the agency's concern, must be avoided.

A formal, written report of the background investigation should be prepared and placed in the applicant's permanent file, on which the final selection decision will be made. It is also useful to have the applicant review the investigator's report and to allow the applicant to submit corrections or objections if necessary.

Whatever selection procedures are used, eventually someone must decide whether an applicant is to be admitted to employment or not. In a multiple-hurdle procedure, this decision may be more or less automatic; those who survive all the hurdles are accepted for training. In a multiple-assessment or assessment-center procedure, after oral interviews and background investigations have been completed, the final decision may be a matter of accepting all applicants whose ratings or rankings are above a certain cutoff point. In any case, if the selection decision is relatively automatic, the personnel officer should inform all candidates, including the unsuccessful ones, as quickly as possible.

In many larger agencies, where the number of qualified applicants exceeds the current vacancies, all applicants who have met the minimum requirements are ranked on an **eligibility list** according to their total scores. The final decision then is made by a selection board, which may or may not consist of the same officers as the oral interview board. The selection board sometimes is given the authority to request additional tests or investigations in questionable or marginal cases.

The stakes in recruiting and personnel selection are high; they concern nothing less than the ultimate success of the police enterprise. Criminal justice professor Peter Horne warns, "If a poor or meaningless selection process exists, then low caliber officers will be recruited and they will perform poorly in the field for, perhaps, a twenty or thirty year career."[24] For the police administrator, recruitment and selection are the means by which the most important resource of all—the human resource—is acquired.

LIEUTENANT LUSK'S IN BASKET

Instructions

In this exercise, you are to assume the role of Lieutenant Dennis Lusk, head of the Personnel and Training Unit. The documents below have been selected from Lieutenant Lusk's in basket. Read them with care. If you need more information about City or its police department, refer to the data bank in the front of the book. After you have studied the documents, complete these steps:

1. State the problem or problems these documents present to Lieutenant Lusk.

2. List as many alternative solutions as you can.

3. Select the solution you think would be best, and give your reasons for choosing it.

CITY POLICE DEPARTMENT
Interoffice Memorandum

FROM:	Chief Abel		
TO:	Lt. Lusk, Personnel		
SUBJECT:	Recruiting	DATE:	15 Aug 19--

Dennis:
    We plan to include funds for ten additional commissioned positions in our budget request for next year. However, I am aware that we have had 3 vacant positions all of the past year. Also, Lt. Boudreau and Lt. Lawrence have informed me that they plan to retire as of October 1.
    The City Manager has asked me to provide him with some assurance that we will be able to fill these new positions if the funds are provided. This means we would have to recruit as many as 15 new people. Considering that we have not hired any new people at all for more than a year, he does not want to budget funds that will not be used. Therefore, please advise me as to the current status of our recruitment effort and how we will be able to increase our force as planned.

Page 2
    Also, Councilman Marcus Anheedus is concerned about the racial balance of the department. He probably will ask about this during budget hearings. Please update the memo you gave me on January 23. Also, do we have an affirmative action plan? If so, has it ever been submitted to EEOC for approval? Please locate a copy of the plan and forward it to me at your earliest convenience.

                                                    E.Z.A.

FROM:	B. Anderson, Patrol, Juvenile Div.
TO:	Lt. Lusk
SUBJECT:	Attached pamphlet

DATE: 22 Aug 19--

SIR:

The attached pamphlet was given to me by the daughter of a friend of mine. She said she found it in a stack of recruiting literature in the counselor's office at City High School. I was very embarrassed over this.

As you can see, this pamphlet for our Dept. is both sexist and racist. I quote, "City Police Dept. offers challenging and exciting career opportunities for young <u>men</u>. As a City Police Dept. patrol<u>man</u>, you will be on the front lines of the fight against crime, guarding the safety of the people you love!"

Also, on page 3, "Our complete training program turns young <u>men</u> into outstanding patrol<u>men</u>. Complete modern facilities and professional training officers will guide you to the peak of <u>manhood</u>." (By the way, WHAT modern facilities?? As far as I know, the only training facility we have is the briefing room!)

Also, there are four photographs at the top of page 3 showing, according to the caption, "City P.D. Officers in Action."

-Page 2-

All of the uniformed officers shown are <u>white males</u>.

The girl who gave me this pamphlet is an outstanding student and had expressed an interest in becoming a police officer. However, I am sure that this awful pamphlet has completely turned her off. Can't you do something about this?

                                        Beth Anderson, Patrol
                                        Juvenile Division

Personal Dept.
City Police Dept.
City, State

                                914 Water St.
                                Riverside, State
                                Aug. 28, 19--

Dear Sir or Maam:

I am a Sergent in the Riverside Police Dept for 18 yrs. of service in this Dept. At this time I am looking for new oppertonities for addvacmunt. I wuld like applie for a posithion of Sergent or Lueitenint in City PD.

I have been a Sergant for 11 yrs. and have been Shift Sup. for the Morning Watch for the past 7 yrs. I am in charge of 2 Patrollmen on this Shift. Before that I was in Detectives for 3 and 1/2 yrs. Before that I was a Patrollman for 7 yrs. and worked on all Watches. Before that I gradatted from Riverside H.S. in the top 1/2 of my class.

Lt. Clark, my supeiror, says that you are looking for a good Sergant or Luietnent for City PD. and that you have hired former Riverside offisers in the past. I wuld like you to concider my out-standing record. Also, I am Region Vise-Pres. of the State Black Police Offisers Assn. and have been an active member for 12 yrs. I think it is expesally important for some of your young Black Patrollmen to have experinced Black leaders. I wuld be ready to come to work for City PD. on 2 wks. of notice.

Thank you for your considderation, I am,

                                Sinsurly yours,

                                Sgt. Otto Goway

IN REVIEW

1. Many police departments recruit continuously because:
   (a) Most applicants are not qualified.
   (b) They are not able to fill their vacancies.
   (c) An unexpected vacancy could occur at any time.
   (d) It is more efficient than an occasional, short-term campaign.
   (e) That is the main duty of recruiting officers.

2. Which of the following techniques should *not* be used to recruit prospective police officers?
   (a) Pamphlets, booklets, and other printed materials.
   (b) Radio and television public service announcements.
   (c) Attractive, imaginative posters.
   (d) Speeches before youth groups.
   (e) All (none of these techniques should be used).
   (f) None (all of these techniques should be used).

3. True or False: Recruiting officers often must make a special effort to correct the misconceptions about law enforcement that people get from the entertainment media.

4. Perhaps the most important factor in appealing to prospective recruits is:
   (a) The general reputation of the agency.
   (b) The salaries and fringe benefits that can be offered.
   (c) The exciting, glamorous image of police work.
   (d) The opportunities for rapid promotions to positions of authority and prestige.
   (e) None of the above.

5. True or False: There is no evidence that a college education contributes to a police officer's performance.

6. An affirmative action plan is:
   (a) A court order requiring an employer to stop discriminating against minorities.
   (b) A plan to increase the proportion of minority individuals and women in the agency's work force.
   (c) A set of quotas specifying the number of minority individuals and women who must be hired.
   (d) A plan to eliminate all standards that favor minority applicants.
   (e) A plan to reduce the number of white male employees in an agency.

7. True or False: Equal Employment Opportunity laws require all female and minority applicants to be regarded as qualified until proven otherwise.

8. True or False: When women are hired as police officers, they should expect to receive exactly the same treatment as all other employees, and should not be allowed to complain about special problems or concerns.

9. Lateral entry refers to:
   (a) An experienced officer's transfer from one agency to an equivalent position in another agency.

(b)   The laws that prevent officers from transferring between different agencies.

(c)   The rule that an officer who transfers from one agency to another must start over as a new recruit.

(d)   The training that all police officers must have before they can be certified.

(e)   None of the above.

10. In principle, all three of the selection procedures described in this chapter are supposed to:

(a)   Be equally cost-efficient.

(b)   Prevent unqualified persons from applying for law enforcement jobs.

(c)   Ensure that all recruits receive adequate training.

(d)   Provide adequate numbers of recruits to fill all of the agency's vacancies.

(e)   Be job-related and have predictive validity.

REFERENCES

1.   John Furcon, "An Overview of Police Selection," in Charles D. Spielberger, ed., *Police Selection and Evaluation*, Washington, D.C.: Hemisphere, 1979, page 7.

2.   Jennie Farley, *Affirmative Action and the Woman Worker*, New York: American Management Association, 1979, page 44.

3.   Farley, pages 57–58.

4.   Jack L. Kuykendall and Peter C. Unsinger, *Community Police Administration*, Chicago: Nelson-Hall, 1975, page 248.

5.   Robert L. Desatrik, *The Expanding Role of the Human Resources Manager*, New York: American Management Association, 1979, page 92.

6.   Desatrik, page 23.

7.   Wayne F. Cascio and Leslie J. Real, "The Civil Service Exam Has Been Passed: Now What?" in Spielberger, pages 118–120.

8.   Farley, page 1.

9.   Farley, page 59.

10.   Farley, page 38.

11.   Farley, pages 109–110.

12.   Peter Horne, *Women in Law Enforcement*, 2nd ed., Springfield, Ill.: Charles C Thomas, 1980, page vii.

13.   Horne, page 32.

14.   Susan Ehrlich Martin, *Breaking and Entering: Policewomen on Patrol*, Berkeley: Univ. of California Press, 1980, page 49.

15.   Terry Eisenberg, Deborah Kent, and Charles R. Wall, *Police Personnel Practices in State and Local Governments*, Washington, D.C.: Police Foundation, 1973, page 27.

16.   Eisenberg, Kent, and Wall, pages 17–26.

17.   Stanley Vanagunas and James F. Elliott, *Administration of Police Organizations*, Boston: Allyn and Bacon, 1980, pages 169–170.

18.   Melany E. Baehr and Arnold B. Oppenheim, "Job Analysis in Police Selection Research," in Spielberger, pages 33–59.

19.   Joseph M. Fabricatore, "Preentry Assessment and Training," in Spielberger, page 79.

20.   Robert J. Filer, "The Assessment Center Method in the Selection of Law Enforcement Officers," in Spielberger, page 212.

21.   Filer, page 224.

22.   Cascio and Leal, pages 124–130.

23.   Kuykendall and Unsinger, pages 254–255.

24.   Horne, pages 52–53.

12 TRAINING AND CAREER DEVELOPMENT

LESS THAN 20 YEARS AGO, THE INTERNATIONAL ASSOCIA-
tion of Chiefs of Police discovered that only about 15 percent of all U.S.
police agencies provided their recruits with any kind of training, or even
required them to receive any training before they were put to work.[1] Police
officials recruited and selected young men (rarely young women), gave
them a badge and a gun, and hoped that they would not get killed before
they learned what they were doing.

Unfortunately, that is still the case for many small police departments,
especially in rural areas, in states that have no mandatory certification
program. Even where certification programs do exist, some states permit
recruits to be hired without training and to be assigned to patrol duties for
up to a year while they complete the certification requirements—if they live
that long.

The lack of training for new police officers usually is explained as a
matter of economics. It is expensive and time-consuming to provide recruits with the training they need. Furthermore, there is a persistent notion
in the minds of some police officials, politicians, and ordinary citizens that
policing is a rather menial task, easily learned by anyone with normal
intelligence in a few weeks of practical experience. The opposite idea—that
policing is an extremely complex discipline requiring practitioners with a
substantial body of knowledge, technical skills, and professional attitudes—
is dismissed by some people as a ploy to justify more money for law
enforcement.

Our own view, which should come as no surprise, is that adequate
training is absolutely vital to the success of any law enforcement agency. No
one is a natural-born police officer, equipped from birth with the knowledge, skills, and attitudes needed to perform this most demanding and
difficult of jobs. We consider it astonishing that some states demand more
education and training of their barbers and undertakers than of their police
officers.

Not only do newly recruited police officers need to be adequately trained
before they begin work, but all police officers, regardless of their rank or
amount of experience, must continuously improve their abilities through
training and education. Education and training are the principal means by
which an individual police officer can advance his or her career, learning
new specialized skills or broader responsibilities. In the past, the individual
officer was left to obtain this advanced training entirely on his or her own
initiative. Today, most police officials recognize that it is at least partly their
responsibility to see that their officers acquire the knowledge and skills they
need, not only to do the jobs assigned to them today but also to fill the
agency's need for specialists and leaders in the future.

But what kinds of knowledge, skills, and attitudes do police officers
need to learn? Who should provide the training (given the fact that it is
costly and time-consuming) and under what conditions? What are the most
effective and efficient ways to provide training? Finally, what should
be the relationship between advanced training and career advancement:
Should promotions be offered only to those who have completed prescribed training courses, or should other factors also be considered? How
can administrators determine which of their officers are most likely to be
successful in higher positions that require more specialized skills or leadership abilities?

TRAINING

Perhaps the first question that needs to be answered is, What do police officers need to know when they begin working as patrol officers and, later, as they seek advancement to more specialized positions or positions of broader responsibility?

This is hardly a new question. Law enforcement authorities have been asking it, and proposing answers, ever since the need for training began to be recognized about a century ago. More recently, in 1965, the International Association of Chiefs of Police advocated a 200-hour basic training course that included academic study of the criminal justice system, judicial procedure, the laws of evidence and arrest, and the organization of law enforcement agencies; and skills training in patrol procedures, the use of firearms, and emergency vehicle operation, among other topics.[2] However, the IACP's curriculum has not been universally adopted. Aside from those agencies that offer no recruit training at all, basic training programs vary from one to two weeks in length (40 to 80 hours) to as much as eight weeks (320 hours), and in a few cases even more. Not only do the lengths of training programs vary, so do the contents, even though training has been somewhat standardized through statewide certification programs.

In principle, any basic training program should be designed to fulfill one objective, succinctly stated by William J. Bopp: "to develop in officers those skills necessary to successfully perform a new job."[3] To accomplish this objective, according to Bopp, "Trainers must be thoroughly familiar with the tasks policemen are expected to perform."[4] In short, the content of the training program should be derived from a close examination of the work that is actually done by police officers. But that is more easily done in theory than in practice; the work of the average patrol officer is so complex and varied that it all but defies analysis.

Basic training for new patrol officers generally occurs in two phases. The first phase, preservice training, may take place either before or after a person has actually been hired by a police agency. The content of the training includes the knowledge and skills that are virtually universal in policing: a basic understanding of criminal law and the criminal justice system; standard procedures in crime prevention, patrol, criminal investigation, traffic law enforcement, and other specialized areas of police science; and similar matters. Ideally, preservice training should be part of a broader educational experience in the social role of policing and in the liberal arts as a whole. Preservice training may be obtained either in a police academy operated by a law enforcement agency or, more frequently, in a community college or four-year university.

The second phase consists of training in the specific policies and procedures of the agency in which the person has been employed. The content of this orientation training might include local criminal ordinances, administrative and operational structure of the agency, and local policies concerning personnel matters, duty assignments, radio procedures, and dozens of other items. By its nature, orientation training must be provided by each agency, in an academy if one exists, or in some other manner in smaller agencies.

Who Should Provide Training

The responsibility for securing adequate training and education must be shared by the individual officers (or, in the case of persons who are not yet employed in law enforcement, the prospective officers) and the police agency. In the past, this responsibility has been borne almost entirely by the individual officer; however, most police agencies today recognize and accept their share of the burden.

There are three possible sources of training and education: individual study (such as the reading of books about law enforcement practices), academic programs conducted by colleges and other educational institutions, and training programs conducted by individual police agencies.

The value of individual study should not be underestimated. Young people who are interested in pursuing a career in law enforcement should be encouraged to learn as much about the field as they can by reading books on the subject (preferably sound academic works rather than just popular fiction). In addition, as we mentioned in Chapter 11, some police agencies have organized volunteer programs for young people that give them limited but valuable experience in police-related activities.

Individual study is just as important for active law enforcement personnel. Every police officer should seek to learn more, to acquire new skills and polish old ones, and to increase his or her ability to perform. However, individual study in law enforcement faces the same limitations as it would in, say, the field of medicine: Reading about brain surgery is not the same as performing an operation. Furthermore, a person pursuing a course of individual study usually lacks the clear objectives and guidance that an organized training program would provide.

Academic programs conducted by two-year community colleges, or by four-year colleges or universities, represent a relatively recent development in the field of law enforcement. Academic programs in criminology (the study of crime as a social phenomenon or as a type of psychological behavior) have existed since the end of the last century, usually within departments of sociology or psychology. Similarly, some universities have offered programs in criminal justice for many years, usually within the departments of political science or law. However, few colleges have offered programs intended specifically for prospective or practicing law enforcement personnel, until about 15 years ago. At that time, the federal Law Enforcement Assistance Administration (part of the U. S. Department of Justice) began to offer funds for grants to educational institutions and scholarships for students to pursue courses in law enforcement and police science. Several hundred two-year and four-year colleges created such programs. Even many high schools began to offer a few elective courses in criminal justice and law enforcement. In 1979, the federal funding for college programs stopped. Nevertheless, many of the programs have continued, since there is little question that they meet a vital need.

The third source of police training is the police academy. All state police agencies and most of the larger municipal police departments operate their own academies. Also, in some cases several police agencies are served by a single regional academy, either operated jointly by the participating agencies or funded through a separate state agency. Generally, the police academy's primary responsibility is to provide basic training for all of the agency's new personnel. In addition, most academies conduct periodic seminars, workshops, and short courses (training programs that last a week or two) for current personnel.

Methods of Training

This text is not the place for an extended discussion of training methods and techniques; information on this subject is readily available elsewhere. However, a police administrator does need to know enough about training methods to permit appropriate planning.

Any training program should begin with an evaluation of existing operations to determine what kinds of training are needed and for whom. Training is not (or should not be) an end in itself, but instead a means of improving the performance of police personnel. Thus, the first step in establishing a sound training program is to examine the performance of all personnel, determine their weaknesses, and decide which of those weaknesses may be corrected through training. For example, if it is found that too many traffic citations are being dismissed by the courts, the reason may be that patrol officers are making technical mistakes in their traffic arrest and citation procedures. Further study may reveal a pattern of particular types of mistakes. A training program then could be organized to correct the error. Or, to take another example, if an evaluation of the agency's current operations reveals the need for a specialized unit to investigate organized crime, a training program ought to be developed to prepare the personnel assigned to the new unit; merely establishing the new unit and assigning personnel to it will not satisfy the need.[5]

A training program does not necessarily involve bringing together a number of people in a classroom under the direction of an instructor. In fact, training programs can be organized and conducted in several different ways. Preservice or recruit training usually does take the form of classroom instruction, preferably with ample laboratory sessions for practice in skills. In-service training of current personnel may take the form of classroom instruction for whatever amount of time may be required, from an hour or two to several days. However, in-service training also may be accomplished through the distribution of printed training bulletins, memoranda, policy statements, and so forth. Short training sessions may be conducted at roll-call at the beginning of each patrol shift. Or, instead of a lecture, instruction may take the form of a discussion involving several officers who are experiencing a common problem in their work.

Each type or form of training has its advantages and disadvantages. Some of the most common training methods are discussed in Table 12.1.

Table 12.1 is not intended to be exhaustive, but instead to illustrate the number of different training techniques that can be used, to suggest their limitations, and to indicate the most beneficial uses of each technique.[6]

Another training technique that is not listed in the table, but that deserves careful consideration, is the use of simulations. Briefly, a **simulation** is any kind of activity that represents a portion of real life. For example, many games are, to some extent, simulations of real-life activities; chess is a very abstract simulation of warfare as it was practiced in medieval times. Another popular board game, Monopoly, is a fanciful simulation of the world of high finance.

Simulations designed for educational or training purposes are not always as entertaining as chess or Monopoly, but, like most popular games, they have the advantage of involving the students or players in an activity that, if the simulation is properly designed, accurately represents some kind of real-life activity.

Table 12.1 Standard Training Methods

Method	Description	Advantages, Disadvantages
Lecture	Instructor presents information to a group (class)	Least expensive method of presenting information to a large group; requires minimal preparation by instructor. Should be used only if all students need the same information and have essentially the same background and preparation, and if the lecture is followed up with practice or application of knowledge. Success depends heavily on ability of the lecturer to get and keep students' interest.
Television, film, etc.	Audiovisual material shown to group or individual	Can be a highly individualized form of instruction; any size group, from one to several hundred, may view a television program or videotape recording, film, slide program, etc.; the best method for showing a procedure, technique, or anything that cannot be brought into a classroom. Relatively expensive; requires careful preparation by instructor, prompt follow-up; content of material, if purchased from external source, may not fit students' needs precisely.
Conference or seminar method	Students (with or without instructor) discuss subject	Excellent for group problem-solving, exploration of issues, modification of attitudes; involvement of students in discussion reinforces learning. Without a skilled instructor, students may learn the wrong information or attitudes. Discussions may be time-consuming and unproductive unless carefully led by the instructor. Limited to small groups (10-15 students) or some will have no chance to participate.
Demonstration method	Instructor shows students	The best way to teach a technique or process. Each student must have a chance to practice immediately after demonstration. Good follow-up to a lecture or use of audiovisual media. Often time-consuming; may require costly specialized training facility or materials for demonstration; requires careful preparation by the instructor. All students must be able to view and participate in the demonstration.
Practice or laboratory method	Students practice techniques or procedures	Most effective form of instruction for learning procedures, techniques. Should be used as follow-up to lecture, demonstration, or use of audiovisual materials. May be costly if many students are given a chance to practice; may require special equipment, facility, or materials. Limited number of students can be supervised by one instructor.

There are a number of different types of simulations, some of which are easier to develop and use than others. The simplest to use in the classroom are role-playing and games.

A role-playing simulation involves assigning two or more students to act out roles in a certain situation. One example of a role-playing exercise was described in Chapter 11, where a student is instructed to conduct a field interrogation and, if necessary, an arrest of a suspicious person who appears to be breaking into a parking meter. Any number of situations can be used as the basis for role-playing exercises.[7] Role-playing can be used not only to give students practical experience in police procedures and techniques but also as a means of exploring (and often changing) attitudes. For example, two students might be assigned to play the roles of a husband and wife engaged in a heated argument; two other students then could be assigned to act as patrol officers responding to a disturbance call who try to break up the argument. The "husband" and "wife" are likely to gain some insight into the strong feelings that law-abiding citizens experience when "outsiders" intrude into their private business; the students assigned to act as patrol officers should learn what is likely to happen in a real-life situation of this type. The exercise would be even more valuable if (1) the four students exchanged roles after a while; (2) the exercise is recorded on videotape and played back (so that the role-playing students can see themselves objectively); and (3) the exercise is carefully discussed afterward by the instructor and the rest of the class.

Games are more elaborate types of simulations. A game should represent a highly abstract set of activities, with carefully designed rules and a preconceived end or goal. Some games are designed for two or more individual players while others are designed for teams of players (often including an entire class of students). The players or teams may be competing against one another, or the game may be designed to require the players to cooperate with one another to achieve their goals. The development of educational games has become rather sophisticated in recent years, involving a great deal of creativity and cleverness. Unfortunately, to the best of our knowledge, there are no educational games designed specifically for police training, and designing them may be too complex and time-consuming for most instructors to undertake.

Finally, real-life situations and activities can be simulated by computer programs. Most of the so-called video games are computer-based simulation exercises, designed for entertainment rather than education. However, computer-based simulations have been developed for training purposes in other fields, notably the training of aircraft pilots. Their potential in law enforcement training is almost limitless.

Field Training

Long before there were any formal training programs in law enforcement, it was the common practice to assign newly hired personnel to patrol a beat for a few weeks in the company of an experienced officer. Even after formal training programs came into being, this practice of on-the-job training continued. Police administrators readily conceded that a formal training program, no matter how well it might be organized and conducted, did not adequately prepare a rookie officer for life on the street.

On-the-job training, more frequently known as **field training**, continues to be the standard practice in most police agencies today. A recruit who has completed the formal training program, either in an academy or in a college, is first hired on a probationary basis for a period of anywhere from one month to two years; more typical probationary periods are 6 to 12 months.

During the probationary period, an officer is subject to being dismissed at any time, usually without notice and without much, if any, right to appeal. Even if the probationary employee is not dismissed, a permanent position is not guaranteed, but depends on an evaluation of the rookie officer's overall performance during the probationary period. The recommendations of the rookie's immediate supervisor usually carry a great deal of weight. Thus a probationary officer is under considerable pressure to satisfy the expectations of his or her supervisors.

There is a long-standing tradition in policing, according to which each rookie officer is told by the experienced officer (field training officer) to whom he or she is assigned, "Now you can forget all that stuff they told you in the academy, because I am going to show you how things are really done." The implication that formal training is irrelevant, unrealistic, and worthless serves to undermine the rookie's confidence and leaves the new officer vulnerable to confusion. Some rookies, eager to please their supervisors, take the advice literally and promptly forget everything they have learned about sound police practices.

It may well be true that some formal training programs are not as relevant and realistic as they ought to be. However, that does not justify dismissing them so lightly. A far better approach, of course, would be to involve experienced officers, at all ranks, in critically evaluating and improving the formal training. But the experienced officers who are given responsibility for the field training of rookies often have no personal knowledge of what is currently being taught in the academy. The experienced officer may have graduated from recruit training five years or more in the past and be completely unaware of major changes in the formal training program since then. In fact, quite often the procedures used by the field training officer are nearly identical to those taught in recruit training.

Furthermore, in many police agencies the assignment of probationary employees to field training officers is completely up to the discretion of unit supervisors (sergeants or lieutenants) who may not realize what an important matter this is. The influence of a field training officer—good or bad—can color a rookie officer's entire career. Clearly, field training officers should be chosen with great care and should be given adequate preparation. They should be exemplary officers whose job performance is as close as possible to the ideal, and they should be informed in detail about the content of the recruit training program. The field training phase itself should not be left to chance. Clear, definite training objectives should be established, and the field training officers should know exactly what is expected of them. Since a major part of field training is the evaluation of the probationary officers' performance, the field training officers should themselves be trained to conduct proper evaluations. Field training should not contradict or undermine the formal recruit training program; instead, field training should be an extension and continuation of the formal program.[8]

Another aspect of field training deserves comment here. The personnel in any police agency naturally form a social group with its own culture; that is, a set of knowledge, ideas, values, and ways of doing things that are, to a greater or lesser degree, shared among all the members. Any newcomer to the group must learn this culture in order to be accepted as a member. Acceptance into the group is vital to any newcomer, since the failure to win acceptance means that the newcomer is shut out of the group's internal, informal systems of communication and social interaction.

The process of learning a group's culture and gaining acceptance as a member is called **socialization**. This process is important in most stable social groups, not just in law enforcement. It actually begins during the recruitment process: Applicants who want to be accepted as recruits attempt to demonstrate the behaviors that, as far as they can tell, will lead to acceptance into the police society. Individuals who do not appear to be capable of learning acceptable behaviors are simply not admitted as recruits. The socialization process continues during recruit training, as the recruits learn more about the specific behaviors that are expected of them and the ideas and attitudes that experienced police officers display. The traditional advice to the rookie to "forget everything you learned in the academy" is so devastating because it amounts to saying, "The knowledge, ideas, values, and attitudes you have tried to master will not help you gain acceptance in the society of real police officers." The field training period is the "final exam" in the socialization process, and this is one exam that every rookie officer must pass.

Socialization is not necessarily a conscious, deliberate process. Often neither the new recruit nor the experienced officer is fully aware that this process is taking place. Recruits are often confused about what is expected of them, what they must do to gain acceptance. Members of the group may reject the newcomer not because of any fault of the recruit, but because of prejudices, fear that the newcomer is a threat to their own jobs, or some other hidden cause.

Administrators and supervisors must be aware of the socialization process and of its significance. They cannot guarantee that every recruit will be accepted into the agency's society, nor should they try to do so. However, they can try to ensure that the process is fair. Discrimination against whole classes of newcomers—such as women or minority members—should not be tolerated; each recruit is entitled to be judged as an individual and given a fair chance to win acceptance. If it appears that experienced personnel are unreasonably hostile toward or fearful of newcomers, the causes should be discovered and corrected. Often it is helpful to make the field training officers themselves aware of, and sensitive to, the socialization process. They should understand that a rookie not only needs to demonstrate technical competence as a professional law enforcement officer but also must fit into the social world of policing. The field training officer, knowingly or otherwise, can either encourage or hinder this vital process.[9]

CAREER DEVELOPMENT

In any bureaucratic organization, both responsibility and rewards are said to flow upward; that is, the person at the top of the organizational pyramid has more of both than anyone else in the organization, and the persons at the bottom have less of both than anyone else.

The members of a bureaucratic organization are supposed to be assigned to their positions according to their individual competence, or merit. In principle, every member of an organization should be the one person who is most capable of performing the specific tasks assigned to him or her. The fact that this is not always the case does not invalidate the principle. People do sometimes attain high positions of responsibility and rewards for which they are not competent. When this happens, whatever the reason may be, the organization as a whole suffers a loss of efficiency and effectiveness. Thus it is very much in the interests of the organization to see that every position is filled by the most competent person.

At the same time, since most people want to receive all the rewards they can, it is in the interests of every individual to achieve the highest position that he or she is competent to fill. But competence is not an inborn, permanent quality of an individual; it is at least partly acquired over a period of time, through the individual's experiences (including the experience of formal and informal training). As a person gains experience, he or she should become increasingly competent to hold higher positions in the organization, up to each individual's natural limits of talent, intelligence, and so on. Again, the organization gains by making the best use of each member's abilities, and the individual gains by holding the highest position for which he or she is competent. Conversely, both the organization and its members suffer when people are prevented from reaching the highest position for which they are competent, especially if some of the higher positions are held by individuals who are less competent.

These principles apply as surely to a police department as to any other government agency, business corporation, or other bureaucracy. To put them into practical terms, police administrators have an obligation to see that both the needs of the agency and the needs of the individuals within it are served by making the best possible use of the agency's human resources. Every member of the agency should be assigned to the one job for which he or she is best suited. Furthermore, every member of the agency should be continuously preparing to advance to the next higher job for which he or she is capable of becoming competent.[10]

If promotions to higher positions of authority are given solely on the basis of seniority (the length of time a person has worked for the agency) or, worse yet, on the basis of the personal prejudices of some higher official, not only will the organization's efficiency suffer but also lower-ranking personnel will become dissatisfied because they will realize that their own abilities are not being properly recognized and rewarded. Dissatisfaction may lead to poor performance throughout the agency, since dissatisfied personnel feel no desire to do their jobs well.

In extreme cases, dissatisfied personnel may engage in destructive acts in a deliberate or unconscious effort to sabotage an agency that they perceive to be unfair.[11] The importance of this principle can hardly be overstated. As Susan Ehrlich Martin points out:

Those individuals who perceive opportunities (although they may be quite limited in reality) will work for them; those who feel blocked (although opportunities may actually exist) will seek alternative sources of satisfaction.[12]

The alternatives may include devoting little or no effort to one's work, or treating the agency's clients (in the case of a police department, the general public) with contempt and hostility, or looking for more satisfying work elsewhere.

Opportunities for promotion are not the only concern of employees. All people need to feel satisfaction in their work: that they are being appropriately rewarded, and that their contributions are recognized and appreciated. One of the most important discoveries of the human relations school of management (see Chapter 2) was that people who feel satisfaction in their work generally are more productive. Traditional, mechanical approaches to increasing productivity—which usually have amounted to finding ways to make people work harder—ignored this vital principle. However, managers of successful enterprises, including law enforcement agencies, realize today that part of their responsibility includes helping all employees to find satisfaction in their work. Later, we will see how this responsibility can be carried out as part of an overall career development program. First, however, we look at the more traditional approach to career development, with its emphasis on evaluating employees' performance and establishing systematic procedures for promotions.

Performance Evaluation

If the most competent employee is to be assigned to each position, then it is necessary to evaluate the competence of every employee. Those who are performing their present jobs successfully are presumed to be most likely to handle a higher job (that is, one requiring more specialized skills or involving broader responsibilities) equally well, and are also presumably entitled to be rewarded for their efforts. The two methods most widely used in law enforcement to evaluate employees' performance are known as work product measurement and trait rating.

Work product measurement simply means counting the amount of work an employee produces. This method works very well in organizations where employees produce tangible products or perform the same kind of operation repetitively. For example, in a factory the assembly-line workers' output might be the number of products assembled in an hour or a day. Even if an employee performs a variety of different tasks, work product measurement is practical if each type of task can be readily measured. A clerical worker's output might consist of so many letters typed, files filed, telephone calls received and transferred, and so forth, per day.

But how can the work of a police officer be measured? Should patrol officers be evaluated on the basis of the number of arrests they make, traffic citations issued, field interviews conducted, and so on? In fact, these items have been used by many police departments. The problem is that there is no real basis for comparing one officer's work with another's, using these "products." One officer might be assigned to a district with little crime while another is assigned to a high-crime area. Even within a single area, the level of police activity may vary from one time of day to another; thus the "product" of officers on different shifts would not be comparable. And it is impossible to measure the intangible, but no less important, work of a police officer in patrolling a beat, counselling citizens, observing traffic and suspicious activities, and many similar activities. Furthermore, merely counting a police officer's products says nothing about the quality of the officer's work. How many of the officer's arrests resulted in convictions? How much of the officer's patrolling prevented crimes in the first place? These factors are ignored in most work product measurement systems.

A **trait-rating system** attempts to look beyond the measurable work and examine the quality of an officer's job performance in terms of the traits, or personal characteristics, a successful officer is supposed to display. In a trait-rating system, supervisors are given a list of the traits that are supposed to be exhibited by police officers. The supervisor is then required to give a numerical rating to each officer for each of the listed traits. The ratings "points" are then added up to arrive at an overall rating for the officer.

The first problem in any trait-rating system is that there is no universal agreement on what traits a police officer ought to display. The trait lists developed by various police agencies show a remarkable diversity. Some trait lists include specific tasks or behaviors, such as, "The officer performs at least 25 field interviews per week" or, "The officer responds to each radio call within four minutes." Other traits concern general characteristics of behavior: "The officer treats all members of the public in a courteous and dignified manner," or, "The officer presents a neat, well-groomed appearance." Still other traits may concern matters that are not readily observable: "The officer is conscientious and diligent in his or her work," or, "The officer has good judgment." Under the best of circumstances, it would be hard for any supervisor to assign numerical ratings to every officer on each of these traits.

In fact, the situation is even more problematic. Most police officers, especially on patrol, work alone or in the company of their regular partner most of the the time. A supervisor has few opportunities to observe officers while they are engaged in actual police duties. Thus, the supervisors' ratings are based not on actual, direct observation but on feelings, impressions, and comments of other officers, and, consciously or unconsciously, personal biases and favoritism.

A few police agencies, recognizing the serious limitations to both work product measurement and trait rating, have tried to develop sound evaluation systems by combining the two methods. Supervisors are required to complete a periodic evaluation of each officer, usually every six months or once each year, that takes into account both the quantity of product (arrests, traffic citations, and so on) an officer has produced and the supervisor's assessment of the officer's personal traits. This combination of methods is certainly better than either method alone, but the original problem still is not entirely solved. The work performed by police officers, especially on patrol, is so complex and varies so greatly from time to time and from place to place that it is nearly impossible to measure in an accurate, objective way.

Another variation of trait rating also has been used with some success: **peer rating**. This merely means that each officer fills out a trait-rating sheet for every other officer in his or her unit. Peer ratings are intended to overcome some of the problems inherent in supervisory ratings. Presumably, peers (that is, other officers of the same rank or level) have more

CHEYENNE POLICE DEPARTMENT
EMPLOYEE EVALUATION REPORT

NAME: _____ Position: _____ Rating Period: _____

KNOWLEDGE OF WORK:
Comments:
Exceeds Standards ☐   Meets Standards ☐   Requires Improvement ☐   Unsatisfactory ☐

QUALITY OF WORK:
Comments:
Exceeds Standards ☐   Meets Standards ☐   Requires Improvement ☐   Unsatisfactory ☐

QUANTITY OF WORK:
Comments:
Exceeds Standards ☐   Meets Standards ☐   Requires Improvement ☐   Unsatisfactory ☐

ATTITUDE & WORK INTEREST:
Comments:
Exceeds Standards ☐   Meets Standards ☐   Requires Improvement ☐   Unsatisfactory ☐

RELATIONS WITH OTHER EMPLOYEES:
Comments:
Exceeds Standards ☐   Meets Standards ☐   Requires Improvement ☐   Unsatisfactory ☐

INITIATIVE:
Comments:
Exceeds Standards ☐   Meets Standards ☐   Requires Improvement ☐   Unsatisfactory ☐

PROMOTION POTENTIAL:
Comments:
Exceeds Standards ☐   Meets Standards ☐   Requires Improvement ☐   Unsatisfactory ☐

SUPERVISORY ABILITY: (when applicable)
Comments:
Exceeds Standards ☐   Meets Standards ☐   Requires Improvement ☐   Unsatisfactory ☐

OVERALL PERFORMANCE:
Comments:
Exceeds Standards ☐   Meets Standards ☐   Requires Improvement ☐   Unsatisfactory ☐

RATER: _____
       Signature   Position   Date

REVIEWER: _____
          Signature   Position   Date
Comments:

REVIEWER: _____
          Signature   Position   Date
Comments:

EMPLOYEE: _____
          Signature   Position   Date
Comments:

White—Personnel
Blue—Division Copy
Pink—Individual

(See Instructions on Reverse Side)

Figure 12-1 A trait-rating personnel evaluation form. (Courtesy Cheyenne, Wyoming, Police Department.)

Please return to coordinator by _____

CITY OF PORTSMOUTH

Performance Evaluation and Counseling Form

PATROL OFFICER

EMPLOYEE NAME	INGRADE PROGRESSION DATE	DEPARTMENT AND DEPARTMENT NUMBER
CLASS SPECIFICATION	EMPLOYEE NUMBER	SOCIAL SECURITY NUMBER
EVALUATION DATE	EMPLOYMENT DATE	SUPERVISOR/REVIEWER

☐ Probationary Employee 1st 6 Month Review　☐ Probationary Employee 2nd Review for Permanent Status & Ingrade Progression　☐ Permanent Employee Annual Review 120 Days Prior to Continuous Service Date　Other (Please Specify) ☐ _____

INSTRUCTIONS

Using the numerical scale below, compare the performance of the employee being rated against the performance criteria listed for each factor. Select the number which best indicates your perception of that individual's performance on each of the criterion and enter it in the box provided. Then enter a number indicating a composite, or overall evaluation for the factor. Your complete evaluation should not necessarily reflect an average of the criteria rating since some criterion are more important than others. Examples of past performance <u>must</u> be cited.

EVALUATION SCALE

```
 O  |  E  |     M     |  B  |  U
 +--+--+--+--+--+--+--+--+--+
 9     8     7  6  5  4     3     2     1
```

(O) <u>Outstanding</u>　　　- Exemplary performance far exceeding performance criteria.
(E) <u>Exceeds Expectation</u>　- Performance which exceeds the level supervisor normally expects.
(M) <u>Meets Expectation</u>　- Generally meets supervisor's expectation on performance criteria.
(B) <u>Below Expectation</u>　- Erratic performance on criteria, falling short of that normally expected .... requires remedial attention.

(U) <u>Unsatisfactory</u>　　- Unacceptable performance which must receive immediate attention.
(NA) <u>Not Applicable</u>　- Evaluation of the factor or criterion is inappropriate for the employee being rated.

FACTOR A: SUPPORT OF UNIT'S OBJECTIVES: PLANNING/TEAMWORK
Performance Criteria:

	Works with supervisor and other officers in planning and building an effective team.
	Officer's objectives, talents and efforts are directed toward the needs of the department and accomplishment of unit's goals.
	Improved methods are suggested and readily tried to improve effectiveness and solve traffic/crime problems.
	New and additional assignments are accepted and performed.
	Composite Evaluation for Factor.

Cite examples of past performance to support your evaluation. _____

FACTOR B: RESPONSE TO RADIO CALLS AND ASSIGNMENTS.
Performance Criteria:

	Radio calls are not missed without valid cause.
	Response is made promptly, safely, and appropriately.
	Further action is rarely required in minor cases.
	Assistance provided is appropriate to the need or problem.
	Proper radio procedures are followed.
	Composite Evaluation for Factor.

Cite examples of past performance to support your evaluation. _____

FACTOR C: INVESTIGATION OF CRIMES OR TRAFFIC ACCIDENTS.
Performance Criteria:

	Appropriate investigative steps are taken.
	Investigations are thorough, and each step properly documented.
	Evidence is properly preserved, collected, and thoroughly described.
	Other divisions or agencies are properly notified as required.
	Composite Evaluation for Factor.

Cite examples of past performance to support your evaluation. _____

FACTOR D: APPREHENSION, ARREST OF CRIMINAL SUSPECTS.
Performance Criteria:

	All necessary information is included in arrest reports and case files.
	No unnecessary force is used.
	Uses correct procedures in effecting an arrest.
	Composite Evaluation for Factor.

Cite examples of past performance to support your evaluation. _____

FACTOR E: ENFORCEMENT OF TRAFFIC REGULATIONS.
Performance Criteria:

	Traffic tickets are issued.
	Actions taken are appropriate to the offense.
	Citations are rarely returned for correction.
	Traffic is controlled as required.
	Composite Evaluation for Factor.

Cite examples of past performance to support your evaluation. _____

FACTOR F: PERFORMANCE UNDER STRESSFUL, EMERGENCY OR UNUSUAL CONDITIONS.
Performance Criteria:

	No serious deviations from expected performance are demonstrated under unusual circumstances.
	Demonstrates ability to take command of emergency situations.
	Composure is maintained under stress.
	No major errors identified by supervisor in post-operation review.
	Composite Evaluation for Factor.

Cite examples of past performance to support your evaluation. _____

FACTOR G: RELATIONS WITH CITIZENS AND THE COMMUNITY.
Performance Criteria:

	Does not antagonize or insult citizens.
	Knows and is responsible to community problems.
	Courtesy is demonstrated in citizen contacts.
	Anger and verbal abuse from citizens does not adversely affect performance.
	Composite Evaluation for Factor.

Cite examples of past performance to support your evaluation. _____

FACTOR H: WORKING RELATIONSHIPS AND COOPERATION WITH OTHER PERSONNEL.
Performance Criteria:

	Valid complaints are not received from fellow officers or supervisory personnel.
	Problems in personal relationships with other personnel do not impair work relationship.
	Readily assists/backs other officers.
	Trains and guides less experienced officers.
	Composite Evaluation for Factor.

Cite examples of past performance to support your evaluation. _____

FACTOR I: PREPARATION AND PRESENTATION OF REQUIRED REPORTS AND INFORMATION.
Performance Criteria:

	Field interview reports are used.
	Reports are legible, concise, grammatically correct, submitted at agreed upon time, with required information.
	Reports and information are rarely returned for correction.
	Evidence is preserved and thoroughly described.
	Composite Evaluation for Factor.

Cite examples of past performance to support your evaluation. _____

FACTOR J: OPERATION, MAINTENANCE AND CARE OF DEPARTMENTAL EQUIPMENT.
Performance Criteria:

	Vehicles are not abused through poor driving habits.
	Specified operating and safety procedures are followed in the use and maintenance of equipment.
	Weapons are checked for cleanliness and serviceability.
	Automobiles are returned clean (interior) and serviced for next shift.
	Equipment wear, malfunctions, damages are identified and reported.
	Composite Evaluation for Factor.

Cite examples of past performance to support your evaluation. _____

FACTOR K: CONFORMANCE TO WORK SCHEDULES, ASSIGNMENTS AND INSTRUCTIONS.
Performance Criteria:

	Instructions are followed and assignments completed on schedule.
	Work does not have to be closely supervised.
	Deviations from instructions and schedules are explained satisfactorily to supervisor.
	Unassigned time is effectively utilized, i. e., maintain citizen contact, proactive patrol.
	Special attention is given to high accident or crime areas.
	Composite Evaluation for Factor.

Cite examples of past performance to support your evaluation. _____

FACTOR L: CONFORMANCE TO DEPARTMENT POLICIES, REGULARITY OF ATTENDANCE AND PUNCTUALITY.
Performance Criteria:

	Policies, rules and regulations are followed as prescribed.
	Appearance meets departmental specifications.
	No unnecessary delays in starting work at specified time.
	No abuse of meal periods, coffee breaks, quitting time, or other special absences.
	Supervisor is given proper notice in advance of absences.
	Composite Evaluation for Factor.

Cite examples of past performance to support your evaluation. _____

FACTOR M: OTHER FACTORS IMPORTANT TO SUPERVISOR. (List any unique duties performed by employee not apparent in Class Specification.)

Performance Criteria:

Cite examples of past performance to support your evaluation. _____

_____

_____

_____

OVERALL PERFORMANCE RATING

Based upon preceding evaluations, but not necessarily an average of the factors since some are more important than others, carefully read the criteria for each of the performance levels and check the term which best describes the employee's overall performance for the evaluation period.

	Outstanding:	Exemplary overall performance deserving special recognition normally occuring in less than 5% of the workforce.
	Exceeds Expectation:	Performance exceeding the supervisor's expectation on nearly all performance factors.
	Meets Expectation:	Performance generally meeting supervisor's expectation on most performance criteria.
	Below Expectation:	Erratic performance falling short of that expected on most factors. Special review recommended in 60 days. USE OF THIS OVERALL RATING REQUIRES COMPLETION OF REMEDIAL ACTIVITIES SECTION BELOW. This rating is not sufficient to deny Ingrade Progression.
	Unsatisfactory:	Unacceptable performance: Ingrade Progression for Permanent Employees may be withheld only upon submission of two unsatisfactory ratings, in accordance with the Pay and Classification Plan. Probationary Employees may be terminated immediately. USE OF THIS OVERALL RATING REQUIRES COMPLETION OF THE REMEDIAL ACTIVITIES SECTION BELOW.

Remedial Activities: Actions which supervisor and employee have agreed upon to correct performance evaluation Below Expectation or Unsatisfactory.

Development Activities: Action which supervisor and employee have agreed upon to further develop employee capabilities and to prepare for greater responsibility.

RATER'S SIGNATURE _____   DATE: _____

COMMENTS OF EMPLOYEE:

SIGNATURE OF EMPLOYEE: _____   DATE: _____

(Signature indicates only that appraisal has been reviewed with employee.)

SIGNATURE OF RATER'S SUPERVISOR: _____   DATE: _____

Figure 12-2 A more elaborate personnel evaluation form with detailed, job-related criteria. (Courtesy Portsmouth, Virginia, Police Department.)

opportunity to observe their fellow officers at work, and therefore their ratings of one another are more likely to be based on actual performance.

Despite all the difficulties we have mentioned, performance evaluation is an indispensable part of police administration. Both work product measurements and trait ratings can be valuable tools in planning, especially in identifying problem areas and making decisions about the deployment of human resources. A trait rating system of some kind is nearly unavoidable if employees are to be evaluated for their current performances and their potential for promotion. However, neither of these tools is perfect. The value of a trait rating system depends first on the quality of the trait lists; the traits to be rated must be selected carefully, to reflect actual, observable performance and not vaguely defined personal qualities. Peer ratings, in addition to supervisory ratings, make trait rating systems even more useful.[13]

Promotional Systems

If it is so difficult to evaluate the performance of individual officers, how can police administrators select those officers who are the best qualified to be promoted?

In the early days of American law enforcement, this posed no problem at all, since assignments and promotions were based almost entirely on political considerations. One of the most important, and most bitterly contested, of the many reforms along the way toward police professionalism was the establishment of **merit systems** for the selection and promotion of officers. A merit system, as the name suggests, simply means that some orderly procedure is used to select recruits and award promotions.

A sound merit system should be objective and free of personal biases; it should allow all qualified candidates to compete fairly for every available position.

Most merit systems are administered not by the police department itself, but by an independent **Civil Service Commission** or similar agency, which may serve the same function for other governmental departments and agencies. The federal Office of Personnel Management (formerly the U.S. Civil Service Commission), for example, supervises the hiring, placement, and promotion of all federal employees in the executive branch (except the military) and independent federal agencies, except those in the highest administrative positions who are appointed directly by the president. Most state and local Civil Service Commissions are organized along similar lines, although there is a great deal of variation from one agency to the next.[14]

When Civil Service merit systems were first introduced, it was widely believed that the most important criterion in choosing candidates for promotion was knowledge about the job to be filled. It seemed that the simplest and fairest way to award promotions would be to require all candidates to pass an examination covering the areas of knowledge that a job involved; whoever obtained the highest score on the examination would be the best qualified for the position. Thus the competitive Civil Service examination became the basis for most merit systems, and this procedure is almost universally used today.

Competitive examinations have the advantage of being, in principle, fair and objective; as long as everyone takes the same test and the tests are scored accurately, it is a simple matter to determine which candidate has the best score and is therefore presumed to be best qualified. But there are several problems with this procedure that are not immediately apparent.

The first problem concerns the composition of the examinations. What questions should be asked? What knowledge is required for a person to be successful in a given job? Who should formulate the questions? In many cases, the task of developing the questions has been left to police administrators, who may have no experience or talent in analyzing the requirements of each position and framing questions that are clear, fair, and accurate in assessing the candidates' abilities. Over the years, the science of developing standard tests, including merit system tests, has progressed to a considerable degree of sophistication. The commercially developed tests used in college entrance examinations, for example, are the product of thousands of hours of work by specialists in psychological testing. Many merit system examinations are made up by small committees or by individual administrators who have no special qualifications for this task.

Several professional organizations, including the IACP, have attempted to improve the quality of merit system tests by developing tests that may be used by local police agencies; some state certification agencies also provide promotional tests for use by local police agencies and Civil Service Commissions. There are also various commercially developed tests intended for this purpose. But local police and Civil Service officials frequently object that these standardized tests are not suitable because they do not take into account local conditions, policies, or requirements. Many police administrators prefer to use a test that has been developed locally, even though its validity (whether it actually measures what it is supposed to be testing) and reliability (whether it consistently produces the same results) may be questionable.

The second problem is even more fundamental: Can any written examination fairly determine whether an individual is capable of performing a given job? It may be true that every job involves applying a given body of knowledge. But the fact that a person has the required knowledge does not necessarily mean that the person can apply it successfully.

Furthermore, it is not clear that any written examination can measure the nonintellectual skills that may be required to successfully perform a certain job. Finally, individuals vary in their ability to do well on written tests. Some people might possess the knowledge and skills to do a job very well, but still receive a low score on a written exam; others may score high on the exam because of their test-taking skill even though they are not really better qualified than some other candidate.

For all of these reasons, the use of competitive examinations as the basis for merit system promotions has come under a growing cloud of controversy and skepticism. But if competitive written examinations are not the answer, how can administrators choose the best-qualified candidates for promotion?

According to the study conducted in 1972 by Eisenberg, Kent, and Wall for the Police Foundation, most law enforcement agencies now use a variety of methods, in combination, to award promotions. Typically, officers who wish to be considered for promotion must first establish their eligibility. Usually they must have been employed in their present position for a minimum period of time (anywhere from one to eight years). Then they must pass a written exam (usually with a minimum score of 70 percent). Some agencies also permit only those officers with the greatest seniority in their current rank to compete for promotions. Oral examinations and ratings by supervisors are also used by some agencies to establish eligibility.

Once candidates have established their eligibility for promotion, a different set of criteria may be used to rank the candidates from "most qualified" to "least qualified." Many agencies continue to use candidates' scores on written exams as one of the bases for ranking. Oral exams and supervisors' ratings are also widely used for ranking. Some agencies ask supervisors to review the list of candidates and estimate each candidate's potential for success if the candidate is promoted; these promotion potential estimates are then considered in the rankings. Seniority in the candidates' present rank and length of service are also taken into account. Finally, two other factors—the candidates' educational achievements and participation in the department's own in-service training program (or equivalent advanced training received elsewhere)—are considered by a few agencies.

The following chart indicates the number of agencies (actually, the percentage of those who responded to the Police Foundation survey) that relied on each of these factors in awarding promotions:[15]

Factors Considered in Awarding Promotions

	For Eligibility (%)	For Ranking (%)
Written exam	55	51
Length of service	56	19
Oral exam	35	39
Seniority in rank	35	20
Supervisor's rating	30	32
Estimate of potential	16	26
Education, training	18	13

The columns of percentages in this chart do not add up to 100 because nearly all police agencies use some combination of factors. It is significant that a little more than half of the agencies responding to the survey reported that they use written exams at all. Nevertheless, the competitive written exam remains the most widely used device to select candidates for promotion, just as it continues to be almost universally used to select recruits. In fact, for most American law enforcement agencies, the promotional system and the recruit-selection system are very similar; the methods used to screen applicants for entry into police employment are used again whenever an employee is being considered for promotion.

Career Development Systems

There is an alternative to the conventional systems of promotion we have just discussed; however, it is considerably more difficult to establish and maintain. A few police departments, mostly large ones, have developed a comprehensive **career development system** that attempts to overcome the drawbacks of the usual promotional system while better serving the needs of both the agency and its employees. One such career development system was developed in the early 1970s by the Los Angeles County Sheriff's Department and reported in a monograph published by the Law Enforcement Assistance Administration.[16]

Briefly, the essential steps in establishing a career development system are as follows:

1. Each position in the agency must be analyzed and a thorough description must be developed, stating the skills and knowledge required for the position and defining the minimum criteria for assignment to it. The analysis may be performed by administrators or, better yet, may be based on information provided by officers who are already serving in each position.

2. An assessment must be made of each employee's attitudes, capabilities, desires, skills, and current performance. These assessments should be based on information from a number of sources: personnel records, supervisors' ratings, scores on standard tests, and the responses to questionnaires completed by the employees themselves.

3. In principle, whenever a vacancy occurs in any position in the agency, the employee records are checked to determine which employees have the experience, skills, and capabilities required. The idea is to match the agency's needs with the human resources available. In all but the smallest agencies, this may require some kind of computerized matching system.

The object of the career development system is not merely to match personnel with vacancies, but to encourage the best use of human resources. Development is the key word here. Each employee must be allowed, and in fact assisted, to reach his or her maximum potential. This is done by treating personnel not merely as jobholders, but as individuals who, over the length of their careers, should be able to progress from one position to another as they gain experience, skill, and knowledge. Since the agency has certain needs, defined by the positions that must be filled (now and in the future), it is to the agency's advantage to ensure that its personnel acquire the abilities they will need to fill those positions.

This is where the employees' attitudes and desires are important. As we noted earlier, most people want to achieve the highest position they are capable of handling successfully, since this will enable them to receive the greatest possible rewards. However, all employees do not necessarily aspire to the same positions. Some patrol officers may be interested in becoming detectives, while others may be more interested in achieving higher ranks in patrol or specializing in traffic enforcement, crime prevention, or some other particular field. The career development system should allow each employee to fulfill his or her individual goals.

The basic mechanism for this purpose is **career counselling**. Experienced officials (usually in supervisory positions, although sometimes specialists in personnel are assigned this responsibility) should discuss with each employee his or her aspirations and should develop a **career development plan** that will enable the employee to become qualified for whatever positions he or she would like to fill in the future. The career development plan for an individual might involve specialized training, or it might involve transferring into a specialized unit (while remaining at the same rank) to gain additional experience. For example, a patrol officer who is interested in traffic law enforcement might be assigned to an in-service training course in that specialty and then reassigned to the traffic patrol unit as soon as a vacancy occurs. Another patrol officer who is more interested in becoming a detective might be encouraged to enroll in a college-level course in criminal investigation, followed by an academy training course in criminalistics.

A career development plan represents an agreement between the employee and the agency. Like any agreement, it is subject to modification if future conditions require it. For example, a patrol officer in 1982 might indicate an interest in becoming a narcotics investigator in the future and might develop a career plan accordingly; but in 1985, it may be apparent to both the officer and his supervisor that the need for narcotics investigators is declining. By the same token, in 1982 an officer might express an interest in traffic law enforcement, but find in 1985 that she is more interested in community relations and crime prevention. In both cases, it makes sense for both the employee and the agency to modify the career development plan.

Career counseling also is an opportunity for a supervisor to discuss an employee's work performance in a nonthreatening, nonpunitive setting. Whatever method is used to evaluate employees' performances, the results should be discussed, confidentially, with each employee. Those who are performing well should be encouraged to continue, of course. Those whose performance is not satisfactory should be counselled on ways to improve. If additional training or a different work assignment might bring about better job performance, those measures can be made part of the employee's career development plan. At the same time, the employee should be told exactly what degree or amount of improvement is expected in a certain period of time; thus the responsibility for improvement is placed on the employee in return for the agency's agreement to assist the employee in carrying out the career development plan.

Career planning is only half of a complete career development program. The other half is job enrichment, an idea that originated in Europe and has become popular in the United States only in the last decade. Briefly, **job enrichment** means that an effort is made to make every job in an organization more intrinsically satisfying and rewarding. People do not enjoy doing routine, meaningless tasks in an unpleasant work setting. According to Robert McGregor's Theory Y (discussed in Chapter 2), most people want to perform jobs that involve meaningful, responsible work; they want to have a substantial degree of control over their own working practices; and they want to know that the results of their work are important.

It might seem, at first glance, that job enrichment is totally unnecessary in a police agency. Surely the vital duties of police officers are meaningful, responsible, and require a high degree of individual control. Unfortunately, that is not always true, especially at the patrol level. In many of the more traditional police agencies, patrol officers are given only the most routine and meaningless duties to perform—such as patrolling endlessly in an area where the most significant criminal act is likely to be jay-walking. Even in high-crime areas, if patrol officers are limited to merely taking reports from complainants and turning cases over to detectives for investigation, much of the patrol officers' time is wasted on trivial tasks.

Throughout a police agency, for both commissioned officers and civilian employees, much can be done to make everyday work more interesting and satisfying. Supervisors and their subordinates must approach this aspect of career development together, in partnership, to identify areas where employees find their work unsatisfying and to make whatever changes are necessary and feasible.

A sound, functional career development system does not come into existence merely because someone wants it to. A great deal of effort must be spent in planning and installing the system. Once the system is in operation, energy must be devoted to making it work, day in and day out, from one year to the next. Training opportunities must exist, either within the agency or through cooperative arrangements with other organizations, not only for new recruits but also for experienced personnel. Performance evaluations must be as thorough, accurate, and fair as possible. Career counselling must be oriented toward satisfying the needs, both immediate and future, of both the agency and its employees. If these criteria are met, the career development system can be one of the most valuable of all the administrative tools for making effective use of human resources.

ASSISTANT CHIEF WILLIAMSON'S IN BASKET

Instructions

In this exercise, you are to assume the role of Assistant Chief Earl Williamson, chief of Administrative Services. The documents below have been selected from Chief Williamson's in basket. Read them with care. If you need more information about City or its police department, refer to the data bank in the front of the book. After you have studied the documents, complete these steps:

1. State the problem or problems these documents present to Chief Williamson.
2. List as many alternative solutions as you can.
3. Select the solution you think would be best, and give your reasons for choosing it.

CITY POLICE DEPARTMENT
Interoffice Memorandum

FROM:	Chief Abel
TO:	Asst. Chief Williamson
SUBJECT:	Training

DATE: 23 Sep 19--

Earl:

It looks like the State Legislature is about to pass the Police Officer Certification Act (POCA) and make it take effect early next year. This will mean that all police officers will be required to have either a bachelor's degree or a minimum of 240 hours of training from an approved police academy. Currently employed personnel will be exempt _if_ they have a minimum of three years of service. Those who have less than three years must meet the standards within one year.

We have got to figure out how we are going to deal with this. I've asked Lt. Lusk to check the records and find out how many of our people will be affected. We also need to decide what to do about new people. Maybe this would be a good time for us to start our own academy. Otherwise, we will have to find some other way for recruits to get the training.

(a)

Page 2

I don't know exactly how many people we would need to train if we start our own academy. As you know, we have set a planning goal of 5 percent annual growth each year for the next ten years. In addition, our normal turnover for the past ten years has averaged 6.5 percent. However, we need to look at our current personnel and see if there is likely to be a change in the turnover rate due to retirements. I don't have any precise figures, but my guess is that half of our turnover in the past has been due to retirements. For the purpose of making a rough estimate, let's assume that any employee who is over 55 years old and has at least 25 years of service is likely to retire sometime in the next ten years. This gives us a basis for figuring the average number of retirees each year, and double that should be about right for annual turnover. This figure plus the growth figure will give us the number of new recruits we will need per year.

Also we will need to have some kind of training facility. I don't know what we will need, but it probably will have to be located somewhere other than our present building, which is already overcrowded. And we will need at least one full-time training officer. I think we can get by with using our present senior officers as part-time faculty for specialized training.

We might be able to work a deal with the County Sheriff's Dept. and possibly Riverside PD to share the costs, or maybe we could train their recruits for a set fee. However, the Sheriff has only 8 deputies, and Riverside's force numbers only 15, so they don't have the same problem we have.

I have discussed our training needs with Dean Eyitt at City University and he was not very interested in starting a police science program. He said he didn't think "training cops" would fit in with their liberal-arts curriculum. However, we might have better luck with the people at State University in Distantburg, since they are always looking for new programs to offer students. The trouble is that it's so far away, I don't know if it would solve our problem.

We need to come up with something on this right away. I have a meeting with the City Manager next Monday and would like to give him some idea of what we want to do. See what you can come up with by Friday, the 28th. Thanks.

EZA

(b)

```
                    CITY POLICE DEPARTMENT
                      Interoffice Memorandum

FROM:      D. Lusk, Lt., Personnel

TO:        Asst. Chief Williamson

SUBJECT:   Training Backgrounds of Personnel    DATE:   25 Sep 19--


    Sir:
        Here is the information Chief Abel asked me to send you.  I have
    listed each person in City PD with three years of service or less,
    their present assignment, and the amount of training they have had,
    if any.  Please let me know if you need anything more.
        Note that all of these personnel are Patrol Officers. We have no
    personnel above this rank with less than 3 years of service. I hope
    this is the information you need.

                                          D. Lusk, Lt.,
                                          Personnel and Training
```

(a)

Officer	Assignment	Training
Aaron, W.	Patrol	None
Barnett, G.	Patrol	2 yrs college
Barrera, R.	Patrol	1/2 yr college
Berman, S.	Patrol	None
Brown, J.	Traffic	20 hrs State Hwy Patrol Schl
Bryant, H.	Patrol	None
Calderon, M.	Patrol	BS, City U.
Castaneda, J.	Patrol	None
Chadwick, J.	Traffic	None
Chapman, E.	Patrol	MA, Political Sci., State U.
Clark, J.	Patrol	None
Davidson, R.	Patrol	120 hrs, Metro City PD academy
Devaney, C.	Patrol	1/2 yr college
Edwards, R.	Patrol	None
Faulkner, M.	Traffic	None
Foster, E.	Patrol	None
Garrison, M.	Patrol	Certified in California
Gibson, J.	Patrol	None
Gilbert, T.	Patrol	None
Gonzalez, G.	Patrol	1 yr college
Hall, G.	Patrol	None
Hall, W.	Patrol	BA, City U.
Hill, D.	Patrol	None
Knox, J.	Patrol	1 yr college
Lawrence, M.	Patrol	Former sheriffs deputy
McPherson, E.	Patrol	None
Roberts, J.	Patrol	None
Robinson, D.	Patrol	2 yrs college
Rush, G.	Patrol	None
Schiller, A.	Patrol	BA, U. of Arizona (History)

(b)

IN REVIEW

1. True or False: State certification programs, where they exist, tend to standardize the training received by local police officers.

2. Which of the following items should be included in basic recruit training?
   (a) Content of the state criminal code.
   (b) Criminal and civil court procedures.
   (c) Duties and authority of the various units of the police agency.
   (d) Personnel matters such as salaries and benefits.
   (e) Driving skills.
   (f) All of the above.
   (g) None of the above.

3. The three primary sources of training are:
   (a) Colleges and other academic institutions.
   (b) Popular fiction.
   (c) Police academies.
   (d) Individual study.
   (e) Experience "on the street."

4. True or False: It is not possible for small agencies to provide training opportunities for their personnel.

5. The seminar method of training means:
   (a) An instructor presents information to a group of students.
   (b) A group of students, preferably under the guidance of an instructor, discuss subject matter.
   (c) Students individually practice techniques or procedures that have been demonstrated in class.
   (d) Students play the roles of participants in police activities.
   (e) Each student pursues an independent course of study.

6. True or False: Simulations are too complicated to be practical in law enforcement training.

7. The final exam in the recruit's socialization process usually occurs during:
   (a) Academy training.
   (b) The recruit selection process.
   (c) In-service training.
   (d) The probationary period.
   (e) Role-playing exercises.

8. The members of a bureaucratic organization are supposed to be assigned to their positions according to:
   (a) Merit.
   (b) Seniority.
   (c) Probation.
   (d) Performance evaluation.
   (e) Natural ability.

9. Work product measurement and trait rating are standard methods of:
   (a) Simulation training.
   (b) Career counselling.
   (c) Promotion.

(d) Performance evaluation.
(e) Determining eligibility for promotions.
10. The purpose of a career development system is to:
(a) Ensure that the agency's personnel needs are met, both immediately and in the future.
(b) Assist individual employees in taking advantage of the career opportunities that are open to them.
(c) Avoid the need for costly, time-consuming training programs.
(d) All of the above.
(e) None of the above.

REFERENCES

1. Jack L. Kuykendall and Peter C. Unsinger, *Community Police Administration*, Chicago: Nelson-Hall, 1975, page 259.

2. Kuykendall and Unsinger, page 261.

3. William J. Bopp, *Police Personnel Administration*, Boston: Holbrook Press, 1974, page 183.

4. Bopp, page 181.

5. Bopp, pages 181–183.

6. John C. Klotter and Joseph Rosenfeld, *Criminal Justice Instructional Techniques*, Springfield, Ill.: Charles C. Thomas, 1979.

7. Joseph M. Fabricatore, "Preentry Assessment and Training," in Charles D. Spielberger, ed., *Police Selection and Evaluation*, Washington, D.C.: Hemisphere, 1979, page 82.

8. Bopp, pages 192–193.

9. U.S. Commission on Civil Rights, *Police Practices and the Preservation of Civil Rights*, Washington, D.C.: U.S. Government Printing Office, 1978, page 42.

10. Law Enforcement Assistance Administration, *Career Development for Law Enforcement*, Washington, D.C.: U.S. Dept. of Justice, 1973, pages 3–4.

11. Law Enforcement Assistance Administration, page 38.

12. Susan Ehrlich Martin, *Breaking and Entering: Policewomen on Patrol*, Berkeley: Univ. of California Press, 1980, page 13.

13. Ernest C. Froemel, "Objective and Subjective Measures of Police Officer Performance," in Spielberger, page 87.

14. George W. Greisinger, Jeffrey S. Slovak, and Joseph J. Molkup, *Civil Service Systems: Their Impact on Police Administration*, Washington, D.C.: U.S. Dept. of Justice (Law Enforcement Assistance Administration), 1979.

15. Terry Eisenberg, Deborah Ann Kent, and Charles R. Wall, *Police Personnel Practices in State and Local Governments*, Washington, D.C.: Police Foundation, 1973, page 28.

16. L. E. A. A., *Career Development*.

13 LEADERSHIP AND DISCIPLINE

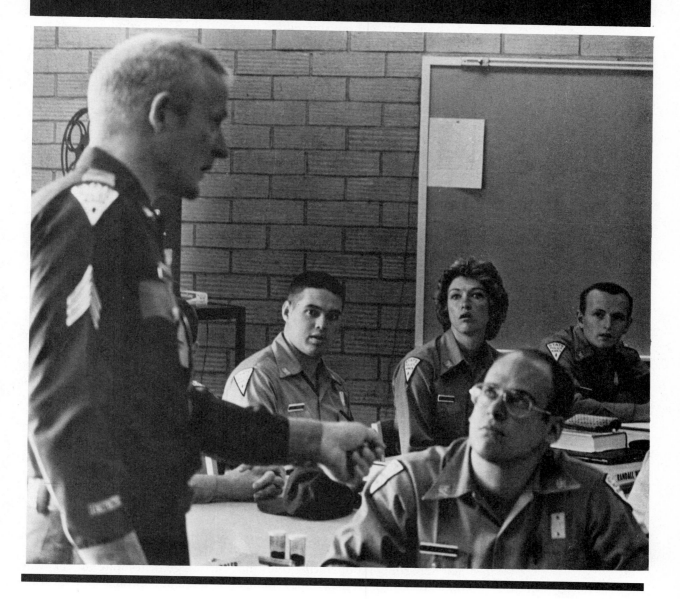

LEADERSHIP

ONE OF THE MOST CRUCIAL CHARACTERISTICS OF ANY police agency is the quality of its leadership. Throughout the course of the police professionalization movement, great emphasis has been placed on improving the quality of leadership exercised by administrators and supervisors, from the highest executive level all the way down to the first-line supervisors (usually sergeants).

This concern for the quality of police leadership is a direct result of the ambiguous nature of law enforcement tasks. If the duties of police officers were simple, clear-cut, and routine, it would be relatively easy to instruct officers in their duties and check to see that those duties were carried out properly. But, as we have seen, the duties of police officers are complex and diverse and often require a good deal of individual judgment and discretion. Furthermore, most police officers perform their duties independently, without immediate supervision. These conditions place a considerable burden on the supervisors to exercise a reasonable degree of control, to promote conformity to the agency's rules and policies, and to obtain reliable information about their employees' performance, by relying on techniques of leadership rather than the more straightforward techniques of management.

What exactly is **leadership** and how does it differ from management? Sociologist Keith Davis defines leadership as "the ability to persuade others to seek defined objectives enthusiastically."[1] The key word here is "persuade." A manager does not need to persuade employees to do their work properly; the manager's authority includes the right to require employees to perform or, if they fail to perform, to face various consequences. As long as the manager is able to determine whether, in fact, the employees are performing as expected, persuasion is not needed; authority alone is sufficient. However, if it is not possible for the manager to exercise such direct supervision, the only alternative is to persuade the employees that it is in their best interests to perform well. And that is exactly the position in which police managers find themselves.[2]

Davis's definition includes two other key concepts: "defined objectives" and "enthusiastically." As we will see, one of the most important duties of a leader is to ensure that employees' objectives are well defined, so that they will know what they are supposed to do. Whether employees perform their jobs enthusiastically or not may seem unimportant at first: as long as the job gets done, what does it matter whether the employees are enthusiastic? But on further reflection, enthusiasm indicates the extent to which employees are motivated to perform their jobs to the best of their ability. Where direct supervision is possible, usually it is enough for employees to perform up to a given, often arbitrary standard. But where a job requires initiative and individual judgment, as police work does, the employees' enthusiasm and desire to perform *better* than the minimum standard assumes greater importance.

The importance of leadership is made dramatically clear when the consequences of poor leadership are considered. As Richard J. Lundman points out, ". . . misconduct by police patrol officers is a complex phenomenon involving . . . at least two elements: illegitimate opportunities and informal departmental operating rules that encourage or tolerate officers who take advantage of these opportunities."[3] Indeed, careful sociological research has demonstrated that wherever corruption, abuse of authority, and other police misconduct exist, the problem can be traced directly to insensitive, inconsistent, and incompetent leadership.

Unfortunately, merely recognizing the importance of leadership does not guarantee that superior leaders will occupy positions of authority in a police agency, or, for that matter, in any other organization. Leadership is an intangible quality attached to individuals. For more than a century, social psychologists and management experts have been trying to define exactly what makes for superior leadership and how superior leaders might be identified.

<table>
<tr><td>

The Functions of Leadership

</td><td>

What exactly do leaders do to exercise leadership? As we have already said, leadership involves several key elements: persuasion, defining of objectives, and promoting enthusiasm.

Each of these elements may require a wide range of specific activities. In Chapter 2, we discussed some of the attempts by social scientists and management theorists to determine how and why some managers are successful leaders while others are not. If any generalization can be made, it is that particular methods or techniques are likely to be successful only for certain leaders, with certain groups of employees (or other subordinates), under certain conditions.[4] No one technique or group of techniques seems to work consistently for all leaders all of the time.

According to Roy R. Roberg, the subordinates' expectations largely determine what leadership behavior will be successful.[5] If employees expect their leader to make forceful decisions, issue orders, and demand strict compliance with arbitrary rules or standards, then a leader who behaves in that fashion will be successful. On the other hand, if employees expect a leader to allow them to participate in making decisions and to give them considerable latitude in carrying out their tasks, then a more authoritarian leader is likely to encounter resentment and resistance.

One of the most important functions of a leader, according to the theory of Robert J. House and Terrence R. Mitchell, is to clarify the organization's objectives and the path by which those objectives may be reached.[6] House and Mitchell, like most contemporary social psychologists, assume that employees generally want to perform their jobs well, since that is most likely to earn them significant rewards (both tangible, such as higher pay, and intangible, such as personal satisfaction). However, employees are often frustrated when the organization's objectives are unclear, or when employees are uncertain about what they are expected to do to reach those goals. Thus it is up to the leaders to make sure that all employees understand the objectives and how to achieve them.

We can see this principle in police agencies. Almost any law enforcement agency will subscribe to some global goals, such as enforcing the law or preventing crime or treating all citizens equally and fairly. But these goals remain little more than noble sentiments until they are translated into specific policies, operating procedures, and programs. The clear fact is that no police agency enforces all laws equally; some laws are essentially unenforceable (either because the agency lacks sufficient resources, or because there is no public support for enforcement), others are enforced only

</td></tr>
</table>

sporadically (for example, traffic laws), and still others are enforced only when there is a public demand for enforcement (for example, some vice laws). If the chief of a police department maintains publicly that the department always enforces the law, while every patrol officer knows that some laws are generally unenforced but is never sure which laws those are, the agency's objectives are ambiguous and confused. Similarly, no one believes that the police can ever prevent all crimes from occurring. For a police administrator to claim piously that preventing crime is a major objective of the department, without specifying what kinds of crime are to be prevented and by what methods, merely leads to cynicism and disillusionment on the part of lower-ranking officers.

The complexity of law enforcement creates a great need for leaders to clarify goals and objectives and to be sure that their employees know what is expected of them. At the same time, employees need to know what rewards they will receive when they attain the agency's goals. Again, these rewards are not necessarily tangible. The approval of fellow officers, praise from superiors, and even the self-satisfying sense of a "job well done" are powerful rewards. By way of contrast, nothing is more discouraging than for an officer to feel that he or she has done a good job or reached some important goal and then be criticized for some trivial, incidental fault.

Leadership Styles

In 1939, three social psychologists conducted a study in which they attempted to learn what kinds of leadership behavior were most effective. The study was designed to test three contrasting leadership styles, which the researchers called autocratic, democratic, and laissez-faire (a French term meaning, approximately, "whatever they like"). Individuals trained to exercise leadership in one of these three styles were assigned at random to carefully matched groups of students, who were then given a relatively straightforward set of tasks to complete. Afterward, the groups' efforts and behavior were compared. The researchers found that, in trial after trial, the group with a democratic leader had the best performance, and that group members expressed the greatest degree of satisfaction with their efforts. The groups with an autocratic leader (one who made all decisions for the group and assigned specific tasks arbitrarily) sometimes performed well and sometimes poorly; group members, no matter how well they had performed, generally expressed resentment and hostility toward their leader and toward one another. The groups with a laissez-faire leader generally performed poorly and the members expressed a great deal of frustration and confusion.[7]

The "three leaders" experiment has been repeated many times with slight variations and almost always has had the same result. However, this kind of study has been criticized on the grounds that it depends on having groups that are carefully selected and matched to be representative of the general population. The critics point out that real-life groups are not always average, and that the characteristics of a particular group might have a bearing on a leader's success. For example, as we pointed out earlier, a group that expects its leader to be more or less dictatorial might perform best under an autocratic leader, and might be very frustrated under a democratic leader who expected group members to contribute to decision-making and to display initiative in carrying out their tasks.[8]

Other theorists have questioned whether there are only three important styles of leadership. House and Mitchell, for example, have identified four leadership styles and have defined them somewhat differently from the conventional three-leaders categories:

1. **Directive.** This style, similar to the conventional autocratic category, is characterized by a leader who makes most of a group's decisions, assigns specific tasks to group members, and enforces conformity to rules and performance standards.
2. **Supportive.** This style, approximately comparable to the laissez-faire style, is characterized by a leader who is concerned solely with the welfare and feelings of group members, who allows group members to make all decisions about policies and performance standards, and who generally exercises no active leadership.
3. **Participative.** This style, similar to the traditional democratic style, is characterized by a leader whose chief concern is to involve group members in decision making.
4. **Achievement-oriented.** This style is characterized by a leader who is concerned solely with achieving the organization's goals; who therefore sets and enforces performance standards and generally enforces the organization's rules and policies, but otherwise leaves group members free to perform tasks in any manner they like.

House and Mitchell, unlike the earlier three-leaders theorists, do not conclude that any one of the four leadership styles is superior to the others. Instead, they conclude (and so do most contemporary social psychologists) that an effective leader may be successful with any of these styles, depending on the characteristics of the group and of the situation in which they must perform. Thus a leader, in order to be consistently successful with all groups and in all situations, must be capable of adopting whichever style is appropriate to the circumstances.[9]

One of the most important findings of research on leadership is that the degree of satisfaction felt by group members is an important factor in determining the group's successful performance. If group members have confidence in their leader, accept the leader's style as appropriate to their needs, believe that the organization's objectives are appropriate and attainable, and believe that they will be properly rewarded for their efforts, they are likely to be successful even in the face of many obstacles. Conversely, if group members lack confidence in their leader, feel that the leader's style is inappropriate, feel that the goals set for them are inappropriate or unattainable, and feel that there is no consistent relationship between their efforts and the rewards available to them, the group's performance is almost certain to be poor. Thus one of the most important functions of the leader, no matter what his or her style might be, is to monitor the group's attitudes and, insofar as possible, correct any of the conditions that are likely to undermine the group's performance. A leader must be especially sensitive and responsive to any grievances expressed by subordinates.

Leadership and Employee Grievances

A **grievance** is simply an expression of dissatisfaction. Since it has long been recognized that dissatisfied employees do not perform well, most modern organizations have attempted to develop procedures to discover and correct the sources of employee grievances wherever possible.

There are two main types of employee grievances: those that are general among employees and those that pertain to a particular individual employee. General grievances are most often the result of working conditions that apply more or less equally to all employees, while individual grievances are more often the result of the personal interactions between the dissatisfied employee and his or her immediate supervisor.

Individual grievances should be, and often are, the easiest to correct. An employee may feel that he or she is being treated unfairly for any number of reasons; quite often, the supervisor is not even aware that these feelings exist. Unfortunately, employees, especially those in the lowest ranks, often feel powerless to do anything about their dissatisfaction; they are afraid to complain to the supervisor, who might retaliate in some way. These fears are not always unjustified; if the supervisor is discriminating against the employee (consciously or otherwise), the employee's complaints are likely to make matters worse rather than better. Unless the employee has some reasonable opportunity to take the grievance to a higher authority, the situation is likely to become progressively worse and may affect not only the dissatisfied employee, but other employees who are aware of the unresolved grievance.

Individual grievances can be a particularly serious problem in a police agency, where employees perform much of their work independently and the organization's success depends so heavily on their individual initiative. A dissatisfied patrol officer or detective is likely to do as little work as possible and to feel little loyalty toward the organization that (in the officer's mind) is treating him or her shabbily. Police supervisors, particularly at the first-line level, must be acutely sensitive to this kind of problem and must be ready at all times to deal with it in a constructive and positive manner.

The first step is to adopt clear policies regarding both the formal and informal resolution of individual grievances. Any employee who feels that he or she is being treated unfairly by a supervisor should have an unlimited right to complain to the supervisor's superior, without any fear of retaliation. When presented with a complaint, the superior must treat the subordinate with courteous attention. If possible, the problem should be resolved informally. The superior officer should investigate the circumstances of the complaint and determine whether, in fact, the supervisor has acted improperly toward the subordinate. If so, usually this is a violation of the agency's policies, and it would be up to the superior to advise the supervisor that such behavior is unacceptable. The superior also must see that the improper behavior stops and that there is no retaliation against the complaining subordinate.

Sometimes the superior's investigation will show that there has been no intentional discrimination, no violation of agency policy, or that the problem falls into the gray area of personal misunderstandings or personality conflicts. In that case, the usual remedy is to bring the supervisor and the subordinate together for a frank discussion of the problem. More often than not, the offending supervisor is unaware that the problem exists or attributes it entirely to the fault of the subordinate. By bringing the conflict out into the open, both parties may be able to see the other's point of view and adjust their behavior accordingly. Again, the superior should not let the matter drop or insist that the two parties "settle this among yourselves." The superior should follow up after a reasonable period of time to see that the problem has been resolved. If it has not, further action might be required, such as specific instructions to the supervisor to correct his or her offensive behavior or a transfer of the subordinate to some other unit of the agency.

These informal procedures should be sufficient to resolve the vast majority of individual grievances. In those few cases that cannot be resolved by the supervisor's immediate superior, it may be necessary for the dissatisfied employee to invoke a formal grievance procedure. Usually, formal procedures are needed only when a grievance is generally shared among a large group of employees throughout the agency.

General grievances (which include those that are held by a number of employees, even though not all) are most often directed at a particular policy or rule of the agency, or at some specific condition or practice that exists throughout the agency. For example, women patrol officers may object to a policy that requires them to be assigned only to two-person patrol units, since this policy implies that they are less competent than male officers (and, since in many agencies there are comparatively few two-person patrol units, also limits their job opportunities). Or a group of minority officers might claim that they are being discriminated against by supervisors who assign them only to the most disagreeable and undesirable duties.

Whatever the cause or nature of a general grievance might be, usually it does not involve the relationship between group members and a particular supervisor, and usually no one manager can resolve the problem. Instead, it must be addressed as a matter of policy throughout the agency (or the subunit that is directly involved). For that reason, a formal grievance procedure is necessary.

Most large police departments have established formal procedures for both individual and general grievances. In agencies that have formal contracts with an employee union or union-like association, grievance procedures usually are spelled out in considerable detail. However, many small and medium-sized agencies have no formal procedures, and often the executives of smaller agencies fail to see a need for them. The need exists even in the smallest agency, since employees who find no appropriate outlet for their grievances invariably become dissatisfied, resentful, and frustrated.

A formal procedure does not have to be so formalized that it becomes a bureaucratic ritual. The important elements of a formal grievance are: (1) the employees must present the grievance as a group; (2) the grievance must be stated in writing; (3) all interested parties (including those who currently benefit from the rule or policy in question) must have an opportunity to respond to the complaint; and (4) there must be a clear, definite resolution.

Even individual grievances should require a group presentation if they cannot be resolved informally. For example, suppose a patrol officer feels that she is being discriminated against by her sergeant. First she should be required to attempt to resolve the problem by appealing to her lieutenant. If the lieutenant's informal efforts are unsuccessful or unsatisfactory, the patrol officer should then be allowed to draft a complaint to higher authorities, but should *not* be permitted to submit the complaint alone. If the agency has a union or union-like employee association, it should submit the complaint on the patrol officer's behalf. If there is no appropriate employee organization, the officer should be required to have her complaint cosigned by several of her colleagues who are aware of the problem and who support the officer's position. The minimum number of cosigners should be established by agency policy; it should be low enough to ensure that employees have a fair opportunity to bring a complaint, but high enough to discourage trivial and frivolous complaints. Naturally, there should be a clear, enforceable policy to prevent any retaliation against any of the cosigners.

The written grievance statement or complaint should include the specific nature of the problem (whether it is an agency policy or an individual supervisor-subordinate conflict) and what action the complainants would like taken. Any evidence in support of the complainants' position should be included. Once the written statement has been submitted, the grievance procedure should concentrate entirely on the problem stated in the complaint, and neither the complainants nor other interested parties should be permitted to bring up unrelated matters.

Formal grievance procedures usually involve a hearing before a board composed of agency officials. In large agencies, the hearing board might be the Civil Service Commission or some other permanently established agency. In smaller agencies where formal grievances are infrequent, it is usually necessary to establish a special hearing board. The board should be composed primarily of high-ranking officials, preferably those who have no immediate interest in the policy at question. The agency's chief executive usually should not be a member of the hearing board, since he or she may be called on to review the board's decision. Within reason, the board should include officers from all of the agency's organizational elements; for example, it might include the chiefs of each of the three major divisions or bureaus. It is also desirable for the board to include at least one member whose rank is the same as that of the complainants.

The hearing procedure does not have to be conducted with all the formality of a court trial, but it should be conducted in a dignified manner. The complainants should be given an opportunity to make their case, including the presentation of any documents, witnesses, or other evidence. Any other interested parties such as officers (of whatever rank) who are opposed to the complainants should then be given an equal opportunity to present their point of view. The entire proceeding should be recorded, at least on audiotape if a stenographic record is impractical.

Usually it is not a good idea for the hearing board to be given the authority to make a final decision. After the hearing, the board should consider the evidence that has been presented (and, if necessary, seek additional evidence), then prepare a recommendation to the agency's chief executive. The action, or relief, requested by the complainants should not be the only option; the board may find an alternative that is more appropriate. The board's recommendation should be made in writing, with a statement summarizing the evidence that has been presented to them, and state what actions the board feels are necessary and appropriate to resolve the grievance.

The board's recommendation must be acted on within a reasonable period of time by the agency's chief executive, and the action should be publicly announced. If the chief executive decides not to accept and follow the hearing board's recommendations, the reasons for that decision should be clearly stated, and the complainants should be given a reasonable opportunity to submit any additional evidence or arguments that may have been overlooked earlier (but not to simply repeat the same arguments indefinitely).

These formal grievance procedures do not guarantee that every grievance will be resolved to the employees' complete satisfaction. Some problems or conflicts simply cannot be resolved, given the limited resources available to police agencies and the complex, often conflicting demands made on them. At least, employees should feel that the formal procedure has given them a fair chance to air their problems and that, even though they have not gotten exactly what they wanted, the final decision is just and reasonable.

Employee grievances are not the only source of problems that test a leader's abilities. In every formal organization there are various rules, policies, and procedures that all members or employees are expected to observe. Employees may violate the rules for any number of reasons, ranging from simple ignorance to malice. Rules in an organization, like laws in a society, are worthless unless they are enforced, unless all members are required to obey them and violators are faced with appropriate consequences. In a police organization, many of the rules are especially important since they are necessary to maintain the agency's integrity and the confidence of the public and, in some cases, to protect the lives of citizens and of police officers themselves. However, in a police agency as in society as a whole, enforcement of the rules must depend to a great degree on the voluntary compliance of all members. The extent of voluntary compliance, in turn, is a product of the degree, kind, and quality of discipline that exists throughout the agency's membership.

DISCIPLINE

Too often, discipline is considered purely in terms of conformity with a strict set of rules and standards and the punishments that may result if the rules and standards are violated. This negative concept of discipline reduces the members of an organization to the level of unthinking, fear-ridden sheep.

A more positive concept of discipline is not only possible, but highly preferable. The very word *discipline* is derived from the same Latin word as *disciple* (follower, or, more specifically, pupil). In its original sense, discipline does not mean blind obedience; it means following the leadership of someone in authority, someone who occupies the role of a teacher.

Discipline is necessary in any organization because it is impractical and unrealistic to expect every member to have enough knowledge and understanding to recognize, and act on, the organization's overall interests. Some members occupy positions of authority and leadership precisely because (in principle, if not in fact) they are most capable of making decisions, setting policies, and assigning tasks that will guide all members to achieve the organization's ultimate goals. Subordinate members are therefore obliged to follow a leader's directions not merely because the leader occupies a position of authority, but rather because the subordinate should be loyal to the organization and its goals.

Most of the rules and policies of an organization concern routine, day-to-day events. The rules themselves are often rather arbitrary. For example, there is no inherent reason that it is better for automobiles to be driven on the right half of the road rather than on the left; the choice is arbitrary, and in fact there are many places (notably Great Britain) where automobiles are driven on the left. However, once the choice has been made and a rule established, everyone must obey it, or there would be chaos on the streets. Similarly, there are a great many ways that patrol officers could be assigned to their beats. However, in every police department one particular method of assignment is established and individual officers are not free to ignore the official routine and choose whatever beat they like (unless that *is* the official routine).

Other rules and policies are designed to deal with extraordinary events in which there may not be time or opportunity for each member to gather information, consider its effects on the organization as a whole, and decide independently on the proper course of action. Instead, the organization's leaders have tried to anticipate these events and have decided on the best way to deal with them. When such an event occurs, members of the organization are expected to respond according to the rules; if the leaders have correctly anticipated the proper course of action, the organization's interests will have been protected. For example, making a traffic stop exposes a patrol officer to a variety of dangers, including the possibility that the motorist will produce a gun and shoot the officer. This is clearly not in the interests of the police department (much less those of the officer!). Therefore, most police departments have adopted specific rules on how traffic stops are to be made. These rules are designed to reduce the officer's vulnerability and give the officer time to recover if the situation suddenly becomes dangerous. An officer who carelessly violates the traffic-stop rules is not only increasing his or her risk unnecessarily, but, indirectly, behaving disloyally toward the entire department.

Finally, some rules and policies are established specifically to protect an organization against the chance that some of its members might be deliberately disloyal and might set out to harm the organization. For example, a police department collects a great deal of information, in the course of its usual work, that could be of great value to criminals. A police officer might inform the operators of a drug-smuggling ring that they were about to be raided by investigators. No doubt the smugglers would be willing to pay well for this information, which would enable them to frustrate the police agency's legitimate work. To avoid this possibility, the department's officials establish policies concerning who may have access to sensitive information and strict rules that forbid stealing and selling the information to anyone outside of the agency.

These few examples merely illustrate the different kinds of rules and policies that exist in police agencies and, for that matter, in all sorts of organizations. The point is that obedience to the rules is not a goal in itself. The rules exist because they are necessary to the proper functioning of the organization. Obedience to the rules should be a product of the members' loyalty to the organization as a whole and their desire to further the organization's ultimate goals.

Blind, unquestioning obedience is not always required. Sometimes rules are made for the wrong reasons, or they produce the wrong results, or they do not apply to the particular circumstances of a given event. In all of these cases, the members' loyalties may lead them to question and even disobey a particular rule, not out of ignorance or malice but out of proper concern for higher goals. When this happens, it is important for leaders to recognize the subordinates' true motives. In a police agency, where individual initiative is demanded, an employee who acts out of a genuine desire to serve the agency's interests ought to be encouraged, even if the employee's actions do not conform strictly to the agency's rules and even if, in a particular instance, the employee's actions turn out to be mistaken or fruitless.

On the other hand, violations of the agency's rules that are a result of thoughtlessness, carelessness, ignorance, or malice cannot be tolerated. Some rules involve interests of the agency that are so overriding in importance that violations cannot be condoned even if the employee's intentions were good.

Thus, for a police administrator, maintaining proper discipline is much more than merely a matter of setting up a system of rules and policies and enforcing them rigidly. Police officers are expected, and must be encouraged, to show initiative in interpreting and applying the rules. When it appears that a rule or policy has been violated, the administrator must consider the intentions and motives of the offending officer and must weigh the violation against the larger interests of the agency. A few rules may be so vital to the agency's interests that no violation is permissible, no matter what the officer's intentions. However, all members of the agency should know which rules are inviolable and under what circumstances they apply.

Finally, as much as possible, the enforcement of rules must be consistent. If some officers are permitted to violate the rules routinely, while others are punished for violating similar rules, respect and loyalty toward the agency and its leaders will be undermined.

Sources of Discipline Problems

Assuming that the personnel of a police agency have been selected for their intelligence, competence, and strong desire to serve the goals of law enforcement, most discipline problems are likely to result from poor management rather than the officers' malice.

The three most common causes of poor discipline are discussed below.

Excessive or Poorly Formulated Rules.   If there are so many rules, policies, procedures, guidelines, orders, and so on that no one can possibly be expected to know, understand, and remember all of them, the inevitable result will be confusion and frequent violations. Rules and policies should be kept to the absolute minimum necessary to maintain smooth operations and to protect the agency's interests in extraordinary situations. Similarly, if rules and policies are so poorly stated that no one understands them, or there is uncertainty about when a particular rule applies, or conflicting rules exist for the same circumstances, proper adherence to the rules may be impossible. Administrators should examine and reconsider *all* agency rules, policies, and procedures periodically, should eliminate those that are not absolutely needed, and should revise those that may be confusing or contradictory.

Inadequate Training.   The English courts, centuries ago, established the principle that "ignorance of the law is no excuse." This principle is observed throughout the American system of justice, but it is balanced by another principle: that no one can be expected to comply with a law until due notice has been given. For example, a legislature must publish the laws it has adopted; no one can be charged with violating an unpublished, secret law.

The same principles must apply to agency rules and procedures. It is the responsibility of administrators to see that all personnel are aware of the rules and policies that have been adopted, and how the rules are to be applied. The more important the rule, the more thoroughly personnel must be trained in its content and application. It is not enough simply to provide new recruits with a "policy handbook" or "manual of orders" and expect them to memorize it. Recruits should be trained to know all of the agency's rules, and all personnel should be retrained periodically, or whenever major new rules are established.

Poor Supervision and Leadership.   Proper supervision involves assisting personnel in carrying out their tasks and checking to make sure that work is performed properly. If supervisors do not carry out their duties diligently and consistently, they have no opportunity to correct their subordinates' mistakes, bad habits, or misinterpretation of the agency's rules and policies.

As we said earlier, the fact that most police officers operate independently and more or less in isolation, rather than under the direct control of supervisors, places a considerable burden on the supervisors. They cannot observe everything their subordinates do. However, they can and must observe subordinates in the field as often as possible, review the subordinates' official reports of actions taken, and occasionally ask subordinates to report informally on how they are doing their work. Furthermore, supervisors can exercise leadership by setting a good example of conformity with the agency's rules and standards and by expecting their subordinates to perform well. A careless, lazy, or incompetent supervisor inevitably will have careless, lazy, and unproductive subordinates.

The remedy for these common problems is fairly obvious. Excessive or poorly formulated rules can be revised or, if possible, eliminated. Personnel can be trained to know the rules, know why they exist, and know when to apply them. Poor leaders can be retrained to make them better leaders, or, if necessary, replaced.

Serious Discipline Problems

There is a certain type of human personality that is sometimes attracted to law enforcement as a career. This personality type is characterized by what psychologists call a high degree of *ego involvement*. This means that the person tends to interpret every kind of event, and every relationship with another person (even the most fleeting ones), in terms of a possible threat to the person's self-image, values, and desires. Such a person tends to be highly aggressive, even combative in the face of the slightest provocation. The Spanish word *macho* is often used to describe this kind of person.

Individuals with this personality type may be excellent police officers. They approach their work with a great deal of energy, dedication, and determination to succeed. Unfortunately, they sometimes carry their zeal to such an extreme degree that they become overly aggressive, careless about following sound police practices, and dangerous to themselves as well as to the public they are pledged to protect. Every encounter with a citizen becomes a confrontation, a test of wills in which the officer's authority and legal power may be used to force the citizen to submit. An arrest or search for evidence may be pursued with no regard for common-sense rules of safety and proper legal procedure.

The macho personality is only one example of what we might call the **insubordinate personality** type. In general, insubordinate personalities are those that cause a person to be incapable of accepting and observing proper discipline. Usually there is the same high degree of ego involvement that we have mentioned, although it may be expressed through different kinds of behavior. A person with this type of personality resists all rules and orders, often regarding them as attacks on his or her rights as an individual.

The causes of the insubordinate personality do not concern us here; that is more a subject for a psychology text. For the police administrator, the insubordinate personality can be a serious problem. A single officer with this type of personality can be a disruptive influence on other personnel and, through improper actions, may undermine the integrity of the whole agency. Several officers who are insubordinate, especially if they are concentrated in key areas such as a high-crime-area patrol district or an investigative unit, can wreak havoc on the agency's ability to perform its vital tasks and on the public confidence that every police agency must have.

Correcting this problem is not easy. Ideally, individuals with insubordinate personality types should be identified and screened out before they ever enter a police agency. Unfortunately, even with extensive and sophisticated psychological testing procedures, the screening process is never foolproof—especially since police agencies want to attract individuals who are dedicated, reasonably aggressive, and determined, all of which are qualities that are displayed by people who might be a problem at some later time. A better opportunity to identify and screen out the insubordinate personality exists during the training process; recruits who are unable to accept direction, who are careless about learning and following correct police procedures, or who are excessively aggressive and heedless of sensible safety precautions should not be allowed to enter the police service. Even so, individuals with insubordinate personalities may get through the most rigorous screening process, or their personality characteristics may become more extreme after they earn a badge. At that point, there are three possible remedies, depending on the seriousness of the individual problem: The insubordinate officer can be retrained to accept proper discipline; the officer can be required to undergo psychological treatment (which may be very costly and time-consuming) to correct the personality defect; or, if all else fails, the officer can be released from employment.

Usually this last step requires a history of violations of agency rules and policies, or a violation so serious and flagrant that dismissal is justified.

Individual officers who are persistently unable to conform to the agency's rules may be not only a problem in themselves, but they may encourage other personnel to disregard proper discipline. In a sense, the insubordinate personality is a kind of "infection" that can weaken or destroy an entire agency. The ultimate result can be systematic corruption of the agency.

Systematic Corruption

Nearly every metropolitan police force in the United States has experienced periodic police scandals in which police officers have been accused of corruption. Invariably these scandals have followed a pattern of events. First there is an arrest of a single officer or a small group, often as a result of an internal investigation started by the agency's administrators or as a result of a citizen's complaint investigated by public officials outside of the agency (such as the district attorney or the city council). The investigation quickly widens; other citizens complain that they have been the victims of corrupt police practices. The news media and politicians carry out their own investigations. Sometimes a special investigative body is formed, made up of elected officials, citizens who have impeccable reputations, and perhaps one or two experts from outside of the community. More police officers, usually those at lower ranks and middle management levels, are arrested, indicted, and drummed out of the agency. Top administrators are swept out (generally they are permitted to resign or take early retirement) and replaced with reform-minded newcomers. The agency is quickly reorganized, during which more managers and administrators are either terminated or transferred to less sensitive duties. After a few months of frantic activity, the community's political leaders announce that all the bad apples have been eliminated and the agency has been purified.

Unfortunately, history indicates that merely changing the administrative structure and replacing a few top officials will not prevent corruption from recurring. Systematic corruption—as opposed to the presence of a few insubordinate individuals—is a product of the attitudes and values held by the members of the police agency.

In 1972, one of the periodic police scandals we have described erupted in New York City. A special investigative body was formed, known as the *Knapp Commission* after its chairman, William Knapp. But unlike most such bodies in the past, the Knapp Commission was given enough authority and investigative resources to go beyond a superficial study of what had gone wrong in the New York Police Department. Some of the Commission's findings, which were published and widely circulated, make clear the sources of systematic corruption.

The Commission found that "group loyalty, . . . stubbornness, hostility and pride" among members of the police force create the circumstances in which corruption can flourish. Even though members of the force are aware that corruption exists, they refuse to do anything about it because of a misplaced loyalty to one another, hostility toward the outside world (that is, the general public), and determination not to permit the agency's reputation to be tarnished. Thus, even high-level administrators and officers who are not themselves corrupt ignore the existence of corruption around them. These circumstances are clearly ideal for those who wish to take advantage of them. New recruits are "invited" to take part by corrupt senior officers; those who decline the invitation find themselves distrusted and shut out of the police society. Those who complain to a superior are ignored or treated as "trouble makers."[10]

The findings of the Knapp Commission in New York have been confirmed by several other studies of police corruption in both large and small departments in every part of the nation. Clearly, the **"bad-apple" theory**, that corruption is caused by a few individual officers, has been thoroughly discredited. In every police agency, Richard Lundman observes, "Police work is exceptionally rich in opportunities for corruption."[11] If the police culture—the set of values and attitudes held by members of the police society—permits corrupt behavior to be ignored and to go unpunished, it will become increasingly widespread and nearly impossible to uproot. It is not enough for administrators to treat particular instances of corruption, such as an officer who is caught accepting a bribe, as mere examples of "bad apples." Administrators must promote a positive police culture, through their personal example and through vigorous enforcement of agency rules.

Dealing with Discipline Problems

Effective administration of a police agency requires a strong and positive attitude toward discipline. Administrators, managers, and supervisors—everyone in the agency above the lowest ranks—must demonstrate by personal example their wholehearted commitment to the agency's goals and their willingness to conform to the agency's rules, policies, and procedures.

At the same time, the police administrator must recognize that perfect discipline is impossible. Some personnel will commit violations of the agency's rules for one or more of the reasons we have cited: ignorance, carelessness, misunderstanding or misinterpretation of the rules or, in the more serious cases, malice or defiance. Violations cannot be ignored or condoned without damaging the agency's morale and public reputation. On the other hand, excessively harsh disciplinary procedures can rob officers of the initiative and sense of personal responsibility they must have to be effective.

What is needed is a range of disciplinary procedures that can be used flexibly, to fit the circumstances of each type of violation, but with enough consistency to maintain a sense of fundamental fairness for all personnel.

A distinction must be made among the various types of disciplinary violations, and among the different degrees of seriousness of violations. The types of violations might be classified in any number of ways, but generally a police agency has four broad classes of rules, policies, and procedures: those that concern purely internal matters of routine administration; those that concern protecting the integrity and security of the agency and its personnel; those that concern proper police conduct in the delivery of law enforcement services; and those that concern clearly illegal acts that might be committed by police officers. Within each of these broad classes, there are degrees of seriousness.

The following list presents a number of examples of actions by police officers that might be violations of specific agency rules, policies, or procedures. The list is by no means exhaustive; in most agencies, it could be expanded considerably. However, it illustrates both the different types of violations that may occur and the different degrees of seriousness; within each class of violations, examples are listed in their approximate order of seriousness, from minor to major.

1. Violations of internal procedure:
   (a) Reporting late for assigned duty.
   (b) Poor grooming; improper wearing of uniform.
   (c) Abuse of privileges such as misuse of sick leave or vacation time, trading assignments without permission, etc.
   (d) Delayed, incomplete, or inaccurate filing of an administrative report.
   (e) Failure to report for duty without excuse.
2. Violations of agency integrity or security:
   (a) Improper disclosure of confidential police information.
   (b) Failure to keep a prisoner in secure custody.
   (c) Careless handling or abuse of police equipment (such as weapons).
   (d) Misuse or theft of evidence, prisoners' property, or police equipment.
3. Improper conduct in performance of police duties:
   (a) Discourteous treatment of a citizen (whether victim, witness, suspect, person requesting assistance, or whatever).
   (b) Failure to obtain a complete report of an incident (crime, traffic accident, etc.).
   (c) Delayed, incomplete, or inaccurate report of an incident involving police service.
   (d) Disregard for safe procedure in carrying out a police service.
   (e) Sleeping, drinking, etc. while on duty.
   (f) Failure to perform an arrest, interrogation, or search for evidence in a legally proper manner.
   (g) Ignoring or condoning an apparent crime known to the officer.
4. Illegal acts of police officers:
   (a) Accepting anything of value from a citizen without proper authorization.
   (b) Physical abuse of a citizen (whether or not suspected of a crime).
   (c) Soliciting a bribe.
   (d) Falsifying a report; soliciting false testimony from a witness, victim, suspect, etc.
   (e) Committing any act that is generally a criminal violation (theft, burglary, etc.).

Again, this list is not intended to be complete, but merely to serve as a list of examples. Depending on local laws and regulations, several of these violations might be regarded as criminal; for instance, physically abusing a suspect may be a crime as well as a serious violation of agency policy.

The disciplinary process requires two steps: (1) violations must be detected; and (2) corrective action must be taken. The process also should operate in two different modes, informal and formal, with regard to both detection and correction.

For example, the informal detection of violations is one of the principal functions of supervisors. By observing their personnel in all phases of their work, supervisors should become aware of many instances of improper conduct. As we have already noted, the fact that much police work occurs out of the supervisors' immediate sight does not (or should not) prevent supervisors from observing their subordinates. Supervisors may use indirect means such as reviewing their officers' reports or questioning officers about their own behavior and that of their colleagues. In addition, supervisors should devote as much time as possible to accompanying individual officers in the field, primarily to observe them at work.

Informal correction should take place as soon as possible after a violation has been detected. Supervisors have a number of methods of informal correction at their disposal, ranging from the simple reprimand or "chewing out" to such techniques as denying privileges (e.g., refusing to approve an officer's request for vacation time), assigning the violator to a less desirable duty (e.g., transferring a motor officer to a foot patrol beat), and so on. Supervisors should not forget that retraining may be the most appropriate response to minor violations, if they are the result of ignorance or carelessness. The retraining may consist of nothing more than the supervisor's explaining the proper procedures or assigning the violator to an appropriate in-service training class.

More formal methods of both detection and correction are required for the more serious violations. Every police agency, even the smallest, should have at least one person specifically designated to conduct internal investigations. In very small agencies (those with fewer than 10 commissioned officers), this person is almost always the chief executive. In small- to medium-sized agencies (up to about 50 commissioned officers), someone other than the chief should be designated as the agency's **inspector**. This person may have other duties as well; often the inspector is the head of a major division. In the role of inspector, the administrator is responsible for investigating any complaints of improper police conduct that come to the agency's attention and reporting the findings of those investigations to the chief executive. In addition, the inspector should take positive steps such as reviewing official reports, questioning supervisors and individual officers, and observing officers in the field whenever possible to discover any improper conduct that might not be the subject of a complaint.

Larger agencies require a full-time, formal investigative system, under the command of an inspector who has no other administrative duties, and with as many additional personnel as the size of the agency requires. The internal investigations unit should be attached directly to the chief executive's office. The head of the investigations unit should hold rank equivalent to captain (or major, in larger agencies), and all members of the unit should hold rank equivalent to lieutenant or above; however, it may be preferable to use the ranks of inspector and chief inspector to emphasize their independence from the agency's administrative hierarchy.

Again, the internal investigations or inspection unit should not only investigate any complaints that are brought to the agency but also should take steps to discover any improper conduct that otherwise would not become known.

In all cases, the results of each investigation carried out internally should be reported first to the chief executive and then, with the chief's approval, to the officers involved and their immediate superiors. In large agencies where many investigations might be conducted, reports of routine matters need not be made to the chief, but only to the officers involved and their superiors.

For minor violations, corrective action may be left to the discretion of the violator's supervisor. Supervisors should be able to apply relatively minor disciplinary measures on their own initiative. These measures might include placing a written reprimand in the officer's permanent personnel file, assigning the violator to extra duty without extra pay, suspending the officer without pay for not more than three days, or transferring the officer temporarily to a less desirable assignment. Supervisors also might be given the authority to apply somewhat more severe measures with the approval of their superiors; examples might be suspension without pay for up to one week, permanent transfer to another unit, temporary reduction in rank for up to six months, or revocation of a probationary promotion. (In most agencies, officers who have been promoted are considered to hold their new rank on a probationary basis for a period ranging from three months to one year.)

The disciplinary measures we have just discussed are formal in the sense that they are applied only following an independent investigation and written report. Still more severe disciplinary measures require an even more formalized process to protect the rights of the individual officers and to protect the interests of the agency.

Whenever an investigation produces evidence that an officer has committed a serious violation of the law or of agency rules, the complete report should be submitted to the chief executive only. The accused violator and his or her superiors should be given notice of the nature of the accusation and of the possible consequences. The officer should be suspended with pay until a final determination is made.

Some agencies use disciplinary hearings only to determine the punishment for a major violation, once guilt has been determined by the internal investigations unit. However, police officers are just as entitled to due process as any other citizen, and a fairer procedure is to submit the entire matter to a hearing.

A disciplinary hearing board should be composed of at least three high-ranking officers who have no direct interest in or knowledge of the subject of the hearing. In smaller agencies, this will be very difficult to achieve, and it may be desirable to include at least one member of the board who is not an official of the agency. For example, an assistant district attorney, or a ranking officer from another agency, or even a civilian who has a high reputation in the community might be appointed to the hearing board along with two ranking officials of the agency.

A disciplinary hearing is not a criminal trial, and there is no legal requirement that the procedures and rules of evidence for a criminal trial be observed. Nevertheless, protection of the interests of both the agency and the accused officer demands that the hearing be conducted in a fair and impartial manner. The accusation and evidence should be presented by the head of the internal investigations unit, and the accused should be allowed

CITY OF MACON

DEPARTMENT OF PERSONNEL

R E Q U E S T   F O R   D I S C I P L I N A R Y   A C T I O N

A P P E A L   O R   H E A R I N G

CITY OF MACON
DEPARTMENT OF PERSONNEL
D I S C R I M I N A T I O N   C L A I M   R E P O R T

NOTE: This form to be used for Alleged Unfair Treatment

NOTE: This form to be used for Pending Discharge

NOTE: This form to be used for Demotion

NOTE: This form to be used for Demotion or Discharge

NOTE: This form to be used for Reprimand, Reduction in Pay, Suspension

NOTE: This form to be used for Reduction in Pay, Suspension

CITY OF MACON

DEPARTMENT OF PERSONNEL

F I N A L   N O T I C E   O F   D I S C I P L I N A R Y   A C T I O N

DATE:_____

TO:_____ CLASSIFICATION:_____
    (Employee)

DEPARTMENT:_____ EFFECTIVE DATE:_____

Three days have elapsed since you were served with a NOTICE OF DISCIPLINARY ACTION.
I have considered any contentions or statements made by you concerning the action
taken, and my decision is as follows:

_____ The action taken is affirmed.

_____ The action taken is rescinded.

If the action taken was a suspension and it was rescinded you will receive back
pay for the days you have been on suspension.

If the action taken was a suspension, and it is affirmed, you may appeal my decision to the Director, Department of Personnel within ten (10) calendar days
of the effective date of the disciplinary notice by filing a notice on the
appropriate form in the Personnel Office.

_____ _____
DEPARTMENT HEAD   DATE

CC: Department of Personnel

PERS: 110

Figure 13-1 A series of different forms are used by this agency for each step in the disciplinary process. (Courtesy Macon, Georgia, Police Department.)

to challenge the evidence, to question the inspectors who have brought the accusation, and to present witnesses or evidence on his or her own behalf. Some agencies permit an accused officer to be represented by an attorney; many agencies do not permit legal representation or place some restrictions on the attorney's role.

The purpose of a disciplinary hearing is (1) to determine whether the accused is guilty of a violation (except in those agencies that allow a hearing only to determine punishment), and (2) if the violation is proven, to assess punishment. In some agencies, especially smaller ones, the findings of a disciplinary hearing board are subject to the approval of the chief execu-

Figure 13-2 Every officer receives a copy of this policy manual, describing in detail the disciplinary procedures. (Courtesy Macon, Georgia, Police Department.)

tive; where this is the case, however, the chief executive thereby assumes full legal responsibility for the consequences. The hearing board (with or without the final approval of the chief) should be able to assess punishments ranging from suspension without pay for up to six months (in some states, the law permits suspension for up to one year), to permanent reduction in rank or, in the most severe cases, dismissal from the force. If the disciplinary board finds the officer guilty of a criminal act, the board's finding should be forwarded to the district attorney for possible prosecution.

In some agencies, the process we have just described is subject to state law and Civil Service rules, which may call for more elaborately formal procedures and may place various restrictions on the composition of the hearing board and the possible outcomes. In other agencies, the contract between the police department (or its parent government) and the employees' union or union-like association contains detailed provisions for the handling of disciplinary matters. However, in general the purpose of a formal disciplinary procedure is to ensure that all serious accusations of police misconduct are thoroughly investigated and that the final disposition is fair to the accused officer, to the agency, and to the public.

Disciplinary procedures are a matter of great concern to all police agencies. Many police officials feel uncomfortable even considering or discussing these matters; there is a widespread belief that serious misconduct is rare (the bad-apple theory) and that any public awareness of these rare incidents will undermine the public's confidence in the whole agency. The truth, however, may be just the opposite. The public's confidence is reinforced, not undermined, when the community knows that police misconduct will not be ignored or condoned, that police officers are expected to maintain the highest standards of integrity and honesty, and that the agency has a vigorous, fair, and consistent system of maintaining discipline.

CAPTAIN AVERY'S IN BASKET

Instructions

In this exercise, you are to assume the role of Captain Mike Avery, chief of the Patrol Bureau. The documents below have been selected from Captain Avery's in basket. Read them with care. If you need more information about City or its police department, refer to the data bank in the front of the book. After you have studied the documents, complete these steps:

1. State the problem or problems these documents present to Captain Avery.
2. List as many alternative solutions as you can.
3. Select the solution you think would be best, and give your reasons for choosing it.

CITY POLICE DEPARTMENT
Interoffice Memorandum

FROM:	R. Fletcher, Sr. Sgt., Patrol
TO:	Capt. Avery, Chief, Patrol
SUBJECT:	Disciplinary action: G. Barnett, P.O. **DATE:** 28 Oct 19--

SIR:

    Lt. Clements has advised me that it is my duty to inform you that I have taken official Disciplinary Action against Patrol Officer Gerald Barnett, for the following reasons.

    First of all, let me say that Barnett has been a real trouble-maker for me for the last six months. He constantly complains about everything, his assignment, his vehicle, and so forth. I have tried to be patient and explain that there is nothing I can do about getting him a better car until the Dept. orders some new ones, at which time his unit will be retired from service (I hope). As for his assignment, I know it is a rough one, but somebody has to do it and the Officers who have more seniority don't want it. Besides, I worked the same beat when I was a rookie, and the way I see it, if a man can't "take it," he shouldn't put on the badge.

    Last Friday night, about 0230, I received a "tip" from a citizen that there was a gambling operation going on in Barnett's

---

Page 2.

district. When he came in at the end of his shift, I asked him about it. He said it "wasn't any big deal," just some people playing poker and craps in an apartment over a warehouse on Vine St. I asked him why he didn't make a report to Vice, or better yet bust it himself. He replied that he was "too busy to be hassling folks all night," and that as far as he was concerned there was "nothing to bust anyone for." I reminded him that gambling is a violation of the state penal code. He cursed at me and told me that he knows what the law is. I then ordered Off. Barnett to write a complete and detailed report on the gambling operation and have it approved by someone in Vice before he went home. He refused to do this and left the station.

    I therefore ordered Off. Barnett suspended without pay for 3 days and told him not to come back until he is ready to be a cop.

    Sir, I sincerely think I would have done exactly the same if Barnett was white. I believe in making my squad toe the line. In my opinion, Off. Barnett is not a "team" player, he is just a hot dog who thinks his college degree entitles him to special treatment. I have discussed this problem with Lt. Clements and he told me that I am the squad commander and it is up to me to handle it. If I am wrong, and Barnett is reinstated to my watch, I would appreciate having him assigned to a different squad.

                             R. Fletcher, Sr. Sgt.

Capt. Michael Avery,
Chief, Patrol Bureau
City Police Department
308 E. Sixth Street
City, State 65901

Dear Captain Avery:

We, the undersigned members of the Black Police Officers' Coalition, hereby formally protest against the suspension of our Brother, Officer Gerald Barnett, on October 26. This suspension was made by Senior Sergeant Richard Fletcher.

Officer Barnett is an outstanding police officer with an outstanding record of police actions over the past year. In spite of being assigned to the toughest patrol beat in City, and in spite of being a rookie patrol officer, Officer Barnett has made sixteen felony arrests during the past eleven months. On June 13, he risked his own life to save the lives of two persons in an automobile accident. There is no doubt that he should be considered for the Chief's Commendation at the end of the year. He has fulfilled to the highest the Department's motto, "We serve and protect."

It is also obvious to us that Sr. Sgt. Fletcher has an attitude problem with regard to Officer Barnett, and possibly to all Black police officers. Sgt. Fletcher has repeatedly given Officer Barnett the most undesirable duty and has repeatedly refused to consider Officer Barnett's requests for a transfer to a different shift. He also routinely refuses to approve Officer Barnett's requests for vacation leave, trading assignments with other officers, and overtime pay (in spite of the fact that Officer Barnett frequently works ten or more hours on his shift to complete investigations and paperwork). Other officers on Sgt. Fletcher's squad are given these privileges all the time.

As far as the incident last Friday is concerned, we would call to your attention the fact that "friendly" poker and craps games go on all the time in certain parts of City. People on the West Side are not hassled over this kind of "gambling," only people in the Riverfront district. We think it is not a coincidence that the people in Riverfront are mostly Black and other minorities. Considering that Friday night is always the busiest night of the week with drunks, stabbings, auto wrecks, and other serious police activity, we believe that Off. Barnett used good judgment in not wasting his time on a "friendly" game.

In conclusion, we respectfully demand that Off. Barnett be reinstated to duty immediately, without penalty for time missed, and that appropriate action be taken to eliminate the discriminatory treatment that has been received by Off. Barnett and other Black patrol officers in this Dept.

Respectfully,

J. Brown

J. Brown, P.O., Traffic

J. Knox

J. Knox, P.O., Patrol

D. Robinson

D. Robinson, P.O., Patrol

(b)

IN REVIEW

1. Concern for the quality of police leadership is a direct result of:
   (a) The clear-cut nature of law enforcement responsibilities.
   (b) The frequent police scandals that have occurred in major cities.
   (c) The low quality of most police personnel.
   (d) The ambiguous nature of the police task.
   (e) The high degree of professionalism expected of the modern police officer.

2. True or False: The crucial concept in a definition of leadership is persuasion.

3. One of the most important functions of any leader is to:
   (a) Clarify the organization's objectives.
   (b) Make forceful decisions and issue clear orders.
   (c) Allow all subordinates a high degree of autonomy.
   (d) Reward employees for their performance.
   (e) Prevent subordinates from making mistakes.

4. The traditional three leadership styles are:
   (a) Participatory.
   (b) Democratic.
   (c) Supportive.
   (d) Laissez-faire.
   (e) Autocratic.
   (f) Managerial.

5. True or False: All employee grievances should be handled through a formal hearing process to ensure that they are properly resolved.

6. The most common causes of discipline problems are:
   (a) Poor rules, ignorance, and lack of leadership.
   (b) Poor rules, overaggressiveness, and unrealistic attitudes.
   (c) Carelessness, ignorance, and egotistical attitudes.
   (d) Lack of leadership, lack of training, and lack of adequate resources.
   (e) None of the above.

7. A person with an insubordinate personality often has a high degree of:
   (a) Professionalism.
   (b) Leadership.
   (c) Ego involvement.
   (d) Ignorance.
   (e) Corruption.

8. According to the bad apple theory:
   (a) Police corruption is entirely the result of improper selection and training of personnel.
   (b) Police corruption is widespread in all large police departments.
   (c) It is impossible to eliminate crime from society because one bad apple infects everyone.
   (d) Police corruption is entirely the product of a few incompetent or malicious officers.
   (e) Police corruption is the result of social forces that may be present throughout an agency.

9. True or False: Group loyalty is one of the factors that make it very difficult to eliminate corruption once it has become widespread in a police agency.

10. The inspections unit of a police agency should be responsible for:
    (a) Ensuring that all personnel are properly equipped and wear proper uniforms.
    (b) Detecting and investigating all instances of improper police behavior.
    (c) Conducting hearings into accusations of improper police behavior.
    (d) Investigating only those complaints of improper police behavior that are submitted in writing by citizens.
    (e) Ensuring that all disciplinary problems are handled within the agency, without attracting unwarranted public notice.

REFERENCES

1. Keith Davis, *Human Behavior at Work*, New York: McGraw-Hill, 1972, 4th ed., page 100.

2. Roy R. Roberg, *Police Management and Organizational Behavior: A Contingency Approach*, St. Paul, Minn.: West, 1979, pages 158–159.

3. Richard J. Lundman, ed., *Police Behavior: A Sociological Perspective*, New York: Oxford, 1980, page 10.

4. Roberg, page 163.

5. Roberg, page 165.

6. Roberg, pages 173–174.

7. Kurt Lewin, Ronald Lippitt, and Ralph White, "Patterns of Aggressive Behavior in Experimentally Created 'Social Climates,'" *Journal of Psychology*, 1939, pages 271–299. Also see White and Lippitt, *Autocracy and Democracy*, New York: Harper, 1960.

8. Fred E. Fiedler, *Leadership*, New York: General Learning Press, 1971.

9. Roberg, page 174.

10. Commission to Investigate Allegations of Police Corruption in New York City (William Knapp, Chairman), *Report*, New York: George Braziller, 1972.

11. Lundman, page 225.

PART FOUR
THE MANAGEMENT OF POLICE OPERATIONS

14 ADMINISTRATION OF PATROL OPERATIONS

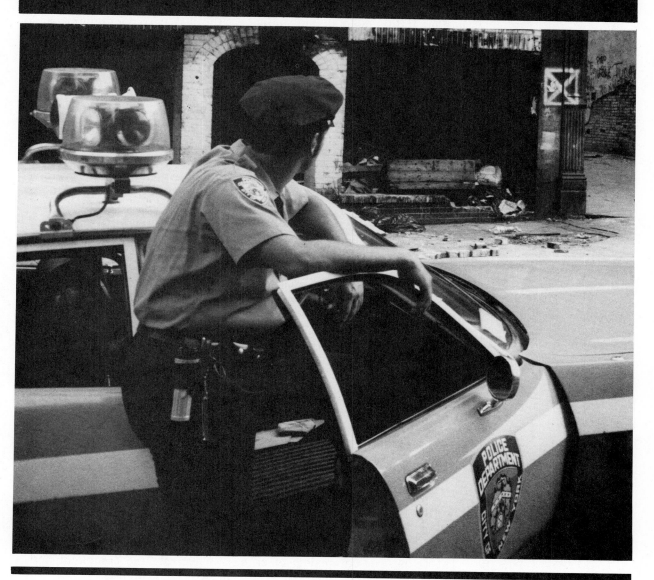

WE HAVE DEVOTED MOST OF THIS TEXT TO THE DISCUSSION of the organization, selection, training, and management of personnel because they are the crucial, indispensable element of a law enforcement agency. Efficient and comfortable facilities, suitable vehicles, and appropriate equipment are all important, but in the final analysis policing is almost entirely dependent on people: the officers and civilian employees of a police agency.

Personnel are also a costly resource. Salaries and personnel benefits generally make up 75 percent or more of a police department's budget. Administrators are responsible for seeing that these human resources are used efficiently, to ensure that as much useful work as possible is obtained for every dollar spent. This does not mean that the agency's personnel should be treated like plantation slaves, under constant pressure to work harder. It does mean that all employees should have a continual stream of work to do, at a pace that allows them to perform at their highest capacity, without either undue strain and pressure or excessive periods of wasted time.

Police administrators have a peculiar problem in trying to establish such a smooth, efficient work flow. By and large, a police agency has little control over the rate at which its most important work must be done. Reports of crimes, traffic accidents, and other police matters simply arrive at random and must be dealt with promptly. This is not true for all police work; some of the tasks of a law enforcement agency, such as preventive patrol, can be scheduled in advance or performed as time is available from less predictable activities such as responding to calls for service. Nevertheless, the fact that a police agency's responsibility includes responding to emergencies that are essentially unpredictable creates a substantial burden on the administrator to arrange the agency's personnel so that at any time, someone will be available to deal with any crisis that occurs.

In almost all American police agencies, the need to have personnel available to respond to emergencies is solved by dividing the agency's personnel into two main forces: the patrol force, whose members are expected to perform a broad range of tasks whenever they occur, and various specialized units, whose members are expected to perform a more limited range of particular tasks at whatever rate is appropriate to the tasks themselves. The precise point at which tasks are divided between the generalists—that is, the patrol force—and the specialists may vary, with important consequences for the scheduling of work and the efficient utilization of the agency's human resources.

PRINCIPLES OF PATROL FORCE MANAGEMENT

Functions of the Patrol Force

Any number of specific functions and duties may be assigned to the patrol force, but this basic element of a police agency generally has four major functions:

1. To answer complaints of crimes, investigate the complaint and, if possible, identify and/or arrest the suspected offender.

2. To assist citizens, other police officers, and personnel of other emergency services (such as the fire department or emergency medical service) to protect lives and property during noncriminal crises.

3. To perform various services that are only indirectly related to law enforcement such as inspecting taxicabs, boarding houses, pawn shops, or other businesses and escorting funeral processions.

4. Observing the people and places in a specific territory for any suspicious activity or indications of a crime (preventive patrol).

In addition to these basic functions, patrol officers also must perform various administrative tasks (such as making reports). A substantial part of a patrol officer's time may be taken up by duties such as transporting prisoners to the jail, presiding over the booking procedure, searching for missing persons, and appearing in court to give testimony. Patrol officers also must be given a certain amount of time while on duty for meals and personal business (not to mention occasional rest breaks!). Finally, patrol officers may be taken off the street to attend training sessions, to have their vehicles or other equipment repaired or maintained, or to perform miscellaneous errands for the agency such as providing chauffeur service for officials or visiting celebrities.

We refer to all the items in the preceding paragraph as nonproductive tasks since they take time away from the patrol force's principal functions. Clearly, the more time spent on nonproductive tasks, the less productive a patrol force will be. However, it is also clear that reducing the time spent on nonproductive tasks to zero is impossible. If nonproductive time can be kept to about 10 or 15 percent of the patrol force's total duty time, administrators may be well satisfied.

The four major functions listed above are not necessarily equal in importance and certainly do not involve equal amounts of a patrol officer's time. Most police administrators (and probably most citizens) feel that the first two functions—responding to criminal complaints and assisting in noncriminal crises—are clearly more important than the latter two, and administrators generally seek to concentrate the patrol force's efforts on these two functions. Administrators typically resist the kinds of tasks we have listed as the third major function (performing services that are only incidentally related to law enforcement).[1] The significance of the fourth major function (preventive patrolling) has become a major point of controversy in law enforcement, largely because of the experiments conducted in Kansas City in the early 1970s.

Preventive Patrolling

We have mentioned the Kansas City experiment earlier in this text, but this is an appropriate point at which to discuss it further. Briefly, the purpose of the experiment was to determine whether conventional patrol techniques are effective in reducing the incidence of crime. Several patrol districts in Kansas City were selected on the basis of having typical and similar characteristics such as population, geographic size, and historical crime rates. The districts were divided into three groups. In one group, the number of patrol units was increased and officers were instructed to devote as much time as possible to preventive patrolling (that is, cruising their beats and observing any indications of criminal activity). In a second group of districts, officers were instructed to spend *no* time on preventive patrol, but to concentrate entirely on responding as quickly as possible to all calls for service. In the third group of districts, no changes were made in the previously existing patrol techniques.

After several months, the number of criminal incidents reported, the number of cases cleared by arrest, the average time of police response to calls for service, and other statistics were compared for the three groups. Officials were surprised to discover that there were no significant differences among the three. Contrary to their expectations, increasing the patrol force's efforts in preventive patrolling had no apparent impact on the number of reported crimes and did not reduce the need for law enforcement services. On the other hand, eliminating preventive patrols altogether also had no apparent effect on crime rates.[2]

Many law enforcement authorities concluded that preventive patrol, despite its appeal to common sense, is in fact a waste of time and resources. However, other authorities have criticized the Kansas City experiment on several grounds and have insisted that the experiment did not provide a valid test of preventive patrols. A decade after the experiment was conducted, very few American municipal police agencies have completely abandoned the practice of preventive patrolling.[3]

Perhaps the most practical assessment of the Kansas City experiment would be that the value of preventive patrolling cannot be assumed, but must be proven on the basis of each police agency's actual experience in its own community and indeed in each patrol district. The concept of preventive patrolling needs to be re-examined in light of the *possibility* that it has little or no value *under certain circumstances*.

The principle of preventive patrolling can be traced back to the original "watchman" function of the earliest municipal police agencies. As we discussed in Chapter 1, it is unlikely that a prospective criminal will attempt to commit a crime if there is a high probability that the attempt will be observed by a police officer. Therefore, placing police officers where they are able to observe the most likely places for crimes to occur should discourage criminals. Since it is impractical to station a police officer at every potential crime location, it is necessary to assign officers to patrol a territory that may contain a number of potential crime locations. As long as prospective criminals are not certain exactly where the patrolling officer will be at any given time, they are discouraged by the possibility that they will be observed.

Placing patrol officers in automobiles increases their mobility and decreases the predictability of their movement. In theory, this should be even more discouraging to prospective criminals than the original practice of foot patrols. The criminal should calculate that a police officer in a patrol car might appear at any time.

Unfortunately, what seems logical in principle may be invalid in practice. Under the best of circumstances, patrol officers cannot spend all of their time patrolling. In most cases, preventive patrolling does not occupy more than about 25 percent of a patrol officer's time; three-fourths of the time, the officer is occupied by other duties, and criminals are therefore unlikely to be observed. Criminals may take a variety of precautions to avoid detection, such as using a police-frequency radio receiver (commonly called a scanner) to keep track of the whereabouts of patrol units, or they may commit crimes out of public view, or they may act so quickly that they are able to complete a crime and leave the scene before there is any possibility that a patrol officer will appear. Criminals also have access to automobiles and other means of rapid mobility.

The crimes that are most likely to be observed by patrol officers are those that are not planned in a calculating manner *and* that occur in public view. It is therefore not surprising that the crimes most often detected on view by patrol officers are public drunkenness, traffic violations, disorderly conduct, and the like.

The administrators of each agency must decide how much of their patrol officers' time should be devoted to patrol, considering the kinds of criminal offenses that are likely to be detected and prevented. If less time is spent on preventive patrols, more time can be devoted to responding to calls for service and assisting in noncriminal crises; or fewer officers will be needed in the patrol force; or patrol officers can be assigned to larger beats without affecting their ability to respond rapidly to calls for service. These decisions must be based on the administrators' best judgment of the needs of the community, public opinion concerning the proper role of the police, and similar factors.

Twenty-Four Hour Service

Usually the first demand of the public is to have police service available 24 hours a day. People feel more secure when they know that competent help is available at all times, no matter what their emergency might be. Indeed, many people unrealistically want a police officer to appear instantaneously whenever trouble occurs. If it takes an officer more than five minutes to respond to a call for help, there will be complaints that the police are not "doing their job."

The problem is especially acute for the very small police agency (those with fewer than 10 commissioned officers). In order to provide 24-hour service, it might be necessary to have only one patrol officer on the street at a time; this would mean three officers on daily shifts and one relief officer filling in on the regular officers' days off. But this arrangement is likely to mean that the officers on duty during the day have more work than they can handle efficiently, while the officer on duty in the middle of the night has little to do.

The usefulness of 24-hour patrol service in rural areas is highly questionable. Few incidents requiring immediate police response are likely to occur between midnight and six o'clock in the morning. In fact, usually the heaviest demand for police service in *any* community occurs between about six o'clock in the evening and midnight; between six AM and six PM, the demand for police service varies considerably. Therefore, it would be more sensible in most cases to assign patrol officers to the daytime shifts, with an extra officer on duty during the evenings, and none at all in the middle of the night. The occasional need for police service late at night can be met by having officers on call, either at the police station or at their own homes. In most communities, the telephone company can arrange to have the police department's telephone calls forwarded to the home of whichever officer is on call. An officer on call would not respond as quickly as an officer who is already on duty, but a somewhat greater response time late at night should be outweighed by the increased quality of service during the day.

In a slightly larger department (one with between 10 and 25 officers), it is likely that the public will insist on having 24-hour service. Again, however, this does not necessarily mean that the same number of officers must be available at all hours. A single patrol officer may be able to handle virtually anything that is likely to arise on the late-night watch, and, again, there could be one or more officers on call for unusual crises.

One-Officer and Two-Officer Patrol Units

One of the most intense areas of controversy in police administration is the question of whether one-officer patrols are preferable to two-officer patrols. Usually the question is stated in terms of efficiency versus safety. It is clear enough that two officers in separate vehicles will be able to patrol a larger area effectively than the same two officers in one vehicle; thus, one-officer patrols are presumably more efficient. However, many police officers believe fervently that two officers working together are much safer than two officers working alone.

The advocates of one-officer patrols claim that two officers working together do not give each other as great a margin of safety as one might think. The reason is human psychology: When two people spend a great deal of time together, they are likely to devote more attention to their personal relationship than to their work. As a result, they may become careless. When a dangerous incident arises, both officers are likely to be inattentive until too late. Furthermore, when two officers work together they may come to rely on one another excessively. An officer may act rashly, precipitating a dangerous situation, in the belief that his or her partner will provide adequate backup. If both officers do this at the same time, each overrelying on the other, both may get into serious trouble.

The safety issue cannot be ignored. Statistics reported by the Federal Bureau of Investigation consistently show that police officers are most likely to be injured or killed in either of two potentially dangerous situations: when responding to disturbance calls (especially family disturbances) and when making an arrest, including routine traffic stops.

Between 1969 and 1978, a total of 1123 law enforcement officers were killed in the line of duty in the United States. Of these, 265 officers were working out of two-officer patrol vehicles and 316 were working alone out of one-officer vehicles. These statistics suggest that the one-officer vehicle is more dangerous. But the figures for the same period also show that only 127 officers were killed when they were working out of one-officer vehicles *but had assistance at the time of the incident*.[3] In other words, two officers, each assigned to a one-officer vehicle but working together, are safer than two officers working out of a single vehicle. The one-officer vehicle is safe—provided officers respond to calls together and back one another up in dangerous situations.

If one-officer vehicles are assigned to separate patrol districts, they may have difficulty in providing backup to one another. On the other hand, putting two officers in separate vehicles and assigning both to the same district reduces the efficiency of one-officer vehicles. A sensible compromise is to assign one-officer patrols to overlapping districts, so that most areas are covered by both officers and they are near enough to one another to provide backup. (See Figure 14.1.)

The use of one-officer vehicles also requires coordination of radio calls. When a dispatcher has a call for any police service that is potentially dangerous such as a disturbance complaint, crime in progress, or suspicious activity, the call should be assigned to the officer in whose district the incident occurs *and* to a backup officer. Similarly, when an officer is about to take an action that could be dangerous, the dispatcher should be notified and a backup should be assigned immediately. No officer should ever initiate any action that has the potential for danger without first notifying the dispatcher; the assignment of a backup then should be automatic, whether or not the officer asks for one.

These policies require a high degree of flexibility on the part of officers and communications personnel. Patrol districts should not be treated as though their boundaries were impassable walls; those boundaries exist primarily as an administrative convenience. Whenever an officer is involved in providing a service that is likely to be time-consuming (investigating a crime or a traffic accident), the rest of the officer's district should not be left vacant while officers in adjacent districts have nothing to do. It should be the responsibility of the dispatcher to see that all patrol areas are covered at all times, by temporarily rearranging district boundaries whenever necessary. Figure 14.2 illustrates how this can be done.

Team Policing

Once upon a time, law enforcement was virtually a neighborhood enterprise. Police officers were recruited "off the street" in the communities they were to serve. Foot patrolmen were intimately acquainted with the shopkeepers, housewives, children, and the criminals on their beats. In the larger cities, the police department often was divided into a number of relatively small precincts, each of which had its own command structure and, for most purposes, operated as if it were an autonomous, independent police agency. Each precinct commander accepted personal responsibility for the protection of the people and property in his precinct, and each patrol officer assumed similar responsibilities for his beat.

In Chapter 1, we mentioned some of the factors that changed the picture of policing in America: the rapid growth of the nation's major urban centers, fueled largely by immigration; the drive toward professionalism in law enforcement; the introduction of new technologies such as the automotive patrol and two-way radio; and the centralization of command in an effort to increase efficiency and eliminate corruption. By the early 1960s, the traditional community-centered personalized police service had all but disappeared in most urban areas.

But traditions die hard and often seem to return from the grave with new names. One consequence of the social upheavals of the late 1960s was a public demand for a return to community-centered policing. The public wanted police officers who were familiar with the community they served, who were accessible to citizens when they needed help, and who were subject to some degree of local control. The police, for their part, desperately needed to reestablish a closer, more cooperative and less hostile relationship with the public. Somehow, it seemed as if the drive for profes-

Figure 14-1 Overlapping patrol beats ensure that backup assistance is readily available to every patrol unit.

Figure 14-2 When patrol beats overlap (see Figure 14-1), it is easier to coordinate beat assignments so that all areas are covered even when one unit (in this case, A-2) is temporarily unavailable.

sionalism had caused the police to lose contact with the people they were trying to serve.

Thus the concept of **team policing** was born in the early 1970s. In its most basic form, team policing simply means that a unit of the police agency is established and given sufficient resources to assume full responsibility for all law enforcement functions within a certain community.

This basic idea is broad enough to cover many variations. Unfortunately, this very flexibility has created a good deal of confusion about exactly what constitutes team policing. Some agencies have used the term to define what amounts to a revival of the antiquated precinct organization, except that the precincts are now called teams. At the other extreme, some agencies have adopted what they called team policing when in fact they have done nothing but instruct their patrol officers to work more closely with one another.

In 1978, the National Institute of Law Enforcement and Criminal Justice (an agency of the federal Department of Justice) funded a study of team policing by the Mitre Corporation. The study was directed by Ellen J. Albright and Larry G. Siegel; their results were published in 1979.

Albright and Siegel found that many police agencies had adopted some sort of team policing program during the early 1970s, but that closer examination revealed great variations in the organizational structure and operating policies of these agencies.

Out of 26 police agencies studied by Albright and Siegel that had adopted one or another form of team policing, 17 had found it successful enough to continue. These 17 agencies ranged in size from 30 to about 2000 commissioned officers.

According to Albright and Siegel, a team-policing system has eight fundamental characteristics:

1. Patrol units, or teams, are assigned to relatively small geographic areas for relatively long periods of time.
2. Interaction and cooperation among team members are encouraged.
3. Specific methods are adopted to facilitate coordination and communication between teams.
4. Communication between team members and the public, within each team's service area, is given a high priority.
5. Each team area is under the full-time control of one supervising officer (usually a lieutenant or captain).
6. As far as possible, each team is given authority to set its own operating policies and procedures.
7. Each team is responsible for the delivery of *all* routine police services.
8. Patrol and investigative functions are combined or integrated as much as possible.[4]

Despite these common characteristics, the exact method of implementing team policing varied considerably. Albright and Siegel defined four common types of team policing:

1. **Basic patrol teams.** In this form of team policing, only the patrol force is affected. Instead of assigning patrol officers to conventional beats and districts, with one officer to each beat, the patrol force is divided

into several teams, each of which is responsible for a "team service area." Each service area is larger than a typical beat, but often smaller than a typical district. The idea is that all members of a team are jointly responsible for all patrol activity in their service area.

2. **Patrol-investigative teams.** Teams are assigned to service areas much like those described above, but each team is responsible for both patrol services and most, if not all, investigations. Usually one or more investigators are assigned to each team, but patrol officers themselves are expected to perform most investigative functions.[5]

3. **Patrol-community service teams.** Patrol officers are not given expanded responsibility for criminal investigations, but they are expected to provide a variety of community services in addition to conventional patrolling such as conducting crime-prevention meetings for residents of their service area and performing crime-prevention inspections of homes and businesses. Often one or two community service officers are added to each team.

4. **Full-service teams.** Within each team service area, virtually all police services are provided by team members: conventional patrols, criminal investigations (except the most complex cases), community services, and so on. In some respects, a "full-service team" resembles an old police precinct.[6]

This diversity in organizational forms indicates that there may be many different goals and purposes in adopting a team policing structure. The most common objectives, according to Albright and Siegel, were these:

1. To improve the management of police services; to make police services more responsive to public demand and to manage the police work load more efficiently.

2. To make policing a more personally satisfying occupation; to expand the role of the patrol officer, say, by giving responsibility for investigations and community services, and to enable patrol officers to work together more productively.

3. To improve the public's degree of satisfaction with its police service; to establish and maintain better relations between the community and the police and to decrease the public's fear of crime.[7]

As with all innovative police practices, of course, the ultimate goal of team policing is to reduce the actual incidence of crime through more effective and efficient law enforcement service.

Establishing a team policing system is no small task, especially in a large agency. There may be resistance from senior officers who simply do not see the need to abandon traditional practices or who are not especially keen on having to learn new ways of doing things. Sometimes the police officers' union or union-like organization will resist any change that might involve increasing the work officers are expected to do or that might have some negative impact on the union's authority, on officers' privileges or benefits (such as the existing system of awarding promotions), or the union's political power. In some cases, poorly informed members of the community, or those with some political interest to protect, may object to team policing on the grounds that it resembles the obsolete precinct system.

The resistance to change can be overcome, but only through concerted and persistent effort. Those affected by the change must be convinced that the new way is superior to the old way and that the change will benefit everyone to some degree. At the same time, administrators must be careful not to raise expectations so high that the results of the new system will prove disappointing. Team policing should not be presented as the solution to every problem of law enforcement. Crime will not vanish from the community as soon as the patrol force is reorganized into teams. Clear objectives, thorough advance planning, and careful implementation are necessary if the change is to be accomplished successfully.[8]

DETERMINING PATROL FORCE REQUIREMENTS

Determining Patrol Force Size

Given the fact that personnel resources are limited in every police agency—no police administrator ever has as many officers as might be desired—what proportion of the force should be assigned to patrol?

First, there is no magic number, and no rule of thumb that can provide guidance. In small agencies, it is not uncommon for 80 or 90 percent of the force to be devoted to patrol; in very large agencies, the proportion might be 50 percent or somewhat less.

The single most important factor is the number and nature of the services that the patrol force is expected to provide. If patrol officers are required to make complete investigations of every criminal incident reported or discovered on their beats, plus respond to all noncriminal crises, plus devote a considerable amount of time to preventive patrolling, plus handle a variety of nonproductive tasks, then certainly a large number of patrol officers will be needed. On the other hand, if the patrol officers' responsibility for criminal investigations is very limited (for instance, if they are expected merely to obtain a preliminary report of the incident and forward the report to detectives), and if the police department assumes only limited responsibility for other kinds of services, then a smaller proportion of the agency will be needed on patrol.

Geographic and population factors also influence the need for patrol officers. If population density is relatively high (for example, in the inner city), a single officer may be kept busy responding to calls for service within a small geographic area. If population density is low (for example, in rural areas), one officer may be able to handle all the calls that arise in a very large area, but response time may be unacceptably large because of the long distances that an officer must travel to respond to a call.

These are not the only factors that affect the size of the patrol force. The basic efficiency of the agency and the productivity of the patrol officers themselves have an important influence. If administrative and operational procedures are designed to assist officers in carrying out their tasks quickly and effectively, and if the officers are competent, well-trained, and highly motivated, fewer officers will be needed to handle a given quantity of work.

But the ruling factor, in practical terms, usually is the size of an agency's budget. Few police administrators are given a budget large enough to hire all the officers they would like to have. Consequently, the usual procedure is to take the agency's overall budget, subtract the nonpersonnel costs, and then subtract the personnel who must be assigned to nonpatrol duties. Whatever is left determines the number of patrol officers available. This base number may be decreased by shifting one or more patrol officers to other duties, or it may be increased by shifting nonpatrol officers to patrol—or by persuading the parent government to increase the agency's budget.

Decreasing the size of the patrol force is not always a bad idea. For example, in a small department it may be the standard practice for patrol officers to perform all of the tasks involved in booking their prisoners: fingerprinting, photographing, assigning to a jail cell, and so on. This may be a time-consuming procedure. At some point, it is likely to be preferable to assign one officer as the full-time booking officer, thereby reducing the amount of time that the patrol officers must spend off the street. Even if this means there will be one less patrol officer on duty, the increased efficiency of the entire patrol force may outweigh the loss. On the other hand, if the agency has a booking officer whose duties are not sufficient to keep the officer occupied full-time, it might be preferable to shift the booking officer to patrol and require the patrol officers to do their own booking of prisoners, or to assign other duties to the booking officer.

Patrol Deployment: Shifts and Beats

Once the base number of patrol officers has been determined, the administrator must decide how the officers are to be deployed: in other words, what geographic area each officer is to patrol and for what period of time.

The conventional procedure is to take the total number of officers available and divide it by four. One-fourth of the total roster is assigned to each of three daily shifts; the fourth group is the **relief shift** that fills in for the other three on their days off. Each shift is eight hours long. Since at any given time, one-fourth of the total patrol force is on duty, the agency's total jurisdiction is divided into that number of patrol districts or beats. The beats usually are laid out to be approximately equal in area, and their boundaries are determined by whatever natural or artificial boundaries (major highways or thoroughfares, rivers, etc.) exist in the community. (See Figure 14.3.)

For example, if the agency has 16 patrol officers, the community would be divided into four patrol beats, usually by simply quartering the town along the major north-south and east-west streets.

This procedure would not be entirely unsatisfactory if the need for police service were more or less constant and evenly distributed. However, that is clearly not the case. Although incidents occur at random, in the sense that they do not invariably occur at the same times and places, there are patterns in the distribution of incidents. Those patterns are not accidental; they are a product of the way people live. Since most people are at home asleep during the late-night hours, relatively few crimes are committed and relatively few noncriminal crises occur between midnight and the early daylight hours. During the morning and early afternoon, most people are either at work or engaged in their individual personal business at home; criminal activity is

Figure 14-3 Conventional patrol beats. The area is simply divided into as many beats or districts as there are patrol officers, with the districts roughly equal in area regardless of the service work load.

comparatively light, although somewhat heavier than late at night, and there are more traffic accidents and noncriminal incidents that require police attention. During the evening hours, many people are involved in family activities at home, and many others are engaged in social activities in public places. The increased social activity (whether at home or in public) creates more situations in which people come into conflict. Also, more people use alcohol during the evening hours. There are therefore more family disturbances, criminal assaults, serious traffic accidents, and other incidents requiring police involvement during the evening hours.

These patterns vary considerably from one community to the next, within a single community, and from one day to the next. Police incidents are more frequent and more serious in areas that have denser populations, where socioeconomic status is lower, where different ethnic groups come into contact, and where young people have limited opportunities for productive recreation or employment. Police incidents are also more frequent and more serious on weekends and on some holidays. In short, what we might call the **natural work load** for the police is not the same from place to place nor from time to time. The efficient deployment of the patrol force must take these variations in work load into account; otherwise, some patrol officers will have too little work to do, while others will not be able to handle all of their work effectively.

Experienced and perceptive administrators may be able to predict the natural work load patterns in their communities with surprising accuracy. However, the most accurate method of determining the work load pattern is to examine the historical record of police activities in the community. (If accurate, complete records have not been kept in the past, considerable effort may have to be devoted to setting up the necessary records system. Usually it is not practical to attempt to recreate the natural work load pattern from haphazard records of past activity.)

The records should show the number of police incidents that have occurred by location, by day of the week, and by the time of day. For each incident, it is necessary to know the number of officers whose services were required and the length of time each officer was involved.

This examination of records should result in three analyses: the geographic distribution of police incidents, the distribution of police incidents over time, and the total work load per patrol officer.[9]

The analysis of geographic distribution can be presented in the form of a map of the agency's jurisdiction, with pins or shading to show the number of recorded incidents in each area. The analysis can be made more thorough by using color codes or some similar device to indicate different categories of incidents, such as crimes (which may be further subdivided into felonies and misdemeanors, or some other categories), noncriminal emergencies, and services indirectly related to law enforcement. Nonproductive tasks should not be shown in terms of their geographic distribution, since they are to be eliminated as far as possible. An example of an incident distribution analysis for our hypothetical City Police Department is shown as Figure 14.4.

The distribution of incidents over time can be presented in the form of graphs. Again, the analysis is improved if different categories are displayed. An analysis for one day is shown as Figure 14.5, and a graph for one week is shown as Figure 14.6.

The average work load for a single patrol officer can be determined by taking the total number of incidents in a given period of time, such as one eight-hour shift, and dividing by the number of patrol officers available on that shift. This number is then multiplied by the average time required to handle each type of incident. The result is the average **service work load** per officer. Time spent on nonproductive tasks and time that is devoted to preventive patrolling must be added to the service work load to arrive at the total work load per officer.

For example, let us suppose that City Police Department has eight patrol officers on duty during the daytime shift on, let us say, Tuesday. According to Figure 14.5, the average number of police incidents during this time period is 56, of which 8 are felony cases, 24 are misdemeanor cases, and the

Figure 14-4 A geographic analysis of incidents for the City Police Department.

Figure 14-5 An incident analysis for an average day in the City Police Department.

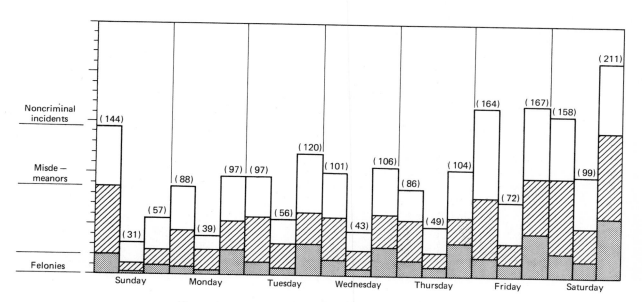

Figure 14-6 An incident analysis for one week in the City Police Department.

rest (24) are noncriminal incidents. The agency's records also show that City Police Department's patrol officers spend on the average 45 minutes on each felony case, 30 minutes on each misdemeanor case, and 20 minutes on each noncriminal incident. On a typical Tuesday, a day-shift officer would spend 45 minutes on one felony case, 90 minutes on three misdemeanor cases, and 60 minutes on three noncriminal incidents. This is a total of 195 minutes, or 3 hours and 15 minutes, in the officer's service work load. To this would be added (again, based on the agency's records) perhaps 2 hours on nonproductive tasks such as meal breaks and administrative duties. Out of an 8-hour shift, there are 2 hours and 15 minutes left for preventive patrolling. (See Figure 14.7.)

However, these figures are based on averages and do not take into account the geographic distribution of incidents. An officer assigned to an area that has a relatively high number of felony incidents might have no time at all for preventive patrolling. Or, on a particular day, the number of noncriminal incidents might be either twice as great, or only half as great, as the average.

For a small agency, it may be possible to adjust patrol beats according to the geographic distribution of incidents by simply shifting the boundaries of the beats. Thus, an officer assigned to a busy area would have a smaller beat to patrol, and an officer assigned to a quiet area would have a larger beat. As long as none of the beats are so large that **response time** (the total time required for a call for service to be dispatched and for the assigned officer to reach the scene of the incident) is not excessive, shifting beat boundaries in this manner is a satisfactory technique. However, in a large agency the problem can become extremely complicated, and merely shifting beat boundaries to achieve roughly equal work loads may be unsatisfactory.

The uneven distribution of incidents over time creates a different set of

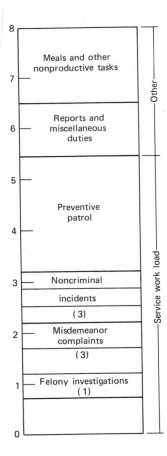

Figure 14-7 The service work load and total work load for one patrol unit in the City Police Department.

problems, even for the small agency. If the day is simply divided into three equal periods, or shifts, and the same number of officers is assigned to each shift, there may be too many officers on duty at some times, and not enough at others. Ideally, there should always be a sufficient number of officers available at any time to handle any incident that might arise. In reality, this ideal is nearly impossible to achieve and would be very expensive if it could be achieved. A more realistic goal is to have on duty at any given time enough patrol officers to handle 80 percent of the predicted peak work load. This means that, during peak periods, there will not be enough officers available to handle every call for service immediately. Some calls will have to be set aside until an officer becomes available. In effect, the natural work load is spread out over time.

For a small agency, if the distribution of incidents over time is not too uneven, adopting a policy of handling calls for service according to a specific system of priorities may solve the problem. At all times, at least one officer should be available immediately to handle first-priority calls or incidents (such as crimes in progress, traffic accidents with injuries, civil disturbances, and so forth). All other calls for service are handled in the order in which they are received, except that when there are more calls waiting to be handled than there are officers available, officers are dispatched according to the priority of the call. Devising a system of priorities is a matter for administrative judgment, based on the community's needs and the kinds of incidents that occur most frequently. Usually, after the kinds of first-priority incidents we have just mentioned, second-priority incidents include felony complaints where the crime is no longer in progress, traffic accidents that do not involve injuries, assistance to other emergency services, and misdemeanor public disturbances; third-priority incidents include all other misdemeanor complaints, minor traffic accidents and any other incidents that disrupt traffic (such as stalled vehicles or malfunctioning traffic signals), and some calls for services that are indirectly related to law enforcement. Any other kind of incident or call for service would be treated as fourth priority.

Assigning priorities to the different types of incidents is certainly better than merely handling all incidents, regardless of their nature, in the order in which they are received. Sometimes, especially in smaller agencies, the use of a system of priorities is sufficient to smooth out the distribution of incidents so that it is not unreasonable to have the same number of officers on duty at all times of the day. In fact, most small- to medium-sized agencies have adopted this practice in one form or another, although the system of priorities often is not worked out specifically, but instead is left to the discretion of the radio dispatchers or their supervisor.

Unfortunately, this approach may not be satisfactory in larger agencies. During peak-work load periods, third-priority and even second-priority calls may stack up to such an extent that unacceptable delays occur. While there are no universal standards of acceptable response time, police administrators generally agree that all first-priority calls should be handled in the shortest possible time, preferably not more than five minutes (total response time); second-priority calls should be handled within 10 to 15 minutes; third-priority calls should be handled in not more than 20 to 30 minutes. Longer response times seriously degrade the quality of service that is being provided to the public and may pose an unacceptable threat to the safety of lives and property.

If calls cannot be handled within an acceptable period of time during peak-work load periods, the only solution is to increase the number of officers available. However, adding more patrol officers to a busy shift does not mean that more officers should also be added to a relatively quiet shift. Each shift should be considered separately and assigned the number of officers that is appropriate to the average work load for that part of the day. In some communities, this may mean that there are twice as many officers on duty during the day as at night and three times as many on duty during the evening as at night. Instead of dividing the total available force into three equal shifts, the total force is divided by six; one-sixth is assigned to the night shift (that is, the early morning hours), two-sixths (or one-third) is assigned to the day shift, and three-sixths (one-half) is assigned to the evening shift. Of course, it is not necessary to divide the total force by any even fraction; if there are 25 patrol officers, three might be assigned to the night shift, eight to the day shift, and 14 to the evening shift.

The starting and ending times for each shift also can be adjusted to accommodate variations in work load. For a variety of reasons, usually it is not practical to vary the lengths of the shifts (so that, for example, the night shift only works seven hours while the evening shift works nine); in any three-shift rotation each shift should be eight hours long. However, the shifts do not have to begin at midnight, 8:00 AM, and 4:00 PM. Depending on the distribution of incidents over an average day, in some communities it might be preferable to start the shifts at 2:00 AM, 10:00 AM, and 6:00 PM. If there are substantial variations in the work load from day to day, it might even be necessary to vary the shift starting times on different days of the week; for example, from Sunday through Thursday the shifts might start at midnight, 8:00 AM, and 4:00 PM, but on Fridays and Saturdays they might start at 2:00 AM, 10:00 AM, and 6:00 PM.

Finally, in some communities the peak-work-load period may be longer than eight hours, or there may be two peak periods. For example, there might be one peak period during the evening rush hour and a second peak period (usually a somewhat smaller peak) between 10:00 PM and 2:00 AM when people are ending their evening's social activities. Since it is impractical to have the entire evening-shift patrol force on duty continuously from 4:00 PM to 2:00 AM, the best solution is to have either staggered shifts or a fourth peak-period shift. In a staggered-shift system, all of the night shift might work from 2:00 AM to 10:00 AM and all of the day shift from 10:00 AM to 6:00 PM. Half of the evening shift might work from 4:00 PM to midnight and the other half from 6:00 PM to 2:00 AM. Thus, the 24-hour schedule might look like this:

Shifts

Period	Night	Day	Evening		Total
			A	B	
Midnight—2:00 AM	0	0	0	7	7
2:00 AM—10:00 AM	3	0	0	0	3
10:00 AM—4:00 PM	0	8	0	0	8
4:00 PM—6:00 PM	0	8	7	0	15
6:00 PM—Midnight	0	0	7	7	14

Of course, once again it is not essential for the staggered shift to be divided equally in half, if it would be preferable to divide it unequally (so that the evening A shift might have nine officers and the evening B shift five, for example).

The use of a peak-period shift is similar to the use of staggered shifts. Instead of dividing one shift into two units, or subshifts, a separate fourth shift is assigned to the peak-work-load period (typically from 4:00 PM to 10:00 PM, although that may vary).

One advantage in the use of either staggered shifts or peak-period shifts is that the shift assignments can be varied considerably from one part of the week to another, merely by changing the shift starting times. For example, the peak-period shift (or one subshift) might work from 4:00 PM to 10:00 PM on weekdays, but from 5:00 PM to 11:00 PM on Fridays and Saturdays, and from 3:00 PM to 9:00 PM on Sundays, if the distribution of incidents in the community requires these variations.

Relief Shifts

One common practice in many agencies, especially smaller ones, is the creation of a fourth relief shift whose members substitute for the regular-shift officers on their days off. Since the eight-hour work day and five-day work week are virtually universal in the United States, most people expect to have two consecutive days off each week. Since law enforcement services must be provided seven days a week, there must be a substitute available to fill in two days a week for each patrol officer. In a three-shift system, if all of the shifts are equal in size, this can be done in the following manner:

Day of Week	Midnight—8:00 AM	8:00 AM—4:00 PM	4:00 PM—Midnight
Sunday	Relief	Shift 1	Shift 2
Monday	Relief	Shift 1	Shift 2
Tuesday	Shift 3	Relief	Shift 2
Wednesday	Shift 3	Relief	Shift 2
Thursday	Shift 3	Shift 1	Relief
Friday	Shift 3	Shift 1	Relief
Saturday	Shift 3	Shift 1	Shift 2

This plan, while simple in concept, has a number of disadvantages. First and foremost, it means that the relief shift must work during a different time of the day every other day, which imposes a severe physical burden on the relief shift officers. Whenever the relief shift is on duty, there is no one from the regular shift present to follow up on uncompleted work from the previous day. Notice also that the relief shift must work six consecutive days and (in the schedule shown above) has only one day off. In some agencies this is in fact the usual practice; the relief shift officers are either the newest recruits or officers who are out of favor with their supervisors, and there-fore are considered to be not entitled to two days of rest each week. An alternative solution is to have all officers on all shifts work six days consecutively, followed by two days off. Thus, in the schedule shown above, the relief shift would be on duty again the following Monday (on the night shift). This means that, for all officers, different days off are taken each week, a situation that can be very disruptive to their personal and family life. Another alternative is to divide the relief shift into two squads and give each squad an additional day off during the week. Thus on, for instance,

Monday, only half the relief shift would replace Shift 3, and on Tuesday only half the relief shift would substitute for Shift 1.

Clearly, none of these arrangements is very satisfactory. A much better approach is to assign a sufficient number of extra personnel to each regular shift to provide the necessary substitutes. Thus, if there are six officers on a given shift, there should be two additional officers assigned to the shift for relief. In large agencies, where the patrol force is divided into precincts or districts, each precinct or district should have its own group of relief officers, so that they will be familiar with the territory in which they are working.[10]

Another problem results from the need to provide 24-hour-a-day police service. Many people, including police officers, consider working in the evenings or at night less desirable than working during the day. In order to accommodate the preference for day-shift assignment, some police agencies have adopted the practice of rotating all shifts periodically. For example, every six months the day-shift officers are reassigned to the evening shift, the evening-shift officers to the night shift, and the night-shift officers to the day shift. Some agencies even include the relief shift in the rotation. Thus, over some period of time (in this case, two years), all officers are required to work on every shift.

This arrangement, however, becomes very complicated when the shifts are not equal in size. Instead of rotating all shifts at the same time, it is necessary to reassign individual officers (since there are more officers on some shifts than on others) at approximately equal intervals. What usually happens, in fact, is that at least a few officers are rotated every week, and the intervals become very unequal; being rotated to a desirable shift becomes a privilege, and being rotated to an undesirable shift becomes an informal type of punishment. Both privileges and punishments may be dependent on the personal favoritism of supervisors, a condition that is often harmful to morale. If seniority is used as the basis for awarding privileges, the result is that the least-experienced officers are assigned to the undesirable shifts for longer periods of time. Unfortunately, the evening and night shifts, while they may be less desirable, are also the times of the day that are often busiest and that impose the greatest demands on the experience and good judgment of officers; loading these shifts with the least-experienced personnel may seriously reduce the agency's effectiveness and productivity.

There is no perfect solution to the problem. Fortunately, some officers actually prefer to work in the evenings or at night, leaving them free to pursue their personal business during the day. As far as possible, these preferences should be encouraged and accommodated. It is not likely that the undesirable shifts can be completely filled with officers who prefer those working hours, and in any case preferences may change from time to time. Rotating all shifts periodically is perhaps the worst solution, since it requires all shifts to be equal in size. Rotation on an individual basis is certainly better, provided the rotation policy does not permit shift assignments to be used unfairly to reward or to punish the individual officers on the basis of supervisors' favoritism, and provided the rotations do not leave the evening and night shifts filled with inexperienced personnel.[11]

Computerized Allocation Systems

So far we have discussed some of the factors that must be taken into consideration in the deployment of the patrol force. In particular, we have emphasized the need to allocate officers to different shifts and beats on the basis of equalizing their natural work load.

In a small- to medium-size agency (up to about 100 patrol officers), the allocation techniques we have discussed can be carried out manually. At least once each year, preferably more often, the agency's records must be analyzed to determine the geographic and time distribution of the service work load in each patrol area. Beat boundaries can then be adjusted and, if necessary, the size of the shifts can be changed to keep work loads even.

In larger agencies, the allocation process becomes increasingly complicated; performing it manually is excessively time-consuming and the results are likely to be less than optimal. Equalizing the work load is not the only goal to be achieved by patrol force allocation; other performance factors also should be taken into consideration. For example, improving response time may be more important than equalizing work loads. In some cases, *unequal* natural work loads may be desirable if they permit officers on some beats to devote more time to preventive patrolling.[12]

Manual systems of patrol force allocation (including those that are based on mathematical formulas for equalizing the work load) simply cannot take into account all of these performance factors, especially in an agency with more than about 50 patrol officers.[13]

Fortunately, there are computerized patrol allocation systems that have been shown to offer several advantages over any manual system. The computerized systems are widely available in the form of standard computer programs that can be run on most computers, including the smaller minicomputers that are used by many police agencies for recordkeeping and other administrative purposes. Any agency that uses computer-assisted dispatching (CAD) certainly has the ability to use a computerized patrol allocation system.

The various computerized systems differ somewhat in their manner of operation and in the number of performance factors they are designed to take into account. However, they all work in a similar fashion. Records of an agency's operations for a given period of time are fed into the computer, which then analyzes the distribution of incidents by geography and time. In the more sophisticated systems, basic information about the agency's jurisdiction (a map of the community, information about population density, and so forth) also is fed into the computer. The computer then produces a set of patrol force assignments to meet either the criteria built into the program (such as equalizing work loads or reducing response time), or, in the more elaborate systems, according to whatever criteria the agency decides to use.

Some systems are designed specifically to be compatible with standard computer-assisted dispatching programs. As the dispatching program records calls for service, these records are automatically accumulated by the allocation program. In essence, the allocation program performs a continuous analysis of the agency's operations. A new patrol force allocation can be called up at any time.

The development of computerized patrol allocation systems is one area in which substantial progress has been made over the past 10 years, and the progress is continuing as more refined and sophisticated programs are being designed and tested. Consequently, it would be futile for us to discuss specific programs here, since the information would become obsolete rapidly. Administrators who are interested in adopting a computerized patrol allocation system should consult with computer system vendors and should seek information in police journals, recent publications of the Police Foundation, and publications of the various research institutions.

AUTOMOTIVE AND NONAUTOMOTIVE PATROLS

As we pointed out in Chapter 7, the use of the automobile for police patrol is probably the single most important characteristic of modern law enforcement. The automobile with its two-way radio has become indispensable to all police services. However, it does not necessarily follow that all patrol services require the use of an automobile. We briefly discussed some of the uses for different types of vehicles such as motorcycles and aircraft, and we mentioned the fact that foot patrols have reappeared in many urban police forces in recent years.

Specifically concerning the patrol force, managers should decide which of many different patrol techniques is appropriate to each patrol assignment and should then allocate the most appropriate type of vehicles. The standard patrol car will continue to be the most widely used vehicle for both general patrol and traffic patrol. An automobile designed or equipped for police service is able to transport from one to five persons (one or two patrol officers, prisoners, witnesses, and so forth) rapidly and comfortably over relatively long distances and is able to carry most of the equipment that a patrol officer might need in various circumstances. The patrol car also can be used in nearly all weather conditions (except those that are severe enough to effectively immobilize the entire community). In areas where the natural work load is relatively low, a single patrol officer in an automobile can cover a beat of 10 or more square miles and still reach the scene of most incidents within a reasonable response time. In rural areas, it is not unusual for a sheriff's deputy or highway patrol officer to cover, by automobile, an area of several hundred square miles.

However, the automobile is less attractive as a patrol vehicle under certain circumstances. For example, in urban areas where traffic is dense, a motorcycle may be preferable because of its much greater maneuverability. Both two-wheel and three-wheel motorcycles are able to cut in and out of traffic lanes where an automobile would be blocked. A motorcycle is able to transport a single officer, with a limited amount of equipment, rapidly over shorter distances. Two-wheel motorcycles usually are capable of being operated at relatively high speeds, making them more effective as pursuit vehicles on urban expressways and city streets.

Motorcycles also have a number of disadvantages. By their nature, they are limited to carrying one person, or at most two if a sidecar is attached (a practice that is so unsafe that it cannot be recommended), and a minimal amount of equipment. Three-wheel motorcycles generally are incapable of being operated at high speeds, and all motorcycles are dangerous to operate because of their inherent instability and the complete lack of protection for the operator. Motorcycles are even more dangerous, and extremely uncomfortable, in poor weather.

Two-wheel motorcycles are probably best suited to traffic patrol (because of their maneuverability and pursuit capability) in urban areas, especially on expressways. Three-wheel motorcycles are limited to low-speed uses such as urban street patrol (both traffic and general law enforcement) and are widely used for the even more limited purpose of parking law enforcement. Wherever motorcycles are used for patrol they must be backed up by automobile patrols for transportation of prisoners and for the delivery of equipment that is too bulky to carry on a motorcycle. Motorcycle officers also must have either the use of an automobile or an alternative assignment for days when the weather prevents the use of cycles.

In very dense urban areas, bicycles should be considered as an appropriate patrol vehicle. A bicycle is even more maneuverable than a motorcycle, especially off the street, in alleys, railroad yards, docks, and other areas where motor vehicles are too cumbersome. A bicycle, although it is obviously a very low-speed vehicle, does allow an officer to travel from one place to another more rapidly than on foot and in some cases permits an officer to reach an off-the-street location more quickly than an automobile.

Finally, as many urban police agencies have discovered, the foot patrol is not entirely obsolete. In dense urban areas, especially in commercial districts that have a very high concentration of potential (or actual) crime sites, foot patrols are considerably more effective than any type of vehicular patrol. A foot patrol officer is able to develop and maintain a personal relationship with citizens, particularly shopkeepers, that would be very difficult for a motorized patrol officer to achieve. An officer patrolling on foot is able to answer citizens' questions and perform countless small,

Figure 14-8 Modern communications and policing techniques have revived the foot patrol, which has come to be recognized as an efficient way for officers to keep in touch with the community. (Photo courtesy Texas Department of Public Safety.)

personal services which may not be closely related to law enforcement, but do help to uphold the agency's public image.

Just as the development of mobile two-way radios made the automobile practical for patrol use, so too the development of compact, efficient portable two-way radios has made the revival of the modern foot patrol possible. With appropriate radio equipment, a foot patrol officer is always accessible to the dispatcher and has rapid access to backup assistance.

Foot patrol officers should be provided with a vehicle of some sort to transport them to their beat, to carry extra equipment they might need while on duty, and occasionally to enable them to transport a prisoner, victim, witness, or some other person to the police station. All but the last of these functions could be served by a motorcycle rather than an automobile.

Combined motor-and-foot patrols are useful in many communities. An officer patrols most of a beat by automobile or motorcycle, but parks the vehicle to walk through a shopping mall or a commercial district of a few blocks. This is clearly the most flexible way to deploy patrol officers in areas where neither the foot patrol nor the automotive patrol is entirely satisfactory by itself.

Foot patrols are rarely needed on a 24-hour-a-day basis. In most cases, foot patrols are effective in commercial areas during business hours and sometimes only during the peak business hours. For most commercial districts, these hours would be between 10:00 AM and 6:00 PM. In an entertainment district, of course, the peak hours occur during the evening. Whatever the local conditions may dictate, it is not necessary for foot patrol shifts to be exactly the same as motorized patrol shifts. For example, the standard day shift might be from, say, 8:00 AM to 4:00 PM, but foot patrol officers on the day shift might work from 10:00 AM to 6:00 PM.

To summarize both this section and the chapter as a whole: The selection of patrol techniques, the choice of patrol vehicles, and the assignment of officers to shifts and beats should reflect an analysis and understanding of the needs of the community an agency is serving. Arbitrary methods of deploying personnel (such as dividing the community into beats of equal geographic size or dividing the patrol force into four equal shifts) are unlikely to provide a close match between the natural work load and the human resources that must handle that work load. Given the fact that all law enforcement agencies are faced with limited resources, administrators must use deployment strategies that make the best and most efficient use of their personnel.

CAPTAIN AVERY'S IN BASKET

Instructions

In this exercise, you are to assume the role of Captain Mike Avery, chief of the Patrol Bureau. The documents below have been selected from Captain Avery's in basket. Read them with care. If you need more information about City or its police department, refer to the data bank in the front of the book. After you have studied the documents, complete these steps:

1. State the problem or problems these documents present to Captain Avery.
2. List as many alternative solutions as you can.
3. Select the solution you think would be best, and give your reasons for choosing it.

CITY POLICE DEPARTMENT
Interoffice Memorandum

FROM:	E. Z. Abel, Chief
TO:	Capt. Avery, Patrol
SUBJECT: Attached letter	DATE: 15 Sep 19--

Mike:
    Please respond to the enclosed letter immediately. I want a full report on this matter before the end of the week. It appears that this citizen has a legitimate complaint. I don't want to see this sort of thing happen again.

EZA

Losten Transit Company

1822 Warehouse Street
City, State 65915

E. Z. Abel, Chief
City Police Dept.
308 E. Sixth St.
City, State 65901

Dear Chief Abel:

On Saturday morning, Sept. 12, at approximately 1:33 A.M., the silent burglar alarm at my warehouse (address above) went off in the office of the Panecky Alarm Company. The guard on duty immediately called your department and was told that an officer would be dispatched to investigate.

I arrived at the warehouse at 2:20 A.M., after being notified by the alarm company. No police officer had arrived at that time. I found the back door open. Officer Castaneda arrived at approximately 2:25 A.M. He entered the warehouse and found no one there. At his request, I checked the premises and discovered that twenty-four television sets, awaiting reshipment to a dealer in Metropolis, had been stolen.

It is beyond doubt that the burglars were present when the alarm went off. It must have taken them at least fifteen or twenty minutes to remove the television sets. In fact, it's surprising that they weren't still there when I arrived. If your officer had gotten there in less than 45 minutes, he might have caught them in the act.

Considering the amount of taxes we pay for police service, it seems to me that the people of City deserve better police protection than this. As a businessman, I consider this situation to be totally unacceptable, and I will inform the City Council about this inexcusable event.

Sincerely yours,

Losten Fonda, President
Losten Transit Company

CITY PD
PATROL ACTIVITY LOG

SHIFT 3	BEAT B-2	NAME J Castaneda	BADGE 376
DATE 9-12	DAY Sat	VEHICLE NO. B-6	

TIME START	TIME END	SERVICE OR ACTIVITY	RESULTS
0005	—	10-8, Patrolling	—
0050	0115	Fam disturb, 626 E Mississippi	No arrest
0145	0205	10-7	—
0205	0245	Burglary, warehse 1820 Warehse St.	Investigated - report
0310	0320.	DWI, 2600 Blk Commerce	Arrested driver
0406	0430	10-7	—
0508	0516	Traff stop (speeding) 400 E Maryland	Cited driver
0516	0530	Prowler, 1200 blk Columbia	Nothing found
0530	0548	T. A., Columbia + Elm	No injury - Report
0605	0640	T.A., 2200 E. Loop	Minor inj - Report
0640	1700	T. A., Main + Maryland	" " Report
0725	0745	Dog barking, 1100 Ohio St	Nothing found
0745	—	10-7 at Station	—

ODOMETER READING: END OF SHIFT 23652

BEGINNING 33321

TOTAL MILEAGE DURING SHIFT 331

OFFICER'S SIGNATURE Jay Castaneda

SUPERVISOR'S SIGNATURE Jerry Davileck, Sr. Sgt.

Form PA-96

CITY POLICE DEPARTMENT
Interoffice Memorandum

FROM:	E. Nash, P.O.	
TO:	Capt. Avery	
SUBJECT:	Request for transfer	DATE: 10 Sep 19--

SIR:
    I have been assigned to the Relief Shift for the past 4 years. I would like very much to be transferred to a regular shift, day shift if possible, at the earliest moment. I would like to work on regular hours and have the same days off as anybody else. I have always done a good job and kept out of trouble. I think I ought to be considered for this transfer as soon as possible. Thank you.

                                        Earl G. Nash, Patrol

CITY POLICE DEPARTMENT
Interoffice Memorandum

FROM:	D. Bailey, Sr. Sgt., Patrol	
TO:	Capt. Avery, Chief, Patrol	
SUBJECT:	Need for additional Patrol Officer	DATE: 16 Sep 19--

SIR:
    Lt. Alexander has asked me to present the following information directly to you. As Senior Sgt. and District Commander for District A on the day watch, it has become apparent that at least 1 additional Patrol Officer is needed in this district. The 2 officers currently assigned to this district are doing as good a job as they can. However, their beats are so large that they are not able to respond to calls in the 5-minute limit. They sometimes take up to 10 minutes even for emergency calls.
    The new construction in the Silver Valley subdivision will mean a major increase in population in the next year in Beat A-2. Probably 500 or more new residents will move into the area.
    I am aware that the budget for the current year has already been submitted to the City Council. However, we still need at least 1 more patrol officer in this District if it means taking one out of another district.

                                        D. Bailey, Sr. Sgt.

IN REVIEW

1. Police administrators face a peculiar problem in trying to establish a smooth, efficient work flow because:
   (a) Police officers vary in their competence and enthusiasm.
   (b) Most police work is extremely dangerous.
   (c) Tasks to be performed occur at unpredictable, random intervals.
   (d) All employees expect to work eight hours a day, five days a week.
   (e) There is never enough money to hire the number of people needed.

2. True or False: Patrol officers should never be allowed to waste time on unproductive activities that are not directly related to their law enforcement responsibilities.

3. Preventive patrol is:
   (a) The use of patrol officers to investigate crimes.
   (b) The modern form of the "watchman" approach to policing.
   (c) The least important function of the patrol force.
   (d) A proven method of deterring criminal activity.
   (e) Practical only because of the development of the automobile.

4. True or False: The crimes most likely to be detected on view by a patrol officer are those that are not planned in a calculating manner and that occur in a public place.

5. The controversy over the use of one-officer patrols revolves around the question of:
   (a) Whether one-officer patrols are as efficient as two-officer patrols.
   (b) Whether patrol officers should assist each other.
   (c) Whether two officers should be assigned to each beat.
   (d) Whether two-officer patrols are safer than one-officer patrols.
   (e) Whether one-officer patrols should be conducted by automobile, by motorcycle, or on foot.

6. True or False: Team policing is nothing more than a variation of the obsolete, corrupt precinct system.

7. The major objectives of team policing are:
   (a) To make police services more responsive to community needs.
   (b) To ensure that preventive patrol is effective.
   (c) To expand the role of patrol officers.
   (d) To improve the relationship between the police and the public.
   (e) To eliminate the need for trained criminal investigators and other specialists.

8. The natural work load of a patrol force includes:
   (a) The number of police incidents that occur in a given community, distributed geographically and over time.
   (b) The total amount of useful work performed by each patrol officer.
   (c) The amount of work an officer is able to perform in a given shift without excessive effort.
   (d) The nonproductive tasks that are unavoidably assigned to each officer.
   (e) Only those incidents that require an immediate police response.

9. Calls may be assigned according to a system of priorities in order to:
   (a) Eliminate time wasted on nonproductive tasks.
   (b) Reduce the number of patrol officers required on each shift.
   (c) Ensure that every officer has adequate backup.
   (d) Spread the demand for services over time.
   (e) Allow each officer to serve a larger geographic area.

10. True or False: Despite several disadvantages, the modern automobile is the only practical, effective vehicle for use by a police patrol force.

REFERENCES

1. O. W. Wilson, *Police Planning*, 2nd ed., Springfield, Ill.: Charles C. Thomas, 1962, page 80.

2. G. Bennett-Sandler et al., *Law Enforcement and Criminal Justice*, Boston: Houghton Mifflin, 1979, pages 101–103.

3. U.S. Dept. of Justice, Federal Bureau of Investigation, *Crime in the United States 1978*, Washington, D.C.: Government Printing Office, 1978, pages 307–311.

4. Ellen J. Albright and Larry G. Siegel, *Team Policing: Recommended Approaches*, Washington, D.C.: U.S. Dept. of Justice, National Institute of Law Enforcement and Criminal Justice, 1979, pages 5–7.

5. Bennett-Sandler, pages 110–111.

6. Albright and Siegel, pages 8–12.

7. Albright and Siegel, pages 1–3.

8. Bennett-Sandler, pages 101–106.

9. Wilson, pages 92–106.

10. Wilson, page 106.

11. Wilson, pages 108–109.

12. R. L. Sohn and R. D. Kennedy, *Patrol Force Allocation for Law Enforcement*, Washington, D.C.: U.S. Dept. of Justice, Law Enforcement Assistance Administration, 1978, page 10.

13. Sohn and Kennedy, pages 5–6.

15 TRAFFIC LAW ENFORCEMENT ADMINISTRATION

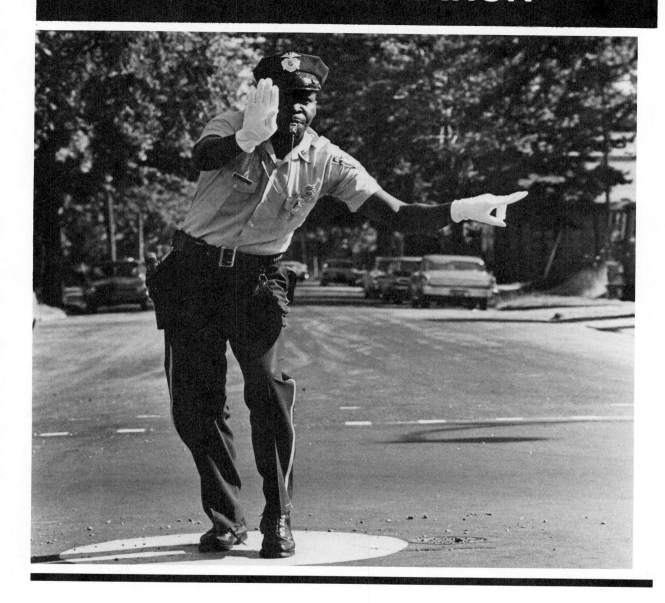

FUNCTIONS OF TRAFFIC LAW ENFORCEMENT

THERE ARE FOUR PRIMARY TRAFFIC LAW ENFORCEMENT functions: (1) to observe the general flow of traffic and, when necessary, remove or direct traffic around any obstructions that would otherwise interrupt the flow; (2) to observe individual motorists and pedestrians for violations of the law; (3) in the event of a traffic accident, to protect the persons and property involved from further harm, and to obtain a report of the incident (for purposes that we will discuss shortly); and (4) to educate motorists, and the public in general, about traffic safety. Many law enforcement agencies also have accepted some degree of responsibility for providing general assistance to motorists, such as providing directions, helping a person with a disabled vehicle to correct the problem or arrange for towing service, and so on; however, some administrators feel that these services are too far removed from the law enforcement function and too time-consuming for their officers to undertake.

Police agencies in this country began to assume responsibility for traffic law enforcement after World War I, when automotive traffic grew rapidly with the introduction of relatively inexpensive, mass-produced vehicles. From the beginning, traffic law enforcement has been a troublesome responsibility for the police. Traffic laws are different from the criminal laws that are the principal concern of the police, in the sense that traffic laws involve the maintenance of public order and the protection of lives and property but not the maintenance of a social code of morality. Exceeding the speed limit or running a stop sign, *if no harm to another person results*, is not an offense against the community's moral code; it is only an offense against a rather arbitrary set of rules imposed to prevent traffic accidents. An armed robbery or a burglary, on the other hand, is an offense against the whole community *whether or not* the immediate victim is substantially harmed.

This is not to say that traffic laws are unimportant. On the contrary: Far more people are injured, and far more property is lost or damaged, as a result of traffic accidents than through armed robberies or burglaries. The national death toll from traffic accidents has been widely regarded as a tragedy and a disgrace for many years.

One important consequence of the distinction between traffic law enforcement and general criminal law enforcement is that the former brings police officers into contact, in the role of authoritarian law enforcer, with many citizens who do not regard themselves as criminals. Anyone who has ever received a traffic ticket will recall the strong feelings of embarrassment and resentment that the encounter provoked. But police officers, too, often have strong feelings about these encounters. On the one hand, citing motorists for violating the law is their duty, and (at least in theory) it is an essential means of preventing the traffic accidents that kill or maim hundreds of thousands of citizens every year. On the other hand, most traffic law violations are not the product of criminal intent, but simply negligence or carelessness. All drivers violate some or all of the traffic laws most of the time, and police officers (whose own driving habits are not always better than those of the general public) realize that only a small minority of the violators are detected and punished. It seems unfair to penalize a few people for actions that are not deliberately malicious, that go unpunished in most cases, and that in most cases result in no real harm to anyone.

Traffic law enforcement also exposes police officers to danger. A motorist stopped for a traffic violation may become so resentful that a violent confrontation develops, or the motorist may have committed some other, more serious offense and may be determined to avoid capture. In recent years, traffic stops have been among the most common situations in which police officers have been assaulted, sometimes fatally.[1]

In short, the police have had several reasons to wonder whether traffic law enforcement is an appropriate responsibility for them to assume and, if so, how to discharge that responsibility effectively without exposing officers unnecessarily to physical danger and to public resentment.

One possible solution is to separate the traffic law enforcement function from the general criminal enforcement function. This can be done to some extent by forming a traffic law enforcement unit within the agency and assigning to it some or all of the traffic law enforcement responsibilities. Most medium-sized and larger police agencies have, in fact, adopted this strategy with varying degrees of success.

Types of Traffic Law Enforcement Units

For the sake of brevity, we refer to the four main traffic enforcement functions as (1) directing traffic, (2) detecting and citing violators, (3) investigating accidents, and (4) safety education.[2]

Small police agencies (those with 25 or fewer patrol officers) generally do not have sufficient personnel to form a separate traffic enforcement unit, and for that matter the natural work load (that is, the pattern of incidents that require police services) for traffic matters is not sufficiently large to warrant a completely separate unit. The first three functions are therefore assigned to the general patrol force. However, all but the smallest police agencies usually have at least one person, often with the rank of lieutenant or above, whose responsibilities include traffic safety education.

Agencies with more than 25 patrol officers vary widely in the size and assigned duties of their traffic units. Some municipal police departments maintain only a small traffic safety education unit with perhaps 5 or 10 officers. Their primary purpose is to collect information on traffic problems in the community (to advise traffic engineers and other local officials), to conduct safety education and promotional campaigns for the general public, and to assist general patrol officers in carrying out the other three traffic enforcement functions.

Other agencies go to the opposite extreme; their traffic enforcement unit consists of a complete patrol force, covering the agency's geographic jurisdiction (often, though not necessarily, on a 24-hour-a-day basis). Traffic patrol officers perform virtually all accident investigations, all planned surveillances for traffic law violators (such as traffic radar stops), and any traffic-directing activities that may be necessary. General patrol officers are relieved of all responsibility for traffic enforcement, except that they are expected to stop and cite motorists for any flagrant violations they happen to observe, and they are expected to assist in any serious traffic accidents that occur on their beats.

Finally, many agencies adopt a middle ground. The traffic unit is principally concerned with safety education and the collection of traffic accident information for enforcement purposes. In addition, the unit has a small patrol force that conducts planned surveillances and that can be called on to direct traffic when necessary. The patrol component may or may not assume responsibility for accident investigations. Whatever functions are not assigned specifically to the traffic unit are left for the general patrol force.

Most police agencies do not assign specific responsibility for general assistance to motorists to either the traffic unit or the general patrol force; rather, any officer who has an opportunity to provide service to a motorist (or any other citizen, for that matter) is encouraged by agency policy to do so.

Allocation of Personnel

The number of officers needed in a traffic law enforcement unit obviously depends on several factors, the first of which is the kind of responsibilities assigned to the unit. The size of the community, the public's demand for services, and the availability of competent personnel are other significant factors.

In the late 1960s, the International Association of Chiefs of Police, under a grant from the National Highway Safety Bureau (now called the National Highway Traffic Safety Administration), attempted to determine a formula for the allocation of personnel to police traffic services, based on the level of service desired, the size of the community, and other factors. The formula was published in 1969. As far as we have been able to determine, very few agencies have attempted to use the formula in their own allocation procedure, partly because it is extraordinarily complicated to use, and also because the formula leaves one significant item out of the equation: the political practicality of obtaining sufficient funds from the local parent government.[3]

OPERATIONS OF THE TRAFFIC LAW ENFORCEMENT UNIT

Traffic Safety Education

The educational function is almost universal among both large and small police agencies, yet the specific methods used to carry out this function are quite diverse. Some agencies rely primarily on the mass media (newspapers, radio, television, and so on) to promote safe driving behavior. Others concentrate on training young people to become safe drivers; traffic safety officers visit schools, organize student safety patrols, promote safety poster contests, and, in some cases, conduct driver training courses.

Nearly all traffic law enforcement officials accept the principle that citing violators is in itself an "educational opportunity." Presumably, a motorist who is given a ticket for a traffic violation is forcefully reminded of the law's existence and is strongly encouraged to obey the law in the future. Some officers conscientiously deliver a brief safety lecture along with the ticket. Unfortunately, the real effectiveness of this kind of education is open to question. People who believe that they have been unfairly punished for doing what almost everyone else does and that their actions have caused no harm to anyone are not likely to be very impressed with this form of education.

The fact that citing motorists for violations may be somewhat ineffective as an educational device does not mean that violators should not be cited. It simply means that the police, if they are seriously interested in educating motorists, must find other means of doing so.

Promotional campaigns, using the mass media, speeches to civic organizations, and so on, certainly have some value. Depending on the skill and ingenuity with which they are prepared and delivered, promotional campaigns can be useful in giving the public information about safe driving techniques and in reminding motorists about the technical details of traffic laws.

Traffic safety campaigns aimed at young people are more likely to be effective. If safe driving habits and attitudes can be taught to young people *before* they begin their driving careers, at a time when they are intellectually and emotionally receptive to being educated, the effects should be substantial and long-lasting. In recent years, there has been some controversy about the effectiveness of driver education courses and some statistical evidence that students who complete these courses are not necessarily safer drivers than students who have not taken the course at all. However, many traffic safety experts believe that the evidence is open to many different interpretations. It may be true that some driver education courses are relatively ineffective, but it has not been proven that all courses are ineffective, or that ineffective courses could not be made more effective.

In most communities, formal driver education courses are the responsibility of the public schools, not of the police. However, if there are no driver education courses available, the police should exercise leadership in trying to get them established and should work cooperatively with school authorities to ensure that the courses being offered are taught by competent teachers.

Similarly, the police should work with the schools to develop and carry out traffic safety programs at all grade levels. These programs may consist of classroom visits by traffic safety officers, the organization of student safety patrols, bicycle safety training, poster contests, and any other activities that will reinforce in students' minds the importance of safe driving.

Traffic safety presentations to school children help to form good safety attitudes. (Photo courtesy Texas Department of Highways and Public Transportation.)

Traffic Accident Investigation

Whenever a motor vehicle collision or other mishap occurs on the streets, most people immediately notify the police. Actually, the laws in many states do not require the police to be notified unless someone is injured or property damage exceeds a minimum amount (generally around $250). Nevertheless, the police are called routinely for even the most minor "fender-benders" and "bumper-bashings."

The responsibilities of a police officer responding to an accident are: (1) to protect the persons and property at the scene from any further harm, (2) to restore the smooth flow of traffic as quickly as possible, and (3) to obtain a complete, accurate report of the incident.[4] The importance of the first responsibility is obvious and requires no further comment here. The importance of restoring the flow of traffic is not so obvious until one considers that any obstruction to traffic increases the danger of further collisions. Motorists passing the scene of even a minor accident are notoriously inattentive to their own driving, as they try to see what has happened, and are therefore all too likely to bend their own fenders. Except for the most serious accidents that may require an extensive investigation, the officer should not hesitate to move the vehicles involved in an accident out of the traffic lanes and to remove any debris from the roadway.

Traffic accident investigation techniques have grown increasingly sophisticated in recent years. There are now computer programs capable of recreating an accident, based on measurements taken at the scene, to demonstrate the movement of each vehicle involved and, thereby, show very accurately how the accident occurred.[5] However, for the great majority of minor collisions, an elaborate investigation is not required. Statements should be taken from each driver, and the names, addresses, and telephone numbers of any witnesses at the scene should be recorded. The exact location of the vehicles and their paths of motion prior to the collision should be recorded.

In general, a police investigation of a traffic accident is *not* intended to determine who was at fault. Under the laws of most states, traffic accidents are primarily a civil matter. Fault, liability, and the payment of damages are issues to be settled between the parties, or, if they cannot agree, to be decided in a civil court. The record of the police investigation may be helpful in settling these issues, but the investigation is not for that purpose. Instead, the primary purpose of the police investigation is to improve traffic safety for the public in general. This purpose is served by analyzing traffic accident records to determine patterns of incidents that may indicate a need for more intensive traffic law enforcement at certain locations or the presence of physical hazards (such as an obstructed view at an intersection) that need to be corrected by engineering means. Thus, the investigating officer's efforts should be devoted to determining exactly *what* happened, not *who* caused the collision.[6]

Most police agencies permit, and indeed encourage, officers to issue citations at the scene of an accident if it appears that one or more of the drivers committed a violation, whether or not the violation directly contributed to the accident. However, this practice has been called into question, and some administrators now discourage their officers from citing anyone at an accident scene unless the evidence of a violation is overwhelming (for example, if one of the drivers is intoxicated). The reasons are: (1)

issuing a citation for a violation that was not witnessed by the officer, but is merely reported by another driver or witness, is legally doubtful (generally, citations for misdemeanor violations are not issued on the basis of hearsay but only on the basis of the officer's own observations); and (2) a citation may be interpreted incorrectly as evidence that the cited motorist caused the accident and therefore bears liability for the damages. State laws and court precedents regarding liability in traffic accidents are extremely complicated, and the fact that one motorist involved in an accident was cited for a violation may confuse the issue more than clarify it.

Traffic Enforcement

In simplest terms, the enforcement of traffic laws means observing violators and arresting them; in that sense, traffic law enforcement is no different from any other type of law enforcement.

However, because most traffic law violations are relatively minor, state laws permit officers to issue citations rather than make physical arrests in most cases. (See Figure 15.1.) Legally, a **citation** is a notice to the motorist that a charge is being filed and that the motorist must appear in court to answer the charge. Most states require a citation to be signed by the motorist, as evidence that he or she is aware that a charge has been filed. Otherwise, it would be possible for police officers to write and file a ticket without the motorist's knowledge.

Figure 15-1 A traffic citation form. (Courtesy Texas Department of Public Safety.)

Whether or not the violator's signature is required on the citation, the police are required to obtain positive identification of the person being charged with a violation. This means that the offender must be stopped and asked to produce identification. In some states, only a valid driver's license can be accepted as identification, and the failure to produce a license is in itself a violation. In other states, a police officer may accept other forms of identification in place of the driver's license, but the motorist must be able to prove to a judge's satisfaction that a valid license was in effect at the time of the offense, or an additional violation will be charged.

In most states, a police officer has some amount of discretion in whether to issue a citation or perform a physical arrest. A physical arrest usually is required for certain serious violations such as driving while intoxicated, reckless driving, or leaving the scene of an accident. Depending on state laws, an officer may be able to make a physical arrest if, in the officer's judgment, the driver is incompetent to operate a motor vehicle, does not have a valid driver's license, poses a continuing danger to other persons, has previously been charged with some number of violations, or is likely to flee to escape the charges. Persons who are passing through the community and who have an out-of-state license (or, sometimes, persons who reside in another county) are often arrested and taken immediately to court. However, a number of states have established an agreement whereby an out-of-state citizen may be given a citation and, if the citizen fails to appear in court or to pay the fine (without contesting the charge), the police in the citizen's home state are authorized to act on behalf of the state in which the citation was issued.

Physical arrest for a traffic violation is, of course, a considerable inconvenience to a motorist. In some cases, especially at night when a judge is not available to settle the charges immediately, an arrest is a greater penalty than the fine that may be imposed. Policies regarding the use of arrest in place of issuing a citation should be worked out carefully and uniformly applied, to be sure that the officers' discretion is exercised consistently and fairly.

Some states' traffic statutes permit officers to issue written warnings for relatively minor violations; where state law allows this practice, local agencies must adopt clear policies governing the use of warnings. Generally, **warnings** are given only for certain kinds of infractions such as operating a vehicle whose safety equipment (a brake light, perhaps) is defective or for violations that involve some degree of judgment on the part of the motorist, for example, entering an intersection after the signal has turned to yellow (when, in the officer's judgment, the driver could and should have stopped). Warnings also may be used for minor violations where there are extenuating circumstances, such as failing to make a complete stop at a stop sign when there is clearly no other traffic approaching the intersection.[7]

Not all police administrators favor the use of warnings. Some feel that if a violation occurs, an officer should issue a citation and let the motorist settle the matter with a judge. Certainly expanding an officer's discretion could lead to abuses and inconsistencies, especially if the agency's policies are not clear and officers are not properly trained and supervised. On the other hand, the use of warnings puts more emphasis on the education of motorists than on merely enforcing the law. In many cases, a potentially unpleasant

HP-3 R-9-80

TEXAS DEPARTMENT OF PUBLIC SAFETY

	DATE	HOUR
		M.

DRIVER NAME	LAST	FIRST	MIDDLE

VEHICLE MAKE & TYPE	LICENSE NO.	STATE	D.L. NO.	STATE

COUNTY	LOCATION & ROUTE

VIOLATION(S)

THIS IS A WARNING ONLY for an infraction of the traffic laws committed to a minor degree or with extenuating circumstances present. No penalty will be assessed and no further action on your part is necessary other than to comply with the traffic laws in the future. This does not become a part of your driving record.

SIGNATURE X _____

This warning is given to you in an effort to secure your cooperation in better observance of the traffic laws thus helping to prevent traffic accidents. The Texas Department of Public Safety believes that good citizens will comply with traffic laws when reminded of their provisions and of the importance of strict compliance with them.

ISSUED BY	SERVICE REGION/AREA	I.D. NO.

MOORE BUSINESS FORMS, INC., AUSTIN, TX. M

Figure 15-2 A traffic warning form. (Courtesy Texas Department of Public Safety.)

confrontation with a hostile motorist can be converted into a productive contact; the motorist is first relieved at not getting a ticket and second (presumably) grateful for the officer's attention and consideration.

If warnings are used, the form should be designed to resemble a citation; there should be appropriate space for the officer to indicate exactly what violation has been observed and for the motorist to sign the warning (as an acknowledgement that it was received). A copy of the warning should be filed at the police agency. If a motorist accumulates several warnings, especially if they occur in a brief period, a letter should be sent advising the motorist that no further warnings will be given; the motorist's name and license number then should be published on a "no-more-warnings" list that should be distributed periodically to all patrol units. (An even better procedure, if the agency has the proper equipment, is to maintain the warnings file in a computer; whenever an officer intends to give a written warning, first the computer file should be checked and, if too many warnings have already been given, the motorist should be cited instead.)

Consistent policies also must be developed concerning the surveillance techniques to be used by traffic enforcement officers. Most police agencies expect all officers to observe traffic whenever they are on patrol and to make a traffic stop and issue a citation (or make an arrest, if necessary) whenever a violation is observed. However, such **casual surveillance** is not enough to form the basis for a thorough traffic enforcement program.

Other surveillance techniques should be applied to specific locations where they are needed. Later, we will discuss the importance of, and procedures for, **selective enforcement**.

Surveillance techniques used in traffic enforcement may be categorized as **overt** or **covert** and as **stationary** or **mobile**. Overt surveillance means simply that the officer is readily visible to motorists; in fact, the officer's visible presence should be sufficient to discourage most violations. Covert surveillance means that the officer is not visible to potential violators, but is able to observe traffic well enough to detect and apprehend violators. A stationary surveillance may be either overt or covert, depending on where the officer is placed and whether that location is in view of passing motorists. Mobile surveillance is almost always overt; the major exception would be the use of an unmarked patrol car, a tactic that has not been used in traffic enforcement very often until the past few years. Covert mobile surveillance is a somewhat controversial technique in some communities, where the public regards it as unfair. For that matter, some motorists regard *any* covert surveillance as unfair, including the placement of radar stops behind bushes, just beyond the crest of a hill or around a bend in the road. Of course, from a law enforcement point of view, the perceived unfairness of covert surveillance is more than outweighed by the seriousness of traffic enforcement and the likely consequences of unsafe driving.

Aerial surveillance, in which either small airplanes or helicopters are used to observe traffic and detect violations, is an extremely effective technique. An airborne officer can spot many violations and report them to a unit on the ground, which then makes the stop and issues a citation. Although airborne units are not actually hidden from view, the fact is that motorists rarely are aware of their presence, and therefore aerial surveillance has many of the advantages of covert surveillance. However, the issue of fairness also has been raised with regard to aerial surveillance, and this technique has been prohibited in some jurisdictions. Aerial surveillance also is a relatively expensive technique, because of the operating costs of aircraft and the need to have one or more ground units available at all times in addition to the airborne unit.

Directing Traffic

Finally, the traffic responsibilities of the police include controlling the flow of traffic, particularly around obstructions or in areas of extreme congestion. At one time, directing traffic was a major function of the police in almost all communities. The development of mechanical and electric traffic signals has reduced the need for this kind of activity, which is extremely expensive because of the personnel time required. Modern traffic signal systems can be controlled by a computer that reacts to the actual flow of traffic much more rapidly and more effectively than any system of direction by officers.

Nevertheless, there are circumstances when officers must direct traffic themselves. Even the most sophisticated traffic signal system may break down. With or without modern signals, traffic congestion may occur at the scene of an accident, near a community event such as a dance or football game, around construction areas, or any place where the volume of traffic exceeds the carrying capacity of the streets (such as downtown intersections during the rush hour).

The techniques of directing traffic are fairly simple and should be learned by all police officers in recruit school. From an administrator's point of view, traffic direction requires some policies concerning the circumstances under which officers will be used for this purpose: who is to have the responsibility of assigning officers to direct traffic and (in cases where traffic must be directed over a large area) how the flow of traffic is to be coordinated.

General Assistance to Motorists

There are two major purposes to this aspect of the traffic law enforcement function: (1) to improve the safe and efficient movement of traffic by removing potential obstacles and (2) to encourage positive contacts between officers and the public.

The kinds of assistance to be offered should be determined by agency policy, which in turn will be influenced by the administrators' perceptions of public demand and by the availability of resources (especially personnel). Usually, police officers should freely offer directions to motorists who are unfamiliar with an area, since people wandering about are especially likely to cause a traffic hazard. Officers also should make some effort to assist motorists stranded by a disabled vehicle. Depending on the circumstances (including the availability of other assistance), an officer might help an elderly motorist change a tire, or might push a disabled vehicle off the road onto a safer parking lot or shoulder, or might even perform simple on-the-spot repairs (such as reconnecting a loose battery wire or advising a motorist on how to correct a flooded carburetor). An officer certainly should be willing to call for a tow truck or other assistance and remain with the disabled vehicle until help arrives.

Some agencies go so far as to equip patrol vehicles with tow chains, emergency tire and fan-belt repair kits, and other special equipment to assist motorists. However, the practice of a few agencies—carrying gasoline in the trunk of a patrol car to help motorists who have run out of gas—should be discouraged because of the safety hazard to the patrol officers.

The Police and Traffic Engineering

In the past, many local law enforcement agencies have been given, or have assumed, responsibility for traffic engineering; that is, designing streets and highways, right-of-way devices (guard rails, pavement markings, signs, and signals), and traffic flow patterns. Today, this function is more often assigned to other governmental agencies at the state and local level. Nevertheless, many police administrators still feel that they should have a role in traffic engineering, and quite a few medium-sized and larger law enforcement agencies have full-time traffic engineering staffs.

Whether this practice is necessary should be decided as a matter of local governmental policy. In our view, the principal responsibility of the police with regard to traffic engineering should be limited to supplying information, based on analyses of the agency's traffic incident records, and offering advice or recommendations. It may be true that smaller communities often cannot afford to maintain a full-time professional traffic engineering department, but in that case the equally limited resources of the police department should not be stretched to make up the deficiency. The proper function of a law enforcement agency is law enforcement, not engineering.

However, this is not to say that the police have no role in traffic engineering. A police agency's records of traffic accidents and patterns of violations should be regarded as a vital resource for traffic engineers. The agency's own traffic law enforcement staff should analyze these records periodically and prepare recommendations to the engineers responsible for street and highway design in the community. If the police agency's staff does not have the expertise (or time) to do the analyses, at least the raw information should be provided to the highway engineers for their use. Quite often, a pattern of accidents or violations may reveal a defect in the street or highway design.[8]

SPECIAL PROBLEMS IN TRAFFIC LAW ENFORCEMENT

The great majority of traffic violations are not very serious. Drivers exceed the legal speed limit, "slide" through stop signs, change lanes without signalling, and otherwise ignore the rules of the road, not out of malice but out of ignorance and carelessness. Enforcement action consists merely of stopping the violator, obtaining identification, explaining the nature of the violation and its possible consequences, and issuing a warning or citation. The motorist generally realizes that he or she is guilty and pays the fine without protest; whether the motorist also changes his or her driving behavior is, as we said earlier, somewhat problematical.

Some violations, however, are considerably more serious, and some traffic situations are considerably more difficult for traffic law enforcement officers to handle.

DWI Enforcement

Perhaps the most serious traffic violation is driving while intoxicated (whether under the influence of alcohol or of drugs, including prescription medication). It is widely believed that about half of all fatal accidents involve one or more persons who are intoxicated.[9] In some communities, intensive campaigns to enforce the DWI laws have had impressive effects on the accident rate.

However, making a case against an intoxicated driver is not always easy. Not all intoxicated drivers are affected by alcohol or drugs to such an extent that their behavior is clearly aberrant. Sometimes it is difficult even to detect the intoxicated state. Furthermore, by the time a motorist cited or arrested for DWI appears in court, usually enough time has elapsed that the person is sober; in the absence of any other evidence, the prosecutor has only the officer's word concerning the motorist's state of intoxication.

The first problem is to detect the level of intoxication (if any) when a motorist is stopped. Whenever a motorist is stopped for any unlawful or dangerous behavior, the officer must consider the possibility that the motorist is intoxicated; however, it is only a possibility. People who are extremely fatigued, ill, suffering from unanticipated side effects of medication, or simply incompetent may behave in the same manner associated with intoxication. Conversely, a motorist may be coherent, able to converse intelligently, and apparently sober when, in fact, he or she is under the influence of alcohol or drugs.

When intoxication is suspected, an officer should require the motorist to leave the vehicle and move to a safe place (either a sidewalk or, on a rural road, well off the pavement). The officer then should conduct a **field**

sobriety test. The test consists of giving the motorist a series of instructions for simple acts, such as closing one's eyes and touching the end of one's nose with the index finger. Several of these tests have been developed and used with varying degrees of success.[10]

In most states, a police officer is authorized to ask a driver to submit to a **breath analysis test**. This test consists of having the subject exhale into a device that performs a chemical analysis to detect the presence of alcohol in the breath. Some breath analysis machines also have been designed to detect certain drugs, such as marijuana, although the effectiveness and accuracy of these devices have not been thoroughly established.[11]

Both the field sobriety test and the breath analysis test are merely screening devices; that is, they neither prove nor disprove the fact that the subject is intoxicated. What matters is not the motorist's score on a field test, but the officer's overall impression of the motorist's behavior (before and after being stopped) and performance on the tests. If a motorist refuses to submit to either a field sobriety or breath analysis test, in most states the officer is empowered to arrest the motorist on suspicion of intoxication. In some states, refusal to submit to a field test may be grounds for suspension of the driver's license.

Whatever the outcome of the field tests, if the officer remains convinced that the motorist *may be* intoxicated, the motorist should be arrested and transported to the police station. At the police station, more thorough tests may be performed. Samples of the subject's urine or blood may be taken by qualified medical personnel; laboratory analysis of the sample will determine the presence and degree of concentration of alcohol or drugs. Again, in some states a person suspected of DWI who refuses to submit to these tests may face license suspension, even if the person turns out not to have been intoxicated.

Persons arrested on suspicion of DWI also should be observed at the police station, and if possible their behavior should be recorded on videotape. Most courts accept videotape recordings, when made under properly controlled circumstances, as evidence; a tape recording showing an intoxicated motorist's behavior often proves to be very persuasive in court.

Practical and effective procedures for gaining convictions of intoxicated drivers do exist. In recent years, a great deal of attention has been devoted to this serious problem. State laws concerning DWI have been tightened, and in many jurisdictions the courts and juries have begun to understand the serious nature of this common violation. If nothing else, the conventional attitude that drunk driving is socially acceptable has begun to change; people are coming to believe that drunk driving is not amusing, and that innocent people are entitled to travel on the streets and highways without being endangered by drunks.

Expressway Enforcement

Expressways, freeways, turnpikes, toll roads—whatever they are called—limited-access, high-speed highways generate several problems for traffic enforcement officers.

In urban areas, expressways are often designed so that the roadway takes up all of the right-of-way; there is little or no space alongside the roadway for motorists to pull off, out of the line of traffic. A disabled vehicle is therefore a major obstruction and safety hazard and must be removed as quickly as possible. Similarly, there is no place for a traffic patrol officer to have a motorist pull out of traffic for an enforcement stop, without creating a serious hazard to other traffic. It may be necessary for the patrol officer to follow the violator to the nearest exit ramp and leave the expressway altogether; since exit ramps may be spaced a mile or more apart, this is not an entirely satisfactory situation.

Expressways are designed for high-speed travel. Many expressways were built before the nationwide 55-mile-an-hour speed limit went into effect and were designed for speeds of 65 or 70 miles per hour. Consequently, motorists often find themselves exceeding the legal speed limit even when they do not intend to do so. Those who deliberately disregard the speed limit may be traveling at 80 mph or more; in light traffic and on rural stretches of expressway, speeds in excess of 100 mph are not uncommon. Stopping a violator who is traveling at such very high speeds is difficult and very dangerous, especially given the relatively inferior performance of most police cars in service today (see Chapter 7).[12]

We will discuss the special problems of pursuit driving shortly. With regard to expressway traffic enforcement, the only practical solution is to use two or more patrol units for speed enforcement. The two units may be spaced about a mile apart on one side of the expressway; the first unit serves as a spotter and the second as an interceptor. When the spotter observes a vehicle in violation of the speed limit, or other traffic laws, a description of the violator's vehicle is radioed to the interceptor. The interceptor should then move onto the highway *ahead of* the violator and, using flashing lights as appropriate, signal the violator to move off the road. (If the interceptor waits until the violator has passed and then pulls onto the highway, a pursuit situation is created, in which case most of the advantage of the two-unit procedure is lost.)

Another problem with expressway traffic enforcement is that, in some communities, jurisdiction over limited-access highways may be divided among several different law enforcement agencies. In some cases, a separate police agency is responsible for enforcement on a freeway, turnpike, or toll road; the local municipal police may not have enforcement authority. In other cases, expressways or freeways that are part of the interstate highway system may be under the authority of the state highway patrol. In yet other cases, the route of an expressway passes through a series of small suburban communities and in and out of the city limits of the central city; thus, jurisdiction may be fragmented among several municipal police departments.

In all such situations, close cooperation among all the affected law enforcement agencies must be arranged at the highest administrative levels and maintained at the operating level. Most states have **"hot pursuit" laws**, under which a police officer in pursuit of a suspected offender (whether for a traffic violation or some other crime) may make a legal arrest beyond his or her proper jurisdiction. However, the precise definition of hot pursuit and the offenses to which it applies vary from state to state.[13] Rather than relying on hot pursuit laws, police officials in adjacent communities, or those who share jurisdiction over limited-access highways, should establish procedures under which an officer in one agency may request and receive assistance from officers in another agency. For example, there should be no legal barrier to using officers from two different agencies as spotters and interceptors for expressway speed-limit enforcement, if mechanisms exist for the spotter (the officer who initially observes the violation) to provide evidence against an offender who is cited or arrested in the interceptor's jurisdiction.

Mandatory Safety Restraints and Devices

Federal laws prescribe the minimum safety equipment that must be present, and in working order, on all automobiles sold in the United States. Many states also have laws regarding minimum safety equipment such as lights, windshield wipers, and horns. A majority of the states require all licensed vehicles to be inspected once a year (in some states, at more frequent intervals) to detect any defective safety equipment. However, the inspection programs do not prevent an officer from enforcing the safety equipment laws if defective equipment is observed on the highway.

At this writing, 49 states require motorists to place children in federally approved **child safety seats** or **restraints**. Unfortunately, there are major variations in the wording and intent of these laws, and they are difficult to enforce. In many cases, it is impractical for officers to enforce mandatory child safety restraint laws on the basis of their observations of passing traffic; only the most flagrant violations, such as a motorist whose small

A child safety seat. (Drawing courtesy Greater Austin Child Passenger Safety Association.)

child is standing on the front seat or sitting in the driver's lap, are readily observable. In most other cases, an officer's only opportunity to observe a violation occurs when a motorist is stopped for some other reason (such as a speed-limit violation), and the officer finds a child in the vehicle without a proper restraint.

Despite the enforcement problems, child safety restraint laws are important; traffic accidents are currently the leading cause of death among children under four years of age in the United States, and child safety restraints are a proven method of reducing this tragic statistic. All officers, and particularly traffic patrol officers, should be thoroughly familiar with the law and should be encouraged to enforce it.

At present, only one state in this country has a mandatory restraint law applying to passengers other than children. Mandatory seat-belt laws also exist in several other countries and have been seriously considered here. If these laws are passed at either the state or the federal level, enforcement will prove to be difficult. Usually enforcement of such laws will take place only when motorists are stopped for other violations, or when an accident occurs and the driver or passenger was not properly restrained.

Unlicensed Drivers

Current law in every state forbids the operation of a motor vehicle on any public road without a valid operator's license or permit. The courts have found consistently that the holding of a driver's license is a privilege granted by the state, and that the state has the right to withdraw, suspend, or revoke that privilege for reasonable cause.

Unfortunately, it is not possible for law enforcement officers to determine whether a motorist is licensed or not merely by observing the motorist's behavior. Thus there are only two possible methods of enforcing the driver's license laws: checking licenses whenever a motorist is stopped for some other violation and conducting periodic license inspections at random roadblocks. The first method is standard procedure for all traffic enforcement. The second method, however, has been successfully challenged in some courts. A few courts have ruled that random stops for license inspections or other purposes violate the constitutional rights of citizens (usually on the grounds that they are unreasonable searches). Other courts have ruled just the opposite: that random stops are permissible *if* all motorists are stopped for the same purpose and the purpose is limited to checking licenses, vehicle safety equipment, and the like. Random stops and inspections for violations of other laws (such as possession of drugs or controlled substances) are less likely to be permitted by the courts, and in some states evidence of criminal offenses that may be found in the course of a driver's license inspection may be inadmissible. Again, however, court decisions on these questions have varied from state to state, and even the federal courts have been inconsistent. Patrol officers must be made aware of the most current applicable decisions, and agency policies must be established accordingly.

Commercial Vehicles

Trucks, vans, buses, taxicabs, and other motor vehicles used to transport people or goods for hire are subject to many laws that do not apply to private vehicles. Furthermore, commercial vehicles generally are on the roads more often, for longer periods of time, than private vehicles. The drivers of commercial vehicles may be under pressure from their employers to do their work as quickly as possible. As a result, commercial drivers sometimes are careless about observing traffic laws.

Traffic law enforcement officers may be reluctant to enforce the laws against commercial drivers, knowing that a driver could lose his or her livelihood as a result of being convicted for one or more violations. Officers may reason that the majority of commercial drivers, because of their special training and extensive experience, are more competent than most other drivers, and therefore their violations should be tolerated to some extent. The dangers in this attitude should be obvious. If commercial drivers are permitted to flout the laws with impunity, other drivers are also encouraged to disregard the rules. Also, it may be true that many commercial drivers are more competent than the average driver, but that is certainly not true in all cases. And commercial vehicles, because they generally are larger and heavier than private vehicles, pose a greater safety hazard; in a collision, the extent of damage and the likelihood of injury are significantly higher when a heavy commercial vehicle is involved.

If anything, traffic enforcement should be even more stringent for commercial drivers than for others. Commercial drivers should be expected to know and understand the laws, and there should be no excuse for their failure to comply. Since their income depends on their holding a commercial operator's license, they should be more conscientious—not less—about observing the law. Traffic officers should not hesitate to cite a commercial driver for speeding, failing to yield the right of way, or other common offenses. Agency policy should demand strict enforcement.[14]

The special laws applying to commercial vehicles also should be strictly enforced. In particular, laws regarding a commercial vehicle's load should receive the attention of traffic officers. It is difficult for traffic officers to determine by casual observation whether a truck is over the legal weight limit, but other loading violations are observable. A load that is too large for the vehicle or that is improperly secured can interfere with the driver's ability to control the vehicle safely, and an improperly secured load may scatter debris into the path of other motorists. These violations have direct, sometimes drastic, effects on the safety of all travelers and should not be tolerated. Overweight vehicles can be detected if the vehicle is clearly unable to maintain a normal speed, if the tires and suspension are seriously strained, or if the driver appears to have difficulty in performing normal maneuvers such as turning, braking, and shifting gears. When an overweight vehicle is suspected, the vehicle should be stopped and the driver questioned; if the officer continues to believe that the vehicle may be overloaded, the driver should be required to proceed to the nearest scale for further inspection. (In some cases, unfortunately, scales may not be readily available. However, the police usually can arrange to use privately owned scales at warehouses, scrap recycling facilities, and other businesses. So-called portable scales, designed to be carried in the trunk of a patrol car, are not very satisfactory: They are heavy, bulky, awkward to use, and in some cases not very reliable. Generally they are useful, if at all, only by officers whose specific responsibility is checking vehicle weights.)

Parking Enforcement

Many municipal police agencies regard parking violations as too trivial to deserve their attention. Parking meters and restrictions on on-street parking seem designed primarily to produce revenue and to protect the privileges of local businesses. Especially where a separate agency has been established to enforce the parking laws, the police may feel free to ignore parking violations.

However, parking violations do have important implications for traffic safety and for the efficient movement of traffic. If metered spaces are monopolized by a few people, other drivers will be forced to waste time and fuel searching for a parking space; as they grow increasingly frustrated, they also become inattentive to their driving. If cars are parked in restricted spaces, they may obstruct moving traffic or interfere with motorists' view of oncoming traffic at intersections. And if people are permitted to leave their cars in no-parking spaces and otherwise ignore the parking regulations, a general attitude of disregard for all traffic laws may be encouraged.

Consequently, all police officers should be expected to observe parking violations and to take appropriate enforcement action. Even in communities where the primary responsibility for parking enforcement has been assigned to a specific police unit or another agency, general patrol officers and, certainly, traffic officers should at least enforce the laws against more serious violations such as leaving an unattended vehicle in the street (double parking), parking in restricted spaces (near a fire hydrant or too close to an intersection), and parking in an unsafe manner (parking on the wrong side of the street, facing oncoming traffic).

Selective Enforcement and STEP

Police officials have realized for many years that it is impossible to enforce every violation of the traffic laws. Most violations go unobserved; they occur when no police officer is present. Many other violations are so minor that taking action to enforce the law would create a greater hazard than tolerating the violation; for example, when a driver changes lanes without signalling in heavy traffic, unless the maneuver seriously and dangerously interferes with another driver, there is little to be gained by pursuing and stopping the offender. Some violations are so common that it is impossible to stop and cite every offender; for example, surveys show that more than half of the drivers on limited-access highways exceed the speed limit by anywhere from 5 to 15 miles per hour.

The only possible course for the police is to enforce the laws selectively. **Selective enforcement** means that a specific effort is made to enforce particular laws, primarily on the basis of evidence that certain violations contribute to the frequency or seriousness of accidents. Enforcement also can be, and usually is, selective with regard to the places where the laws are enforced.[15]

For example, an agency will analyze its records of traffic accidents and citations to determine what patterns exist. The analysis might show that an abnormally high number of accidents have occurred at a certain intersection, and that the cause of a majority of the accidents has been the failure of drivers to heed a stop sign or traffic signal. This analysis would provide the basis for a selective enforcement effort; officers would be assigned to observe traffic at that intersection and to concentrate on right-of-way violations.

A traffic accident analysis, developed by engineers from accident report data. (Courtesy Texas Department of Highways and Public Transportation.)

Selective enforcement can be a powerful tool in achieving traffic safety goals. For this reason, the National Highway Traffic Safety Administration (NHTSA), an agency of the U.S. Department of Transportation, has established a special program to encourage police agencies to adopt selective enforcement projects. The **Selective Traffic Enforcement Program (STEP)** provides federal funds to support these projects. The funds are allocated to every state on the basis of a formula that takes into account population, number of registered motor vehicles, accident rates, and other factors. These funds, in turn, are parceled out by a state coordinating agency (which may be within the Office of the Governor, or under the state highway department, or may be an independent agency). Any law enforcement agency may apply for a STEP grant. In some states, the competition for STEP funding is intense; in other states, there are ample funds available.

Ordinarily, STEP grants are used to pay overtime for officers who conduct selective traffic enforcement projects in addition to their normal duties. Because STEP funds are limited, usually they are not available to purchase extra equipment or to hire additional personnel. Also, STEP grants are limited to one year, even though a STEP project may be planned for a two-year or longer period; the reason is that there is no assurance that federal funds will be available for more than one year at a time. STEP projects are intended to be demonstration projects; the purpose is to show that selective enforcement, even using a limited number of officers on an overtime basis, can be effective in improving traffic safety. Once the effectiveness of the project has been demonstrated, it is hoped that the local government will be able to provide adequate funds for a permanent selective enforcement program. (In many cases, STEP projects have demonstrated not only that selective enforcement reduces accident rates, but that the revenue from fines paid by offenders exceeds the cost of the program. Although the production of revenue should not be the goal of any law enforcement activity, this fact is sometimes more persuasive to local political officials than the reduction of accident rates. When the savings from reduced accident incidence are also shown—savings due to reduced property damage, personal injuries, and personnel time to attend to accident victims and perform investigations—the cost effectiveness of selective enforcement may be overwhelming.)[16]

PURSUIT DRIVING

One of the major areas of controversy in traffic law enforcement, and in patrol administration generally, is the practice of pursuing fugitives at high speed. We have referred to this issue several times in this text. The controversy has been greatly heightened in recent years by the gradual deterioration of police vehicle performance (which we discussed in Chapter 7). Today it is by no means certain that a patrol car will be able to overtake and stop a fleeing vehicle.

High-speed pursuit is an exceedingly dangerous kind of police operation. It is dangerous not only for the police officer and the fugitive, but equally so for innocent citizens who happen to be in their path. Once a high-speed pursuit begins, it is unlikely that the fugitive will stop voluntarily; from the fugitive's point of view, there is nothing to be gained by stopping as long as the police are unsuccessful in the pursuit. More often than not, a high-speed pursuit ends only when either the fugitive or the officer is involved in a collision, often a fatal one.

If the likelihood of being able to overtake and stop a fugitive vehicle is doubtful, the rationale for beginning a high-speed pursuit is absent. In other words, patrol officers should not continue to pursue a fugitive if it is apparent that the fugitive will merely increase his or her speed and that the patrol vehicle is incapable of overtaking the fugitive rapidly.

Does this mean that police officers should merely look the other way and let the fugitive go? Of course not. It means that a different set of techniques must be used.

When a fugitive vehicle is observed, the patrol officer should make one attempt to stop it. If the fugitive flees at high speed, the patrol officer should follow at a safe, reasonable speed, keep the fugitive in sight, and report the incident at once. In many cases, the dispatcher will be able to direct other patrol officers to intercept the fugitive.

Experienced patrol officers will see two major difficulties with this procedure. First, the fugitive, by making a series of rapid turns, may escape from the pursuing officer's observation. Second, it often takes more than one police vehicle to intercept a fugitive since one car cannot control the entire width of a street. If the fugitive is unwilling to stop—which must be assumed—the intercepting officer may be forced to block the roadway. A patrol car is not large enough to block an entire road and is not a very satisfactory tool for this purpose.

The first problem may not be as serious as it seems. Even if the fugitive vehicle escapes from sight, the pursuing officer at least knows the general vicinity and direction of travel before the pursuit began. Most often, once the fugitive loses the pursuing officer, he or she will once again head for his or her original destination. Intercepting officers may still be able to head off the fugitive. If the pursuing officer is able to get the license number of the fleeing vehicle, an officer might be waiting on the fugitive's doorstep when he or she arrives home. This is by no means a perfect solution, since the prospects of capturing the fugitive remain uncertain, but it is still better than chasing at high speeds until someone is killed.

The second problem is more difficult. A patrol car makes a poor blockade at best, and two or three cars may be needed to control the entire width of a street. Getting several patrol cars into the proper position ahead of a vehicle traveling at high speed requires an extremely well-coordinated operation.

Airborne surveillance, using a helicopter or small airplane, is most useful for this kind of situation. An airborne officer can maintain constant surveillance of a fleeing fugitive and can direct intercepting officers no matter what path the fugitive takes. In many cases, the fugitive will be unaware of the airborne surveillance and will slow down as soon as the pursuing patrol car is out of sight. Again, this kind of air and ground operation requires a high degree of coordination among the airborne officers and patrol officers on the ground.

Even these admittedly imperfect techniques are preferable to high-speed pursuit. Police officers do not have the right to endanger themselves and innocent citizens by driving with reckless abandon. There is no rational justification for taking the lives of innocent bystanders even in the process of apprehending the most dangerous of criminals.

The "chase-at-all-costs" attitude has been fostered not by sound police philosophy, but by the romantic notions and clever techniques of television and movie producers. Hollywood may take deserved credit for promoting excellent police practices and a positive image of law enforcement through many films and television series. However, Hollywood also must share the blame for the deaths of many police officers and innocent citizens. The fact is that neither police vehicles nor any other ordinary automobiles will perform the way they appear to in TV shows and movies. The cars used in Hollywood stunt work are carefully, ingeniously prepared—sometimes built from the ground up—for each separate stunt. Often what appears on the TV or movie screen as one car going through a series of hair-raising flights, crashes, and careening turns was, in fact, several different cars, each built and prepared specifically for one stunt. The stunts are filmed separately and edited together into a continuous sequence. Quite often a single stunt destroys the stunt car; what appears in the next shot is actually a different car. Since these facts are not common knowledge, many people (even police officers who should know better) sometimes try to drive their ordinary cars in the manner of Hollywood stunt cars, with catastrophic results.

Police officers should be trained in high-performance driving not to encourage recklessness, but to ensure that they are competent to operate a vehicle under extreme conditions in an emergency. Nevertheless, *even when an emergency exists*, a police officer must operate his or her vehicle in the safest manner possible, with full regard for the safety of other motorists and pedestrians. Continuing a high-speed pursuit, heedless of the danger involved, is every bit as inappropriate and senseless as shooting at a fugitive on a crowded sidewalk.

LIEUTENANT YOUNG'S IN BASKET

Instructions

In this exercise, you are to assume the role of Lieutenant Joe Young, chief of the Traffic Law Enforcement section. The documents below have been selected from Lieutenant Young's in basket. Read them with care. If you need more information about City or its police department, refer to the data bank in the front of the book. After you have studied the documents, complete these steps:

1. State the problem or problems these documents present to Lieutenant Young.
2. List as many alternative solutions as you can.
3. Select the solution you think would be best, and give your reasons for choosing it.

CITY POLICE DEPARTMENT
Interoffice Memorandum

FROM: W. Sloan, Sgt. Traffic

TO: Lt. Young

SUBJECT: Need for new Patrol Car   DATE: 1 Oct 19--

SIR:

I understand that some new Patrol Cars are going to be bought from this year's budget. Please see if one of them can be bought for Traffic. As you know, if weather is so bad that the Traffic Patrol Officers can't use their motorcycles, they have to take my Patrol Car, and I don't have any transportation. Or else the Patrol Officers have to stay in the office so I can be out on the street. Either way, it is not very efficient for us. THank you.

William Sloan, Sr. Sgt.
Traffic

CITY, STATE
City Hall

City Council Memorandum

TO: Chief Abel, Police Dept.

DATE: Sept. 15, 19--

Dear Chief:

This is the third time I have inquired about this. I would like to know immediately what you are going to do. I am referring to the series of auto wrecks that have occurred at the intersection of Golden Valley Drive and Massachusetts Ave. There was another one yesterday, and this is at least the seventh or eighth one that I know about this month. Luckily, nobody has gotten killed yet, but it is just a matter of time. It is apparent to me that your Dept. is not doing an adequate job of enforcing the traffic law at this intersection. I have reminded you about this serious problem repeatedly ever since my car was hit back in February. I think it's about time you did something.

Paul Iticoe, Member
City Council

CITY POLICE DEPARTMENT
Interoffice Memorandum

FROM: J. Rader, Lt., OC/Vice

TO: Lt. Young, Traffic

SUBJECT: Training for SWT Team   DATE: 27 Sep 19--

Joe:

    You'll be glad to hear that plans for the SWT team are going forward. I expect to have Chief Abel's approval any day now, and I am certain that the City Council will okay the money.

    Please arrange for two members of your unit, Sgt. Bailey and Sr. P.O. Chambers, to be released from their regular duty for SWT training. The training will begin about 2 weeks after we get approval and is planned for a total of 325 hours (7 weeks including overtime on weekends).

    I am surprised that Bailey and Chambers are the only people from Traffic to volunteer for this. I thought you guys were all behind it. However, we have to start somewhere. I hope you will encourage more of your people to get with the program in the second training cycle.

    Thanks for all your help and support.

        Johnny Rader

CITY POLICE DEPARTMENT
Interoffice Memorandum

FROM: G. Cantrell, Sr. Sgt., Traffic

TO: Lt. Young

SUBJECT: Release of personnel for SWAT training   DATE: 29 Sep 19--

SIR:

    Sgt. Bailey and Off. Chambers want to take SWAT training for seven (7) weeks. This would be if Lt. Rader gets his SWAT project approved, which a lot of people say is very unlikely. However, if it is approved, I don't see how we can let two (2) of our people go for seven (7) weeks! We would even have to pay them overtime out of our own budget! We don't have enough people as it is. Also, I am not sure that Bailey and Chambers are qualified for this kind of program, as I am sure you will understand. If we have to give up two (2) people for this business, we should at least pick the ones to go. Personally, I don't see why Traffic should get involved in the SWAT thing anyway. We have enough work to do of our own. I respectfully request that you do not give your OK for them to participate. Thank you.

        G. Cantrell, Sr. Sgt.
        Traffic

CITY POLICE DEPARTMENT
Interoffice Memorandum

FROM:	Sr. Sgt. R. Gordon, Parking Enforcement
TO:	Lt. J. Young, Traffic
SUBJECT:	Interference by Traffic Officers

DATE: 28 Sep 19--

SIR:

Yesterday afternoon, at approximately 1400 hrs., one of your officers (P.O. Chadwick) was observed by Meter Maid A. Bell, putting a parking ticket on a car in the 1700 blk. Holly Street.

We have discussed this matter before and I thought we had a clear understanding about this. Your officers should not interfere in the duty of the Meter Maids. As I explained before, it is important for the Meter Maids to get proper credit for their enforcement activity. When your people start ticketing cars, they are preventing the Meter Maids from fulfilling their productivity standards.

I have checked with Capt. Lewis and Chief Williamson and they agree with me. Besides, it seems that your Traffic officers ought to have more important things to do. Please remind them that if they see improperly parked cars in the Downtown district, they should leave them for the Meter Maids to worry about. Thank you.

Bob Gordon, Sr. Sgt.
Parking Enforcement Section

Lt. Young: I would like to have your approval to give our Traffic Safety Education puppet show, "Punch Wrecks His Bike," at Western Hills Jr. High School this coming Thursday at 1500 hrs. I have already cleared this with the Principal, and he said I am always welcome at any time.

Also, would it be okay if I took the puppets to get them repaired? They are both more than 5 yrs. old and starting to get kind of ragged. However, the kids always seem to like the show and I think it gets across some important safety messages. I try to give it at least once each year to the 6th, 7th, 8th, and 9th grades in every school.

Also, since the presentation at WHJHS will go from 1500 hrs to 1600 hrs and my regular shift ends at 1400 hrs, I would like you to approve 2 hours of overtime for me.

Les Reese, Patrol, Traffic

IN REVIEW

1. Traffic laws are different from criminal laws in the sense that:
   (a) Traffic laws are more difficult to enforce.
   (b) Most people do not regard violating the traffic laws as a moral offense.
   (c) Traffic violations rarely cause harm to anyone.
   (d) Criminals do not usually violate traffic laws.
   (e) Criminal violations are always more serious.

2. The four main functions of traffic law enforcement are:
   (a) Investigating accidents.
   (b) Directing traffic.
   (c) Parking law enforcement.

(d) Detecting and citing violators.
(e) Assisting disabled motorists.
(f) Safety education.
(g) Routine patrol.

3. True or False: Nearly all traffic law enforcement officials accept the principle that citing violators is an educational opportunity.

4. The primary purpose of traffic accident investigation is:
    (a) To detect violators of the traffic laws.
    (b) To restore the smooth flow of traffic as quickly as possible.
    (c) To assist the citizens involved in the accident in settling any claims they may have against each other.
    (d) To gather information for use in planning selective enforcement and engineering improvements.
    (e) To remove the vehicles from the streets before they cause further hazards to other motorists.

5. True or False: Whether an officer arrests a traffic violator or simply issues a citation is determined by state laws; the officer has no discretion in this regard.

6. Covert surveillance means that:
    (a) Officers are hidden from motorists' view.
    (b) Officers use aircraft to observe traffic.
    (c) Motorists are hidden from officers' view.
    (d) Officers observe traffic from their own moving vehicles.
    (e) All police officers should observe traffic and arrest or cite offenders.

7. True or False: A police agency should not assume any responsibility or duty with regard to traffic engineering.

8. A _____ can be used to screen a motorist who is suspected of driving while intoxicated.
    (a) Blood sample analysis
    (b) Videotape recording
    (c) Written examination
    (d) Field sobriety test
    (e) Written warning

9. True or False: It is reasonable for traffic law enforcement officers to be more tolerant of the minor violations of commercial vehicle operators, since they are usually more competent than other drivers.

10. A STEP project is intended to:
    (a) Recognize exceptional traffic officers for their efforts by granting them extra pay.
    (b) Increase the revenue from traffic fines.
    (c) Demonstrate the value of selective enforcement.
    (d) Reduce traffic accidents by eliminating most common violations.
    (e) Ensure that frequent violators are punished more severely than occasional, minor violators.

REFERENCES

1. U.S. Dept. of Justice, Federal Bureau of Investigation, *Crime in the United States*, Washington, D.C.: Government Printing Office, 1980, page 302.

2. *Police Traffic Responsibilities*, (Highway Safety Program Management Series, Volume II) Washington, D.C.: International Association of Chiefs of Police, 1976, pages 25–28.

3. *Police Traffic Responsibilities*.

4. *Introduction to Police Traffic Services Management*, (Highway Safety Program Management Series, Volume I) Washington, D.C.: International Association of Chiefs of Police, 1976, pages 51–52.

5. Two of the best sources of information on accident investigation procedures are: the Traffic Institute, Northwestern University, Evanston, Illinois; and The Texas Transportation Institute, Texas A&M University, College Station, Texas.

6. O. W. Wilson, *Police Planning*, 2nd ed., Springfield, Ill.: Charles C. Thomas, 1962, page 157.

7. *Introduction to Police Traffic Services Management*, pages 161–164.

8. President's Task Force on Highway Safety, *Mobility Without Mayhem*, Washington, D.C.: Government Printing Office, 1970.

9. *Alcohol Enforcement Countermeasures*, (Highway Safety Program Management Series, Volume IV) Washington, D.C.: International Association of Chiefs of Police, 1976, page v.

10. L. P. Watts, *Some Observations on Police-Administered Tests for Intoxication*, Chapel Hill, N.C.: Univ. of North Carolina Press, 1966.

11. *Testing the Drinking Driver*, Chicago: National Safety Council, 1970.

12. R. Dean Smith and David A. Espie, *Guidelines for Police Services on Controlled-Access Roadways*, Washington, D.C.: International Association of Chiefs of Police, 1968.

13. E. F. Hennessy, T. Hamilton, K. B. Joscelyn, and J. S. Merritt, *A Study of the Problem of Hot Pursuit by the Police*, Washington, D.C.: U.S. Dept. of Transportation, National Highway Safety Bureau, 1970.

14. Bedford M. Crittenden, *Truck Violation Survey*, Sacramento, Calif.: California Highway Patrol, 1965.

15. *Introduction to Police Traffic Services Management*, pages 43–46.

16. *Introduction to Police Traffic Services Management*, pages 19–21.

16 ADMINISTRATION OF CRIMINAL INVESTIGATION

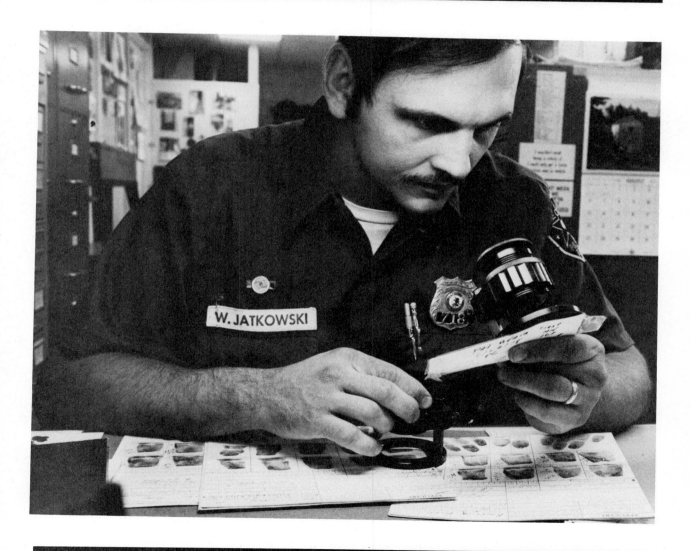

THE THOROUGH, SCIENTIFIC INVESTIGATION OF CRIME WAS not a function of the earliest police departments in this country. As investigative techniques began to be developed in France and Britain, around the middle of the last century, a few American cities established completely separate patrol and investigation departments. After the Civil War, however, the investigative function was more often assigned to a detective bureau within the municipal police department, and that is the usual arrangement in nearly all American police agencies today.

FUNCTIONS OF CRIMINAL INVESTIGATION UNITS

In simplest terms, the mission of a criminal investigation unit is to discover, for every crime that comes to the attention of the police, what crime was committed, by what means, and by what person or persons.[1]

This mission can be divided into a series of specific functions that must be performed, to some degree, for each crime that is investigated. First, a crime must become known to the police. Occasionally a police officer on patrol will observe a crime in progress or will happen upon a crime scene; however, it is relatively rare for crimes to become known to the police in this manner.

The police go to great lengths to become aware of certain types of crimes; this becomes one of the principal functions of certain investigative units. Officers in organized crime units, vice units, drug abuse units, and sometimes juvenile crime units devote most of their time to discovering what crimes are being committed and by whom. The principal technique used for this function is undercover investigation, in which officers conceal their identity in an attempt to penetrate the criminal activity. Once the nature and extent of that criminal activity have been learned, the investigation can focus on gathering sufficient evidence to charge offenders with specific crimes.

The vast majority of crimes that come to the attention of the police are discovered through a report or complaint from a victim, witness, or other person who has knowledge of the crime. Usually the initial report is made by telephone to the police emergency switchboard; occasionally a victim or other person with knowledge about a crime will visit the police station in person to file a report. This initial report, however it is made, becomes the basis on which the police begin their investigation, and therefore it has great significance for the prospective success of the investigation. From now on, we refer to the initial report of a crime (or possible crime) as a **complaint**, regardless of how or from whom it is received.

Before we continue this discussion, we should note that, according to numerous surveys, only a small fraction of all crimes ever become known to the police.[2] Naturally, criminals take whatever steps they can to avoid the discovery of their offenses. Unfortunately, victims and witnesses, who presumably would have an interest in letting the police know that a crime has occurred, frequently fail to complain. Some research indicates that for every crime that becomes known to the police, perhaps 10 or 20 crimes go undiscovered. The reasons for nonreporting of crime are difficult to pin down; some people seem to distrust the police, while others are so traumatized by the criminal event that they are psychologically incapable of responding to it in a positive manner, and still others are fearful of retaliation by the criminal if they report the matter. Since the police cannot do anything about a crime until they know of its existence, nonreporting is a serious problem and police administrators must do whatever they can to encourage prompt reporting of all crimes.

Once a crime becomes known to the police, a series of actions may be taken. If the crime is fresh—either still in progress, or recently committed—usually a patrol officer is dispatched to assist the victim, protect the crime scene so that further investigation is possible, and make an initial or **preliminary investigation**; if the offender is still on the scene, of course, the patrol officer is expected to make an arrest. If the crime is not fresh (for example, when the victims return home from vacation and discover that their home has been burglarized sometime during their absence), an urgent response is not necessary, but either a patrol officer or a detective is assigned to conduct the preliminary investigation.

The purpose of the preliminary investigation, no matter when it is done or by whom, is to determine the circumstances of the crime and to gather as much information as possible about how it was committed and, if known, the identity of the perpetrator. The quality of the preliminary investigation often is the most significant factor in determining the prospects for a successful investigation; the information and evidence obtained in this step usually provide the basis for any further investigation of the crime. According to some studies, the majority of crimes are solved only if the identity of the perpetrator is learned during the preliminary investigation (either because the victim knows who committed the crime, or physical evidence leading to the perpetrator is found at the scene).[3]

Even so, many criminal investigations must continue beyond the preliminary stage. If the identity of the perpetrator is known, it may still be necessary to obtain and develop evidence to prove that the suspect committed the crime. If the perpetrator is not known, but there is sufficient information or physical evidence to give some hope that the criminal's identity can be discovered, or if the crime is sufficiently serious to warrant an all-out attempt to identify the perpetrator, further investigation is necessary. Whether the follow-up investigation is conducted by patrol officers or specialist investigators depends largely on the policies and organizational structure of the police agency.

Finally, a successful investigation ends when the suspected perpetrator is not only identified but also located and arrested, and sufficient evidence is assembled to obtain a conviction in court. Again, both patrol officers and specialist investigators may have a role at this point, depending on agency policy and structure.

Summarizing the investigative process, there are four distinct phases or stages:

1. Receiving the initial report or *complaint*.
2. Conducting a *preliminary investigation*.
3. Conducting a *follow-up investigation*, if necessary.
4. Concluding the investigation by arresting the accused perpetrator and assembling evidence for presentation in court.

Types of Investigative Units

The relationship between the general patrol force and the criminal investigation element is one of the most important characteristics of a modern law enforcement agency. Briefly, three common patterns are found in American police departments.[4]

Specialized Investigation.   The general patrol force has very limited responsibility for criminal investigations. Patrol officers responding to a crime complaint are expected to make an arrest if a suspect is present at the scene; otherwise, the patrol officer merely obtains a report from the victim or witnesses and forwards the report to the agency's investigators. In some serious cases, or if it appears that substantial physical evidence is available at the scene, the patrol officer may notify investigators by radio or telephone and protect the scene until an investigator or evidence technician arrives. Virtually all felony cases and most serious misdemeanor cases (other than those in which the offender is present at the scene when patrol officers arrive) are the responsibility of investigators. The investigators are divided into a number of specialized organizational units according to categories of crimes, so that each investigator concentrates on a particular type of offense.

Integrated Investigation.   The general patrol force is responsible for most preliminary investigations. The patrol officers responding to a crime complaint are expected to obtain a thorough report from the victim or witnesses and to collect any physical evidence that can be found at the scene. The report and evidence (if any) are turned over to specialist investigators for follow-up. Evidence technicians and other technical specialists may be available to assist the patrol officers. Investigators may be divided into a number of organizational units, according to crime categories, or they may be consolidated into two or three relatively large and generalized units (such as "crimes against persons," "crimes against property," "vice," and so on). In either case, investigators retain most of the responsibility for completing the investigations of most felonies and serious misdemeanors, although they are encouraged to involve the patrol force whenever possible (for example, in searching for suspects, seeking informants, and so on).

Patrol-oriented Investigation.   The patrol force is responsible for completing most investigations. After obtaining the preliminary report, patrol officers notify the investigators of their findings, but the responsibility for most follow-up activities is left with the patrol unit. The investigators' function is primarily one of support for the patrol force: advising patrol officers on investigative techniques and procedures, assisting with records checks, and analyzing information from a number of sources. Investigators may assume full responsibility only for the most serious or complicated cases that would be too time-consuming or difficult for patrol officers to pursue to completion.[5]

Thus, the nature of the investigators' responsibilities and the organizational structure of the investigative element of a police agency depend mostly on the extent of the patrol force's responsibilities for investigation. If the patrol force performs very little investigation, the investigative unit must be relatively large, and usually is divided into some number of specialized subunits. If the investigative unit is kept small and its personnel serve primarily as technical advisors, the bulk of investigative work must be done by the patrol force.

Until fairly recently, the specialized pattern described above was by far the most common among medium-sized and larger American police agencies. Only small agencies, because of their limited human resources, expected patrol officers to assume any responsibility for criminal investigations. Most police authorities assumed (perhaps correctly) that patrol officers were too inexperienced and limited in technical competence to be trusted with such important tasks. Furthermore, as we discussed in Chapter 3, specialization was assumed to be valuable in itself. By specializing in specific types of investigations, detectives presumably would become more knowledgeable and skillful. Many police authorities believed that typical criminals tended to specialize in committing certain types of crimes, and therefore that specialized investigators should become familiar with the habits and personalities of the offenders with whom they would have to deal.[6]

However, these assumptions and widely held beliefs are not necessarily valid. Since the beginning of this century, most American police departments have worked hard to upgrade the capabilities of their patrol forces. Today, entry-level officers are, on the average, better educated and more highly motivated than their predecessors, and they receive better training in all aspects of police science; there is less reason than ever before to assume that a patrol officer is incapable of performing a sound, thorough investigation. There are also several reasons to regard specialization as a mixed blessing. Although specializing may indeed permit an investigator to reach a high level of knowledge and skill in a certain type of investigation, it also tends to narrow the range of the investigator's competence. It is simply not true that typical criminals specialize in specific types of crimes. Some do, but many others do not, and it is not unusual for one person to be responsible for several different types of property crime. Also, some criminal incidents are not so easy to categorize. If an incident involves both a burglary and an armed robbery, or if it is not clear which type of crime has occurred, who should be given the responsibility for investigating it: the burglary detective or the robbery detective?

Specialization also creates administrative problems in the management of the natural work load. At one time, there might be many more burglaries than armed robberies to be investigated, while at another time the reverse might be true. Thus, in the first instance the burglary unit would be overworked and the robbery unit might have too little work, while in the second instance the robbery unit would be overworked and the burglary unit idle.

For these and many other reasons, police administrators in recent years have tended to despecialize their investigative units. What we have called the integrated pattern has become more common: Patrol officers are given more responsibility for the early stages of most investigations, while investigators are given responsibility for a broader range of the more serious and complicated cases. Some agencies, especially the smaller ones, have gone even further, adopting the patrol-oriented system.

Both the integrated and patrol-oriented systems demand more of the patrol force's time. In an integrated system, a patrol officer may spend an average of about an hour in the preliminary investigation of a serious misdemeanor or felony. In a patrol-oriented system, the patrol officer might spend from an hour to an hour and a half in the preliminary investigation of the same incident, plus another hour or two on follow-up investigation; more serious cases could require even more time for follow-up. Both systems, therefore, depend on having more patrol officers than the conventional specialized system, in which detectives would perform most of the preliminary investigation and virtually all of the follow-up work. On the other hand, the integrated and patrol-oriented systems also require fewer detectives, fewer specialized units (each of which requires its own administrative mechanisms for supervision), and more flexible arrangement of work loads.

Technical Support for Investigation

No matter which organizational system is used, the fundamental techniques and procedures of criminal investigation are essentially the same; the basic steps we described earlier must be carried out either by patrol officers or specialist investigators, or by both to some degree.

Most of these steps should be within the capabilities of any police officer. Every officer should be trained to complete at least the preliminary investigation of a crime, including the completion of a basic crime report form and the interviewing of the victim, witnesses, or complainants. Similarly, every officer should be able to perform a legal arrest once a suspect has been identified.

However, the search for, acquisition of, and analysis of physical evidence involves a great array of technical skills that may not be possessed by all officers. The laws that govern searching for evidence are complicated and subtle. The actual search for physical evidence may involve such varied skills as those of a photographer, those of a chemist, and those of a physicist. Much of the evidence that might be found at a crime scene must be examined and analyzed in a laboratory. These are all areas that seem to demand the experience, knowledge, and skills of specialists.

Investigative technical specialists can be considered in two general categories: crime scene technicians and laboratory technicians.[7] The former might include photographic technicians, fingerprint acquisition technicians, and physical evidence technicians. Laboratory specialists might include chemists, physicists, fingerprint examination and identification specialists, firearms examination specialists (sometimes called ballistics technicians), and photo analysts. All of these technical specialists may be called *criminalistics technicians* or, more simply, **criminalists**. Another type of specialist, the polygraph examiner, also should be considered a criminalist, although the use of the polygraph (and other so-called lie-detection techniques) does not actually involve physical evidence.

The number of technical specialists available to support criminal investigations depends primarily on the size of the police agency and secondarily on the extent of the training and skill possessed by other personnel. The table below suggests the distribution of personnel and the various ways that technical support for investigations may be provided in police agencies of varying sizes.

Small agency (under 10 officers)	No criminalistics specialists; all officers are trained in basic evidence acquisition techniques; assistance is requested from county or state police in complicated cases; laboratory work is done in a regional cooperative lab, state police lab, or, in some cases, the FBI lab in Washington, D.C.
Small-to-medium agency (10–25 officers)	One or two officers (patrol officers or detectives) receive special training in such technical fields as police photography, fingerprint examination, and firearms examination; laboratory work is done elsewhere.
Medium-sized agency (25–50 officers)	One or two full-time evidence technicians may be available to assist in relatively complex cases; a small laboratory may be available for photography, fingerprint examination, and some routine evidence processing, with more complicated work done elsewhere.
Medium-to-larger agency (50–100 officers)	Two or more evidence technicians may be available, some with a high degree of special training in photography, fingerprints, or firearms; a small laboratory with one to five full-time criminalistics technicians may be available for most routine work, with more complicated work done elsewhere.
Large agency (more than 100 officers)	Approximately one evidence technician for every 10 patrol officers on duty; technicians specialize in various types of evidence collection; extensive laboratory facilities with a number of criminalistics technicians, capable of handling nearly all types of evidence examination procedures.

The extent to which technical support personnel are needed also depends partly on the capabilities of the patrol force and regular investigators and on the extent to which they are assigned responsibility for carrying out their own investigations. Obviously, if all patrol officers and detectives are thoroughly trained in such matters as crime scene photography, fingerprint acquisition, evidence collection, and so on, there is less need for full-time specialists. However, if patrol officers are expected to perform time-consuming evidence searches, more patrol officers will be needed to make sure that there is adequate coverage.

As noted in the table above, medium-sized and smaller agencies generally cannot support a full-time criminalistics laboratory. There are several alternatives: three or four small agencies may establish a cooperative regional laboratory; a smaller agency may rely heavily on a laboratory operated by the state police agency (or, in a few cases, by the county sheriff's office); or evidence that requires elaborate analysis may be sent to the FBI's laboratories in Washington.[8] Another option is to use the resources of a nearby college or university for some of the more complex kinds of evidence analysis that require expertise in chemistry, physics, or other scientific disciplines; however, this practice introduces problems in maintaining the integrity of the evidence, and care must be taken to ensure that non-law enforcement personnel, acting as technical resource specialists, understand the full legal significance of their participation.

Agencies that do have their own criminalistics laboratory usually do not place it under the administrative supervision of the criminal investigations unit. More often, the lab is placed as an element of a technical services bureau or equivalent division, along with other support elements (communications, fleet services, and so on). If the lab provides services for the patrol force, traffic law enforcement, and perhaps special investigative units, as well as the investigations unit, this organizational structure is appropriate. However, closer coordination can be achieved by placing the lab directly under the authority of the investigations unit if that unit accounts for nearly all of the lab's work load.

THE ORGANIZATION OF CRIMINAL INVESTIGATION UNITS

Traditionally, criminal investigation units have been divided into more and more specialized subunits, following the principle expressed by O. W. Wilson: "Specialization in detective assignments should be the invariable rule."[9] Even a small agency with only four or five detectives would divide them into at least two subunits, a Crimes Against Persons Unit and a Crimes Against Property Unit. Larger agencies would further subdivide the detective bureau into as many small units as possible, each with a distinct and specific category of crimes to handle. There might be a Homicide Division, Theft Division, Burglary Division, Robbery Division, Auto Theft Division, Fraud Division, and so on and so on. Each division, in a very large agency, would be further subdivided into subsections, sometimes called "details": the Theft Division might have a Larceny Detail, Shoplifting Detail, Pickpocket Detail, and so on. Each detail might contain anywhere from one to a dozen detectives.

In an integrated structure, in which both the patrol force and the detective force are involved in most criminal investigations, such elaborate specialization is neither necessary nor justified. An investigations unit with a total of 20 officers or less may be divided into two, or at most three, sections: Crimes Against Persons, Crimes Against Property, and perhaps a separate unit for Organized Crimes. Larger agencies may find it useful to divide these sections into subsections according to broad categories of crime; for example, the Crimes Against Persons Section could be divided into a Homicide Unit, Sex Crimes Unit, and Assault Unit.

In a patrol-oriented investigations system, where patrol officers perform virtually all investigative functions and the detectives serve primarily as resource consultants to the patrol officers, there is little need to divide the detective force into more than two or three sections. Any further subdivisions would simply encourage the kind of specialization that patrol-oriented investigation is intended to overcome.

Organized Crime Investigative Units

The kinds of organizational structures we have just described are appropriate for investigative units that are concerned with, for lack of a better term, "common" crimes. However, some police administrators feel that a different structure is necessary for investigative units that are concerned with organized crimes.

Organized crime is not a precise term. Usually it includes the various categories of crimes that are called vice: prostitution, pornography (to the extent that it is still a criminal offense), gambling, some liquor law violations, and violations of narcotics and controlled-substances laws.[10] The key elements that set these crimes apart from common crimes are: (1) the criminals engage in these activities primarily for profit, sometimes as their principal source of income; and (2) the "victims" are willing participants, usually as consumers of illicit goods and services. (Whether the consumers should be regarded as victims or as contributing offenders is a matter of some debate.) These are organized crimes in the sense that the perpetrators have established themselves in an illegal business, in which they engage over some period of time, and which requires some degree of cooperation and coordination among a number of participants. For example, a successful gambling operation requires one or more banks, where money is collected, odds are established, and bets are paid off; usually several books where bets are recorded; and any number of runners who deal directly with the customers, accepting bets and payments and, for the lucky few, making payoffs. The operation also may require one or more enforcers to collect money from losers. Well-established gambling operations often have several functionaries who are responsible for placing bribes and maintaining liaison with corrupt police officers and officials. Many gambling organizations also maintain profitable loan-sharking operations to accommodate heavy gamblers who are otherwise unable to pay their debts. Thus, a gambling organization might involve anywhere from a dozen to several hundred individuals, some on a full-time basis and many others on a part-time or occasional basis.

Other vice operations are similarly organized. Drug trafficking may involve importers who bring huge quantities of illegal substances into the country, distributors who process and adulterate the drugs, and dealers who sell small quantities to individual users (many of whom also resell even smaller quantities to their friends).

Vices are not the only crimes that lend themselves to organization. Stolen goods, whatever their nature, must be sold in order for the thief to realize an income from his or her work. Since the trade in stolen goods is itself illegal, some degree of organization is necessary to protect the traders from discovery. Sometimes the trader, or "fence," organizes groups of thieves to steal specific kinds of goods for which a ready market exists. Auto theft rings, for example, have been known to accept orders for specific makes and models of cars—sometimes with optional accessories also specified! —to be delivered to their customers. The order is then assigned to experienced, professional thieves who scout parking lots for the desired vehicle, steal it, modify it to meet the specifications if necessary, and deliver it. Auto parts, electronic consumer and industrial products, jewelry, clothing, medical supplies, and any number of other goods are traded by well-organized fencing operations.

Since all of the participants in organized crime—the organizers, the street-level functionaries, and the consumers—are willing participants and go to great lengths to avoid discovery, law enforcement authorities cannot wait for a complaint before they investigate. Instead, active investigation is necessary just to discover what crimes are being committed and by whom.

The principal police technique in all organized crime investigations is undercover surveillance performed by an **undercover agent**. Police officers pose as prospective customers or as minor participants; they attempt to infiltrate the criminal organization in order to gather evidence about the kinds of crimes being committed and identities of the major participants. Understandably, if an undercover investigator's true identity is revealed, the agent's usefulness is lost—and, more important, his or her life may be in jeopardy. Therefore, extreme secrecy is essential to the undercover investigator's work.

Organized criminals are well aware that an active police force will attempt to discover their activities. The criminals rely on two approaches to protect themselves. If possible, they use bribery, blackmail, and similar methods to corrupt the police and criminal justice officials.[11] If corruption fails, the criminals may attempt to infiltrate the police agency itself and discover whatever information they can about current investigations. Usually organized criminals do not resort to overt violence, since that simply calls attention to their activities and gives the police more opportunity to arrest the key individuals. (Violence is used to enforce discipline within some criminal organizations, however. Usually the organization hires a professional enforcer, not otherwise associated with the criminal organization, for this purpose.)

Because of the need for secrecy to protect the undercover agents and because of the need to protect sensitive information and to prevent the criminals from sabotaging the investigative effort, special measures must be taken to maintain security. Those measures may be reflected in the agency's entire organizational structure. For example, in many agencies the organized crime investigative unit is completely separate from the criminal investigations unit. The organized crime investigators are placed under the direct supervision of, and are responsible only to, the agency's chief executive. In larger agencies, the identities of the undercover investigators may be unknown even to other police officers. In smaller agencies, such extreme secrecy usually is not practical; nevertheless, undercover agents are discouraged from frequenting the police station and associating with other officers, and their identities are protected as far as possible.

Reasonable measures to protect organized crime investigators are essential, both in the interests of effective law enforcement and in the interest of protecting the agents' lives. However, there is a danger that the undercover officers and the entire organized crime unit may evolve into a privileged elite of secret agents who, because of the secretive nature and great importance attached to their work, are permitted to operate in ways that would not be tolerated among the conventional force. For example, the niceties of preparing detailed, accurate reports of investigative activities may be ignored; agents may be permitted to use tactics whose propriety, and even legality, are doubtful; constitutional guarantees of freedom from unreasonable searches and improper arrests may be overlooked. Abuses such as the excessive use of force, the entrapment of suspects (by inducing them to participate in crimes for the sole purpose of catching them red-handed), and the commission of criminal acts by agents to gain the confidence of suspects may be tolerated.

These dangers exist even in agencies that otherwise scrupulously avoid any taint of corruption or impropriety. Undercover investigation is, to be sure, difficult and dangerous. Even the most conscientious administrator may be tempted to make allowances when an overzealous or frustrated investigator goes beyond the bounds of proper police technique. The temptation is even greater when the impropriety is obscured within a secretive organizational structure. As long as no one else knows what is being done, it is easy for the administrator to look the other way or to rationalize that the ends justify the means.

Precisely because of these dangers, and the ultimate consequences that may result from them, it may be a serious mistake to remove the organized crime investigative unit from the built-in chain of accountability in the agency's conventional administrative structure. If the abuses we have mentioned are tolerated, the likely consequences include the corruption of undercover officers and, eventually, other members of the force. If improper police actions become public knowledge, the agency will suffer a devastating loss of public confidence. These dangers must be weighed against the sensitive nature of the task and the need for security.

It also may be a serious mistake to overlook the need for close coordination between the organized crime unit and other elements of the agency. Undercover agents usually do not participate in arrests, since that would reveal their identity as police officers. Therefore, at some point the undercover agents must rely on regular investigators and patrol officers to complete their work. In some cases, the undercover agent will gather sufficient evidence to justify a raid on a crime site (such as a house of prostitution or a gambling bank); the raid itself will be carried out by patrol officers and other investigators. Conversely, the activities of regular investigators and patrol officers may affect undercover agents, if the regular officers are not aware of the undercover agents' activities. For example, a patrol officer who happens to observe suspicious activity might interrupt a drug deal that has been painstakingly arranged by an undercover agent through months of work.

In short, regular investigators and patrol officers must be aware of undercover investigations, at least to the extent that the regular officers will not accidentally interfere with the undercover agents. This awareness can only come through the exchange of information among the patrol force, regular investigators, and organized crime investigators. Coordination and the free exchange of information are infinitely easier when the agency's organizational structure does not place unnecessary barriers between the various elements. In simple terms, this means that the organized crime investigative unit should not be separated from the rest of the agency's criminal investigations element. Organized crime investigations may be—probably should be—treated as a specialized element, but it also should be placed within the agency's administrative structure to permit proper coordination and supervision.

Special Crimes Unit

Depending on the nature and needs of the community, many law enforcement agencies have established special investigative units to deal with crimes that demand unique investigative skills and techniques.

For example, the police in a state capital may have jurisdiction over any illegal acts performed by officials of the state government, including legislators and other elected officials. In a community whose economy is dominated by a particular type of industry—perhaps mining, heavy industry, finance, oil and gas production, or maritime trade—the police may be concerned with certain types of crime that are peculiar to that industry.

In recent years, many American law enforcement agencies have assumed new responsibilities for the investigation of illegal acts that once were considered private matters, subject only to civil laws. For example, business crimes such as embezzlement, industrial espionage and sabotage, consumer fraud, and other so-called white-collar crimes formerly were regarded as civil disputes between the parties involved; today they are more likely to be regarded as crimes that require police intervention. Similarly, offenses that were once considered purely family matters such as child abuse and incest are now very much the concern of the criminal justice system.

Each type of crime we have mentioned requires unusual investigative skills and techniques. That is one reason the police traditionally have been reluctant to involve themselves in these areas. Public pressure, in some cases very intense pressure, has brought about a change of attitudes in many communities, and today the police cannot ignore the demand for enforcement activity.

The particular skills and techniques needed for the successful investigation of special crimes depend on the nature of the crime being investigated. For example, the investigation of political crime (that is, offenses such as interference with an election, bribery of a legislator or other public official, misapplication of the laws for private gain, or misuse of public property) requires extraordinary discretion. The mere fact of an investigation may have serious consequences for the person being investigated, which may be unfair if the person turns out to be innocent. Powerful officials (whether they are innocent or guilty) may use their power to retaliate against the police.

The investigation of political crime generally involves conventional investigative procedures: interviewing victims and witnesses, collecting documents, and so on. Occasionally, unconventional techniques may be required; in the Abscam series of cases in the late 1970s, the FBI and other law enforcement agencies used agents who posed as Arab sheiks and offered bribes to members of Congress and other officials. The offers were made in a series of specially arranged meetings; the meetings were recorded on videotape. The spectacular results included the conviction of a few corrupt officials and the destruction of the political careers of several others.

Business crime investigations also require a high degree of discretion and, in some instances, special techniques. More often, the major requirement is special knowledge of the business practices that are being criminally attacked. Embezzlement, for example, often is perpetrated by accountants, bookkeepers, cashiers, and sometimes financial officers who are intimately familiar with the cash-handling and bookkeeping procedures of their company. Their crimes can be discovered and evidence acquired only by investigators who understand thoroughly how the financial records are kept. Since virtually all companies (and governmental agencies) now use computers to keep their financial records, knowledge and understanding of computer systems also may be required. Few police officers are trained in bookkeeping and accounting, much less the esoteric practices of, say, the banking industry. In order to investigate such crimes, the police may require the assistance of experts. However, once again discretion is required. Expert consultants not only must be competent in their field of expertise but also must be made aware of the full legal significance of their participation. In particular, consultants who are asked to assist in an investigation must understand that their involvement is absolutely confidential, no matter what the results (except that they may be called on to testify in court). If an investigation fails to produce enough evidence to bring charges against the offender, it is conceivable that the police and their consultants could be sued for slander, invasion of privacy, or other civil offenses.

The widespread use of computers has opened up whole new fields for criminal activity, fields that are filled with landmines for investigators. Computers can be used as tools to commit crimes, or the computers themselves and the information they contain can be the objects of criminal attack.[12]

In the motion picture *Superman III*, the character played by Richard Pryor uses a computer to embezzle money from his employer, by ordering the employer's computerized accounting system to transfer to his own account the fractions of a cent that are otherwise omitted from the employees' expense accounts. In a few days, the embezzler's account is credited with several hundred thousand dollars. The movie makes the embezzlement appear amusing, but in fact the fictional account is based on several real-life incidents. Criminals with access to computers have gained entry to bank computers and have ordered them to transfer to their own accounts the fractional cents that arise from the calculation of interest. When depositors' interest is computed, often the amount of interest to be credited to each account includes some part of one cent; since it is not possible to pay a fractional cent in cash, the computer is programmed to set aside the fraction. But in order for the bank's books to balance, the fractional cents must be accounted for; the amount may accumulate into the hundreds of thousands of dollars in a large bank. A knowledgeable criminal may be able to penetrate the computer system and divert the fractional-cents account into his own account, withdraw the money periodically, and disappear before anyone realizes what has happened.[13]

This particular crime is not especially common, and most computerized accounting systems now have safeguards to prevent it. However, it is a good illustration of the complexity of many business crimes, and it is easy to see that detecting and investigating such a crime would be quite difficult.

The difficulties are even greater when the object of criminal activity is not money but information. State and federal laws are inconsistent on the basic question of whether information is property. If it is property, it belongs to the person (or company) who possesses it, and stealing it is a crime. If information is not property, it cannot be stolen; a person who takes it without authorization is not a thief. Nevertheless, it is certainly true that information has value, sometimes an enormous value. The owners or managers of any business would gain a significant advantage if they knew the sales plans, product designs, and other information possessed by their competitors, suppliers, or customers. Some people are sufficiently dishonest to steal such information if they can, and the use of computers to produce and store information may create the opportunity to do so. Many computers are connected to telephone and other communications systems for the exchange of information between terminals and processors, or between computer systems at different sites. It may be possible for an intruder to gain access to the communications system and then into the computers themselves, and then remove information without leaving any trace of the intrusion. (Of course, information can be stolen without the involvement of computers at all; a thief may enter a business and steal or copy plans, business documents, and so forth, or may be able to obtain information from dishonest or naive employees.)

Clearly, detecting and investigating these instances of espionage require an intimate understanding of the nature of the information, the way the information is created and stored (whether or not computers are involved), and the methods used to steal it. Even when these facts can be ascertained, a criminal offense may or may not be involved, depending on the exact content of state and federal laws.[14] In some cases, industrial spies who have been found guilty of stealing information worth millions of dollars have been punished only for the misdemeanor offense of taking the pieces of paper or the computer tapes on which the information was recorded.

Consumer fraud is another area of law enforcement that has grown rapidly in recent years, but that poses special difficulties. A dissatisfied purchaser of goods or services may complain that the product was misrepresented (it could not do what the seller claimed), or that it was defective (it did not do what it was supposed to do, or it caused some harm when it was used). The seller, however, may claim either that the purchaser misunderstood what the product or service was supposed to do or misused the product and is therefore responsible for its failure and any harm that may have resulted.

Consumer protection laws are the result of legislation at the federal and state level and of numerous court decisions (mainly in civil courts, although the criminal courts also have dealt with this subject). Some consumer frauds may involve criminal violations; others remain purely civil matters; still others may involve both. Prosecuting a consumer fraud may require an understanding of such terms as "puffery," "merchantability," "implied representation," "contributory negligence," and other technical concepts. An accusation of consumer fraud might be merely the result of a misunderstanding between an honest merchant and a dissatisfied customer; in a few cases, the "victimized" customer is actually attempting to bilk the merchant by claiming damages that never occurred!

The most important investigative tool in consumer fraud cases is the investigator's open mind. Some cases are very clear-cut, as when an advertiser offers a product with certain claimed features, but actually delivers a cheap substitute. Far more often, the investigator must determine not only whether the product is in fact defective, but whether there was any criminal intent (such as deliberate misrepresentation) on the part of the merchant, or whether indeed the customer is the one with fraudulent intent. At the same time, a fraud investigator must be thoroughly familiar with the laws and court decisions that affect this kind of situation. What begins as a criminal investigation may wind up as a civil matter, or vice versa, or may be settled privately between the parties involved.

Crimes within a family are among the most difficult of criminal matters for the police. Traditionally in our society, family relationships have been considered purely private and not subject to interference by outsiders. But in recent years, growing evidence of violent abuse within the family has brought about a change in public attitudes. Many people now believe that society has a right and a need to protect the innocent from abuse, wherever that abuse occurs, and that abusers cannot draw a veil of privacy over their crimes. New laws have been enacted to spell out the kinds of abuses that are deemed criminal and to require the police to intervene.

Again, the presence of criminal intent is an important issue. Most state laws regarding child abuse (whether the abuse is violent, sexual, or even emotional) explicitly disregard the question of intent; even unintentional abuse, caused perhaps by ignorance, neglect, or the emotional problems of the abuser, is criminal and must be prosecuted. However, intent is very much an issue when the victim of abuse is an adult—either spouse or parent. Thus, the investigation of alleged abuses within a family must determine not only what happened and who caused it, but why it happened and whether there are extenuating circumstances.

In summary, the investigation of these special crimes usually requires (1) experienced and sensitive investigators who are aware of the need for discretion and due regard for the delicate nature of each situation; (2) extensive knowledge of the legal and technical aspects of the alleged criminal acts; and (3) an unusually open-minded attitude and ability to conduct the investigation without prejudging the parties involved. Great ingenuity may be needed to develop investigative procedures that fit the circumstances. Expert consultants may be called on to advise the investigator or to participate in discovering the nature and methods of the criminal activity; if consultants are used, they must be closely supervised to ensure that they do not compromise the investigation or the integrity of the law enforcement agency.

We have discussed these matters in some detail because of the implications for the administrator. Special crimes demand special treatment. In particular, special crimes units require close administrative supervision. Personnel assigned to these units must have personal qualities that are different from (not necessarily superior to) those required in regular investigators or even organized-crime investigators. Extensive training may also be required, and frequent opportunities for continuing training and education are necessary. For all of these reasons, the investigation of special crimes usually demands the establishment of separate investigative units. As in the case of organized crime units, the special crimes units usually should be under the administrative authority of the detective bureau (or whatever the investigative element is called); the requirements of coordination and close supervision are the same.

THE ADMINISTRATION OF INVESTIGATIVE OPERATIONS

Administrators are particularly concerned with four aspects of the operations of all investigative elements:

1. The assignment of cases for investigation.
2. The coordination of investigative activities.
3. The collection and distribution of information.
4. The legal implications of investigative activities.

Case Assignment

Every incident that comes to the attention of the police may require investigation. Some cases are generated by the investigative units themselves; this is most often true for organized crime investigations. Other cases are usually the result of a complaint.

If the investigative unit is highly specialized, the nature of the alleged crime usually determines the unit to which the case is assigned. Thus, a complaint of a theft is assigned to the theft division. Assignment to cases within each specialized unit may be left to the discretion of the unit's supervisor or manager or may be based on some mechanical principle such as assignment by rotation.

In a patrol-oriented organization, case assignment usually is based on geography; that is, each officer is responsible for investigating every case, regardless of the nature of the alleged offense, that occurs within his or her beat. For the administrator, this means that beats must be carefully designed to equalize the patrol officers' work load; otherwise, one officer may be assigned an excessive number of cases while other officers have little or nothing to do.

Case assignment is a major concern in what we have called an integrated organizational structure. The initial investigative steps, such as the preliminary investigation, may be assigned to patrol officers on the basis of geography, but further investigation usually is assigned to detectives. The key question here is whether there is some standard procedure for making these assignments (for example, the investigators also may be allocated to geographic districts, with each detective responsible for every investigation within his or her district; this system is sometimes a feature of team policing structures), or whether the responsibility for case assignment is given to some individual (such as the chief of the detective bureau). In the former system, the assignment procedure must be designed to ensure the reasonable equalization of work loads and cases must be given to investigators who have the appropriate training and ability to perform successful follow-up investigations. If a supervisor or manager is responsible for making assignments, there must be some assurance that the assignments are made in a fair and reasonable manner; favored investigators should not be given all of the easiest or most interesting cases, while others are given an overwhelming number of cases that are either dull and routine or unlikely to be successful.

Coordination of Investigative Activity

Criminal activity does not occur in a vacuum. Some criminals (especially those involved in organized crime) tend to specialize in certain types of crime, but many others commit a variety of offenses, depending on what opportunities arise. Thus it is not unusual for an individual to be involved in a series of burglaries, thefts, armed robberies, assaults, and miscellaneous other offenses.

If investigative cases are assigned to specialized units, and within each unit are assigned to detectives on the basis of some mechanical principle such as rotation, it is easy to overlook the possibility that a suspect in one case may be involved in a number of other crimes. According to at least one study of criminal investigation practices, investigators rarely discuss their cases with one another unless there is some specific procedure that encourages or requires them to do so.[15]

In an integrated or patrol-oriented system, the need for coordination is more obvious; investigators and patrol officers cannot do their work successfully unless they cooperate with one another. The means for achieving and maintaining that cooperation must be provided, partly through the organizational structure itself and partly through administrative policies and regulations.

Some very basic policies should be adopted by every law enforcement agency. First, no case under investigation belongs to any individual officer (whether patrol officer or investigator). Every case must be assigned to someone, who serves as the principal investigator and who is responsible for bringing the case to conclusion. However, it should be possible for any other officer to contribute information that might influence an investigation, and every officer should be able to gain access to the information that an investigator has obtained.

A second basic policy should be that enforcement activities directed toward related criminal activities must be carried out in a coordinated manner. Earlier we pointed out the urgent need for coordination between conventional and undercover investigative units. Patrol officers and regular detectives need to know what kinds of undercover investigations are in progress, so that they will not inadvertently interfere with the undercover agents' work. In fact, the efforts of all units should be directed to reinforce one another.

In general, the coordination of activities among several elements of an organization is the responsibility of the managers. Certainly it is much easier for the managers in a small agency to know what all of their subordinates are doing; in a larger agency, a greater effort must be expended to ensure that each manager has the necessary information and acts on it. Operating-level personnel (patrol officers and detectives) must be encouraged to share information and to cooperate with one another; it is the responsibility of their supervisors and managers to see that they do so.

Collection and Distribution of Information

Every police investigative unit is, in a sense, an information-processing machine. Investigators (whether they are called patrol officers or detectives) collect information from victims and witnesses, obtain information from physical evidence, compare information from different cases, and process information to arrive at an understanding of how a crime was committed and by whom.

The administrators' chief concern is that all of this information be collected and processed in an efficient manner. At a crime scene, the patrol officers, detectives, and evidence technicians must collect all of the information that is available. Once collected, the information must be fully and accurately recorded. Once recorded, the information must be reported—fully and accurately—to everyone who may need it, including investigators who are responsible for follow-up investigations and managers who are responsible for coordinating investigative activity.

In Chapter 9 we pointed out the importance of maintaining a single, central record of all crime-related information, and we discussed what kinds of records should be kept. We also discussed some of the ways that information-processing equipment such as computers could be used to make the investigative process more efficient and effective. Naturally, administrators must be deeply involved in planning such a system; much thought and effort will go into designing the entire information-processing system, purchasing the necessary equipment, and training all personnel to use it properly. Beyond that, administrators must enact appropriate policies and procedures to be sure that the system is used as it was intended.

We are especially concerned that the investigative units of a police agency have direct, immediate access to any computerized information system. In the past, police communications and information systems have been designed primarily to serve the needs of administrators and of the patrol forces. Criminal investigators' specific needs have not gotten much attention. In our view, the best information system is one that gives every investigator immediate, direct access to every scrap of information possessed by the agency.

Legal Implications

It should not be necessary to warn administrators that every police activity has potential consequences and implications affecting the legal and constitutional rights of citizens. Unfortunately, experience suggests that too many administrators are either ignorant of these implications or overlook them in favor of what they regard as "efficient police practices."

A moment's reflection on history (see Chapter 1) will help one to understand why Americans traditionally have distrusted police authority and have gone to great lengths to limit the privileges of the police. In the most sweeping terms, every citizen has the right to be let alone by the police. To put the matter another way, the police have no right or authority to act against the interests of any citizen unless there is compelling evidence that the citizen has committed, or knows something about, a particular crime.

Even victims and witnesses cannot be forced to give information (although many states have laws that place an obligation on citizens to cooperate with the police). When an officer begins an interview with a complainant, the officer must be aware that the complainant has a right to remain silent about anything other than the particular crime being investigated. If the officer wants to search the crime scene for physical evidence, either the consent of the property's owner must be given or a court order must be obtained. If an arrest is to be made, the specific rights of the suspect must be observed; otherwise, not only will the suspect go free and the crime go unpunished, but the police themselves may wind up defending a civil suit.[16]

Police officers cannot reasonably be expected to know and understand every fine interpretation of every law that applies to common police procedures and techniques. Administrators have a duty to inform their officers of the most basic and significant laws that affect their work; this information should be conveyed to each new officer during training and to all personnel through in-service training and the distribution of periodic bulletins. However, there will remain large areas of legal uncertainty concerning the particular applications of the law to particular cases. In every police agency, someone should be responsible for keeping current with court decisions and new legislation in the areas of suspects' rights, the laws of search and seizure, the laws of arrest, and the liability of police officers for improper acts. Ideally, an agency should have the benefit of a trained, experienced legal counsel; either an in-house attorney should be employed by every agency or, if that is impractical, at least the agency should have access to an assistant city attorney, a member of the attorney general's staff, or (as a last resort) a private attorney. Whenever officers, especially investigators, are considering any action that goes beyond routine, conventional police procedures, the advice of a qualified attorney should be solicited.

CHIEF ABEL'S IN BASKET

Instructions

In this exercise, you are to assume the role of Chief of Police E. Z. Abel. The documents below have been selected from Chief Abel's in basket. Read them with care. If you need more information about City or its police department, refer to the data bank in the front of the book. After you have studied the documents, complete these steps:

1. State the problem or problems these documents present to Chief Abel.
2. List as many alternative solutions as you can.
3. Select the solution you think would be best, and give your reasons for choosing it.

CITY POLICE DEPARTMENT
Interoffice Memorandum

FROM:	Capt. Frank Edwards, Chief, Organized Crime Bureau	
TO:	Chief Abel	
SUBJECT:	Recommended Commendation for Lt. J. Rader	DATE: 12 Oct 19--

SIR:

It is my pleasure to recommend that Lt. John Rader, head of the Organized Crimes Bureau, Vice Section, be awarded the City Police Dept.'s highest commendation for heroism above and beyond the call of duty.

On Friday, 9 Oct, at approximately 1900 hrs, Lt. Rader was enroute to his home, having completed his normal shift, and was driving along the 2900 block of Western Hills Drive when he observed a City PD patrol unit, A-1, parked in front of Big Charlie's Pawn Shop. Lt. Rader, knowing that the pawn shop was the subject of an on-going investigation as a site of illegal bookmaking, took the initiative to determine whether his assistance might be required. He therefore entered the pawn shop and found Patrol Office Edwin Chapman engaged in a heated discussion with the proprietor of the pawn shop, known to Lt. Rader as "Big Charlie." Recognizing that Off. Chapman might be in danger, Lt. Rader immediately drew his handgun and announced that he was a police officer.

According to Lt. Rader's confidential OC Report, "Big Charlie" leaned over the pawn shop counter, grabbed Off. Chapman around the neck, and, using

RECOMMENDED COMMENDATION - PAGE 2 of 2.

Off. Chapman as a shield, withdrew into the back room of the pawn shop, shouting, "Get outta here or I'll kill this (expletive deleted)!"

Lt. Rader immediately went to Off. Chapman's patrol vehicle and called in a "hostage situation, officer needs help" report. However, Lt. Rader realized that, since his proposal for a SWT team had never been approved, no clear procedure for this kind of situation existed. Again seizing the initiative, Lt. Rader went to the laundromat next door to the pawn shop and, at his own expense, telephoned four members of the Organized Crime Bureau and the Detective Bureau who had previously volunteered for the SWT unit. These officers--Lt. Sam Courtney, Sr. Sgt. Lee Brooks, Sr. Sgt. Edward Gifford, and Sgt. David McIntyre-- responded to the scene within twelve minutes. By that time, two other Patrol units (A-2, Off. Thomas Amberg, and B-], Off. John Fowler) had arrived. Lt. Rader instructed the two patrol officers to cover the rear entrance of the pawn shop but to take no further action. As soon as the rest of the SWT unit arrived, Lt. Rader instructed them to assist him in rescuing Off. Chapman. Lt. Rader led the four other officers into the pawn shop, where they were met with gunshots from the back room. Disregarding the danger to his own life, Lt. Rader led Lt. Courtney and Sgt. Gifford to the door to the back room, which the suspect by that time had locked and barricaded. Lt. Rader personally kicked in the door and led the way into the back room, where the suspect was hiding behind a filing cabinet. Lts. Rader and Courtney and Sgt. Gifford fired several rounds from their service revolvers, at least three of which struck the suspect, fatally wounding him. They found Off. Chapman wounded on the floor near the door. Fortunately, Off. Chapman's wounds were not serious and he is expected to recover.

In my opinion, the bravery and initiative displayed by Lt. Rader are in the highest tradition of the City P.D. The other four senior officers involved also deserve commendation for their prompt response and courageous action to assist a fellow officer.

Furthermore, it appears to me that this incident demonstrates the need for the SWT unit that Lt. Rader previously proposed. This kind of incident requires the degree of rapid response, coordinated action, and highly disciplined application of effective police response that were shown by Lt. Rader and the others. I hope you will reconsider your recent decision to hold back on approving the SWT proposal.

Capt. Frank Edwards, Chief
Organized Crime Bureau

Chief E. Z. Abel   October 12, 19--
City Police Department

Sir:

    At your request, here is my report of what happened the other
night.
    While on regular patrol on Beat A-2, I observed an automobile
parked illegally at the fire hydrant in the 2900 block of Western
Hills Drive. I went into a store, "Big Charlie's Pawn Shop," to
see if anyone knew whose car it was. The man behind the counter, whom
I knew to be the owner of the place (he is called "Big Charlie"), told me
that the car belonged to him. I asked him to please move it out of the
no-parking zone near the fire hydrant. "Big Charlie" objected to
this, saying that it was "convenient" to him to leave the car where
it was.
    While "Big Charlie" and I were discussing this matter, another
person entered the store behind me. I have since learned that this
person was Lt. John Rader, a vice detective for City P.D. Before
I knew what was happening, this person started waving around a
handgun. As far as I can recall, the only words he said, in a loud
voice, were "Freeze before I blow your blankety-blank-blank off!" I
turned around and started to pull my own weapon, thinking that
this person was about to rob the store. Suddenly, "Big Charlie"
grabbed me around the neck and pulled me over the counter,
dragging me into a back room. He was choking me so hard that I
lost consciousness for a few seconds. The next thing I knew, I
heard several sirens and a lot of shouting from the front of the
building. "Big Charlie" drew my revolver from my holster and pulled
me with him behind his desk. I tried to talk him into giving up the gun,
and I might have succeeded but suddenly there was a lot of noise
in the front of the store. That's when I decided to take action to
protect myself, and I tried to wrestle the gun away from "Big Charlie."
Unfortunately, I was not successful, and he fired at least two shots
that struck me in the shoulder and rib cage. I immediately lost
consciousness and do not know what happened after that, until
I woke up in the hospital.
    As soon as I get out of the hospital, I will file a complete
official report of this incident on the proper forms. I hope
this is the informatin you asked me to give you. Again, I
appreciate very much your visit this morning was a real morale-
booster. Thank you for your concern.

                                        Sincerely,

                                        Edwin Chapman

                                        E. Chapman, Patrol

CITY POLICE DEPARTMENT
Interoffice Memorandum

FROM:	T. Bowen, Capt., Chief of Detectives	
TO:	E. Z. Abel, Chief	
SUBJECT:	Resignation	DATE: 14 Oct 19--

SIR:
    I hereby tender my resignation from the City Police Dept., effective October 31 or at any earlier date convenient to you.
    I have already explained to you my reasons for resigning. For the record, I feel that my ability and authority to command the Detective Bureau have been seriously undermined, and there is no point in my continuing to hold this position.
    I have been a member of this Dept. for 26 years, and have been Chief of Detectives for 11 years. I was opposed to the establishment of the Organized Crimes Bureau when the Dept. was reorganized by Chief Ellis in 1964, when I was just a Patrolman. When I became Chief of Detectives, I proposed that OCB and the Detectives Bureau be combined, and my proposal was denied. I felt then, and I still feel, that having 2 separate investigations units in our small Dept. is unnecessary and inefficient.

Page 2.
    The incident that occurred last Friday night was the last straw for me. Lt. Rader of OCB involved two of my people, Sr. Sgt. Brooks and Sgt. McIntyre, without my authorization and approval. In my opinion, the actions taken by Lt. Rader were very poor police work that results in the death of a suspect and the wounding of an officer for no good reason. Furthermore, the suspect, "Big Charlie," had been under surveillance for more than two months on suspicion of receiving stolen goods. Thanks to Lt. Rader's interference, that investigation has now been ruined, and we probably will not be able to recover most of the stolen merchandise that "Big Charlie" bought and sold over the past several weeks. When I learned that Lt. Rader has been recommended for a medal, I felt like I must be in the wrong business.
    I sincerely regret any inconvenience my resignation will cause you or the Dept., but I feel that I have no choice, and I hope you will approve without delay.

        Thomas Bowen, Captain,
        Chief of Detectives

IN REVIEW

1. True or False: One of the principal functions of a police agency's investigative unit is the discovery of certain crimes that otherwise would not be reported.

2. The four stages of the investigative process are (list in the correct order):
   (a) The preliminary investigation.
   (b) Undercover surveillance.
   (c) Concluding the investigation.
   (d) Convicting the perpetrator.
   (e) Receiving the complaint.
   (f) The follow-up investigation.
   (g) Coordination with other units.

3. In an integrated investigative system:
   (a) Investigators are divided into specialized units that are responsible for specific types of crimes.
   (b) Patrol officers perform nearly all investigations.
   (c) All investigators assist in each case that is investigated.
   (d) Investigators are responsible for most follow-up investigations.
   (e) Cases are assigned according to the ethnic background of the complainant.

4. A *criminalist* is:
   (a) A person who engages in crime for monetary gain.
   (b) A technical specialist in the discovery, collection, and analysis of evidence.
   (c) Anyone who investigates a crime.
   (d) Anyone who reports a crime.
   (e) An expert in the psychology of criminals.

5. The key elements that distinguish organized crimes from common crimes are:
   (a) Organized criminals engage in crimes primarily for profit, and the victims are willing participants.
   (b) Organized criminals are less violent than common criminals, and organized crimes are more difficult to detect.
   (c) Organized crimes are offenses against society's moral standards, and organized criminals make a special effort to avoid being identified.
   (d) Organized crimes result in profit to the criminals and involve large numbers of people.
   (e) Organized crimes are businesslike and require investigators to have an understanding of how businesses operate.

6. True or False: Because undercover agents must operate in great secrecy, it is necessary to allow them to use police techniques and procedures that might be questionable in other investigations.

7. Special crimes units may be required:
   (a) When the incidence of crime exceeds the ability of regular investigators to manage.
   (b) To deal with crimes that demand unique investigative skills and techniques.
   (c) To prevent organized crime from infiltrating the criminal justice system.
   (d) To resolve noncriminal disputes between citizens.
   (e) To determine whether certain incidents are really crimes or merely misunderstandings.

8. True or False: Expert consultants should never be used because their lack of understanding of the criminal justice system is likely to compromise the investigation.

9. Administrators are particularly concerned with the following aspects of the investigative operation:
   (a) The use of standardized reporting techniques.
   (b) The assignment of cases for investigation.
   (c) The legal implications of investigative activities.

(d) The effects of crime on its victims.
(e) The coordination of investigative activities.
(f) The use of specialized investigative techniques.
(g) The collection and distribution of information.

10. True or False: In general, the coordination of activities among several investigative units is the responsibility of the officers directly involved.

REFERENCES

1. Alfred R. Stone and Stuart M. DeLuca, *Investigating Crimes*, Boston: Houghton Mifflin, 1980, page 44.

2. Ronald J. Waldron et al. *The Criminal Justice System*, Boston: Houghton Mifflin, 1976, pages 356–357.

3. Peter W. Greenwood, Jan M. Chaiken, and Joan Petersilia, *The Criminal Investigation Process*, Lexington, Mass.: D. C. Heath, 1977, page 121.

4. Greenwood, pages 17–23.

5. Stone and DeLuca, pages 39–40.

6. O. W. Wilson, *Police Planning*, 2nd ed., Springfield, Ill.: Charles C. Thomas, 1967, page 114.

7. Jay Cameron Hall, *Inside the Crime Lab*, Englewood Cliffs, N.J.: Prentice-Hall, 1974, page 16.

8. Richard H. Fox and Carl L. Cunningham, *Crime Scene Search and Physical Evidence Handbook*, Washington, D.C.: U.S. Dept. of Justice, National Institute of Law Enforcement and Criminal Justice, 1973.

9. Wilson, page 113.

10. Donald R. Cressey, *Theft of the Nation*, New York: Harper & Row, 1969.

11. Cressey.

12. Donn B. Parker, *Fighting Computer Crime*, New York: Scribner's, 1980.

13. Parker, page 107.

14. David Stamps, "CPU Crime Laws Weak," *MISWeek*, September 28, 1983, page 12.

15. Greenwood, page 15.

16. J. Shane Creamer, *The Law of Arrest, Search, and Seizure*, 2nd ed., Philadelphia: W. B. Saunders, 1975.

17 MANAGEMENT OF AUXILIARY AND SUPPORT UNITS

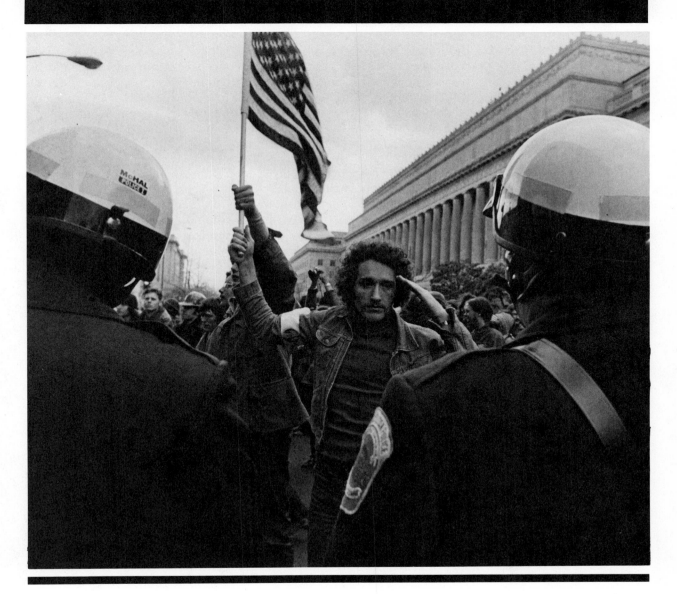

THE PATROL, TRAFFIC, AND CRIMINAL INVESTIGATION units are the backbone of the police service in any law enforcement agency. Their functions include all of the major aspects of the police mission. Many smaller agencies consist entirely of those three elements, plus a fourth very small administrative element.

Larger agencies may have an array of specialized units to provide police services for which the public (through its elected officials) has expressed some demand, or for which the administrator perceives a need. Larger agencies also require more extensive technical and administrative support, if only to provide for the routine "housekeeping" tasks that are necessary to keep the agency in operation. In this chapter, we consider some of the different special operational units and technical support elements that are found in many police agencies.

SPECIAL OPERATIONAL UNITS

Before the turn of the century, many progressive police administrators recognized that neither the watchman concept of crime prevention nor the trooper concept of maintaining public order by suppressing crime was sufficient to ensure the safety and well-being of the public. Law enforcement agencies, in order to fulfill their fundamental mission, would have to take action to identify and, as far as possible, correct those conditions in society that contribute to lawlessness.

This thinking led to the establishment of a range of services that, in retrospect, seem rather peculiar. Some police departments set up soup kitchens, transient shelters, employment offices, and other social-welfare units, in a well-meaning but ultimately futile attempt to attack crime by getting at its sources: poverty, unemployment, and social deprivation in general. Most of these welfare-oriented services fell by the wayside as later police reforms concentrated on professionalizing the law enforcement functions.[1]

One part of the social-welfare program remained within many police agencies, however, and continues to this day: the juvenile crime prevention unit. Partly because of the unique structure of the American juvenile justice system, and partly because of the philosophy that diverting juveniles from crime is a crucial means of preventing future adult crime, most police agencies continue to treat juvenile crimes in an entirely different manner from adult crimes.

Juvenile Crime Units

A typical juvenile crime unit is designed not to identify and arrest offenders, but to identify young people who are (or might be) involved in criminal activities so that they can be rehabilitated and diverted into law-abiding citizenship.

In every state, laws specify at what age a person is regarded as an adult for various purposes. All states presently allow citizens to vote at age 18; most states permit young people to obtain motor vehicle licenses at age 16 (sometimes with the qualification that they must have passed a driver education course); some states permit alcoholic beverages to be bought at 18, while others set the minimum drinking age at 19 and a few have left the drinking age at 21. In some states, young people may marry without their parents' consent at age 14; in others, the age of consent is 16 or even 18. In most states, young people may enter into binding contracts, including contracts for debts and for the purchase or sale of automobiles, at age 18; in a few states, the minimum age is 16.

Similarly, the age at which a person who commits an offense is treated as an adult varies from state to state. In most states, an offender is an adult at age 16; in some states, at age 17 or 18. Several states leave the decision to a judge or jury; in Texas, for example, anyone under the age of 18 who is accused of a criminal offense must be certified as an adult before he or she can be tried. Offenders as young as 14 years old have been certified as adults.

Persons who have, or may have, committed criminal offenses but who are not legally adults are diverted into the juvenile justice system. The accused offender is not tried and cannot be convicted; however, the offender may be the subject of a hearing to determine what kind of rehabilitative treatment is appropriate.[2] The treatment may include assignment to an institution (variously called reform school or rehabilitation center, among other terms) or release into the custody of his or her parents or some other responsibile adult. Some imaginative judges have "sentenced" young offenders to various sorts of community-service work such as cleaning up trash along roadways or assisting in the emergency room of a hospital; other judges simply impose fines, which are most often paid by the offenders' parents.[3]

The role of the police in the juvenile justice system is, in a word, ambiguous. On one hand, the police have a general duty to enforce the law and prevent crime. On the other hand, when the criminals are juveniles, the usual crime-suppression tactics are not available.

Most police authorities agree that, in principle, children cannot be held responsible for their antisocial behavior, even when that behavior includes violent crimes; second, it is more important to rehabilitate juvenile offenders than to punish them; and third, the formalities of the adult criminal justice system are not entirely appropriate for application to juveniles.

Nevertheless, the fact remains that juveniles commit crimes, that rehabilitation is very far from foolproof, and that diversion from the adult criminal justice system often seems to mean wandering in a quagmire of good intentions, confused motives, and uncertain results.

All of which means, in practical terms, that the functions and activities of the juvenile crime unit are considerably different from those of the patrol and criminal investigation units. Officers assigned to the juvenile unit must be thoroughly familiar with the laws relating to juvenile offenses and with the workings of the juvenile justice system.[4]

Juvenile offenders come to the attention of the juvenile crime unit in any of several ways. Some juveniles are taken into custody by regular police officers in the course of investigating a crime; others are reported by victims or witnesses. Most juvenile crime units also take active measures to identify juvenile offenders. Officers from the juvenile unit attempt to maintain contact with youth gangs (which are not necessarily involved in criminal behavior) and organizations that cater to young people such as recreation centers. Whenever possible, juvenile crime officers attempt to identify offenders before they are arrested, preferably even before they become involved in serious crimes.

The first step in dealing with a juvenile offender (or prospective offender) is counseling with both the child and his or her parents. The object of counseling the young offender is twofold: (1) to discover whether there is some reason, such as emotional illness, for the antisocial behavior; and (2) to persuade the young person to devote his or her energies to productive, lawful activities. Counseling with the parents also has a dual purpose: to determine whether the child's problem is symptomatic of more serious social or psychological problems in the entire family, and to persuade the parents to accept responsibility for their child's behavior.

On the whole, the success rate for these counseling efforts is not very high. By the time young people come to the attention of the police, it is not likely that they will be persuaded to mend their ways. Still, many juvenile crime officers are very successful in their counseling. Even if the success rate is not very high, *any* success is better than none.

If counseling fails, or if in the officer's judgment it is hopeless to begin with, the next step is to turn the young offender over to the juvenile justice system. Usually this means that a social worker will assume responsibility for the child's custody (although in many cases the child will continue to live at home) and a hearing will be held before a judge or juvenile magistrate.[5] At this point, the only role of the police is to provide information concerning the young offender's record.

This brief outline of the police role in the juvenile justice system should not be taken as anything more than an introduction. The field of juvenile justice is exceedingly complex, and any thorough discussion of it would require much more time and space than we can devote to it. In most states, juveniles are subject to any number of noncriminal laws that would never apply to adults. Juveniles may be arrested, taken from their parents' custody, and sentenced to institutions for such noncriminal offenses as being truant from school, running away from home, or violating a local curfew ordinance. The custody of children where the parents are divorced or legally separated also involves the juvenile justice system in many states.

Crime Prevention Units

Juvenile crime units and crime prevention units are often one and the same. Many police administrators adhere to the idea that the only really effective method of preventing adult crime is to divert young people from criminal activity.[6] Therefore, the only element of the police agency whose specific responsibility includes crime prevention is the juvenile unit (except to the extent that patrol officers are supposed to engage in preventive patrolling).

In recent years, however, a different philosophy of prevention has developed in American law enforcement. Police administrators and law enforcement theorists have concluded that most citizens can protect themselves from crime if they are taught how to do so. Educating the public to prevent crime therefore becomes the responsibility of the crime prevention unit.

The crime prevention measures usually advocated by the police include such elementary matters as securing one's home or business by installing better locks on doors and windows. An extensive literature has developed on the subject of residential and commercial security; in fact, a whole industry has grown up to make and sell door locks, "burglar bars," and alarm systems. Some crime prevention units have become little more than salespeople for the vendors of commercial security systems.

Crime prevention units also may be concerned with teaching people how to deal with violent attack. Some police departments go so far as to conduct workshops and courses on self-defense techniques or the use of self-protection devices. Special workshops are often conducted for particular segments of the public such as women and the elderly.

Most of these efforts are entirely appropriate for a police agency. In some instances, the crime prevention officers may become a bit overenthusiastic and promise more than they can deliver. No security system, no matter how elaborate, will protect a home or business from an experienced and determined intruder; some of the commercial systems offered to the public are notoriously unreliable. By the same token, all the self-defense and self-protection lessons in the world will do little good when a citizen is confronted by a determined, armed attacker. If false expectations are raised and citizens are given false confidence, the results might be even more disastrous than if the citizen had never attended the workshops.

The point is that establishing a crime prevention unit is eminently worthwhile, if there is a public interest to be served and if the crime prevention officers maintain a modest attitude toward the results of their efforts.

More effective methods of crime prevention certainly need to be developed, and we may reasonably hope that as they are developed, more police agencies will share them with the public through educational campaigns, workshops, and other methods. In the last analysis, for reasons that we have discussed earlier, the police themselves can never hope to be entirely successful in preventing crime. The more responsibility for crime prevention is assumed by individual citizens, the more successful the police will be and the less crime-ridden our communities will become.

Community Relations Units

Despite the fact that modern American police agencies are not likely to be involved in the kinds of social-welfare schemes that were common before the turn of the century, it is still true that crime is a social problem, not just a legal problem, and the source of all crime is the community in which people live. For those reasons, the police continue to have a legitimate concern for social conditions in the community they serve. Although they do not operate soup kitchens, transient shelters, and employment offices, many police agencies do offer some services to assist the people in their community to improve their social welfare.

At the same time, the police urgently need to be aware of social conditions in their community. They may be able to do little about slum housing and chronic unemployment, but they need to know which slum landlords fail to provide their tenants with heat in the winter and which unemployed laborers are reaching the breaking point of desperation. This kind of knowledge can be gained only by establishing and maintaining close, continual contact with the community.

Both social services and what we might call community intelligence functions are sometimes assigned to a **community relations unit**. In fact, all kinds of non-law-enforcement services and functions may be assigned to the community relations unit; one danger in establishing this organizational element is that it may become a grab bag of assorted, miscellaneous operations.[7]

A community relations unit often operates "storefront police stations" in minority neighborhoods and other areas where it is especially important to maintain good relations with the community. The function of a storefront operation is primarily to assist citizens in their dealings with the police and other public agencies, and generally to build a favorable image for the police. Storefront community relations officers have one mandate: to help people in any way they can without compromising the primary police mission. They might help a young mother fill out an application for food stamps or counsel a young man on how to apply for a job. They might act as interpreters for a person who is qualified for free medical assistance but is unfamiliar with the bureaucratic procedures of a public clinic or hospital. They certainly would offer advice on crime prevention and self-protection and might assist a citizen in filing a complaint against a noisy neighbor.

Community relations units often sponsor youth groups such as Boys Clubs or Police Athletic Leagues and adult volunteer organizations such as Citizens Band emergency monitoring clubs, "police buddy" organizations, or neighborhood crime watches. In some instances, the community relations unit is responsible for administering the agency's police cadet program.

Again, the specific objective of any of these activities may have relatively little to do with criminal law enforcement, but the ultimate goal is to keep open the lines of communication between the police and the community.

Tactical Units

Not all special operational units are concerned with services that are only indirectly related to law enforcement. Some police departments have established special units to concentrate on very specific types of criminal activities. These units, often called tactical squads or tactical patrols, are similar in concept to the selective traffic enforcement operations we discussed in Chapter 15.

Tactical units are most likely to be effective in large agencies serving metropolitan areas. If the agency is able to identify a particular pattern of criminal activity, the tactical unit can be assigned to take whatever action is appropriate.[8] For example, if there has been a series of armed robberies of convenience stores in one part of town, tactical units might be assigned to patrol that area intensively.

The specific actions taken by a tactical unit should be based on the type of crime. In some cases, intensive patrol of an area may be appropriate, using standard, marked patrol vehicles. In other cases, patrolling in unmarked vehicles might be more effective. In yet other cases, tactical officers might stake out businesses that are likely crime targets. The choice of tactics depends on the amount of information that is available about the type of crime being fought.

The value of a tactical unit depends largely on the fact that criminals, individually and collectively, often commit offenses in a series or pattern. If a person is successful in holding up a liquor store, he or she is encouraged to hold up a second liquor store, then a third and a fourth, and to continue until he or she is caught or moves on to some other crime. Furthermore, if one person is successful in holding up several liquor stores, other people may try their hand at it.

To be sure, not all crimes occur in series, and not all criminal activity exhibits a clear pattern. Many crimes occur because of a unique opportunity or because of the personal relationships between the offender and victim; these crimes are less likely to be repeated. Some criminals are either not clever enough or too clever to follow any particular pattern of activity.

Nevertheless, when a clear pattern emerges from the daily flood of crime, the police have an opportunity to choose a specific tactic to disrupt the pattern. Often the only tactic necessary is to inform patrol officers or investigators and encourage them to concentrate their efforts on a specific enforcement goal. However, patrol officers and investigators may already have a heavy work load, or the organizational structure may not permit the kind of flexibility needed to assign officers to intensive patrolling or other specific tactics. In such cases, the formation of a tactical unit may be effective. Members of the tactical unit (which may vary in size from three or four officers to 15 or 20) usually are drawn from the general patrol force and typically are among the more experienced and successful patrol officers.

The assignment of a tactical unit to a particular task may come from the head of the patrol force, the head of the investigations element, or (more rarely) the head of a crime analysis or intelligence unit. The head of the tactical unit should be an experienced patrol commander with an excellent record for leadership. For each tactical assignment, the commander and other unit heads should determine exactly what tactics are to be employed, where, by whom, and for what period of time. These instructions then are given to the tactical officers; the instructions should specify whether marked or unmarked vehicles are to be used, whether officers are to be uniformed or in plainclothes, what actions are to be taken when criminal activity is observed (whether an individual officer should make an immediate arrest or simply observe the suspect and call for backup assistance), and anything else concerning the mission.

As with selective traffic enforcement, a tactical unit can be an extremely effective weapon against certain kinds of crime. There is a large body of evidence to show that a majority of crimes are committed by a minority of criminals. These are the people who commit essentially the same crime repetitively. The very fact that they are able to repeat their crime indicates that routine patrol and investigative techniques are unsuccessful. Tactical units, because they are not limited to a single geographic patrol area nor to the time-consuming, after-the-fact approach of conventional investigation, intensify the enforcement effort and focus it on those criminals who are otherwise all too likely to escape detection.

Special Situations Units

Some police agencies, especially in the major metropolitan areas, have established another kind of specialized operational unit, known variously as **Special Weapons and Tactics (SWAT)** teams, **Special Weapons Units**, and **Special Situations Units**. Whatever they are called, these units are organized to provide rapid police response to certain kinds of critical events, usually of an emergency nature.

A special situations unit may be organized on a permanent basis, or may be established on an on-call basis. In the latter case, members of the special situations unit are regular patrol officers and investigators who have received advanced training in special-situations techniques. Ordinarily they are assigned to their usual patrol or investigative duties. However, when a special situation arises, the unit is activated and members report to a prearranged point for their special assignment.

What constitutes a special situation? That is the first and perhaps most important question to be answered before a special situations unit is established. Generally, these units are called up for some or all of the following kinds of incidents:

1. A hostage-taking, barricaded suspect, or other situation in which a criminal has taken refuge in some location that is not readily accessible, or has taken one or more innocent citizens as hostages.
2. Sniper incidents, where the criminal is in an inaccessible location and is firing a weapon at police officers or innocent bystanders.
3. VIP security, where a public official or other celebrity requires special protection, usually because the celebrity is a controversial person, or because the celebrity's safety has been threatened.

Special situations units also may be used as the primary force, supplemented by regular officers, in such situations as riots and other major civil disturbances, parades or demonstrations that have a potential for violence, or any other incident that, because of its magnitude and potential for violence, is beyond the capabilities of the regular patrol force.

Members of a special situations unit usually are trained in a variety of advanced skills and techniques, including the use of both lethal and nonlethal weapons, hand-to-hand combat, and techniques for gaining access to inaccessible locations (such as rappelling). They also should be trained in crowd-control and riot suppression techniques and in the psychology of hostage situations.

In our City Police Department simulation exercises, we have presented a fictional proposal for a SWAT team that, for purposes of illustration, was somewhat exaggerated. We have deliberately made our Lieutenant Rader overzealous in his efforts to establish the SWAT unit. However, we do not mean to suggest that special situations units are never justified or effective. There is a danger in letting an overly aggressive leader turn a special situations unit into some kind of private army. The proper response to this danger, of course, is to limit the unit's mission to those carefully defined types of incidents that are most likely to occur in the community, for which extensive special training is justified. With those limitations, a special situations unit can be an effective means of augmenting a police agency's ability to respond to crisis situations.

SUPPORT SERVICES

Every police agency, large or small, requires a certain number of housekeeping and supportive services that do not directly involve law enforcement, but are nevertheless necessary for the law enforcement officers to do their jobs. In addition, a police agency usually requires certain technical support services to be performed in order to carry out the primary law enforcement functions. These functions may be assigned to a single element, often called the technical services unit or auxiliary support unit. A partial list of these auxiliary support functions would include:

1. Building maintenance and custodial service.
2. Vehicle maintenance.
3. Secretarial, clerical, and office management.
4. Financial management (bookkeeping, accounting).
5. Personnel management (recruitment and selection, management of the promotion system, recordkeeping, administration of contracts with unions or union-like police organizations, administration of benefit programs, etc.).
6. Purchasing and property management.
7. Communications and information services.
8. Public information, relations with news media.
9. Legal counsel concerning both law enforcement and non-law enforcement matters.
10. Personnel training services.
11. Criminalistics (evidence collection and analysis).
12. Crime analysis, intelligence, and planning.
13. Jail operations.

Some of the support services listed here are often provided by the parent government of small and medium-sized agencies. Larger agencies, however, generally prefer to assume responsibility for their own support services, thereby giving the agency's administrators better control over their own resources.

In the past, many medium-sized and larger police agencies assigned police officers to these auxiliary functions. There were two reasons for this practice. The police, like an army, preferred to be entirely self-reliant. By entrusting even the most menial housekeeping tasks only to fellow officers, police administrators kept "civilians" at bay and maintained a police mystique, according to which all police work was necessarily secretive and dangerous.[9]

A second reason was that most lower-level police officers were so poorly paid that it was simply cheaper to use patrol officers, and even sergeants, as secretaries and mechanics, rather than hiring "civilians" for these functions and paying them competitive wages.

Modern police practice has changed considerably. Today, "civilians"—that is, personnel who are not commissioned law enforcement officers—are found throughout most police agencies, performing most of the auxiliary support services listed above. There is a straightforward, practical reason for this change: Today's police officers, even at the entry level, cost too much to be assigned to menial tasks. In almost all police agencies, even the smallest ones, an entering patrol officer's salary is several thousand dollars higher than a typical clerk's or mechanic's salary. In addition, a patrol officer represents a considerable investment in training that should not be wasted on tasks more suitable to noncommissioned personnel.[10]

Aside from these practical considerations, there also have been changes in the attitudes of most police administrators. Maintaining the police mystique is no longer seen as necessary, or even desirable. Modern administrators are more interested in building bridges between the police and the public—not in stocking the moat with alligators. By bringing noncommissioned personnel into the agency at all levels, the administrator helps to break down the fortress mentality that once permeated police thinking.

Noncommissioned personnel also bring to their jobs a broader range of skills and talents than are likely to be found among police personnel. People with special ability and experience in, say, computer programming can make a substantial contribution to a police agency.

However, noncommissioned support personnel usually require some training in law enforcement and police policies if they are to apply their particular skills successfully. For example, a secretary should know enough about basic police procedure to decide whether "filed," "filled," or "field" is the correct word in this sentence:

Officer Jones submitted a _____ interview report on this subject yesterday.

The basic training needs of noncommissioned auxiliary support personnel may be satisfied by providing a fairly brief orientation course through the agency's own academy or by encouraging new noncommissioned personnel to enroll in an introductory course on the criminal justice system at a local community college. In addition, all new noncommissioned personnel should be given a planned on-the-job training program under the supervision of a commissioned police officer (usually the officer who will supervise the new employee).

There are some disadvantages in using noncommissioned personnel in auxiliary support roles. Personnel turnover is generally higher than it is among police officers. In addition, since noncommissioned employees have not gone through the rigorous screening and selection process applied to police recruits, the noncommissioned personnel are likely to have (on the average) lower qualifications in terms of educational levels, work experience, and personal backgrounds. They may be somewhat less resistant to the opportunities for corruption that are unavoidably present in law enforcement. Since they have no legal authority as law enforcement officers, it may be necessary to protect some sensitive records and police activities from them. Finally, commissioned officers may resist accepting direction from noncommissioned employees, which means that the latter are restricted to subordinate positions.

Nevertheless, despite the disadvantages, the practical benefits of using noncommissioned personnel in most auxiliary support roles are so great that this practice is likely to grow. Upgrading the qualifications and abilities of police officers is one of the highest priorities of modern police administrators, but one of the side effects is that highly qualified, professionally trained officers are simply too valuable to waste on routine housekeeping tasks.

Some of the support services listed above demand the special training and qualifications of commissioned law enforcement officers. At the very least, an experienced senior officer should manage such technical elements as communications, personnel training, crime analysis, and the jail. In some states, all jail personnel must be either commissioned law enforcement officers or certified correctional officers.

Building Maintenance and Custodial Services

If this function is not served by the parent government or, in the case of rented facilities, the owner of the building, the police agency must employ a custodial staff and some maintenance personnel. The skills required include those of an electrician, plumber, and carpenter; however, it is sometimes possible to find individuals who have two or more of those skills and who are able to handle the agency's work load. The building maintenance and custodial staff should be under the supervision of the police administrator responsible for administrative services; in a small agency, this is likely to be the agency's chief executive.

Vehicle Maintenance

We have previously discussed police fleet maintenance (see Chapter 7). Usually it is preferable to use noncommissioned personnel for this function; they should be under the supervision of the official responsible for administrative or technical services.

Secretarial, Clerical, and Office Management Services

Most police agencies have a secretarial and clerical pool whose members provide basic office services to all personnel as needed. Larger agencies may have a few secretaries assigned to individual administrators or to units such as records and identification. Pool employees should be supervised by the chief of administrative services; secretaries or clerks assigned to specific officials or units should be supervised by them.

Financial Management Services

This is one function that is almost always provided by the parent government. Nevertheless, every police agency (except perhaps the very smallest ones) should have at least a bookkeeper to maintain, on a day-to-day basis, accurate accounts of expenditures. Larger agencies may require a separate accounting staff to handle revenues from various sources, payroll accounting, and purchases and other disbursements. These personnel should be under the supervision of the chief of administrative services.

Personnel Management

Again, this function often is provided by the parent government and sometimes by a completely separate civil service or merit system agency. Still, every police agency should have at least a personnel clerk, and preferably a staff of experienced personnel administrators, to plan and carry out recruitment and selection campaigns, to maintain records of promotions and other personnel actions, to supervise the administration of union contracts, and to ensure that personnel benefits (such as health insurance and pension plans) are properly administered. The personnel management function should be supervised by the chief of administrative services or by the agency's chief executive.

Purchasing and Property Management

Since we discussed this function at considerable length in Chapter 10, there is no need to repeat it here. Purchasing and property management services should be supervised by the chief of administrative services; the management of evidence, found property, and other personal property that does not belong to the agency should be at least supervised by a commissioned officer.

Communications and Information Services

Again, these functions were described in Chapter 9. Because of their technical nature and vital importance to effective police operations, communications and records services must be under the direct management of experienced police administrators. Many administrators feel that only commissioned officers should act as radio dispatchers, partly because of the sensitive information that must be handled and partly because the dispatcher actually serves as the *de facto* commander of most routine patrol operations. However, many agencies have had great success in using noncommissioned personnel as dispatchers, provided that an experienced commissioned officer is constantly present to supervise the dispatching operation and assume command in emergencies.

Public Information

Police activities and criminal incidents are of constant interest to the general public, and the news media demand access to information about these matters. Every police agency should have one designated senior official who is authorized to act as the official spokesperson for the department. In addition, except in very small agencies, the public information officer should make a positive effort to inform the community, through the news media, of significant activities and events. Larger agencies, especially those in major metropolitan areas and those whose jurisdiction is statewide, may require a staff of public information specialists: writers, audiovisual materials producers, and others. The latter do not need to be commissioned officers, but should be under the direct supervision of an experienced officer.[11]

Legal Counsel

Every police agency should have access to the services of the city or county attorney or the state attorney general for legal counsel. However, those individuals are not always readily available when an urgent question arises. Arrangements can be made to employ a private attorney on a retainer basis (a regular fee is paid, entitling the client to a certain amount of service). This may be a satisfactory solution for many small and medium-sized agencies. Larger agencies usually should have at least one qualified attorney on the agency's staff. Very large agencies may require several attorneys, along with their own support personnel. Usually the department's attorney or chief legal counsel is considered an administrative officer and is responsible directly to the chief executive.

Personnel Training

Both preservice and in-service training of all commissioned and noncommissioned personnel should be provided by a permanent training staff; in smaller agencies, this function may be combined with the personnel management function. Training staff members should include experienced police officers. However, special expertise in training and education is also needed and may be provided by noncommissioned personnel; in some agencies, the training staff is directed not by a senior police officer but by a qualified educator. Whatever the composition of the training staff may be, they should be supervised by the official responsible for administrative services.

Criminalistics Services

Evidence technicians and laboratory personnel do not need to be commissioned officers; conversely, however, there is no reason that commissioned officers with special interests in criminalistics cannot be assigned to that function. As we noted in Chapter 15, agencies that are too small to maintain a full-time criminalistics staff may rely instead on a regional laboratory or some other cooperative arrangement. Criminalistics should be under the command of the chief of technical services or the head of the agency's criminal investigations unit.

Crime Analysis, Intelligence, or Planning Services

Earlier we discussed the use of tactical units to attack specific types of crimes, on the basis of analyses of criminal activity.[12] Those analyses may be performed by a technical staff, sometimes called the **crime analysis unit**; other terms for the same function are **intelligence unit** and **planning unit**. In some agencies, the intelligence unit is concerned primarily or exclusively with information about organized crime, a field that is considerably narrower than that of a crime analysis unit.[13] Also, in some agencies, the planning unit is responsible for a broader range of functions than a crime analysis unit; planners may not only collect and analyze information about criminal activities, but also develop plans for long-range programs, special projects, personnel development, and budgeting.

Regardless of the administrative structure adopted, the crime analysis, intelligence, or planning unit should be commanded by an experienced police officer. Other members of the staff do not need to be commissioned officers; often it is preferable to employ technical specialists such as demographers (persons who study population trends), computer operators, statisticians, and so on. Depending on its specific responsibilities, the unit may be supervised by the chief of the criminal investigations element, by the head of the organized crimes unit, by the official responsible for the administration of technical services, or by the chief executive of the agency.

Jail Operations

Most municipal police agencies are required to operate some kind of detention facility to hold persons who have been arrested and are awaiting a hearing before a magistrate. Prisoners awaiting trial who have not been released on bail may be held either by the municipal agency or, more often, transferred to a county or state facility. Usually prisoners in a city detention facility are held only for a short period, as little as one or two hours and not more than a week.

Prisoners in county and state facilities are more often held for longer periods, either awaiting trial or serving a sentence. A county jail or state prison is not merely a detention facility, it is a correctional institution whose responsibilities include (to some degree) the rehabilitation of inmates.[14]

The requirements of both short-term detention facilities and long-term correctional institutions are spelled out in state laws and, increasingly, federal laws and court decisions. In the most general terms, the operators of a jail or prison have two major duties: to prevent prisoners from leaving and to protect the prisoners' health and welfare while they are being detained. The specific means of discharging both responsibilities are far too complex to discuss here.

As noted earlier, most states require that custodial personnel in jails and prisons be either commissioned law enforcement officers or certified correctional officers. Other jail staff members (cooks, rehabilitation specialists, librarians, and so forth) usually are not commissioned officers. Any detention facility operated by a municipal police department must be under the immediate management of a senior police official, often the chief executive.

This brief overview of support services is intended only to suggest the kinds of services that are required by most police agencies and the kinds of administrative and management structures that are likely to be successful. However, each law enforcement agency has its own needs, and police administrators have their own preferences. The organization of support services is one area in which there are no universal rules; administrators should apply their creativity and ingenuity to provide for necessary services in the most effective and efficient manner possible.

CHIEF ABEL'S IN BASKET

Instructions

In this exercise, you are to assume the role of E. Z. Abel, chief of the City Police Department. The documents below have been selected from Chief Abel's in basket. Read them with care. If you need more information about City or its police department, refer to the data bank in the front of the book. After you have studied the documents, complete these steps:

1. State the problem or problems these documents present to Chief Abel.
2. List as many alternative solutions as you can.
3. Select the solution you think would be best, and give your reasons for choosing it.

CITY POLICE DEPARTMENT
Interoffice Memorandum

FROM: Lt. W. Lawrence and Lt. H. Washington

TO: Chief Abel

SUBJECT: Proposed Crime Prevention Program   DATE: 4 Nov 19--

SIR:

As commanders of the Crimes Against Persons and Crimes Against Property Sections of the Detective Bureau, we are very much aware that many of the crimes reported to our Dept. could have been prevented, if people had just used some common sense and simple prevention methods. It appears to us that the general public is not aware of these methods. We have read about successful crime prevention programs based on the Neighborhood or Citizens' Crime Watch concept in other cities, and we would like to set up that kind of progam in City. As far as we know, it has never been tried here, but we think it would work.

We talked about this to Lt. Smith of the Crime Prevention Section and he said he just doesn't have the staff for this kind of program. We also discussed it with Captain Bowen and he told us to present it directly to you. It is our feeling that if this project is

Page 2.

left to Lt. Smith and his people, it will never get done. Therefore, we would like to set it up under our direct control.

We would need probably two or three Patrol Officers and at least one Sergeant to plan and carry out the program. At this time, we do not have a specific, detailed proposal, but we would like to know if you are interested before we go any farther. Thank you in advance for your consideration.

William Lawrence, Lieutenant
Henry Washington, Lieutenant
Detective Bureau

CITY POLICE DEPARTMENT
Interoffice Memorandum

FROM: Sgt. Lloyd James, Community Relations

TO: Chief Abel

SUBJECT: Request for Reassignment   DATE: 6 Nov 19--

SIR:

I respectfully request transfer to one of the operating sections of the Criminal Investigations Bureau. I have discussed this request with Lt. Smith, my superior, and he said he has no objection.

The reason for my request is that I feel my training and experience are being wasted in my present position. As the only member of the Community Relations Unit, there is nothing much I can do, and Lt. Smith has said several times that there is no chance of getting more personnel for this Unit. I have tried to keep in touch with community leaders and advise other Units of any problems or concerns in the community, but it seems that the other Units in this Dept. are not especially interested in my advice and information.

Page 2.

I have a very good record from the six years I served in Patrol, including two Commendations from Chief Ellis. For the last three years, I feel like I have been spinning my wheels, so to speak, in Community Relations, and I would like to get back to doing real police work.

I will be very grateful for your favorable consideration of this request.

Lloyd James, Sergeant
Community Relations Unit

Police powerless as Hills Burglar strikes again

City Police officials have expressed frustration and despair in the wake of the eighth commercial burglary this month in the Western Hills area.

Last night, Hillside Drugs at 1807 Hillside Drive was burglarized. The amount of the loss was not disclosed, but the burglar's methods were similar to those used last Friday night in the burglary of the Columbia Gems Co., a jewlery store at Hillside and Columbia Blvd.

Police detective Sgt. Jeffrey Anderson told reporters, "We think the same guys are doing all these, but we don't have enough evidence to find them." According to Anderson, in six of the eight burglaries in the Western Hills area, the burglars entered through a back door by removing the lock, after disabling the burglar alarm system. "These guys obviously know what they're doing,"

Anderson said. He added, "With just two patrol cars in that part of town, we can't be everywhere."

Lt. Henry Washington, commander of the Property Crimes Section of the Police Dept., said, "We're dealing with some real pros here. Most of the places have had good security. I don't know how we're going to stop them."

Police Chief E. Z. Abel was not available for comment.

Vic Timms, owner of Hillside Drugs, commented, "I'm not really too surprised. I figured it was just a matter of time before they got around to my place. Now I'm wondering what this will do to my insurance rates." He said the thieves took an undetermined quantity of drugs and merchandise, but no cash. "I don't keep money in the store, not with all these burglaries," Timms said.

CITY POLICE DEPARTMENT
Interoffice Memorandum

FROM:	M. Lewis, Capt., Tech. Svcs.	
TO:	Chief Abel	
SUBJECT:	Vacation Leave Policy	DATE: 7 Nov 19--

SIR:

With the Christmas holiday season approaching, I would like to call your attention to a problem we have had in past years.

Chief Ellis always prohibited any commissioned officers from taking leave or vacation time during the holidays because it is a very busy time. However, this policy only applied to officers in Patrol and Criminal Investigations. It did not apply to personnel in Technical Services or Administrative.

Because of this policy, we have always had a lot of conflict over when people are going to take their leave. Last year, both Sgts. Matthews and Davis wanted to take off the same week (the week before Christmas). This would have left us without any Fleet Maintenance. I allowed Sgt. Matthews to go the week before Christmas and Sgt. Davis the week after. By the time they were both back on duty, the backlog of work was twice as big as usual. At the present time, they were still way behind on getting cars back on the street.

Page 2.

Fleet is not the only problem. The people in Communications, Records, and Traffic also want to takeleave during the holidays. Last year I let the Traffic people take their leave 2 weeks before Christmas or the week after New Years, so most of them were here during the busiest period. However, I had to let Lt. Young take his vacation the week after Christmas. I also had a real problem juggling the leaves for the Sergeants in Jail Operations.

Would you please consider prohibiting all commissioned personnel from taking vacation during the holidays? This would make my life a lot simpler.

M. Lewis, Captain
Technical Services

1. The primary purpose of a juvenile crime unit is:
    (a) To obtain sufficient evidence against juvenile offenders that they will be convicted for their crimes.
    (b) To remove juvenile offenders from the influence of their parents, peers, and others who are responsible for their antisocial attitudes.
    (c) To identify the victims of juvenile crimes.
    (d) To identify juvenile offenders so that they can be rehabilitated.
    (e) To prevent adults from committing crimes against juveniles.

2. True or False: The criminal laws that apply to juvenile offenders are precisely the same as those that apply to adult criminals.

3. Community relations units generally are:
    (a) Ineffective in promoting a positive image of the police.
    (b) Designed to deliver social-welfare services to the poor and oppressed minorities.
    (c) Intended partly to provide the police with information about social conditions in the community.
    (d) Established to provide the news media with accurate information from the police point of view.
    (e) Organized only as a response to pressure from community political leaders.

4. Tactical units may use a variety of techniques, including:
    (a) The use of unmarked patrol vehicles.
    (b) Fixed surveillances (stakeouts) of potential crime sites.
    (c) Counselling with offenders and their parents.
    (d) Marked patrol vehicles.
    (e) "Rappelling" to gain access to a sniper or barricaded suspect.

5. True or False: A special situations unit may consist of regular patrol officers and investigators who respond to crises on an on-call basis.

6. Noncommissioned personnel are often employed in police agencies because:
    (a) Commissioned officers are too valuable to use for routine housekeeping chores.
    (b) Noncommissioned personnel often have special skills or talents that are not available among the commissioned officers.
    (c) Noncommissioned personnel usually are paid less than commissioned personnel.
    (d) Personnel turnover is often lower among noncommissioned staff.
    (e) Noncommissioned personnel are usually better educated and more highly motivated than regular police officers.

7. The functions of a personnel management unit include:
    (a) Maintaining records of promotions and other personnel actions.
    (b) Planning and conducting recruitment campaigns.
    (c) Administering employee contracts with unions or union-like organizations.
    (d) Administering health insurance and other employee benefit programs.

    (e)   All of the above.

    (f)   None of the above.

8. A retainer may be used:

    (a)   To guarantee that highly trained personnel will not leave the agency unexpectedly.

    (b)   To secure a minimum level of services from a private attorney.

    (c)   To ensure that a city or county attorney will be available at all times to answer questions.

    (d)   To protect a police agency from any legal problems that might arise.

    (e)   To reduce the need for commissioned officers to be assigned to non-law-enforcement duties.

9. True or False: The duties of a crime analysis unit, intelligence unit, or planning unit are essentially the same in all police agencies.

10. The major responsibilities of jail administrators are:

    (a)   To prevent prisoners from leaving.

    (b)   To operate the jail as economically as possible.

    (c)   To assist police officers in making legal arrests.

    (d)   To protect the health and welfare of prisoners.

    (e)   To deliver prisoners promptly to the courts for trial and sentencing.

REFERENCES

1. William J. Bopp, "Police History and Social Consciousness," in William J. Bopp, ed., *Police Administration: Selected Readings*, Boston: Holbrook Press, 1975, page 77.

2. Charles D. Hale, *Fundamentals of Police Administration*, Boston: Holbrook Press, 1977, page 142.

3. *Task Force Report: Corrections*, Washington, D.C.: President's Commission on Law Enforcement and the Administration of Justice, 1967, pages 23–24.

4. Hale, pages 144–146.

5. *Reports of the National Juvenile Justice Assessment Centers: The Shadows of Distress*, Washington, D.C.: U.S. Dept. of Justice, Law Enforcement Assistance Administration, 1980, pages 34–43.

6. Hale, page 142.

7. Arthur Niederhoffer and Alexander B. Smith, *New Directions of Police–Community Relations*, San Francisco: Rinehart Press, 1974, pages 2–6.

8. Jerry L. Carlin and Colin L. Moodie, "A Comparison of Some Patrol Methods," in Bopp, pages 251–252.

9. William J. Bopp, "The Traditional Approach to Police Organization," in Bopp, pages 79–80.

10. Robert D. Pursley, "Traditional Police Organization: A Portent of Failure?", in Bopp, pages 83–85.

11. E. M. Davis, "A Press Relations Guide for Peace Officers," in Bopp, pages 44–53.

12. Richard H. Snibbe, "A Concept for Police in Crime Prevention," in Bopp, pages 204–210.

13. Hale, pages 167–169; see also Donald O. Schultz and Loran A. Norton, *Police Operational Intelligence*, Springfield, Ill.: Charles C. Thomas, 1973.

14. *A Handbook on Jail Administration*, Washington, D.C.: National Sheriffs' Association, 1974, pages 9–10.

EPILOGUE
THE POLICE AND THE COMMUNITY

THROUGHOUT THIS BOOK WE HAVE BEEN CONCERNED principally with the internal operations of police agencies, particularly with the duties of administrators to ensure that their agencies operate effectively and efficiently. We have not taken the time to examine the relationship between a police agency and the community it serves, except when that relationship has an immediate bearing on the workings of the agency.

That relationship certainly deserves closer scrutiny; in fact, it needs to be explored in a complete, separate text. The police-community relationship is too complex to be given once-over-lightly treatment; it is too vital to be regarded as merely the concern of the police community relations unit or public information staff. Every police administrator, manager, supervisor, and officer must be aware of, sensitive to, and responsive to the needs, interests, and demands of the community, however they might be expressed.

Without going into great detail, we will try to summarize some of the main concerns of police administrators with regard to the external environment (the term sometimes used to encompass the various segments of the community).

THE POLICE AND LOCAL GOVERNMENT

The first and most important characteristic of every American community is that its government is organized along the lines of a representative democracy. This means that the citizens choose individuals to represent their interests; the elected representatives, in turn, appoint other individuals to manage the day-to-day affairs of government. Among the officials who are usually appointed are the chief executives of law enforcement agencies; an important exception is that most sheriffs, and a few heads of state police agencies, are themselves elected by the citizens.

Police executives, whether appointed or elected in their own right, are subject to the authority and supervision of elected officials in all three branches of government. The head of the executive branch (mayor, county commissioner, or governor) is responsible for seeing that the laws are properly enforced; the legislators (city council or aldermen, county supervisors, and state legislators) enact the laws that are to be enforced, enact laws that define how enforcement agencies are to be organized and operated, and provide the public funds that are required by law enforcement agencies. The judicial branch—the judges and, to a lesser extent, prosecutors—determine the manner in which law-enforcement authority is to be exercised.

It is hardly any wonder that police administrators often find themselves resentful of the politicians who have authority over law enforcement. The chief executive of the parent government, the legislators, and the judicial officers often have very different ideas about how the law-enforcement mission should be carried out and often make different, even conflicting, demands on the police. In many municipal governments, yet another element—the city manager, appointed by the city council—has authority over the police department. Ever since the police reform movement began in the late nineteenth century, police administrators have tried to remove themselves from political influence, to give themselves as great a degree of freedom as possible to carry out their duties as they see fit.

Removing the police from the political system is impossible. Without the police, the political system would have no means of enforcing its decisions; without the political system, the police have no reason to exist. What is possible, and indeed necessary, is to ensure that the political system does not influence the police in ways that are contrary to the interests of the public. No sensible person wants to go back to the kind of political domination of the police that existed a hundred years ago (and that still lingers, in a few places, to this day).

The police are subject to the authority of the executive branch of government because that branch has the legal responsibility of carrying out the decisions made by the legislative branch.

The police are subject to the authority of the legislative branch of government because that branch has the legal responsibility of making decisions; among those decisions are the enactment of laws and the provision of public funds for public purposes.

The police are subject to the authority of the judicial branch of government because that branch has the legal responsibility of ensuring that the laws are enforced fairly and of protecting individual citizens from the improper exercise of political authority.

Any attempt by the police to remove themselves from the authority of any of the three branches of government would be a direct repudiation of the principles of representative democracy. The police are not, and cannot be, a law unto themselves.

Unfortunately, it is possible for any of the three branches of government to become corrupt and for members of the three branches to exercise their authority improperly. A member of the executive branch may have a personal, selfish interest in seeing that certain laws are not enforced at all, or are enforced unequally. The mayor's brother-in-law might be a slum landlord who is not interested in having his property condemned by the building inspectors. The governor might be receiving bribes in return for awarding contracts to crooked highway contractors. Members of the legislative branch may be improperly influenced to enact laws—or not to enact certain laws—that favor the interests of one or another segment of the public. Members of the judicial branch may believe, in all sincerity, that their personal ideals are superior to the dictates of the law, and that their own interpretations of right and wrong are more important than the constitutional rights of citizens.

The police often find themselves aware of, and sometimes directly or indirectly involved in, abuses of the political system. For the police administrator, any such situation presents a powerful dilemma. The administrator may be under considerable pressure to overlook, tolerate, or even participate in corrupt practices. Failure to go along may bring some form of retaliation. A corrupt political official, given the opportunity, will not hesitate to fire a police administrator who is uncooperative. More subtly, a corrupt public official may find indirect ways to obstruct, even cripple, the effective operation of the law enforcement agency. Laws can be passed, or administrative regulations enacted (which often have the full force of laws), to limit the ability of the police to carry out their duties.

Fighting political corruption is, from the police administrator's point of view, fraught with danger. On the other hand, *not* fighting corruption is an abdication of the police duty and inevitably leads to even more corruption and abuse. A person cannot live in a burning house by choosing not to breathe.

The solution is not to abandon the burning house but to fight the fire *with the help of others*. Even in the most thoroughly corrupt government, there are individuals whose integrity and concern for justice have not been impaired. A police administrator must locate and identify those individuals, whether they are in positions of power or not. With their help, evidence of corruption must be gathered, just as it would be for any other crime.

The aid of the public also may be solicited. Once sufficient evidence has been gathered to ensure that there is a reasonable likelihood of convicting the corrupt individuals, the existence of an investigation should be made public through the news media. Details of the investigation and of the evidence do not have to be revealed, and in fact usually should not be revealed any more than they would be for any other criminal investigation. However, by making the fact of an investigation known to the public, and proceeding openly toward prosecution, the police administrator reduces a corrupt official's opportunities to retaliate.

These are not easy steps to take. Any accusation of corruption or abuse by a public official is bound to stir up controversy. Political supporters of the accused official may themselves attack the accuser, especially if the accused is popular or very powerful. If prosecution of the accused official fails, the consequences for the police administrator are likely to be devastating.

Political corruption is not the only danger facing a police administrator. Elected officials often bring to office their own perceptions of the way government should operate; they also may have obligations to their political supporters. Conflicts between the ideologies and the political interests of different officials may catch the police in a web of controversy, intrigue, and political maneuvering. One faction may demand stronger enforcement while another faction demands more economical government; the first faction may insist on assigning more police to vice enforcement, while the second faction may cause the agency's budget to be cut.

Within reason, these conflicts are legitimate; after all, the basic idea behind representative democracy is that citizens have different ideas about what kind of government they want, and those differences should be resolved through the democratic process. However, these noble principles are not much comfort to the police administrator caught in the cross fire.

The most dangerous course for a police administrator to take is to follow the dictates of whichever faction appears to have a momentary advantage. The second most dangerous course is to ignore the political battle altogether.

A police administrator's first duty, and first loyalty, must be to the public, not to the politicians. Currying the favor of any one political faction is likely to arouse the hostility of all others. Instead, the administrator must rely above all on the fundamental principles of criminal justice, expressed in the federal and state constitutions, that define and limit police authority; second, the administrator must gain and keep the confidence of the public. Politicians, no matter what their ideology, are less likely to attack an agency that enjoys a general (and deserved) reputation for efficiency, effectiveness, and fairness.

Police practices themselves are sometimes the subject of political controversy. When the budget for police service or the techniques of law enforcement are under attack, the best defense is the truth—preferably truth for which there is ample evidence. Facts about the incidence of crime, about the organization and operating policies of the agency, and about the agency's achievements are far more powerful than appeals to political interests or ideologies. An administrator must be capable of explaining precisely why the agency needs the resources contained in its budget; if a budget cannot be defended, it does not deserve to be funded. An administrator also must be capable of giving clear, reasonable explanations of the agency's organization and operations; otherwise, political leaders and the public as a whole are justified in losing confidence in the police.

The details of managing a police agency—buying supplies, recruiting and training personnel, assigning patrol beats, reviewing investigations—are not the crucial tasks for the police administrator. As much as possible, those duties should be delegated to others. The most important duty of the administrator is to represent the agency before the public and its elected representatives. If the administrator fails in that duty, all the rest will count for very little.

POLICE UNIONS AND UNION-LIKE ORGANIZATIONS

Strictly speaking, the members of a police officers' union or union-like organization are the personnel of the police agency and are therefore internal to it. However, we have decided to consider them as part of the external environment because (1) a union or union-like organization is an entity in itself, with interests and resources that may be (and usually are) completely separate from those of the police department; and (2) the relationship between police administrators and the police officers' organizations is much like that of police administrators and other segments of the community.

We have used the cumbersome phrase, "unions and union-like organizations," because historically the police and other public employees have been discouraged (if not actually prohibited) from joining the labor union movement.

The first recorded effort of American police officers to form or join a union occurred in Cincinnati in 1918. Several hundred members of the Cincinnati police force joined the local Central Labor Council and went on strike to protest the arbitrary firing of four fellow officers. The strike lasted only a few days; the officers were persuaded to return to work, and their labor union activity soon dissolved.[1] A year later, Boston police officers formed a union affiliated with the American Federation of Labor and attempted to negotiate collectively for better working conditions (which were, at the time, deplorable). Nineteen officers were immediately suspended for their participation in the union; a few weeks later, about three-fourths of the police force went out on strike. Looting and rioting followed. After four days, the striking officers were fired and replaced; departmental working conditions and salaries were later improved, but the police officers' union was destroyed.[2]

Other police unions were formed before World War I and generally were met with the same intransigent response as in Boston. The public believed, and political leaders declared, that public employees—especially police officers—had no right to form unions or hold strikes. During the 1920s and 1930s, few police officers dared to risk their livelihoods by openly joining unions.

However, there was an alternative route for police officers: forming nonunion associations, such as the Fraternal Order of Police (FOP) and the Patrolmen's Benevolent Association (PBA). The FOP was founded in 1915 to work for the welfare of police officers. PBA's, each independent and autonomous, were formed after World War I, partly as social organizations and partly to promote better working conditions and benefits.

After World War II, established labor unions—mainly under the American Federation of Labor—again attempted to organize police unions, this time with more success. Public attitudes about police unions had relaxed, and union leaders were less inclined to use threats and inflammatory rhetoric to promote their cause. Some police unions renounced the right to strike. By the early 1960s, federal and some state laws prohibiting public employees from forming unions were overturned; as of the end of the 1960s, some 20 states had specific provisions for collective bargaining by public employees, and similar laws have been enacted in most states since then.

There remains a good deal of public concern about the possibility that the police will go out on strike, leaving a community defenseless against criminals. The Boston strike is almost always cited as the cautionary example. However, studies of more recent police strikes indicate that looting and rioting do not immediately break out when the police walk off the job.[3] Usually a police strike is the desperate act of officers who have found no other way to overcome the refusal of political leaders to consider their demands. Usually, too, there is ample time for police administrators to develop a contingency plan which, once the strike occurs, will provide at least a minimal level of police service. (It is not true that criminals "go on holiday" when the police strike. However, it does appear to be true that during a police strike only the most serious crimes are reported; consequently, the official crime rates often go down drastically.) In short, the fears of the public are somewhat exaggerated, if not entirely groundless.

It is important to realize that the police administrator can do little to prevent police officers from joining unions. Police officers have the same right to associate as any other citizens; even if unions are prohibited, they will form fraternal orders or benevolent associations that eventually act like unions. In fact, many Police Benevolent Associations have affiliated with the AFL-CIO and other labor organizations.

It is also important to understand that the police administrator cannot, singlehandedly, prevent officers from going on strike. Once a strike occurs, there is very little that the administrator can do about it, other than to put into effect a contingency plan to keep the community from being defenseless.

A police administrator is merely another public employee. He or she usually does not have the authority to either grant or refuse the officers' demands; that authority is held by the parent government and is exercised by the elected political officials. They may delegate authority to negotiate with the union, but ultimately the administrator can neither give nor withhold what the union wants.

In point of fact, most police administrators do not even have the authority to negotiate with employee organizations. Probably this is for the best. Negotiations between employees and employers tend to involve controversial issues; both sides typically approach negotiations as adversaries. Resentment, frustration, and hostility are not uncommon. The police administrator who takes an active part in union negotiations must step out of the role of leader and into the role of opponent. Whatever the outcome of the negotiations, it may be difficult for the administrator to take up the role of leader again; there may be a residue of bitterness that will poison the relationship between the administrator and officers for years to come.

Since the political officials (including, in many cases, the city manager) have the authority to grant whatever benefits the union is demanding, they are the ones who should conduct negotiations, or at least they should assume the responsibility for negotiations conducted by their immediate subordinates. If negotiations fail and the union calls a strike or other job action (such as encouraging officers to call in sick), the administrator is well advised to let the political officials resolve the matter. The police administrator's duty is to see that essential police services are delivered, no matter what. This may require using managers and other ranking officers as temporary substitutes for field officers; in extreme cases, it may be necessary to request assistance from the state police or National Guard. Otherwise, the administrator should refrain from making public statements or taking any action that will further inflame the situation.

Fortunately, police strikes are rare; usually they last only a few days; and the consequences are not as disastrous as the public fears. In most cases, they are also futile: The striking officers do not get what they wanted, and sometimes a temporary victory leads to retaliation by the political officials that is more costly than the union leaders anticipated.

THE POLICE AND THE NEWS MEDIA

The news media occupy a special place in American society. Even before the right of a free press was guaranteed in the First Amendment to the Constitution, a tradition of journalistic freedom and independence had begun to evolve. In its modern embodiment, this tradition is expressed not only by print journalists but also by broadcast journalists as well.

One of the elements of that tradition is the right of journalists to investigate, question, and criticize the actions of government. Any police officer or administrator who feels that law enforcement should be immune from that right is sadly mistaken. Journalists not only have a right to question the police but, according to their traditions, a duty to do so.

This does not mean that the police and the news media are necessarily enemies. It does mean that they are not necessarily friendly. The best relationship between the police and the news media is one based on mutual respect, cooperation when appropriate, and understanding of one another's needs.

The police do need the news media. The public has a great interest in the activities of the police, not only because some people find police activities exciting and glamorous, but because citizens naturally want to know how well they are being protected from crime. By providing full, accurate information about police activity to the news media (who then are responsible for conveying the information to the public), the police can reassure the community that criminal behavior is being dealt with effectively.

By the same token, the police often need the active assistance of the public. Very few crimes occur without someone (other than the perpetrator and the victim) having some knowledge about them. Citizens may observe a crime without realizing the significance of what they have seen, or may be reluctant to get involved. Appeals to the public for information and assistance, whether concerning a specific crime or criminal activity in general, are often remarkably effective. The most efficient way to make such an appeal is through the news media.

The techniques available to the police for developing and maintaining a satisfactory relationship with the news media are too numerous to describe here. Public information is a discipline in itself; valuable texts on the subject are widely available.

However, we are concerned about the attitudes of police administrators toward the news media. Those attitudes seem to range from a naive belief that the news media exist to promote law enforcement, to an attitude of suspicion and hostility.

The news media do not exist to promote law enforcement or any other governmental function. They exist to inform the public about anything, including the activities of government, that is of interest to the public. How, and how well, they discharge that function is not the concern of the police.

Nor do the news media exist to discredit the police. Contrary to the belief of some police administrators, most journalists take seriously their duty to report information fully and accurately. Whether that information is favorable or unfavorable to the police, their duty is to report it. In the long run, newspapers or broadcasters do not profit by waging war on the police or any other governmental agency.

Not all journalists are conscientious and responsible, any more than are all police officers. It sometimes happens that a newspaper editor or a broadcast news director, for whatever reasons, will campaign against the police. When that occurs, the police administrator may feel defensive and frustrated; there are few weapons available to counterattack the news media. However, even in small communities, it is rare for any one news medium to have an absolute monopoly. There may be only one newspaper, but there usually is at least a radio station, if not a television station, serving the same community. Even in rural counties, there are often two or more newspapers that circulate throughout the county and usually radio and television stations in nearby communities.

In other words, if one news medium treats the police unfairly, the administrator should seek other ways of getting full, accurate information to the public. Any effort to retaliate against the unfair medium is likely to be ineffective and probably counterproductive.

Withholding information from the news media is also ineffective and counterproductive. Competent journalists know that they can get the information they want from any of several different sources. If a police administrator refuses to provide the information they need, for whatever reasons, they will find another source.

Sometimes this puts the administrator in an awkward situation. Detailed information about a criminal investigation should not be made public, since this may hinder the investigation and is likely to interfere with the prosecution of the offender. In such cases, the administrator has a legal duty to withhold information that journalists may feel strongly about. The only recourse for the administrator is to release as much general information as possible and explain candidly why additional information cannot be made public. Again, the majority of journalists will act responsibly; they realize that it is not in their own interests to interfere with the criminal justice system.

Police administrators need to learn as much as they can about the workings of the news media in their own community: what deadlines are imposed on reporters, which reporters and editors are conscientious and responsible in their work, which media are most successful in reaching different segments of the population. This knowledge will give the administrator the considerable advantage of being able to cooperate with the most competent and reliable members of the media and, through them, to ensure that full and accurate information reaches the public.

THE POLICE AND COMMUNITY SERVICE ORGANIZATIONS

The French journalist who visited America in the early 1800s, Alexis de Tocqueville, observed that Americans were a nation of organizers and joiners. It seems to be characteristic of people in our society that they form committees, clubs, and associations for every conceivable purpose.

In every community, large or small, there are numerous organizations devoted to providing some sort of service to the public. These organizations can be a valuable resource to the police.

Every law enforcement agency requires the support of the public. The funds to operate the agency come ultimately from taxes paid by the public, and consequently the public has a considerable interest in how those funds are spent. Beyond that, the public can either comply with the law voluntarily or, by refusing to comply, increase the work load of the police; the public can either assist the police by voluntarily giving information about criminal activity or, by refusing to come forward, hinder police efforts to suppress crime.

Community service organizations contain, among their members, citizens who are active in community affairs and, in many cases, citizens who influence the attitudes and opinions of others. At the very least, it can be valuable for the police administrator to enlist the support of community service organizations in promoting positive attitudes toward the police.

The members of community service organizations also may be in a position to support the police in many other ways. They may endorse the position of the law enforcement agency with regard to pending legislation. They may help to distribute crime-prevention literature and information. They may help to set up neighborhood crime watches and other police-assistance organizations. In Chapter 9, we discussed the possibility of calling on the operators of radio-equipped fleets and other two-way radio operators (such as Citizens Band operators) to report crimes and other incidents that require police services.

Some community service groups may be organized specifically to provide volunteer help for the police. Many police departments sponsor law enforcement "posts" of Explorer Scouts (affiliated with the Boy Scouts of America) and similar youth groups. Some agencies have had success with "police buddy" and police reserve groups. Sometimes, especially in smaller communities, volunteer help might simply take the form of unpaid, part-time clerical workers to maintain a satisfactory records system.

The point is that every police administrator should take the initiative in reaching out to all segments of the community for support and assistance. Community service organizations, whatever their primary purpose, offer a vehicle for the administrator to solicit the good will and support of the community. It is up to the administrator to create and seize this opportunity. The potential benefits are immense, and the costs are virtually none. Few other activities offer that kind of cost-benefit ratio.

REFERENCES

1. John H. Burpo, *The Police Labor Movement*, Springfield, Ill.: Charles C. Thomas, 1971, page 3.
2. Burpo, pages 4–5.
3. *Police Strikes: Causes and Prevention*, Washington, D.C.: International Association of Chiefs of Police, 1979.

GLOSSARY

A **Academy:** A training and educational institution operated by a law enforcement agency or cooperatively by several law enforcement agencies.

Account: In bookkeeping and budgeting, the heading or category under which all entries of the same type are recorded.

Accountability: In a hierarchical organization, the principle that each subordinate must report to his or her superior and account for his or her actions.

Administration: In any organization, the element that is responsible for making and enforcing policies, allocating resources, and coordinating activities to fulfill the organization's primary goals or purpose.

Aerial surveillance: The observation of people or things from the air, as from an airplane or helicopter.

Affirmative action plan: A plan, usually but not always submitted for approval to the *Equal Employment Opportunity Commission*, stating an organization's goals for achieving equal employment opportunities and how those goals are to be accomplished.

Amortization: The distribution of a capital expense over the useful life of the item; see *capital budget*.

Assessment center method: A method of evaluating applicants for police jobs, by administering a series of tests (often including *simulation tests* and *performance tests*), each of which is separately assessed by two or more evaluators; often but not necessarily involving a testing site chosen and prepared specifically for this purpose.

Attrition: Loss due to normal causes; for example, the loss of personnel due to retirement, voluntary termination, death in service, etc.

Audit: A careful review of financial (or other) records to determine their accuracy and completeness.

Authority: In any organization, the right of an individual to make certain decisions and/or to require subordinates to perform certain tasks.

Auxiliary support unit: In a police agency, any element whose primary responsibility is to support law enforcement activities by providing various technical or housekeeping services.

B **"Bad apple" theory:** The theory (generally discredited) that nearly all police officers are honest, and that any dishonest or corrupt activity within a police agency is attributable to a few dishonest employees.

Bailiff: Originally, a local English official, appointed by the nobility, whose principal responsibility was to maintain order and settle local disputes; in modern usage, a law enforcement officer assigned to the courts.

Basic training: The training given to new police officers, usually after they have been accepted for employment but before they are assigned to actual duties.

Behavioral theory: In management science, the theory that increased productivity and superior employee performance can be obtained by accommodating the employees' personal motivations and needs.

Body armor: A device (often called a bulletproof vest) consisting of a vest or jacket filled with a shock- and impact-absorbing material, designed to protect the wearer from the impact of bullets or other projectiles.

Breath analysis test: A test to determine the approximate concentration of alcohol in a person's body by having the subject breathe into a device containing chemicals that react to the presence of alcohol in the breath; generally used for a *field sobriety test*.

Budget: A plan for the receipt and expenditure of funds for any number of specified purposes over a specified period of time (usually but not necessarily one year).

Budget cycle: The series of events that include the development, approval, execution, and evaluation of a *budget*.

Bulletin: An official document, issued periodically, summarizing a police agency's activities during a preceding period (such as one day or one week) and including other essential information for use by the personnel of a police agency.

Bureaucracy: Any organization, structured into a hierarchy consisting of specialized elements, each responsible for a specific part of the organization's overall tasks; the theory of organization developed by Max Weber, a German sociologist.

C **Calling number display:** In a telephone system, a special feature that displays the telephone number of the person who is calling, so that if necessary the call can be traced.

Capital budget: The budget for the purchase of items that have an expected useful life of more than one year.

Career counselling: In a *career development system*, a specific procedure whereby each supervisor advises or counsels each of his or her subordinates on their current job performance, and offers suggestions for improving performance and methods of attaining individual career goals.

Career development plan: An agreement between an employee and the agency, whereby the employee is assured of certain career opportunities (contingent on such uncontrollable factors as the availability of budgeted funds) in return for the employee's agreement to undertake specified training or other steps to attain a certain level of competency.

Career development system: A system for coordinating the career aspirations of employees with the agency's human resource needs, through *career counselling*, career planning, *job enrichment*, and other methods.

Case report: The complete record of the initial report of a crime and of all police activities taken to identify and apprehend the perpetrator.

Casual surveillance: Incidental observation, by a police officer while carrying out other duties (such as patrol), of the general public for any signs of suspicious or criminal activity.

Certification: Official recognition, such as by a state agency, that an individual has attained a specified level of proficiency by completing a required training course or by similar means.

Chain of command: In any hierarchical organization, the system of relationships between superiors and subordinates through which *authority* and *accountability* pass.

Chain of custody: In reference to evidence, the record of the whereabouts of an item of *physical evidence* from the time it was discovered until it is presented as an exhibit in court.

Chemical Mace: A trademark for a chemical substance, similar to tear gas in its effects, packaged in an aerosol pressure cannister.

Chief: In a police agency, specifically the highest administrative officer or *executive*; often used informally to mean the head of any element of the organization such as chief of detectives.

Child safety restraint: A device intended to protect a child while being transported in a motor vehicle by restraining the child in the event of an accident; usually a special padded seat, held in place by seat belts or other devices.

Citation: A written notice that a person is accused of a misdemeanor offense, such as a traffic violation, and is required to answer the charge in court; used in place of a physical arrest.

Civil Service Commission: An agency, usually established by state law but often organized at the local level, responsible for ensuring that the best available qualified personnel are employed in public agencies; in some cases, also responsible for administering employment contracts between unions or other employee organizations and the public agencies; in some cases, responsible for adjudicating employee *grievances* and other employee matters.

Command vehicle: A police vehicle, usually unmarked, used by plain-clothes officers and administrators.

Commodity: Any item used routinely or continuously, usually purchased in large quantities or on a contract basis for a period of several months to a year.

Communication: The transfer of information over time (by recording) and/or space (by transmission).

Community-centered policing: In principle, the maintenance of a cooperative and mutually supportive relationship between police officers and the community they serve; sometimes taken to mean control of a police agency by politically active individuals in the community.

Community relations: The promotion of positive attitudes between the community and a law enforcement agency.

Community service officer: A person other than a commissioned police officer who assists officers in certain duties (such as *community relations* and crime prevention programs); in some cases, paid, part-time or full-time employees; in other cases, unpaid volunteers; in some cases, applicants for police employment who have not yet met all of the requirements for employment.

Complaint: A report from a citizen that a crime has been, or may have been, committed; generally, any request for police assistance.

Computer-aided dispatching: A system whereby dispatchers are assisted in assigning cases to patrol officers by a computer-based procedure; often, though not necessarily, a system in which communication between the dispatchers and patrol officers (and sometimes other field officers) takes place over a computer-based communications system, with messages received on a mobile computer terminal in police vehicles.

Constable: In medieval England, the person employed to care for the stables who, when the noble's guards were out of the village, acted as a watchman and caretaker; today, an elected county official with limited law-enforcement responsibilities.

Contingency plan: A plan for dealing with certain unusual events such as natural disasters or large-scale disturbances.

Contingency theory: The theory that an effective leader is one who is able to use whatever style or method of leadership is most appropriate to a given group or situation.

Coordination: In any organization, the act of providing for the performance of several tasks or a series of tasks in proper order and relationship to one another.

Corporate model: The general model of organizations in which a *hierarchy* of *authority* and *responsibility* is established and in which specific tasks are assigned according to the principle of *bureaucracy*.

Cost-benefit analysis: A comparison of the costs of a proposed plan of action with the benefits that may be reasonably anticipated if the action is successful.

Cost-benefit assessment: The comparison of several proposed plans of action, all with the same or similar objectives, on the basis of a *cost-benefit analysis* of each proposal.

Covert surveillance: The observation of the public, by a police officer who is hidden from public view, to detect suspicious or illegal activity; often used in traffic law enforcement.

Crime: The violation of any law or local ordinance, so designated by a legislature.

Crime analysis: The study of information about criminal incidents to detect patterns or trends of criminal activity that may be used to predict the need for specific police techniques, such as intensive surveillance of a given geographic area.

Criminal investigation: The use of particular techniques and procedures to identify and apprehend the *perpetrators* of crimes and to gather evidence to demonstrate the perpetrators' guilt in court.

Criminalist: A person, such as an *evidence technician*, who practices *criminalistics*.

Criminalistics: The gathering, processing, analysis, and evaluation of *physical evidence* (and, by extension, the use of polygraphic techniques to evaluate *testimonial evidence*).

Criminology: The scientific study of crime, including such matters as the nature and sources of criminal behavior.

Cross-training: The training of employees who are ordinarily assigned to different tasks, such that each is able to perform the others' work when necessary.

D **Data bank:** In a computer system, an electronic or mechanical file containing a number of *indexed* records.

Debt service: In budget administration, the periodic payment of debt (both principal and interest).

Delegation: In administration, the act of assigning a specific portion of one's *authority* to a subordinate, to enable the subordinate to carry out certain tasks.

Demography: The study of the characteristics of a given population such as rates of births and deaths or rates of migration.

Deployment: The distribution of certain resources, such as personnel, to ensure the performance of a task or the attainment of an objective.

Depreciation: The loss of value of an item, over a period of time, because of its use and normal wear and tear; the value of an item reduced in proportion to the spent part of its expected useful life.

Design constraint: Any preexisting condition that acts to restrict the range of choices that may be exercised in a design process (such as in designing a new building).

Disbursement: Any payment of budgeted funds.

Discipline: Adherence by subordinates to the policies and rules of an organization; originally, obedience to a teacher or leader.

Discretion: The act of making decisions or engaging in activities on one's own initiative and, implicitly, assuming *responsibility* for the consequences.

Dispatcher: In a police organization, an employee (who may be a police officer or not) whose principal duty is to communicate, usually by radio, with field personnel.

Dominance: In the social sciences, the condition in which certain individuals exert influence over the other members of a group by persuasion, force, or otherwise.

Driving while intoxicated (DWI): The crime of operating a motor vehicle while under the intoxicating influence of alcohol, drugs, or any other substance.

E **Efficiency:** The accomplishment of the greatest amount of work for the smallest expenditure of resources.

Ego involvement: The extent or degree to which a person invests with personal significance his or her work and job performance; in cases of excessive ego involvement, any criticism of one's work (expressed or implied) is regarded as an attack on one's person.

Element (of an organization): Any part of an organizational structure; a group of members of an organization who are assigned a given task, or set of tasks, and who have a particular relationship to the rest of the organization.

Eligibility list: In a police agency, the list of persons who have qualified for employment or promotion.

Enforcement: The application of legally given authority to ensure the compliance of other persons with certain laws, rules, or policies.

Equal Employment Opportunity Commission (EEOC): A federal agency authorized by Congress to enforce federal laws that prohibit discrimination in all aspects of employer and employee relationships on the basis of race, ethnic origin, nationality, language, creed, gender, age, or other specified personal characteristics.

Evidence: In law enforcement, anything that bears or conveys information about a criminal act.
Physical evidence: Any physical item that has or may have evidentiary value.
Testimonial evidence: The reports or statements of persons who have or may have knowledge about a crime.

Evidence technician: A person whose assigned job is to discover and collect *physical evidence*.

Executive: In *administration*, the highest position in a *hierarchy*; the person who has *authority* over, and *responsibility* for, all elements of the organization; in government, the branch that is given the duty of enforcing the laws established by the legislature.

External funds: Funds available to a police agency from a source other than its parent government.

F **Feedback:** In communications, a message or series of messages transmitted in response to a previous message.

Field interview report: A report made by a police officer recording an encounter with a citizen who is not known to be connected with a particular crime and including the identity of the citizen and any information given by him or her.

Field sobriety test: Any of several procedures used by police officers to determine whether it is likely that a person suspected of *driving while intoxicated* is, in fact, intoxicated.

Field training: That portion of a training program that takes place outside of an *academy* or other formal classroom setting and that includes actual experience in police activities by the trainee, usually under the immediate supervision of an experienced officer.

Flat structure: An organizational structure with a minimum of hierarchical levels.

Flow-through requirements: Any conditions or requirements imposed by the source of funds that are transmitted through intermediary agencies; for example, rules for the use of funds originating in a federal grant that is administered by a state planning agency and that apply to the use of those funds by a local police department.

Forecast: In planning, a prediction of future conditions, based on historical and present conditions and the trends that have been deduced from them.

Functional assignment matrix: A procedure in which the functions of an organization are distributed among the several individuals, or groups of individuals, who are members of the organization.

Functional title: The title given to a position in an organization which describes the duties or functions assigned to that position, without regard to its placement in an organizational *hierarchy*.

G **Goal:** The stated condition that an organization is intended to achieve at some future time; an objective.

Grievance: An expression of dissatisfaction by an employee or group of employees, through specific formal or informal methods to give notice of the grievance to superiors.

H **Hierarchy:** In any organizational structure, an arrangement of elements such that some are superior to others, typically in a pyramid in which one person has the *authority* and *responsibility* of an *executive*, there are some number of intermediate levels of *managers* and *supervisors*, and *operational personnel* are *subordinate* to all others.

"Hot pursuit" law: A law that permits police officers to act under their legal authority outside of their usual jurisdiction if they have directly pursued a suspected criminal who has fled from the original jurisdiction.

Human relations theory: In management science, the theory that worker performance is influenced by the personal relationships among workers.

Impact weapon: A nonlethal weapon designed to subdue a subject by inflicting a forceful, sometimes painful, impact on the person's body.

Incremental method: In budgeting, a presentation of proposed expenditures in which only the changes (increases or decreases) from the previous period's budget are explained.

Independent police station: A police facility that contains all elements of the agency, including administrative, technical, support, and operational units.

Index: A directory to the location of specific items of information contained among the records of a file.

Information: The content and product of human minds; that which may be communicated from one person to another, or stored or transmitted (see *communication*).

Information system: Any set of devices and procedures for acquiring, recording, storing, and/or transmitting *information* for a particular use or purpose.

In-service training: Training provided to employees, usually but not necessarily including formal classroom training, to improve their job performance or increase their range of competencies.

Inspector: Generally, a police rank, usually superior to that of captain; also, a functional title in a police agency: a commissioned officer (usually holding the rank of lieutenant or higher) whose duty is to detect, investigate, and report any instances of improper behavior on the part of other agency personnel.

Institutional cable channels: Communications channels in a cable television system, designed and reserved for use by governmental agencies, commercial organizations, and other institutions, as opposed to channels designed primarily to convey entertainment to the public.

Insubordinate personality: A person characterized by an emotional or psychological inability to accept a reasonable degree of discipline and an inability to assume responsibility for one's own behavior.

Integrated investigations: An organizational structure in a police agency in which both patrol officers and detectives jointly investigate most criminal incidents.

Intelligence unit: An element of a police agency whose principal task is to collect and analyze information about criminal behavior, often limited to organized crimes.

Interaction matrix: A planning device, used principally in designing a building, showing the interactions that occur among the various elements of an organization and between those elements and the general public.

Inventory: An accurate record of items, such as equipment, furniture, and supplies, owned by an organization.

Invoice: A claim for payment, issued by a vendor to a purchaser on the delivery of goods or services.

Item order: The purchase of a single item or group of related items that are not bought on a continuous basis; see *commodity*.

J Job enrichment: In a *career development system*, efforts directed toward making employees' work more satisfying and personally rewarding, usually but not necessarily by providing for a greater degree of *discretion* and autonomy among employees.

Job-related selection criteria: Standards for the selection of new employees that are based on the actual skills, abilities, and personal characteristics needed to perform a given job.

K Kansas City study: An experiment conducted by the Kansas City, Missouri police department to determine the efficiency of various types of preventive patrol, which seemed to show that no one type of patrol is any more effective than any other type in preventing crime.

Knapp Commission: A commission appointed to investigate reports of corruption in the New York City Police Department in the early 1970s and whose conclusions indicated that the *"bad-apple" theory* is not valid.

L Lateral entry: The transfer of a person from one police agency to a similar rank and position in another police agency.

Law Enforcement Assistance Administration (LEAA): An agency of the U.S. Department of Justice, established under the Omnibus Safe Streets and Crime Control Act of 1968, among whose responsibilities was the awarding of funds to state criminal justice planning agencies and, in some instances, directly to local police agencies; the agency was severely reduced in 1979 and effectively abolished thereafter.

Leadership: The act or quality of inducing other persons, usually by persuasion, to attain certain goals or purposes; also, those persons who collectively provide leadership in an organization (usually those who hold administrative positions).

Lexan: A trademark for a product consisting of a plastic, usually transparent, that resists breaking under very high impacts.

Lexow Committee: A committee appointed by the New York State legislature, named for its chairman, Clarence Lexow, appointed in 1894 to investigate complaints of corruption in the New York City Police Department; the Committee's findings were an important stimulus to the first major efforts to reform urban police in the United States.

Limited-access highway: An expressway or other highway designed for high-speed travel, with access permitted only at designated points and with grade-level intersections eliminated as much as possible.

Load-bearing structure: That part of a building which is designed to support the floors above and the roof.

M Mainframe computer: A large, high-speed computer system consisting of one or more high-speed central processing units, various kinds of memory devices, and devices for the entry and retrieval of information; see *microcomputer* and *minicomputer*.

Maintenance contract: A contract with a vendor to provide any needed repairs or maintenance on an item of equipment.

Management by objectives (MBO): In management science, the theory that effective and efficient management requires specific procedures by which administrators and other employees establish goals or objectives and evaluate their performance in terms of these goals or objectives.

Management information system: An *information system*, usually but not necessarily including computers and electronic communications systems, designed primarily to provide *managers* and *administrators* with information about the performance of their organization.

Manager: In any bureaucratic organization, an employee who is assigned the *authority* and *responsibility* to provide *coordination* among a number of employees or *elements* of the organization; a position that is superior to that of the *supervisor* and equal to or somewhat subordinate to that of the administrator.

Marshal: An appointed law enforcement officer; at one time, often the title of the principal police officer in a town or county, but used today only as the title of certain law enforcement agents of the federal court system.

Medium (of communication): The means by which *information* is recorded, stored, or transmitted in a *communications* system.

Merit system: A set of procedures and methods designed to ensure that the best-qualified persons are appointed to positions in public agencies; usually administered by a *Civil Service Commission* or similar agency.

Message: A unit of *information*, especially in the act or process of *communication*.

Metro channel: In a police radio system, a channel or frequency that is available to all police and public safety agencies in a city or other area, to permit the coordination of their activities.

Microcomputer: A small computer system in which the central processing unit, a limited amount of memory, and (usually) devices for the entry and retrieval of information are housed in a single unit, often designed for desk-top use, and to which additional memory or other devices may be attached; specifically, a small computer system that uses a single semiconductor device (or in some cases two such devices) to contain all of the central processing and logic elements.

Middle management: The intermediate levels of an organizational *hierarchy*, consisting of *supervisors* and *managers*.

Minicomputer: A medium-sized computer system consisting of a central processing unit, one or more memory devices, and one or more devices for the entry and retrieval of information, generally contained in two or three units; a computer system intermediate in size between a *mainframe computer* and a *microcomputer*.

Minority: A member of an ethnic group that historically has been the victim of discrimination; in federal law, specifically members of the Negro race, persons of Hispanic national origin, persons of Oriental national or ethnic origin, persons of Native American (Indian) and Alaskan native ethnic groups, and certain other specified populations.

Mobile surveillance: The police technique of observing the public for suspicious or possibly criminal behavior from a moving vehicle such as a patrol car.

N **National Crime Information Center (NCIC):** An agency of the federal government, administered by the U.S. Department of Justice, whose responsibility is to collect, index, store, and (under certain conditions) disseminate information about criminal incidents and persons identified as criminals.

National Law Enforcement Telecommunications System (NLETS): A communications system, relying principally on a teletype network, organized and administered by the U.S. Department of Justice, for the communication of information concerning criminal incidents and other law-enforcement matters among federal, state, and local police agencies.

Natural work load: In a police agency, the average amount of work required to be performed by each police officer (or each officer in a specific unit such as patrol) as a result of reports of criminal incidents and other matters that require police attention and services.

911 system: A telephone system in which the directory number, "9-1-1," is reserved for emergency calls, such as calls for police service, fire service, or emergency medical service; usually based at a single location (the 911 center) at which all such calls are received and routed to the appropriate agency.

Nonlethal weapon: Any device intended to exert physical force on persons, such as belligerent subjects, without causing permanent injury or death.

O **Object-of-expenditure budget:** A *budget* in which only the items to be purchased (such as the services of employees) are listed and explained.

Operating budget: A *budget* containing all expenditures for the operations of an agency during a particular period of time, excluding the *capital budget* but including such capital-related items as *amortization* or *debt service*.

Operational definition: A statement of a *goal* or objective in terms that readily permit evaluation of the extent to which the goal or objective is achieved.

Operational personnel: Those members of an organization who are assigned to carry out the specific functions or tasks necessary to achieve the organization's major goals or purposes; the lowest level of a bureaucratic *hierarchy*.

Operational plans: Those plans that concern the routine, day-to-day work of an organization and that are intended to ensure the accomplishment of necessary work.

Organization chart: A graphic display of the structure, such as the bureaucratic *hierarchy*, of an organization.

Organizational theory: In management science, the theory that the structure of an organization is the most important influence on its effectiveness or efficiency.

Organized crime: The criminal activity of persons who engage in crime as a major source of personal income and who cooperate and coordinate illegal activity with one another; often involving the production, sale, and delivery of illegal goods and services such as prostitution or prohibited drugs.

Orientation training: The training given formally or informally to new employees to acquaint them with the rules and policies of the organization and any local conditions that will affect their work; often the final stage of *basic training* or the first stage of *field training* in a police agency.

Overt surveillance: The observation of the public by a police officer, in plain sight of the public, to detect any suspicious or criminal activity.

P **Packing density:** The characteristic of any system or device for recording and storing information that determines the quantity of information that can be stored or recorded in a given amount of space.

Paramilitary: Similar to, but not actually a part of, a military organization.

Patrol-oriented investigation: A type of police agency organizational structure in which nearly all *criminal investigations* are carried out by patrol officers, and detectives serve primarily as technical advisors.

Patrol vehicle: An automobile or other vehicle, usually clearly marked as a police vehicle, used by patrol officers for transportation and as a mobile platform for *preventive patrol*.

Patrol wagon: A large vehicle, often a van or bus, used to transport prisoners from the point of arrest to a jail or other detention facility.

Peer rating: A *performance evaluation* system in which employees evaluate one another's work performance.

Performance budget: A *budget* showing the quantity of work to be produced as a result of each expenditure of funds.

Performance evaluation: A systematic means by which the quality and quantity of work performed by an employee or group of employees are evaluated; a specific instance of the application of this system (that is, the evaluation of the work of a single employee).

Performance test: A procedure used to evaluate applicants for police jobs by requiring them to perform actual or simulated activities similar to those that police officers are expected to perform; generally, any test that measures the actual performance of a person, such as an applicant, rather than the personal qualities or characteristics of the person.

Perpetrator: The person who has committed an act such as a crime.

Planning: The act or process of choosing goals to be attained in the future, methods of attaining those goals, the allocation of resources to carry out those methods, and methods of determining the extent or degree to which the goals are attained.

Planning criteria: The considerations that must be taken into account during a planning process, such as the design of a new building, and that will be used as standards to evaluate whether the plan or design is satisfactory.

Planning-programming-budgeting system (PPBS): A procedure for planning an organization's activities in which the selection of *goals*, the process of *planning*, the development of a *budget*, and the selection of methods of evaluation are coordinated and expressed in a single document.

Police academy: See *academy*.

Police aide: A person, either a paid employee or an unpaid volunteer, who is not a commissioned police officer but who performs various routine tasks to assist and support the work of a police agency; see also *community service officer* and *police cadet*.

Police cadet: Generally, a person who is being trained to become a commissioned police officer; often used to mean specifically a trainee who is assigned to certain minor police tasks, such as directing traffic, under the direct supervision of a commissioned officer, for purposes of training; sometimes used to mean a person appointed to a police position on a probationary status.

Police commission: (1) In some municipalities, an official body consisting of one or more commissioners, either elected or appointed, who individually or collectively act as the *executive* of a police agency; and (2) the legal authorization given to certain persons to act with the *authority* of a police officer.

Precinct: A geographic area within a larger jurisdiction such as a city or county; a portion of a city defined as the area of administrative jurisdiction for a section of a police agency.

Predicted peak work load: The estimated greatest amount of work that must be performed by an individual employee or element of an organization, within a specified geographic area and during a specified period of time.

Predictive validity: In reference to a test or system of evaluation, the extent to which the results of the test accurately indicate the future performance of the person or thing tested.

Preliminary investigation: The initial investigation of a report or complaint of a crime, by the officer responding to the report or complaint (whether detective or patrol officer).

Preservice training: Any training given to a person before he or she is employed by a police agency or, after the person has been employed, before he or she is assigned to regular police duties.

Prevention (of crime): Any effort or activity designed to discourage persons from engaging in criminal behavior, for example, by protecting possible sites of criminal attack or by conspicuously observing persons who might be engaged in criminal activities.

Preventive maintenance: Periodic examination and testing of equipment to determine the extent of wear and need for repairs or replacement, usually on a scheduled basis, as a method of ensuring that the equipment is kept in proper operating condition.

Preventive patrol: A police technique in which patrol officers, when they are not responding to a report or complaint of a crime or otherwise engaged in specific police services, observe the public for any suspicious or criminal activities.

Probation: (1) In corrections, a status to which a convicted offender may be assigned by a court, in which the offender is required to report regularly to an official (probation officer) and to avoid any further illegal behavior, as an alternative to being incarcerated or required to pay a fine; (2) in regard to employees, a status in which a person is employed or assigned to a rank or position temporarily, subject to dismissal or reassignment to a former rank or position if the person's performance is unsatisfactory.

Professionalism: The principle that members of an occupational group (such as police officers) are expected to observe and maintain certain standards of behavior, in exchange for certain privileges accorded by society, including a high degree of autonomy and *authority*.

Program: In *planning* and *administration*, a specific activity or group of activities, to which personnel and other resources have been allocated, which is intended to continue for an indefinite period of time and to accomplish specific goals or purposes.

Program budget: A *budget* in which costs are shown for each of an agency's or organization's *programs*.

Programmatic plans: In *planning*, those plans that define an organization's activities directed toward the achievement of specified goals or purposes; see *program*.

Project: In *planning* and *administration*, an activity or group of activities intended to be carried out within a definite, limited period of time; see also *program*.

Public information: An activity carried out by a police agency or other organization to transmit information about the agency's operations to the general public, and particularly to the news media.

Public record: Any document or other record of the operations and activities of a public agency that, by law, must be accessible to the general public; also, the totality of all such records kept by an agency.

Purchase order: A contract between a purchaser and a vendor, authorizing the vendor to deliver a product or service at an agreed-upon price and committing the purchaser to pay for the item upon delivery.

Purge: With regard to an *information system*, the removal of obsolete, inaccurate, or unneeded records.

Pursuit driving: The police technique of operating a motor vehicle to overtake and arrest a fugitive who is fleeing in another motor vehicle.

Q R **Radio frequency bandwidth:** A portion of the electromagnetic energy spectrum used to transmit intelligible signals; the information-carrying capacity of a given system of radio communications; a particular group of radio channels.

Radiotelephone: A communications system in which voice messages and other information are transmitted over radio frequencies.

Random access memory (RAM): In a computer system, that portion of the system into which programs and data are recorded temporarily and retrieved in no particular order (or in whatever order is dictated by the computer program).

Rank: In a police agency or other organization, a position in the *hierarchy*, indicating a person's degree of *authority* and *responsibility* and usually implying the person's entitlement to certain benefits and privileges such as a given level of compensation.

Recruiting: The activity of seeking qualified applicants for employment.

Relief shift: In a police agency, a group of employees who have no regular duty assignment, but who substitute for other employees (such as patrol officers) when they are absent for any reason.

Request for proposals (RFP): In purchasing, a document published by a prospective purchaser, intended to solicit proposals from prospective vendors, usually for items that are relatively complex and expensive.

Requisition: In purchasing, a document requesting that specified goods or services be obtained, explaining their intended use or the reason they are needed, and stating that adequate funds for the purchase are available.

Research: In *planning*, any activity designed to collect or evaluate information, in preparation for deciding what future activities may be needed or desired.

Response time: The total amount of time between the receipt of a report or complaint of a crime, or other request for police service, and the time a police officer arrives to investigate the report or provide the requested service.

Responsibility: In *administration*, the duty a person has to perform certain acts as a necessary consequence of the *authority* assigned or delegated to that person.

S   **Scientific management:** A management theory based on the principle that there is "one best way" to perform any given job or task, and that establishing the most efficient method of performing each task will increase the overall *efficiency* of an organization.

Selective Traffic Enforcement Program (STEP): A program administered by the federal National Highway Traffic Safety Administration, in which funds are granted to local police agencies (through state planning agencies) to support selective traffic law enforcement projects.

Selective traffic law enforcement: The police technique of identifying specific needs for traffic law enforcement activities on the basis of records of collisions and previous observed violations of the traffic laws.

Sergeans: In medieval England, a watchman assigned to guard a town's or castle's gates; the origin of the military title, *sergeant*.

Service work load: The total volume of work required to be performed by a given police officer or group of officers during a given period of time, including all police services and related duties to be performed, but excluding nonproductive activities.

Sheriff: The principal law enforcement official of county government in most states; usually elected by the public; see also, *shire reeve*.

Shire reeve: In medieval England, the chief official of a town or village, appointed by the local noble to keep the peace, adjudicate local disputes, and administer the noble's laws and regulations; the origin of the modern term, *sheriff*.

Simulation: Something that represents, and appears in a form similar to, something else; in personnel training, an activity that is intended to represent, and be similar to, an actual police task or procedure, used to give trainees practical experience or to evaluate their response to realistic situations.

Socialization: The process by which an individual learns to exhibit the culture of a group to which the individual is a new member.

Source list: In purchasing, a list of possible vendors for a particular type of product or service.

Span of control: The number of subordinate employees or organizational elements that are subject to the control and authority of a particular individual.

Special fund budget: A budget *account* containing funds that may be used only for certain defined purposes.

Specialization: The principle that each employee should be assigned only to specific tasks, which the employee should learn (through training and experience) to perform in a highly effective and efficient manner; therefore, the principle that all of the work of an organization is to be divided into as many specific tasks or types of tasks as possible.

Specialized building network: A number of buildings, designed to serve the total needs of an agency for various kinds of physical facilities, by designing, constructing, or locating each building to serve one or more specific purposes.

Specialized investigation: A system in which most crimes are investigated by detectives who specialize in specific types or categories of offenses.

Special situations unit: An element of a police agency whose assigned duty is to respond to unusual crises in which unconventional police techniques and skills may be required; see also *special weapons and tactics* and *special weapons unit*.

Special weapons and tactics (SWAT): A *special situations unit*, usually made up of officers who have other routine assignments, but who have advanced training in the use of unconventional weapons and police tactics and who are available for use in unusual crises.

Special weapons unit: Another term for a *special weapons and tactics* unit.

Squad car: Originally, an automobile used to transport several police officers (a squad) to the scene of a disturbance or to their foot-patrol beats; an obsolete term for a police patrol vehicle.

Staggered shifts: In patrol allocation, a procedure in which the personnel of one regular shift are divided into two (or more) subshifts to accommodate variation in the service work load during a part of the day.

Standardization: The principle that all personnel assigned to similar duty should have essentially the same uniform and equipment.

Stationary surveillance: A police technique in which one or more officers remain at a fixed location to observe a person or place for suspicious or criminal activity.

Strategic plan: In *planning*, a general plan defining a series of methods or activities that are intended to attain a major goal or purpose, usually over a relatively long period of time.

Subordinate: In any *hierarchy*, a position that is lower than another position (and, by implication, the person in the lower position).

Supervisor: Any person whose assigned duties include observing, evaluating, and, when necessary, correcting the performance or behavior of subordinate employees; more generally, the first level of management above the *operational personnel* in an organization.

T **Tactical unit:** An element of a police organization, sometimes formed on a temporary basis, assigned to perform specific tasks or to use particular police techniques to prevent or detect specific criminal activities.

Tall structure: An organizational structure with a large number of hierarchical levels; see *flat structure*.

Team policing: A system of law enforcement in which one of several organizational schemes is used other than the conventional structure of generalist patrol officers and specialist detectives; usually, a system in which a group of officers, or team, which may include patrol officers, detectives, and sometimes other support personnel, are assigned joint responsibility for all police services in a given area.

Tear gas: Any of several chemicals, usually stored in liquid form and released as an aerosol liquid or gas, that have the effect of disorienting and disabling any person who inhales the substance; a nonlethal weapon.

Technology Assessment Program (TAP): A program sponsored by the International Association of Chiefs of Police to test various kinds of police equipment for their effectiveness, safety, etc.

Teletype: Any of several communications systems in which a typewriter-like device is used to generate coded telegraph signals which are transmitted by wire or by radio-frequency broadcast to receiving units that display the messages on a printer or television-like screen.

Telex: Trademark for a communications service offered by the Western Union Corporation providing for the two-way transmission of *teletype* messages between any two points (terminals) connected to the Western Union network.

Ten-code: Any of several systems of coded messages, usually transmitted by voice, in which each message is preceded by the spoken number, "Ten," and a second number conveys the sense of the message; for example, the ten-code adopted and endorsed by the Association of Public Safety Communications Officers.

Terminal: A device in a communications system for sending and/or receiving messages, usually under the control of an operator.

Trait-rating system: A method of evaluating employees by rating them on a list of "traits" or personal characteristics.

U **Undercover agent:** A police officer assigned to investigate known or suspected criminal activity by posing as a prospective "customer" or as a participant in such activity in order to gain the confidence of criminals and thereby collect information.

Undercover vehicle: An unmarked police vehicle used by an undercover agent, intended to resemble the sorts of vehicles that ordinarily would be associated with the kind of person the undercover agent portrays.

Underrepresentation: With regard to personnel, the condition in which a particular population segment, such as an ethnic minority, is found among the members of an organization or employees of an agency in a smaller proportion than the group's representation among the general population of the community.

Uniform Crime Reporting System (UCRS): A system for recording, collecting, and analyzing information about criminal activities and other law-enforcement matters, originally developed by the International Association of Chiefs of Police, and currently administered by the Federal Bureau of Investigation under the supervision of an advisory committee composed of representatives of IACP and various law enforcement agencies.

Unity of command: The principle that each employee in an organization should be directly *subordinate* and *accountable* to only one superior.

V **Vice:** Any of various types of crimes that involve offenses against the community's moral code, but that generally do not involve attacks against persons or property, and thus are sometimes regarded as victimless crimes; the commerce in illegal goods and services.

W **Ward:** In urban politics, a geographic portion of a city, defining the constituency of an elected official (such as a city council member or alderman).

Ward boss: An official of a political party whose duty is to promote the party's interests in a *ward*.

Warning (traffic): An official notice, given by a police officer to a motorist, advising the motorist that he or she has violated the law but that, in this instance, no formal complaint will be filed.

Watch: In police organization, a term sometimes used to define an organizational element or the period of time that a particular element (such as a patrol shift) is assigned to duty.

Watchman: A person (either a hired employee or an unpaid volunteer) who has been assigned the duty of observing a particular place or area for suspicious or criminal activity; one conception of the basic technique of crime prevention.

Work product measurement: A technique for evaluating the performance of employees by counting the amount of work they have performed in a given period of time.

X Y Z **Zero-base budget:** A *budget* in which all proposed expenditures are presented as if each type of activity had never been performed before, usually showing several variations in the amount of activity to be performed, the benefits presumably to be obtained, and the cost for each level of activity.

Zoned security: In the design and construction of a building, the principle that different kinds of facilities and activities require different degrees of protection from attack, and that similar facilities or activities should be grouped together in areas that are designed and built to provide the correct degree of protection.

BIBLIOGRAPHY

Ackoff, Russell L., *A Concept of Corporate Planning*. New York: Wiley-Interscience, 1970.

Albright, Ellen J., and Larry G. Siegel, *Team Policing: Recommended Approaches*. Washington, D.C.: U.S. Dept. of Justice, National Institute of Law Enforcement and Criminal Justice, 1979.

Alcohol Enforcement Countermeasures, Highway Safety Program Management Series, Volume IV. Washington, D.C.: International Association of Chiefs of Police, 1976.

Ascher, William, *Forecasting: Appraisal for Policy-makers and Planners*. Baltimore: Johns Hopkins University Press, 1978.

Bates, Alan P., and Joseph Julian, *Sociology: Understanding Social Behavior*. Boston: Houghton Mifflin, 1975.

Bennett-Sandler, G. et al. *Law Enforcement and Criminal Justice*. Boston: Houghton Mifflin, 1979.

Blake, Robert R., and Jane Srygley Mouton, *The New Managerial Grid*, 2nd ed. Houston: Gulf, 1978.

Bopp, William J., ed., *Police Administration: Selected Readings*. Boston: Holbrook, 1975.

———— *Police Personnel Administration*. Boston: Holbrook, 1974.

Burpo, John H., *The Police Labor Movement*. Springfield, Ill.: Charles C. Thomas, 1971.

Burton, Alan, *Police Telecommunications*. Springfield, Ill.: Charles C. Thomas, 1973.

Carroll, Arthur B. et al., *Computer-Aided Dispatching for Law Enforcement Agencies*. Champaign, Ill.: Community Technology, Inc., n.d.

Chambers, John C., Satinder K. Mullick, and Donald D. Smith, *An Executive's Guide to Forecasting*. New York: Wiley, 1974.

Commission to Investigate Allegations of Police Corruption in New York City (William Knapp, Chairman), *Report*. New York: George Braziller, 1972.

Creamer, J. Shane. *The Law of Arrest, Search, and Seizure*, 2nd ed. Philadelphia: W. B. Saunders, 1975.

Cressey, Donald R., *Theft of the Nation*. New York: Harper & Row, 1969.

Crittenden, Bedford M., *Truck Violation Survey*. Sacramento, Calif.: California Highway Patrol, 1965.

Dale, Ernest, *Management: Theory and Practice*, 3rd ed. New York: McGraw-Hill, 1973.

Davis, Keith, *Human Behavior at Work*, 4th ed. New York: McGraw-Hill, 1972.

Desatrik, Robert L., *The Expanding Role of the Human Resources Manager*. New York: American Management Association, 1979.

Eastman, George D., ed., *Municipal Police Administration*, 2nd ed. Washington, D.C.: International City Management Association, 1969.

Eisenberg, Terry, Deborah Ann Kent, and Charles R. Wall, *Police Personnel Practices in State and Local Governments*. Washington, D.C.: Police Foundation, 1973.

Farley, Jennie, *Affirmative Action and the Woman Worker*. New York: American Management Association, 1979.

Farrell, Paul V., *Aljian's Purchasing Handbook*, 4th ed. New York: McGraw-Hill, 1982.

Fiedler, Fred E., *Leadership*. New York: General Learning Press, 1971.

Fogelson, Robert, *Big City Police*. Cambridge, Mass.: Harvard Univ. Press, 1977.

Fox, Richard H., and Carl L. Cunningham, *Crime Scene Search and Physical Evidence Handbook*. Washington, D.C.: U.S. Department of Justice, National Institute of Law Enforcement and Criminal Justice, 1973.

Goldsmith, Jack, and Sharon S. Goldsmith, eds., *The Police Community*. Pacific Palisades, Calif.: Palisades Publishers, 1974.

Greenwood, Peter W., Jan M. Chaiken, and Joan Petersilia, *The Criminal Investigation Process*. Lexington, Mass.: D.C. Heath, 1977.

Greisinger, George W., Jeffrey S. Slovak, and Joseph J. Molkup, *Civil Service Systems: Their Impact on Police Administration*. Washington, D.C.: U.S. Dept. of Justice, Law Enforcement Assistance Administration, 1979.

A Guide—Scheduled Preventive Maintenance. Washington, D.C.: Technology Assessment Program, International Association of Chiefs of Police, 1981.

Gulick, Luther, and Lyndall Urwick, eds., *Papers on the Science of Administration*. New York: Institute of Public Administration, 1937.

Hale, Charles D., *Fundamentals of Police Administration*. Boston: Holbrook, 1977.

Hall, Jay Cameron, *Inside the Crime Lab*. Englewood Cliffs, N.J.: Prentice-Hall, 1974.

A Handbook on Jail Administration. Washington, D.C.: National Sheriffs' Association, 1974.

Hannah, Donald G., and John R. Kleberg, *A Police Records System for the Small Department*, 2nd ed. Springfield, Ill.: Charles C. Thomas, 1974.

Hennessy, E. F., T. Hamilton, K. B. Joscelyn, and J. S. Merritt, *A Study of the Problem of Hot Pursuit by the Police*. Washington, D.C.: U.S. Dept. of Transportation, National Highway Safety Bureau, 1970.

Hicks, Herbert C., and C. Ray Gullett, *The Management of Organizations*, 3rd ed. New York: McGraw-Hill, 1976.

Horne, Peter, *Women in Law Enforcement*, 2nd ed. Springfield, Ill.: Charles C. Thomas, 1980.

Introduction to Police Traffic Service Management, Highway Safety Program Management Series, Volume I. Washington, D.C.: International Association of Chiefs of Police, 1976.

The Kansas City Preventive Patrol Experiment. Washington, D.C.: Police Foundation, 1974.

Klotter, John C., and Joseph Rosenfeld, *Criminal Justice Instructional Techniques*. Springfield, Ill.: Charles C. Thomas, 1979.

Kuykendall, Jack, and Peter C. Unsinger, *Community Police Administration*. Chicago: Nelson-Hall, 1975.

Lee, Robert D., Jr., and Ronald W. Johnson, *Public Budgeting System*. Baltimore: University Park Press, 1973.

Leonard, V. A., *The Police Records System*. Springfield, Ill.: Charles C. Thomas, 1970.

Lewin, Kurt, Ronald Lippitt, and Ralph White, "Patterns of Aggressive Behavior in Experimentally Created 'Social Climates'." *Journal of Psychology* 1939:271–299.

Lundman, Richard J., ed., *Police Behavior: A Sociological Approach*. New York: Oxford Univ. Press, 1980.

Maclay, George, and Humphry Knipe, *The Dominant Man*. New York: Delacorte, 1972.

Martin, James, *Telecommunications and the Computer*, 2nd ed. Englewood Cliffs, N.J.: Prentice-Hall, 1976.

Martin, Susan Ehrlich, *Breaking and Entering: Policewomen on Patrol*. Berkeley: Univ. of California Press, 1980.

Maslow, Abraham H., *Motivation and Personality*. New York: Harper & Row, 1954.

McGregor, Douglas M., *The Human Side of Enterprise*. New York: McGraw-Hill, 1960.

Muir, William Ker, Jr., *Police: Streetcorner Politicians*. Chicago: Univ. of Chicago Press, 1977.

National Clearinghouse for Criminal Justice Planning and Architecture, *Guidelines for the Planning and Design of Police Programs and Facilities*. Urbana, Ill.: Univ. of Illinois Press, 1973.

Newman, William H., and E. Kirby Warren, *The Process of Management*, 4th ed. Englewood Cliffs, N.J.: Prentice-Hall, 1977.

Nicholas, Alex, *New York Cops Talk Back*. New York: Wiley, 1976.

Niederhoffer, Arthur, and Alexander B. Smith, *New Directions of Police-Community Relations*. San Francisco: Rinehart Press, 1974.

Parker, Donn B., *Fighting Computer Crime*. New York: Scribner's, 1980.

Police Body Armor. Gaithersberg, Md.: Technology Assessment Program, International Association of Chiefs of Police, 1978.

Police Personal FM Transceiver Report. Washington, D.C.: Technology Assessment Center, International Association of Chiefs of Police, 1981.

Police Strikes: Causes and Prevention. Washington, D.C.: International Association of Chiefs of Police, 1979.

Police Traffic Safety Responsibilities, Highway Safety Program Management Series, Volume II. Washington, D.C.: International Association of Chiefs of Police, 1976.

President's Commission on Law Enforcement and the Administration of Justice, *Task Force Report: Corrections*. Washington, D.C.: U.S. Government Printing Office, 1967.

President's Task Force on Highway Safety, *Mobility Without Mayhem*. Washington, D.C.: U.S. Government Printing Office, 1970.

Reinke, Roger W., *Design and Operation of Police Communications Systems*. Washington, D.C.: International Association of Chiefs of Police, 1964.

Roberg, Roy R., *Police Management and Organizational Behavior: A Contingency Approach*. St. Paul, Minn.: West Publishing Co., 1979.

Schultz, Donald O., and Loran A. Norton, *Police Operational Intelligence*. Springfield, Ill.: Charles C. Thomas, 1973.

Seulig, Barbara, *You Can't Eat Peanuts in Church and Other Little-Known Laws*. Garden City, N.Y.: Doubleday, 1975.

Shanahan, Donald T., *Police Administration*. Boston: Holbrook, 1975.

Smith, R. Dean, and David A. Espie, *Guidelines for Police Services on Controlled-Access Roadways*. Washington, D.C.: International Association of Chiefs of Police, 1968.

Sohn, R. L., and R. D. Kennedy, *Patrol Force Allocation for Law Enforcement*. Washington, D.C.: U.S. Dept. of Justice, Law Enforcement Assistance Administration, 1978.

Souryal, Sam, *Police Administration and Management*. St. Paul, Minn.: West Publishing Co., 1977.

Spielberger, Charles D., ed., *Police Selection and Evaluation*. Washington, D.C.: Hemisphere, 1979.

Stamps, David, "CPU Crime Laws Weak." *MISWeek*, September 28, 1983.

Stone, Alfred R., and Stuart M. DeLuca, *Investigating Crimes*. Boston: Houghton Mifflin, 1980.

Testing the Drinking Driver. Chicago: National Safety Council, 1970.

Troan, Arthur B., Jr., *Using Information to Manage*. New York: Ronald Press, 1968.

U.S. Commission on Civil Rights, *Police Practices and the Preservation of Civil Rights*. Washington, D.C.: U.S. Government Printing Office, 1978.

U.S. Department of Justice, Federal Bureau of Investigation, *Crime in the United States*. Washington, D.C.: U.S. Government Printing Office, annual.

U.S. Department of Justice, Law Enforcement Assistance Adminstration, *Career Development for Law Enforcement*. Washington, D.C.: U.S. Government Printing Office, 1973.

———— *Reports of the National Juvenile Justice Assessment Centers: The Shadow of Distress*. Washington, D.C.: U.S. Government Printing Office, 1980.

Vanagunas, Stanley, and James F. Elliott, *Administration of Police Organizations*. Boston: Allyn and Bacon, 1980.

Waldron, Ronald et al., *The Criminal Justice System*. Boston: Houghton Mifflin, 1976.

Walker, Samuel, *A Critical History of Police Reform*. Lexington, Mass.: D.C. Heath, Lexington Books, 1977.

Watts, L. P., *Some Observations of Police-Administered Tests for Intoxication*. Chapel Hill, N.C.: Univ. of North Carolina Press, 1966.

Weber, Max, *Theory of Social and Economic Organization*. tr. A. M. Henderson and Talcott Parsons. New York: Oxford Univ. Press, 1947.

White, Ralph, and Ronald Lippitt, *Autocracy and Democracy*. New York: Harper, 1960.

Wilson, O. W., *Police Planning*, 2nd ed. Springfield, Ill.: Charles C. Thomas, 1967.

———— *Police Records and Their Installation*. Chicago: Public Administration Service, 1942.

Wilson, O. W., and Roy C. McLaren, *Police Administration*, 3rd ed. New York: McGraw-Hill, 1972.

Wolinsky, Fredric D., *The Sociology of Health*. Boston: Little, Brown, 1980.

INDEX